WORLD WAR I

THE AFRICAN FRONT

WORLD WAR I
THE AFRICAN FRONT

★ ★ ★

EDWARD PAICE

PEGASUS BOOKS
NEW YORK

WORLD WAR I
THE AFRICAN FRONT

Pegasus Books LLC
80 Broad Street
5th Floor
New York, NY 10004

First Pegasus Books cloth edition 2008
First Pegasus Books trade paperback edition 2010

Library of Congress Cataloging-in-Publication Data is available.

ISBN: 978-1-60598-080-5

10 9 8 7 6 5 4 3 2 1

Printed in the United States of America
Distributed by W. W. Norton & Company, Inc.
www.pegasusbooks.us

To Stephanie

CONTENTS

LIST OF ILLUSTRATIONS

29. Spicer-Simson signalling from the deck of *Netta*
30. HMS *Fifi* at anchor
31. A German column makes its way across the *pori*
32. A *Königsberg* gun is manhandled into position
33. 1st King's African Rifles occupying Longido
34. The 2nd Rhodesia Regiment entrains
35. Von Lettow-Vorbeck observing troop movements on the Kilimanjaro front

(BETWEEN PP. 280 AND 281)

36. 'The Girls They Left Behind' – King's African Rifles recruits leave for the war
37. Portuguese troops embarking at Lisbon for East Africa
38. Allied troops prepare to advance by motor, horse (39), and train (40)
41. South Africans bring their guns into action
42. *Königsberg* gun during the retreat down the Usambara Railway
43. German prisoners being led into captivity
44. Concert hall performance at the Fort Napier prison camp in South Africa
45. Belgian troops commanded by General Tombeur (46) advance towards Tabora
47. The capture of Tabora
48. Northey's troops capture Fort Namema before converging on Iringa
49. Ras Tafari and Wilfred Thesiger after the defeat of Lij Iyasu in Abyssinia
50. No let-up in the fighting in German East Africa
51. German *askari* playing cards in camp
52. Nigerian gunners wrestling
53. Discipline for malefactors was harsh
54. Ratings on the *Kinfauns Castle*
55. HMS *Hyacinth* tilted to fire inland at German positions

(BETWEEN PP. 376 AND 377)

56. British and South African troops cross the Ruaha
57. British airmen celebrate Christmas
58. 1917 brought the worst rains in living memory
59. Von Lettow-Vorbeck's troops remained as elusive as ever
60. General Hoskins paid the price for the lack of Allied progress
61. *Askari* of 15 *Feldkompanie* in camp
62. One of von Lettow-Vorbeck's indomitable NCOs
63. Max Wintgens remained on the loose until mid 1917
64. Belgian troops capture Mahenge
65. L59, the airship sent with supplies to the beleaguered German troops

The author wishes to express his thanks to the following for their kind permission to reproduce photographs:

Bodleian Library of Commonwealth and African Studies at Rhodes House (1, 32, 36, 38); Mrs Ruth Rabb (2); Der Bildbestand der Deutschen Kolonialgesellschaft – Universitätsbibliothek Frankfurt am Main (4, 6, 7, 31, 35, 42, 51, 61, 62, 69, 73); the National Army Museum (8, 9); Bundesarchiv Koblenz – Walther Dobbertin Collection (10, 50, 59); the Imperial War Museum (13, 16, 21, 29); Australian War Memorial (20); the Gurkha Museum (23, 24, 25); The National Archives (39); the Peter Liddle Collection, Brotherton Library, University of Leeds (40, 53, 54, 55); the Syndics of Cambridge University Library (52, 66); South African National Museum of Military History (56, 70); Missionari d'Africa Archives (63); Kenya National Archives (76); the Royal Geographical Society for the endpapers.

All other photographs are either in the author's collection or appeared in many contemporary publications and the copyright holders have been impossible to identify.

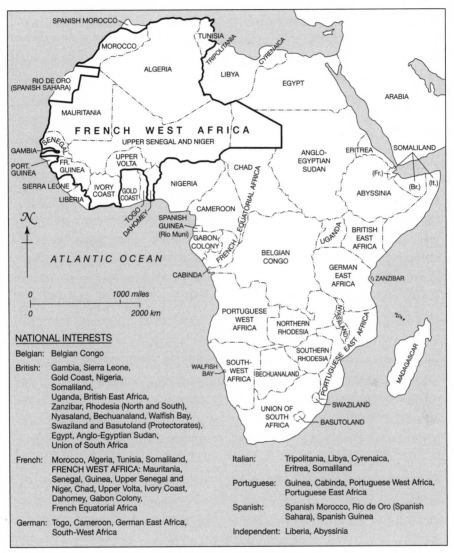

Colonial Africa in 1914

Theatre of War: Central and Eastern Africa

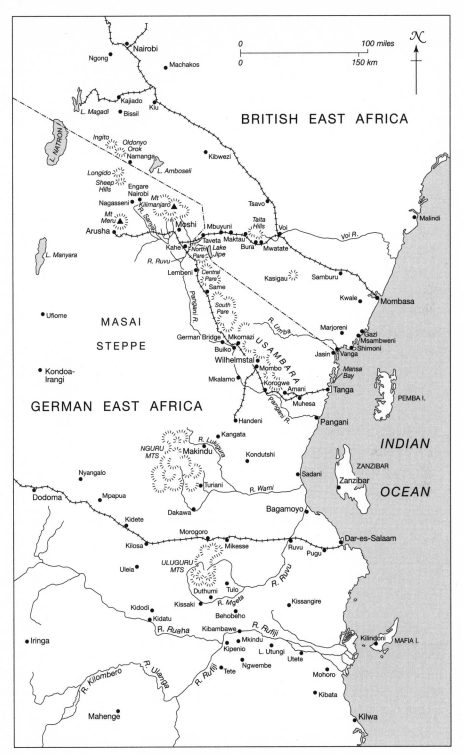

The Campaign in the North-East

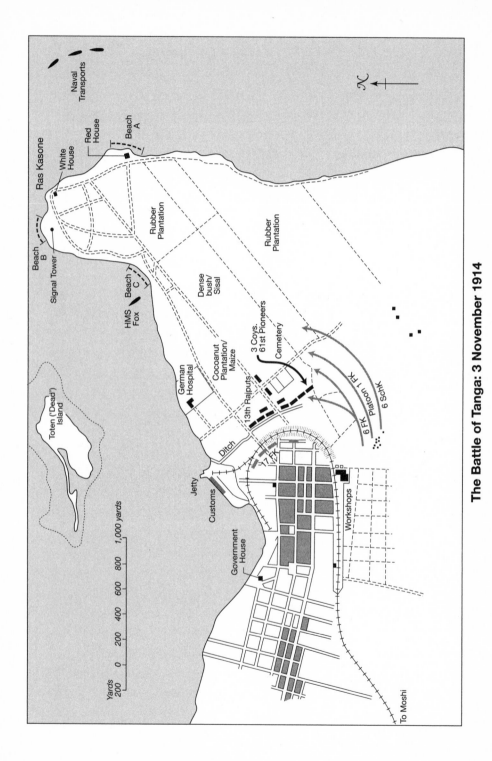

The Battle of Tanga: 3 November 1914

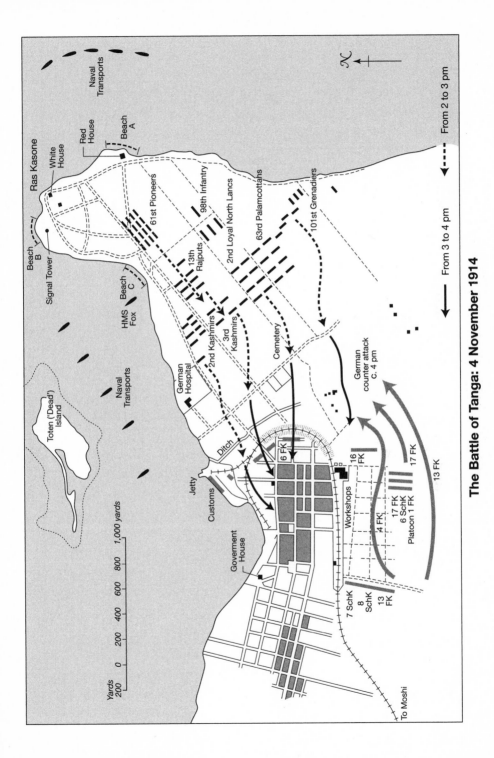

The Battle of Tanga: 4 November 1914

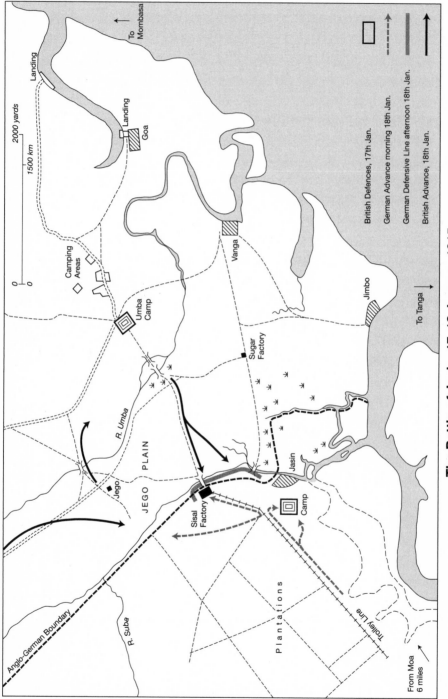

The Battle of Jasin, 17–18 January 1915

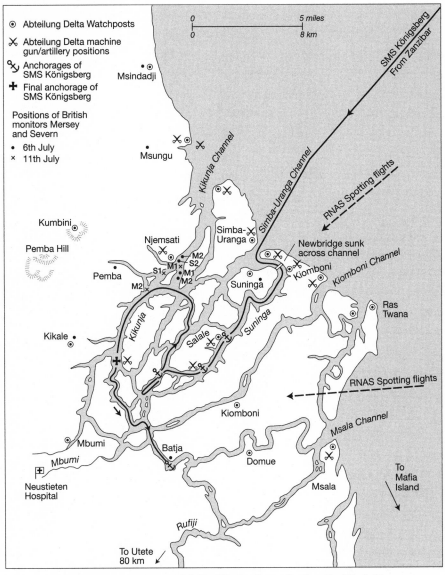

Operations against SMS *Königsberg* in the Rufiji delta

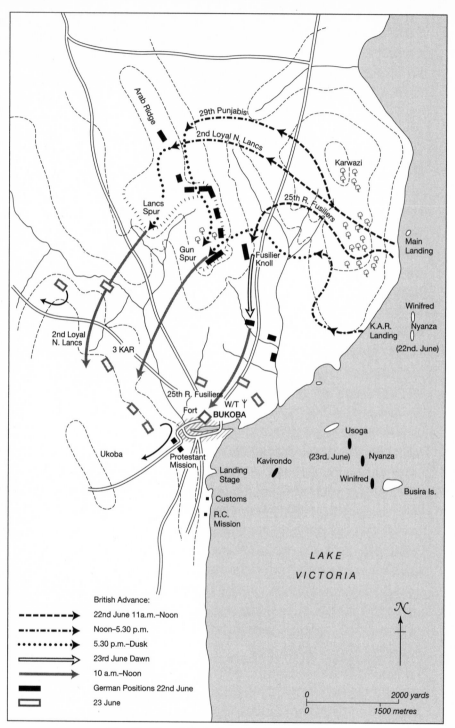

The Battle of Bukoba, 22–23 June 1915

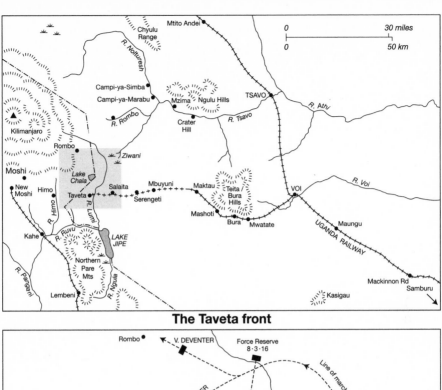

The Taveta front

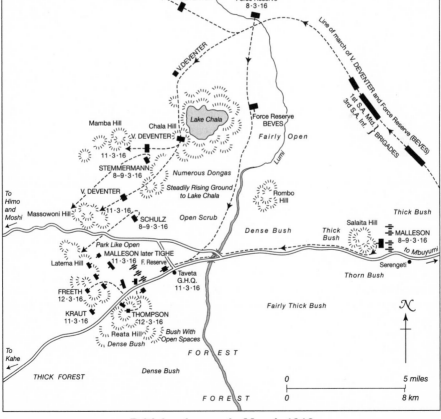

British advance in March 1916

The Campaign in the West and North-West

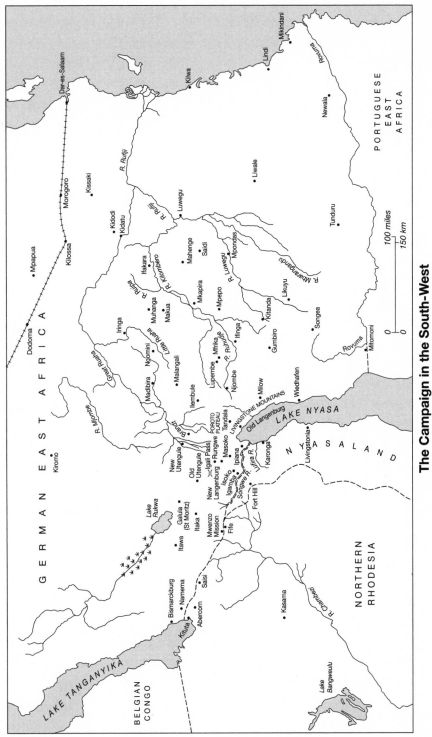

The Campaign in the South-West

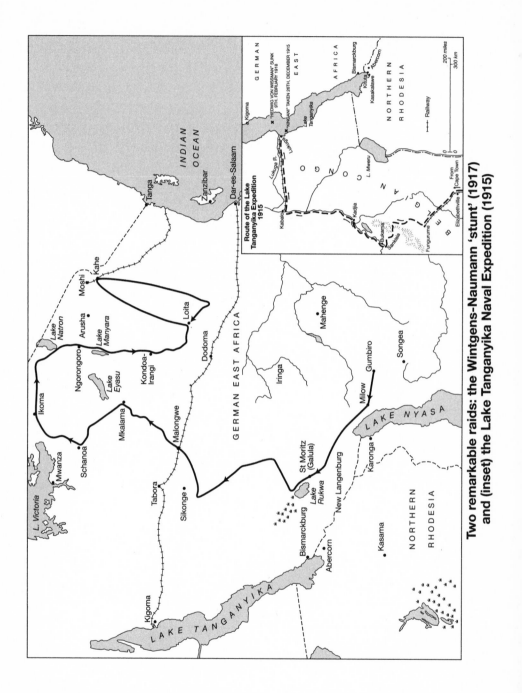

Two remarkable raids: the Wintgens-Naumann 'stunt' (1917) and (inset) the Lake Tanganyika Naval Expedition (1915)

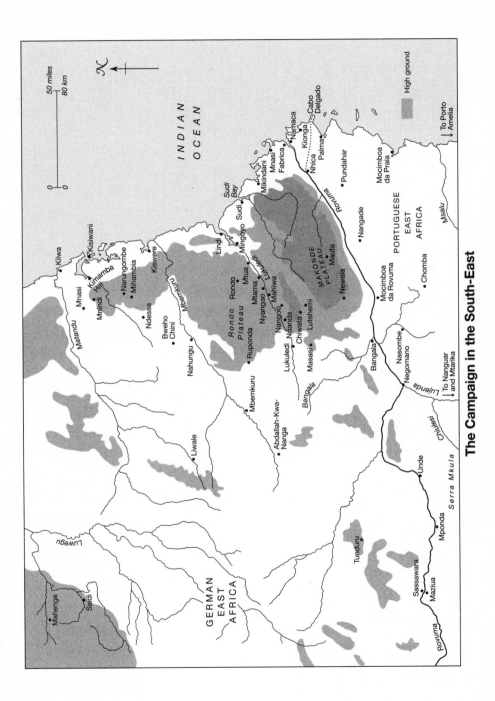

The Campaign in the South-East

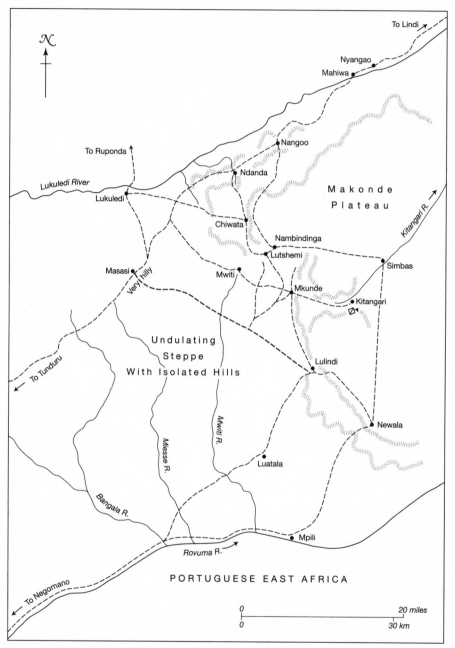

Von Lettow-Vorbeck's escape route, November 1917

ACKNOWLEDGEMENTS

I would like to thank Duncan Robinson (The Master), Professor Eamon Duffy (President), Dr Ronald Hyam and the Governing Body of Magdalene College, Cambridge for welcoming me so warmly as a Visiting Fellow for the academic year 2003–4. I can imagine no better home in which to have begun the final stages of the work on *Tip and Run*.

Many people in Africa and Europe have provided pertinent advice or a place to stay and I am especially grateful to: Alliy Abadou, Richard Ambani, David Anderson, Karen Attar, Rennie Barnes, William Boyd, Anthony Cheetham, Peter Colmore, Alec Cunningham, Tom Donovan, Daniel Fearn, Mark and Lyn Ferguson, David and Sheila Foster, Chris Flatt, Tony and Glenda Lederle, Alan Linsell, John Lonsdale, Daniel M'kimathi, M'Ithiria Mukaria, Phil McComish, David McLennan, Peter Merrington, Bill Nasson, Álvaro Nóbrega, Tom Ofcansky, Ngaiyok Olengunin, Andrew Onyeagbako, Oliver and Natalie Nicholson, Solomon and Ruth Rabb, Rachel Rowe, David Read, Gerald Rilling, Tony Seth-Smith, Aylward Shorter, Keith Steward, June Sutherland, Philip Warhurst, Sara Wheeler, Jeremy Withers-Green and Rashid Yahaya.

One of the great joys of undertaking a project such as this is being the recipient of so many kindnesses from archivists, institutions and a plethora of experts of one sort or another. I would like to thank the following:

In Britain: The Naval Historical Branch, Ministry of Defence; The Royal College of Nursing Archives (Kate Mason); Special Collections, Birmingham University (Phillipa Bassett); Cambridge University Library; British Library; The Peter Liddle Collection, Brotherton Library, University of Leeds (Richard Davies and Jill Winder); The Churchill Archives Centre; The National Archives (William Spencer and Mandy Banton); Royal Air Force Museum (Gordon Leith); the Royal Geographical Society (Eugene Rae); Bodleian Library of Commonwealth and African Studies at Rhodes House (John Pinfold and Lucy McCann); Imperial War Museum; National Army Museum; Gurkha Museum (Gavin Edgerley-Harris).

In Portugal: Biblioteca Nacional; Instituto Superior Naval de Guerra; Arquivo Histórico-Diplomático do Ministério do Negócios Estrangeiros; Serviço

Biblioteca e Documentaças Diplomática do MNF (Maria Helena Neves Pinto), Arquivo Histórico Militar; and the Contemporary Portuguese History Research Centre.

In Italy: Fr. Ivan Page and Fr. Johannes Tappeser at the Missionari d'Africa archives in Rome.

In Germany: Bundesarchiv/Militärarchiv (Freiburg im Breisgau); Bundesarchiv/Reichskolonialamt (Koblenz); Staatsbibliothek zu Berlin – Preussischer Kulturbesitz (Dorothea Barfknecht); Stadt- und Universitätsbibliothek (Frankfurt am Main); Deutsches Historisches Museum (Berlin); Traditionsverband ehemaliger Schutz- und Überseetruppen; Wolfgang Führmann.

In Africa: The South African Library, Cape Town; University of Cape Town Libraries, Manuscripts and Archives Department (Lesley Hart); The South African National Military History Museum (J.F. Keene, Betty de Lange, Rowena Wilkinson and Gerda Viljoen); Joan Marsh of the South African Military History Society; the South African National Archives; Professor Rodney Davenport; M. Musembi, Eliakim Azangu, Evanson Kiiru and Philip Omondi at the Kenya National Archives; the Zimbabwe National Archive and Nicholas Vumbunu.

In Australia: National Archives of Australia; National Library of Australia (Ian Morris); Sea Power Centre, Australian Defence Organisation (Brett Mitchell); Australian War Memorial Archive.

Also: Pascale Bouzanquet (International Hydrographic Bureau, Monaco); Alan Cobley (Senior Lecturer in African History and Dean, University of the West Indies); David H. Gray (Canadian Hydrographic Service); Wenda L. Meyers and Pat Hollis at the journal *Field Artillery*; Melville J. Herskovits Library of African Studies, Northwestern University, Illinois (David L. Easterbrook).

Special thanks are due to Ion Trewin, Anna Hervé and Bea Hemming at Weidenfeld & Nicolson for their ever-wise counsel; to Georgina Capel; to Linden Lawson; to cartographer David Hoxley, indexer David Atkinson and proof-reader Jane Birkett; to Terry Barringer; to my mother, who sadly died before she could scrutinise the draft text with the enthusiasm and sagacity with which she had tackled my previous works; and to my wife, Stephanie, for her extraordinary patience, support and unflagging good spirits. This book is dedicated to her.

GLOSSARY

FOREIGN WORDS

Abteilung – detachment (German)
askari – soldier (Swahili)
baraza – meeting (Swahili)
boma – enclosure, government or police station (Swahili)
bundu – wild region, bush (Swahili)
cacimbo – dry season morning fog and drizzle (Portuguese)
cipais – policeman (Portuguese)
donga – ditch, watercourse (Afrikaans)
dop – brandy (Afrikaans)
impi – regiment (Zulu)
kopje – hill (Afrikaans)
machila – hammock slung between poles (Portuguese)
matoke – plantain, banana (Swahili)
miombo – woodland of trees of Brachystegia genus (Swahili)
nek – pass (Afrikaans)
oom – uncle, term of respect (Afrikaans)
pombe – beer, often distilled from millet (Swahili)
pori – wild uninhabited country, bush (Swahili)
prazo – term, lease (Portuguese)
Reichskolonialamt – Colonial Office (German)
ruga-ruga – levy, mercenary (Swahili)
Schutztruppe – colonial troops (German)
shamba – farm, homestead (Swahili)
slim – cunning, sly (Afrikaans)
subadar – sergeant (Indian Army rank)
taal – vernacular Afrikaans
tenga-tenga – carrier, porter (Swahili)

MILITARY ABBREVIATIONS

British

ADC –   *aide-de-camp*
BSAP –   British South Africa Police
CPO –   Chief Petty Officer
DCM –   Distinguished Conduct Medal
DSO –   Distinguished Service Order
EAMR –   East African Mounted Rifles
GSO –   General Staff Officer
IEF –   Indian Expeditionary Force
KAR –   King's African Rifles (1/KAR – 1st Regiment KAR; 1/3KAR – 1st Battalion of 3rd Regiment)
MC –   Military Cross
NCO –   Non-commissioned Officer
NRP –   Northern Rhodesia Police
QF –   Quick-firing (artillery)
RNAS –   Royal Naval Air Service
RNR –   Rhodesia Native Regiment
RNVR –   Royal Naval Volunteer Reserve
SAFA –   South African Field Artillery
SAH –   South African Horse (10/SAH – 10th Battalion South African Horse)
SAI –   South African Infantry (7/SAI – 7th Battalion South African Infantry)
SAMC –   South African Medical Corps
SAMR –   South African Mounted Rifles
SAR –   South African Rifles
VC –   Victoria Cross

German

FK –   *Feldkompanie*, Field Company (17/FK – 17th Field Company)
ResK –   *Reservekompanie*, Reserve Company
SchK –   *Schützenkompanie*, Rifle Company

For German military ranks and their British equivalents, see Appendix One

COLONIAL COUNTRY NAMES AND THEIR MODERN EQUIVALENTS

Belgian Congo – Democratic Republic of Congo
British East Africa – Kenya
Cameroons – Cameroon
German East Africa – Tanzania
German South-West Africa – Namibia
Northern Rhodesia – Zambia
Nyasaland – Malawi
Portuguese East Africa – Mozambique
Portuguese West Africa – Angola
Southern Rhodesia – Zimbabwe
Togo/Togoland – The Togolese Republic

Note on Place Names

The spellings adopted for place names in the text and on the maps are those most commonly used by contemporary British and South African sources.

DRAMATIS PERSONAE

Adler, Otto – retired infantry officer, *Schutztruppe* company commander

Aitken, Arthur – General Officer Commanding, Indian Expeditionary Force 'B'

Amorim, Pedro Massano de – commanding officer 1st Portuguese Expeditionary Force (1914), Governor-General Portuguese East Africa (1917–18)

Apel, Hans – gunnery officer of the *Königsberg*

Arning, Wilhelm – retired infantry officer, *Schutztruppe* medical officer

Aumann, Heinrich – *Schutztruppe* company commander

Baumstark, Paul – *Schutztruppe* detachment commander

Belfield, Henry Conway – Governor British East Africa

Berrangé, C.A.L. – brigade commander, South African forces (1916)

Beves, Percival Scott – brigade commander, South African forces (1916–17)

Bock, Heinrich Freiherr von – retired infantry officer, *Schutztruppe* detachment commander

Bock von Wülfingen, Wilhelm – *Schutztruppe* company commander

Bockmann, Walther – Engineer Officer on the *Königsberg*, *Schutztruppe* company commander

Boell, Ludwig – *Schutztruppe* company commander/staff officer, unofficial historian of the campaign

Boemcken, Julius von – active infantry officer returning to Germany in August 1914, *Schutztruppe* detachment commander

Botha, Louis – Prime Minister of the Union of South Africa

Botha, Manie – mounted brigade commander, South African forces (1916)

Brandis, Ernst von – Chief of Police, Dar-es-Salaam, *Schutztruppe* company commander (1914–16), staff officer *Westtruppen* (1917)

Braunschweig, Friedrich – *Schutztruppe* company commander

Bridgeman, R. – Flag Commander HMS *Hyacinth*

Brits, Coen – divisional commander, British/South African forces (1916)

Burne, N.H.M. – commanding officer 11th South African Infantry (1916)

Byron, J.J. – commanding officer 5th South African Infantry (1916–17)

Capell, Algernon Essex – commanding officer 2nd Rhodesia Regiment

Castro, Álvaro de – Governor-General Portuguese East Africa (1915–18)

Caulfield, Francis – Captain HMS *Fox*

Chappuis, Udo von – *Schutztruppe* company commander

Charlewood, C.J. – naval reservist commanding various small craft

Charlton, E.F.B. – Commander-in-Chief Cape Station (1915–17)

Chilembwe, John – missionary, leader of 1915 uprising in Nyasaland

Christiansen, Karl – Captain of blockade-runner *Kronborg* (1915)

Chwa, Daudi – *Kabaka* (king) of Baganda

Clayton, C. – commanding officer 2nd Cape Corps (1917–18)

Codrington, H.W. – commanding officer 13th Rajputs (1914)

Cohen, 'Sos' – Chief Scout, British forces in Portuguese East Africa (1917–18)

Collyer, J.J. – Chief of Staff to Jan Smuts (1916)

Crewe, Charles – South African politician and newspaper proprietor, commanding officer 'Lake Force' (1916)

Crowe, J.H.V. – commanding officer British/South African artillery (1916)

Cull, J.T. – RNAS aviator

Cunliffe, F.H.B. – commanding officer Nigerian Brigade

Dennistoun, G.H. – commander Lake Nyasa flotilla

Deppe, Ludwig – *Schutztruppe* medical officer

Doering, Robert – *Schutztruppe* company commander

Drew, A.B.H. – commanding officer 29th Punjabis

Driscoll, Daniel – commanding officer 25th Battalion Royal Fusiliers

Drought, J.– commanding officer Nandi Scouts ('Skin Corps')

Drury-Lowe, Sydney – Captain HMS *Chatham*

Dyke, P.H. – 30th Punjabis, column commander (1917)

Edwards, A.H.M. – Commandant-General Rhodesian forces

Edwards, W.F.S. – former Inspector-General Uganda Police, Inspector-General Lines of Communication (1916)

Eliott, F.A.H. – commanding officer 4th South African Horse

Enslin, B.G.L. – mounted brigade commander, South African forces

Fair, 'Jock' – column commander, 'Norforce'

Fairweather, J. – commanding officer South African Motor Cyclist Corps

Falkenhausen, Konrad von – naval reservist, *Schutztruppe* detachment commander

Falkenstein, Walter von – *Schutztruppe* company commander

Fischer, Erich – *Schutztruppe* detachment commander

Fitzgerald, T.O. – commanding officer 3rd King's African Rifles (1916–18), column commander (1918)

Flindt, R.L. – 2nd South African Rifles, column commander, 'Norforce' (1916)

Franken, Gotthold – retired infantry officer, *Schutztruppe* company commander

Freeth, J.C. – commanding officer 7th South African Infantry

Frobenius, Leo – German anthropologist, envoy to Abyssinia (1916)

Fullerton, E.J.A. – Captain HMS *Severn*

Giffard, George – commanding officer 2nd King's African Rifles (1916–18), column commander, Portuguese East Africa (1918)

Gil, Ferreira – commanding officer 3rd Portuguese Expeditionary Force (1916)

Gordon, R. – RNAS aviator

Göring, Karl – adjutant in Dar-es-Salaam (1914), *Schutztruppe* company and detachment commander

Grawert, Gideon von – *Schutztruppe* detachment commander

Grogan, Ewart – British liaison officer with Belgian forces (1914–15 and 1917)

Gudowius, Eberhard – *Schutztruppe* reservist commanding Bukoba district

Hannyngton, Arthur – commanding officer 129th (DCO) Baluchis

Hasslacher, Heinrich – civil servant, *Schutztruppe* company commander

Hauer, August – *Schutztruppe* medical officer

Hawkins, Brian – battalion and column commander, 4th King's African Rifles (1916–18)

Hawthorn, George – commanding officer 1st King's African Rifles (1914–1917), commanding officer Nyasaland forces (1917–18)

Haxthausen, Wilhelm von – *Schutztruppe* company commander

Hazleton, P. – senior officer, Supply and Transport British/South African forces (1916–17)

Henry, Josué – *Commissaire-Général* Eastern Province, Belgian Congo

Hering, Albrecht – retired artillery officer, commander of *Schutztruppe* battery

Herm, Walter – Captain of the German steamer *Somali*

Hertzog, J.B.M. – leader of the South African National Party

Heyden-Linden, Eckard von – Governor's adjutant (1914), *Schutztruppe* company commander

Hinrichs, Herbert – Navigating Officer on the *Königsberg*, *Schutztruppe* company commander

Hoskins, Reginald – former Inspector-General King's African Rifles, divisional commander (1916), Commander-in-Chief British/South African forces (1917)

Hübener, Franz – retired infantry officer, *Schutztruppe* recruiting officer and detachment commander

Huyghé, Armand – regimental commander, Belgian *Brigade Nord* (1916), Commander-in-Chief Belgian forces (1917)

Ingles, J.A. – Captain HMS *Pegasus*

Jollie, F. – commanding officer 17th Cavalry

Jourdain, C.E.A. – commanding officer 2nd Loyal North Lancs (1914–17)

Kaiser, Paul – retired infantry officer, *Schutztruppe* company and detachment commander

Kaltenborn-Stachau, Roland von – artillery officer sent by Berlin on blockade-breaker *Marie*

Kempner, Franz – civil servant, *Schutztruppe* company commander

Kepler, Arthur – senior staff officer, Dar-es-Salaam

King, Norman – British Consul, German East Africa (1914)

King-Hall, Herbert – Commander-in-Chief Cape Station (1914–15)

Kirkpatrick, H.J. – commanding officer 9th South African Infantry

Klinghardt, Rudolf – retired infantry officer, *Schutztruppe* company and detachment commander

Koch, Georg – First Officer of the *Königsberg*, *Schutztruppe* detachment commander

Kock, Nis – crew member of the blockade-breaker *Kronborg*

Köhl, Franz – *Schutztruppe* company commander

Kornatzki, Friedrich von – *Schutztruppe* company commander

Kraut, Georg – commander *Schutztruppe* northern border forces (1914–16), Mahenge forces (1916), staff officer (1916–18)

Krüger, Franz – reservist, *Schutztruppe* company commander

Küdicke, Robert – *Schutztruppe* medical officer

Langen, Peter – *Schutztruppe* company commander

Langenn-Steinkeller, Erich von – *Schutztruppe* company commander (1914), commander of Urundi detachment (1915–16)

Lettow-Vorbeck, Paul von – Commander-in-Chief German forces in East Africa

Lieberman, Eberhard von – on hunting trip in GEA in 1914, *Schutztruppe* company commander

Lincke, Friedrich – Deputy Chief of Police (1914), *Schutztruppe* company commander

Linde-Suden, Harald von – *Schutztruppe* company commander

Looff, Max – Captain of the *Königsberg*, *Schutztruppe* detachment commander

Lyall, R.A. – commanding officer 2nd Kashmirs

Lyncker, Otto Freiherr von – *Schutztruppe* company commander

MacDonell, Errol – British Consul in Portuguese East Africa

Mackay, J.D. – senior Intelligence officer, Indian Expeditionary Force 'B'

Malfeyt, Justin – Governor of Belgian-occupied German East Africa (1916)

Malleson, Wilfrid – Inspector-General of Communications Indian Expeditionary Force 'B', brigade commander (1915–16)

Meinertzhagen, Richard – deputy chief of Intelligence Indian Expeditionary

Force 'B' (1914), Chief of Intelligence British forces (1915–16)

Meixner, Hugo – *Schutztruppe* Chief Medical Officer

Mendes, Moura – commanding officer 2nd Portuguese Expeditionary Force

Merensky, Albert – retired infantry officer, *Schutztruppe* company commander

Mitchell, W.J. – commanding officer 40th Pathans

Molitor, Philippe – commander Belgian *Brigade Nord*

Molyneux, G.M. – commanding officer 6th South African Infantry

Montgomery, J.W.V. – commanding officer 10th South African Infantry

Moon, E.R. – RNAS aviator

Morris, G.A. – commanding officer 1st Cape Corps

Moulaert, Georges – commanding officer Belgian forces Lake Tanganyika

Muller, Emmanuel – regimental commander, Belgian *Brigade Nord*

Müller, Erich – staff officer (Ordnance) in Dar-es-Salaam (1914), *Schutztruppe* company and detachment commander

Müller, Paul – *Schutztruppe* medical officer

Murray, Ronald – column commander, 'Norforce'

Musinga – paramount chief of Ruanda

Naumann, Heinrich – *Schutztruppe* company commander

Northey, Edward – Commander-in-Chief 'Norforce'

Nussey, A.H.M. – Chief of Staff to General van Deventer, mounted brigade commander (1916)

O'Grady, H. de C. – Brigade Major, Indian Expeditionary Force 'B' (1914), column commander (1916–17)

Olsen, Frederik – commander Belgian *Brigade Sud*

Oppen, Werner von – *Schutztruppe* company commander

Orr, G.M. – staff officer Indian Expeditionary Force 'B' (1914), column commander (1917)

Otto, Ernst – *Schutztruppe* company and detachment commander

Phillips, Charles – battalion and column commander, 2nd King's African Rifles (1916–18)

Poppe, Max – *Schutztruppe* company commander

Pretorius, Piet – King-Hall's Chief Scout in the Rufiji delta operations against the *Königsberg* (1915), Smuts's Chief Scout (1916)

Price, Charles – commanding officer 130th (KGO) Baluchis (1915–16), column commander (1916–17)

Ridgway, R. – column commander, British/South African forces (1917)

Rodger, E. – commanding officer 2nd South African Rifles and column commander, 'Norforce' (1916)

Rose, Richard – Commandant Gold Coast Regiment (1916–18)

Rothe, Wilhelm – Postmaster-General, *Schutztruppe* detachment commander

Rothert, Paul – retired infantry officer, *Schutztruppe* company commander

Routh, G.M. – senior officer (Ordnance) Indian Expeditionary Force 'B' (1914)

Ruckteschell, Walter von – reservist, *Schutztruppe* company and detachment commander

Sabath, Hermann – civil servant (1914), battery commander (1915–18), company commander (1918)

Scherbening, Otto von – reservist, *Schutztruppe* company commander

Schimmer, Karl – active infantry officer, Acting Administrator and commander of *Schutztruppe* Urundi

Schnee, Heinrich – Governor of German East Africa

Schönfeld, Werner – retired naval officer, commander of *Schutztruppe* Rufiji delta defences (1914–15), commander of sabotage forces on northern border and Lake Tanganyika (1915–16)

Schulz, Hans – *Schutztruppe* company and detachment commander

Sheppard, S.H. – Chief of Staff Indian Expeditionary Force 'B' (1914), divisional commander (1916–17), chief staff officer to van Deventer (1917–18)

Shorthose, W. – battalion and column commander 4th King's African Rifles (1916–18)

Smith-Dorrien, Horace – appointed Commander-in-Chief British/South African forces (1915), resigned due to ill-health in January 1916

Smuts, Jan – Cabinet minister in Union of South Africa (1914–15), Commander-in-Chief British/South African forces (1916)

Solf, Wilhelm – Colonial Secretary in Berlin

Sorenson, Conrad – Captain of blockade-runner *Marie* (1916)

Sousa Rosa, Tómas de – commanding officer 4th Portuguese Expeditionary Force

Spangenburg, Walter – *Schutztruppe* company commander

Spicer-Simson, Geoffrey – Senior Naval Officer, Lake Tanganyika Expedition (1915–16)

Sprockhoff, Leonhard – merchant marine officer, commander Kilwa detachment (1916)

Stemmermann, Paul – *Schutztruppe* company commander

Stewart, James – commanding officer Indian Expeditionary Force 'C' (1914), commanding officer Namanga forces (1915), divisional commander (1916)

Stosch, Hans Freiherr von – *Schutztruppe* company commander

Stuemer, Willibald von – retired artillery officer, civil servant

Sykes, A.C. – Captain HMS *Astraea*

Tafel, Theodor – *Schutztruppe* staff officer in Dar-es-Salaam, company commander (1914), staff officer (1915–16), commander of *Westtruppen* (1917)

Taute, Max – *Schutztruppe* medical officer

Taylor, A.J. – commanding officer 8th South African Infantry

Thornley, G.S. – commander Lake Flotilla (Lake Victoria)

Tighe, Michael – brigade commander, Indian Expeditionary Force 'B' (1914), Commander-in-Chief British forces (1915–16), divisional commander (1916)

Tombeur, Charles-Henri – Commander-in-Chief Belgian forces (1916)

Tomlinson, A.J. – commanding officer Rhodesia Native Regiment

Vallings, H.A. – commanding officer 29th Punjabis

van Deventer, Jakobus – divisional commander, British/South African forces (1916), Commander-in-Chief British/South African forces (1917–18)

van Nieuwenhuizen, Piet – von Lettow-Vorbeck's Chief Scout

Wahle, Kurt – retired general visiting family (1914), *Schutztruppe* logistics officer and Commandant of Dar-es-Salaam (1915), commander *Westtruppen* (1915–17), detachment commander (1917–18)

Wapshare, Richard – brigade commander, Indian Expeditionary Force 'B' (1914), Commander-in-Chief British forces (1914–15)

Watkins, O.F. – Director of British East Africa Military Labour Bureau (1916–18)

Weck, Wolfgang – *Schutztruppe* medical officer

Wenig, Richard – officer on the *Königsberg*, *Schutztruppe* battery commander

Whittall, W. – RNAS armoured car commander (1916)

Wilson, R.A. – Captain HMS *Mersey*

Wintgens, Max – Administrator of Ruanda and commander of its *Schutztruppe*

Wolfram, Ernst – retired infantry officer, *Schutztruppe* company commander

Zimmer, Gustav – Captain of survey ship *Möwe*, commander of naval force on Lake Tanganyika

Zingel, Joseph – magistrate in Bismarckburg (1914), *Schutztruppe* company and detachment commander.

INTRODUCTION

A frica *mattered* to the European powers at the beginning of the twentieth century. The preceding two decades had witnessed a process of colonial expansion as rapid, unseemly, and fraught with rivalry as any that the world had ever known; and by the mid 1890s it was evident that 'the stew pan of Africa was simmering and liable to froth over at any moment'.[1] Bismarck had warned – long before Germany even joined the so-called 'Scramble for Africa' – that 'the attempt to found colonies in regions claimed by other states, no matter whether with or without legitimacy', would cause 'manifold, undesired conflicts';[2] and when Joseph Chamberlain, the British Secretary of State for Colonies, considered the very real possibility of an imperial war in Africa in May 1896 he warned the House of Commons that such a conflict would be 'one of the most serious wars that could possibly be waged . . . It would be a long war, a bitter war and a costly war . . . it would leave behind it the embers of a strife which I believe generations would hardly be long enough to extinguish'.

Three years after Chamberlain's warning war did break out in Africa, and although it pitted Britain against the Boer republics of South Africa rather than a rival European power, it was unmistakably imperial in character. Far from being the rapid and immediately profitable pushover envisaged by British imperialists, the conflict cost 'the greatest show on earth'[3] over £200m (*c.* £12bn in today's money), involved the mobilisation of more than 400,000 British and colonial troops, and left South Africa in ruins. 'In money and lives', wrote Thomas Pakenham, 'no British war since 1815 had been so prodigal.'[4] The bill was fully ten times the value of the output of the Transvaal gold mines for 1899; British casualties exceeded even those of the Crimean War half a century earlier; and the toll wrought on Afrikaner and African alike was equally immense. Control of the Nile (and therefore the Suez Canal and the maritime route to India), control of South Africa's vast reserves of gold and diamonds, Cecil Rhodes's dream of linking the Cape with Cairo by railway and lake steamer – these were issues that preoccupied Whitehall rather more than the 'self-centred, ethnocentric and frequently arrogant presuppositions' of liberal imperialists' 'civilizing mission ideology'[5] by the turn of the century.

None of Britain's European rivals intervened to counter her aggression in South Africa. But it earned the opprobrium of Germany, France and Russia, and developments elsewhere on the African continent exacerbated an already tense and recriminatory atmosphere. A simultaneous war between Britain and France over an incursion by the latter into the upper reaches of the Nile, thousands of miles to the north of Kruger's Transvaal, was only averted by the narrowest of margins. Germany's *Weltpolitik* called for a doubling of the size of her Navy and the establishment of naval bases in all her African colonies (thereby posing a threat to the Royal Navy's control of the high seas). Belgium and Portugal were suspicious to the point of paranoia that Britain, acting in concert with France and Germany, meant to dispossess them of their vast African empires. The message was clear: if rivalry in Africa was not checked it would soon constitute a threat to peace in Europe.

By 1914 the idea of a second 'White Man's War' in sub-Saharan Africa had all but disappeared. Rivalries certainly persisted as the first phase of the Scramble for Africa drew to a close, but the spectacle of the Anglo-South African War, a common desire to develop (or exploit) rather than fight over (and devastate) their African colonies, and a common determination to safeguard racial 'prestige', had fostered increasing rapprochement among the colonial powers. Nowhere was this more evident than in relations between Britain and Germany. In 1884 *The Times* had declared that 'Englishmen are too little enamoured of Africa to grudge Germans the privilege of seeking their fortunes on its vacant shores',[6] and this sentiment survived the jingoism and 'colonial mania' of the ensuing two decades sufficiently intact to provide some common ground between the two countries. At a time of escalating tensions between Britain and Germany in Europe this entente in Africa was doubly paradoxical. Both countries had established their vast African empires – a quarter of the map of Africa was painted red and German Africa encompassed an area five times the size of the Fatherland – in spite of the scepticism with which Gladstone and Bismarck had regarded colonial ventures in the 1880s; and even as war clouds gathered over Europe they were on the verge of increasing their respective domains still further by concluding an amicable agreement for a future redistribution of certain Portuguese and Belgian colonial possessions. In the opinion of the British Secretary of State for Colonies, Lord Harcourt, Africa was where Germany might be 'distracted'; and Dr Solf, his German counterpart, was willing to accept that Germany's ambitions in Africa would be best served by assuming the role of 'England's junior partner'.[7]

In August 1914 Anglo-German entente in Africa, and the shared belief that a European war in Africa was a concept as risible as it was inadvisable, evaporated overnight. The first British shots of the Great War were fired not in Europe but by a regimental sergeant-major of the West African Frontier Force in (German) Togoland, as Britain moved to neutralise the threat to shipping lanes posed by the wireless stations and ports of Germany's African colonies. Undisputed control of African waters was rapidly secured, but in addition to eliminating Germany's ability to deploy commerce raiders against Allied shipping Britain's strategy called for action against German troops on African soil, and as the *Schutztruppe*, the German colonial defence force, had no intention of surrendering without a fight, Britain and Germany began a land war which both sides were certain would be little more than a short, sharp affair concluded by Christmas 1914. In a manner reminiscent of the Anglo-South African War, the short war proved to be anything but short. Indeed Britain and Germany did not formally agree to cease hostilities in East Africa until two weeks after the Armistice was signed in Europe in November 1918; and in the intervening four years Britain, India, South Africa, Belgium, Portugal and Germany were sucked into a maelstrom which radically altered the lives of millions of Africans and would result in a complete redrawing of the map of colonial Africa.

The financial cost to the Allies of the Great War in sub-Saharan Africa was immense. The expense to the British Treasury of the East Africa campaign alone, the focus of this book and by far the largest of the African campaigns, was unofficially estimated at more than £70m (*c.* £2.8bn in today's money). On the face of it this was 'only' one third of the cost of the Anglo-South African War; but it was a sum equivalent to Britain's entire defence expenditure for 1913 or the cost of the eight million new items of clothing required by the British Army in 1918, and was one third greater than the value of the currency in circulation in Britain in 1914. Furthermore, when the contributions of India, South Africa and Britain's African colonies were included the bill, in the words of one senior colonial official, 'approached, if it did not actually exceed that of the Boer War',[8] and the *Cape Times* of 3 February 1919 commented that it was 'said to exceed £300m'.

The 'butcher's bill' was equally colossal. The death toll among African soldiers and military carriers recruited from British East Africa alone exceeded 45,000 – or one in eight of the country's adult male population; and among all British imperial combatant and support units who took to the field in the East Africa theatre of war the official death toll exceeded 100,000 men. This equated to the number of British soldiers killed in the carnage on the Somme between July and November 1916, or to America's total war dead in the Great War; and the true figure may have been as much as double the official tally. Such was the astonishing cost in human life of a campaign which one official historian described as 'a war of attrition and extermination which [was] without parallel in modern times'.[9] At the Versailles Peace Conference in 1919

George Beer, Chief of the Colonial Division of the American delegation, remarked that he had 'not seen the tale of native victims in any official publication', and speculated that 'it may be too long to give to the world and Africa';[10] while at the Pan-African Conference that same year William DuBois lamented that 'twenty centuries after Christ, black Africa, prostrate, raped and shamed, lies at the feet of the conquering Philistines of Europe'.[11]

Despite its cost in men and money the campaign in East Africa was, and is, often referred to as a mere 'sideshow'. It is certainly true that there was never any question of the conflagration in Africa affecting the outcome of the 'main show' in Europe, but it is also true that there were many who regarded it as the very epitome of the 'selfish imperialism' which had caused the Great War in the first place. Jan Smuts, commander-in-chief of the British troops in East Africa during 1916, articulated this view when he declared that it was 'not difficult to foresee that the East African campaign, while apparently a minor side-show in the great world war, may yet have important bearings on the future of the world';[12] DuBois went further still when he remarked that 'in a very real sense Africa is a prime cause of this terrible overturning of civilization which we have lived to see [because] in the Dark Continent are hidden the roots, not simply of war today but of the menace of wars tomorrow';[13] and Sir Harry Johnston, the famous African explorer and administrator, was convinced 'that the Great War was more occasioned by conflicting colonial ambitions in Africa than by German and Austrian schemes in the Balkans and Asia Minor'.[14] Their point was this: that the war in Africa put imperialism itself, and all the highfalutin talk of the European Powers' 'civilizing mission', on trial; and in so doing it exposed the unremitting ambitions of the colonial powers to a degree of scrutiny unsurpassed since the very beginnings of the Scramble for Africa. Above all it was this that made the East Africa campaign, which spread as rapidly as a bush fire to engulf much more than just the 'East' of the continent, 'a campaign of importance'.[15]

This fact may not have been appreciated by those in the British War Office for whom the campaign was never anything more than an extreme nuisance, a fiendish and remote war that drained British money, shipping tonnage and men from the 'main shows'; and even among a majority of British government ministers the fate of the German colonies in Africa was 'one of the lesser concerns' during the first two years of the war. But the longer the war dragged on the more apparent it became that 'the issue was inextricably bound up with the fundamental hopes, fears and changing expectations of the British Empire at war';[16] and by 1916 British politicians and Whitehall officials recognised that the war in East Africa – though still referred to as a 'sideshow' in military circles – was a vital 'part of the stakes for which the belligerents are now fighting'.[17] Furthermore, Britain's allies never sought to downplay the military significance of the campaign. The Belgian and Portuguese governments knew from the outset that they were fighting for the retention of their African colonies, South Africa harboured ambitions for territorial expansion and an 'all red route' to Cairo, and many India Office officials saw the possibility of securing part of German East Africa as an outlet for Indian emigration as a prize that justified considerable sacrifice. As for Germany, the military authorities in Berlin deemed the conflict sufficiently important to risk sending two supply ships and – incredibly – a zeppelin to its beleaguered forces in East Africa. One British newspaper editor even went as far as saying that 'to the German, Africa is the key continent of the world. Its owners will possess the balance of power between the old world and the new.'[18]

There was, arguably, a hint of denial about the dismissive attitude among the British 'top brass' to what they were wont to refer to as the 'bow-and-arrow fighting', or game of 'tip and run', in Africa. Many a British general of the Great War had cut his teeth on the African continent – Kitchener, Haig, French, Roberts, Hamilton, Allenby, and Smith-Dorrien, to name but a few – and yet the collective experience of the British military establishment had not resulted in many lessons being learnt about African warfare (whether against 'natives' or another European power). It was as if the Anglo-South African War was an aberration, a 'White Man's War' in Africa that could not possibly recur and therefore need not be exhaustively pored over for lessons for the future. But the German General Staff studied that same war closely, with the result that German *Schutztruppe* commanders and NCOs in Africa were instructed to become well versed in fighting 'mobile', as opposed to static, wars and dealing with the Sisyphean logistical and medical challenges inherent in such warfare.

It was ironic that German commanders sought to master the art of 'African' warfare so much more actively than their future enemies when it was a Briton, Colonel Charles Callwell, who had written the classic manual *Small Wars: Their Principles and Practice*. Indeed in the first decade of the twentieth century, while the rest of the world turned a blind eye, German colonial troops honed scorched earth and bush warfare tactics against the indigenous inhabitants of German South-West Africa and German East Africa with a single-mindedness that Kitchener had been neither willing nor able to contemplate in the Anglo-South African War – with results that can only be termed genocidal. Such thoroughness also ensured that Germany's larger African colonies, in marked contrast to Britain's, had mobilisation procedures in place which in 1914 would prove every bit as effective at countering aggression from a colonial neighbour as they had for suppressing indigenous uprisings.

Among the German officers to have served in the campaign which virtually exterminated the Herero and Nama peoples of German South-West Africa in 1904–7 was one Paul von Lettow-Vorbeck, who by 1914 had risen to the rank of Colonel and commander-in-chief of the *Schutztruppe* in German East Africa. Von Lettow-Vorbeck's four-year defiance of overwhelmingly superior forces – more than 150,000 Allied troops and one million military carriers were engaged during the campaign in trying to bring to heel a foe one tenth the size – earned him the reputation among friend and foe alike as 'one of the greatest guerrilla leaders in history'[19] and the embodiment of all that was deemed 'admirable' about Prussian militarism in the pre-war era. His obduracy and success in playing 'a lone hand to the last card in a hopeless game'[20] were certainly extraordinary. Von Lettow-Vorbeck exploited to the full the advantages that could, with appropriate weaponry and skill, be found in defence, and he had a much greater understanding than his opponents of the insignificance of conventional objectives in African warfare. The loss of individual towns, ports, mountain ranges, and railways – prized by Allied generals desperate to register tangible successes – were of little consequence to him: all that mattered was keeping the Imperial flag flying *somewhere*, and causing maximum inconvenience to the enemy. But after the war there were also many who believed, with the benefit of hindsight, that von Lettow-Vorbeck's 'extreme sense of duty ... bordered on fanaticism';[21] and the appalling consequences of his strategy, however justifiable in his own eyes, were subjected to close examination at Versailles in 1919. Once again the future of Africa mattered, and although von Lettow-Vorbeck's reputation as 'one of the few German commanders ... who have fought clean throughout'[22] and who had 'played the game'[23] survived the Peace Conference largely intact, Germany's reputation as a colonial power did not. Amid universal condemnation of the 'frightfulness' of German rule in Africa, Germany was summarily dispossessed of her colonies and the dreams of creating a vast second Fatherland in Africa – a fundamental war aim – lay in ruins.

Despite the great importance attached to 'colonial questions' at Versailles, very little was known in Europe about what exactly had happened in the East Africa campaign: when the editors of the *Cape Times* called (unsuccessfully) for the instigation of a Commission of Enquiry in 1919, they complained that it had been conducted behind 'an almost impenetrable veil of secrecy'.[24] No newspaper had published handy sets of maps and flags for children to follow the progress of this war, as they had done for the Anglo-South African War and the war in Europe. In some respects this was unsurprising. The war in Europe inevitably dominated the public consciousness. But one booklet boldly (and correctly) ventured the opinion that 'if there had been no war in Europe the campaigns in the German colonies would have compelled the interest of the whole world'.[25] Using any yardstick but the war in Europe, the scale and scope of the conflict was gargantuan; and it produced cameos of extraordinary courage and preposterous improvisation on land, on sea, and in the air, that rivalled anything witnessed in the 'main shows'. Furthermore, the accounts of many a former combatant would attest to the fact that 'there is no form of warfare that requires so much inherent pluck in the individual as bush fighting'; to the terrible loneliness which 'tested the nerves of the bravest';[26] and to the horrors of fighting through the rainy season of early 1917, when the conditions made men question 'if any of the millions who took up arms between 1914 and 1918 ... endured much greater hardships'.[27] This was a war which 'involved having to fight nature in a mood that very few have experienced and will scarcely believe'.[28] It was really only the 'bush humour' (a counterpart to the 'trench humour' of the Western Front), the *absurdity* of fighting a war in as hostile an environment as could be imagined, and the odd episode of high adventure that were destined to permeate the public imagination (and provide the inspiration for C.S. Forester's *The African Queen*, Wilbur Smith's *Shout At The Devil*, William Boyd's Booker Prize-nominated *An Ice-Cream War*, and even *The Young Indiana Jones and the River of Death*, *Tarzan The Untamed* and *Tarzan The Terrible*).

The voices and memorials of the Great War in East Africa are predominantly European. But African combatants and carriers called upon to march twenty miles a day for months on end, in searing heat and through pouring rain, subsisting on minimal rations and with only the most rudimentary medical resources, would undoubtedly have concurred with the sentiment expressed by one young British officer. In 1914 Lieutenant Lewis had witnessed the slaughter of every single man in his half-battalion on the Western Front and had experienced all the horrors of trench warfare. Yet sixteen months later, in a letter sent to his mother from the East African 'front', Lewis wrote 'I would rather be in France than here'.[29]

Imagine a country three times the size of Germany, mostly covered by dense bush, with no roads and only two railways, and either sweltering under a tropical sun or swept by torrential rain which makes the friable soil impassable to wheeled traffic; a country with occasional wide and swampy areas interspersed with arid areas where water is often more precious than gold; in which man rots with malaria and suffers torments from insect pests; in which animals die wholesale from the ravages of the tse-tse fly; where crocodiles and lions seize unwary porters, giraffes destroy telegraph lines, elephants damage tracks, hippopotami attack boats, rhinoceroses charge troops on the march, and bees put whole battalions to flight. Such was German East Africa in 1914–18.

H.L. Pritchard (ed.),
History of the Royal Corps of Engineers, Vol. VII, p. 107

PART ONE

1914

OFFICER'S VOICE IN THE OFFING: 'Pass the word down, Corporal
Higginbotham, to advance in rushes of twenty paces, not firing till ordered and
not exposing yourselves to danger.'

(Corpl. Higginbotham wishes himself somewhere in – France.)

Steam down to Tanga
Over the briny main
See our Major-General
And his brilliant train.
Three brigade commanders
Colonels, staff galore;
Majors count for little,
Captains they ignore.

Earnestly they study
Each his little book
Which, compiled in Simla,
Tells him where to look.
Local knowledge needed?
Native scouts of use?
For so quaint a notion
There is small excuse.

See them shortly landing
At the chosen spot,
Find the local climate
Just a trifle hot.
Foes unsympathetic,
Maxims on them train
Careful first to signal
Range to ascertain.

Ping, ping, go the bullets
Crash! Explode the shells,
Major-General's worried
Thinks its just as well
Not to move too rashly
While he's in the dark
What's the strength opposing?
Orders re-embark.

Back to old Mombasa
Steams B force again
Are these generals ruffled?
Not the smallest grain.
Martial regulations
Inform us day by day.
They may have foozled Tanga
But they've taken BEA.

Poem by W. Monson,
a government official in British East Africa.

ONE

'The Germans Open the Ball'[1]

———•———

'Tipsified Pumgirdles Germany Novel' was the wording of the telegram
which had Mr Webb reaching for his code book on 5 August 1914. As
District Commissioner at Karonga, the headquarters of the Ross-Adam
Trading Company in northern Nyasaland, he had been told a few days earlier
that he might receive just such a message. A minute later he was certain of
its meaning, and began despatching messengers to all outlying European
settlements in his district. On the shores of Lake Nyasa one of the less fortunate
ones was received with 'ribald suggestions'[2] from two planters whom he had
surprised midway through a gargantuan drinking session. The news he
brought seemed barely credible: Webb had been informed that a state of war
existed between Britain and Germany.

All across East Africa the initial disbelief soon gave way to shock. In
Dar-es-Salaam, the capital of German East Africa, the thousand or so European
residents had spent weeks putting the final touches to preparations for a grand
exhibition to mark the twenty-fifth anniversary of the *Schutztruppe*, and the
completion of the 780-mile Central Railway which now connected the capital
with Lake Tanganyika. Regattas, sailing matches, beer evenings and an open
day on the railway were all part of the plans which were to have culminated
in a Grand Ball on 30 August. Crown Prince Wilhelm himself was to have
been patron, an aeroplane had been shipped from German South-West Africa
to do aerial displays, and the 6,300-ton SS *Feldmarschall* had arrived laden
with provisions – but the advent of war had now ruined what should have
been the greatest month in the life of the colony. It had also come as a rude
'interruption' to colonial life in Nairobi, the capital of British East Africa. The
Muthaiga Club had opened that summer, boasting the best cellar in Africa, a
shop which sold dreamy luxuries like Charbonnel et Walker chocolates, and
a head chef from the Bombay Yacht Club. At its first fancy dress ball, attended
by no fewer than 150 guests, Miss Henderson had been much admired for her
Apache outfit, as were Mrs Hodgkinson (as Bo-Peep) and Mrs Gilkes (who
came as a magpie). In the small towns of both colonies the prospect of
hostilities was initially greeted with sceptical humour: the clenched fist of

German East Africa was, after all, surrounded by hostile British territories (British East Africa, Uganda, Northern Rhodesia and Nyasaland), an ocean over which the Royal Navy held sway, or colonies of ostensibly neutral European Powers (Belgian Congo and Portuguese East Africa) whose sympathies were thought unlikely to be pro-German.

Neither colony was on a war footing, although British settlers would subsequently speculate that their German neighbours' cancelled celebrations had been nothing more than a smokescreen for stocking the colony with war materials; and their respective Governors were both aware that the 1885 Berlin Act excluded the colonies of the so-called 'Congo Basin' from any 'universal war', not least on the grounds that the spectacle of a war between European states on African soil might undermine white 'prestige' and lead to 'native unrest'. Above all, it seemed impossible that war would break out for the simple reason that neither colony appeared to have the prerequisite resources for a fight. There were just seventeen companies of the King's African Rifles (KAR) in British East Africa and Uganda, comprising 2,400 officers and *askari*; the full complement of German East Africa's colonial troops amounted to 216 officers and 2,540 *askari* (see Appendix One); and the purpose of all these troops was the maintenance of internal security in the three principal colonies of East Africa, which encompassed almost three-quarters of a million square miles.

On the eve of war tension between British and German settlers, even between British and German colonial governments, simply did not exist. As one Nairobi wag put it, British East Africa 'was not prepared. Why should it have been, with a German colony cheek-by-jowl across the border? Had German East Africa . . . been removed some thousands of miles away it is just possible that elaborate military arrangements would have been made years ahead in contemplation of a raid from it in the future. But German East Africa was much too near to be dangerous. Just a handful of comrades who spoke German, over the border as it were . . . So nobody worried. There was nothing to worry about.'[3] But the war in Europe immediately created a climate of fear and suspicion, and by mid August it had ignited outright hostilities in eastern Africa.

The catalyst for this improbable strife was a single nine-year-old German light cruiser, the 3,600-ton *Königsberg*, which had put to sea from Dar-es-Salaam on 31 July (and was rumoured, among the port's civilian population, to be bound for the Mediterranean). Her captain, Max Looff, had been warned of the possibility of war and had no intention of being trapped by the Royal Navy in German East Africa's 'Haven of Peace'. According to one of his signalmen, Looff told his crew that he 'would not seek battle' but that they should all be at the ready 'to defend ourselves if necessary'.[4] The escape was timely: that night the *Königsberg* passed within a few thousand yards of two British cruisers from the Cape Station on their annual 'East Coast summer cruise'. In the darkness Looff showed the older British ships a clean pair of heels but, as a midshipman on HMS *Hyacinth* later suggested, it would only have required 'one nervous gunlayer to press his trigger and [the First World War] might have started four days earlier'.[5]

Although he was at sea, and not trapped in port, Captain Looff's predicament was an unenviable one. The German Imperial Navy had never displayed any great enthusiasm for the Kaiser's colonies, which had been acquired for reasons that had little to do with its own strategic interests, and colonies were a nuisance. In a bygone era it had been required to enforce the anti-slavery blockade of East Africa (acting in conjunction with the Royal Navy); and on two occasions serious rebellions against German rule had called for a naval presence. But since Germany had abandoned its strategy of using its colonies as *Stützpunkte* – bases – for numerous commerce raiders a decade earlier, in favour of a concentration on the Home Fleet, the Imperial Navy had ceased to present much of a threat to the British Empire in distant waters. In August 1914 only a handful of German warships therefore roamed south of the Equator, and Looff's sentiments mirrored those of Admiral von Spee, commanding Germany's South Atlantic squadron: 'I am quite homeless', wrote the latter, '[and] cannot reach Germany. We possess no other secure harbour. I must plough the seas of the world doing as much mischief as I can, until my ammunition is exhausted, or a foe far superior in power succeeds in catching me.'[6]

On 5 August Heinrich Schnee, German East Africa's Governor, closed the door on Looff and the *Königsberg*. On 23 July he had been informed by the *Reichskolonialamt* – the Colonial Office – in Berlin that 'the Imperial Navy [did] not intend to protect places on the coast of the German Protectorates' in the event of war and his instructions were explicit: to ensure 'that no pretext . . . be offered to hostile naval forces for the bombardment of our undefended maritime places'[7] by declaring his colony's ports 'open'. This he duly did. A floating dock was sunk in the narrow entrance to Dar-es-Salaam harbour to prevent its use by any warship, he gave undertakings to the Royal Navy that all German vessels in the harbour would be considered British prizes, ordered the company of troops garrisoning the capital to abandon the town, and made preparations to move his seat of government 100 miles inland to Morogoro. All in all, Schnee *seemed* to be carrying out his task meticulously and allowing a 4,900-ton collier, the *König*, to leave port with coal for the *Königsberg* may have been nothing more than the result of an oversight which was quickly rectified by the Royal Navy when the *König* was turned back to port. But further 'oversights' followed. Two pinnaces from the SS *Feldmarschall* and a steamer, the *Rovuma*, were not intercepted as they made their way south to the Rufiji delta laden with coal and other supplies to await a possible rendezvous with the *Königsberg*; in ordering the mobilisation of the colony's

Schutztruppe Schnee made Dar-es-Salaam's railway station, which would facilitate troop movements along the Central Railway, a legitimate target for the Royal Navy; and he did nothing to disable the city's high-powered wireless installation, which was capable of communicating with the *Königsberg*. Schnee certainly resented the Royal Navy's overbearing presence, and the conditions created by war were chaotic. But he was a lawyer by training, fully conversant with the definition of an 'open port' contained in the 1907 Hague Convention, and he was therefore either acting naïvely or taking considerable risks in his interpretation of the Convention. As he was a man who, according to his Anglo-Irish wife, took decisions 'after judging the risks ... with calm consideration, displaying iron will and vigour',[8] Schnee's actions were almost certainly in the latter category.

Had the *Königsberg* been swiftly apprehended by the Royal Navy, whose orders were to neutralise all threats to shipping in the southern hemisphere, Schnee's brinkmanship would have mattered little. On 6 August, however, the *Königsberg* captured the *City of Winchester*, newly built at a cost of £400,000 (£20m in today's money), in the Gulf of Aden. It was the British Empire's first merchant shipping loss of the war, confirmation that Looff's vessel was a menace to Allied shipping in the Indian Ocean, and as such implicated its most recent home port – Dar-es-Salaam – in an act of war if it had not satisfied the 'open port' conditions of the Hague Convention (which it had not). Reprisals were immediately planned by the Royal Navy, and on 8 and 9 August Dar-es-Salaam's wireless installation and railway station were subjected to bombardment by HMS *Pegasus* and HMS *Astraea*. Schnee's reaction was variously described as one of surprise and one of complete outrage as he ordered the destruction of the wireless station and the scuttling of an armed survey ship, the *Möwe*, in a belated attempt to achieve full compliance with the 'open port' rules.[*] It was a disingenuous response. Dar-es-Salaam was no more open than Dover. But the naval bombardment was seized upon by German East Africa's military and civilian authorities as an unprovoked act of aggression on a par with Belgium's refusal to allow the free passage of German troops into France.

With the bombardment of Dar-es-Salaam, and the reaction it provoked

---

* The Royal Navy's bombardment of Dar-es-Salaam was defensible under the stipulations of Chapter 1 of the *Memorandum Concerning the 2nd International Hague Peace Conference of 1907* (the 'Hague Convention'). Schnee's decision to destroy the wireless station was attributed by von Lettow-Vorbeck to 'a rather excessive fear of its falling into the enemy's hands' (Lettow-Vorbeck (1), p. 27). It was soon rendered serviceable again by Chief Postmaster Rothe, who erected a new aerial disguised as a palm tree, but contact with Berlin became more problematic and intermittent after the intermediate station in Togo was captured and the one at Windhuk, in German South-West Africa, was destroyed.

among the more bellicose quarters in German East Africa, the likelihood of the war at sea spreading to land suddenly became a very real possibility. Indeed this had already occurred in West Africa where, on 7 August, Regimental Sergeant-Major Alhaji Grunshi had gained lasting notoriety by being the first British soldier to fire a shot in anger in World War I as joint operations commenced to eliminate any naval threat emanating from Togo and destroy the German colony's high-power wireless station at Kamina. As far as German East Africa was concerned Schnee's orders from Berlin stipulated that, having established the neutrality of the colony's ports, he should mobilise the *Schutztruppe* for 'a defence of the rest of the Protectorate'[9] in the event of attack and intern all British subjects in the colony. Schnee had followed these instructions to the letter, and issued a decree on 5 August telling the colony's 5,000 or so Germans that it was 'expected that we too [defend] to the death the soil of German East Africa entrusted to us'.[10]

With that he had summoned Major Kepler, the acting commander of the *Schutztruppe* in Dar-es-Salaam, and Colonel von Lettow-Vorbeck, the commander-in-chief of the *Schutztruppe*, for consultations. Schnee's principal concern was that no action should be taken that would jeopardise the bright future he envisaged for German East Africa, which had generated revenue of 120 million Marks (£330m in today's money) in the decade prior to 1914, or compromise internal security. There had been two major rebellions in the colony's short history, the most recent only a decade previously; and Schnee recognised, rather prosaically, that a number of tribes among German East Africa's eight million indigenous population had 'a certain tendency towards belligerence'.[11]

As forty-two-year-old Schnee was the supreme authority in the colony, he had every justification for expecting that his plans for defence would be obeyed without question. But in suggesting that 'the exact orders for the troops in the event of them having to be mobilised' were 'to be left to the discretion of the Governor as well as the commander [of the *Schutztruppe*][12] his superiors in Berlin had unwittingly placed Schnee in 'an extraordinarily difficult position'[13] due to the character of his 'commander'. Von Lettow-Vorbeck, 'tall, sinewy and blond with blue-grey eyes',[14] was a career soldier who had served in China during the Boxer Rebellion; had played a leading role in the 'pacification' of German South-West Africa in 1904–6, during which he lost the sight in his left eye;* and had commanded the Marine 2nd *Seebataillon* at Wilhelmshaven

---

* Legend had it that von Lettow-Vorbeck had a glass eye which, on one occasion, he lost in the bush. An *askari* returned it to him and enquired why the colonel had removed it. Von Lettow-Vorbeck's reply was that he had 'placed it there to watch that *askari* were doing their duty' (*The Nongqai*, May 1919, p. 202).

before his appointment as German East Africa's commander-in-chief in 1913. Schnee, far from being the slightly weak, 'quiet and peace-loving'[15] character portrayed by some accounts of the war, was a ruthlessly efficient, zealously patriotic and cunning official; but in von Lettow-Vorbeck he had met his match.

As a Prussian of the old school von Lettow-Vorbeck believed implicitly that the military was the First Estate, the buttress upon which the future of an embattled Fatherland rested. 'Military measures are exclusively military matters' was von Lettow-Vorbeck's dictum in dealing with Schnee, and from the outset he repeatedly reminded the Governor that he was 'not the leader of the *Schutztruppen*'.[16] A battle of wills that would even involve shouting matches had begun, as von Lettow-Vorbeck's 'lack of understanding for the administrative necessities of an overseas colony changed', in the opinion of Dr Solf, the German Colonial Secretary, 'into a blatant grudge against the Governor'.[17] Both men were in complete agreement that it was their 'duty ... to do all in our power for our country'.[18] But they disagreed vehemently about how this should best be done. Von Lettow-Vorbeck's opinion on ceding control of German East Africa's ports to the Royal Navy was that such a strategy, and Berlin's assertion that 'their eventual seizure may be without influence on the defence of the rest of the Protectorate',[19] were absurd; and that the pre-war mobilisation plan, involving a retreat to the interior, was not an appropriate response to the advent of 'universal war'.* He was also convinced that it was only a matter of time before Britain invaded the colony, and that its interpretation of 'defence' should therefore be rather more Machiavellian than that envisaged by Schnee.

To begin with, von Lettow-Vorbeck, by his own admission, 'did not succeed in interesting all authorities'[20] in his plans, and the civilian population was distinctly non-belligerent. But he pressed on with preparations to defend the *coast* even if Schnee insisted that *ports* remain open. On 8 August a British internee, Mr Russell, watched as a trainload of concrete destined for coastal fortifications collided with one carrying cattle at Pugu station, just a dozen miles inland from Dar-es-Salaam; and later that day the naval bombardment of Dar-es-Salaam considerably strengthened von Lettow-Vorbeck's hand. In the ensuing mêlée, Russell managed to escape in a canoe and reach safety aboard HMS *Pegasus*, where he was able to report the words of a German officer he had encountered at Pugu: 'we take war just as serious[ly] as an

---

* Von Lettow-Vorbeck was convinced that an open port policy meant that 'Dar-es-Salaam and Tanga ... the termini of our railways and the obvious bases for hostile operations from the coast towards the interior, would fall into the enemy's hands without a struggle' (Lettow-Vorbeck (1), p. 21).

Englishman takes his golf'.[21] Bombardment or no bombardment, von Lettow-Vorbeck was endeavouring to imbue the colony with what he described as the 'warlike spirit without which the fulfilment of our task was simply impossible'.[22]

Schnee offered no objection to von Lettow-Vorbeck's plan to move seven companies to Konduchi, a day's march north of the port, in order to oppose any attempt by the Royal Navy to land British troops there; nor did he object to the opposition offered by Lieutenant von Chappuis's 17th *Feldkompanie* (17/FK) to a Royal Navy inspection party when it tried to land at the ancient slaving port of Bagamoyo on 23 August; and he personally authorised the *Somali* to leave Dar-es-Salaam on 13 August with coal and provisions for the *Königsberg*. All in all there was seemingly no difference of opinion between the two men about the need to defend German East Africa – but the source of their mutual antagonism was von Lettow-Vorbeck's obvious determination to 'assume control of the [civilian] executive'[23] and sole responsibility for conducting any 'negotiations with the enemy'.[24] A palace coup was under way, mounted by von Lettow-Vorbeck against the man he began sarcastically to refer to as 'the holder of supreme power'.[25]

On 15 August the German commander-in-chief decided to 'open the ball' on land by ordering reservists Captain Tom von Prince and former artillery officer Captain Albrecht Hering to capture Taveta, a 'valuable sally-port'[26] a dozen miles inside British East Africa, with a force of *askari* and European volunteers 300-strong.[*] In so doing, Herr Bröker, a government forester, became the first casualty of the war on enemy soil; but that was the only cost to von Lettow-Vorbeck in seeing off Mr La Fontaine, Taveta's Acting District Commissioner, and securing control of the corridor between the foothills of Mt Kilimanjaro and the North Pare Mountains into German East Africa. The operation was no 'raid'. Once they were in Taveta, von Lettow-Vorbeck intended his troops to stay – ostensibly to 'defend' German settlements in the north-east of his colony and, in particular, the 278-mile Usambara Railway which ran from the port of Tanga to Moshi through the principal area of German settlement in the colony. By the end of the month, the deserted mission at Taveta was extensively fortified; a new bridge had been constructed over the Lumi River; and Salaita Hill, ten miles further into British territory and commanding the main approach to

---

[*] Ada Schnee, for one, believed that British troops from Uganda had invaded German territory south of the Kagera River before Taveta was seized (Ada Schnee, p. 16). This was untrue. An incursion into German East Africa at Buddu by 300 troops and 1,000 levies from Uganda did not take place until 17 August, two days after the 'Taveta Affair'. Other German sources cited the action against the *Hermann von Wissmann* on Lake Nyasa as predating the Taveta offensive, which was also not the case.

Taveta, had been seized and entrenched. As the topography of the area so favoured defence, von Lettow-Vorbeck knew that thenceforth he would require no more than a couple of hundred troops to prevent any attempted incursion by British troops from Voi, seventy miles to the east on the Uganda Railway, even by a force many times larger.

Schnee thought that his commander-in-chief must have taken leave of his senses before invading British East Africa. But within twenty-four hours von Lettow-Vorbeck's belief that the British were not only preoccupied with squaring the *Königsberg* was seemingly vindicated. A thousand miles south of Taveta, Dr Stier, the administrator at Neu Langenburg, was still unaware that a state of war existed between Britain and Germany for the simple reason that his principal means of communication with the outside world was via Nyasaland's telegraph – and the connection had been cut. But he had heard dark rumours and on 15 August sent a runner across the border to seek clarification from Mr Webb, his British counterpart at Karonga. His message read:

> Thanks to your extreme kindness in preventing the forwarding of despat-ches into our Colony, I am not clear whether England is at war with Germany or not. But I understand that you are mobilising your available forces ... If you therefore wish to attack our province, I must most cour-teously remark that we are prepared to greet you in a somewhat unfriendly fashion. The position decidedly needs clearing up and therefore I beg you most politely and urgently to let me have a clear answer.[27]

The next day the position was indeed clarified for Stier, though not by Mr Webb. On Lake Nyasa, the intense blue 'steamer parish'[28] of missionaries galore, a red-haired British skipper by the name of Captain Rhoades, who was renowned for his 'Rabelaisian wit' and 'unprintable songs', steered the 340-ton *Guendolen* into Sphinxhaven Bay, at the German end of the lake, and disabled the *Hermann von Wissmann* with a single shot from a range of 2,000 yards. His erstwhile drinking partner, the *von Wissmann's* Captain Berndt, immediately rowed out to the *Guendolen* to remonstrate with Rhoades, bel-lowing 'Gott for damn, Rhoades, vos you drunk?'[29] as he pulled alongside. Rhoades was not. His orders were to seize control of Lake Nyasa, and in so doing he scored what *The Times* hailed as the British Empire's first naval victory of the Great War. Berndt and his crew were, somewhat apologetically, 'put in the bag'.[30]

Von Lettow-Vorbeck's suspicions that British aggression would not be confined to offshore and onshore naval operations were in fact correct. If Sir Henry Conway Belfield, the fifty-seven-year-old Governor of British East Africa, seemed to share neither the enthusiasm for war displayed by the hundreds of settlers who had converged on Nairobi to enlist in the first week of August nor their bombastic reaction to the attack on Taveta, it was for good reason. He knew that the Committee of Imperial Defence in London had met on the first day of the war and approved a military expedition against Dar-es-Salaam as just one of five against German colonies around the globe.[*] Such a move, it was argued, would safeguard shipping lanes vital to the Allied war effort and provide colonial 'hostages' which would be of value when the war ended before Christmas. Belfield voiced his 'strong support' for these 'offensive measures'[31] and then sat back to await developments. It was true that his colony had been 'in a measure caught napping'[32] but, having only arrived in 1912, he did not consider that to be any fault of his; and as recently as July he had proposed a review of the colony's official Defence Scheme only to have to defer it because of the absence on leave of the 3rd King's African Rifles' commanding officer. He wasn't even sure that offensive measures would be necessary. Like many of his fellow officials, Belfield thought there was a good chance that the 'native issue' would soon prove the undoing of German East Africa if the country's troops and police were moved from their peacetime garrisons. His Director of Public Works, an old Africa hand, said as much when writing home on 7 August: 'the Germans have made such bloomers in the past that I guess they are now in the last stages of funk as to native uprisings in their country'; and ten days later he reported having heard rumours that 'the Governor of German East Africa is likely to make overtures to [British East Africa] to take his country over on account of the fear of native risings – which must be a very acute nightmare just now'.[33]

Schnee was not entertaining any thoughts of asking Belfield 'to take his country over', but when von Lettow-Vorbeck ordered *Schutztruppe* veteran Major Georg Kraut to begin concentrating troops in the north-east of the colony he did become extremely concerned about the possible consequences for internal security. Schnee's reaction to this potential threat, given the hostilities that had already occurred, was both surprising and audacious: citing 'native interests' as his chief concern, he secretly appealed to Walter Page, America's Ambassador in London, to broker a restoration of neutrality in all East African colonies in accordance with the 1885 Berlin Act. This was not the initiative of a pacifist liberal, but a shrewd lawyer and diplomat. It is inconceivable that Schnee expected any action by Page, but he knew that publication of his appeal could be extremely advantageous to Germany after

---

[*] Churchill, First Lord of the Admiralty, remarked on the anomaly of 'respectable Liberal politicians sitting down deliberately and with malice aforethought to plan the seizure of the German colonies in every part of the world . . . the whole world was surveyed, [and] six different expeditions approved' (see Forster, p. 75).

the war. If there was a 'native uprising', it could be blamed on British intransigence; if there was an escalation in the hostilities, it could be blamed on British aggression against 'peace-loving' Germany's presence in Africa; and if, by some extraordinary turn of events, a restoration of peace was brokered it would enable Schnee to reassert his authority over his commander-in-chief.

Von Lettow-Vorbeck was not informed of Schnee's neutrality initiative, although he was aware that 'many people believed that ... we were bound to remain neutral'.* As far as he was concerned neutrality would be to his enemies' advantage and he continued with his plans to 'threaten the enemy in his own territory',[34] thereby drawing off as many Allied troops as possible from other theatres of war and inflicting on them as much damage as possible. It was a strategy that Schnee considered grossly over-ambitious as the colony was cut off from any source of military and other vital supplies. But von Lettow-Vorbeck remained determined, stubborn and completely unperturbed about the possibility of insurrection.

One week after the 'Taveta Affair' and Captain Rhoades's attack on the *Hermann von Wissmann* von Lettow-Vorbeck turned his attention to German East Africa's still-neutral neighbours. He had rushed part of the crew of the scuttled *Möwe* 800 miles across the colony by rail to Lake Tanganyika in order to arm the 60-ton *Hedwig von Wissmann* with their ship's four pom-pom guns, and on 22 August the *Hedwig* attacked Lukuga, the principal lake port of Belgian Congo. Lieutenant Horn's orders were to destroy the only Belgian steamer on the lake, the *Alexandre Delcommune*, a mission he finally accomplished after two further raids. With that, German mastery over the 400-mile-long stretch of water on German East Africa's western border was secured. The neutral stance of the Belgian colonial authorities began to waiver, and by the end of the month their embattled government-in-exile in Le Havre had not only ordered the Congo's 15,000-strong paramilitary police force, the *Force Publique*, to assist British troops in their defence of Northern Rhodesia but also to undertake whatever *offensive* measures were deemed necessary for the maintenance of the territorial integrity of the Congo.

On 24 August it was the turn of Portuguese East Africa (today's Mozambique) to have its neutrality violated when German *askari* led by Staff surgeon Dr Weck attacked Maziua, a remote post 250 miles inland of Porto Amelia on the Rovuma River. Its commanding officer, Sergeant Costa of the military medical service, and a dozen Portuguese *askari* were killed in the

---

* Lettow-Vorbeck (I), p. 29; see also p. 19. 'The Congo Act ... only says that in case of conflict between two of the Powers concerned, a third Power may offer its good services as a mediator. But as far as I know this step was not taken by any Power. We were therefore not obliged to restrict our operations out of regard for any agreement.'

attack, a '*horroroso espectáculo*'[35] which caused immediate outrage in Portugal and was cited as definitive proof 'that war was the national industry of the Prussian'.[36] Dr Weck, who claimed to have found himself at Maziua while conducting a sleeping-sickness survey from nearby Sassawala, maintained that he had no idea that a war had broken out between the European Powers and had attacked because he thought Maziua had been overrun by 'rebels'.[37] The Portuguese government received an official apology from Berlin, but von Lettow-Vorbeck ordered 3/FK and 800 *ruga-ruga*, Angoni levies, to move south from the port of Lindi to the border with Portuguese East Africa just in case Portugal entertained any thoughts of exacting reprisals. Continuing nervousness on the part of the Portuguese was justifiable. Despite remaining neutral, on the other side of the continent in Portuguese West Africa (today's Angola) a frontier post was also attacked by a force from German South-West Africa in late October, and in December a full-scale battle was fought inside Portuguese territory at Naulila.

In the last week of August a German patrol was caught trying to blow up British East Africa's railway, which ran for a distance of almost 600 miles from Mombasa to Lake Victoria, at Mile 78; and other raids were launched towards Vanga (south of Mombasa), to the Ingito Hills (south-west of Lake Magadi), and forward to Bura from Taveta. However improbable it had seemed a month earlier, it was obvious that a war between the tiny European populations of East and Central Africa was under way.

Captain Looff had had a lean time of his foray in the Indian Ocean since capturing the *City of Winchester*. Reuters credited him with having sunk a dozen merchant ships off the coast of Arabia, and even with shelling the railway line running from French Somaliland to the highlands of Abyssinia. The truth was more prosaic: the *Königsberg* had found no further prey and the question of where to coal had become a recurring nightmare for Looff, eventually driving him south as far as Madagascar in the hope of finding a German collier or a coal-laden British merchant vessel. By the end of August his supplies of coal, and even meat and beer, were almost exhausted – despite having reprovisioned at sea from four German merchant vessels. He also urgently needed to undertake repairs somewhere onshore. But Dar-es-Salaam was no longer an option, and since the *Emden*, the sole German cruiser loose in the eastern Indian Ocean, had bombarded Madras earlier in the month the Royal Navy was likely to be more vigilant than ever. What was required, Looff concluded, was not so much a port as a hiding place.

On 3 September Ulrich Dankwarth, director of the forestry service at Salale in German East Africa's Rufiji delta, was considerably alarmed when his young African workers warned him of an imminent intrusion by a British cruiser into his otherwise peaceful existence. As a lieutenant in the colony's reserve, he grabbed his two hunting rifles and revolver and rushed to ascertain the nature of the intrusion. His alarm was unfounded: the 'British' warship soon identified itself as the *Königsberg* and Looff assured Dankwarth that he had no desire to disturb (or be disturbed). The timing of his arrival was fortuitous. Although the First Lord of the Admiralty, Winston Churchill, had ordered that the *Königsberg* be attacked wherever she was found, 'without regard to neutral waters',[38] HMS *Pegasus* had been left as the sole vessel patrolling the German East African coast and her skipper had his hands full simply policing the dhow traffic between Zanzibar and the mainland.

Two days later, by authorising that every assistance be given to Looff during his stay in the Rufiji delta, Schnee demonstrated the insincerity of his neutrality initiative. His letter had just reached Walter Page in London, but Page found that his initial soundings on its contents met with little enthusiasm. Attention in Britain was firmly focused on the German advance on Paris, only stopped at the River Marne in the second week of September, and Whitehall was convinced that neutrality in Africa would simply let Germany 'off the hook'. The Belgian government-in-exile was equally dismissive, having just had its country overrun and witnessed extensive atrocities committed against its civilians; so too was France. All in all 'colonial issues' were very low down European governments' lists of war priorities, and it was not until three months later that the British Foreign Secretary, Sir Edward Grey, wrote to Page saying that, in the light of the fighting that had already taken place, Schnee's proposal was no longer practicable. It was recognised for what it was – a *canard* (at best) or a cynical ruse – as Grey knew only too well: in early September his own brother Charles was severely wounded during a German assault on Kisii, on the British side of Lake Victoria, and before the campaign was over a second brother was killed by a lion while on active service.

Schnee's invocation of 'native interests' did, as he knew it would, attract *some* humanitarian interest in London and the prominent Fabian barrister R.C. Hawkin was still pressing for an end to the fighting in East Africa as late as the summer of 1915. On 30 June he wrote to *The Times* calling on the colonial powers to 'stop this suicidal policy of introducing our quarrels into Central Africa, and beware how we deal with a country which Nature has marked out as the home of the African'. But a note on the relevant Colonial Office file dismissed 'the idea that all warlike operations in Central Africa could be stopped at this stage' as being 'so manifestly ridiculous that it does not require much argument'.[39] More bizarrely, in answering a question on the subject in the House of Lords, Lord Cecil stated that 'the Berlin Act remains in force, except [in] so far as it has been abrogated'.[40]

It would later transpire that humanitarian interests could never have prevailed. Even as Schnee framed his proposal, his political masters at the *Reichskolonialamt* in Berlin were pursuing a very different tack to that of their representative in German East Africa. By 28 August 1914 Dr Solf, the Colonial Secretary, had drawn up a list of substantial annexations to be sought by Germany after winning the war. German intentions were clear: further colonial expansion, through the creation of a 'second Fatherland' in *Mittelafrika*, had become a fundamental war aim of Germany before Walter Page received Schnee's missive.

TWO

Phoney War

———◆———

Sir Henry Conway Belfield, the Governor of British East Africa, had not only the appearance but also the dwindling faculties and preoccupation with health matters of a much-loved grandfather. After a long career in the Malay States Nairobi was an exacting posting for a man in the twilight of his career. Its climate was infamously enervating, and the persistent (and vociferous) demands of its European settlers were a source of more or less continual friction with the Colonial Office. War simply complicated Belfield's life still further, and his role as commander-in-chief was not one to which he took with alacrity. His principal wish was that sufficient troops would be sent by the mother country to subdue his increasingly aggressive Teutonic neighbours swiftly. Then his life could revert to normal.

In the meantime the lack of authoritarianism and dynamism displayed by Belfield was in marked contrast to that of Schnee and von Lettow-Vorbeck. Although a lawyer by training, his enforcement of martial law was extraordinarily lax. Mail went largely uncensored during August and September, and the process of deporting German civilians resident in the colony did not begin until October. In German East Africa, a Greek discovered sending signals to British troops from the slopes of Mt Kilimanjaro was hanged within days of his capture. But a report of the existence of a German 'cell' operating from Kijabe Sanatorium, which overlooked the Uganda Railway less than fifty miles from Nairobi, was not followed up by the British authorities for months; even then the spies were merely deported, despite having been caught in possession of 20,000 rounds of ammunition and twenty-one assorted firearms. Belfield's oversights could not be attributed to British policy: on Zanzibar the censorship of civilian mail, and the rounding up and hanging of spies, began on the very first day of the war.

Given the overwhelming numerical superiority of German troops and weaponry, Belfield's initial refusal to let any government officials enlist was also ill-judged. Settlers, many of whom were former army officers or registered reservists, had emerged from the bush to sign up in droves in the first week in August, much to the Governor's surprise as he had no idea there were so many 'active, intelligent, and adventurous young officers . . . stationed on our side of the frontier'.[1] Yet even by the end of the month, when volunteers accounted for more than a third of the 1,622 rifles available for the colony's defence and the civilian population was well on the way to being fully mobilised, only a handful of officials with skills desperately needed by the newly formed intelligence, medical and veterinary corps had been released for military duty.* Meanwhile the majority of civil servants continued to draw their salaries and to take leave as the first settlers fell in combat. The antagonism this caused was considerable, the more so as the entire European population of British East Africa was no greater than 4,000 men, women and children – the size of a small town at 'home'.

Belfield's lackadaisical attitude and his overarching confidence in the imminent deliverance of a 'knock-out blow' to German East Africa soon became infectious. Mr Bremner, a mechanic in the railway workshops in Nairobi, wrote to his mother as early as 20 August telling her that 'we are going to take over German East Africa . . . eight battalions are coming from India to do the job';[2] and a Boer War veteran who had remained on his farm was roundly dismissive of German tactics in a letter to his sister written soon after the 'Taveta Affair'. 'I don't understand the German scheme of campaign in these parts,' he wrote; 'they seem to be sending small forces here there and everywhere – more like sort of raiding forces than forces attacking with any idea of conquest. I suppose they have been told by their Colonial Office to fight, and think that any old sort of fighting will do, knowing that it will all be the same in the long run.'† Most damaging of all was Belfield's failure to encourage reconnaissance across the border at a time when forays were still just possible.

Belfield's confidence was not entirely fanciful. On 25 August Germany lost its first colony in Africa when Togo surrendered to an Anglo-French expeditionary force, and on 1 September the 29th Punjabis, the first of more than 2,000 troops comprising Indian Expeditionary Force (IEF) 'C', arrived in Mombasa. The force was commanded by Brigadier-General 'Jimmie' Stewart, a former Commandant of the 5th Gurkha Rifles with a reputation for being 'a safe pair of hands'; and by 6 p.m. that same evening the first troops of the 29th Punjabis were already on a train bound for Voi accompanied by a 12-pdr naval gun from HMS *Fox*. Four companies of each of the Jhind,

* The 1911 census listed 2,022 European males (including children) as resident in British East Africa, of whom 632 government officials, railway staff and missionaries were excluded from military service. The male population had not increased significantly by 1914.
† RCS/Arnold Paice, letter to his sister, 30 August 1914. Paice expressed rather greater interest in this letter in the fact that a pig on a neighbouring farm had just, most unusually, devoured a mare.

Bharatpur, Kapurthala and Rampur Imperial Service Troops – the armed forces of independent Indian potentates – a Volunteer Maxim Gun Company, the Calcutta Field Battery and the 27th Mountain Battery followed, and by mid September had been ordered to take up positions protecting the Uganda Railway. (See Appendix Two.) IEF 'C' was not quite what Belfield had hoped for: due to the more pressing requirements of the war in Europe and the Middle East the invasion of German East Africa, originally planned for 28 August, had been delayed until more troops could be mustered in India. But it was sufficient for Belfield to declare the situation 'entirely satisfactory'[3] pending the despatch of a larger invasion force which would have 'every prospect of success'. His 'period of great anxiety'[4] seemed to be over.

The arrival of IEF 'C', of which he was fully aware, provided the final confirmation for von Lettow-Vorbeck that Britain intended to 'quietly snaffle'[5] German East Africa; and if his principal foe was underestimating both his resolve and ingenuity, that suited him well. In addition to his previous experience of campaigning in Africa von Lettow-Vorbeck had been entrusted by the Imperial General Staff with conducting a study of the military requirements of Germany's African colonies a decade before; and on arrival in German East Africa he had immediately set off on a reconnaissance of the entire country with a view to ensuring that its defence scheme was on a proper footing. With a trained force of just over 5,000 police and *askari* even before he had mobilised German East Africa's civilian reservists, he not only had a considerable superiority over British East Africa in manpower but also in machine-guns and artillery.* But the task of mobilising them to best advantage was fraught with complications as the troops were spread all over a colony encompassing almost 400,000 square miles – an area twice the size of the German *Reich* – whose borders were 'almost half as long again as all the [future] battle-fronts in Europe put together'.[6] Von Lettow-Vorbeck was therefore barely exaggerating when he claimed that to move a single company 'required about the same consideration as would a division in Germany'[7] and, although he had persuaded Schnee to agree to moving 'the bulk of our forces to the north-east',[8] he was yet to convince the Governor that the only role for the civilian government in war was one of unquestioning support for his strategy.

---

* According to Boell (1), p. 28 the *Schutztruppe* comprised 218 European officers and NCOs (of whom 130 were combatant and the remainder non-combatant medical and support services) and 2,542 *askari* (including two officers and 184 NCOs). In addition there were fifty-five European officers and NCOs and 2,160 *askari* in the paramilitary police, 1,670 European registered reservists, and the sailors from various *Deutsche Ostafrika-Linie* merchant vessels in Dar-es-Salaam who were rapidly incorporated into the *Schutztruppe*. The total male population of German East Africa listed in the 1913 census was 3,536, of whom most were German by birth.

By mid August the German field companies stationed at Dar-es-Salaam, Ujiji, Tabora, Usambara and Kissenyi were concentrated at Pugu, outside Dar-es-Salaam, and those from Kondoa-Irangi and Arusha at Moshi, to the south of Mt Kilimanjaro. But the next phase, marching the former grouping north, could not possibly be completed before September. Communications systems between HQ and the newly deployed units needed to be set up; a line of supply established from Morogoro to the north-east; roads had to be built from Morogoro to Korogwe, from Dodoma to Kondoa-Irangi through to Arusha; and a trolley-line built from Mombo to Handeni via Mkalamo.* All this took time, completely precluding a full-scale attack during August and providing the answer to a question posed subsequently by the editors of Nairobi's *The Leader*—namely, why 'the Germans did not take full advantage of their opportunity and wreck the Uganda railway, destroy the telegraph and occupy Voi and Mombasa, thus cutting off [British East Africa and Uganda] from outside help'.[9]

While all these preparations were under way, with increasingly enthusiastic assistance from civilians and government officials alike, von Lettow-Vorbeck was determined not to let the British consolidate their defences across the border. During September Taveta was used as the launch post for a multitude of daring German raids across waterless terrain to the Uganda Railway. Armoured trains were placed on the line and British troops patrolled the most vulnerable stretches closer to the coast as best they could, and sharp engagements occurred on the Tsavo River, at Mzima Springs and at Campi Ya Marabu between rival forces numbering hundreds of rifles. At night the task of the British patrols was particularly exacting, not least due to the presence of huge numbers of lions, and many of the German raids went undetected.

The closest that any incursion to British East Africa came to resembling a full-scale invasion was the advance of Captain Baumstark's 15/FK, 16/FK and 17/FK towards Mombasa in late September, wreaking havoc throughout the southern coastlands. Baumstark's 600 men were accompanied by the 'Arab Corps' of Mbarak, a slave trader whom the British had expelled some years earlier, and they began by attacking a British fort at Majoreni on 25 September. After putting up a stout defence its small garrison fell back on Gazi, only twenty-five miles south of Mombasa, to await reinforcements; and until they arrived the safety of Mombasa rested solely in the hands of Captain Wavell's British 'Arab Corps', 300 or so Swahilis raised from Mombasa jail and the bazaars of Malindi and Lamu.† For ten days Wavell and a small detachment

---

* When completed, a 'train' of thirty trucks, each carrying eight soldiers, and pushed by six men, could complete the sixty-mile journey in thirteen hours.
† Wavell was a former officer in the 60th Rifles who had made the pilgrimage to Mecca disguised as a Zanzibari and suffered imprisonment by the Turks in Yemen. He wrote *A Modern Pilgrimage to Mecca*, and was later regarded as 'British East Africa's T.E. Lawrence'.

of 3rd King's African Rifles (3/KAR) recently shipped by sea from Jubaland, the north-eastern province of British East Africa, resisted all German attempts to push on to Mombasa; but women and children were moved inland from the port, all specie was packed up, the Uganda Railway's rolling-stock was removed, and the Town Guard prepared for a visit from the *Königsberg*. On 8 October Baumstark launched what was to be his final attack on Gazi, only to be foiled by the arrival of Captain Hawthorn with three companies of 1/KAR. In the ensuing battle Wavell and Hawthorn were both severely wounded, but Baumstark was denied his 'golden opportunity'* to march on Mombasa and British troops pursued his force right back to Majoreni and Vanga. For the time being Mombasa, British East Africa's principal port and the railhead of the Uganda Railway, was safe.

September also witnessed attacks far to the west, the most alarming occurring when Captain Wilhelm Bock von Wülfingen, an officer who was visiting the colony from the *Schutztruppe* General Staff in Berlin, led 7/FK from Bukoba district and marched straight into British East Africa to seize the undefended British *boma* at Kisii, in the hills to the east of Lake Victoria. A prompt response by Captains Thornycroft and Lilley with three companies of 4/KAR saw Kisii retaken after a very fierce battle which cost Thornycroft and seven *askari* their lives, but grave concerns lingered about the likelihood of a follow-up attack on the Uganda Railway's terminus on Lake Victoria at nearby Kisumu.

In Uganda the situation was considered equally precarious. Even by comparison with British East Africa, it had been unprepared for participation in an inter-colonial war: in August 1914 two of the colony's four companies of 4/KAR were mounting an expedition against the Turkana in northern British East Africa and its tiny settler population was in no position to raise a volunteer force comparable to that of neighbouring British East Africa. The first three months of the war were therefore adjudged 'somewhat critical'¹⁰ in Uganda as the military authorities endeavoured to defend their 180-mile boundary with German East Africa with 200 European and Indian volunteers and 3,000 Baganda spearmen (with a further 15,000 in reserve). In contrast to the situation in British East Africa, a majority of government officials were also released for military service, and the combined defence force had succeeded in driving a large German detachment back over the Kagera River at the end of August. An elaborate system of watchposts along the river was then developed, and much-needed reinforcements were finally made available by the arrival of IEF 'C' in British East Africa. But even then Uganda's

---

* *The Leader*, 13 March 1915. That Mombasa was Baumstark's objective appears to be confirmed by German sources, for example the *Deutscher Kolonial-Atlas mit Jahrbuch 1918* (p. 23).

commanding officer judged the colony's defence plan with the words 'so much for the idea'.[11]

Not all the raids launched by German troops were at the direct behest of von Lettow-Vorbeck, who was fully occupied in effecting his troop concentration in the north-east. His personal diary merely noted the casualties resulting from Baumstark's action on the coast, and German officers in the more distant reaches of the colony continued to act with a considerable degree of independence.[*] One such action, led by *Schutztruppe* veteran Major Erich von Langenn-Steinkeller, exactly mirrored von Lettow-Vorbeck's capture of Taveta, a dozen miles inside British East Africa; and if equally successful it would have resulted not only in the seizure of control of the whole of British Nyasaland but would also have avenged the disabling of the *Hermann von Wissmann.*

Von Langenn-Steinkeller's sights were set on Karonga, whose District Commissioner, Mr Webb, had had a worrisome time since the 'naval victory' on Lake Nyasa. Nyasaland's entire European male population, in a country of one and a quarter million Africans, was just 500, so there was not much of a volunteer defence force to augment the presence of a company of 1/KAR as rumours of an impending attack from across the border grew increasingly persistent: the total number of men available to Captain Barton, commanding the company of 1/KAR, was only about 400. But on 7 September Barton decided on a sally towards the border, deliberately avoiding the main track along the lakeshore, to see if he could ascertain the intentions of the enemy's 5/FK stationed near Neu Langenburg.

At exactly the same time von Langenn-Steinkeller was leading 5/FK, supported by 500 African levies, across the Songwe River into Nyasaland at Ipiana. Part of his force, led by Lieutenant Aumann, looped to the west while von Langenn-Steinkeller headed straight down the lakeshore track. Eighteen miles of flat plain lay ahead of him and at some point on 8 September, with Barton's Nyasaland Field Force moving through wooded country a little to the west, the two passed within a mile of each other. Barton, unlike his German counterpart, learnt of the proximity to the enemy; but for reasons that would long be hotly debated he pressed on northwards leaving von Langenn-Steinkeller to continue on his way and attack Karonga, where Barton had left Lieutenant Bishop and a garrison of just seventy rifles, the next morning. The battle, like that at Kisii, was surprisingly fierce in the opinion of many a volunteer who had been lamenting that they seemed 'right out of the way of

---

[*] See, for example, Lettow-Vorbeck (1), p. 71. Von Lettow-Vorbeck seemingly only became aware of 'the existence' of what he called 'small bodies of troops' at Mwanza, Kigoma and Lindi 'after a considerable time'.

all the fun that [was] going on at home'.[12] Some would later say that it was an aged muzzle-loading cannon in Karonga which swung the tide, although its first shot had only 'carried the length of a tennis court';[13] altogether more decisive was the fact that when Barton first heard gunfire from the direction of Karonga he immediately despatched a relief column there. The reinforcements fell on the German force, over 800 strong, among the long grass and banana groves outside the settlement, and forced von Langenn-Steinkeller to retreat. On the road north his troops ran straight into Captain Barton's other columns, well concealed in the thickets either side of the road. The German force was routed: casualties among the African native levies were severe, but those incurred by 5/FK were a staggering seventy per cent. Among them, von Langenn-Steinkeller was himself seriously wounded and later lost the use of one eye. British casualties amounted to thirteen killed and forty-nine wounded in this rare example of a battle fought as both commanders were returning to base; and Lieutenant Bishop won the first Military Cross to be awarded in East Africa.

Northern Rhodesia was also seriously threatened for the first time in September, and its capacity for defence looked even more precarious than that of Nyasaland. As a British territory administered by the British South Africa Company, as opposed to the Colonial Office, it was not allowed to maintain a standing defence force and the outbreak of war with Germany found it with just five companies of African paramilitary police and two of district police – a total of 800 men – with which to counter any incursions. It was a tall order: Northern Rhodesia encompassed 275,000 square miles and its border with German East Africa, running from Abercorn to Fife, was 200 miles long. Nor were there many volunteers available as fewer than 2,300 Europeans resided among the country's 850,000 Africans.

The first attack on Northern Rhodesia came from the direction of Lake Tanganyika, controlled by the Germans since the sinking of the Belgian steamer the *Alexandre Delcommune*. As was the case at Kisii, the simultaneous assault was led by a chance visitor to German East Africa: retired General Wahle had recently arrived from Europe on the SS *Feldmarschall* and was enjoying a holiday with his son when war broke out. Now, having offered his services to von Lettow-Vorbeck, Wahle found himself leading a force of 100 *askari* and 250 *ruga-ruga* against Abercorn. Wahle's first attack was beaten off by the garrison's forty Northern Rhodesia Police *askari*, commanded by Lieutenant J.J. McCarthy, but the German troops then put Abercorn under siege and only after Major Stennett arrived with 100 reinforcements on 9 September – having completed a ninety-nine-mile march from Kasama in just sixty-six hours – was the town's safety assured. Stennett was awarded the DSO for his feat, and after Wahle was chased back across the border he was summoned to the north-east by von Lettow-Vorbeck to oversee the immense and complicated logistical requirements of the main German force.

Despite the success of the Northern Rhodesia Police *askari* in countering Wahle's incursion, it was clear that they would be unable to withstand a more determined attack. The Belgians in the Congo's mineral-rich Katanga province were therefore asked to provide assistance, and Major Olsen soon arrived with 500 *askari* of the *Force Publique* to bolster the Northern Rhodesian defences. Hundreds of miles to the south, where Northern Rhodesia marched with German South-West Africa along the so-called Caprivi Strip, the NRP also moved to counter any threat to Victoria Falls by seizing Schuckmannsburg in late September in a joint action with Southern Rhodesia's British South Africa Police. It was a horrifying outpost to have to occupy: Lieutenant O'Sullevan of the NRP lamented that the Caprivi bred 'the largest, most vindictive, and venomous mosquitoes I have seen ... in the wet season it is a swamp and unhealthy; in the dry weather the heat is terrific, whilst the sand is deep and uncomfortable to walk in';[14] but by the end of December, to the great relief of its garrison, the possibility of an attempt by German troops in South-West Africa to link up with their compatriots in East Africa appeared to have diminished.

The Belgians' decision to help their beleaguered British neighbours marked a significant watershed in their attitude to the mounting tensions in eastern Africa. The Congo's neutrality 'in perpetuity', enshrined in the 1885 Berlin Act and violated by the German attack on Lukuga, was becoming less maintainable by the day; and with the capture of Kwidjwi Island by German raiders on 24 September, an act which robbed Belgium of control of Lake Kivu, it became a dead letter. On 4 October Belgian troops launched their first overtly offensive action of the war, an unsuccessful attempt to oust German troops from Kissenyi, on the north shore of Lake Kivu.

These early battles in East Africa were described by Lewis Harcourt, the British Secretary of State for Colonies, as 'all very thrilling'. It was still widely assumed – on both sides – that the war in Europe would be over by Christmas and that a process of a political horse-trading would then see Germany's soon-to-be-invaded colonies handed back to their 'rightful owner'. But beneath its Gilbertian veneer the fighting had assumed a seriousness which few would recognise until much later. Longstanding, and intense, imperial rivalries had been rekindled; colonial ambitions were being reappraised; and the insouciant atmosphere of the first weeks of August was fast evaporating. At an engagement at Ingito Hills, south-east of Nairobi, the volunteer East African Mounted Rifles suffered twelve casualties in defeating – and inflicting substantially higher casualties on – a German raiding party led by Captain Tafel; and at Karonga British and German settlers had killed men with whom they had formerly shared a drink on the shores of Lake Nyasa or exchanged opinions on the forthcoming harvest. This made what Harcourt called 'the deadly work'[15] of the conflict a great deal more intimate than was true of the fighting in Europe, even if it was not on a comparable scale. Furthermore, African troops ostensibly raised for peacekeeping duties (and an increasing number of African civilians) were rapidly finding themselves involved in a fray which flew in the face of lofty European claims to be 'civilising' and developing Africa – and about whose origins they knew nothing.

While the fighting intensified on land the crew of the *Königsberg* made the most of their arrival in the Rufiji delta. Fresh fruit and vegetables aplenty were brought to Salale by German settlers, and news of the war in Europe was digested and then discussed for hours by the crew as they were given opportunities to relax on land after their month-long cruise. Swimming, however, was not popular as the Rufiji was swarming with crocodiles and hippos.

After a few days coal from Dar-es-Salaam and other ports began to arrive in an assortment of small craft sent by Schnee. This not only illustrated the ongoing 'flexibility' of his 'open port policy' but also involved considerable risk: the coal might be seized by the Royal Navy or, worse still, the whereabouts of Looff's cruiser might be detected. By the morning of 19 September, however, Looff had sufficient coal on board to enable him to put to sea again; and that same day he learnt that a lone British cruiser had put in to Zanzibar. It was just possible, he thought, that she had discovered the proximity of the *Königsberg* and was awaiting the arrival of other vessels before launching an attack. If that were the case, Looff decided that his best course of action would be to attack first.

The *Königsberg* was readied for battle in double-quick time, carefully navigated the shallow waters of the delta, and entered the open sea. Passing the Makatumbe lighthouse, at the entrance to Dar-es-Salaam harbour, Looff was able to fix his exact position one final time before darkness fell and was reminded of the indignity inflicted on the port by HMS *Astraea* and HMS *Pegasus*'s bombardment in August. He then checked the *Königsberg*'s speed to ensure that neither flames nor excessive smoke emanated from her funnels and set a course for Zanzibar.

The protection of Zanzibar's harbour, and of the aged 2,135-ton cruiser HMS *Pegasus*, was entrusted to two small government steamers, *Cupid* and *Khalifa* (which had formerly provided a ferry service between Aberdeen, the Shetlands and Orkney). Four navigable channels led to the harbour and at sunset every day the steamers began a nocturnal vigil on the seaward side of the two channels that were buoyed. On the night of 19 September *Cupid* was occupied transporting the clove harvest from the neighbouring island of Pemba to Zanzibar and had been replaced by a recently captured German vessel, the *Helmuth*, commanded by Lieutenant C.J. Charlewood. A Cape Horner at the age of seventeen and in peacetime an officer with the British India Line, Charlewood had felt 'some uneasiness' ever since *Pegasus*'s sister ship, HMS *Astraea*, had departed for the Cape five weeks earlier. At the start of the war it had been 'generally thought that the two cruisers in action together would prove more than a match for the *Königsberg* but that the enemy would not hesitate to engage either singly with a fair prospect of success'; yet now *Pegasus* was not only alone but undergoing repairs to her boilers.

At 5 a.m. the following morning *Helmuth* was on her way back to Zanzibar when a 'large vessel' was spotted approaching from the south. In the gloom Charlewood reckoned it must be the Union Castle liner he was expecting, although all merchant shipping had been instructed to use the northern approach to Zanzibar, and he changed course to meet the new arrival. As he did so dawn turned to daylight and he realised, to his horror, that the vessel had three funnels. He knew immediately, even before 'the German colours were broken from the foremast head and the peak of her gaff',[16] that he was staring straight at the rapidly approaching *Königsberg*.

The *Königsberg*'s crew had spent a tense night, even passing close by an unidentifiable British ship just after midnight. Looff did not think he had been spotted; at any rate no wireless message was sent from the ship to Zanzibar. By dawn the palm trees of his destination were visible to the naked eye, as was Tchumbe lighthouse, and then finally the port. The whole panorama was described to him by Walter Herm, the skipper of the *Somali*, who had volunteered to pilot the *Königsberg* on her mission through waters he knew well. To Looff's slight consternation a second large ship was docked near *Pegasus*, one of whose identity he was uncertain. But there was no time to dwell on it: he was now committed to his attack and a fraction of a second after his command – 'Salve! Feuer!' – his five starboard 4.1-inch guns opened fire from a distance of about six miles. Looff had no way of knowing that the *Pegasus* was immobilised while undergoing repairs, but when no answering fire came until he had loosed his seventh salvo it was clear that 'the surprise was total'. Under the command of Gunnery Officer Apel salvo after salvo was directed at the static target, the starboard gun-barrels 'reddening little by little' until Looff commenced a turn to bring his port guns to bear.

Less than half an hour after the commencement of the one-sided engagement Apel reported that he thought he saw a white flag being hoisted from

Pegasus, now enveloped in smoke and with flames shooting skywards from her deck. Apel's observation was received with incredulity by Looff who, convinced that 'Jack Tar' would not contemplate such 'ignominy', gave no quarter. White flag or no white flag,* after loosing off some fifty shells *Pegasus's* fifteen-year-old guns fell silent, and Looff finally realised that victory in the first duel of the war between British and German cruisers was his. He was ecstatic, subsequently invoking the words of Baron Börries von Münchhausen in his diary: 'The most powerful of all things is war! The most magnificent of all good things is victory!'[17]

The destruction of the *Pegasus* placed the *Helmuth*, and Charlewood, 'in a very unenviable position' as Looff surveyed Zanzibar harbour for other targets. Apel's first shell fell short of the *Helmuth* and the second went high. Charlewood 'did not wait for the third', and ordered all hands overboard. It struck him as 'humorous that I should be swimming in the sea while a naval battle was being waged in my immediate neighbourhood', but the deafening noise of *Königsberg's* exhaust and guns, the death of his Indian engineer for refusing to jump ship, and the fact that he was two miles from shore were anything but 'humorous'. His predicament worsened still further when the German cruiser turned and headed straight towards the floundering crew. It passed within feet, but just as Charlewood contemplated his imminent demise he heard a voice call out 'are you all right?'[18] – and a lifebuoy landed in the water nearby.

Looff stuck to his task for a few more minutes, shelling Zanzibar's wireless mast and other onshore targets and lobbing sand-filled petrol drums overboard to create the impression that he was laying mines.† For some inexplicable reason he left alone the 4,000-ton collier *Banffshire*, the vessel he had been unable to identify at dawn; and, had he but known of their existence, 30,000 cases of kerosene in a warehouse right on the harbour front presented another excellent target. Time was Looff's great concern: he knew he could not afford to linger a moment longer than necessary within Zanzibar's inner waters, especially with one engine having broken down and smoke suddenly visible

---

* Looff (1), pp. 57–8. The debate about whether a white flag was hoisted or not, implying that Looff had continued to fire on a vessel after the event, raged for years. Looff could not be certain, for the simple reason that 'as the flag came up the masthead it was gathered into a little box that served as gun control position for Hattersley-Smith, the gunnery lieutenant, and so subsequently for each sheet or pillowslip that was hoisted' (see IWM/McCall, a midshipman on *Hyacinth*). This caused the appearance, disappearance and reappearance of the flag which, given the smoke and flames pouring from the stricken *Pegasus*, understandably caused confusion.

† The *Königsberg* was entered in naval lists as a minelayer but, according to Looff, carried no mines at the time of the attack.

on the horizon. The approaching vessel, it later transpired, was only the *Gascon*, a Union Castle liner, and she fled back to Mombasa immediately after receiving a warning signal from Zanzibar.

By 3 p.m., having expended more than 270 irreplaceable shells from a magazine of 1,500, Looff had returned the *Königsberg* and his jubilant crew to their lair in the Rufiji delta. In his wake he left a scene of utter chaos. More than fifty of the crew of the *Pegasus* had been killed or wounded, the Admiralty wanted to know why Captain Ingles had not obeyed the order to ensure that his ship was never without steam 'on at least one engine',[19] and when smoke was seen off Mombasa a few days later one member of the Town Guard was heard to remark to another, 'now *we're* for it at last, old boy'.[20] Worse still for the Royal Navy, the news of *Pegasus*'s fate reached the Cape Station on the very same day as that of the sinking of the cruisers *Aboukir, Cressy* and *Hogue* by a German U-boat in the North Sea.

At the end of the first week in October German incursions into neighbouring territories all but ceased. The most obvious reason for this was that von Lettow-Vorbeck's strategy was, for the time being at least, a busted flush. Not one of the *Schutztruppe* company commanders had succeeded in routing their opponents, and half a dozen of his most senior officers had been seriously wounded during September – Schulz and Rothert at Tsavo, Tafel (at Ingito Hills), Wintgens (at Kissenyi), von Langenn-Steinkeller (at Karonga) and Bock von Wülfingen (at Kisii). Many of their attacks were simply badly planned and badly executed, and running battles tended to preclude taking advantage of the *Schutztruppe*'s overwhelmingly superior number of machine-guns. A further factor, however, was destined to be largely over-shadowed by a myth of invincibility that later surrounded the German *askari*: namely that the well-trained *askari* of the King's African Rifles excelled themselves on countless occasions in these early battles. Sergeant Gizau Wol-demariam of the Abyssinian company of 3/KAR won a bar for his DCM at Upper Rombo in August 1914; Sergeant Miyoiyou of 4/KAR was awarded the DCM at Kisii; Colour Sergeant-Major Sumani assumed command of his company of 1/KAR at Gazi after its two British officers were wounded, and was recommended for the same award; as was Sergeant George Williams for his reconnaissance work at Tsavo. At Campi Ya Marabu the conduct of Hagenas Abdul Ferag and Mohammed Fadulla was mentioned in despatches; and Lance-Corporal Ismail Takir proved himself a lethal force on a Maxim gun at Mzima. The list of examples of outstanding bravery was extensive.

Man for man the King's African Rifles, and the European volunteers who had taken to the field, had proved themselves the equals of their German opponents.

Von Lettow-Vorbeck also needed a pause in the hostilities while completing the complex process of concentrating troops in the north-east. General Wahle was appointed to establish the lines of communication from Morogoro, on the Central Railway, to Handeni; the light railway, or trolley-line, connecting Handeni to the Usambara Railway at Mombo had to be completed; Major Kraut, who knew the Kilimanjaro borderlands as well as anyone, having worked on the pre-war Anglo-German boundary commission, had to organise and redeploy the five field companies and 500 or so reservists in the Kilimanjaro area; and Captain Baumstark needed to regroup after the bruising experience of his thwarted advance towards Mombasa. Meanwhile von Lettow-Vorbeck established his headquarters at Moshi and set about reconnoitring Tanga district, with Captain Otto Adler, a retired officer of the 33rd Fusilier Regiment managing a sisal plantation near Tanga, and the District Commissioner, Dr Auracher. So certain was he that the imminently expected British invasion would occur there that only one company, Inspector of Police von Kornatzki's newly raised 18/FK, was left watching Dar-es-Salaam.

Although communications with the outside world had 'to all intents and purposes been cut off',[21] and the September battles had proved a harsh initiation for many a German reservist, morale in the colony rose considerably as von Lettow-Vorbeck's preparations neared completion. The sinking of the *Pegasus* was a further boon, as was the absence of 'unrest' which Schnee had feared the war might trigger among the Wahehe in the centre of the country or the Wachagga in Kilimanjaro district. 'Our troops have behaved courageously throughout', read a despatch of Schnee's which attested to the mood among the European population,

> [and] the supply of provisions and medical stores has worked well. A Red Cross Committee under the direction of Frau Schnee has collected considerable sums and have shown themselves very active. The health of the troops and population are on the whole favourable. The natives with the exception of the usual cattle looting expeditions from Warundi, which are being dealt with, have remained quiet. Their attitude has been with a few exceptions loyal; the Mohammedan population have shown themselves enthusiastic for German victory and have prayed for victory in the mosques. The supply of recruits from all parts of the colony was greater than could have been anticipated.[22]

Across the border in British East Africa no attempt was made to exploit the relative inactivity of the enemy. Both Belfield and Captain Cadell, an

Intelligence officer with IEF 'C', were so convinced that the imminent invasion of German East Africa would not encounter strong resistance that they made little effort to ascertain what, if anything, might be happening behind the German front lines around Taveta and on the coast; and government officials continued to conduct their business as if the war was no affair of theirs. News that the main expeditionary force was about to leave India was finally received in the second week in October and by the 12th even the manager of the Gazi Rubber Plantation Company knew that invasion of German East Africa was about to begin. It looked as if the 'East Africa Affair' would be over in a matter of weeks.

After countless delays and substantial last-minute alterations to its composition, the bulk of IEF 'B' sailed from Bombay in sweltering heat on 16 October. Their fourteen transports constituted only one third of the whole convoy which, escorted by HMSs *Goliath*, *Swiftsure* and *Dufferin*, was continuing the process of denuding India of troops; and yet more ships joined from Karachi two days later, creating 'a most impressive sight, the whole ocean being dotted with ships as far as the eye could see'.[23] Neither the War Office nor the Imperial General Staff were involved in the planning for the invasion of German East Africa. The principal responsibility lay with the Committee of Imperial Defence, the India Office and the Colonial Office; and the plan to seize Tanga before operating later against Dar-es-Salaam and the Central Railway was, in the words of one senior staff officer with IEF 'B', 'extremely ambitious'.[24] Above all, success would depend a great deal on the intelligence provided by Belfield, Captain Cadell, and Norman King – the former British Consul in Dar-es-Salaam; and that, as would soon be revealed, was far from comprehensive.

As the transports carrying IEF 'B' made their way towards East Africa, von Lettow-Vorbeck completed his troop deployments in the north-east. Two companies of European volunteers, the 7th and 8th *Schutzkompanie* (SchK), were based at Taveta; Major Kepler's *Abteilung*, or detachment – consisting of 4/FK, 8/FK, 9/FK and 13/FK – was based at Rombo, on the slopes of Mt Kilimanjaro; and at headquarters in New Moshi were Lieutenant Merensky's 1/FK, 6/FK and 6/SchK. A hundred miles north-west of Kilimanjaro Major Kraut held the mountain stronghold of Longido with 10/FK, 11/FK, 21/FK and 9/SchK; on the coast Captain Baumstark kept watch on the border and Tanga with 15/FK, 16/FK and 17/FK; 4/SchK and 5/SchK patrolled and protected the Usambara Railway, which ran through the north-east connecting the port of Tanga with Moshi, 190 miles distant. With these 3,500 men, all of whom could be rushed to the defence of others by the railway, von Lettow-Vorbeck awaited the arrival of up to 10,000 Indian troops.

THREE

'The Action of a Lunatic'*

The fourteen transports carrying Indian Expeditionary Force 'B' to East Africa peeled off from the rest of the convoy on 19 October and, with *Goliath* and *Hardinge* as escorts, shaped a course for Mombasa. (See Appendix Two.) The invasion force was over 8,000-strong and commanded by Major-General Arthur Aitken, who was wont to describe himself as a 'Red Hot Imperialist'. A cavalryman since 1882, Aitken had no experience of joint operations or of campaigning in Africa. Nor had he even met one of his two brigade generals, Brigadier-General Richard Wapshare, until just prior to departure; and Wapshare had never seen two of the four battalions in the 27th Bangalore Brigade under his command until the day before embarkation. The other half of the force comprised an Imperial Service Brigade, commanded by Brigadier-General Michael Tighe, who also had little previous knowledge of any his battalions. Four and a half of the expeditionary force's eight infantry battalions were deemed to have good reputations; but the 63rd Palamcottahs, 98th Infantry and 61st Pioneers were regarded as 'suspect' for being drawn from less 'martial' peoples of India. Whatever truth underlay these judgements, there was no escaping the fact that the force was very much a 'scissors and paste' affair whose agglomeration resulted from higher priorities in Europe and the Middle East. One senior officer, surveying it prior to embarkation, remarked that 'this campaign will either be a walk-over or a tragedy'.[1]

IEF 'B' appeared to be distinctly under-equipped for any major battle. It was issued with just fourteen machine-guns, and its small artillery capability consisted of just six guns of the 28th Mountain Battery. There were also countless anomalies in what had been provided: one transport, the *Rheinfels*, was laden with rolling-stock and two Railway Companies for the intended advance up the Usambara Railway, yet the expeditionary force lacked even a single regular company of sappers and miners.[2] But whatever its shortcomings, the force was colossal by comparison with what was thought to oppose it.

* RH/Bremner, letter of 11 November 1914: 'to land a large force without reconnaissance to see whether any of the enemy were about appears the action of a lunatic'.

With the exception of the Boer War it was, in fact, the largest British military expedition to have landed in sub-Saharan Africa since the 30,000-strong Napier Expedition had been sent to 'subdue' the Abyssinian emperor Theodore at Magdala in 1868.

The two-week voyage had been little short of a nightmare. The transports were grossly overcrowded and the swell nauseating at the convoy's cruising speed of seven knots. On the *Homayun*, carrying 1,000 men of the force's 'coolie corps' although its capacity was 800, the medical officer was appalled that there 'was barely room for the men to lie down side by side on the decks';[3] and as they had not been subjected to a medical inspection before leaving Karachi sickness, especially dysentery, spread through the ship in no time. On the *Assouan*, the 63rd Palamcottah Light Infantry had been on board and awaiting departure since 30 September, which meant that by the time the convoy was met by HMS *Fox* off Mombasa on 30 October the battalion had been at sea a full month. Even then their ordeal was not over. At a conference ashore with Belfield and recently promoted General Stewart, Aitken decided to proceed immediately against the port of Tanga on the north-east coast of German East Africa, without disembarking his force to recover from their voyage and reorganise, while Stewart prepared a diversion on the German border north-west of Mt Kilimanjaro. The intelligence gleaned from Norman King, the former British consul in Dar-es-Salaam (and designer of Tanga's nine-hole golf course), and Colonel Mackay, the senior Intelligence officer of IEF 'B', indicated that there was no reason to suppose that their assessment of the position in August needed reappraisal: it was still assumed that Tanga would be undefended, and that any resistance would only be encountered during the advance up the Usambara Railway through the heartland of German settlement towards Mt Kilimanjaro.

During the conference at Mombasa Captain Caulfeild, commanding HMS *Fox*, suggested to Aitken the possibility of splitting his force, effecting landings at Tanga and Dar-es-Salaam simultaneously.* This strategy, as von Lettow-Vorbeck later admitted, was what the German commander feared most because he had opted to leave Dar-es-Salaam virtually undefended. But HMS *Goliath* was experiencing engine trouble and, with no other reliable warship available to accompany a second landing, Aitken dismissed the suggestion. So great was his sense of urgency, having discovered that his mission was 'more or less

---

* Caulfeild had caused some concern to Brigadier-General Stewart when IEF 'C' had landed in East Africa in September. 'He was a rather strange fellow', wrote Stewart, '[who] assured me that he was fully acquainted with the situation, that there was no urgency about our arrival ... His appreciation of the situation proved very incorrect for a landing at Mombasa on Sept 1st: I found affairs were in a critical position and our Intelligence service, though rapidly improving, was rather vague.' (See Gurkha Museum/Stewart/5RGR/Appxi/14, p. 54.)

public property'* in British East Africa, that he also refused an offer of the services of a company of King's African Rifles and rejected a plan to blow up the Usambara Railway south of Moshi to stop German reinforcements being sent from Kilimanjaro to meet the landing at Tanga. Either might have served IEF 'B' well, but Aitken was set on following instructions from the Colonial and India Offices originally issued in August rather than displaying any great imagination or initiative; and he hoped that by executing them as rapidly as possible he might yet surprise his enemy.

A minor inconvenience was introduced when Caulfeild informed Aitken of his need to observe the 'open port' rules, which were being treated with rather greater respect by the Royal Navy than by Schnee. The Admiralty had never formally ratified the naval truce, but it had agreed unofficially that any warship in East African waters should always give notice to the German civilian authorities of any intention to bombard a port. The Royal Navy had no desire to stand accused of slaughtering innocent European civilians, and the likely effect of inflicting unnecessary casualties among the African population was an even greater concern: when German East Africa was invaded the Colonial Office wanted its African population loyal, not embittered. Aitken protested but agreed that Caulfeild could allow Dr Auracher, the senior administrator in Tanga, one hour in which he could decide whether he would surrender or face the consequences.† The British convoy would, after all, be out of sight of land when such a parley took place, and there would be no need to reveal to Auracher that a full-scale invasion was in the offing.

Before dawn on 2 November, the convoy carrying IEF 'B' reached a point fifteen miles off Tanga and Caulfeild ordered it to heave to while he took HMS *Fox* inshore. By the time Dr Auracher came on board under the white flag it was light. To the west the peaks of the Usambara Mountains were clearly visible, rising to heights of more than 7,500 feet above the coastal plain; the luxuriant vegetation of this humid stretch of coast extended as far as the eye could see to the north and south; and directly before Caulfeild lay the low coral cliffs on which stood the little port of Tanga, set in the midst of 'a

---

* It is a curious anomaly that while Aitken was told to expect no resistance the Governor of Nyasaland was being told that he need not fear another German invasion as all von Lettow-Vorbeck's troops were concentrated in the north-east of German East Africa (see IWM/Aitken report and TNA/WO/106/573).

† The consequences of observing the truce were to be greatly exaggerated by Aitken later. He already knew that the arrival of IEF 'B' was no secret in East Africa and had everything else gone according to plan one hour's notice was not going to make any difference. Hordern, the official historian of the campaign, was misled by Aitken's 'propaganda' when recording that it was 'a factor vitally affecting his plans' (p. 73). Besides, Aitken was not expecting any resistance and if he had been he could have ordered a landing at some other spot not covered by the truce, such as Mansa Bay to the north.

mighty grove of coconuts'.[4] Auracher was informed that if he did not surrender the port it would be bombarded. He was also asked if the harbour was mined, a question he refused to answer. At 8.30 a.m. he left HMS *Fox*, saying that he had to confer with his seniors before making a formal response, and returned to his office. There he donned his reservist's uniform, and telegraphed von Lettow-Vorbeck and Schnee to inform them not only of HMS *Fox*'s demands but also that, despite Caulfeild's precautions, a substantial convoy had been spotted proceeding down the coast at dawn and was known to be lurking offshore.

Auracher's change of clothing was evidence of the considerable extent to which von Lettow-Vorbeck had proved successful in subordinating the civilian authorities to the military. All over the colony a majority of Schnee's government officials now viewed von Lettow-Vorbeck as 'the supreme commander': the Postmaster-General, Wilhelm Rothe, and Government Secretary Franz Krüger had built the trolley-line connecting Handeni to Mombo (which was intended to facilitate a speedy retreat of the forces in the north-east to the area favoured by von Lettow-Vorbeck for the decisive battle); Schnee's personal secretary, Lieutenant Eckhard von Heyden-Linden, had abandoned him to rejoin the *Schutztruppe*; his former adjutant, Captain Alexander Freiherr von Hammerstein-Gesmold, had done likewise. It was therefore von Lettow-Vorbeck, not Schnee, who was going to decide the response to Caulfeild's ultimatum and, during his reconnaissance of Tanga in October, he had assured Auracher that he would 'assume the responsibility for any consequences that might ensue'[5] from defending the port. By 9.30 a.m. Auracher had given no answer to Caulfeild, and HMS *Fox* departed without bombarding Tanga: Aitken had no wish to see his base for the invasion of German East Africa razed to the ground.

However 'leaky' Aitken had discovered British East Africa to be, von Lettow-Vorbeck did not know beforehand that 2 November would be the day that HMS *Fox* and fourteen transports appeared off Tanga; and when, at 6 a.m., the convoy was first sighted by coastal lookouts attached to 17/FK the company's Standing Orders for the day stipulated that two of its platoons were to march to Mvumoni, near the border with British East Africa, leaving only a single platoon under reservist Lieutenant Kempner in the immediate vicinity of Tanga. After the appearance of HMS *Fox*, however, the orders were quickly altered by Captain Baumstark, commanding the German troops on the north-east coast. 17/FK marched straight to Tanga's police headquarters instead of Mvumoni while Kempner's platoon made its way to Ras Kasone, the spit at the eastern end of Tanga Bay, the better to observe the convoy from near the red-roofed house of Herr Böhm, the manager of a contiguous rubber plantation. When HMS *Fox* anchored half a mile offshore for its parley with

Auracher, Kempner, 'more and more certain that the enemy was contemplating a landing',[6] withdrew almost a mile to the south-west and then took up defensive position in the railway cutting east of the town. Fellow reservist Hans Baldamus, a road engineer, was sent forward on Kempner's left, from where he could keep a watch on the *Fox*. After the British warship departed the rest of the day was spent barricading the three bridges over the railway cutting, organising a firing line of two platoons in the cutting, and positioning the third platoon with two machine-guns behind its centre while some European volunteers from the town dug in behind the right wing. Kempner placed no troops in the town itself so, just as Aitken had been informed it would be, Tanga was to all intents and purposes undefended at dusk against any landing in its harbour. Just one German company of police led by Dr Auracher – now *Lieutenant* Auracher – and a handful of volunteers remained in the town to maintain public order, as they were allowed to under the terms of the naval 'truce'. The atmosphere in the European quarter of town, where just a few weeks earlier 'contented Germans' had enjoyed sitting in the squares 'placidly smoking and quaffing huge glasses of beer',[7] was tense.

Von Lettow-Vorbeck took some time to decide upon his course of action, and only Schnee's intervention put paid to a plan to destroy twenty-five miles of the railway running from Tanga inland to Moshi. He was concerned that the appearance of HMS *Fox* might be a feint, and that the convoy might proceed down the coast to attack Dar-es-Salaam or even land at both ports at the same time. But his hunch that he would have to stand and fight near Handeni in the north-east rather than on the Central Railway persisted, and after hours of consideration he dismissed the idea of a feint. It was a colossal gamble, albeit a calculated one: had Aitken opted to split his force, as Caulfeild had suggested, von Lettow-Vorbeck's name would probably have been soon forgotten. In mid afternoon, however, he issued orders for his troops in the north-east to converge on Tanga by forced march and rail. Not everything went as smoothly as he wanted. The telephone connection with Kraut's HQ at Longido, far to the north-west, was broken, and the Usambara Railway could only move one company at a time along its 190-mile narrow-gauge track. Logistical constraints therefore determined that only one and a half companies stationed at Moshi and the companies on railway guard duty were in a position to reach Tanga in less than twenty-four hours. If the British landed and deployed rapidly, von Lettow-Vorbeck's position was precarious. The best he could hope for was three or four companies, perhaps 700 rifles, to disrupt the landing of a force ten times the size.

Von Lettow-Vorbeck did not believe he had the slightest chance of actually preventing the landing of 8,000 British troops on German soil. But his lines of communication across the north-east were now in reasonable working order and, as a former commander of II *Seebataillon* at Wilhelmshaven, he was as familiar with landing exercises as he was experienced in colonial warfare. The opportunity clearly beckoned to disrupt the British landing as much as possible before withdrawing inland to fight where the terrain better suited him. Around Handeni one flank was protected by the Masai Steppe to the north-west, the other by the Usambara and Pare mountain ranges; and it took a substantial leap of the imagination to envisage General Stewart's troops being able to advance from Longido as far as the railhead of the Usambara Railway at Moshi, let alone to Handeni district, in less than a week.

No manual existed for joint operations such as Aitken and Caulfeild were attempting to undertake on an unfamiliar shore. But an inordinate length of time elapsed before the landing commenced. The process of observing the truce was not in itself a major delaying factor, HMS *Fox* having returned to the convoy through the notoriously treacherous reefs off Tanga by noon; nor was the ensuing conference between Captain Caulfeild and Aitken, which was over by 2.30 p.m. (after which Aitken spent the rest of the afternoon reading a novel on deck); nor was the one and a half hours it took to begin transferring troops from the transports to lighters; nor was the time taken by Lieutenant Charlewood's tug *Helmuth*, which had miraculously survived the *Königsberg*'s raid against Zanzibar, to sweep Tanga's inner harbour for mines. Taken cumulatively, however, these gave the impression of there being no sense of urgency whatsoever (for which Aitken would later lay the blame squarely at the feet of Caulfeild). Certain precautions had to be taken by the Royal Navy, but in insisting on altering the formation of the convoy prior to commencing the disembarkation process and only allowing three transports to be brought in at a time, Caulfeild's caution began to be viewed as excessive even by his own officers. Not until 10 p.m., six hours after leaving the anchorage out to sea, did the first troops board their lighters and make for the landing place on the seaward side of the promontory known as Ras Kasone (which had been chosen as an alternative landing place to the two beaches in the harbour itself until the *Helmuth*'s task was complete). Ras Kasone was well known to Lieutenant Ismail who, as a former manager of a rubber plantation outside Tanga, was the invasion force's only Intelligence officer with intimate pre-war knowledge of the town, and it had the advantage of being out of sight of Tanga. On the other hand its distance from the town, and the nature of the intervening terrain, were soon to prove distinctly disadvantageous.

By midnight Lieutenant Charlewood had finished his sweep for mines in

Tanga's inner harbours to the accompaniment of sporadic fire from a lone machine-gun onshore and increasing concern in some quarters about the slow pace of the operation. No enterprise was shown in attempting to land troops in the harbour that night, a task that would have been easy, whereas landing at Ras Kasone, designated Beach 'A', proved laborious even with the benefit of a bright moon: the 13th Rajputs and 61st Pioneers had to struggle on wobbly sea-legs through chest-high water and mangroves onto a beach only a couple of hundred yards wide, and then up a coral cliff face fifteen to twenty feet high. It was not until 4 a.m. that the 13th Rajputs, ably marshalled by Captain Seymour, were ready to advance on the town from Böhm's 'Red House' while a patrol of the 61st Pioneers occupied the nearby signal tower.*

Although the landing had encountered no serious opposition, a single volley of rifle fire being quickly silenced by the Rajputs' machine-guns and HMS *Fox*'s guns, further doubts about the conduct of the operation started to be felt. Captain Evans of the transport *Karmala*, for example, was not alone in speculating that 'if the enemy had been at all enterprising they might have mounted their Maxims on the cliffs above the beach and wiped out the whole force';[8] and there was frustration among the troops that little seemed to have been achieved in the twenty-four hours since the convoy's arrival off Tanga. But the situation could hardly be described as ominous. During the night Lieutenant Ismail and Lieutenant Russell, the former internee from German East Africa who had escaped from Dar-es-Salaam in August, had reconnoitred the ground between Ras Kasone and Tanga and although Ismail had been killed by a German patrol near the hospital, Russell had returned to his ship by 3 a.m. with the information that there was only one company of police in Tanga with three or four German officers or NCOs. As a result of his intelligence Aitken still regarded a bombardment of the town as unnecessary. Indeed he was so confident of snaffling the town without a fight that he took the decision for Tighe to advance when only one and a half of the three battalions allotted to take the town were ashore. They would, he was certain, be 'sufficient for the time [being]'.[9]

Mickey Tighe was an Irishman and a 'thruster' who had earned a fine reputation as a field commander in his thirty-one years in the Indian Army (and was the only general with IEF 'B' to have campaigned in East Africa before). It was said that 'the mere mention of a fight made his blue eyes sparkle with hope'.[10] By dawn he had established his headquarters at the 'Red House',

---

* The house had still been occupied earlier that night. According to Colonel Macpherson, commanding the Kashmiris, lamps were still burning, dinner was still on the table and there was an ice chest with cold beer and other drinks in it as well as parcels of 'comforts' ready for despatch to German troops in the north-east. These were 'promptly commandeered' (see NAM/Macpherson).

near the signal tower at Ras Kasone, and by 5 a.m. had ordered his troops to advance. The 13th Rajputs, half a battalion forward and the other half in reserve, were considered 'fighters' but the 61st Pioneers, also in reserve, were not. As pioneers, their task was the preparation of a base that would receive the main body of troops and their deployment in the initial advance was a further indication that Aitken expected no resistance (as was his failure to order the establishment of an ordnance field park at the landing place). Field Service Regulations ordered that such units should be used in combat 'only in an emergency, as a last resource'. Furthermore all the troops, combat and technical alike, had had a sleepless and exhausting night and were confronted by terrain of a type with which they were wholly unfamiliar. But 'all' they were required to do was establish themselves in Tanga and cover the landing of the main force in the harbour, after which the roll-up of von Lettow-Vorbeck's troops in the north-east could begin in earnest.

During the night Captain Adler had arrived at Mvumoni to take command of 17/FK, and it was he who had sent forward a single platoon from Tanga's railway cutting as the British landing commenced. The platoon was, as Captain Evans of the *Karmala* had feared, in possession of two machine-guns but after firing their volley of rifle shots and coming under fire from HMS *Fox*, it had retreated to its position above and behind the railway cutting. Only later did Adler realise his men had witnessed the first signs that British troops were 'making serious endeavours to land'[11] en masse, as opposed to merely reconnoitring, and when it dawned on him what might be occurring he immediately contacted Captain Baumstark, the district commander at Muhesa, twenty-five miles up the Usambara Railway, to say he would need immediate reinforcements. Adler was then told that 16/FK were at Amboni, just a few miles north-west of Tanga, and would be with him between 5 a.m. and 6 a.m. – just as Tighe began his advance towards Tanga.

Half an hour after setting out through the rubber plantation and some African dwellings interspersed with patches of cultivation, a Rajput patrol led by Captain Seymour had advanced a distance of some 2,000 yards to emerge right in front of the right wing of Adler's defences in the railway cutting. Their approach through 'dead ground'* had gone undetected but as soon as they were in the open they came under fire from the German defences and the Rajputs were forced to take cover. A report sent back to Tighe that there were two machine-guns in the railway cutting was 'received with scepticism',[12] and the order was given for the advance to resume.

---

* NAM/17/FK Field Report. By 'dead ground' Adler meant the cover afforded by the rubber plantation, the African village and the deep ditch on its western boundary which ran parallel to the railway cutting 200 yards distant.

Adler's company was well protected by the embankment and had 200 yards of open ground in front of it, but when the Rajputs' entire firing line began to emerge from the dead ground and the firing started in earnest he knew that he was outnumbered by a factor of at least four. To make matters worse rain set in, hampering his observation of the advancing enemy and causing the smoke of his men's antiquated black powder rifles to hang in the damp morning air in front of his dispositions. But the *askari* of 17/FK maintained a rapid fire until their ammunition was almost exhausted, an hour and a half later, and in so doing they forced Tighe to deploy his reserve of four companies of Rajputs and three companies of 61st Pioneers so that his firing line extended all the way from Adler's left on the sea to his right at the south end of the cutting. At this critical juncture a runner appeared to tell Adler that 16/FK had arrived from Amboni and were now engaged on his right, halting the flanking movement of the Rajputs; and, to his considerable relief, he was also informed that the first troops of Lieutenant Merensky's *Abteilung* – comprising 1/FK, 6/FK and 6/SchK – had arrived on a train from Moshi.

The appearance of 16/FK in the German defensive lines had serious consequences for the Rajputs: when Colonel Codrington, the regiment's commanding officer, and two other officers climbed a knoll in order to try and ascertain its exact disposition they were mown down by machine-gun fire. Worse still, a German counter-attack also robbed the 61st Pioneers of their commanding officer and the troops buckled. Although there were individual acts of great courage among their number during the retreat, the men had never faced machine-gun fire before, let alone trained properly with the machine-guns which had only recently been issued to them. Many fled back to the landing place near Ras Kasone just as rapidly as they had moved up an hour earlier and by 8 a.m. Tighe's left wing had collapsed, the counter-attacking force almost forming a right angle with Adler's line in the railway cutting. While Tighe called for reinforcements, Adler, seeing the speed of the British collapse on his right and mindful of the danger of firing on his own advancing men by accident, ordered his *askari* to push forward out of the railway cutting. This move threatened to outflank Tighe's centre and right and, at the sight of Adler's men emerging from the cutting as if from the earth itself, the Rajputs hastily retired while a reserve double company of the 61st Pioneers which had only landed at 8.30 a.m. stubbornly checked the German advance on Tighe's left. In the centre, Adler pressed on unhindered until he reached a position south of the two-storied Government Hospital and gave the order to halt.

During his advance Adler could quite clearly see HMS *Fox* in the harbour between the hospital and Ras Kasone. At 7.40 a.m. she had fired about a dozen shots into the rubber plantation, killing only retreating Rajputs and Pioneers, but now, two hours later, she began shelling Tanga itself. Adler was undeterred, and was just about to resume his offensive when two new orders arrived from Baumstark. They read: 'when bombardment begins, disengage and retire' and 'Tanga Detachment. The Detachment will retire to Kange Station, I have taken up position there.' At the same time he also received a report from the harbour that three 'strongly manned' lighters were landing further troops there – and with that Adler 'gave the order to stop the fight and to begin the march to Kange as far away as possible from the town'. 'By degrees,' he later reported, 'the noise of the fighting got fainter.'[13]

When Tighe's troops were able to muster back at the 'Red House', above the beach whence they had started out at dawn, their number was depleted by casualties of almost fifteen per cent.* The last company of 61st Pioneers had not even landed until 10 a.m., by which time the folly of Aitken's order to advance before Tighe had all three of his battalions at the ready was already obvious. In an increasingly recriminatory atmosphere, the setback was blamed on Captain Caulfeild's insistence on sweeping the inner harbour for mines a second time before he would contemplate HMS *Fox* taking up a position there to cover the landing of troops on its two beaches. This exercise was not completed in time to respond to Tighe's call for reinforcements: four double companies of the 2nd Loyal North Lancs – observed by Adler's scouts – did not clear their transports until 9.30 a.m. Deemed the best troops in the expeditionary force, the Loyal North Lancs landed on Beach 'B', by the signal tower, and were immediately ordered to entrench a 900-yard line covering Beaches 'B' and 'A' (the landing point of the night before). Near their landing point a house was being hastily converted into a hospital to care for the morning's casualties, a sight not calculated to boost morale, while out to sea on the *Karmala* Captain Evans judged that Caulfeild's caution of the previous day had turned into a case of outright 'cold feet'.[14]

Tighe was considerably shaken, and somewhat embarrassed, by the failure of his troops to take Tanga and he sent 'grave reports'[15] to Aitken about the morning's events. His natural instinct was to attack again immediately, but he

---

* 13th Rajputs' casualties – five out of twelve officers, and forty-nine out of 690 other ranks; 61st Pioneers' casualties – two officers, and ninety-one out of 400 other ranks. Three other attached officers were killed, including Lieutenant Ismael the previous night. Hordern remarks: 'the casualties had not been excessive' (p. 82).

thought better of it: a further rebuff might mean the end of the whole operation. As a result a second day passed without IEF 'B' securing its initial objective. In pouring rain that afternoon the landing of troops continued on the two beaches in Tanga's inner harbour. Their combined frontage was no more than 400 yards, creating considerable congestion, but there was no resistance from the now-absent enemy. No attempt was made to land troops at Tanga's main jetty under cover of HMS *Fox*'s guns, a huge oversight, nor even to send a patrol towards the town to try to ascertain if such a move would be opposed. At 5 p.m. on 3 November Aitken himself set foot on shore for the first time. He was still sure that real resistance would not be met until he began advancing up the Usambara Railway; and the last three battalions of IEF 'B' did not land until the following morning.

That night, under another brilliant moon, Lieutenant Russell, accompanied by three Indian soldiers, again found his local informant and was assured that no German troop concentration was under way 'in the town' (although it was rumoured that troops 'were expected very soon').[16] Russell was not the only furtive visitor to Tanga in the hours of darkness. Von Lettow-Vorbeck had moved his headquarters forward from Moshi to Muhesa on 3 November and interviewed the German wounded in its hospital. The most senior among them, Lieutenant Albert Merensky of 1/FK, who sported an enormous red beard, was of the opinion that the British were defeated and would not attack again. Von Lettow-Vorbeck then took the train to Kange, arriving at 3 a.m. to consult Captain Baumstark, who took a rather more pessimistic view, believing that Tanga could not be held against another attack. It was these contradictory opinions that decided von Lettow-Vorbeck on taking a look at Tanga himself, cycling through its deserted streets to the harbour with his old friend Captain von Hammerstein-Gesmold and Dr Lessel, and pushing out small patrols towards Ras Kasone as he went. On the harbour front he saw the blaze of lights from the British transports and wished that Captain Hering's two field guns had arrived from Kilimanjaro. Next they rode further towards Ras Kasone itself and, leaving the bicycles at the German hospital, climbed down to the waterside. It was a courageous, if foolhardy action: just before dawn an exchange of shots between opposing patrols was heard nearby.

Von Lettow-Vorbeck decided, as a result of his nocturnal foray, that he would ignore Schnee's instruction 'to avoid a bombardment of Tanga at all costs' and would 'meet the attack'. 'To gain all we must risk all'[17] was his maxim, despite the only too obvious numerical advantage of IEF 'B', and he issued his orders accordingly. Lieutenant Max Poppe's trusted 6/FK, whose peacetime garrison was at Ujiji on Lake Tanganyika, was detailed to defend the broad eastern front of the town (held by Captain Adler the day before). Behind it, and to its right, he positioned 16/FK under Lieutenant Ernst von

Brandis, Adler's 17/FK, and a composite company. To their right rear were Tom von Prince's two companies of reservists, 7/SchK and 8/SchK with three machine-guns. Lieutenant Oppen's crack 13/FK were deployed with four machine-guns on the Tanga–Pangani road, with a view to delivering a powerful 'right hook' counter-attack. The formation was reminiscent of that favoured by the Zulus in the previous century and was deemed ideal by von Lettow-Vorbeck for taking advantage of the propensity for British troops, as he had observed in China during the Boxer Rebellion, to be 'moved and led [with] clumsiness'.[18] There was more than a touch of irony in such a tactic: Aitken *was* modelling his assault on the methods used by the British Army in the Boxer Rebellion and von Lettow-Vorbeck meant to inflict on him just the sort of drubbing that the Zulus had on Lord Chelmsford at Isandhlwana in 1879. Von Lettow-Vorbeck rued the fact that 4/FK and 9/FK were, like his artillery, still to arrive. But eight and a half companies, a total of 935 rifles with fifteen machine-guns, were in carefully prepared positions by noon on 4 November. There was nothing else to do but wait. Drinks were brought out to the troops from the town and Master Butcher Grabow bustled about delivering hot sausages.

By the early afternoon von Lettow-Vorbeck was beginning to doubt whether Aitken would attack at all that day. The 63rd Palamcottahs, 98th Infantry and 101st Grenadiers had finally made it ashore by 9.30 a.m., and the guns of the 28th Mounted Battery were at the ready on the deck of the *Bharata* in the harbour, but it was not until just before noon that Aitken ordered his troops to advance. It took some time before any evidence of the advance was discernible to Tanga's defenders because it was conducted at a snail's pace. The previous day it had taken the 13th Rajputs just half an hour to advance all the way to the open ground in front of Tanga's railway cutting; but on 4 November it took fully two and a half hours before the first British troops even encountered German outposts just one mile inland. Some caution was understandable in the light of the setback of the previous day; but it was as if the whole of IEF 'B' were on a painstaking search for four-leaved clovers rather than seeking to overrun a town just 2,000 yards away which Aitken still believed to be undefended. All units had to negotiate various natural obstacles – the rubber plantation, tall bush grass, sisal – but this was only really problematic because of Aitken's insistence that his seven battalions advance in one long line, 'a formation which', in the words of one Intelligence officer, 'staggered me and reminded me of days long past'.[19] Von Lettow-Vorbeck's anticipation of his enemy's methods had proved spot on. It was just fortunate for the British rank and file that not all of Aitken's officers were to prove quite so inflexible that day.

On the British left, Wapshare's orders were for his 27th Brigade to extend far enough south of the town to cut off that line of retreat to the Germans. The Loyal North Lancs on his right and 101st Grenadiers on his left, the latter veterans of the Somaliland campaign a decade earlier, had the 'untrusted' 63rd Palamcottahs sandwiched between them,* and the 98th Infantry followed the Loyal North Lancs. On Aitken's right wing, extending to the sea, were Tighe's one and a half battalions of Kashmiri troops, supported by the battered Rajputs; and behind them the equally battered 61st Pioneers, who had been working hard all night, formed the only reserve. Three companies of the 3rd Gwalior Infantry were detailed for guard duty at Ras Kasone. Four parallel tracks led through the various natural obstacles towards the town, but even with these for guidance gaps appeared in Wapshare's line, inter-communications were poor, and German snipers 'roosting in trees'[20] greatly unnerved the troops. To make matters worse, pits had also been dug in the rubber plantation which were 'skilfully covered over again so that there was nothing to show their existence'; when the odd inattentive soldier 'stepped upon the top covering it gave way and [he] was precipitated onto sharp stakes several feet below'.[21]

At 2 p.m. a general halt was called to allow the Loyal North Lancs to fill a gap to their right caused by the Kashmiris inclining towards the sea. Half an hour after that both battalions were in action and the battle finally began in earnest. German outposts were successfully driven back by the Kashmiris, but at the first sound of unfamiliar machine-gun fire the 63rd Palamcottahs panicked and 'as a fighting unit ... ceased to exist'.[22] The demoralising sight of many of the Palamcottahs fleeing past the 98th Infantry was not made any better by the equally alarming appearance of swarms of angry bees, disturbed in their tree hives by the gunfire. In the course of the afternoon they displayed no differentiation between British and German units and some men were to be stung more than a hundred times. The 98th Infantry, which had a fine reputation for musketry but had not been in action for decades, apparently scattered (although this is not the impression created by their War Diary); and by the time it had regrouped the battalion had lost touch with the rapidly advancing Loyal North Lancs in front.[†]

---

* To add to the misery of over a month on board ship, the 63rd Palamcottahs had spent the whole of the previous evening awaiting embarkation. Finally they were put in lighters at 11 p.m., only to be ordered back on board shortly after with orders to land by 7 a.m. the following morning. As a result they had 'had little sleep or food before landing to take part in the action' (Hordern, p. 83, note 3).

† In his report of 9 November (TNA/CO/533/146) Aitken also mentions that the 98th Infantry were ordered by him to fill the gap left by 63rd Palamcottahs and support the 101st Grenadiers. The 98th Infantry War Diary records the orders it received, but makes no mention of this one (which would have been contrary to its initial order to support the Loyal North Lancs). It is

Despite these setbacks the Kashmiris (famed for being 'as steady as any troops could be'),[23] the Loyal North Lancs (who were also hit by bees), and some 13th Rajputs pressed forward determinedly and charged with fixed bayonets across the railway cutting into the town, capturing a machine-gun in the process. As they came on, naval reservist Lieutenant Werner Besch of 17/FK rushed with eight men from the railway workshops past the main position of his company to check whether it was being outflanked on the seaward side. After ten minutes observing the scene from the upstairs of a house on the north-east corner of the town, he caught sight of Max Poppe's 6/FK retreating from the railway cutting, Poppe and Lieutenant Bergmann having been wounded, and received a message ordering his detachment to engage the troops entering the town. Although separated from the bulk of his company by two high fences which enclosed the railway station, he pressed back into the town, coming under a heavy crossfire from a side street which ran down to the harbour. He then hurried on to the offices of Miller & Company and there was able to join up with a detachment of Germans who were subjecting pockets of Kashmiri troops to a withering fire. Rallied by the Rajputs' determined Captain Seymour, some Kashmiris succeeded in occupying the Kaiserhof Hotel and lowered the two German flags flying from its roof. But at street level their comrades around the Marine Monument and in the market-place were encountering heavy fire from von Prince's two companies of European reservists positioned in the surrounding houses. At 3 p.m. they had been ordered into the town by von Lettow-Vorbeck, demonstrating that he was prepared to risk a street fight even if such a strategy invited shellfire from HMS *Fox* and the mountain guns aboard the *Bharata*.

On the British left the disintegration of the 63rd Palamcottahs completely isolated the 101st Grenadiers on the south side of Aitken's battlefront and, with the battalions to their right inclining towards the sea, they too were forced north in an attempt to gain touch with the Loyal North Lancs. Wapshare was still confident that he was on the brink of rolling up the German right, however, and that is what might have happened if the 101st Grenadiers had maintained the direction of their advance rather than wheel to the north. This would have brought them to a position which outflanked the troops gathering at the railway station and workshops to deliver von Lettow-Vorbeck's 'right hook'. Instead the gentle arc being followed by the 101st Grenadiers as they pushed on through thick bush and scattered African huts brought them

distinctly possible that Aitken invented this order, as he did other details in his reports, to protect himself from the question why one of his best regiments was sent out with only the 'untrusted' 63rd Palamcottahs alongside them, the flight of the latter leaving the Grenadiers to sustain the worst casualties of the whole battle.

to a position directly in front of the workshops, where they encountered heavy fire from the entrenchments of von Brandis's 16/FK. Major Tatum was killed in the advance, but his two senior Indian officers immediately ordered a charge by the battalion's double company of Dekhani Mahrattas which was only halted twenty-five yards from the German trenches. The casualties inflicted by charging two machine-guns were appalling enough; but four more machine-guns were suddenly brought to bear by 1/FK and 17/FK on the 101st Grenadiers' left. This was the moment that von Lettow-Vorbeck had been waiting for. He ordered his 'right hook' counter-attack to commence, and Oppen's 13/FK threw themselves on the Grenadiers' open and battered left flank. In a matter of minutes all of the battalion's British officers, five Indian officers and a third of the rank and file in the front line were dead. They contested every inch of ground, the two machine-guns on their left wing being supported by two machine-guns of the 63rd Palamcottahs whose crews had not joined in the flight of most of the rest of their battalion. But the survivors of the mauling received in front of the workshops were forced to pull back gradually and by 4 p.m. were scattered in isolated pockets in the bush. Any vestigial hope of reversing the German counter-attack was gone, and the remnants of Aitken's left were in very real danger of annihilation.

In the vicious street-to-street fighting taking place in Tanga itself, the Loyal North Lancs were still without support from the 98th Infantry and had received no orders from HQ since the start of the advance. After the attack by bees the latter had regrouped and moved a little forward and to the right. But there they stayed, rigidly true to their initial orders to maintain a distance of 300 yards between themselves and the Loyal North Lancs, until Colonel Ward received the order from Wapshare to enter the town at 4.30 p.m. It came too late. A brief bombardment of the town by HMS *Fox* at 3.45 p.m. had failed to make the slightest dent in the German resistance.* From the decks of the *Bharata*, the six 10-pdr guns of the 28th Mountain Battery also fired 150 shells in the direction of the town but as their commanding officer, Major Forestier-Walker, was not permitted to send a man ashore to spot for the guns they were firing blind and by 4.30 p.m. the German defence had been stiffened by the arrival of 4/FK, led by Karl Göring and Maximilian Dransfeld. The Loyal North Lancs were pushed to the very edge of the town, forming a defensive line between the railway and the cemetery alongside a number of

---

* When the guns of the 28th Mountain Battery fired their shells into Tanga from the transport *Bharata*, 1,000 yards offshore in the harbour, they could not see the effect or on whom they were firing. Hordern points out that 'at this date forward observing officers had hardly been instituted' (p. 88 note 1), and spotting, such as it was, was done by Major Forestier-Walker up the mast. HMS *Fox* was also firing blind, and one shell even hit the German hospital, halfway between its position off Beach 'C' and the town.

Kashmiris, Rajputs and the machine-gunners of 61st Pioneers who had advanced undaunted all the way from the rear, past retreating comrades, for the second time in two days. The first contact between the Loyal North Lancs and the belatedly advancing 98th Infantry finally occurred just as the first two companies of the former began to retire. Soldiers from all three battalions that had earlier gained a foothold in the town now began streaming past the 98th Infantry which, 'finding [itself] apparently isolated and a general retirement in progress',[24] also began to withdraw at 5.30 p.m.

Closer to the sea the Kashmiri and Rajput units, which had fulfilled their supporting role in a way that the 98th Infantry seemingly had not, were also retiring towards the Customs House. They had suffered considerably in the street fighting, and as they withdrew the Germans shifted their positions to Kaiser Street and Mascher's house before opening fire on the Customs buildings and a boat conveying wounded Kashmiris to the nearest transport in the harbour. At 5.13 p.m., when all British troops had vacated the town, HMS *Fox* finally opened fire on Kaiser Street – but even then Caulfeild was instructed by the ever-optimistic Aitken 'to avoid the railway'.[25] Lieutenant Besch and most of the German defenders retreated hastily to the vicinity of the Bismarck Monument and the Miller & Company offices, taking up positions on the top floor to cover any attempted landing at the jetty by British troops (which might usefully have taken place earlier in the day). They fired at a heavily laden lighter, forcing it to retire, and no further attempt was made to use the jetty.

Aitken's order to HMS *Fox* demonstrated that even with his invasion force in full retreat, and a mutiny taking place among Greek crewmen on the transport ship *Laisang*, he persisted in believing that he was going to need the railway to advance into German East Africa. But it was not the shelling of the town that emptied Tanga and saved the remaining Kashmiris and Rajputs clinging to the waterfront from being driven into the sea. A German *askari* bugler suddenly blew the *Sammeln*, the same command as had been used the previous day to order the German troops to withdraw when *Fox* had bombarded Tanga, and from all across the battlefield German troops began to make their way back to the assembly point at Muhesa. The command had not been ordered by von Lettow-Vorbeck, and its effect was to deprive him of any troops with which to pursue the retreating enemy.[*] Equally fortunate for Aitken was that Hering's two guns had now arrived from Taveta and were just about to enter Tanga when the call for the German withdrawal was sounded. As darkness fell on what Wapshare described as 'altogether a most terrible

* See Lettow-Vorbeck (1), p. 43: 'In some inexplicable way the troops imagined a Headquarters order had been issued that they were to return to their old camp west of Tanga.'

day',[26] this was a godsend for the five brightly lit transports in the harbour; and it was 3.30 a.m. on 5 November before von Lettow-Vorbeck managed to get the first German companies back into position in Tanga. A single 'inexplicable'[27] bugle call had seemingly caused his force to relinquish certain victory in a fashion reminiscent of the battle of Cannae.

Aitken's bubble of optimism was finally burst in the early evening by the reports of his commanders. Wapshare's 27th Brigade was no longer a cohesive force at all but widely dispersed pockets of stubborn 101st Grenadiers and a few Palamcottahs, the last of whom did not appear at Ras Kasone until 6 a.m. the following morning. Tighe, a man 'without an atom of physical fear',[28] who had himself experienced being shot through his trousers, was adamant that his Imperial Service Brigade could not attack again without reliable reinforcements. There were none. Water and food were also scarce and before 8 p.m. Aitken considered that he had no choice but to re-embark IEF 'B'. When news of his decision reached the front line the reaction among many was one of shock and disgust. The Loyal North Lancs, Kashmiris and Rajputs were all set to launch a new attack but were ordered instead to withdraw to a line covering the beaches on the seaward side of Ras Kasone. Huddled on those beaches was a rabble of wounded, frightened and exhausted soldiers, and some 2,000 terrified African porters and Indian Army followers. At 11 p.m. the final orders were issued for re-embarkation the following morning, and a very nerve-wracking night ensued. Two thousand yards away, Tanga lay empty of enemy troops.

Heavy rain fell for an hour or so after dawn on 5 November as Aitken took a further momentous decision: that in order to retire with maximum speed and minimum risk to life, all heavy stores were to be left behind, the machine-guns disabled. In the harbour the final indignity was suffered by the *Laisang*, which was hit by a German field gun and forced to depart in flames as von Lettow-Vorbeck deployed his troops to meet the new attack he was certain would come. Captain Otto's 9/FK had extricated itself from an engagement near Mzima, more than 200 miles away in British East Africa, and finally arrived from Kilimanjaro; and von Chappuis's 15/FK had also marched 100 miles from Bagamoyo, to the south of Tanga, bringing the German strength to about 1,500 rifles. But von Lettow-Vorbeck had decided, after the return of strong patrols sent out towards the British defensive lines, that 'it was not now advisable to advance'.[29] It was, in hindsight, a curious decision to have made. German casualties did not exceed ten per cent of the total strength at von

Lettow-Vorbeck's disposal, a tally he regarded as 'insignificant'.[30] On the other hand nine officers had been killed, including his old friend Tom von Prince, the son of an English policeman whose prominent role in Germany's conquest of its East African colony had made him a legendary figure, and if the *Schutztruppe* were ordered to advance through the plantations and bush to the east of Tanga they would be exposed to the possibility of a vigorous counter-attack by an enemy which was now hidden from the view of his patrols (and a bombardment from HMS *Fox*). The fact that von Lettow-Vorbeck chose not to risk an advance was a godsend for the British troops on the beaches south of Ras Kasone. In mid morning Hering's pair of antiquated field guns briefly fired on HMS *Fox* near the jetty, but otherwise little happened while IEF 'B' and the Royal Navy waited for the tide on which to depart the battlefield.

Behind the natural protective screen, and the defensive line held by the Loyal North Lancs, the Royal Navy's Commander Headlam ordered the re-embarkation to commence at 1 p.m. The Indian Army followers and African carriers waded out to the waiting lighters first, followed by the troops who had suffered most in the battle of the day before. A volley of rifle fire from the defensive perimeter at a German patrol caused total panic at one point, with Headlam being required to restore order 'not without difficulty and violence'.[31] On the other hand the departure of the Loyal North Lancs and Kashmir Rifles was calm and orderly, and by 3.20 p.m. the evacuation was over without von Lettow-Vorbeck having gained an inkling that it was even under way. A disembarkation that had taken fifty-four hours to complete had been reversed in less than two and a half, a feat for which Headlam and Colonel Sheppard, Aitken's senior Staff officer, were largely responsible. For Captain Evans of the *Karmala* the final indictment of Caulfeild's 'perfectly disgraceful and badly managed' landings occurred when HMS *Fox* had 'fairly bolted out of the harbour ... leaving the troops uncovered'[32] when she had come under fire in the morning.

On the evening of 5 November British Intelligence officer Captain Richard Meinertzhagen landed under a flag of truce to negotiate the removal of the wounded with von Hammerstein-Gesmold, von Lettow-Vorbeck's senior Staff officer, and only then did the German commander realise that IEF 'B' had re-embarked. That night, the British officers charged with organising the evacuation of the wounded were the guests at a distinctly bizarre dinner with their German counterparts. 'Of all the supper parties within my experience', wrote Lieutenant Charlewood of the *Helmuth*, 'this was the strangest ... The food, which comprised soup, fish and steak, all out of tins, was well cooked, and the conversation astonishingly bright. The Germans', he added, 'said they thought the war [in Europe] would soon be over because they expected the

French to give in, and then of course it would be useless for Britain to continue the struggle.'[33]

Forty-nine men too seriously wounded to be moved had to be left behind on shore, along with booty galore for von Lettow-Vorbeck: eight serviceable machine-guns, 455 rifles, half a million rounds of ammunition, telephone gear, coats, blankets and even uniforms. There is no record of whether the 30,000lbs of pickles which had been brought from India by the Loyal North Lancs were among the abandoned supplies. The official tally of British casualties would eventually list 817 men dead, wounded or missing – about fifteen per cent of the invasion force – of whom the Germans buried 159 on the edge of the rubber plantation. Most significant in the context of Aitken's decision not to attack again were the losses among the 101st Grenadiers, Loyal North Lancs and Kashmiris.* The toll among British and Indian officers in the force – thirty-one dead and thirty wounded – was such that one survivor wrote home ruefully 'the officer man gets so much individual attention that at times it becomes embarrassing not to say annoying'.[34]

As the British ships sailed away, leaving the appropriately named *Toten* (Dead) Island in their wake, the German troops gradually realised that at the cost of some 125 casualties they had inflicted 'such a beating [on the British invasion] that they jolly well won't try it again'.[35] The *askari* were as jubilant as their German officers, pouring scorn on the 'Indian she-goats'. All that was left on shore of Aitken's effort, apart from the wounded and the booty, was the 'terrible cadaverous smell [which] hung' over the little town of Tanga.[36] 'So ended,' wrote the intrepid Lieutenant Russell, who had escaped from Dar-es-Salaam and twice been sent to reconnoitre Tanga at night, 'one of the most ignominious defeats ever inflicted on a British Army'.[37]

---

* Total casualties among the 2nd Loyal North Lancs – 115; 101st Grenadiers – 222; 2nd Kashmir Rifles and half-battalion 3rd Kashmir Rifles – sixty-two. As late as 7 November Aitken still believed that he had lost 417 Grenadiers; there was no senior officer left alive or not in hospital to correct him.

FOUR

The Aftermath

———◆———

The description of the battle of Tanga in the British official history of the campaign as 'one of the most notable failures in British military history'[1] echoed the judgement of Lieutenant Russell, and even the Director of Military Operations at the War Office was forced to concede that the failure to invade German East Africa at the first attempt was 'a setback on a small scale perhaps, but as decided a one as [the British Empire] met with during the war'.[2] The battle was also much 'celebrated' in verse, and for decades after the Great War the sequence of events at Tanga would be analysed in minute detail in British Staff colleges.

The immediate consequence of the failure to seize Tanga was to force the hard-pressed War Office to relieve the Colonial and India Offices of their responsibility for military affairs in eastern Africa. It was simply no longer possible for the British High Command to ignore what it had previously dismissed as a 'local affair'. Across the border in German East Africa, on the other hand, Ada Schnee observed that after Tanga 'the confidence of the colony ... soared'.[3] Von Lettow-Vorbeck's astonishing victory was to earn him lasting fame, and there would be more German accounts of *Die Schlacht bei Tanga* than any other battle in the years ahead.

News of the rout spread through British East Africa within days. On 5 November, when the disaster was not even quite complete, *The Leader* revealed that 'a telegram has been received to the effect than an attempt to land troops at Tanga met with strong opposition and that operations in that area have been temporarily deferred'. But the editors were then gagged; not until late December did any further detail appear in print, and then it was in the South African *Pioneer Mail*, rather than an East African or British newspaper. In Britain, Prime Minister Asquith did not inform King George V until 11 November, three days after the shattered remains of IEF 'B' landed at Mombasa, by which time his government had decided that such a 'grave setback'[4] was best covered up. Even as august a figure as Lord Curzon, former Viceroy of India, was swiftly rebuffed in the House of Lords when he asked for a clarification of rumours that had begun to circulate. Was Tanga 'a big thing or a little thing,' he enquired, 'because we know nothing at all about it'.[5] That was how it remained. 'Keep secret for the present'[6] had become government policy and, despite Curzon's protestations, 'not one word of information [was] vouchsafed to the British public'.[7]

Concern about Tanga's depressing effect on British morale was not the only justification behind the cover-up: it took a considerable time for Whitehall to ascertain the details of what had happened. At the Colonial Office the first indication that all was not well in East Africa was contained in a telegram sent from Nairobi at 10.02 p.m. on 5 November, causing a state of alarm which mounted with the receipt of each subsequent missive from East Africa. 'This makes very bad reading', 'a good bit of a muddle', and 'a sorry story' were some of the remarks scrawled in red ink across Aitken's 'woolly' despatches.[8] The hapless commander of IEF 'B' appears to have been in a state of shock. Although one account credits him with 'generously [placing] all the blame upon himself'* as his force withdrew, his despatches soon became viciously defensive as the magnitude and implications of the 'reverse' dawned on him. He was not only vituperative on the subject of the 'deplorable state of more than half my force',[9] demanding that the 63rd Palamcottahs and 98th Infantry be immediately sent home to India in disgrace, but imaginative. In one despatch he claimed that his defeat had been at the hands of a solely European force which included 1,000 Germans who were thought to have arrived from Australia and China on the *Zieten* in early August; and in another he grossly overestimated the manpower available to von Lettow-Vorbeck at the time of the battle, putting it at 5,000 Europeans and 9,000 *askari*. Aitken also roundly criticised the Royal Navy as he cast around for scapegoats, singling out the *canard* of Caulfeild's observation of the naval truce as a critical factor in the defeat, as well as the inordinately long time it had taken to execute the landing of his troops; and he lambasted those responsible for the lack of up-to-date intelligence about German troops' dispositions. Such intelligence would not have affected the outcome at Tanga – Aitken had been warned that von Lettow-Vorbeck might use the Usambara Railway to ferry troops to Tanga – but it was certainly true that Norman King, the former British Consul at Dar-es-Salaam who had been so intimately involved in the planning of the expedition, and Colonel Mackay and Captain Cadell of the Intelligence Departments of IEF 'B' and 'C' respectively, had not exactly distinguished themselves.

Despite his best efforts to deflect, or at least spread, the blame, Aitken's

---

* Wynn, p. 67. Wynn added: 'Defeat had carried him to unexpected heights. He was cheery, calm, and courteous, winning the affection and sympathy of all. Lack of soldiership rather than of character was what had brought about his downfall.'

leadership attracted universal condemnation in Whitehall. The War Office censured him for not conducting adequate reconnaissance of his own, and was certain that his decision to send Tighe towards Tanga with a force of only one and a half battalions on 3 November (and its resultant rebuff) was instrumental in leading to the 'reversal' the following day. Above all, Aitken's military superiors were amazed that he had not landed his troops for reorganisation and rest at Mombasa after their debilitating voyage from India. He could then have denounced the truce from a distance, not risked a 'hasty and haphazard attack', and left von Lettow-Vorbeck to worry about when – and where – the invasion would take place.

The Military Secretary at the India Office, Sir Edmund Barrow, was equally forthright about the execution of what he described as a 'premature, haphazard and aimless' operation. Barrow had been personally involved in the preparation of IEF 'B', but he was shocked at Aitken's 'entire inability to grasp the situation and to adapt his measures to fit it' and 'not surprised that some of [Aitken's] regiments failed him'. In Barrow's opinion, Aitken should have landed troops at Tanga's jetty as soon as the harbour had been swept for mines and put the 28th Mountain Battery onshore where it could have made its presence felt. At the Admiralty, Sir Henry Jackson concurred with Barrow that it was sheer madness for IEF 'B' not to have recuperated in Mombasa while a feint across the border or against Dar-es-Salaam paved the way for the main attack. Jackson did admit that Caulfeild's insistence on observing the naval truce may have caused confusion, but considered that his 'honourable'[10] conduct had had no significant bearing on the outcome of the invasion attempt. Churchill, on the other hand, disagreed with Jackson's support for Caulfeild's 'unauthorised' observation of a truce, considering it 'incredible that *Fox* should not have supported the infantry',[11] and dismissed Caulfeild's claim that he had undertaken a 'heavy bombardment of the town'[12] as risible.

In the inter-departmental stakes the Colonial Office was found to be 'primarily responsible for the disaster', closely followed by the India Office for providing 'indifferent' troops. The latter by and large accepted the charge levelled at it; the former was more equivocal, claiming in its defence that after the arrival of Indian Expeditionary Force 'B' it no longer had any responsibility for military matters and that its remit was the future administration of German East Africa (not the invasion). This was technically true, but also disingenuous; and the India Office's riposte was to accuse Belfield of being almost as culpable as Aitken for devoting 'more attention to dividing the lion's kin than slaying the lion'.[13] Amid all the recriminations there were two points on which civil servants and military top brass were able to agree unanimously: namely that Aitken's despatches read like 'a crushing indictment of himself', and that what was now required in East Africa was 'not so much reinforcements as a new general'.[14] On 4 December Aitken, who was suffering from malaria after neglecting to sleep under a mosquito net, was informed that he was being relieved of his command. The Colonial Office noted on the despatch 'Good', and the sentiment of most of the officers and men of IEF 'B' was that their departing general bore with him 'the blessings of nobody'.

Aitken was to spend the best part of a decade trying to clear his name, a campaign which met with only partial success.* He was neither the first nor the last British general to be found lacking by an unfamiliar challenge during the Great War and, as one of his officers later remarked, he was 'a good soul, honest and well meaning. It was only tragic ignorance of his profession that had made him so woefully incompetent for waging war'.[15] His failure was all the more tragic because, whatever his shortcomings and those of some of his troops, victory had only just eluded him. The realisation that this was the case greatly disturbed some of his commanders. In January 1915 General Wapshare wrote in his diary: 'the more I think of the Tanga battle the more disquieted I am. We *ought* to have got in even with the troops we had. But for bad generalship there were of course other excuses but nothing can excuse what we did.'

Although 'Old Wappy', as he was affectionately known among the troops, lamented how 'very sickening' it was to have been 'mixed up in an affair of this sort'[16] he vetoed a suggestion by the commanding officer of the 98th Infantry that an independent account of Tanga should be submitted to the War Office by the senior officers of IEF 'B'; and he left it entirely to the War Office to decide what to do next to preserve Britain's status as 'the paramount country in central and southern Africa'.[17] The repercussions throughout the Empire of failing to prevent a German invasion of British East Africa, an event the War Office now considered 'not improbable',[18] were certainly unthinkable; and providing two divisions to finish the job properly – as Aitken suggested – was equally unthinkable given the requirements elsewhere. The only possible solution seemed to lie in persuading South Africa to help. But as South Africa was already embroiled in trying to defeat German troops in South-West Africa while simultaneously tackling a rebellion among the Boer population, it was with some trepidation that a telegram was despatched to Lord Buxton, the Governor-General, in Cape Town.

---

* TNA/CO/533/147. Kitchener refused to grant an audience to Aitken on his arrival in London, and the latter was not employed again for the duration of the war. After the war he was eventually exonerated in Parliament of personal blame for Tanga but compensation for damage to his career was refused. He died of a 'seizure' in 1924 at the age of sixty-three, on a train in Italy.

Tanga was not the only military setback in East Africa in the first week of November. At the conference in Mombasa prior to Aitken's departure for Tanga, General Stewart had agreed to launch a simultaneous 'demonstration' across the border some 250 miles to the north-west. The aim was to create a diversion which would prevent German troops from being rushed down the Usambara Railway to Tanga. Stewart had personally reconnoitred the borderlands in October with Colonel Drew of the 29th Punjabis, and Masai and settler scouts had kept watch on German comings and goings in the area for weeks – even spotting the huge wagons of Boer ox-trains bringing supplies up to the front in the last week of October. He was therefore confident that only 200 Germans and 200–300 *askari* held his chosen objective, the isolated volcano of Longido. Had the telephone line connecting Major Kraut, commanding Longido, with von Lettow-Vorbeck's HQ at Moshi been in working order, this would probably have proved to be an exaggeration as many, if not all, of the troops would have been summoned to Tanga. But the telephone line was out of order, and Kraut's force was not only much stronger than expected but also entrenched in positions which fully exploited Longido's natural defensive advantages.[*]

The 'decisive attack column' led by Colonel Drew and Major Haslehurst of the 29th Punjabis left camp on the Namanga River in the afternoon of 2 November with a mounted escort from the volunteer East African Mounted Rifles. Their objective was to seize the main German camp high up on Longido while Major Laverton, who set out three hours later with the main body of EAMR and the Kapurthalas of IEF 'C', launched a simultaneous frontal attack on the mountain. The combined strength of the 'invasion force' was 1,500 rifles, and it was accompanied by four guns of the 27th Mountain Battery.[†]

At 1.30 a.m. that night, just as Tighe's troops were landing at Tanga, Drew's column arrived at the south-east spur of Longido under the full moon. Up close the thickly wooded volcano looked a good deal more imposing, and defensible, than from twenty miles away at Namanga. Its perimeter measured twenty-five to thirty miles and the main German camp was thought to be in the heart of the crater, 2,000 feet above the plains. But Drew had surprise on his side, his force was large and mostly reliable, and if he could reach his objective – Sandbach *kopje* – he would be in a commanding position well

---

[*] Kraut's force: 10/FK, 11/FK, 21/FK and 9/SchK – a total of eighty-six Germans and 583 *askari* with six machine-guns.

[†] 29th Punjabis less two companies (475 men), half-battalion Kapurthala Infantry (378 men), and five squadrons EAMR (360 men); 27/MB less one section, two machine-guns of the Volunteer Maxim Company, Masai Scouts.

above the camp. By dawn Drew's 29th Punjabis had covered five miles in their ascent towards Sandbach *kopje*. A dense mist hung all about Longido's heights, making signalling to the plains impossible, and the mass of ravines and gullies, covered in dense undergrowth, made for tough going. But with sunrise the damp air slowly began to clear and the gunners of the 27th Mountain Battery could finally see enough to open fire on the German camp and an entrenched ridge between the opposing forces. In less than an hour the main spur overlooking the camp was taken by a double company of the 29th Punjabis advancing along it by rushes and the enemy were cleared from their trenches on the ridge.

Down in the foothills to the north Laverton's column was not proving so successful in the frontal attack. The EAMR and Kapurthalas – the 'Coppertails' – met determined resistance as they tried to push through a *nek* formed by the lower sections of Longido's two main watercourses, and Laverton reluctantly concluded that he had insufficient troops with which to assault the well-positioned German trenches and four Maxim gun posts which he was unable to locate. A stalemate ensued while, to the south, two squadrons of EAMR which had been sent round the base of Longido were faring even worse. Their mission was to find the enemy's water supply, known to exist somewhere on Longido's southern side, and to cut off any enemy troops attempting to retreat south towards Moshi or Arusha. But Captain Bingley could find no water supply in the dark – it was a well-concealed spring in the rocks – nor any sign of a German camp guarding it; so he rode off in search of a second, larger water source known to exist at 'Longido West'. That proved equally elusive and, as the light started to improve, Bingley's flying column retraced its steps to search again for the first spring. With dawn the danger of being detected increased markedly, the dust kicked up by the horses' hooves being visible for miles around, and Bingley ordered one troop of his men to gallop south to watch the track leading from Meru to Longido for the approach of enemy reinforcements and to try and cut the telephone line.

It was from their distant vantage point on the Meru track that the detached troop, having cut the German telephone line, spotted enemy troops on horseback riding up Longido's southern slope. It later transpired that they were a detachment of Captain Stemmermann's 11/FK who were returning from repairing the telephone line which Bingley's men had just disabled again; more importantly, their appearance revealed the exact location of the spring that Bingley had been told to capture. Bingley ordered an immediate attack, but in next to no time found his troopers pinned down by rifle fire from Longido's southern slope; and when Stemmermann's much larger force began to outflank the EAMR mounted troopers Bingley ordered a hasty retreat to a *kopje* beside the Meru track. Nine of his men had been killed in the sharp engagement with 11/FK, and six more were seriously wounded.

The failure by Laverton and Bingley to threaten the enemy in front or in the rear made Drew's task of overrunning the main German camp all the more challenging, and at 2 p.m. German reinforcements – who had scaled the southern escarpment after seeing off the EAMR – suddenly appeared *above* his positions. Two hours later his predicament worsened still further when the rate of fire from the entrenchments of the main camp increased markedly and Drew noticed that in the distance Laverton had begun to retreat out of Longido's northern foothills and across the plain to a *kopje* five miles to the north-east. The 29th Punjabis were seemingly being left high and, quite literally, dry: their water-carrying mules had bolted earlier in the day, and all watercourses on the mountain were enfiladed by the enemy.

As a small detachment worked its way unobserved into a position on the Punjabis' left flank, enabling them to fire directly into his main positions, Drew took the decision to withdraw. The new threat was successfully countered by the machine-guns of his Volunteer Maxim Company and a single company of Punjabis, but as darkness began to fall the British troops found themselves under attack from almost every direction and the gunners of the 27th Mountain Battery were forced to set their fuses at zero. There was, in marked contrast to the scene simultaneously unfolding at Tanga, no panic, and Drew's men fought their way back down the mountain with commendable composure. During the night all the British troops made their way back to Namanga, having sustained fifty or so casualties – a similar number to that inflicted on the enemy. One EAMR trooper wrote of the day's fighting: 'I have no ambition to repeat the experience again if it can be avoided . . . I failed to see anything funny about it nor am I likely to in the future'; and as his comrades straggled back to British East Africa it was as clear to them as it was to Aitken's troops at Tanga that 'the taking of German East [was] not going to be child's play'.[19]

General Stewart's 'reconnaissance in force', as the attempt to capture Longido was subsequently referred to, attracted criticism in some quarters for being a day late. But having only agreed to the attack on 30 October, at the conference with Aitken in Mombasa, such criticism was manifestly unfair. Furthermore, the combined effect of the broken German telephone line and the British attack was to prevent Kraut sending troops to join von Lettow-Vorbeck – Stewart's prime objective – and his troops bore thirty-eight hours of continuous marching and fighting without food or water remarkably stoically. On 17 November Kraut abandoned Longido and a combined force of EAMR troopers and 29th Punjabis took over the former German positions. The mountain was 'not apparently a *point d'appui* for anywhere, and covers nowhere';* but on Christmas Day 1914 a company of the 2nd Loyal North Lancs which had been posted there held the dubious distinction of being 'the only company of British regular infantry occupying German territory ... in any part of the world'.[20]

Although it was clear, as one government official in Nairobi put it, that victory in 'the first round [lay] *completely* with Mr Squarehead'[21] there was an intriguing Intelligence coup in late November when an anonymous 'British' agent, probably a Boer living in German East Africa, managed to reconnoitre Tanga. His report revealed that von Lettow-Vorbeck had inspected new gun positions at Ras Kasone, that extensive new entrenchments had been dug, and that all the houses in the European quarter of the town now had loopholes for use by concealed marksmen. Mines had also been laid on the outskirts and the all streets barricaded. The agent sensed that the mood in Tanga was 'anxious'[22] – and that von Lettow-Vorbeck was undoubtedly expecting another visit.

* TNA/CAB/45/43 (Routh, *An Ordnance Officer in East Africa, 1914–1918*, p. 69). Kraut realised the difficulties of holding Longido for any prolonged period of time and made Ngare Nairobi, between Mt Meru and the border with British East Africa, his forward position for the 1,200 troops on this front.

FIVE

Marking Time

———◆———

One piece of good news emanated from British East Africa in early November. The sinking of the HMS *Pegasus* in Zanzibar harbour had caused such a furore that finding the *Königsberg* had rapidly scaled the British Admiralty's priority list. Churchill now deemed her destruction to be 'a matter of the highest importance' and swiftly despatched the cruisers *Chatham*, *Dartmouth* and *Weymouth* to East Africa. Their captains were told 'Do not miss your opportunity on any account'.[1]

At the end of September, soon after Looff's return to the Rufiji from destroying *Pegasus*, the crew of HMS *Chatham* spotted a German shore party on the islet of Komu, but despite capturing documents indicating that the *Königsberg* might be hiding at Salale, no immediate investigation of the delta was undertaken. In the third week of October, *Chatham* was still in pursuit of clues along an unfamiliar coast when she mistook the wireless masts of one of the German merchant vessels in Dar-es-Salaam harbour for those of *Königsberg* and shelled her until the mistake was realised. By then the *Königsberg*'s whereabouts had remained a perplexing mystery for over a month. But a few days later *Weymouth* intercepted the German steamer *Adjutant* making a break for Beira, in neutral Portuguese East Africa, and papers found on board connected her with the port of Lindi, some 250 miles south of Dar-es-Salaam. *Chatham* steamed there post-haste and during a search of the German liner *Präsident*, which appeared to have been converted into a hospital ship and was flying the Red Cross flag, evidence was found of her lighters having taken coal to the Rufiji delta. The net was closing on the *Königsberg*, and valuable intelligence received from the skipper of a Zanzibari dhow also pointed the Royal Navy in the direction of the Rufiji delta.

At the start of the war Captain Sydney Drury-Lowe and HMS *Chatham* had been part of the 'watchdog fleet' charged with preventing the German warships *Goeben* and *Breslau* from finding a safe haven with Turkey. They had failed, and Drury-Lowe was keen to avoid a second 'mishap'. On 30 October he put a landing party ashore at the mouth of the Rufiji and local inhabitants confirmed that there was indeed a *manoari ya bomba tatu* – a warship with three funnels – at Salale, about six miles inland up the Simba Uranga channel. Later that day *Chatham*'s masthead also reported sighting two masts inland. *Chatham* was not a moment too soon: the *Königsberg*'s faulty engine had been repaired and Looff was preparing to leave his lair for the high seas. 'The first visit was different, the second as we thought,' noted Signalman Ritter on board the *Königsberg*; 'this time the Englishman is coming to pay us a visit'.[2] Immediate congratulations were wired to *Chatham* from Churchill – 'Well done! Hold her and fight her without fail'[3] – and HMS *Fox* was ordered to join *Chatham* off the delta.

Finding the *Königsberg* was one thing, destroying her quite another. The mouth of the delta was about forty miles wide, with a number of channels extending up to a dozen miles inland to the Rufiji and Mohoro Rivers, and the Royal Navy knew very little about it as much had changed since a survey conducted in the 1880s.[*] Drury-Lowe was initially loath to take the *Chatham* within five miles of the delta, assuming that its mouths would be mined and that the inshore waters were too shallow for his warship. But Churchill reiterated an earlier command to destroy the German light cruiser 'without fail' and, as his obsession with the *Königsberg* grew, he even began suggesting that troops should be landed in a plethora of small craft and attack the German trenches protecting the delta. At the time all troops, and HMS *Fox*, were on their way to Tanga and any vessel approaching the shore would be a potential target for a torpedo attack by one of the small German craft known to be lurking in the delta.[†] But Churchill was undeterred, and on 2 November *Weymouth* and *Dartmouth* joined *Chatham* off the delta.

On a spring tide on which Looff had intended to make good his exit, *Chatham* did manage to navigate through the treacherous approaches to within just over a mile of the delta. The last three miles were in only three to four fathoms of water, but she was then able to give *Königsberg* 'a good pounding'[4] at a range of just over 14,500 yards. This time it was Looff's turn to 'sit idle and watch' as his guns were outranged by *Chatham*'s, and when the bombardment ceased Signalman Ritter declared it 'an absolute wonder' that his ship had not been hit as 'the shells fell close in front and behind us the whole time'.[5] The 2,600-ton German collier *Somali* was also shelled, but as the tide ebbed *Chatham* was forced to make for deeper waters. On each of the next five days Drury-Lowe shelled the delta mouth, and the *Somali* was

* On the other hand the German survey ship *Möwe* had rather fortuitously completed a survey just months before the outbreak of war.
† CHAR/13/38/21. Churchill wondered whether HMS *Fox*'s 6-inch guns might reach the *Königsberg*. But *Fox* drew five feet more than *Chatham*, the range of her guns was some 400 yards less than those of *Weymouth*, and he was told that she was 'unavailable'. He had seemingly not been informed that she was the escort ship to IEF 'B'.

finally sunk at her berth near Salale. But insufficient damage was inflicted on the German shore defences to prevent them from beating back a flotilla of small craft endeavouring to launch a torpedo attack on the *Königsberg*, so Drury-Lowe altered his tactics. Churchill had decided that if the *Königsberg* would not come out then he 'must block her in',[6] and on 10 November the British collier *Newbridge* was sunk across the Suninga entrance to the delta by Commander Fitzmaurice – a dangerous venture which cost the lives of five naval ratings from HMS *Chatham.*

That very day news reached the British ships that HMAS *Sydney* had registered the nascent Royal Australian Navy's first victory at sea, and it was a very significant one indeed: she had caught Captain von Müller's *Emden* by surprise off Direction Island and, after a short action carried out at full speed, the *Emden* was destroyed on the reef off North Keeling Island. *Sydney* had rid the Indian Ocean of a menace that had bombarded Madras in September, had sunk twenty-two ships in three months, and had been one of the causes of both the delayed departure of IEF 'B' from India and the elevation of its task of invading German East Africa to one of 'high priority'. But von Spee's South Atlantic squadron, having sunk *Good Hope* and *Monmouth* at Coronel on 1 November, was still on the loose and it would take another month for it to be hunted down and destroyed off the Falkland Islands. The Royal Navy was being stretched to the limit in the southern hemisphere, with the result that no sooner had *Weymouth* and *Dartmouth* arrived off East Africa than they were ordered to the Cape to face the potential threat from von Spee. *Chatham* was also ordered to leave for Gibraltar and it was only after Drury-Lowe pointed out to the Admiralty that Churchill – the First Lord of the Admiralty – was daily cajoling him to eliminate the threat posed by the *Königsberg* that his ship was allowed to remain in East Africa. Meanwhile Looff craftily took the opportunity presented by *Chatham*'s concentration on the delta's shore defences to shift his berth even further upriver. This made *Chatham*'s task well-nigh impossible and the only compensation for the radical reduction in the strength of the blockading fleet was that the tides rendered a break-out by Looff equally impossible.

The Admiralty's most protracted and, in its way, complicated task of the Great War had begun, and within six months more than twenty British ships of varying tonnages and types would be employed in assaulting Looff's Rufiji delta fortress. With hindsight Churchill might have been better off leaving Looff and the crew of *Königsberg* to stew in the appallingly debilitating tropical conditions of the Rufiji. But inaction was not in his nature, and a plethora of documents attest to the extent of Churchill's obsession with his prey: soon he was even professing to have 'gone further into the question of destroying

Königsberg by fire' – by flooding the Rufiji with burning pitch, oil and other combustibles.*

Looff made two determined attempts in late November to evade the blockade by reaching Kikale, whence he might escape to the open sea through the delta's southernmost mouth. On both occasions *Königsberg*'s draught proved too great, as did a sally in the direction of the northern Kikunya mouth, but it was clear by then that Churchill's hunch that something unusual would need to be deployed to harm the winkle in its shell was correct. Just such a thing now presented itself. An aeroplane had never before been used in operations against a naval vessel but this was the ingenious solution proposed by Drury-Lowe and Rear-Admiral King-Hall, commander-in-chief of the Cape Station. What's more they knew where to find one, and in no time Herbert Dennis Cutler was commissioned in the Royal Naval Volunteer Reserve and left Durban on the newly armed 15,000-ton Union Castle liner *Kinfauns Castle* with his demonstration 90hp Curtiss seaplane and jerry-built bombs of blasting gelatine.

Captain Denis Crampton of *Kinfauns Castle* took to his innovative mission with relish, remarking that 'it *will* be jolly if we go into action'; and on 19 November Cutler was ready for his first dawn flight over the Rufiji from Niororo Island. It was not an auspicious start to the aerial operations against *Königsberg* because he did not return. At one o'clock he was sighted on Okuzi Island way to the south of Niororo and rescued. Cutler seemed 'quite undisturbed although on a desert island' with his aeroplane 'adrift' and two days later was airborne again, with Crampton himself as observer. This time Cutler succeeded in staying airborne and was rewarded for the feat: the *Königsberg* was spotted about twelve miles upriver, 'hauled in close to the bank of a small island and hidden by high trees so that she could not be seen until the hydroplane was almost over her'. Looff had also struck her topgallant mast and attempted to hide her topmast with branches of trees; and although it was safe to assume that *Königsberg* was 'unable to escape ... even if the river [was] not completely blocked', it was also realised that her 'destruction [was] impracticable by any means, except by means of bomb attack'.[7] The 12-inch guns of HMS *Goliath* could not reach her and even fitting *Goliath*'s guns on the armed merchant cruiser *Duplex*, a former cable-laying ship with shallower draught, was dismissed as being too risky an undertaking in light of the strength of the German shore defences.

Cutler's third daring flight, in the first week of December, was unfortunately his last of the war. His plane came down about a mile upriver and he began

* CHAR/13/38/80. Experiments were carried out at Whale Island by Sir Boverton Redwood. Churchill minuted reports of the findings with a simple 'I like it'.

three grim years as a POW in the bush for his efforts.* Only prompt and courageous action by Lieutenant Charlewood's tug *Helmuth* saved his plane from falling into the hands of the shore defenders as well; but it sank while being hooked onto *Kinfauns Castle* and, though salvaged, was deemed irreparable. The loss of the indefatigable Cutler, who in his short period of active service had proved not only a great source of excitement but also extremely popular, was keenly felt; and the loss of the plane meant that other than hoping for 'the most unhealthy river' that was now home to the *Königsberg* to do its worst to crew and cruiser alike, there was seemingly nothing to be done except wait for the wherewithal with which to attempt the first ever aerial bomb attack of a naval vessel.

In the meantime the Royal Navy's attention reverted to the other tasks involved in blockading the East African coastline, and relations between Drury-Lowe and many of his officers took a turn for the worse. Captain Crampton considered him to be 'rather a little fool' and demanded to know 'how the Devil he expected me to stop the *Königsberg* coming out when my speed can't touch hers and my guns have 600 yards less range'. He was also not alone in believing that Drury-Lowe was running 'grave risks' in his conduct of the *Königsberg* operation, and after a timid reconnaissance of Tanga Crampton's frustration boiled over. 'Give me patience and preserve me from such warfare,' wrote Crampton, 'why on earth doesn't he go in, or let me, and smash up their trenches'.[8] The criticism was only partly justified: Churchill had rescinded an earlier order to 'lay Tanga in ashes'[9] for fear of harming British 'prestige' among the African population; but it echoed the remarks directed at the *Fox*'s Captain Caulfeild six weeks earlier at the very same place. East Africa was proving to be a singularly testing and nerve-wracking theatre of operations for 'Jack Tar', and by the end of November suspicions were mounting that Dar-es-Salaam required another close inspection.

On 28 November *Fox*, *Goliath* and armed merchantman *Duplex* anchored off the German East African capital with the intention of searching the 8,000-ton German liner *Tabora* – which was newly painted in the livery of a hospital ship – and the smaller liners *Feldmarschall* and *König*. Acting Governor Humann was not at all happy with the request, or the expressed intention to disable the *Tabora*'s engines, and he asked if the inspection craft would be flying the white flag. The answer was negative and Humann departed, ostensibly to confer with his superiors. But before he left he went to considerable

---

* See Jones, p. 5: 'there may be more striking incidents in the history of naval aircraft in the war; there are few which, for quiet gallantry, can beat this story of an under-powered flying boat, patched and repatched . . . operating in monsoon weather, from the beach of a tropical island over jungle swamp'.

lengths to explain that *if* the capital was about to be bombarded the Royal Navy should be aware that the town's women and children would be between the Evangelical Mission House and the Cathedral. It was a portentous declaration, the full significance of which apparently eluded the Royal Navy, as did the implications of Humann's refusal to guarantee that no resistance would be encountered if the German ships were searched. The naval truce covering Dar-es-Salaam had been formally revoked by HMS *Chatham* on 21 October, and it was only out of a desire to appear 'honourable' that Humann was forewarned of the Navy's intentions on this occasion. In the meantime, however, von Lettow-Vorbeck had had enough of having to conduct 'fresh negotiations every time . . . we wanted to escape a threatened bombardment'[10] and just two days earlier General Wahle had succeeded, at his commander's behest, in persuading Schnee that Dar-es-Salaam should be vigorously defended the next time the Royal Navy called.

The consequences of this 'misunderstanding' were calamitous. The *Helmuth* visited the *Feldmarschall* and *König*, taking the crew of the latter prisoner and disabling her engines, while Commander Ritchie took *Goliath*'s steam pinnace up the palm-fringed creek to the *Kaiser Wilhelm II* to destroy her engines as well. But finding no one on board the *Wilhelm II* made Ritchie extremely suspicious and he fastened lighters abaft and to both beams of his pinnace for his return journey. Meanwhile, Lieutenant-Commander Paterson, having finished his demolition work on the *Feldmarschall* and *König*, ordered *Helmuth* to put a search party under naval surgeon Holtom on the *Tabora*, and then to return to *Duplex* with the two boatloads of prisoners from the *König*. The crew of the *Helmuth* assumed that Paterson would be picked up by Ritchie as he returned from the *Wilhelm II*.

As this merry-go-round of small craft neared its conclusion in the sweltering heat of a tropical afternoon, the captain of the *Goliath* – still anchored offshore – decided to inspect Dar-es-Salaam's floating dock (which had been sunk in the harbour entrance in August). But when his cutter approached the harbour the sharp crack of rifle fire was heard emanating from the exact area in which Humann had said the town's civilians would be concentrated. Two white flags still fluttered in the breeze, but the rifle fire intensified as *Helmuth*, with its boatloads of prisoners, also approached the harbour neck from the opposite direction; and after *Helmuth*'s gun was put out of action by a lucky rifle shot, *Duplex* was ordered to open fire on Dar-es-Salaam with her 12-pdr. With that, the guns of *Fox* and *Goliath* joined the fray and as *Helmuth* passed the harbour neck her crew were gratified to look back and see 'portions of Government House flying over trees',[11] the more so as their vessel now had the appearance of 'a porcupine below the gunwale and a nutmeg grater above it'.[12]

Back in the harbour, Ritchie's pinnace had still to run the gauntlet and was unable to pick up Holtom from the *Tabora*. German field guns were now in action and by the time Ritchie had reached the harbour neck he had been wounded seven times. Once through it he was hit again, in the leg, and by the time his pinnace reached the *Fox* seven of her crew were also wounded. Only then did it become clear that in addition to Holtom being stranded on the *Tabora*, Paterson's demolition team was still on the *König* and had taken cover below decks.* By the end of the day a total of thirty-five British officers and ratings had been rounded up by German troops, and the only consolation for the Royal Navy for its losses in the ambush was the awarding of nine decorations to men in the boats that had entered the harbour. Most prestigious among these was the Victoria Cross conferred on Commander Ritchie, the Royal Navy's first such award of the Great War.

The flimsy pretext for the attack on the British vessels was – according to Humann – that neither the intrusion of more than one pinnace into the harbour nor the disabling of the German ships' engines had been agreed to. As for the white flags which flew throughout the conflict, Humann claimed in response to an official letter of protest that they could not be lowered 'owing to the intense fire'.[13] The truth of the matter was that von Lettow-Vorbeck, having seized the initiative at Tanga, had no intention of relinquishing it. The more trouble he was able to cause, the more successful he would be in his attempt to force Britain to divert men and materiel to the campaign in East Africa. Churchill's response to the news from Dar-es-Salaam was to order the Royal Navy to 'bombard it severely and then offer not to renew if officers and men are surrendered'.[14] At 10.30 a.m. on 30 December the Navy put its demands to Humann, no British prisoners were handed over, and in a systematic thirty-salvo bombardment shells further wrecked the Governor's Palace and Bismarckstrasse, the railway station and coaling depot, and the signal station on the beach. Many naval officers were at a loss to understand why any warning was given, especially as fifty or more soldiers and a field gun were clearly visible near the harbour at the time. The only possible explanation lay in a desire to avoid being accused of 'atrocities', but if this was the intention it failed. In Dar-es-Salaam the bombardment was painted as an outrage against 'a poor little crowd of human beings, exposed to the fury of a force which cannot be compared for sheer terror to any natural force'; and it further kindled the 'warlike spirit' that von Lettow-Vorbeck sought to instil in the colony. One resident of the town proudly declared that 'the timidity [had] gone' from the civilian population of Dar-es-Salaam, and expressed great satisfaction that 'now at last our government has shown some backbone,

---

* German accounts alleged that Paterson's men were 'getting drunk in the saloon' when captured by Lieutenant Soethe (see Ada Schnee, p. 24).

reawakening the idea of a greater Germany'.[15] The fact that Pilsen and French champagne were still available in any hotel in the town even after four months of being blockaded by the Royal Navy was a further boost to morale.

Von Lettow-Vorbeck need not have worried unduly about the possibility of a further attack on Tanga. With the War Office in the process of taking over responsibility for the campaign from the Colonial and India Offices, and Aitken being replaced by Wapshare, his opponents were neither able nor willing to do anything other than mark time. The deployment of IEF 'B' was the first priority, and it had a very marked effect on administrative and civilian life in British East Africa. Belfield suddenly found himself superfluous to requirements and, after being subjected to 'a few electrics'[16] by the military establishment, he complained of feeling 'a bit neuralgic in Nairobi' and retired to the coast. 'Nobody knows what [the military] are up to', he lamented in a despatch to Lord Harcourt, and he was largely correct. An 'air of mystery and secrecy'[17] prevailed, compounded by the fact that Wapshare seemingly gave Tighe (at Mombasa) and Stewart (at Bissil, fifty miles south of Nairobi) a free rein to run military affairs in their respective zones. This caused a good deal of confusion, and tensions soon arose between Belfield's government officials and their military counterparts.

Supply issues proved particularly contentious. Captain Routh, a supply officer with IEF 'B' whose enterprise was attested to by his having bicycled from Port Said to Ostend in 1906, was astounded at the 'hyper-parochialism' of Belfield's officials and derided them as 'men of fifteen years' accumulated EA inertia, unspoilt by the race for life now disturbing [them] so distressingly'.[18] When he needed new telephone lines for Longido he was told by the Postmaster-General that there were none available because the Post Office only had ten spares and 'several new subscribers were coming on the exchange';[19] and when Belfield was asked for a rebate on customs duty on all stores purchased locally by the troops since August 1914, the Governor refused, thereby claiming a 'profit to the Protectorate at the expense of Imperial War Funds'.[20] In similar vein, when Ewart Grogan, the owner of British East Africa's largest timber concern, offered the military 100 tons of desperately needed timber for nothing the offer was blocked by the government as constituting 'an unfair risk'[21] to its own Public Works Department. Routh's overall impression was that the government 'didn't take the war too seriously', and that any vestigial interest had 'evaporated since Force "B" arrived'.[22] 'The atmosphere', he wrote, 'was "we have done very well up to now" – which was true, but I consider something more than smug complacence and an empty market was required.'[23]

Routh's observations regarding official inertia would have come as no surprise to British East Africa's settler population. A marked antipathy had characterised settler – official relations in the decade before the war, engendered by the settlers' clamour for greater participation in running the country and the Colonial Office's perceived aversion to 'development', and the settlers were unimpressed by the fact that officials had not yet participated in the war. Leslie Tarlton, Bellasis, Kay-Mouat, Sandbach, Le Page – these were the names of just a few of the settlers who had died for their country during the first three months of war, and yet civil servants were conspicuously absent from the roll of honour. But any hopes that Wapshare's General Staff was about to embrace the settlers with open arms were soon dashed. A 'Poona-Poona' attitude to using civilians in the field prevailed among Indian Army officers, who regarded 'the local obsession . . . that any pack of fools can use guns'[24] with derision. All in all, the conclusion was that 'settlers are great fellows in a bar, and some few outside it, but they make one quite nervous fighting'.[25] Settlers were also *expensive*, and in an effort to trim India's share of the costs of the campaign, which had mushroomed to £400,000 (£20m in today's money) against a budgeted £100,000, only 130 men were retained in the volunteer East African Mounted Rifles by the end of the year. Meanwhile their comrades were given the choice of returning to their peacetime occupations or joining other units.

Amid the 'sanity and a solid settling down to the job in hand'[26] in December came a realisation that Britain was now playing for high stakes in East Africa. 'To the German,' wrote the editors of *The Leader*, 'Africa is the key continent of the world, and its owners will possess the balance of power between the old world and the new.'[27] The military situation therefore remained extremely nerve-wracking and *real* martial law was finally declared in December in an attempt to keep secret a planned expedition to the Umba Valley – a vast plain of ebony trees, baobabs and euphorbia on the coastal borderlands between British and German East Africa – whose Wadigo inhabitants had requested British protection from German raids. The spectre of invasion again loomed large, not only on the coast but also on Uganda's weakly defended Kagera 'front'.

The job of clearing the Umba Valley of German troops and 'Arab' levies fell to Mickey Tighe. This time he made quite sure he had sufficient troops for the purpose – 1,800 rifles in all[*] – and a simultaneous 'demonstration' north

---

[*] Tighe's force: 2nd Kashmir Rifles, 101st Grenadiers, two companies of 3/KAR, four companies of 3rd Gwalior Infantry, 100 Wavell's 'Arab' Scouts, the 28th Mountain Battery and six machine-guns.

of Tanga was arranged by the Royal Navy. By Christmas Eve a new coastal headquarters had been established at Msambweni to replace the one at Gazi (which had become so unsanitary that a smallpox epidemic had broken out); and Tighe's troops had occupied Vanga, on the border with German East Africa. Just for good measure Tighe then ordered the two companies of 3/KAR and the 101st Grenadiers to attack Jasin, a few miles the other side of the border, on Christmas Day. The German garrison withdrew after a short scrap, and the post was then garrisoned so as 'to ensure ample warning of any German advance from the south'.[28]

By New Year Wapshare was able to report to London that for the time being British East Africa was 'clear of the enemy'.[29] But the real significance of the Umba Valley operation lay in Tighe's choice of combat and support personnel. Although Aitken had refused an offer of the use of 3/KAR at Tanga, it was *askari* of this regiment that fought alongside a company of the 101st Grenadiers to seize Jasin; and the mobility of the whole Umba Valley force depended on 5,500 African porters. After Tanga *The Leader* had remarked that it was 'of course ... an understood rule that in these wars the natives are not brought into the row', and the paper's editors accused von Lettow-Vorbeck of 'ignoring all the rules of civilised war'[30] by deploying his *askari* in the battle. Yet two months later it was quite clear that any absurd aspirations to limit the participation of East Africa's indigenous population had been dispensed with by Britain as well, and the campaign was destined to become no more a 'White Man's War' than the war between Britain and the Boer Republics a decade and a half earlier. The Great *African* War had begun.

PART TWO

1915

SNIPING NOTE FROM EAST AFRICA
'Picking off the enemy'

Perhaps the blokes in Flanders our little bit will scorn,
'Cos we've never had an order that gas masks must be worn,
And have never heard a 'nine point five' or a Hymn of Hate at morn.

But how'd you like to tramp it for a solid month on end,
And then go on another month till your knees begin to bend,
Or when you're out on picquet hear a lion answer 'Friend'?

And what about a scrapping up a mountain three miles high,
A-swearing and a-panting till you thought your end was nigh,
And then to bump a Maxim gun that's dug in on the sky?

And would you like anopheles and jigger-fleas and snakes
To 'chivvy' you from dusk till dawn, and fill you up with aches,
And then go on fatigue all day in a heat that fairly bakes?

There wasn't any Blighty, no, nor mails in twice a week:
We had no concerts 'hind the lines; we got too bored to speak,
And there was no change of rations; and our water bottles leak.

So don't despise our efforts, for we've done our level best,
For it wasn't beer and skittles, those two years without a rest,
And though the world forgot us we think we stood the test.

From 'The Return of the Cohort' by Owen Letcher

SIX

The Coast

———— ◆ ————

Tighe's success in clearing German troops from the Umba Valley enabled British East Africa's European population to enjoy a relatively untroubled Christmas. Marquees and tents lit with Japanese lanterns were rigged up overlooking Mombasa harbour, creating an ambience that could have been mistaken for that 'at the White Hart, Hendon Way'; and in Nairobi festive season gossip – including the observation that 'whilst skirts retain their fullness and evince signs of becoming wider as the winter advances, the bodices appear to get plainer and tighter'[1] – was as prominent in the pages of *The Leader* as news of the war.

Hundreds of miles to the south, even the naval ratings keeping watch on the *Königsberg* were able to make light of their dreary, debilitating task. Coffin-shaped floats with lanterns were launched into the Rufiji delta bearing such seasonal greetings as 'Try our Christmas pudding – large six inch – small size four point seven',[2] and the humour was reciprocated. Looff had moved his cruiser to a 'new hiding place' on 20 December, and felt sufficiently secure to celebrate onshore, where long tables laden with beer, cigarettes and gifts from all around the colony were set around a small mango tree; and a week later the German sailors were celebrating in similar fashion when HMS *Weymouth* sent them a wireless message which read 'we wish you a happy New Year and hope to see you soon'. Looff replied: 'Thanks for the message, if you wish to see us we are always at home'.[3]

The season of goodwill proved to be short – and illusory. Tighe's success could not mask the fact that there were only 4,000 'reliable' troops in British East Africa, backed by a reserve of 1,000 rifles whose performance in combat was considered rather less reliable.[*] Further advances southwards from Jasin or from Voi, on the Uganda Railway, towards the German stronghold at

———

[*] See TNA/WO/106/573. The 'reliable' troops were listed as: 600 2nd Loyal North Lancs, 600 29th Punjabis, 520 101st Grenadiers, 660 Kashmiris and 1,000 KAR. The 98th Infantry and 63rd Palamcottahs were regarded as 'useless', and the 61st Pioneers were dismissively referred to as being 'only fit as labourers'.

Taveta were therefore out of the question until such time as a substantial numerical advantage could be assured and the necessary supply and transport arrangements put in place. But to do nothing was as unappealing a prospect as suffering another resounding defeat; and when Tighe, a man who was 'appalled by administrative detail'[4] and treated anyone less optimistic than he 'like a naughty schoolboy',[5] became alarmed by a bizarre rumour that Belgian troops from the Congo had advanced 300 miles into German East Africa and captured Tabora, he succeeded in goading Wapshare into action.

The unlikely target of British attentions was Mafia – a small, malarial island of about 13,000 inhabitants that had once been a favoured haunt of coastal pirates and in 1890 had been swapped with Germany for the strip of land connecting Lake Nyasa with Lake Tanganyika that became known as the Stevenson Road. Thereafter it had become the focus of an unsuccessful attempt by a few intrepid German planters to break the British monopoly of the clove industry, centred on Zanzibar and Pemba; otherwise its significance had remained slight – until its position ten miles off the Rufiji delta presented Wapshare with a relatively risk-free opportunity to raise British morale and secure a more proximate base than Zanzibar from which to conduct further operations against the *Königsberg*.

The 'invasion' of Mafia by four companies of 1/KAR and one company of the 101st Grenadiers – 500 troops in all – began on 9 January 1915. Resistance was only encountered two days later at a hillock near the village of Ngombeni, where three Germans and thirty *askari* led by reservist Lieutenant Erich Schiller held out for a couple of hours before being persuaded to surrender. The following day the German administrator at Kilindoni followed suit and, at the cost of fewer than a dozen casualties, the Union Jack was raised over Mafia after an absence of twenty-five years. The success of the joint operation – in which HMS *Fox*, HMS *Weymouth* and the *Kinfauns Castle* took part – was scarcely compensation for the failure at Tanga, but there was considerable relief in the ships' wardrooms that, whatever the growing doubts about Drury-Lowe's merits as Senior Naval Officer, at least Captain Caulfeild's 'footling orders' and 'mis-management'[6] had been dispensed with. On 12 January the invasion force re-embarked for Mombasa, leaving only Colonel Mackay, the former senior Intelligence officer of IEF 'B', and a single company of the 63rd Palamcottahs to atone for their respective 'sins' at Tanga by garrisoning the sweltering hell-hole that was Mafia.

At exactly the same time as Mafia fell into British hands, von Lettow-Vorbeck began the preparations for his next move. A message from the Kaiser had recently arrived and, emboldened by the knowledge that 'the Fatherland

[was] proud of its sons'* in East Africa, the German commander-in-chief decided that Tighe's occupation of Jasin needed to be countered immediately. It might, von Lettow-Vorbeck suspected, be a prelude to an advance down the coast to Tanga and with that in mind he ordered 4/SchK and 15/FK to reconnoitre the defences of Jasin's fort and a nearby sisal factory on 12 January. The prompt arrival of British reinforcements from the Umba Valley camp, just three miles north of Jasin, forced the German troops to retreat and a further probe four days later was also seen off. These encounters furnished von Lettow-Vorbeck with valuable information about how British troops would deploy in the event of an attack, and within a week he had concentrated fully nine companies to the south of Jasin in readiness for the execution of a classic 'horns of the bull' assault of the sort once favoured by the Zulus. Captain Otto was to assault Jasin fort frontally with 9/FK and the irregular 'Arab Corps', supported by a battery of two guns under reservist Bruno Fromme; Major Kepler was to advance on Otto's right with 11/FK and 4/FK; and Captain Adler was to lead 15/FK and 17/FK on the left flank. Meanwhile a trolley-line from Tothovu, seven miles to the south of Jasin, would enable von Lettow-Vorbeck speedily to deploy his force reserve – 1/FK, 6/FK and 13/FK led by Captain Schulz, Demuth's 7/SchK of European reservists, and Hering's two C73 field guns – wherever they were required. Von Lettow-Vorbeck's determination to regain German supremacy over the coastal bor-derlands was self-evident: his attack force was larger than that which had concentrated at Tanga by 5 November the previous year.[†]

The terrain over which the German troops advanced at dawn on 18 January was even less favourable than that encountered by the British troops to the east of Tanga. Dense vegetation and a multitude of streams criss-crossed the battlefield, hampering progress and robbing the initial attack of the advantage of complete surprise, and by the time German troops appeared within range of the fort SOS rockets had been fired to call for reinforcements from Umba, and Colonel Raghbir Singh's garrison of Kashmiris and Grenadiers all stood at the ready. What ensued was hardly the introit that von Lettow-Vorbeck had

* TNA/CAB/45/10 (Gerlach). One German officer was moved to write that 'there was no one left among all of us, who, when the message reached us, did not solemnly repeat to himself the oath to preserve faithfully, and to give the last drop of blood and breath to help what is German land to remain German so that the confidence which the Kaiser has put in his people here will not be misplaced'.
† The German attack force comprised 244 Europeans, 1,350 *askari* and 400 'Arab' levies, armed with twenty-three machine-guns and four field guns. The British garrison at Jasin fort comprised one company of 101st Grenadiers (138 rifles), one and a half companies of Kashmiris (144 rifles) and a KAR machine-gun detachment. The sisal factory was held by forty-four men of the 2nd Kashmir Rifles.

hoped for: Otto's frontal attack was stopped in its tracks by disciplined and accurate fire from the fort, Major Kepler was killed in the first hour of fighting on the German right, and when the elite 13/FK was sent to reinforce Otto it lost its three senior officers – Spalding, Langen and Oppen – in just ten minutes.

Captain Adler's simultaneous attack on Jasin's sisal factory 1,000 yards north of the fort fared rather better. Although one company of 1/KAR, led by Captain Giffard, arrived promptly from Umba it was unable to break through to the factory and by 9 a.m. the garrison of forty Kashmiris was surrounded. For two hours the Indian troops stood their ground 'with great spirit' against 'very heavy rifle and machine-gun fire'[7] from Captain Adler's *askari*; and when their ammunition ran out Subadar Mardan Ali led a bayonet and *kukri* charge at the German lines which resulted in three-quarters of his men reaching safety. But with their departure, Adler's two companies were able to turn their full attention to preventing any British reinforcements from reaching Colonel Singh's garrison in Jasin's now-isolated fort.

During the morning two companies of 3/KAR from Umba had managed to secure a foothold south of the Suba River in the hope of reinforcing the fort, but after two hours of intense fighting they, like their comrades attempting to get to the sisal factory, had been forced to retire. Von Lettow-Vorbeck had used the intelligence gained during his earlier probes against Jasin well: this time the police *askari* of Adler's 17/FK were dug in on a ridge overlooking the river and from this commanding position were able to oppose any British troops approaching from the north. By noon, however, four companies of 1/KAR, two companies of Jhind Infantry and a section of the 28th Mountain Battery had been ordered to attack the captured sisal factory and cross the Suba River for an advance on the fort. Once again it proved impossible to do more than establish tenuous footholds south of the river, and the Jhind Infantry suffered particularly heavy casualties in the process – of their 120 men who crossed the river thirty-six were killed and twenty-one were wounded. Among others the conduct of Major-General Natha Singh of the Jhinds was singled out for special mention by Tighe, as was that of Effendi Said Abd-el-Rahman of 3/KAR; and Colour-Sergeant George Williams, also of 3/KAR, who had already won the DCM for his conduct at Tsavo in September, saved a Maxim gun after its ammunition ran out and succeeded in extricating his company from a position while under intense fire.[*]

---

[*] Williams was recommended for the VC but was eventually awarded a bar to his DCM. For an explanation of why, as an African soldier, he was not given the former see Keith Steward, 'An African Hero Who Deserved the Victoria Cross', *The Orders and Medals Research Society Journal* (March 2005), pp. 19–26.

By mid afternoon it was clear that the situation was a stalemate and Tighe decided that any new attack would have to wait until HMS *Weymouth* arrived offshore the following day to provide naval support. Tighe's decision was based upon a belief that the garrison at Jasin would be able to withstand a siege lasting a week. This may have been true as far as comestibles were concerned, but in mounting such a solid defence most of the ammunition – 300 rounds per man – had been expended by nightfall. Worse still, the sole machine-gun in the fort was no longer working, and Captains Hanson and Turner of the 101st Grenadiers reluctantly gave the order to surrender.

The capture of almost 300 Kashmiris and Grenadiers, and the thwarting of any imminent advance on Tanga that Tighe might have been planning, prompted von Lettow-Vorbeck to declare that his attack on Jasin had been 'completely successful'[8] (and that the enemy had sustained more than 700 casualties). News of the victory was immediately despatched to Berlin in the hope that it might even arrive in time for the Kaiser's birthday on 27 January. But the price of success was considerable. Von Lettow-Vorbeck's troops had expended 200,000 rounds of ammunition; his senior Staff officer, Major Kepler, had been killed; and a further six officers and eighteen German NCOs also lay dead, including the German leader's great friend, Freiherr Alexander von Hammerstein-Gesmold, and many officers who had distinguished themselves at Tanga. Total German casualties amounted to almost 300, and even von Lettow-Vorbeck had suffered the indignity of being shot through his bush hat and in the arm. On the face of it, Jasin was less like an outright 'victory' than a rather costly exercise prompted by a rush of blood to the German commander's head, an irresponsible initiative by a man who after Tanga entertained thoughts of invincibility and was even prepared to risk fighting *offensively* over terrain that neither he nor his senior officers, with the sole exception of a reservist who had once worked on the sisal plantation at Jasin, knew at all well. On the other hand Jasin was entirely consistent with von Lettow-Vorbeck's strategy of inflicting as much damage on his enemy as possible before the 'decisive' battle – which he remained convinced would take place in the near future around Handeni – and, in that context, his casualties and the use of irreplaceable materiel were justifiable. Besides, neither side expected the war to last much longer and a second major victory in German East Africa could only strengthen Germany's hand at the negotiating table.

Von Lettow-Vorbeck did recognise, amid the jubilation of his troops, that 'such heavy losses as we had suffered could only be borne in exceptional cases', and that he 'could at most fight three more actions of this nature'. Materiel was one constraint, but even that paled in comparison with the problem of manpower. There was no problem recruiting *askari* aplenty. The difficulty after Jasin was finding sufficient officers and NCOs among the colony's European population to train and lead them: by the end of January 1915 one third of the *Schutztruppe*'s thirty-three officers with the rank of *Oberleutnant* and above had already been killed or severely wounded. It was this alarming fact that not only forced von Lettow-Vorbeck to authorise a round of instant promotions but also to modify his tactics. There would be no attempt to repeat the blows struck at Tanga and Jasin in 1915. But this did not signify any diminution in the resolve of the German commander, who heard in February that his brother had been killed on the Western Front during the first month of the war: his new tactic was simply to concentrate on causing maximum disruption to British East Africa's lifeline – the Uganda Railway.

The limitations imposed on von Lettow-Vorbeck by the battle at Jasin were as nothing when compared to those immediately imposed on Wapshare and Tighe by the War Office. Even though Tighe did not regard his clearance of German troops from the Umba Valley and the occupation of Jasin as offensive measures, or even a prelude to offensive measures, Lord Kitchener viewed them as 'risky expeditions'[9] of a type which he had expressly forbidden. As a result all British positions south of Gazi and Msambweni were abandoned and by the second week in February Tighe's force, having sustained some 500 casualties, was back where it had started before Christmas – a move which made it abundantly clear to his demoralised and debilitated troops that the invasion of German East Africa had been postponed 'for some time to come'.[10]

Looff had discussed the possibility of joint operations with Major Kepler just prior to the outbreak of war, but the German Navy had always forcefully resisted any subordination to colonial land forces and the captain of the *Königsberg* had largely been left to his own devices by von Lettow-Vorbeck. As January drew to a close he was frustrated that the enemy cruisers off the delta never came within range of his guns, but took considerable pride in the fact that by 1915 'there [was] not one [other] German cruiser operating by herself in the whole world ... All the others have preceded us in honour and in death.'[11] Like von Lettow-Vorbeck he recognised that the best he could do was 'to engage the greatest number of the enemy'[12] and all incursions by the plethora of smaller British craft were forcefully opposed by the delta's defence force, commanded by retired naval officer Werner Schönfeld.

Looff's greatest concern, other than keeping the *Königsberg* ready to pounce at the slightest opportunity for a break-out, was the health of his men. Malaria was rife among his crew, despite the best efforts of Dr Eyerich's staff at the hospital on the nearby plantation of Neustieten. By Looff's own admission morale was also poor, the men fatalistic, and although the welfare of a baby hippo kept everyone occupied for the fifteen days that it survived, diversions were few. Work continued on trying to rig torpedoes to one of the small craft in the delta, but this initiative proved as frustrating as the occasional attempt to send a steamboat to Dar-es-Salaam. Always thwarted by the vigilance of the Royal Navy, such attempts only served to emphasise the degree to which the German sailors were now well and truly imprisoned.

An *official* blockade of the East Coast was declared on 28 February, begging the question as to what state of affairs had existed before, and a week later the bushy-eyebrowed, monocled Admiral Herbert King-Hall arrived from the Cape to take direct command of the East Coast operations, flying his flag on board HMS *Hyacinth*. King-Hall had started his naval career in 1874 at the age of twelve, weighing five stone and measuring just under four feet four inches in height. Four decades later one petty officer remarked that he still 'didn't stand as high as six of coppers' and added that he had 'seen a better looking monkey in a zoo'[13] – a fact readily admitted by King-Hall, who took great pride in introducing himself to people as 'the ugliest man in the British Navy'. Appearances aside, he was a forceful and bustling officer, and his appointment was an indication that Churchill wanted an end to Drury-Lowe's 'woolliness' even if it meant dealing with a man as opinionated and self-assured as himself. The one blot on King-Hall's war record thus far had been the failure of his squadron to deal with the *Königsberg*, but as HMS *Weymouth* was 'the only really efficient modern vessel in the whole pack'[14] at his disposal he did not consider such allegations at all justified. Either way King-Hall meant to put the record straight. Like Churchill he possessed an innovative mind: the Cutler seaplane expedition, however short-lived, attested to that, as did the planning of a new aerial initiative.

Cutler's fate had in no way deterred King-Hall from using the new weapon of air power and in January No. 4 Squadron of the newly formed Royal Naval Air Service was detailed to East Africa. Led by Flight Lieutenants Cull and Watkins, the party numbered twenty in all, including a mechanic lent by Sopwith and two men from the propeller manufacturer Messrs Lang. They and their two Sopwith 807 100hp seaplanes were collected from Bombay by the *Kinfauns Castle* and arrived at their secret base on Niororo Island, about 100 miles south of Zanzibar, on 20 February. A single, fleeting look at their new 'desert island' home would have dispelled any thoughts of living up to the RNAS's reputation for being 'Rather Naughty After Sunset'. With only the island's headman and thirty-strong family as astonished onlookers they commenced trials immediately, and no sooner had they done so than their respect for Cutler's 'brilliant feat'[15] of reconnoitring the Rufiji delta soared. *He* had at least managed to get airborne in the thin tropical air which proved quite beyond the new Sopwith machines, the more so when loaded with bombs. Eventually, after one of their planes was irreparably wrecked, these pioneer aviators, or 'chauffeurs of airplanes' as Churchill was somewhat pompously wont to refer to their ilk, discovered that flight could be achieved on days of high humidity – but only with one hour's fuel and only to a height of no more than 1,500 feet. The squadron agreed that 'something had to be done',[16] not least in order to save face in front of Niororo's inhabitants, all of whom turned out to watch each doomed trial.

Flying, or the lack of it, was not the squadron's only problem. When the one remaining serviceable plane took to the water its floats had an alarming tendency to peel off and the plane would start to sink; and with the onset of the monsoon from the north-east sharks appeared inshore, adding further excitement to the process of launching or beaching the Sopwith. Furthermore, none of the airmen appeared to be at all aware of the dangers of sunburn, and as clothing was largely dispensed with at their secret base many were destined to spend sweltering days and nights swaddled in bandages of picric acid. Yet for all their tribulations the airmen had the complete backing of King-Hall and his Flag Commander, the Hon. Richard Bridgeman. The enthusiasm, kindness and sheer pizzazz of the latter 'was everything to us', reported Cull, as were the services of intrepid Midshipman Gallehawk (who soon secured a transfer to the RNAS); and by the end of March help was on its way in the shape of three Short seaplanes from Britain. These were sent in response to the discovery that only 'exceptionally powerful machines'[17] would defy the exacting climatic conditions. But Cull was soon to discover that the planes brought out by the Cunarder *Laconia* were in fact well known to him from the RNAS base at the Isle of Grain: they were old Short Folders, and their lamentable condition seemingly put paid to any thoughts of destroying the *Königsberg* from the air.

The 'ugliest man in the British Navy' had another trick up his sleeve, however, bringing from South Africa in his wake one Piet Pretorius. Pretorius was 'thin, lithe, and coloured brown from continual bouts of malaria'.[18] Descended from the Boer *Voortrekker* Andries Pretorius, he had achieved celebrity status in southern Africa as an elephant hunter and adventurer before finding himself on an island in the Rovuma River, the border between German and Portuguese East Africa, when news of the outbreak of war reached him. Three testing months had ensued, in which this intrepid 'Africa hand' had escaped from the infamous Dr Weck – the leader of the German patrol which had attacked the border post of Maziua in neutral Portuguese East Africa in August 1914 – despite his right leg being shattered by a bullet; been arrested by the Portuguese and escaped their clutches at Negomano; and trekked for a month to the safety of an English mission on Lake Nyasa. When he had finally recovered from his ordeals, Pretorius had then made his way to South Africa where he soon received a summons from King-Hall.

King-Hall's interest in Pretorius was prompted by the latter's unrivalled knowledge of the Rufiji delta. Years earlier he had owned a cotton plantation there, but the German authorities had dispossessed him of this and his hunting licence in controversial circumstances. Pretorius's response to his treatment had been stubborn and uncompromising: he had set about recouping all his losses by poaching ivory. But even when he had succeeded in exacting his revenge, he retained a very considerable grudge against the German colonial authorities (and remained on German East Africa's 'most wanted' list). To Pretorius, all Germans were possessed of an 'arrogant attitude' that was 'bred in the national character';[19] and, although the Rufiji was where he had lost everything, including a young bride, he agreed, to King-Hall's huge sat-isfaction, to return to this place of sad memories and become his chief scout in the delta. Pretorius made his base on Mafia, selected six 'of the biggest rogues on the entire coast'[20] as his henchmen, and set about his task with relish. He sensed in King-Hall a man who 'when he struck meant to kill'.[21]

While Pretorius began to reconnoitre the defences of Schönfeld's 'Delta Force', King-Hall and Churchill continued their jousting contest. Churchill wanted to land two battalions of 'jollies' – Royal Marines – with six 12-pdr guns in the delta, but was told by the Admiralty that there were no jollies to spare; while King-Hall proposed sending a small boat armed with torpedoes upriver, to which Churchill's damning reply read: 'I do not think the chance of a rowing boat with spar torpedo going 12 miles up a creek past a fortified port with numerous trenches and trying to attack a ship with searchlights and modern guns is likely to be very rosy'.[22] King-Hall was not so easily rebuffed, however, and countered Churchill with the idea of a night attack to attach charges to *Königsberg's* hull combined with an attempt to fire the ship with petrol. 'Not approved' came the reply, with a renewed suggestion to mine as many mouths to the delta as possible. 'Not possible' answered King-Hall, citing scarce resources and pointing out that German troops guarding the delta would most probably raise the mines and re-lay them in the hope of sinking one of the Royal Navy's own vessels.

Amid the sparring, the merry-go-round of Royal Navy vessels blockading the delta continued unabated. During March 1915 *Weymouth, Hyacinth, Chil-ders* and *Echo* patrolled off the main entrances while *Pioneer, Duplex* and *Pickle* covered the northern approaches and *Pyramus* and *Fly* the southern. *Goliath,* the largest of the fleet, and *Kinfauns Castle,* the mother ship to the RNAS seaplanes, operated further offshore. *Fox* had left for a refit in Bombay, *Chatham* had been recalled to the Mediterranean, *Goliath* was ordered to leave for the Dardanelles (where she would meet her doom), and Lord Kelburn's *Pyramus* was soon forced to leave her station for her engines to be repaired in Cape Town. With each passing week, the conditions exacted a larger toll. Navigation in shallow waters strewn with sandbanks, mudbanks and reefs was extremely testing (one channel off Niororo that had to be frequently used was just 200 yards wide and *Hyacinth* only cleared the bottom by nine inches at low water), underwater fittings rapidly deteriorated, and condenser tubes and inlets became choked and corroded at a much quicker rate than was normal. Plates also became distorted in the heat, and keels were torn on reefs, but the worst job of all was the ghastly, messy, suffocating process of coaling every ten days or so.

Many hoped that the arrival of Captain Thomas Biddlecombe's HMAS *Pioneer* might be a favourable portent. The fledgling Royal Australian Navy had already indirectly played an important part in the East African campaign when HMAS *Sydney* had rid the Indian Ocean of the *Emden* in November; and *Pioneer* was, like the New Zealand Navy's *Pyramus*, a sister ship of the ill-fated *Pegasus*. But the state of repair of this aged *Pelorus*-class light cruiser put paid to such optimism: her below-decks conditions were so appalling that in recent years 'clinker-knockers' – stokers – had deserted her in droves and they exacerbated the suffering of ratings required to maintain a heavy – and mind-numbingly dull – workload off the delta. Indeed sheer boredom was the greatest challenge confronting the officers and men on blockade duty. Many of their ships were destined to be under weigh for more than 250 days in 1915, and in *Pioneer*'s case the tally reached an astonishing 287 days, (during which she cruised almost 30,000 miles). Shore leave was seldom for long and, except in the case of a refit in one of South Africa's ports, where all the womenfolk would turn out to give ships a traditional 'colonial welcome', unexciting. The diet was execrable: *Pioneer* and the older ships had no bakery or refrigerator and were seldom able to find adequate quantities of preserved meat, pickled pork, condensed milk, biscuits, tinned fish, eggs, bacon, or even dried fruit in the markets of Zanzibar and Mombasa. And to cap all the discomfort, cockroaches infested the decks (where temperatures seldom fell below 85°F) and even engine rooms (where the temperature frequently reached 125°F). Mails – the most vital source of succour to the crews – were at best infrequent.

In such conditions cynicism abounded. In one edition of *Pioneer*'s shipboard magazine, *The Observer*, 'Disappointed VC' contributed the following stanza to the 'Deaths Column':

> Our enthusiasm has died since coming to this country.
> Glory we sought
> But won it not.

East African settlers report to Nairobi's recruitment office in August 1914 . . .

. . . and take to the field

The execution of spies in Zanzibar

SMS *Königsberg*, commanded by Max Looff (inset), at Dar-es-Salaam

German lookout posts were swiftly constructed along the border with British East Africa, and formidable entrenchments were dug around many towns

Arthur Aitken, the commander of Indian Expeditionary Force 'B'

After the disastrous setback at Tanga Aitken's two successors, Richard Wapshare (left) and Michael Tighe (right), were charged with preventing a German invasion of British East Africa

The transports carrying IEF 'B' approach Tanga in November 1914

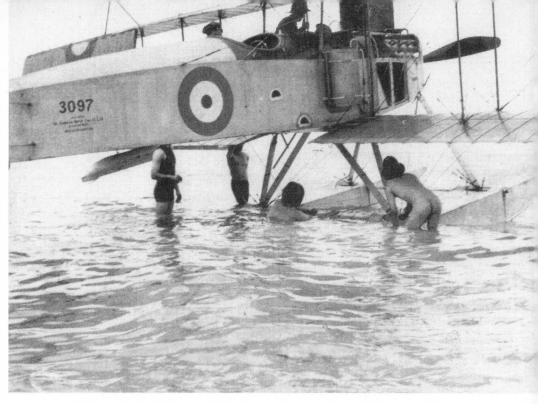

Men of the Royal Naval Air Service prepare one of their seaplanes for take-off

German shore defences guarding the approaches to the *Königsberg*'s lair in the Rufiji delta

Askari of 4th King's African Rifles watching over a wounded comrade awaiting evacuation near Mzima

An attempt by troopers of the East African Mounted Rifles to disguise a pony as a zebra

A halt is called by a Belgian Cyclist Company

Indian gunners in action on the Longido front

British troops prepare to resist an attack on the Uganda Railway
(painted by Philip Dadd)

'Loyal *askari*'
(painted by Fritz Grotemeyer)

Discomfort, not laurels
Is all we got.

And in April *The Observer* noted that 'Once again we are back at the old Rufigi. On every hand one hears such ejaculations as "she'll come out tonight", "by Jove I wish something would happen", "we hear that *Königsberg* has moved".' In the column 'For Our Intellectual Readers' a challenge was even posed: 'If the *Königsberg* advances up the river at the rate of 3 yards a week, how long will it take the *Pioneer* to sink her firing at the rate of 5 rounds per hour (perhaps).' Social highlights such as a cricket match against *Hyacinth*, or the first dismal performance of *Pioneer*'s brass band were rare. All in all, there was no disguising the fact that sinking the occasional unarmed dhow was not really the stuff that had made 'England's glorious name resound through the ages'.[23]

Boredom and hardship were inevitably attended by sickness. The Fleet Surgeon on *Hyacinth*, Robley-Browne, recorded no fewer than 3,638 sick days from 603 cases among a crew of 625 in 1915. The vast majority of these were classified as 'routine' – influenza, ear infections, septicaemia associated with minor work injuries (everything turned septic in the sweaty heat); and most common of all were respiratory problems, which were treated in surprisingly progressive fashion, through the use of massage. Uncommon 'incidents' often posed a greater challenge. When Robley-Browne was confronted by a stoker with a sore on his genitals, he was unconvinced by his patient's claim that 'this was due to an accident with a match while lying in his hammock' and assumed that the 'obvious explanation' lay in 'some visits to Zanzibar'. Due to the lack of conventional combat, the only casualty in the year was the unfortunate crewman bin Ali who, while on duty on the tug *Salamander*, was 'struck on the head by a shell' from the delta's shore battery, a misfortune which Robley-Browne noted had 'immediately fatal results'.[24]

Under the circumstances it was little short of miraculous that the Royal Navy was able to stick with its thankless task, or that any Germans remained alive in the Rufiji delta. By the end of March, however, morale on both sides suddenly took a turn for the better when the real reason for the declaration of an official blockade became common knowledge: it wasn't a belated formalisation of the blocking-in of all German vessels but a response to rumours of a 'visitor' from outside. Towards the end of February an impounded British steamer of almost 4,000 gross tons, formerly the SS *Rubens* of the Frederick

Bolton Steamship Company, had slipped quietly out of Wilhelmshaven – von Lettow-Vorbeck's base in his days with II *Seebataillon* – and into the North Sea. Sailing under the Danish flag as the *Kronborg* she passed north of the Shetland Islands, south of the Faroes and, one month later, Cape Verde. Eluding detection was a feat in itself. 'True, Britannia ruled the waves,' wrote Nis Kock, one of the predominantly South Jutland crew, 'but here and there you can still find one or two not quite under control, and we sailed on those.'[25] Her destination was East Africa, and she was laden with huge quantities of supplies and materiel – and 1,600 tons of prime coal to facilitate the *Königsberg*'s return to Germany. Her skipper, Karl Christiansen, told his crew that their mission might mean the difference between capitulation and survival for German East Africa. 'One rifle in Africa', he pointed out, was 'worth as much as a big gun'[26] on the Western Front.

The Admiralty was on to the *Kronborg* quickly, having intercepted wireless signals from Nauen, Germany's principal wireless station, to a mystery vessel with the call-sign 'DH'; and as the blockade-runner neared the East African coast, the Royal Navy also began picking up signals from the *Königsberg*'s wireless. Looff was only able to send signals to Germany on the odd occasion when weather conditions were exceptionally clement, but he could receive them, and when he was informed of the *Kronborg*'s proximity he began trying to contact the blockade-runner. His intention was to attempt – rather too conspicuously for Christiansen's liking – to confuse the Royal Navy as his first real chance for a break-out loomed, and in the second week in April contact was established with the *Kronborg* herself during a two-day stop at the Aldabra Islands. The final, most testing leg of her epic journey lay ahead. Looff rejected the possibility of effecting an offshore rendezvous between the *Kronborg* and the *Königsberg* but ordered Christiansen to make for Tanga, where he could pick up a pilot to guide him to Mansa Bay. There, it was hoped, he would be able to unload his cargo undetected by the Royal Navy; and when the precious coal reached the *Königsberg* Looff would be able to take advantage of the next favourable tide to make an escape attempt. It was a bold scheme, and unbeknownst to either German vessel, the details of its execution were all intercepted by the Royal Navy. Back in London, Churchill could barely contain his excitement: 'this is your opportunity,' he told King-Hall, adding a placatory 'I am very glad you are on the spot at this critical moment'.[27] So determined was he to nab the *Kronborg*'s cargo that King-Hall was even instructed to inform her crew at the first opportunity that 'if they scuttle or damage the ship they will be left to drown' (although Churchill was adamant that King-Hall should 'on no account ... carry out this threat').[28]

For five days in the second week of April *Hyacinth* combed the approaches to Tanga for her prey, her gun crews sleeping at their stations and flames ten feet wide spurting from her funnels as she reached speeds of up to 19 knots. At dawn on 14 April the patience of her crew was finally rewarded when the *Kronborg* was spotted close inshore, twelve miles north of the Tanga lighthouse. But disaster struck as King-Hall ordered the chase to begin. *Hyacinth*'s starboard engine gave out, and by the time she had reached the bluff protecting Mansa Bay the *Kronborg* had, as one midshipman put it, 'disappeared up the creek'.[29] A bombardment over the bluff began immediately, but as the guns were firing blind and the *Kronborg* was still over five miles distant the chances of sinking her seemed remote.

In the frenzied half-hour breathing space that *Hyacinth*'s seizure gave Christiansen he had managed to put the crew ashore, open his vessel's portholes and douse the decks in petrol. When *Hyacinth* hove to at the entrance of the almost enclosed bay *Kronborg*'s deck and coal bunkers were ablaze and she was listing badly to port. But the subterfuge did not spare the *Kronborg* from further attention: she was shelled from close range and the crew were subjected to shrapnel fire as they made their way on all fours away from the beach. Christiansen and a number of others were wounded as they struggled towards the high ground a mile inland, but when they at last had a view of the bay they were considerably heartened by the scene unfolding there. German machine-gun fire from the shore defences had forced three small craft from *Hyacinth* to abandon their inspection of the *Kronborg* and soon the British warship could be seen preparing to depart. But then a final salvo burst from the *Hyacinth*. One shell hit the *Kronborg*'s deck aft, sending flames halfway up the mainmast, another hit the waterline, and in minutes she began to sink. Young Nis Kock and the *Kronborg*'s crew 'stared at the ship which had carried us so long and so well' and, 'seeing her whole superstructure gutted by fire',[30] knew at that moment that there would be no 12,000-mile homeward journey. As *Hyacinth* weighed anchor three huge explosions shook the *Kronborg* and a plume of smoke visible twenty miles away rose into the otherwise clear morning air.

By 9.15 a.m. *Hyacinth* was at anchor in Zanzibar harbour, and King-Hall was certain that his job was done (despite the breakdown of his flagship's starboard engine). He assumed that the final explosions on board the *Kronborg* were caused by ammunition below-decks and that, whatever his regrets at not being to salvage the cargo, nothing of any use to von Lettow-Vorbeck or Looff could possibly have survived intact. A thorough search of the blockade-runner had not been possible due to the heat, but he promised Churchill that he would return in a few days to carry out a further inspection. No such follow-up was to occur for ten weeks: intelligence reports indicated that mines had been laid at the entrance to Mansa Bay and that after two days' work the *Kronborg*'s crew had given up trying to rescue any cargo.

In the second half of April the Royal Navy's attention reverted to the *Königsberg*. Looff's suspicions that the Royal Navy must possess the 'Reserve Key "A"' cipher had mounted during the *Kronborg*'s dash for Tanga and he was determined to put those suspicions to the test by sending out messages declaring that he was about to leave the delta to rendezvous with another German blockade-runner. The result was exactly as he expected: *Hyacinth* and *Pioneer* spent weeks watching an area off Mikindani, far to the south; and when that proved fruitless they moved to search the waters south of Lindi and Lindi harbour itself. Only when the *Königsberg* remained in the delta after the high tide of 28 April did the two ships return to the delta and by then news of an even more successful and productive ruse was starting to spread through German East Africa.

For a single day in late April the Tanga harbourmaster's log recorded the recovery of 239 rifles, 375,000 rounds of ammunition, one field gun, four machine-guns, 100 4.1-inch shells and 150 3.5-inch shells from the *Kronborg*.[31] Much of her above-decks superstructure had indeed been blown to pieces, but Christiansen's ploy of dousing his ship in petrol had made the damage to his vessel seem far worse than it really was – and below her thick timber decks much of the cargo was salvageable. Some ammunition was damaged, as was some coal. But within two months the *Kronborg*'s crew, working with divers from the *Königsberg*, had rescued 2,000 Mauser rifles, five million cartridges, a light battery, 1,000 shells for *Königsberg*'s guns, a vast quantity of high explosive, telephone equipment, foodstuffs and vital medical supplies. At the end of June the salvage camp was abandoned and the men of the *Kronborg* were distributed among the land forces. They had been told at the outset that their mission would 'take six months or until the end of the war'.[32] None among the thirty-strong band of South Jutlanders and Germans could have envisaged that that might entail fighting on African soil for up to three and a half years let alone, as would be the fate of most, dying there.

When the Royal Navy finally inspected Mansa Bay on 22 July it reported that there was 'no indication that any salvage had taken place'[33] and King-Hall was to be considerably embarrassed when the truth became known – the more so as it coincided with the discovery that one of the small German steamers in the Rufiji delta had managed to slip the blockade and reach Dar-es-Salaam. But he remained as ebullient as ever, dismissing those who criticised his handling of the *Kronborg* 'incident' for possessing 'a singular ignorance of the use of men-of-war'.[34] It was a strangely rigid retort from a man commanding a naval station on which the changing nature of naval warfare was as evident as anywhere; and if they were to square the *Königsberg*, King-Hall would require still greater ingenuity on the part of his 'men-of-war'.

SEVEN

The War in the West

———◆———

While von Lettow-Vorbeck set about putting extreme pressure on British East Africa's Uganda Railway – nearly fifty separate raids were to be launched in a year, reducing the railway 'to the verge of collapse'[1] – the situation to the far west was equally perplexing for the Allies. Belgium had only taken over responsibility for the Congo in 1908, when the country was 'removed' by an international outcry from the personal clutches of King Leopold II: during the decades in which he had run it as a personal fiefdom between five and eight *million* Africans were reckoned to have lost their lives at the hands of the most cruel and exploitative colonial system that would ever be seen in Africa. The Belgian Congo had been the Africa of Joseph Conrad's *Heart of Darkness*, and the outbreak of war on the eastern borders of a country eighty times the size of Belgium was the last thing the Belgian government-in-exile in France needed as it sought to put its colonial house in order.

Not surprisingly, given their predicament in Europe, the Belgians had considerable problems in preparing for Anglo-Belgian co-operation on the Congo front. At the outset, however, both sides were unusually fortunate in being able to secure the involvement of a man who knew the Ruanda-Urundi borderlands as well as any alive. Ewart Grogan, British East Africa's most prominent business magnate and political firebrand, had passed through them on his great Cape-to-Cairo trek which had made him famous throughout the British Empire some fifteen years earlier; and by a fortunate coincidence one of the Belgian district administrators he had met at that time had been Commandant Josué Henry, now *Commissaire-Général* of the Belgian Congo and commander-in-chief of the Belgian troops in Kivu district.

By the end of October 1914 Grogan, completely unbeknownst to Governor Belfield but with General Stewart's approval, had set out on a mission to establish contact with the Belgian High Command and successfully reached his former stomping grounds around Lake Kivu. En route, he had crossed Lake Victoria at a time when the German steamer *Muansa* was still able to maraud at will, made his way right along the 200-mile Kagera front (the boundary between Uganda and German East Africa), and crossed 100 miles of German territory. It was a remarkable achievement for a man almost in his forties, accompanied only by a few porters and Ibrahim, his fiercely loyal Somali headman, and he eventually found Henry at Kibati, about five miles north of the lake. When Grogan appeared out of the blue he was received by his somewhat astonished old friend with 'the greatest possible cordiality and consideration'.[2]

Henry's position was a difficult one. Belgium had abandoned its hopes of keeping the Congo neutral after repeated German incursions across its borders, but getting sufficient troops to those borders had taken time and a very great deal of effort. By the time Grogan arrived some 2,000 Belgian *askari* had succeeded in marching from Stanleyville in just two months to join Henry at Kivu, and bolster the numbers of the 1,500 men of the *Force Publique* already on garrison duty on the Congo's eastern borders. Henry's dilemma was what to do with an 'army' that was exhausted and desperately short of both ammunition and provisions, and he turned to Grogan for advice on how to improve morale. Grogan responded with a whirlwind of activity, and by the end of November he had led shooting parties to obtain hippo meat from Lake Edward, opened a supply line to Mbarara (100 miles away in south-western Uganda), and persuaded Henry to move his camp north to the healthier climes of Rutchuru (midway between Lake Kivu and Lake Edward). He then requested further instructions from Nairobi and at a meeting at Lake Kivu in January 1915 – attended by Henry, Grogan and Colonel Malleson, a former senior Staff officer with IEF 'B' – closer co-operation was agreed between the two allies. A telegraph line was laid which would put Henry in (almost) direct contact with Nairobi, and Grogan agreed to provide 100 ox-carts from his timber yards for a Belgian advance into German territory that was assumed to be imminent.

Grogan was assured by Henry that 'without wishing to commit the Belgian government in respect of any *post bellum* adjustments of frontiers ... [its] policy specifically excludes any intention of territorial gain aggrandisement or war of conquest'; and the Belgian commander added that he assumed that 'it was the policy of the British Government to annex German East Africa'.[3] All he asked for was clarification of his ally's military plans and a simplification of communications – being required to deal with several Whitehall ministries and the civilian and military authorities in Nairobi had already been the cause of countless misunderstandings. To Grogan, these seemed like perfectly reasonable requests and Henry's desire to be as co-operative as possible was evidenced by the despatch of 500 Belgian troops to Uganda's Kagera front and Belgium's affirmation of ongoing assistance in protecting the Northern Rhodesia border. Such support was vital: on the Kagera front the ravages of disease were proving so great that one in four men of a company of the 2nd Loyal North Lancs posted there in January were in hospital within a matter of weeks, while in Northern Rhodesia British troops were bracing themselves for another German invasion attempt.

In the first three months of 1915 Belgian troops had succeeded in repelling a number of further incursions from German East Africa, even beating off a determined assault by Captain Schimmer on Luvungi, between Lake Tanganyika and Lake Kivu, and killing the German commander in the process. Confidence rose steadily as a result of these successes, and by March Henry suggested that his troops should invade Ruanda and Urundi while British troops simultaneously attacked Mwanza – a move which might well cause German troops to abandon Bukoba and the whole of the western littoral of Lake Victoria. On paper the plan looked attractive, as did a second initiative discussed by the Belgian and British governments for joint operations against Neu Langenburg and Bismarckburg. But at this critical juncture Anglo-Belgian co-operation began to falter as the expectations of the Belgian government-in-exile became increasingly unrealistic.

Henry's call for an immediate offensive was made at the behest of Jules Renkin, Belgium's ambitious Colonial Minister in Le Havre, who was determined to ensure that if the war ended soon Belgium would not take her place at the negotiating table empty-handed. There was no imminent likelihood of ending the German occupation of Belgium – but if Belgian troops occupied the rich and fertile German colonies of Ruanda and Urundi, Renkin would at least possess a valuable bargaining counter. Such bellicose intentions caused a good deal of suspicion in Whitehall: on the Western Front Belgian troops had played no part in the battles at Ypres or the spring offensive of 1915 which had cost hundreds of thousands of British and French lives; and in spite of the useful propaganda value of King Albert and the 'poor little Belgians', Belgian self-interest began to arouse increasing indignation. Furthermore, Belgium's troops in the Congo were entirely dependent on Britain for their supplies of military hardware; and the War Office was adamant that it could not approve, or provide the wherewithal for, any more 'risky expeditions' by Wapshare and Tighe for the foreseeable future even in the name of Anglo-Belgian co-operation.

The Belgian government's response to what it perceived as British stubbornness was to pursue as independent a course of action in Africa as Europe. This started to become evident when Henry was subordinated to General Tombeur, the Vice-Governor of Belgian Congo's copper-rich Katanga province and a former aide-de-camp to King Albert. His instructions were to ensure that Belgian troops were on German soil as fast as possible, and as he set about preparing for an independent offensive he declared that 'Belgium is not only taking the most appropriate stance to maintain the integrity of her colonial domain; it is intended that her resolve will demonstrate once more to the world her indomitable spirit and unshakeable vitality'.[4] Jules Renkin had seemingly prevailed, but the magnitude of the challenge confronting Tombeur made a mockery of his ambitions. The deployment of his troops for an all-out offensive against German East Africa, Ruanda and Urundi could not be effected in less than seven months (and, according to the Belgian official history, eighty-four steps); and there was no prospect of Britain finding spare shipping tonnage to provide the necessary arms and ammunition before the end of 1915. Furthermore, all Belgian attempts to capture Kissenyi – a vital precursor to any offensive – in the period May–September 1915 were successfully beaten off by the German garrison commanded by Lieutenant Peter Langen, who had recovered from a severe wound inflicted at Jasin. In other words Tombeur's 'offensive' was a figment of the imagination of his political masters, and his refusal to acknowledge the practical difficulties inherent in his proposed strategy caused further political ructions with Britain.

Poor communications, and Tighe's reservations about Tombeur's strategy, compounded the mounting confusion. A telegram from Rutchuru to Nairobi took anything up to ten days, by which time Nairobi had often heard of the response of the Belgian government-in-exile in Le Havre to the matter currently under discussion; and after Tombeur began his four-month journey from Katanga to Kivu he was barely contactable, which meant that his order for the three Belgian battalions which were assisting with the defence of Northern Rhodesia to proceed northwards was ignored by their commanding officer, Major Olsen, pending its clarification. Indeed for much of 1915, most of Tombeur's commanders remained completely unaware of their roles in his 'grand plan'.

As 1915 wore on King Albert further distanced himself from his British and French allies and, on several occasions before the war was over, Belgium would consider the possibility of concluding a separate peace with Germany. But amid all the political horse-trading there was *one* offensive measure on whose merits both Britain and Belgium agreed wholeheartedly, namely the need to wrest control of Lake Tanganyika from the enemy. Even Tombeur recognised that as long as the Germans held the lake his troops would not be able to advance without exposing their flanks to the depredations of General Wahle's *Westtruppen* or the German *askari* companies in Ruanda and Urundi commanded by the fiercely competent Captain Max Wintgens; and the British military authorities recognised that without a Belgian advance from the west any eventual offensive of their own would surely be doomed to failure.

The vast Rift Valley lakes – Victoria, Tanganyika and Nyasa – represented the entire theatre of war in microcosm in as much as supremacy could be maintained by possession of a single craft which would not have attracted attention on any of the principal lakes or rivers of Europe. There was something faintly ridiculous about this fact but supremacy, as both sides knew, was vital. The lakes were not only the highways along which troops could be transported long distances at speed and reasonable cost, but with each passing month they assumed greater political significance. Command implied possession and, with all the colonial powers anticipating a rich commercial future for Central Africa, possession would convey an advantage when the hostilities in Europe ceased.

British supremacy on Lakes Nyasa and Victoria had already been achieved. On the former, although there were bouts of periodic nervousness that the Germans would succeed in refloating the crippled *Hermann von Wissmann* and arm her with a *Königsberg* gun, this did not occur until 1918 (when she took to the water flying British colours and renamed the *King George*). In the meantime Lieutenant-Commander Dennistoun ran what he described as 'a sort of maritime Pickford's Carrier service ... up and down the Lake',[5] and it was well-nigh invincible after the *Guendolen* had been armed with two 6-pdrs from *Pegasus*. The contest for Lake Victoria, Africa's largest lake with a surface area of some 27,000 square miles, was also settled with relative ease when the elusive 80-ton German steamer *Muansa* was finally sunk in March 1915; and even after she was refloated her two 7-pdr guns were no longer a match for the armaments placed on board the British 'fleet' of six steamers (the largest of which were the *Nyanza* and the *Usoga*, each displacing 1,000 tons) and three tugs.

Lake Tanganyika, covering an area of approximately 400 miles by thirty, was a challenge on an altogether different scale. The sinking of the Belgian *Alexandre Delcommune* early in the war had robbed the Belgians of any mobility on the lake; and in November 1914 a German raid had disabled the African Lakes Corporation's steamer, the *Cecil Rhodes*, burnt the British company's stores and seized 150 miles of telegraph wire which was then used by the Germans to lay a line connecting Neu Langenburg with Iringa. After that Belgian caravans straying too close to the lakeshore were frequently attacked and relieved of their loads, further huge quantities of Belgian telegraph wire were 'appropriated', and even the Belgian harbour defences at Lukuga were regularly bombarded. In December, German troops from Neu Langenburg also attacked Fife on two occasions and, although the British defences held firm, the attacks led to growing concerns about British 'prestige' among the African population on the 200-mile border, particularly the 'warlike'* Angoni who had rebelled

---

* See Hordern, p. 183: 'in the interests of British prestige among the warlike tribes on the northern border ... it was imperative that the Germans should not be permitted to penetrate into Rhodesian territory'.

against British rule in 1897–8 in the Fort Jameson area, and steps were taken to bolster its defences. Among those detailed to the border was a column of Northern Rhodesia Police from Schuckmannsburg, in the Caprivi Strip, commanded by Major J.J. O'Sullevan, who marched 430 miles in torrential rain through Katanga to arrive in Abercorn just twenty days later. O'Sullevan was then sent to establish a garrison at a farm thirty miles east of Abercorn where the Stevenson Road crossed the Saisi River.

In April, with the Belgians and British still locked in protracted negotiations, an extraordinary solution to the problems caused by the German attacks on the shores of Lake Tanganyika and Northern Rhodesia presented itself to the Admiralty in the shape of John R. Lee, professional big game hunter, veteran scout of the Boer War and infamous 'old Africa hand'. Lee had become aware in February that the Germans were in the process of launching a very large steamer, the *Goetzen*, on Lake Tanganyika. Its construction had been undertaken at a cost of £20,000 (£1.1m in today's money) at the Meyer shipyard in Papenburg under the approving eye of the Kaiser himself and, once complete, the vessel was disassembled, packed into 5,000 crates and shipped to Dar-es-Salaam. From there she had been transported across German East Africa on the Central Railway and, for three months, by porter to Kigoma where she had been reassembled by her three shipwrights. The completion of such a journey was some achievement. The crates were hardly designed for shouldering by porters, the propeller shaft was damaged by fire en route, and the shipwrights were required to direct operations in an environment with which they were wholly unfamiliar. But on 5 February 1915 engineers Wendt, Tellmann and Rüter completed the structural work on their ship, which measured 220 feet in length by $32\frac{1}{2}$ feet in the beam and displaced 1,575 tons, and she was ready for arming by Friedrich Hübener, a retired infantry colonel renowned for his engineering skills. Originally intended as the flagship for German commercial enterprise in Central Africa, the *Goetzen*'s sheer size threatened to make Germany's control of the lake unassailable.

Lee explained to the Admiralty that the *Goetzen* would be capable of supporting 'raiding operations' into Northern Rhodesia and the Belgian Congo 'with impunity' and he insisted that 'the effect of this on the native mind' would be 'a very serious matter indeed'. Among 'the old hands of North Rhodesia' it was already believed that 'a general rising of the natives north of the Zambezi may take place at any moment' and that what was required was an immediate display of 'the power of the [British] Empire'. The possibility of 'native uprisings' and the obliteration of Belgian forces in the Congo were highly charged issues in Whitehall and Lee's warnings were heeded. But naval resources were severely limited, the more so as the preparations for an attempt to seize the Dardanelles were well advanced, and the Admiralty was initially unsure what it could provide at such short notice that might be of use.

Lee's solution to the problem was as modest as his scheme was outrageous. He suggested that the German feat of manhandling the *Goetzen* from Europe to Central Africa should be trumped by sending a motor boat capable of 15 knots and with a gun ranged to more than 7,000 yards. He was convinced that such a craft could both outrun and outgun the *Goetzen*. On the other hand, the gunboat would have to be transported from Cape Town by rail, traction engine, and human porterage – but Lee declared himself to have 'a wide experience of heavy steam transport' as well as being 'a first class handler of small craft'. With that confident assertion he requested permission to proceed immediately to Northern Rhodesia to establish contact with 'long-standing loyal African friends'[6] and assure them that the British Empire was not going to let the German supremacy of Lake Tanganyika last long.

Britain had a long tradition of sending gunboats to parts of the British Empire about whose exact location the Admiralty was far from certain, and Lee seemed exceptionally well informed about recent developments on Lake Tanganyika. After rapid consultation with the Belgians, the Army Council, and Tighe, Lee's plan was approved and he set off for Cape Town bearing the rank of Lieutenant in the Royal Naval Volunteer Reserve. Meanwhile the Admiralty started to cast around for an appropriate vessel to send after him – and some unlikely character to lead the ambitious expedition.

Lieutenant-Commander Geoffrey Basil Spicer-Simson had not had a particularly remarkable naval career, but he was about as cosmopolitan an officer as the Admiralty could wish to find at such short notice. The brother of the world-famous medallion portrait artist, Theodore, Geoffrey had spent his childhood in Tasmania, France, Germany and at Stubbington Royal Naval College. His father had a great love for the sea and had himself served in the mercantile marine before becoming a stockbroker for Rothschild's in India, a sheep farmer in Tasmania and a businessman in Le Havre. As a result of this peripatetic upbringing Spicer-Simson was fluent in French and German, had broad horizons, and was tenacious. He had recently completed a four-year survey of the Gambia River in West Africa, and this mission had furthered his already extensive knowledge of small craft, of leadership of tightly knit crews, and of operating in 'the tropics'.

Spicer-Simson's approach to the war was also personal. HMS *Good Hope*, sunk at Coronel by Admiral von Spee the previous year, had once been the command of his cousin Sir Willmot Fawkes; and he had learned his German at the Moravian school in Neuwied-am-Rhein under the threat of the punishment of *Stillstrafe*, the strict imposition of silence on any pupil caught speaking English. To his delight, his appointment was confirmed by the end of April and he was given free rein to find suitable craft and the requisite personnel for 'The Lake Tanganyika Expedition'. Spicer-Simson's first challenge was to find men with appropriate skills who were available, and it was the RNVR, the 'Wavy Navy', that came to the rescue by providing twenty-seven of 'the strangest and queerest characters'.[7] Spicer-Simson was equally fortunate that two appropriate motor boats were unearthed by Messrs Thornycroft, part of a consignment of eight built for the Greek government before the war.

It did not take long for Spicer-Simson's crew to discover that their commander was more than mildly eccentric: when undergoing a crash-course in naval lore at the RNVR training camp at Crystal Palace, it was revealed that he had named the expedition's two motor boats *Mimi* and *Toutou*.* But during the 'sea trials' on the River Thames of these forty-foot craft, capable of achieving a speed of 18–19 knots, he also showed his ingenuity. Extensive modifications were carried out on *Mimi* and *Toutou*, and by 29 May – just three weeks after receiving their orders – the 'road-making' advance party left England on the first leg of a 10,000-mile journey to Lake Tanganyika. All the men were sworn 'not to divulge, even to their nearest and dearest, where they were bound nor what was their mission'.[8]

---

* One member of the expedition claimed that the names 'Dog' and 'Cat' were rejected by the Admiralty as being 'rotten names' for gunboats so Spicer-Simson, having had 'a vision of the Luxembourg Gardens in Paris, and a child playing with a cat and dog and calling out to them by their names', proposed the French alternative. See 'Leviathan', p. 176.

EIGHT

'A Brilliant Affair'

In April 1915, Brigadier-General Wapshare was promoted Major-General and transferred to command the 33rd Division in Mesopotamia, a move which caused him 'great anxiety'[1] in case it should be viewed as censorious of his time in British East Africa, and Brigadier-General Mickey Tighe took the helm. This was a mixed blessing. As a 'fighting man' Tighe was undoubtedly popular with the troops, but his tendency to blow hot and cold and to eschew all forms of administrative work was regarded by Staff officers as a liability. He also loathed sitting on the defensive, as the War Office instructed after the very costly defence of Jasin, and was certain that if his troops remained inactive the ravages of disease would soon reduce their fighting capability to nought.

Nowhere was this more evident than on Uganda's Kagera front, where the local defence force had succeeded in holding its own until reinforcements – the 13th Rajputs and two companies of 4/KAR – became available towards the end of 1914. If Tanga had proved unfamiliar in terrain and clime to the rank and file of the 13th Rajputs, the Kagera line was an altogether different, and menacing, planet. A considerable proportion were invalided at any one time by malaria and dysentery and by the end of the year ninety-five per cent were ordered to take three months' rest and undergo intensive malaria treatment. Elsewhere, almost one in five of the 900 men of the Loyal North Lancs were also on the sick list by March 1915, a further one in seven required daily hospital treatment, and their generally debilitated state forced Tighe to order the evacuation of Longido in early April. Similarly, the 2nd Rhodesia Regiment, which arrived in March and assisted in the withdrawal from Longido before being posted to Tsavo and Voi, soon found itself in need of large, regular drafts to keep its strength above 500 men.* As for further new regiments, 'bits and bobs' were about all the hard-pressed War Office was able

---

* A total of thirty-six officers and 1,006 rank and file would serve in the ranks of the 2nd Rhodesia Regiment during its twenty-one months in East Africa; during that period the regimental records showed 2,272 admissions to hospital and 10,626 sick cases (of which malaria accounted for about one third).

to provide. One squadron of the 17th Cavalry was sent from India; the 130th Baluchis ('Jacob's Rifles') arrived from Rangoon, their reputation as a 'fighting regiment' with first-class marksmanship somewhat battered by two recent mutinies among the Mahsuds, tribesmen from the North-West Frontier, in its ranks; and the appearance of the 25th Battalion ('Legion of Frontiersmen') Royal Fusiliers gave Tighe the use of what was without doubt the most colourful – and one of the most courageous – units to take to the field in the entire campaign.

The Legion of Frontiersmen was only a decade old, having been founded by Roger Pocock as a body of 'colonial territorials . . . of good character who have trained in wild countries, at sea, or in war'.[2] The General Council included Sir John French, Rider Haggard and Sir Arthur Conan Doyle, among other well-known names, while its members were drawn from all walks of life, from aristocrats to trappers; one of them even listed his previous occupations as 'soldier, explorer, prospector, mining engineer, mail rider, freighter, cowboy, horse-breaker, rancher, veterinary surgeon, scout to Lord Roberts in South Africa'. The Frontiersmen were not without former combat experience as a distinct unit – in 1906 2,000 of them had volunteered at a moment's notice to assist the South African government to suppress the Zulu 'Bambatha' rebellion in Natal – and by 1914 there were more than 10,000 Frontiersmen spread across the globe. Within months, 7,000 had tired of waiting for the War Office to allow them to form their own unit but by the spring the persistent entreaties of Colonel Daniel Patrick Driscoll, DSO, a veteran scout of the Boer War with a voice like a fog-horn, finally secured the formation of a battalion under the umbrella of the Royal Fusiliers.

The news that it was destined for East Africa did not meet with universal approval. One of Tighe's more 'Poona-Poona' Indian Army officers spoke for many when he wrote: 'Driscoll threatens to arrive. God help us! Fancy being reduced to rescue by a curly-headed buck-nigger who couldn't even get into the Mandalay Club. I suppose they hope for loot!'[*] Such snide remarks were to persist, even after 1,500 ANZAC Frontiersmen and all but eighteen of 600 Frontiersmen who joined Princess Patricia's Canadian Light Infantry died at Gallipoli. In the meantime, Driscoll set about combing Britain for members of the Legion who had not already signed up with other units, and a remarkably heterogeneous rank and file soon emerged. Youngsters who in peacetime were Post Office clerks in Bolton and book-keepers from Sheffield joined the music hall comedians, border gunmen, university professors, Moroccan bandits, ex-MPs, cowboys, prize fighters, and acrobats; and there was even 'a member of

---

* NAM/Davidson. The racist reference was prompted by Driscoll's dark appearance, thought to be attributable to mixed parentage.

Six Brothers Luck, a vaudeville team, who could climb stairs on his head'.[3] The recruitment campaign appealed for 'any young and fit men who would like to participate in what undoubtedly will be a great trip, chock full of glorious incident and adventure,'[4] to report to a Mr Banning in Sheffield immediately; and the mention that such famous 'Africa hands' as photographer Cherry Kearton, and 'white hunters' George Outram and F.C. Selous, were also part of the 'adventure' was greeted with considerable enthusiasm. To Selous, the most famous 'white hunter' of them all, belonged the distinction of being the oldest soldier in the British Army: he was sixty-three at the start of the war, but still 'as active as a cat and hard as nails'.[5]

All in all the battalion was 'the oddest crew',[6] and so great was its expertise presumed to be that no training took place before departure for East Africa. In fact almost half its number had never fired a rifle, and the initial reaction of some of the 'old-timer' Frontiersmen to the new recruits was not always positive. 'The conversation among the Yorkshiremen and Londoners is vile', wrote Canadian Private Angus Buchanan; 'I've been among rough men before but never among such a debased, thoughtless lot as this – generally speaking I am ashamed of them – and ashamed of the England that mothered them'.[7]

Whatever the misgivings inside and outside the ranks of the Frontiersmen, their arrival was a huge boon for Tighe. Although the majority of his troops were in a seriously debilitated state he was desperate for an opportunity to do something decisive to restore morale in East Africa – and the Frontiersmen provided the necessary additional manpower. Rather surprisingly, given what had happened at Jasin, permission was secured from the War Office to attack Bukoba, thirty miles south of the Uganda border on the German side of Lake Victoria, with a view to relieving pressure on the Kagera front and severely denting German 'prestige'. A further consideration was that the naval conflict on Lake Victoria was also getting increasingly 'dirty', with the Germans accusing the British fleet of steamers of bombarding undefended settlements and the British accusing the Germans of leaving booby-trapped piles of tempting firewood by the lakeshore. A demonstration 'for destructive pur- poses'[8] at Bukoba would, it was hoped, underscore British supremacy on the lake once and for all and put paid to German 'shenanigans'.

The town of Bukoba, the peacetime garrison of 7/FK, lay straddling the Kanoni River on a small marshy plain surrounded by grassy hills and colossal limestone *kopjes*. Its importance to the enemy was twofold. Not only did it possess a high-power wireless transmitter, which if destroyed would increase the isolation of the north-west corner of the German colony; but its sur- rounding district was thickly populated and of considerable economic import- ance. Coffee, much desired by the colony's European population, grew in abundance; and a lively trade was carried on with Ruanda and Urundi in hides and skins, large quantities of which were required by the *Schutztruppe*. Disruption of these supplies had long been an aim of the British General Staff; but only after the sinking of the German steamer *Muansa* in May 1915 and the arming of the British steamers *Winifred, Usoga, Nyanza, Rusinga, Kavirondo* and *Percy Anderson* with guns from HMS *Pegasus* and other warships did an attack on Bukoba become a realistic possibility.

Tighe deputed General Stewart to lead the attack. It was to be fully supported by the armament on the British ships of the lake flotilla and was intended to be rapid: although the German garrison commanded by Major Willibald von Stuemer numbered only 300, five times that number of enemy troops were thought to be within three days' march of Bukoba. Stewart took with him 1,500 of the best troops available: detachments from the Loyal North Lancs, the newly arrived 25th Royal Fusiliers, 3/KAR with two guns of the 28th Mountain Battery, a full machine-gun section from the East Africa Regiment, and the four machine-guns of the Volunteer Maxim Company.[*] Before dawn on 22 June, under the light of a half-moon, the ships carrying the troops put them ashore a few miles north of the town in a bay surrounded by a semicircle of hills. The landings were a conspicuous success by comparison with those carried out at Tanga: although an early-warning post on Busira Island had spotted the British flotilla and raised the alarum, the British force had caused confusion by splitting. *Nyanza* executed a feint towards Bukoba's Customs House where, 100 yards offshore, she and *Winifred* narrowly missed being hit by a German gun; while other ships executed the landings far enough away from the town to prevent any advance guard from opposing them in any force. Despite most of the ships' guns being 'a decade behind the times'[†] over 1,000 shells were fired on Bukoba during the landings.

Once onshore at Kiaya Bay the Frontiersmen were ordered to scale the first ridge, Rwonga Hill, before pushing on through a *matoke* plantation and swampland to secure Karwazi Hill without opposition. There they halted to cover the disembarkation of the rest of the force. The relative ease with which this first phase of the attack was executed was attributable not only to the confusion caused by the plethora of British ships offshore, but also to von Stuemer having split his force. The day before the attack, responding to a British 'feint' on the Kagera River, he had marched eighty *askari* thirty miles to the river's Kyaka ferry crossing in anticipation of a simultaneous thrust on

---

[*] The approximate strengths of the British infantry battalions were as follows: 2nd Loyal North Lancs – 300 rifles; 25th Royal Fusiliers – 400 rifles; 3/KAR – 450 rifles; 29th Punjabis – 200 rifles.

[†] Anon (2), p. 297; among the diverse armaments on board the ships were a 12-pdr 12cwt gun from an armoured train in India (on *Winifred*); and four guns from the ill-fated *Pegasus* (on *Usoga, Nyanza* and *Winifred*).

Bukoba from there, while Lieutenant Eberhard Gudowius was left to defend Bukoba with just 150 rifles. Gudowius was therefore alone in Bukoba when the attack was launched and, although his *askari* fought stubbornly, they were forced to cede ground as the British landings continued throughout the day. By the time von Stuemer returned to Bukoba that evening the Frontiersmen had fought their way, sometimes chest-high in water, across more swampy ground and taken another ridge, 'Fusilier Knoll'; while to the north the Loyal North Lancs and 29th Punjabis had taken 'Arab Ridge'. As the German troops withdrew they deployed the field gun which had nearly hit the *Winifred* earlier in the day against the British advance. But by dusk Stewart's force commanded the heights overlooking the town.

At dawn on 23 June the advance from the heights resumed in torrential rain. The ships' guns forced the two German guns shelling the advancing troops in the open to shift positions several times, but German resistance remained fierce until all its troops had been pushed back to the outskirts of the town. Fearing the annihilation of his troops, von Stuemer then ordered his men to retreat over the hills to the west and in the early afternoon 3/KAR and the Frontiersmen were the first to enter Bukoba. The honour of lowering the flag flying above the German *boma* fell to Lieutenant Dartnell, an Australian Frontiersman, and it was soon realised that whereas von Stuemer had sustained fifteen per cent casualties among his 350 men Stewart's force had captured Bukoba at a cost of just ten men killed and about twenty wounded. As one naval officer remarked, 'the whole operation would hardly constitute an incident in a larger campaign, but at the time it was the first undisputed success we had achieved in the country'.[9] Even Lord Kitchener, who had never been keen on British troops becoming embroiled in East Africa, sent a telegram to Tighe and Stewart congratulating them on 'the brilliant success of the Bukoba operation', while *The Leader* trumpeted that 'the Germans are not allowing natives to enter the ruins of Bukoba for fear of the moral effect it will have'.[10]

In what remained of daylight on 23 June Bukoba's wireless mast was dismantled and destroyed by the Faridkot Sappers and a German field gun was removed, only to fall off the lighter transporting it to the British flotilla into the lake. An apology was also given to Père Barthélemy of the White Fathers' Mission, in whose grounds one of the German guns had been positioned, and whose chapel was consequently damaged by responding fire from the *Nyanza*. Other than Barthélemy, a fellow missionary and a handful of relieved British subjects, the town was almost deserted; even the bishop, Mgr Sweens, had recently been ordered out by the Germans.[11] Something then occurred that would not perhaps have pleased Kitchener so much, and was not mentioned in the public plaudits for the victory: Bukoba was thoroughly and systematically sacked. One Frontiersman watched as fellow members of his regiment went 'through homes, picking up loot of all kinds'[12] while another, with champagne in hand, witnessed a comrade emerging from the governor's house with 'a lady's toilet set in ivory' and another with 'the governor's ceremonial helmet'.[*] Colonel Driscoll regarded all this as part and parcel of colonial warfare and the incident contributed greatly to the creation of the Fusiliers' new moniker – the 'Boozaliers'.

When the British troops departed that evening every house in which ammunition had been found was burned to the ground; one officer remarked that it was a 'spectacular but somewhat sad sight to see such beautiful houses destroyed'.[13] Von Stuemer did not authorise his troops' return to the town until the following evening. By then local Africans had also been on the rampage – an occurrence that *was* recorded by the newspapers – and a returning German officer described the scene thus:

> The darkness of the night only allowed us to see that which could be seen at close distance. In our mission station, all that was left were beds. As far as we could see, wardrobes, commodes and chests had been broken into and their contents had been stolen. Whatever hadn't been taken lay torn or damaged on the ground. We were, however, just happy to at least have our Bukoba back. Beds and rest places were prepared with care for the ill and injured. The buildings of the mission remained unscathed apart from the storeroom, which had been hit by an incendiary grenade. In the town itself all the regional administrational buildings as well as most of the housing had been burnt down. Pictures of the Kaiser had been broken by the enemy and at times stabbed through with bayonets.[14]

The largest haul of loot, which included the uniform of a German soldier mortally wounded in the attack, was found at the house of the chief Muntu. He was imprisoned, but chief Ntale was publicly hanged in front of the Post Office, and von Stuemer placed Lieutenant Gudowius – known locally as *bwana lazima* ('you must') – in charge of the town.[15] The Frontiersmen, meanwhile, were sent straight to border duty in British East Africa, interpreting this as 'punishment for the misdeeds'[16] of some of their number.

Tighe was jubilant at the much-needed boost to morale provided by Bukoba, even to the extent of crowing about the success to his Belgian allies. It was through Bukoba district that any Belgian advance was likely to proceed, and in the wake of the British victory Tighe informed the War

[*] Liddle/Shaw. The Field Diary of the 2nd Loyal North Lancs also recorded that 'there was a regrettable amount of looting and thoughtless destruction of property in which the North Lancs took no part' (see TNA/WO/95/5339).

Office that Tombeur's troops could now invade Ruanda 'whenever they want', and would stand 'every possibility of success'. At the time, however, Tombeur was completely out of contact not only with his government but even his own troops as he made his way north from Katanga; and while Belgian troops continued to probe the German defences at Kissenyi it was obvious that there was no immediate prospect of breaking through. Tighe's remarks may have been provocative and even critical – he considered that no matter how bellicose the declarations of the Belgian government, 'the local inertia is considerable'[17] – but they were also correct. The fact remained that a Belgian advance was still a figment of the imagination. Belgian troops on the Kagera and Kivu fronts would remain wholly dependent for supplies on British East Africa until the end of September, and arms and ammunition being shipped from Europe were being delayed by Britain's dire shortage of shipping tonnage.

A further complication also arose as a result of the Uganda Railway's difficulties in handling tonnages which had been unimaginable in peacetime – difficulties that were greatly exacerbated by the ever-increasing number of German raids on the line. The appropriation by the railway administration of new engines and 160 wagons ordered before the war by the Magadi Soda Company for its private branch line certainly helped, as did the arrival of more rolling-stock from India. But the demands of the military continued to escalate by the month and so huge were the quantities of fuel, for example, arriving at Mombasa that new storage facilities for 2¾m gallons had to be built there and at Kisumu. At the same time the tonnage of coffee available for export doubled, and that of cotton rose by almost a fifth, with the result that by November 1915 'the incidence of the war was making it more and more difficult to maintain the economic life of the Uganda and East African Protectorates'.[18] Under these circumstances, it was not surprising that Tombeur's demand that his materiel should receive priority requirements was disregarded.

Unbeknownst to both Tombeur and Tighe, a Belgian advance through Ruanda and Urundi in July would indeed have had, as Tighe had put it, 'every possibility of success'. This was not because the attack on Bukoba had inflicted irreparable damage on the German forces in the north-west, but because the number of companies facing the Belgians was considerably fewer than was thought: at exactly the same time as Tighe was planning the Bukoba raid von Lettow-Vorbeck was preparing to strike a blow against Northern Rhodesia. In April von Lettow-Vorbeck ordered 18/FK and 23/FK to proceed to Bismarckburg from Dar-es-Salaam, where they would join 22/FK and newly formed 29/FK from Kigoma. Von Langenn-Steinkeller was put in charge of the initial concentration, but when he set off for Neu Langenburg with three of these companies in May Wahle arrived from Dar-es-Salaam with 24/FK and 10/SchK to direct the whole offensive. On 17 June Wahle sailed from Kigoma to Bismarckburg.

The timing of the offensive was excellent. Colonel Tombeur had issued orders for the three Belgian battalions co-operating with British forces on the border to proceed north for his planned advance into German East Africa – but only one had actually begun its trek up the west side of Lake Tanganyika. The other two, under the overall command of Major Olsen, remained at Abercorn and Pweto (on Lake Mweru), considerably strengthening the British defence force of 1,000 *askari* of the Northern Rhodesia Police, 250 Northern Rhodesia volunteers and 350 Europeans of the British South Africa Police. Soon after arriving at Bismarckburg Wahle, aided by the launch of the *Goetzen* on Lake Tanganyika, was ready to move forward, and the point at which he decided to probe the Anglo-Belgian defences was Major O'Sullevan's outpost at the little farm at Saisi. On 28 June 24/FK, 29/FK and the European reservists of 10/SchK – a force 700-strong – launched their attack in dense mist before dawn. Neither the initial bombardment by two 1873 field guns nor the subsequent advance against Saisi's formidable network of trenches and fort-ifications yielded any result; Karl Proempeler, the company commander of 24/FK, was killed; and the following morning all German troops had with-drawn back over the border. But when dummy graves dug by the retreating Germans were discovered to contain ammunition it became clear that the attack was no more than a reconnaissance, that the enemy 'would make more serious attempts to occupy Rhodesia'.[9]

For a month only minor skirmishing occurred along the border. Then, on 25 July, the main attack began, led by Wahle himself; and for a week the 450 British and Belgian troops at Saisi were under siege from a force more than twice the size. The fighting was almost continuous, day and night, for four days. On 28 July Belgian troops from Abercorn, led by Major de Koninck, were prevented from breaking through to their beleaguered allies, and three days later Wahle called on Major O'Sullevan to surrender. Despite an acute shortage of water, which could only be collected at night from between the lines, and the fact that the German forward positions had reached to within 600 yards of the British trenches, O'Sullevan refused. At 7.30 p.m., just after dark, Wahle launched another determined attack with some troops advancing as close as sixty yards from the trenches. But still the Anglo-Belgian defences held, and during the night of 2–3 August the German troops slipped away.

Saisi had been held, an achievement for which O'Sullevan was to win the DSO, and the Northern Rhodesia border was not attacked again in 1915 on any scale. Many British officers thought at the time that Wahle's incursion was a last-ditch attempt to break through to German South-West Africa, but

Wahle knew that the German colony had surrendered to South African forces a few weeks earlier and his attack had been launched for defensive purposes. As early as February 1915 von Lettow-Vorbeck feared that 'the enemy appeared to be preparing to attack'[20] across his south-western border, and it was this that explained the increase in German strength there to almost 2,000 rifles, von Langenn-Steinkeller's return to Neu Langenburg after a number of months in Urundi, and Wahle's decision to pull his attack on Saisi when his artillery and attempt at frontal assault failed to make any impression on its defences. In Wahle's opinion, Saisi did not constitute a defeat; rather it ensured, at a cost of about sixty German casualties, that no British advance from Northern Rhodesia was possible 'until the middle of 1916'.[21] No such advance was envisaged; but Wahle's aggression did have the effect of delaying the departure northwards of Olsen's two remaining Belgian battalions until November.

Olsen's decision to keep the Belgian I *Bataillon* and III *Bataillon* on the Rhodesian border 'for the time being',[22] a decision taken independently of Tombeur, had proved exceptionally fortuitous. But the attacks on Saisi had again demonstrated that no Belgian advance would be possible while German vessels still controlled the waters of Lake Tanganyika; and unfortunately Lieutenant Lee's obsession with 'native uprisings' was working directly contrary to the paramount need for secrecy of the Admiralty's Lake Tanganyika Expedition. On reaching Northern Rhodesia and Katanga, in the company of Frank Magee, an American journalist with the appearance of a prize-fighter, he appears to have launched a one-man propaganda campaign to restore faith in the British Empire in the area. In July reports were received by the British High Commissioner in Cape Town that Lee and Magee, who'd started his career at *The Daily Mirror* under the famous journalist (and spiritualist) Hannen Swaffer, had 'given the whole business of the expedition away all the way up the line'.

The enthusiasm of Lee and Magee for their task was considerable, but their reputations were soon called into question. Both men were said to have been reported by the police to the civilian authorities in Katanga for being drunk and patronising 'the lowest haunts' in Elizabethville; and when asked for his opinion of Lee the British Vice-Consul in the town reported that his 'antecedents were questionable' and confirmed rumours that Lee had been 'convicted of drunkenness, had been employed in a local bar, and still owed considerable debts in town'. As a result of such conduct the Belgian authorities 'considered [Lee's] appointment a direct insult to them',[23] but Spicer-Simson was not prepared instantly to terminate the involvement of a man whose local knowledge was so important to the expedition.

The transportation of *Mimi* and *Toutou* on cradles from Cape Town to the lakeshore was an epic feat beside which even the *Goetzen*'s own journey to Lake Tanganyika paled; in the words of one member of the expedition, it made

'Fiction look like Truth's shabby sister'.[24] The rail junction at Elizabethville was reached easily enough on 26 July and in a bar which went by the name of 'Le Chat Noir' the crew discovered just how widely Lee and Magee had publicised their impending arrival: Lee's fondness for 'the lowest haunts' meant that people 'knew as much about [the mission] as, if not more than, we did'.[25] The services of Magee, as official scribe to the expedition, were retained and his monkey Josephine became the official mascot; but Lee was quietly recalled to Cape Town in the hope of avoiding further 'talk and scandal'[26] in Katanga. His departure was euphemistically attributed to 'sunstroke and fever'.[27]

Whatever Lee's personal shortcomings he had reconnoitred, and begun to construct, a 150-mile route for *Mimi* and *Toutou* to progress through mile upon mile of bush and over the formidable Mitumba Mountains from the railhead at Fungurume, 100 miles north-west of Elizabethville, to Sankisia. But its completion now passed to another member of the crew with local knowledge, Arthur 'Ginger Dick' Davison. Snow-blindness affected many as the surface soil was full of mica, over 150 bridges needed to be built, the temperature regularly reached 118°F in the shade, and 'wandering' swamps of water cabbage and forest fires moving at 30–40mph had to be negotiated on this first stage of the journey 'proper'.

While Lieutenant 'Paddy' Wainwright, an irascible Irish rancher from Rhodesia, took charge of the convoy of 130 tons of supplies, a lorry and trailer with the boats' guns and ammunition, and *Mimi* and *Toutou* on two traction engines with a predilection for finding ant-bear holes, his commander busied to and fro on a bicycle. On 8 September the summit of the Mitumba Mountains, 6,400 feet above sea level, was attained and, having descended with immense difficulties to the valley of the Lualaba River, the expedition had just thirty-five miles to go before *Mimi* and *Toutou* could be launched into their more natural environment. With the river in sight, however, water became so scarce that the men and their 400 porters had to subsist in the searing heat on a daily ration of just half a pint per man. The traction engines were the first priority, but just as they came to a 'full stop' scouts reported water nearby and hundreds of local women were 'bribed with some gaudy waist-cloths' to bring it in.* All the while scribe Magee noticed that 'a fine example was set by the commander. He went around encouraging his officers and men with a kindly word (and sometimes a curse) and so got things done.'[28] His charm and joviality also kept the porters willing, although all the crewmen were occasionally taken aback by their choice of marching tunes which included a vigorous, mission-inspired rendition of 'Now the Labourer's Task is O'er'.

---

* Spicer-Simson (1), p. 758; Magee (p. 337) observed that 'the work in this country is [all] done by women ... sad yet true'.

Tick fever and jiggers were a constant problem for the crew, and at night their encampments were invariably surrounded by lions, whose roaring would keep the men awake until the small hours. But at 2.30 p.m. on 28 September 1915 the expedition eventually reached Sankisia. It had taken six weeks to cover the 150 miles from Fungurume, an average of just four miles per day, and there, in the absence of any cranes or hoists, *Mimi* and *Toutou*, each weighing $4\frac{1}{2}$ tons, were manhandled onto railway trucks for the fifteen-mile run to Bukama on the Lualaba River. As the dry season was drawing to a close time was running short. Furthermore, the Lualaba was so low that Captain Mauritzen, a Danish pilot sent by the Belgians to assist the expedition, reported that his riverboat, the *Constantin de Burlay*, had been unable to navigate the river any closer than fifty-eight miles downriver. There was no alternative but to paddle *Mimi* and *Toutou* the intervening distance, an exhausting and frustrating task. On a single day the two gunboats ran aground fourteen times in just twelve miles, which Spicer-Simson wryly speculated was 'a record, I think, for HM ships',[29] but the *Constantin de Burlay* was finally spotted on 11 October and *Mimi* and *Toutou* loaded onboard her lighter. Regular groundings still occurred in the crocodile-infested Lualaba, while by day the men 'were baked alive' and by night were 'tormented by all the flying pests of the Congo'. But after seventeen days on the river the town of Kabalo was reached, everything was manhandled onto yet another railway and, after all that had gone before, the 175-mile run to Lake Tanganyika seemed 'but a stone's throw'.

With the exception of Lee and Lieutenant Hope, who had (genuinely) succumbed to sunstroke, all the men were in astonishingly rude health and the expedition doctor had 'had a far busier time treating natives and their children than attending to members of the expedition'.[30] The privations had been great but the only one that had caused 'considerable despondency and consternation' was the exhaustion of the supply of Pusser's naval rum with which the men had daily toasted 'Simson's Circus' (also known as 'The Tanganyika Tits').[31] At Lukuga, or Albertville, on the lakeshore Spicer-Simson was met by Commandant Stinghlhamber, the commanding officer of the Belgian garrison, on 24 October. The expedition, its two valuable charges and crew intact, had completed their 3,000-mile journey from Cape Town, using almost every terrestrial means known to man, in under four months. They had also beaten the rains, and could now commence in earnest the task of robbing Germany of dominance on the lake. It was a signal achievement.

NINE

The End of the *Königsberg*

————◆————

After a tremendous amount of work Cull's aviators finally rendered the 'new' flying machines sent from Britain serviceable. An aerial bombardment of the *Königsberg* was no longer regarded as a realistic possibility, but on 25 April – the day that the Gallipoli landings commenced – Cull reached a height of 1,200 feet and a speed of 60mph on his maiden flight before down bumps over the entrance to the delta forced him back to 800 feet. Soon afterwards he was rewarded for his efforts: below him was the *Königsberg*, 'looking as though she had been newly painted, her side screens and awnings spread, [and] smoke was issuing from her funnels'. His conclusion was that the German cruiser looked 'very spick and span',[1] though he was forced to beat a hasty retreat when the *Königsberg* and the shore defences opened fire on him. Given the nature of *Königsberg*'s armament, firing at planes was akin to 'throwing stones at swallows',[2] but a lucky burst of shrapnel punched a hole in Cull's air intake and his engine packed up half a dozen miles from Mafia. He brought the plane down safely and 'very satisfactory' aerial photographs of the *Königsberg* were the prize for his hair-raising escapade.

In the course of the next few weeks the difficulties encountered by the airmen were legion. During one flight a bullet passed clean through the cap of Flag Commander Bridgeman, who regularly volunteered to accompany Cull as his observer; Flight Lieutenant Watkins was forced to ditch his plane in the water after a bullet hit the rudder; and any aviator deposited in the Indian Ocean was wont to have an anxious wait of many hours before being picked up. The lack of spares was also a constant worry and in May Cull wrote to their Air Department to give his superiors 'some idea of the state of affairs': 'glue not holding on any propellers, wood only for one more propeller. Has India rubber tubing been sent as all ours has perished? No fabric and few spares left.'[3]

While the RNAS maintained its watch on the *Königsberg* to the best of its abilities, Admiral King-Hall continued to urge Churchill to authorise a night torpedo attack using the RNAS's motor boat with a jerry-built 'super-silencer' or an electric launch from England. Bridgeman, Cull and Watkins had devised the plan, working in league with officers on board *Hyacinth*, but to their 'great disappointment' Churchill vetoed it. He did, however, inform King-Hall that two monitors and four 'really modern aeroplanes'[4] were on their way to East Africa. News of the Admiralty's munificence caused an immediate stir. Cull began moving his men to Mafia to start construction of a new aerodrome, a fine corrugated iron hangar was built in Zanzibar and shipped down to Mafia in sections, and on 18 June HMS *Laurentic* joined the throng off the East African coast bringing not only the biplanes – two Henry Farmans with Canton Unne engines and two Caudrons with Gnome engines – but Squadron Commander Gordon, seven officers and CPOs, and eight mechanics. In just thirty-six hours the new arrivals were ready to fly and more regular reconnaissance of the delta began. WT signalling tests were made, bomb-dropping was again practised, and confidence soared. After eight months of effort and the expenditure of '*vast* sums of money'[5] an end to the *Königsberg* operations finally seemed to be approaching. All that was required was confirmation that the monitors were as ready as Cull's airmen.

The monitors *Mersey* and *Severn* were two of triplets, their sister ship being the *Humber*. But these were not their original names: they had been commissioned as *Javary*, *Solindes* and *Madeira*, *Solimões*-class river gunboats for the Brazilian Navy. Their war had been an active one, taking part in the action at Ostende covering the retreat of the British Expeditionary Force, and the Dunkirk raid. April had found *Mersey* and *Severn* in Lazzaretto Bay, Malta, charged with sailing up the Danube as the Dardanelles were 'forced'. It is the clearest measure of any of the magnitude of the Admiralty's obsession with destroying the *Königsberg* that Churchill saw fit to order them to East Africa instead. On 6 May *Mersey* and *Severn* were towed through the Suez Canal by the tugs of their parent ship, *Trent*, and set a course for Mafia where they arrived on 3 June. Measuring 265 feet in length and displacing 1,260 tons, monitors were essentially mobile gun platforms drawing just five to six feet; their armament consisted of two 6-inch guns, two 4.7-inch guns, four 3-pdrs and six machine-guns. Deployed in appropriate conditions they were truly formidable craft.

On arrival in East Africa the monitors' hulls and decks were fitted with steel boiler-plates, empty kerosene tins by the thousand were placed below-decks to maintain buoyancy if hit, and sandbags were piled around the conning towers, quarter-decks and fo'c's'les. Different shades of green paint, a rudimentary attempt at camouflage appropriate to conditions in the delta, were daubed all over; and by the end of June joint operations were practised with the planes that were to spot for them during their attack on the delta. It was an anxious time. The crews of the blockading vessels were becoming increasingly impatient, as one rating's shanty indicated:

Ar I loodle I Loodle I tay
I loodle
From aeroplane island to *Königsberg* Bay
We do a trip just 3 times a day
But what we are doing no one can say
From aeroplane island to *Königsberg* Bay.[6]

Furthermore, one of the new Caudron planes and one Henry Farman had already been wrecked, and the vital intelligence regarding the delta that would be essential to the success of the attack was still incomplete.

For two months Pretorius, King-Hall's chief scout, had made repeated incursions into the delta from Koma Island, he and his men making their way stealthily past Werner Schönfeld's shore defences. On at least two occasions he observed the *Königsberg* from a distance of 300 yards; he captured prisoners who were taken back for interrogation; and he learnt just in time of young Lieutenant Richard Wenig's plan to launch one of his five torpedoes at a British cruiser if one ventured too close to the delta mouth. Pretorius's most arduous challenge began when it was confirmed that monitors were to be used against the *Königsberg*: he was the only man to whom the vital task of charting the delta could be entrusted. So began weeks of manoeuvring a dugout up and down the various entrances at night taking soundings with a pole, the only relief to the monotony and discomfort being 'a sense of adventure brought by the possibility of a Teutonic face suddenly peering at me out of the bush'.[7] Before the rains broke the heat and mosquitoes at night were appalling, the danger of being caught in the glare of searchlights constant; after they broke he was permanently soaked to the skin. Eventually he found to his satisfaction that the northern channel would be navigable for the shallow-draught monitors for a distance of seven miles; and from there he walked to the *Königsberg* to confirm that she would then be within range of the monitors' 6-inch guns. His final task even Pretorius described as 'a simply ghastly job': it was to measure the tides at the entrance to the channel for a whole month. During his comings and goings Pretorius made a huge impression on all who came across him. One naval volunteer on *Laconia* described the 'awe and anticipation' of meeting him 'fully justified', adding that he 'learned also, for the first time, the quality and understanding of a great man, possessed of fine qualities and great experiences himself, towards lesser mortals. He was a quiet, gentle person who was genuinely more interested in enquiring about one's own background and comparatively short and mediocre experience of life than in talking about himself.'[8] Armed with Pretorius's charts and invaluable intelligence – for which he would be awarded the DSO – King-Hall was now ready for the fray.

Captain Looff knew what was in store for his ship, but other than continuing to work on successfully launching a torpedo there was little he could do to frustrate King-Hall's preparations. On 24 June, he sent a despatch to Berlin stating that 'all is well on board', confirming that 'the unloading of the cargo of the auxiliary ship [*Kronborg*] is completed', and informing his superiors that he was sending the *Kronborg*'s debonair Captain Christiansen to South Africa so that he could 'make a report on the situation and to order additional auxiliary ships in case the war lasts long'. This would seem to indicate that he had no fear of the monitors, of whose presence he had been informed by spies in Zanzibar, and his statement that 'after the conclusion of Peace the *Königsberg* must be sent home to undergo a thorough overhaul'[9] was equally optimistic. It was true that in spite of the ravages of disease during the rains on his depleted crew Looff was once again in a position to move his vessel: many of the 105 sailors from the German vessels *Planet*, *Khalif* and *Zieten*, interned in Portuguese East Africa, had begun arriving in dribs and drabs and had replaced a similar number of ratings who, led by Lieutenant Angel, the *Königsberg*'s torpedo officer, had been detailed for onshore service by von Lettow-Vorbeck earlier in the year. But on the other hand, most of his crew had long since given up hope of breaking out of the delta and many were certain that the arrival of the monitors meant that the Royal Navy was about to come at them, in the words of a signalman on the *Königsberg*, 'in real bloody earnest'.[10]

King-Hall's orders to the blockading fleet were issued amid worsening relations between him and the many captains on his station. Captain Crampton, who had assumed command of *Weymouth* after its previous incumbent returned home with a 'bad carbuncle', remarked on the plethora of 'extraordinary general memo[s]' from his admiral and concluded that King-Hall was 'mad'.[11] Captain Fullerton of the *Severn* was inclined to agree, especially after King-Hall chose 6 July for the decisive attack in response to his own request for the attack to take place on 3 or 4 July. To make matters even worse, Fullerton and Commander Wilson of *Mersey* heard that Churchill was insisting that the monitors should attack up two different channels of the delta. As this would render them unable to protect each other the order was ignored.

There was no moon on the night of 5–6 July as King-Hall's plethora of vessels took up their positions. *Laurentic*, *Barjora* and a collier steamed north to execute a feint landing at Dar-es-Salaam at dawn; *Hyacinth* stood off the centre channel into the delta, *Pioneer* off the southern with *Trent*, and *Weymouth* and *Pyramus* covered the north. The monitors anchored ten miles off the northernmost Kikunja mouth of the delta at 11 p.m. At 4 a.m. they started for their destination, flying ensigns eighteen feet by twelve, and reaching the mouth just before light at 5.45 a.m. At much the same time a plane dropped four bombs near the *Königsberg* as a diversionary measure and at 6 a.m. the monitors were in the channel. The tide was low, making any torpedo attack less likely, but small weapons fire opened from both banks and a well-concealed German field gun on the starboard side fired three blanks to signal the alarum before directing its fire at *Severn*. In the dim light the men on the monitors 'saw very little with the exception of a few men in trees and bullets ... pattering against the ship's side'.[12] A small boat, suspected of housing a torpedo, was sunk about half a mile up the channel, and at 6.30 a.m. the monitors anchored in their intended positions five to six miles into the delta.

Severn fired first at *Königsberg* at a range of 10,600 yards and was immediately answered with one or two guns until the *Königsberg* found her range; and soon after 7 a.m. she straddled *Mersey* with all five starboard guns. On board *Echo* Lieutenant Charlewood, the fortunate survivor of *Königsberg*'s foray to Zanzibar, remarked on hearing 'the sharp crack of [her] salvoes': 'I had heard that sound before and was not likely to forget it.'[13] In the *Königsberg*'s control tower Lieutenant Apel, the gunnery officer, rapidly increased the rate of fire to five or six salvoes per minute. One shell pitched just two feet short of the *Mersey*'s quarter-deck; another hit a motor boat tied to her quarter abaft the steel plating; and finally one hit the shield of her 6-inch forward gun. One gunner's head was left in its ear protectors while the rest of his body disintegrated. The gun-layer lost four fingers and had his throat skinned. The gun-trainer and breech-worker were killed instantly. For a matter of seconds the survivors watched aghast as the charge that was being loaded just at the moment of impact caught fire, the fire spreading to another charge and then jumping down to the monitor's magazine. Had the petty officer below had a charge in his hand *Mersey*, by the admission of her skipper, 'would almost certainly have blown up'.[14] Even then *Mersey*'s ordeal was not over. The crew had donned their kapok life-vests as protection against shrapnel splinters but these caught fire, severely burning two men, who would die later in the day; the rapid deployment of a hose only just saved a third horrifically burnt rating. Wilson slipped the *Mersey*'s anchors, a shell landing with a great spout of water just where he had been moored, and ordered full speed ahead to a position 700 yards downriver to assess the damage while Apel turned his attention to *Severn*.

In the air all was not going to plan either. Cull, with Flight Lieutenant Arnold observing, had been circling over the delta since 6.17 a.m. – the first time in the history of naval warfare that planes had been used to spot the fall of shots from battleships – but there were problems with the two-letter signalling system used to communicate with the monitors. When both monitors were firing at once he also had difficulty in spotting which were whose shells. At 8 a.m. Arnold did manage to signal that *Severn* had hit *Königsberg* and *Mersey* moved back upriver, anchored on the opposite bank and commenced firing with her aft gun to try and draw fire from *Severn*. *Severn* then moved towards *Mersey*, and the latter succeeded in registering another hit on the *Königsberg* whose fire, using just two guns in an effort to conserve valuable ammunition, became more erratic. Apel had been seriously wounded, and when *Mersey* put a 4.7-inch shrapnel shell and three 6-inch high-explosive shells over a German observation platform watching the monitors, he also had to fire blind: in the main lookout on Pemba Hill, Lieutenant Georg Schlawe, a retired naval officer, could not assist as the monitors were hidden from view.

After a pause in the hostilities Cull took to the air again at 11.50 a.m., and at 1.30 p.m., in the searing heat of the delta, *Mersey* shifted closer to her prey and recommenced firing. But again the signalling system vital to the monitors' indirect firing broke down and a stalemate ensued. The *Königsberg* was still only firing intermittently when, at 3.30 p.m., the monitors retired from the delta, firing ferociously at the shore defences on both banks as they went and in turn again coming under accurate fire from a German field gun. As they emerged into the open sea, Charlewood remarked 'what a relief it was to see those ungainly craft! There had been a time when we had thought that our ships stood no chance of surviving *Königsberg*'s fire. The sight of these two vessels as they drew slowly towards us, wrapped in smoke and belching fire ... and the ever-increasing volume of sound, are impressions that time failed to erase from my memory.'[15] At dusk the monitors passed through the fleet and the crews returned in sombre mood to Tirene Bay on Mafia. The six dead and dying men on *Mersey* represented almost a third of her complement, while the airmen were so cold they had to be lifted from their machines. Using the only two serviceable biplanes at their disposal they had stuck at their task despite the signalling difficulties, logging fifteen hours of flying time and a distance of 970 miles. Their final flight over the *Königsberg*, with Flag Commander Bridgeman as observer, confirmed the worst: only one of the cruiser's 4.1-inch guns appeared to have been put out of action, despite the monitors having scored six hits in all. 'From all points,' noted Cull, 'the day had been discouraging.'[16]

On board the *Königsberg* the crew collapsed on deck, exhausted. Looff, Apel and one other senior officer were wounded; and young Wenig, who had been striving unsuccessfully for so long to improvise a torpedo attack against a British cruiser, had lost his left foot. Among the ratings five lay dead and seven wounded. But the cruiser was most certainly not destroyed and Apel's control of the guns had, even in the estimation of his adversaries, been 'splendid'. For one officer, however, the strain of months of virtual imprisonment had proved too much. The minute the monitors opened fire reserve Sub-Lieutenant Josef Jaeger had shot himself; 'the cause of his suicide [was] presumed to have been insanity', but among his shipmates a rumour circulated that he had been exposed as a spy and that 'he was the reason why our attempts to torpedo the English had always failed'.[17] The crew were aware that they had not seen the last of the monitors, and Looff ordered all inflammables removed from the ship.

Out to sea the atmosphere among the blockade captains and King-Hall worsened at the post-mortem. King-Hall hurriedly telegraphed the Admiralty to say that 'the task of the monitors was an extremely difficult one, on account of the jungle and the difficulties of accurate spotting'.[18] But recriminations directed by him against Fullerton, the captain of *Severn*, were not popular. Crampton wrote that 'Fullerton like all the rest of us is fed up with K-H ... and he cannot talk to him without the little man being thoroughly rude ... everyone is fed up with the little man's methods, and indeed incompetence'.[19] The only good news, received three days after the attack, was that German South-West Africa had capitulated to General Botha's South African forces – a victory that made the destruction of the *Königsberg* all the more important to the pride of those serving on the East Africa Station.

As the darkness lifted on 11 July, Pretorius counted sixteen 'smidges' on the horizon – the British fleet – backed by an 'angry dawn'.[20] His reconnaissance of the Kikunja channel had proved invaluable for the monitors, but they had still had to work principally from a captured German chart which Wilson deemed 'the most inaccurate thing one could ever want to use ... nothing appeared to resemble anything'.[21] Undaunted, Wilson, Fullerton and Cull resolved that this time the monitors would take it in turns to fire to make spotting the results from the air less confusing. At 8 a.m. the monitors left Mafia, pulled by their tugs, for the twenty-mile journey to the delta. There could be no surprise about this second attack. By the time they arrived off the river bar at 10.40 a.m. the temperature in the engine rooms was 125°F, and the reception that awaited them as they entered the delta forty minutes later was equally 'hot'. The German field gun ranged on *Severn* and then hit *Mersey* twice, wounding three men manning her 6-inch gun aft. But once past the reception committee the monitors' captains had the distinct impression that the banks were less well guarded than during their previous visit and they were able to anchor successfully at their firing position fifty minutes later. The true explanation for this relative tranquillity was that on this occasion the cruisers supported the monitors with a proper bombardment of the shore defences and Lieutenant Schlawe's observation position on Pemba Hill; and the greater participation by the offshore fleet in this second attack also thwarted an attempt by the *Wami*, one of the *Königsberg*'s tenders, to torpedo one of the monitors. On board *Hyacinth*, bombarding the Simba Uranga and Kiomboni channels with *Pioneer*, Pretorius looked on in awe as 'orders were sung out to the men already at their stations, and our guns spoke … all previous noises faded to insignificance as salvo after salvo belched out'. Yet another cruiser, HMS *Challenger*, had also arrived to assist in the attack, and what struck Pretorius most was 'the nonchalance of the English sailors' in the heat of battle. 'One group', he noticed, 'not engaged in the firing, were calmly sitting on the deck mending their boots, and others were stitching canvas just as if nothing untoward were happening. They did not even trouble to watch the bombardment.' For him, however, this was the culmination of months of clandestine handiwork and the excitement was 'terrific'.[22]

As *Mersey* swung broadside on to *Königsberg*'s position and opened fire the incoming shells soared overhead at first and then began to fall short – the erratic pattern being due to the ferocity of the fleet's bombardment of the German observation posts. Meanwhile *Severn* moved 100 yards further upriver, drawing *Königsberg*'s fire in the process, and when she was ready to commence firing *Mersey* ceased. On board *Severn* the atmosphere was one of controlled bedlam. Apel had found his range at last and his salvoes were turning the water around the monitor into a vortex – forty-seven shell fragments would later be found strewn across her deck. But with communications with the planes now working smoothly, and only *Severn* firing, *Mersey* also began to close in on her prey. Wilson's first direct hit was scored at

12.35 p.m. and *Königsberg*'s accuracy immediately started to falter. Arnold, Cull's observer, signalled two more hits from *Severn* and soon afterwards noticed that only three of *Königsberg*'s guns were still firing. Just before one o'clock, however, one of *Königsberg*'s last two QF shrapnel shells exploded right in front of Cull and Arnold's plane, even though it was almost in the black clouds 2,400 feet overhead. Arnold coolly signalled the hit to *Mersey*, and continued signalling on the descent, his last message informing *Severn* that 'all hits are right forward'. The plane crashed into the water not far from *Mersey*. Arnold was flung twenty-five yards clear on impact but Cull still wore his belt and was somewhere beneath the upturned plane. It was some time before, to their great relief, Wilson and the crew of *Mersey* saw him emerge from underneath and struggle clear, having 'swallowed a good deal more than his fair share of the Rufiji'. Both men were safely picked up, all crocodiles having moved off when the firing had first started, and Cull and Arnold were congratulated on what Wilson considered to be 'one of the most gallant episodes of the war'. Meanwhile *Severn* was scoring hit after hit on the *Königsberg*, nine from fifteen shots in twelve minutes; and *Weymouth* and *Pyramus* had – for the very first time – crossed the bar at the entrance to the delta and were 'fairly giving both banks "Tommy Up The Orchard"'.[23]

Three minutes after the airmen came down a huge explosion could be heard from the *Königsberg*, followed soon after by two more. *Mersey* now took up the gauntlet and closed in for the kill. Passing *Severn* at her anchorage between Gengeni Island and the west bank, Wilson skilfully manoeuvred his cumbersome craft to within 7,000 yards of *Königsberg* and anchored only when her passage upriver was barred by a shoal which Pretorius had warned seemed to stretch the whole width of the river. The German cruiser was still out of sight but a vast column of smoke rose into the sky from her decks and further explosions could be heard. Wilson ordered *Mersey*'s gunners to open fire and a hit was registered with her third shot. He continued firing until 2.45 p.m., also destroying on the riverbank what he suspected was a torpedo boat whose crew had bolted, and an observation post in a tub submerged in the mud just thirty yards away. By then it was clear to all that '*Königsberg* was no more', and the order was given to cease fire and to retire on the falling tide. Flight Lieutenant Watkins's Caudron, which had taken over spotting for Cull and was now the sole serviceable British plane, returned to Mafia where it landed in the swamp at the end of the runway, throwing Watkins clear but leaving his observer upside down with his head in the grime.

As the monitors passed through the fleet to a colossal cheer, there was pandemonium on board the *Königsberg*. Looff proudly recorded that when the attack had started his crew 'did not sleep like *Pegasus* people'. But this second attack was 'the straw that broke the camel's back'. He was short of ammunition after loosing off 150 shells from four starboard guns, and at last was forced to recognise that 'we would never leave the delta'. The *Königsberg*'s decks were strewn with wreckage and the fallen, fire was spreading through the ship, and the magazines had to be flooded. A 'shake of the hand, some brief words' were all he could offer as the wounded staggered past and just before 1 p.m. he had finally ordered Oberleutnant Georg Koch to blow up the ship with a torpedo warhead. The noise, though clearly audible to his assailants, was 'more feeble than we had thought it would be, almost like the distant thunder of the enemy's guns'. *Königsberg* juddered, listed to starboard and sank in the shallow water to the level of her upper deck. From her mainmast the Imperial Navy's pennant still flew, but the fire on board had spread to the shore and it was only thanks to the timely and energetic assistance of Ulrich Dankwarth, the government forester at Salale, that the wounded were guided to safety. One of the longest continuous engagements in naval history was at an end.

'Was this a victory?' Looff asked himself. 'Certainly not'[24] was his defiant answer. His guns were not irreparable, the 125 wounded crewmen would mostly recover, and in the eight months of manning the shore defences only four members of Schönfeld's 500-strong Delta Force were thought to have been killed. All of the *Königsberg*'s crew were awarded the Iron Cross 2nd Class, thirty-two of them posthumously, on the Kaiserin's birthday in October; and Looff won the Iron Cross 1st Class and the even more prestigious *Pour le Mérite*. On the other hand the abandonment of the *Königsberg* was not carried out in as orderly a fashion as Looff would later claim: there were still men on board when the torpedo warheads were detonated, and the Chief Engineer 'behaved abominably, pushing away all the crew who stood in his way into the water'[25] as he made for the shore. Furthermore 'Das Ende der *Königsberg*' was not a story that was run by German newspapers until April 1916. Monitors were not deemed good for morale, as a captured letter written by one of the crew subsequently made clear. 'Those were hard days here', it read, 'if you never have any dealings with monitors you will have to congratulate yourself, dear Hans, they are beastly things and not to be trifled with … The *Königsberg* was shot to pieces as if she had been in a mousetrap.'[26]

As *Severn* and *Mersey* anchored off Mafia their captains assessed what it had cost in ordnance to finish the *Königsberg*. In the two attacks they had between them fired 943 6-inch shells, 389 4.7-inch shells, 1,860 3-pdr shells and 16,000 rounds from their machine-guns. 'So,' remarked Wilson, 'you can imagine what one's hearing was like at the end of the day.'[27] For the airmen, led by Gordon and Cull, there was considerable pride in their indispensable and courageous spotting during the second attack, and the knowledge that they were the first aviators in history to participate in the destruction of a warship. DSOs were awarded to Fullerton, Wilson, Gordon, Cull and Arnold; while six DSMs were won by the crew of *Severn*, three by *Mersey*'s men and one by Air Mechanic Boggis for his unstinting efforts to keep the British planes in the air.

The Royal Navy had more than twenty warships of various types and sizes off the delta on 11 July. There was a strong feeling on board most of them that a lot of trouble, and tremendous cost, could have been saved but 'no one had the resolution to go after [*Königsberg*] at once'.[28] This was not entirely fair, but King-Hall was generally blamed. An utterly fed-up Captain Crampton on *Weymouth* was disgusted at the 'misplaced hot air'[29] talked by his admiral in the debrief of 12 July. A young lieutenant on *Hyacinth* also suggested that 'had we served under more inspired leadership than we had from King-Hall I am sure we would have left with a different feeling, for we had taken part in a campaign that was to say the least unusual'.[30] All felt that it had, even at the end, been 'a narrow squeak' and that 'the luck was all on our side and entirely against the Germans'.[31]

Of those naval officers who took part four, including Fullerton, were destined to become admirals. But for the man who had commanded them, there was considerable disappointment. Having overseen what he described as 'a very neat job',[32] King-Hall left the East Africa Station on 18 July. He was refused an active command at sea and ended the war in command of the Royal Naval base at Scapa Flow. And *his* superior, Churchill, was – for the time being – brought down by the debacle at the Dardanelles.*

For six days after the events of 11 July the weather was rainy and misty, preventing aerial assessment of the exact extent of the damage inflicted on the *Königsberg*. But on the seventh the weather cleared and Pretorius led a landing party to take a look up the delta. 'One

---

* Following his resignation from the Cabinet, Churchill offered to take command of a squadron of armoured cars in East Africa. The offer was declined by the War Office.

would scarcely have known what she had been,' he wrote; 'for here, beside the bush-crowded edge of the small island against which she had been moored, lay little more than a vast disorder of tortured steel.'[33] Within two weeks, while the wounded recovered in the care of Dr Eyerich and Dr Seitz at Neustieten, Koch led the fit crewmen of the *Königsberg* off to Dar-es-Salaam to begin their war as soldiers rather than sailors and Franz Köhl, a Bavarian gunner, began the salvage of the ship's ten guns. Only fifteen of the *Königsberg*'s original crew would ever see Germany again, and by then the wreck of their former vessel had been bought for £200 by none other than Commander Ingles, the skipper of the *Pegasus*.

TEN

'The Lion and the Springbok'[1]

The surrender of German South-West Africa to South African troops in July 1915 was an event of considerable significance. It was the second German colony in Africa to fall, following the capture of Togo in the first month of the war, leaving only the Cameroons and German East Africa still to be 'squared', and it had been achieved at an acceptable cost of £15m (£675m in today's money). More importantly, however, it constituted the first major Allied victory of the entire war and was regarded as a welcome boost to morale midway through a year of disastrous setbacks in Europe and at the Dardanelles.

That victory should have been secured by the popular South African Premier Louis Botha – a man recently described as 'a sort of Sir Edward Grey on horseback'[2] – was equally reassuring to the War Office. Little more than a decade had passed since the end of the Anglo-South African, or 'Boer', War in which Botha and his deputy, Jan Smuts, had been prominent 'enemy' generals. But from a position of total defeat these two men had vigorously supported union between the formerly British South African territories and the old Boer republics of Transvaal and the Orange Free State; and when this was finally achieved in 1910 the South African electorate had voted for an Afrikaner majority in parliament. This remarkable outcome, which seemed to indicate that it was Boer not Briton who had finally won the war, was not the one anticipated by the British government; but any fears about a renewal of hostilities were allayed by Botha's firm conviction that South Africa's interests would be best served by a future within the British Empire.

At the outbreak of war, Botha had reaffirmed South Africa's loyalty to the Crown, much to the relief of those in Britain who feared the possibility of a declaration of neutrality or even tacit sympathy with Germany. Such fears were not unjustified. Germany had supported Kruger during the Anglo-South African War, and the threat posed to British shipping by German South-West Africa's ports and its high-powered wireless station at Windhuk *might* have been construed by Botha to have been no concern of South Africa's (even after a relatively minor German cross-border incursion). Furthermore, there were tens of thousands of German settlers living in South Africa. But Germany's growing belligerence, and the implicit threat to South African interests of the Kaiser's doctrine of 'Unser Feld ist die Welt' – 'The whole world is our playing field' – determined Botha's course of action; and by the end of August 1914 the seven British infantry battalions and one cavalry regiment stationed in South Africa were able to begin making their way to Europe as a result of his declaration that the country would assume responsibility for its own defence.

Botha's decision was a bold one. It was taken against a background of immense internal strife in South Africa, and in no time old grievances between Afrikaner and Briton, Afrikaner and Afrikaner, and Briton and German were resurgent. The tension among Afrikaners was the greatest concern. For the moderates, led by Botha and Smuts, allegiance to Britain was accepted as both a *de iure* and a *de facto* obligation for the ultimate greater good of South Africa. But there were 'as many kinds of Dutchmen as there are nations in Europe'.[3] Some were resolutely pro-British, believing that if Botha and Smuts thought it best to fight for the British that was good enough for them, no matter how great their grievances against the *verdomde rooineks* – 'damned rednecks' – had been after the Boer War; some were all for participating in the war but, like General Coen Brits, who had accepted his call-up from Botha with the words 'who do we fight, Germans or English?', were unsure where South Africa's allegiance would lie; and there was a substantial faction of Afrikaner *bitter-einders* – the 'bitter-enders' – who either vigorously opposed South Africa's incorporation within the British Empire or accepted it only grudgingly. The republican and nationalist sentiments of this latter group found a spokesman in a man who, like Botha and Smuts, was a former Boer general. James Barry Munnik Hertzog possessed 'a dangerous face, that of a fanatic, brooding, intense and rather cruel',[4] and was described by his many enemies as 'a good hater', 'a rigid martinet', and 'narrow in the extreme'.[5] In short he seemed – to his detractors – to embody the most despicable characteristics of the extremist wing of Afrikaner society, and in 1912 he was even left out of Botha's Cabinet.

In spite of, or perhaps because of, his objectionable personal traits and invective, Hertzog's parochialism appealed to the concerns of the deeply conservative, the dispossessed, the malcontent, the reactionary, and the plain ignorant elements of Afrikaner society; and he wasted no time in making his views on the war known. Hertzog saw no merit whatsoever in siding with Britain against those whom he regarded as the Boers' 'fellow Teutons', and his virulent criticism of *de Engelse* knew no bounds. *Afrika voor de afrikander* ('Africa for the Afrikaner') was his relentless cry, a concept from which not only black Africans were excluded but also the likes of Botha and Smuts, whom he cast as 'turncoats', scourges of 'Afrikaner culture'. Hertzog may have been 'a hysterical dunderhead',[6] but he was a dangerous one; and the fact that parliament was not in session during the first month of the war gave him ample opportunity to foment sedition.

By the time the Royal Navy and South African troops captured the German South-West African port of Lüderitz on 15 September 1914 the criticism of Botha's pro-British stance had reached fever pitch in Nationalist circles, despite the invasion of the German colony being retrospectively approved by a massive parliamentary majority. General Beyers resigned as Commandant General of the Defence Force in protest at Botha's rejection of neutrality and he, General Koos De la Rey and Hertzog embarked on a campaign to air their grievances in those sections of Afrikaner society where they would be received most favourably. This was more than just filibustering; and when De la Rey, as big a hero of the Boer War to the Afrikaner population as was Lord Roberts to the English, was accidentally shot at a police roadblock near Johannesburg on the very day that Lüderitz fell a full-scale rebellion erupted.

Whitehall received the first reports of fratricidal hostilities in South Africa with considerable consternation. There was no telling how many Afrikaners might take up arms, especially as the rebellion was exclusively led by former heroes of the Anglo-South African War. Christiaan De Wet, the Boer 'Pimpernel' of that conflict, occupied towns in the Orange Free State which soon contributed three-quarters of the rebel commandos; General Beyers organised resistance in the Transvaal; and in the northern Cape Colonel Solomon 'Manie' Maritz and 1,000 troops joined their erstwhile enemies in German South-West Africa and commenced operations against the Union. All in all, Admiral King-Hall, who at the time had not yet departed to take charge of the operations against the *Königsberg*, was not exaggerating when he warned Churchill that the situation was 'very grave',* and it worsened when rumours began to circulate that German missionaries were encouraging the Zulus to rise up as well. All loyal troops were either campaigning in German South-West Africa or deploying against the Afrikaner rebels, leaving only the police to face this new threat to peace. One of them anticipated that 'if the Zulus do rise ... it will be *bon soir* for us all';[7] but fortunately the rumours proved exaggerated.

As 'tribal leader', Botha acted decisively. Martial law was proclaimed, operations in German South-West Africa were suspended, and the South African Premier personally led 40,000 predominantly Afrikaner troops

---

* CHAR/13/38/295. On 12 October Churchill replied that *he* did not consider 'the use of the expression "very grave" to be warranted'. On 22 October King-Hall reiterated that it was 'undoubtedly grave'.

against their mutinous brethren. Beyers was defeated at Rustenburg in December, and drowned while crossing the Vaal River to escape his pursuers. Christiaan De Wet was defeated and captured at Mushroom Valley the same month. 'Manie' Maritz remained in German South-West Africa and was joined, after a remarkable crossing of the Kalahari, by rebels led by Major Jan Kemp; but in February 1915, Maritz fled to Portuguese West Africa and Kemp surrendered. By the end of the month the remnants of the 'Ten Bob Rebellion', so called because of the token fine subsequently levied on De Wet, were all rounded up.

The relative ease with which the rebellion was put down could not disguise its potential danger to Botha's government and to the British war effort. Indeed so great was the concern in Britain that the War Office had made contingency plans to divert 30,000 Australian and New Zealand soldiers en route for Europe to South Africa. Nor did the suppression of the rebellion preclude the possibility of further insurrection. Union in South Africa had only been achieved through compromise on the part of a deeply divided society, and the fact that just 12,000 men had actually taken up arms against the state was no cause for optimism. In 1913 imperial troops had had to be called upon to extinguish widespread strikes, and a severe drought in 1913–14 had been a contributory factor to a general strike a few months before the war that had required the mobilisation of the Union Defence Force. In other words, South Africa was markedly unstable even before the war, and the outbreak of war had simply exacerbated that instability. From a British point of view it was therefore 'fortunate indeed', as King-Hall put it, that 'General Botha, supported by his brilliant colleague, General Smuts, was the one political power at this time', because he was by common consent the only man who commanded sufficient respect to counter the 'well-nigh insuperable'[8] divisions in South Africa's white population.

Neither Botha's physical appearance, nor his reputation for being 'a man above the ordinary',[9] suggested that he might be a sensitive man. But he was greatly troubled by the sight of Afrikaner fighting Afrikaner, and deeply hurt by the treachery of former close friends and the 'abusive and threatening letters which were showered upon [him]'[10] by rebel sympathisers. However he showed extreme leniency to the rebel commanders, only one of whom was executed (for having failed to resign his commission in the Defence Force before joining Beyers); and, in King-Hall's words, 'his eye remained fixed on the Pole Star of duty'[11] even when he suffered from a chronic attack of dysentery while campaigning in German South-West Africa. Having committed South Africa to fight alongside Britain, Botha meant to see it through, and as soon as the German South-West campaign was over he undertook not only to despatch the 5th Battery of the South African

Mounted Rifles to bolster the defences of Nyasaland but also to raise a full brigade for 'overseas' service.*

The South African victory over her German neighbour and Botha's promise to raise further troops for the Empire's war effort soon prompted the War Office to devote serious attention to its options in East Africa where, in the words of Major-General Callwell, the Director of Military Operations in London, 'the enemy enjoyed such initiative as there was and the situation was an eminently unsatisfactory one'. Ever since Tanga the vexing question of 'what was to be done' had gone unanswered, not least because of more pressing priorities elsewhere, but now the possibility of deploying South Africans to '[come] to the rescue on the farther side of the Dark Continent, and of their getting our Indian and native African contingents ... out of the scrape they were in'[12] seemed to give genuine cause for optimism.

The problem for Britain (and Botha) was that an election was approaching in South Africa, and the rebellion had not only made martyrs of its defeated commanders but involved the death of some 350 of their followers. At first glance this was hardly an extensive casualty list, but it was comparable to that of the entire German South-West Africa campaign and was therefore sufficiently long for Hertzog's purposes. With renewed vigour he set about appealing to the many paranoid and 'bully-boy' elements of the South African electorate, and focused on undermining Botha by heaping vitriol on his more authoritarian, austere deputy, Jan Smuts.

During the campaigning Smuts told his wife that he was certain that he must be 'the most hated man in South Africa'. Labourites resented his handling of the economy and the strikes in 1913 and 1914 (when Smuts had been Minister of Finance), Nationalists accused him of having the blood of Afrikaner 'heroes' on his hands, and death threats arrived at his home almost daily. But this brilliant scholar and lawyer who had risen to be Kruger's Attorney-General at the age of just twenty-eight, and had helped Botha to forge the Union, was as steely (and humourless) as Botha was jovial. He did not enjoy the loneliness and abuse, professing at one point that he 'would like nothing better than to get out of this hell into which I have wandered',[13] but his determination to raise South Africa above the pettiness of fratricidal turmoil was as great as his ambition for the country. Like Hertzog, Smuts would never forget the 'grievous wrong' and 'great misery'[14] wrought by Britain during the Anglo-South African War. But like Botha, he was adamant that a 'Greater South Africa' could only

---

*The 1st South African Infantry Brigade was recruited in August and September 1915 and comprised four battalions: 1st South African Infantry (Cape of Good Hope) Regiment; 2nd South African (Natal and Orange Free State) Regiment; 3rd South African (Transvaal and Rhodesia) Regiment; and 4th South African (South African Scottish) Regiment. Brigadier-General Lukin was appointed commander-in-chief of the 160 officers and 5,648 other ranks.

be created alongside the British Empire, and that the German political system was 'a menace to the world even worse than Bonapartism'.[15]

Botha and Smuts carried the election, their South African Party winning fifty-four seats to the Nationalists' twenty-seven. The predominantly 'British' Unionist Party took second place with forty seats. The result seemed like an overwhelming display of support for their stance on the war, and Botha immediately began to plan for a still greater South African involvement. Two high-ranking South African officers were despatched to appraise the military situation in East Africa and the situation that confronted them was distinctly gloomy.

The 'Brilliant Affair' at Bukoba had been but a temporary fillip. Within a week of the destruction of the *Königsberg*, British troops had been given a severe bloody nose when they tried to eject a German force numbering between 600 and 800 rifles and commanded by Captain Vorberg and Lieutenant Merensky, from Mbuyuni, twenty miles east of Taveta. Mbuyuni was the German forward post for raids against both the Uganda Railway and a new military railway being constructed to support an eventual advance by British troops from Voi towards Taveta. By the end of June this line had reached Maktau, within a day's march of Mbuyuni, and Tighe decided that Mbuyuni needed to be cleared of the enemy. Brigadier-General Malleson, who had nearly been killed during a patrol towards the German positions during May, and was only saved by the intervention of Subadar Ghulam Haidar of the 130th Baluchis, was ordered by Tighe to lead the attack on 14 July. Malleson was given 1,200 reliable troops – men from the Loyal North Lancs, 130th Baluchis, 29th Punjabis, KAR and the 2nd Rhodesians – with whom to seize Mbuyuni, but the attack went badly wrong. Colonel Vallings, commanding the 29th Punjabis, was killed, and on learning that British casualties were well in excess of 100 men the prevailing opinion among those who had taken part was that there had been 'no military reason, tactical or strategical, for undertaking this hazardous attack on a known prepared position'. Tighe's 'impatience ... [and] desire to do something' attracted as much criticism as Malleson's handling of the operation, which had achieved nothing more than 'the strengthening of the already fine morale of the enemy'.[16]

More 'reverses' followed soon afterwards. In August a British post on the mountain of Kasigau, thirty miles from Voi, was overrun; and the following month an attempt to retake Longido by a force 450-strong, led by Colonel Jollie, commanding officer of the 17th Cavalry, was beaten off after incurring heavy casualties. This latest Longido 'Affair' was immediately hushed up, for fear of further damaging the morale of British troops buckling before the 'aggressive attitude of the enemy's advanced troops',[17] the raids on the Uganda Railway and the effects of disease. At the end of August Tighe admitted to the

War Office that although the ration strength of his force had swelled to almost 15,000 men over the summer, only 4,000 British and Indian troops and 3,600 *askari* of the KAR were actually fit for duty – a combined strength no greater than that of IEF 'B' almost a year earlier. Certain regiments, like the 13th Rajputs, had been so decimated by malaria and dysentery that Tighe had to declare them unfit for any further action; of the 1,100 men who had seen action with the 2nd Loyal North Lancs fewer than one in four had not been admitted to hospital at some point; while among the 2nd Rhodesia Regiment, for example, 'nerves stretched to breaking-point [were causing] many break-downs'.[18] In Tighe's estimation, the greatest strike force he could put into the field in British East Africa would comprise 2,500 infantry with eighteen field guns and thirty-five machine-guns; and he concluded that 'against such odds as I have now to meet, if all my troops were fit, I could probably hold my own ... [but] should the enemy make an advance on the [Maktau-Mzima] lines, a contingency which I regard as quite possible, the situation would be serious'. Furthermore, he warned Whitehall that the *Königsberg's* guns had mostly been refurbished and were being deployed, as were the millions of rounds of ammunition, six field guns and modern rifles salvaged from the *Kronborg*. Given the circumstances, it is perhaps unsurprising that the courageous and determined, but hapless, Mickey Tighe began to earn a reputation for sporadic bouts of bibulousness.

Von Lettow-Vorbeck, on the other hand, had every reason to be optimistic. By mid summer a recruitment drive for *askari* had raised the number of indigenous troops in the *Schutztruppe* to nearly 9,000 and the full mobilisation of German East Africa's reservists had put some 2,000 European combatants into service on the various fronts. British Intelligence, which had improved considerably since Tanga under the direction of Captain Richard Mein-ertzhagen, reckoned that von Lettow-Vorbeck could actually field as many as 20,000 troops; and German armaments – sixty-six machine-guns and sixty field guns – gave their troops a considerable superiority in firepower. Thanks to a superior medical establishment and number of trained medical staff, who drew on the knowledge gained by German doctors in the course of two decades of experimentation and innovation in Africa, sickness rates among the German troops, European and African alike, were also considerably lower than those afflicting the British ranks.

Meanwhile, Schnee's administration was proving highly adept at coping with the shortages caused by the British naval blockade. In time, there would be almost nothing for which scientists working in laboratories at Amani, in the Usambara Mountains, and Dar-es-Salaam could not create a substitute. Candles were fashioned from beeswax; salad oil was made from pressed peanuts; soap was manufactured using charcoal, or soda from Lake Natron;

ships' lifebelts, euphorbia wood and corn cobs provided the wherewithal to make 'cork'; and *kifefe*, a soup of salt and beef fat favoured by many *askari*, was found to be a potent balm for ridding dogs of fleas. Most important of all, a foul-tasting quinine known as 'Lettow-schnapps' began to be locally manufactured from the bark of *cinchona* trees (and the Schulze brewery in Dar-es-Salaam had sufficient stocks of hops to see it through 1915). Efficient supply networks were also established to bring huge quantities of foodstuffs from all around the colony to Korogwe, Mombo and Neu Moshi, whence they were distributed to the front lines in the north-east. The resourcefulness and ingenuity of both von Lettow-Vorbeck and Schnee soon became known in the British ranks, and a rumour that they were even about to launch their own 'home-made' submarine began to circulate. Fanciful though this idea may have been, it was quite clear that German East Africa had no intention of capitulating in the same way as German South-West Africa; and Schnee publicly declared that 'we won't allow ourselves to surrender here – we shall fight to the last man'.[19]

The prognosis of the two South African officers inspecting the situation in East Africa was mixed. Many aspects of the conduct of the campaign thus far were criticised, but their report concluded that von Lettow-Vorbeck could be defeated if sufficient numbers of South African troops could be raised for the task. In the meantime, however, Tighe had to consider the possibility that it might be his colony that faced imminent invasion, and his thoughts turned to persuading British East Africa's settlers to take to the field once again. Settlers had done rather well, however, since most of them had been encouraged to return to their farms and businesses at the end of 1914. Certainly there were hardships: German East Africa was now a closed market, machinery was difficult to obtain from overseas, and many input prices had soared. *The Leader* even remarked in April that 'women who were quite pretty in normal times suddenly became plain and uninteresting-looking', developing what it called 'knitting faces'.[20] But African dominance of the agricultural sector was rapidly being eroded by the settlers, partly due to substantial investment made before the war, and partly due to a plentiful supply of labour: as the military labour requirement for Africans began to rise, exemption for those willing to squat on European farms and hire out their work became a popular way of avoiding military call-up. In order to lure the settlers back to the front, Tighe therefore needed help from someone who had real authority in the settler community; and he called on the services of Ewart Grogan.

'Cape-to-Cairo' Grogan had already distinguished himself as the British Liaison Officer with the Belgian forces, and was not only the most prominent businessman in British East Africa but also its finest orator. He readily agreed to make a 'call to arms' on Tighe's behalf and his presence on 7 September

1915 at Nairobi's Theatre Royal guaranteed a packed house for what would subsequently be heralded as 'the greatest meeting in the history of British East Africa'. The evening began with a stirring performance from the orchestra and the singing of patriotic songs. Then Grogan, immaculate in his captain's uniform, rose to his feet and the cheer from the 1,500-strong audience was deafening. Many minutes elapsed before he could begin his hour-long speech, delivered, as was his wont, without the assistance of a single note.

Grogan began with a resumé of the war. He fulsomely praised the 'magnificent work' being done by fellow colonists from Australia, New Zealand, Canada and South Africa – a compliment which brought further cheers – and reminded his audience that the conflict in East Africa was 'but a small part of the whole'. Many in the protectorate, he declared, had done what was expected of them, whereupon he singled out the exemplary bravery and loyalty of the *askari* of the King's African Rifles. But many, he added, fixing on his audience a rapier-like gaze, had not. Indeed there were settlers who were 'chaffering in the market, dodging about attending to twopenny-halfpenny bits of business and thinking of *shambas*' instead of fighting, and there were officials happily tending their gardens and playing tennis on the Hill while continuing to draw salaries far in excess of the bob a day to which enlisted men were entitled. It was possible, Grogan mocked, 'to walk into any club and see half a dozen men between twenty and twenty-five passively reclining in chairs with illustrated papers on their knees'; and he poured scorn on the Public Works Department, accusing it of doing nothing to help anyone at the front. Given the situation, in which so many were behaving like 'white rabbits', he asked whether it was any wonder that Andrew Bonar Law, leader of the Conservative Party and Colonial Secretary in Asquith's coalition government, had pointed out that British East Africa was the only protectorate in the Empire that had called on outside help. This deplorable state of affairs, thundered Grogan, had to change.

His rebuke was met – paradoxically – with ecstatic acclaim. Then, carrying the crowd with him, Grogan turned to exhortation. It was time for everyone to realise that 'these were times of war, war – red war; not games'. *Everyone*, he stressed, had to be prepared to assume responsibility for some part of the war effort: conscription should be imposed, Provincial Commissioners should help to run the farms of absent settlers, and women should play their part to the full since it was well known that they were indispensable 'if you want anything well done'. In short, it was time for sacrifice by all. With that, Grogan gestured to the chairman of the meeting, an American millionaire with a sixty-three-inch sword-belt called Northrup McMillan, and pointed out that he had offered Chiromo – a grand Nairobi home which he had leased from Grogan – as well as his farm at Juja for use as hospitals; and Grogan declared that he was ready to follow this magnificent example by offering his estate at Turi as a camp for women and children.

Grogan saved his most emotive appeal for last: he asked everyone to realise that they were facing the 'ultimate challenge' and to ensure that 'when the history of the war comes to be written and the children ask "what did your Daddy do in the war?", let no man shrink from having the question asked. When we pass on our account of what we have done, let us be sure the answer from home will be "Well done thou babe of Empire".'[21] It took several minutes for the clapping, hollering and stamping of feet to abate, causing Mr Radley, the manager of the Theatre Royal, to worry that the roof might cave in. The meeting was then thrown open to the audience. Affirmations of loyalty were given by leaders of British East Africa's Indian and Goan communities, three cheers were given for Grogan and, with a rousing rendition of the National Anthem, the meeting drew to a close. 'I look on this moment as being the turning point in the history of British East Africa,' Captain Meinertzhagen wrote in his diary. 'The colony has found itself.'[22]

By the end of 1915 1,000 settlers and over 300 officials were again on active service; and of the 1,200 adult males who were not, half were either unfit or too old for the rigours of bush fighting. 'Stokers' – those who kept the home fires burning with an eye to personal gain – became few and far between. Many years later, after Churchill's famous exhortations during World War II, old men and women would look back to that night in the Theatre Royal and bestow upon Grogan the title of 'Kenya's Churchill'.

By the end of November Botha had promised the War Office the services of five batteries of artillery, one mounted and one infantry brigade and a battalion of the Cape Corps (a unit of 'coloureds' raised in the Cape) for the East Africa campaign; and within a month the force was greater still. As an avid lover of auction bridge, Botha's motto was 'never make an original trump declaration unless you have either the ace or king of the suit',[23] and he meant to provide it. It was an act of considerable brinkmanship: a closer inspection of the election results showed that the South African Party had only polled 18,000 votes more than the Nationalists' 77,000, and it was not long before rumours of a second rebellion began to circulate. Even the loyalty of the small Boer community in East Africa came under suspicion when one of their number, a Captain Wessels who had served in the East African Mounted Rifles, was found to have been spying for the enemy and was hastily deported to Ceylon.

Encouraged by Botha's optimism, and anxious to find some front on which it could secure a rapid and decisive victory, the War Office finally began to pay attention to Tighe's reports of a 'radically altered'[24] situation in East Africa. If von Lettow-Vorbeck launched an offensive prior to the end of the year, and

Tighe's ravaged troops gave way at Taveta and on the coast, the Germans could easily cut the Uganda Railway. Such a move, in the opinion of the War Office, 'would probably be decisive';[25] and it would inflict irreparable damage on British 'prestige' in Africa. But there was nothing that could be done to counter it except 'thrash [the situation] out thoroughly',[26] and await the arrival in East Africa of the first South African troops in the hope that they were not too late.

On 12 November 1915 – almost exactly a year after Tanga – the Committee of Imperial Defence formalised its plan for a second attempt at invading German East Africa. Lord Kitchener wanted 'nothing to do with it' because he 'looked on sideshows with no kindly eye', the more so after the Dardanelles fiasco, and believed that humiliating Germany in the colonies would be to the detriment of any peace agreement. But his influence in the British War Cabinet was on the wane, and the prevailing view was that 'this sideshow, even if it had begun in the interests of protecting British sea-power, had become both necessary and unavoidable'.[27] The plan hastily drawn up by Whitehall required Botha to find at least 10,000 South African troops, a realistic possibility as recruitment was proceeding well; and also required him to approve the appointment of a commander in whom those troops would have confidence. This was not so easy for the South African Premier. The political future of Botha and Smuts, indeed the whole future of South Africa as a part of the British Empire, rested on a swift and decisive victory being achieved in East Africa at a cost in men and money comparable to that of the German South-West Africa campaign.

ELEVEN

A Velha Aliada – 'The Old Ally'

———•———

The South African conquest of German South-West Africa and its mobil-isation for deployment in British East Africa was accompanied by Portuguese East Africa (Mozambique) joining the fray. Portugal remained officially neutral, both in Europe and Africa; but the Portuguese government, like the Belgian government, was gravely concerned about its position in the event of any new, post-war carve-up of Africa. As early as January 1915 there were signs of Portugal's intent – 20,000 Mauser-Vergueiro rifles and 12 million rounds of ammunition were provided to South Africa for use in the German South-West Africa campaign, and troops from Portuguese East Africa were sent to the Nyasaland border to assist Britain in quelling a 'native uprising'; by the end of the year Portuguese neutrality had, *de facto* if not *de iure*, largely been abandoned.

Portugal's insistence on playing a proactive part in the campaigning in eastern and southwest Africa was to plunge the country into a nightmare, because its domestic political situation was even less stable than that of South Africa. Four years before the outbreak of war a revolution had forced King Manuel into exile in Twickenham and Portugal had been declared a Republic. But no diminution in the violence and factionalism which had led to its creation ensued, and by 1926 no fewer than forty-five governments had held power. The outbreak of war exacerbated the instability, as did Portugal's parlous financial state; and it vastly complicated the process of dealing with Portugal's predicament in Africa, where the Republic had inherited a colonial domain the size of western Europe whose beginnings predated the 'Scramble for Africa' by more than four centuries. Determining a course of action in relation to its vast African 'possessions' was to prove a Sisyphean challenge, with adverse consequences for all of Portugal's allies as they sought to defeat von Lettow-Vorbeck.

The birth of the Republic had placed particular strain on the 'old alliance' between Britain and Portugal which dated back to 1373. In the nineteenth century Britain had exercised 'trusteeship' over Portugal during the Peninsular War against Napoleon and remained treaty-bound to 'defend and protect all conquest of colonies belonging to the Crown of Portugal against all his enemies, future as well as present'. But there was no longer a monarchy, and the altered state of affairs was recognised by a Foreign Office memo of 1910 which declared that 'many of the clauses of the old treaties are ... now obsolete, because referring to conditions which have passed away', and pointed out that Britain had never 'in more recent times ... admitted that she is necessarily bound to espouse all Portugal's quarrels'.[1] Two years later, when considering Anglo-Portuguese treaty obligations in the event of a European war, British policy had hardened. Given that the prevailing view in Whitehall was that 'neither the Portuguese Army, nor Treasury, has any effective war value that could strengthen the position of Great Britain', it was decided that Britain reserved the right 'to judge for herself in every case whether a *casus foederis* has arisen'. An Admiralty War Staff memo expressed this position even more bluntly: however old the alliance existing between Britain and Portugal, there were now 'no direct advantages' accruing from it to Britain 'as regards strategic considerations';[*] and by 1914 it was admitted that if Britain 'had to choose between the friendship of Portugal and the friendship of Spain, that of Spain is of the greater value'.[2]

Republican Portugal was keenly aware of British attitudes, and strong suspicions were aroused about the intentions of the *velha aliada Gran-Bret-anha*. In theory Portugal could have ignored them and maintained absolute neutrality on the outbreak of war. But in practice this was not a viable option. The new Republic feared that exclusion from the war might prove catastrophic for the country's interests, and possibly even for Portugal's very existence. Portugal's keenness to participate in the war mystified many in Whitehall who thought that Portugal's interests would be best served by non-participation; and the result was the exposure of successive republican regimes to four years of almost constant indignity suffered at the hands of her oldest ally. Even those British officials who understood the Portuguese predicament had little patience with it. In their opinion it was of Portugal's making, and if Portugal insisted on assuming a role in the war for its own reasons then the country's leaders would have to be told what to do and be kept on a tight leash.

The man charged with 'running' the Portuguese was Sir Lancelot Carnegie, the British Minister in Lisbon (and a son of the 9th Earl of Southesk). As a skilled diplomat, Carnegie was always scrupulously polite in his dealings with the Portuguese and frequently emphasised the need for an understanding in Whitehall of Portugal's internal crises. He was also always quick to praise in public Portugal's desire to comply with ancient treaty obligations. But his task

---

* TNA/FO/371/2105, December 1912. 'Nor', the memo continued, 'could the use of Portuguese Colonies facilitate the operations of our forces under any reasonably probable contingencies.'

was complicated by the fact that the issue of Portugal's participation or non-participation was not one of overarching importance to anyone but the Portuguese; and conveying official policy that was high-handed to an extreme when he towered over most of his Portuguese counterparts was far from easy. Portuguese pride was frequently pricked, creating further paranoia and jealousy among political elites in Lisbon who – though they would never admit it – were only too well aware that once-mighty Portugal was no longer a world power. British imperiousness also played into the hands of Portuguese monarchists, whose leanings tended towards being pro-German, and even alienated many politicians who were resolutely pro-British. 'Britain is very close to Portugal,' began an old saying in Portugal; 'close enough to screw us.'

The British 'instruction' to the Portuguese to declare neither neutrality nor belligerence in 1914 failed to take account of the fact that stasis was one course of action no Portuguese government could afford to follow. It might help to assuage Portuguese nervousness about Spain's reaction to her neighbour siding openly with Britain, but it neither enhanced the international prestige or confidence of the new Republic nor helped to quell the destabilising faction-fighting which characterised it.[*] So 'quasi-neutrality' was adopted as the only viable option, despite British concerns that it might facilitate Germany's use of Portuguese ports in Africa. Outright belligerence on the part of Portugal was not deemed practicable at the outset: the Portuguese Army was not keen to be involved as a pawn in the republicans' political manoeuvrings, was of suspect loyalty, and had 'a capacity to make war ... so limited as to be almost non-existent'.[†]

Amid the confines imposed by quasi-neutrality, Portugal placed a far higher importance on defending its African colonies than Britain initially did. The new Republic viewed their preservation as a matter of its own life and death, and central to the nation's *mundovisão*. This explains why Portuguese rhetoric continued to defy their reputation as the *cafres da Europa* ('the kaffirs of Europe'), and to concentrate firmly on the glories of centuries gone by. The European Powers seemed to have ceased to understand Portugal's existence – except as a rather unimportant European offshoot of its colonies – reinforcing

---

* Portugal's fear of Spanish aggression in the event of the former's entry into the war on the side of Britain was acute. The British were sceptical about such an eventuality and judged Spain to be 'quite incapable of absorbing Portugal, nor could she even temporarily administer it without recourse to those Spanish methods of government which have lost Spain her own colonies' (TNA/FO/371/2105, August 1914, Crowe to Churchill).

† Vincent-Smith, p. 210. See also TNA/FO/371/2105: 'it must be borne in mind that if Portugal assumes the status of our active ally in war, all her Dominions and interest become objects of possible attack by the enemy ... and Portugal would be unable to defend her Dominions against the attacks of any but a minor adversary'.

a nagging belief in Portugal itself which dated back at least as far as the loss of Brazil in 1825 that 'Portugal' was nothing but a '*grande ilusão*', an '*império teórico*'.[3] Africa offered a possible solution to this parlous state of affairs. In the sixteenth century African gold, slaves and ivory had vastly increased Portugal's wealth, which flowed into Lisbon as fast as emigrants left for Brazil. The African colonies also provided a potential palliative to the deep-seated nostalgic yearning for the glories of the past – *saudade* – which permeated Portuguese society. But if the African colonies were to do so again, and replace the wealth that Brazil had once brought to Portugal, they had to be firmly in Portuguese hands.

There was another reason why Portugal felt the need to affirm its attachment to its African colonies. Ever since its own interests in Africa had started to multiply Britain had continually thwarted Portugal's expansion on the continent. In 1889–90, Britain aggressively blocked Portuguese 'incursions' in Mashonaland (Southern Rhodesia) and Shire (Nyasaland), regarding them as part of an attempt to join Portuguese West Africa (Angola) and Portuguese East Africa; and by 1898 Britain and Germany began negotiating for the redistribution of the Portuguese colonies in the event that Portugal was no longer able to bear the financial burden of its overseas commitments. Portugal had succeeded in clinging on to her colonies, but in 1912–13 Britain and Germany had re-examined the possibility of carving up Portugal *ultramar* – Portugal's colonies – and a new agreement had only been frustrated by the outbreak of war and Germany's insistence on keeping the negotiations secret.

The new negotiations between Britain and Germany were attended by a propaganda campaign which stiffened Portuguese resolve to enforce the 'defence of [her] colonial rights'[4] still further. Britain had grown increasingly condemnatory of Portuguese colonial rule, and by 1914 Portugal's African colonies were depicted as 'derelict' and 'sinks of iniquity'. The Portuguese government stood accused of condoning a thinly disguised slave trade, and of administering its colonies cruelly and inefficiently. Even the alleged 'degeneracy' of Portuguese colonial officials' 'domestic arrangements'* and their predilection for miscegenation came under fire as Portugal was painted as the inheritor of King Leopold's mantle. Portuguese rule *was* appalling by any standards, but the pre-war call from Britain and Germany for Portugal to improve her administration or risk losing her colonies altogether only served to increase Portuguese paranoia. All in all, Anglo-German machinations and propaganda had ensured that the war in Africa was even more important to

---

* See, for example, Rider Haggard, p. 253: 'Their domestic arrangements seem to be of a peculiar description.' He was referring in particular to the widespread practice of taking African mistresses.

the Portuguese than the war in Europe; and the Republic fully intended to call upon the *tradição de heroismo* of as many troops as necessary in its attempt to safeguard the African colonies. But, as one historian put it, 'the consequences of the attempts to ignore both the limitations of their resources and the lack of belligerence in the nation were to be discord, counter-revolution and impoverishment at home, and very strained relations with her ally abroad'.[5]

The bulk of the First Expeditionary Force sent by Lisbon to Portuguese East Africa, some 1,500 troops, arrived in Porto Amelia on 1 November 1914[*] – just days before IEF 'B' attempted to take Tanga. The port was ostensibly the headquarters of the *Companhia do Niassa*, to whom the north of the colony was 'subcontracted'; and as the company was controlled by German share-holders it was hardly surprising that not a single preparation had been made for receiving troops. Indeed little had even been done to repair the damage wrought by a cyclone earlier in the year: the main pier was still a ruin, all trees were stripped of their leaves, and the houses remained unroofed. The scene was not reassuring to a force which, by the admission of most of its own officers, was 'badly trained, badly equipped, badly clothed and badly organized',[6] and which had endured an appalling sea voyage from Europe. Furthermore, Lieutenant-Colonel Massano de Amorim, the expedition's commanding officer, was unsure how to conduct a mission the very existence of which seemed to have a lot more to do with politics at home than securing any meaningful military objectives, and his force simply languished. Proper health facilities did not exist, good food was unobtainable, and the men slept outside without using mosquito nets. When the rains came, and Porto Amelia was transformed into a swamp, the result was inevitable: sickness became rife.

In the wake of the overthrow of General Pimenta de Castro's government in May 1915, a campaign objective was finally suggested by Lisbon: the invasion of the German-held Quionga 'triangle' to the north of Porto Amelia. Amorim regarded this as a poor joke. His force had long since been robbed of any offensive capability: in six months they had suffered disease-related casualties in excess of twenty per cent without his troops even having left Porto Amelia

---

* The First Expeditionary Force consisted of 3rd Battalion 15th Infantry (based in Tomar); 4th Battery Mountain Artillery; 4th Squadron 10th Cavalry; and engineering, medical and administrative staff. Total strength: 1,527 men. Before this force arrived the colony's garrison consisted of twelve African companies of 282 men each (nine of which were stationed in Mozambique province), an artillery battery, the 460-strong Republican Guard, one *companhia disciplinar*, and various support units; total strength: 3,250–3,750 men. The *Companhia de Moçambique* and *Companhia do Niassa* also maintained private police forces. Source: *Anuario de Moçambique*, 1917.

or fired a shot in anger. Survival was Amorim's principal concern, followed by the likelihood of a 'native uprising' directed against his static and crippled garrison. In his opinion a whole division of new troops would be required before any thrust into German territory could be considered.* In the meantime he was incapable even of obeying an order to reinforce the 600-mile northern border of the colony. Not only was there little in the way of a Portuguese presence along the Rovuma River to 'reinforce', but, in the absence of even the most rudimentary tracks, he had no way of moving any sizeable bodies of troops to the few isolated posts manned by indigenous troops. Amorim's main achievement, no mean feat under the circumstances, was his attempt to rectify the latter. Before his force was recalled in late 1915, he had succeeded in opening a 200-mile 'road' and telegraph line running inland across the Makonde plateau to Mocímboa da Rovuma.

In November the Second Expeditionary Force, of comparable size to its predecessor, arrived under the command of Major Moura Mendes.† His orders were to hold the Rovuma 'front' and create a network of posts along the river stretching from the Indian Ocean to its confluence with the River Lujenda. But Mendes was a political appointee with no experience of warfare in the colonies. He ignored Amorim's dire warnings of the enormity of the task being asked of the Portuguese forces by Lisbon, and completely neglected to address the problem of the appalling conditions in Porto Amelia. Even had he known how to make progress, Mendes was also hampered by being one step removed from Lisbon: the colony's new Governor-General, thirty-six-year-old Republican stalwart Álvaro de Castro, insisted on issuing the orders of the fifth government of the year in Lisbon from the relative comfort of Lourenço Marques, over 1,000 miles away to the south. But the South African victory in South-West Africa, and German incursions into Portuguese West Africa, had imbued the metropole with an increasingly belligerent spirit and Mendes was ordered to prepare to occupy Quionga and co-operate with British troops as soon as possible. Mendes protested that he was not capable of advancing anywhere, but was told by Castro that he simply hadn't studied the military situation at the front properly: Lisbon was not interested in what was possible, only in glorious victories.

Throughout 1915 the border between German and Portuguese East Africa scarcely attracted von Lettow-Vorbeck's attention and only a single company

---

* Amorim's insistence that the division should include ten companies of African troops, each 180-strong, illustrates that it had not taken him long to realise the absolute necessity of involving indigenous troops.
† The Second Expeditionary Force comprised 5th Mountain Battery, 4th Squadron of the 3rd Cavalry, 3rd Battalion of the 21st Infantry (based in Penmacor), 2nd Battery of 7th Group QF. Total strength: 1,543 men.

of troops, the newly raised 20/FK, was based at Lindi to watch it.[*] Such, as one German combatant put it, was 'the deep respect which one accorded to the Portuguese as a war power'.[7] Von Lettow-Vorbeck was, of course, pre-occupied with operations in the north of the colony, where he believed the fate of German East Africa would be determined; and he knew full well that no Portuguese force, no matter how sizeable, was likely to cause him any real problem. On the other hand, Britain grew increasingly aware that the situation south of the Rovuma was far from satisfactory. The reports emanating from Lisbon sounded convincing enough – successive governments asserted that Portugal would defend her borders against any German incursions and was building a semblance of an infrastructure to enable it so to do – but the evidence on the ground was far from convincing.

The Foreign Office had good reason to be sceptical of Portuguese official communiqués. History seemed to be repeating itself: Portugal's interest in her East African colony had twice waned because her vast northern territory had proved unconquerable, and it was blindly optimistic to assume that this time would be any different. The reasons for the previous failures, in the sixteenth and nineteenth centuries, remained as seemingly insoluble as ever: the hostile environment and the lack of even the most rudimentary natural lines of communication which could facilitate the rapid movement of troops and supplies. The skill and strength of indigenous resistance, during both the sixteenth-century attempts at conquest and four disastrous campaigns under-taken in 1865–8 in Zambezia, was a further factor which unnerved Whitehall. All in all, far from learning that in Africa, 'the objectives to be achieved are of a different order from those in a conventional European war' and that 'warfare itself [therefore] assumes a wholly different character',[8] Portugal showed all the signs of committing the same mistakes as she had done before, obsessed by prestige and the need to 'dignify' the new Republic.

The biggest irony underlying Portugal's grandiose military aspirations, abundantly clear to all the troops languishing in Porto Amelia, was that the government's authority in the north – and much of the rest of her colony – was minimal. It was the *Companhia do Niassa* which 'governed' the 100,000 square miles between the Lurio and Rovuma Rivers, and the *Companhia de Moçambique* which 'governed' all territory between the Zambesi River and latitude 22 degrees south. Both did so in a fashion as predatory and cynical as could be imagined with the result that, at best, Lisbon's claims to be implementing any sort of strategy were fanciful; and, at worst, they would be

---

[*] Captain Doering's 3/FK formed the peacetime garrison at Lindi but had been ordered to Morogoro, on the Central Railway, as part of von Lettow-Vorbeck's concentration of troops in the north-east of the colony. 20/FK was also supported by 'W' Company, a unit of African levies.

deliberately stymied by commercial companies whose loyalty was suspect. In fact the Portuguese East Africa controlled by Lisbon really only comprised the Ilha de Moçambique and the larger coastal towns between Beira and Lourenço Marques. The rest of the country was mostly the domain of private charter companies or labour recruiters from the mines of Southern Rhodesia and South Africa.

During 1915 the Foreign Office also became unnerved by mounting evidence that Portuguese East Africa was 'leaky', and far from being neutral in the sense that Britain had envisaged. As late as August mail for German East Africa passed freely through the colony; the *Deutsche Ostafrika-Linie* was active in trans-shipping essential supplies across the border; and the infamous Dr Weck, who had 'mistakenly' overrun a Portuguese border post in August 1914, encountered few difficulties in visiting Palma to receive war news from the German Vice-Consul at Porto Amelia, and to revictual. Furthermore, the *Empreza Nacional de Navegação* continued to ferry German passengers travelling on false papers to sign up in German East Africa and, even as late as April 1916, it remained relatively easy for Schnee 'to continue to communicate with the German government'[9] via Portuguese East Africa. This was deemed a lamentable state of affairs by Sir Lancelot Carnegie. 'So long as German officers and agents have a free hand in the northern part of the Portuguese colony, it renders the blockade of German East Africa practically a dead letter',[10] he wrote in August 1915 – and that very month Karl Christiansen, the captain of the blockade-runner *Kronborg* which had landed north of Tanga earlier in the year, was arrested in Johannesburg having trekked from the Rufiji delta to Portuguese East Africa and then boarded a steamer to Lourenço Marques.[11]

All that could be done initially was for the British Consul-General in Lourenço Marques, Errol MacDonell, to keep close tabs on German comings and goings. This he did with quite outstanding efficiency and enterprise. One of his agents, Alan Black, established among other things that the Portuguese-German firm of Oswald Hoffman was in regular contact with the German Legation in Lisbon, that a German missionary wireless station in Port Nyassa was relaying news to German East Africa, that the *Deutsche Ostafrika-Linie* was stockpiling mangrove bark, and that in November a vessel belonging to the *Empreza Nacional de Navegação* was despatched by a German agent in Lisbon to Portuguese East Africa carrying medicines, leather, boots, socks and other vital supplies for the German war effort. But a letter sent in August by the manager of the Philippi shipping company in Beira to his superiors in Hamburg illustrates what MacDonell was up against. 'The latest news I have received from German East Africa,' it read, 'states that our friends fighting there are well and cheerful. As you will have seen from the official news, things in the Colony are going well for us. The lack of munitions need now no longer be feared since the successful arrival of the Norwegian steamer [the *Kronborg*]. As far as I can judge, it seems certain that we shall manage to keep the colony.'[12]

Schnee's boldest attempt to exploit the neutrality of his neighbours to the south was thwarted by MacDonell. In November 1914 Schnee had despatched an agent, Lothar Bohlen, to Portuguese East Africa with cables for Berlin, £1,500 in gold and a letter of credit for one million rupees (£50,000). His instructions were to open a supply line for khaki, petroleum, flour, chemicals and surgical materials, boots, 1,000 rifles and a million cartridges. What is significant about his mission was not the small quantities of these supplies which undoubtedly found their way into German East Africa before Bohlen was rumbled, but the way in which it was stymied by the British. Alarmed by the hot air emanating from Lisbon, Britain simply tightened the noose around Portuguese East Africa and by the end of 1915 the man who ran the colony, inasmuch as anyone ran it, was Errol MacDonell, supported by his agents and the Royal Navy. Bohlen, an employee of the *Deutsche Ostafrika-Linie*, found the Governor-General of Mozambique province 'not inimically inclined towards the Germans, but his hands were tied on every side'; Britain owned the only cable between the province and Lourenço Marques; every ton of coal entering and leaving the colony had to be accounted for to MacDonell; and as the naval blockade became more effective the sea routes to German East Africa and from India – even for large dhows – were effectively closed. Bohlen's pessimistic conclusion was that MacDonell 'ruled autocratically in the colony' over the *verrottet* – 'degenerate' – Portuguese, and that even exploiting Portuguese officials who were not 'expressly inimical'[13] to Germany would be fraught with difficulties.[14] Although Palma remained 'a centre of German intrigue', and German influence continued to be 'very strong'[15] in the territory controlled by the *Companhia do Niassa*, inland from the coastal ports German smuggling effectively ceased.[16]

By late October 1915 MacDonell's actions had proved so successful that, amid a crescendo of protests at the restriction of the free passage of mail through Portuguese East Africa, a German incursion into Portuguese East Africa was a distinct possibility. Even the infinitely resourceful MacDonell was not up to stopping a military threat single-handed, but at his behest HMS *Hyacinth* and an armed merchantman, the *Laconia*, were immediately ordered to stand by off Palma. For their part, the Portuguese were as worried about an 'invasion' from South Africa as one from German East Africa: rumours were rife that Botha was about to land a force at Palma which would attack von Lettow-Vorbeck's southern flank in conjunction with a British force from Zanzibar.

TWELVE

'Swallows and Amazons'

———◆———

In December 1915, the key question for Spicer-Simson was whether the Germans knew about the arrival of his 'secret weapons' on Lake Tanganyika. For over a year Captain Gustav Zimmer's 130-strong naval detachment, drawn from the crews of the survey ship *Möwe* (scuttled in Dar-es-Salaam harbour in the first week of the war), the *Königsberg* and *Deutsche Ostafrika-Linie* merchant ships, had held sway over Lake Tanganyika with just two small craft, the 60-ton gunboat *Hedwig von Wissman* and the 38-ton tug *Kingani*. It was these vessels, armed with the *Möwe*'s six guns, which had sunk the Belgian steamer *Alexandre Delcommune* and the British steamers the *Cecil Rhodes* and the *Good News* in 1914, and since then they had caused endless trouble to the Allies with forays from the fortress port at Kigoma.

In June 1915 German supremacy on the lake was further enhanced by the launch of the magnificent *Goetzen*, the Kaiser's Central Africa flagship, and as fine a craft as would ever be seen on African inland waters. Her main importance lay in being large enough to ship 800–900 troops at a time anywhere on the lake, and her presence was felt by the Allies almost immediately. In September, she enabled General Wahle, still commanding von Lettow-Vorbeck's *Westtruppen* – Western Force – in spite of the rebuff of his attack on Saisi, to move six companies in double-quick time along the Central Railway to Kigoma and then up the lake to Usumbura, from where they struck north towards Luvungi, the key Belgian position on the Rusisi 'front'. On the night of 27 September the German force, led by Captain Schulz, crossed the Rusisi in pirogues and pounced on the Belgian garrison, defended by fewer than 200 men. All day the battle raged, and had Major Muller not been camped two hours to the west with a similar number of men from the Belgian II *Bataillon*, Schulz would almost certainly have succeeded in driving a wedge between Belgian troops around Lake Kivu and those stationed on Lake Tanganyika. The attack was eventually beaten off, but Luvungi was bombarded twice in October and intense pressure was maintained by the German troops on the Rusisi front even when the attack force was withdrawn and only two companies – von Langenn-Steinkeller's Urundi

Company and the 14th Reserve Company – were left facing the Belgians.

The speed with which half a dozen German companies from elsewhere in the colony had concentrated for the attack on Luvungi caused huge alarm to the Belgian military authorities; and when the *Goetzen* had been used in similar fashion in the attack on Saisi in July, the British also discovered just how vulnerable the Northern Rhodesia border was to amphibious operations launched with rapidity from Lake Tanganyika. German naval supremacy on the lake in effect conferred supremacy over German East Africa's entire western borderlands, and when Major Olsen began moving the Belgian I and III *Bataillons* north from their positions covering the Northern Rhodesia border in November the German advantage in mobility became all too obvious: his troops would take two months to reach the Rusisi front on foot, whereas German troops could be moved the entire length of Lake Tanganyika in just four days on the *Goetzen*. The men of Zimmer's naval detachment, the *Möwe Abteilung*, were proving their worth: though few in number they had responded to their wartime role with alacrity, and Zimmer's network of African spies along the lakeshore was so extensive that he was always one step ahead of any attempt by the Belgians to counter his next foray. Furthermore, if Zimmer *did* know about *Mimi* and *Toutou's* arrival on the lake there was a substantial risk that they would be attacked before they were even launched.

Zimmer would later claim to have heard a rumour about Spicer-Simson's expedition as early as March 1915 (before John Lee had even suggested it to the Admiralty). Although his memory of the exact date may have been erroneous, Belgian telegraph messages intercepted in November and December confirmed growing suspicions that something was going on at Lukuga, the principal port on the Belgian shore of Lake Tanganyika. It appears that by then Zimmer had forgotten about the earlier rumour of a British naval expedition, or dismissed it as unlikely to pose any threat to the *Goetzen*; and his main concern was whether the Belgians were close to completing their own large steamer, the 700-ton *Baron Dhanis*. Such a sizeable vessel would not threaten him in his own lair at Kigoma, especially as two of the *Königsberg's* guns had arrived by rail to protect the port. But Zimmer did not want anything to challenge the *Goetzen's* freedom of movement on the lake itself, and decided to mount one of the *Königsberg* guns on board, thereby rendering her practically invincible. With that, he turned his attention to discovering what exactly was happening at Lukuga so that he could institute what he described as 'counter-measures'.[1]

Zimmer's curiosity produced some extraordinarily daring exploits in late November. On one night he sent Lieutenant Odebrecht in a dinghy full of dynamite up the Lukuga River, and on another Lieutenant Rosenthal and Leading Seaman Müller even tried to enter the Belgian camp from the land side disguised as Africans. Both ruses were thwarted by Belgian and British vigilance, and Rosenthal's subsequent capture of a patrol boat manned by a Belgian *askari* merely confirmed what Zimmer 'already knew'[2] – that work was proceeding apace on the *Baron Dhanis*. What he wanted were *details* and on I December the intrepid Rosenthal, an officer from the *Königsberg*, returned to Lukuga on the *Hedwig* and succeeded in photographing Lukuga at dawn from a distance of one cable. A building slip was clearly visible, but Rosenthal was forced to beat a hasty retreat before any further information could be gleaned as the six huge guns of the Belgian shore defences opened fire on the *Hedwig*. Undeterred, Rosenthal returned the next night and braved the storm surf and crocodiles to swim to within sixty yards of Lukuga's slipway. When he was ready to leave, however, he was unable to see the *Hedwig* through the darkness and had to remain in the water until dawn; and when he finally spotted his boat it was steaming off to the north out of range of the Belgian guns. Rosenthal was left with no alternative but to swim ashore, into captivity; had he returned successfully from his mission, on the other hand, the existence of *Mimi* and *Toutou* would have been revealed. In addition to the *Baron Dhanis*, Rosenthal had also seen 'the shapes of two motor boats at the slip' – information which he recounted in urine on the back of an innocuous message which he succeeded in persuading the Belgians to send to Zimmer. The message did not reach Kigoma until months later, however, and the existence of the secret 'addendum' was not discovered until some time after that. Luck was once again on Spicer-Simson's side.

By Christmas, Spicer-Simson had abandoned Lukuga for a new harbour he had been building at Kalemie, three miles south of the Lukuga River. Relations with his Belgian hosts had become strained after he was denied the opportunity to interrogate Rosenthal, and he had also decided that Lukuga was a highly unsatisfactory port. With the onset of the rains spectacular storms often blew up on the lake, and Kalemie offered much better shelter from the prevailing winds while still being protected by the Belgian shore defences. The weather was not Spicer-Simson's only source of concern: the rains also brought more frequent bouts of malaria among his men, and disenchantment with life in grass huts, subsisting on a staple diet of bully beef and raisins, began to escalate. Spicer-Simson was sympathetic up to a point but reminded his crew that it *was* wartime – and that he had coped with far worse during three years on the Upper Yangtze. His stories, some taller than others, about his life on the ocean (and river) wave were by now a feature of camp life. So too was the khaki drill kilt that he had adopted as his 'uniform', the macabre tattoos from his time in the east which revealed themselves at bath-times, the mono-grammed cigarettes, and a host of other idiosyncrasies.

Despite the daily discomfort, and the hard graft involved in constructing the new harbour at Kalemie, *Mimi* and *Toutou* were finally launched on Lake Tanganyika in the week before Christmas. It was a triumph for what would later be recognised as Spicer-Simson's 'indefatigable energy and inexhaustible resourcefulness',[3] and the tenacity of his team. Christmas Eve was spent mounting the guns fore and aft, 'a long, hard day's work', and in trials the newly armed *Mimi* and *Toutou* were found to be capable of 13.5 knots. As this was fast enough to enable them to outrun the *Goetzen* and any other German vessel they might encounter, the news was greeted with considerable relief and the expedition celebrated with 'a really good Christmas'.[4] Spicer-Simson spliced the mainbrace – in the absence of Pusser's Navy Rum a double tot of whisky was issued – and was pleased to learn that his Belgian counterpart, Commandant Goor, had decided to recognise his talents by placing all Belgian small craft at Lukuga under his command.

It was just as well that full watches were maintained throughout the festivities. Rosenthal's capture had alerted Spicer-Simson to the possibility that 'the enemy knew we were up to something',[5] and in somewhat unfestive spirit Zimmer had in fact despatched Captain Werner Schönfeld and his team of explosives experts across the lake. They had proved instrumental in defending the Rufiji delta during the *Königsberg*'s incarceration, and since the sinking of the German cruiser had been orchestrating the demolition raids against the Uganda Railway. But German supremacy on Lake Tanganyika was deemed so important by von Lettow-Vorbeck that he decided Schönfeld should be sent to assist Zimmer in putting paid to whatever the Belgians were up to at Lukuga; and at 6 a.m. on 26 December, just as Spicer-Simson was conducting Sunday prayers, the *Kingani* was spotted reconnoitring offshore. The service was hastily concluded, Spicer-Simson ordered the beat to quarters, and at 11 a.m. *Mimi* and *Toutou* were launched into the choppy waters of the lake. After a dogfight lasting just eleven minutes their first combat was over. Sub-Lieutenant Junge and four of the crew of the *Kingani* had been killed by the time she hove to, and at that moment the months of hardship borne by the men of the Lake Tanganyika Expedition suddenly all seemed worthwhile.

When the captured German vessel had successfully been beached Commandant Goor greeted Spicer-Simson with a kiss on both cheeks. 'His embarrassment was extreme, so was our amusement',[6] wrote one of the British crew. A guard of honour was drawn up by Lukuga's Belgian officers, buglers played a fanfare and the guns from one of the shore batteries fired a salute. Frank Magee, the expedition's scribe, recorded that people 'had flocked to the coast from inland villages to watch a spectacle they had never seen before ... they covered every hill-top and crest along the coast, and when it became known that the German ship had been captured, their excitement knew no bounds'. Spicer-Simson was hailed as a 'Great White Chief', and clay models of him were suddenly to be found everywhere.[7] 'Simson's Circus' had seemingly confirmed its entertainment value as well as its commander's unstinting optimism, and a message arrived from London which read: 'His Majesty The King desires to express his appreciation of the wonderful work carried out by his most remote expedition.'

After the German dead were buried with full military honours much valuable intelligence – about Kigoma, about the impress of African carriers, and about the forces ranged against him – was gleaned from his prisoners by Spicer-Simson. Not a word was said about Schönfeld and his team of explosives experts on board the *Hedwig*, which, in Zimmer's words, 'failed to get near [Kalemie]'[8] and fled at the first sound of gunfire. But Salimu, usually the *Hedwig*'s stoker, confirmed that only the *Hedwig* and *Goetzen* now opposed Spicer-Simson and that 'no ships [were] being brought up'[9] from Dar-es-Salaam. Lieutenant Junge's 'boy', an Angoni who'd been with him at Dar-es-Salaam, Tanga and in the Rufiji delta, also provided the disquieting news that the *Goetzen* now possessed a gun from the *Königsberg*. Armed with this information, there were to be no German 'surprises' for Spicer-Simson as had so often occurred elsewhere in the campaign. But he was now aware that the *Goetzen* could, if Zimmer so chose, heave to well offshore and systematically obliterate Lukuga and Kalemie.

It was fortunate for Spicer-Simson that Zimmer did not choose this course of action. Why he did not is a mystery, but his fears that the *Baron Dhanis* might have been made ready may well have acted as a deterrent, and the recall of Schönfeld's explosives team by von Lettow-Vorbeck put paid to any prospect of blowing up Lukuga in a commando operation. It was also strange that Zimmer did not immediately investigate the disappearance of the *Kingani* – the only possible explanation being that the *Goetzen* was too busy transporting troops and supplies to Usumbura and the Rusisi Front and that he dared not risk sending the *Hedwig*: January was the storm season on Lake Tanganyika and the offshore waters would have been off-limits to any vessel smaller than the *Goetzen*. In the meantime, Spicer-Simson's secret weapons remained secret and were soon joined by *Fifi* (the French equivalent of 'Tweet-Tweet'), as the *Kingani* had imaginatively been renamed, which had her 6-pdr gun moved aft and a 12-pdr semi-automatic gun from a shore battery mounted on the foredeck. Measuring twelve feet in length, the gun's recoil had the effect of stopping fifty-six-foot *Fifi* dead even when she was cruising at full speed.

Only on 8 February did Zimmer finally order the *Hedwig* to investigate the disappearance of the *Kingani* off Lukuga – and she too promptly vanished. In the morning of the following day distant gunfire was heard by the crew of the *Goetzen*, which was waiting at an offshore rendezvous, and when there was still no sign of the *Hedwig* at 1 p.m. the *Goetzen* steamed back to Kigoma.

Zimmer would later write that 'as we still knew nothing of any hostile [British] vessels, it was assumed that the *Hedwig* had approached too close to the shore batteries and had been destroyed by them'.[10] What had really happened was that Spicer-Simson had unleashed four craft against the *Hedwig* – *Mimi*, *Toutou*, a Belgian motor boat known only as *Vedette*, and *Fifi* – the minute the alarum had been raised at Lukuga. In blisteringly hot and hazy conditions a thirty-mile chase had ensued, the *Hedwig* sometimes appearing to its British pursuers only 'as a dark blob suspended above the horizon'.[11] It was *Mimi* which first caught up with the *Hedwig* and, buzzing around her quarters like a mosquito and firing repeatedly, forced her to make continual changes in direction. In so doing, the *Hedwig* lost speed and came within the 7,500-yard range of *Fifi*'s heavy gun, capable of firing twenty-eight rounds a minute. At 11.15 a.m. the *Hedwig*, commanded by Lieutenant Odebrecht, went down in flames with the loss of seven of her crew. *Fifi* had scored forty direct hits out of sixty shells fired and *les cruisers Spicer-Simson*, as the Belgians referred to them, had won their second decisive victory on Lake Tanganyika.

An intercepted Belgian wireless message confirmed the destruction of the *Hedwig*, but Zimmer remained unaware of exactly how this had occurred. What he *did* know was that his supremacy on Lake Tanganyika was now 'seriously threatened'. The *Wami*, a former tender to the *Königsberg* in the Rufiji delta and sister ship to the *Kingani*, and the *Adjutant* arrived by rail in February and could have restored the balance of power. But Zimmer did not use either of them and ordered Kigoma 'put into a state of defence'.[12] He never revealed why he did not send the *Goetzen* across the lake to investigate the loss of his two vessels. He may have feared encountering the (unbuilt) *Baron Dhanis* in a trap; or he may have been under strict orders that the *Goetzen* could only be used for the transport of troops. Either way, when Spicer-Simson caught a glimpse of the *Goetzen* for the first time the day after sinking the *Hedwig* and decided that he could not attack it under any circumstances, a stalemate ensued.

Stalemate was a good enough situation for the Allies. Spicer-Simson attracted accusations of an attack of cold feet from some Belgians, whose single-mindedness seemed to have increased as a result of America's suggestion that Belgium might consider selling the Congo to Germany as part of a compromise peace, but his decision was undoubtedly correct. Lake Tanganyika was not the Thames. Sudden squalls of immense ferocity were common and the British motor boats did not provide reliable gun platforms in choppy waters. Furthermore, a single shell from *Goetzen*'s guns would have vaporised any of his craft, and Spicer-Simson knew that Kigoma's shore defences were formidable. His decision also disappointed some of his crew who, under his leadership, had begun to believe in their own invincibility: one remarked that 'it seemed that [the *Goetzen*] was as windy of us as we were of her'.[13] But Spicer-Simson knew that the right decisions are not always the popular ones, and was unperturbed by any mutterings of discontent. The mere presence of his gunboats was obviously sufficient to enable Allied troops to use Lake Tanganyika again – if only a ship large enough to ferry them could be found – and that was all that he had been asked to achieve.

Spicer-Simson and his crew were credited by the Belgians, despite the carping about cold feet, with 'a remarkable performance of which England should be justly proud'.[14] But their failure to complete the *Baron Dhanis* grated with the British commander, and the atmosphere at Lukuga began to sour. Spicer-Simson had always found his Belgian naval opposite number, Commandant Goor, easy to work with; it was Belgian bureaucracy that had proved a nightmare both to the British and the Belgian servicemen on the lake ever since he arrived. Colonel Moulaert, who assumed command of the Belgian *Brigade Sud* in February 1916, admitted as much when he observed how much time 'had been lost in hesitations and vain discussions'[15] about the *Baron Dhanis*. In fact its construction had been largely abandoned when the British expedition arrived the previous October, but subsequently the Belgian government changed its mind and Moulaert was charged with overseeing its completion as fast as possible. In the meantime he informed Spicer-Simson that his government had secured the use of four (British) Short seaplanes which would put paid to the *Goetzen*. Moulaert and Spicer-Simson, both proud men and zealously protective of their own authority, quickly – and unsurprisingly – fell out; and, rather than trust any longer in an ally who had let him down on countless occasions, Spicer-Simson set off at the end of February with Commandant Goor to search for a lake steamer that could take the place of the *Baron Dhanis* if, as he guessed might happen, she was never completed.

When Spicer-Simson began his antics on Lake Tanganyika in December 1915, the South African preparations for an invasion of German East Africa were well under way, and the identity of the man appointed to lead the expedition was revealed. Given the uncertain political climate in South Africa Smuts was forced to declare himself unavailable, but he and Botha were confident that the War Office's suggestion of General Sir Horace Smith-Dorrien was a good one. Smith-Dorrien was widely respected both in Africa (having fought in the Zulu War in 1879, Omdurman and the Anglo-South African War), in India (where he had commanded the 4th Quetta Division), and in Britain (where he was credited with having played the leading role in saving the British Expeditionary Force at Le Cateau in 1914). Furthermore, he was not entirely ignorant of the conditions that would confront him in East

Africa as his wife was a goddaughter of Sir Donald Stewart, a former Governor of the protectorate.

From the outset, however, Smith-Dorrien was beset with difficulties stemming from the War Office's neglect of the East African campaign. Lord Kitchener, the Minister for War, persisted in his belief that no matter how parlous the situation confronting Tighe the diversion of materiel and men to East Africa was undesirable; and he was well aware, from his Boer War days, of the immense cost that warfare in Africa could entail. The Colonial Secretary, Andrew Bonar Law, did not agree – and he soon proved a powerful ally to those in the War Office who were working to circumvent Kitchener. When Kitchener visited the Near East in November, the War Office '[brought] the whole thing to a head', with the result that when 'the Chief' returned 'the business was practically settled'. Kitchener was 'by no means enthusiastic' about the news that greeted him but despite his reservations 'he accepted the situation'.[16]

Kitchener's acquiescence removed one obstacle, but Smith-Dorrien's task remained daunting. He was very short of time, and encountered problems at every turn in securing the particular types of weaponry – and sufficient shipping tonnage – to ensure a quick victory in East Africa at an acceptable cost. The strain was immense, and it was exacerbated by acute seasickness and an attack of pneumonia during his voyage out to Cape Town in December. Over New Year Smith-Dorrien 'hovered between life and death' for three days during a stop at Madeira; but despite his illness he continued to take on a heavy workload for the remainder of the voyage and after reaching South Africa. He was in constant consultation with Botha and Smuts and the volume of telegrams transmitted during January between his headquarters, East Africa, India, and London attested to the gathering pace of the build-up. Draught and pack mules from Buenos Aires, Ford chassis suitable for water-carrying, units of armoured cars, a 5-inch howitzer battery and further mountain batteries, specialist railway companies, two British officers fluent in Urdu to act as Foremen of Works, a first consignment of the nine million rounds of Mark VI ammunition, sixty miles of railway track with fifteen engines and 100 wagons from India *by March* – the list of Smith-Dorrien's requests grew daily. But after three weeks Dr Hugh-Smith tapped the general's lungs and 'drew off 4½oz of rank poison'. Smith-Dorrien wrote in his diary 'self not worth much'.[17] His weight had fallen to just nine stone and at the end of January he finally had to admit that he was, quite simply, 'all done in'. 'It would have killed him to have gone to East Africa', wrote Sergeant Castle, his clerk of five years; and he expressed the great disappointment of all members of Smith-Dorrien's Staff: 'No one could have worked harder to make [the expedition] a success . . . I shall always think of Sir H. with all his peculiar and hard-to-get-used-to ways as a great man, a fine soldier and a God-fearing gentleman.'[18]

Kitchener expressed his regrets at the news but by 12 February, when Smith-Dorrien was graciously seen on board the *Balmoral Castle* by Louis Botha, 'the Chief' had still not taken the trouble to inform him of the identity of his successor. Rumours that Smith-Dorrien was dead may have been wide of the mark but he had, so far as the War Office was concerned, ceased to exist; and what followed created 'the sensation of the campaign'.[19] Smuts was again offered the supreme command in East Africa and, though he regretted the loss of a man in whom the Union Government had the utmost confidence, this time he and Botha felt that the political situation in South Africa was stable enough for him to accept. On the evening of 11 February, Smuts left Pretoria bound for East Africa. *The Star* reported that 'the feeling of the countryside in regard to ... East Africa is distinctly optimistic',[20] but Smuts's enemies in the Nationalist camp pounced on the new opportunity to condemn his 'jingoism' and question why South African 'boys' had to go to East Africa at all. Hertzog's mouthpiece, *Die Burger*, openly accused Smuts of running away from his party's embattled predicament at home.

In East Africa the reaction was also mixed. The ever-enthusiastic Mickey Tighe had greeted Smith-Dorrien's appointment as evidence that the War Office was at last taking his campaign seriously and would give him a fighting chance of finishing it. The change of commander-in-chief bothered him not one jot. But among some of his 'Red Tab' officers Smuts's appointment was greeted more cautiously. In their eyes Smuts was an 'amateur' whose reputation as a soldier was not proven; and the campaign in German South-West Africa had not been on a scale that established the South African generals as the masters of strategy they thought they were. Furthermore, Colonel Victor Franke, the German commander in German South-West Africa, was no von Lettow-Vorbeck. It was admitted that Smuts had acquired a certain notoriety for his brave but ultimately futile 1,000-mile raid into the Cape in the closing stages of the Anglo-South African War; and word had it that his planning skills had proved invaluable to the suppression of the Afrikaner rebellion and the campaign in German South-West Africa. But such military skills as he possessed were self-taught, and first and foremost Smuts was regarded as a politician. It is not surprising that Smuts's appointment as field commander of a force which might exceed 25,000 troops caused some astonishment but on the other hand, as one of his Staff officers pointed out, the British 'dug-outs ... had not been very successful'.[21]

With plans for what would become known as 'the first Salaita show', the start of the offensive in German East Africa, already so advanced, Smuts's first real test would have to wait. As a prelude to the advance proper Longido was reoccupied before the end of January, and General Malleson succeeded where he had failed in July 1915 when he pushed four battalions and eighteen guns forward to Mbuyuni, less than twenty miles from Taveta. A few days later Serengeti, four miles further on, was wrested from the Germans and the military railway from Voi – now dubbed 'the crazy line' on account of the obvious results of the rapidity of its construction – was extended to this new British camp. The advance also compelled a strong German force commanded by Captain Doering to abandon the mountain of Kasigau, thirty miles to the south of Voi, and when they did so German raids on the Uganda Railway became much more hazardous to execute and therefore less frequent. Resistance to these cautious moves was slight. British troops suffered serious casualties in an incident on the coast, when Major Wavell and thirty men of his Arab Corps were killed in a scrap with a much larger German force near Mwele Ndogo; and a 'demonstration' near Bukoba might well have resulted in the annihilation of a detachment of 98th Infantry had it not been for the support of the Lake Victoria flotilla. All in all, however, the British preparations seemed to reveal no insurmountable causes for concern other than the continuation of average *monthly* wastage rates – due to disease – of approximately ten per cent; and the embarkation of the first troops from South Africa helped to create the impression that the situation in East Africa was at least 'stable'.

The preparations for an offensive did not escape von Lettow-Vorbeck's notice. As early as the beginning of December German prisoners were telling their captors that they knew the Boers were coming, and their commander was determined to 'encourage the enemy' so that as many troops as possible would be 'diverted from other and more important theatres of war'.[22] The South Africans, even those with combat experience in the Boer War or in German South West-Africa, had scant idea of the conditions that awaited them; and until their commander-in-chief arrived they were in the hands of British generals whose abilities had been sorely tested – and frequently found wanting – during the first sixteen months of the war.

THIRTEEN

The African War

'The outbreak of war came as an unexpected shock to the natives as a whole,' wrote Charles Hobley, the Provincial Commissioner of British East Africa's Coast Province; 'like most of our countrymen,' he added, 'the natives naturally had no conception of the magnitude of the struggle or its possible duration.' This much was certainly true at the outset, as it was of civilians in Europe, and during the first eighteen months indigenous communities in eastern Africa responded in a multitude of different ways. War quite simply presented an opportunity both to individuals and to groups keen to vent old grievances against the government and to settle old scores with neighbours.

British East Africa had been conquered with remarkable ease and lack of bloodshed by comparison with the sub-Saharan colonies of Britain's colonial rivals. There had been fewer than thirty 'punitive campaigns', many of which amounted to little more than patrols, in the two decades preceding the war; and only two of these involved African casualties in excess of 1,000. The relative paucity of casualties did not, however, connote complete acquiescence on the part of the conquered. Certain tribes, such as the Kikuyu, quickly adapted to the arrival of Europeans in their midst and even to the taxation – hardly a new concept to any African society – that accompanied it. Others did not. The coastal Giriama people, renowned as traders of slaves and ivory and as skilled manufacturers of arrow poison, numbered some 60,000, and although their society was highly decentralised they had retained a strong sense of identity and a distinctive spiritual life through centuries that witnessed the comings and goings of the Portuguese and Arabs. When the British appeared as the latest in this line of 'visitors' the Giriama had simply responded in time-honoured fashion, resisting any attempts to incorporate them into the emerging colonial economy. After 1912 relations with the government began to come to a head over persistent labour and tax demands, both of which the Giriama regarded as eroding their way of life and wealth, and on 4 August 1914 the tribe rose in revolt.

Many British government officials suspected German agents of encouraging the uprising, given the historic connections between the Giriama and German East Africa through ivory-trading, but such suspicions were wide of the mark. The timing of the revolt was sheer coincidence, its main trigger being the destruction that day of the principal Giriama shrine, the *Kaya Fungo*, south of Kilifi. Once started, however, it was clear to those involved in the rebellion that it was to their considerable advantage that the British were preoccupied with the wider war: as one British administrator put it, the Giriama 'were told we were at war and that we were powerless to retaliate'.[1] After a number of incidents prompted by the government's demand that the Giriama vacate their fertile lands north of the Sabaki River, KAR troops were despatched to put down the uprising. The ensuing 'pacification' was carried out by the end of August 1914. Casualties were not heavy, not least because the Giriama sensibly succumbed to what one of their opponents called 'chilled abdomen, an African variety of the disorder known as cold feet'.[2] But the resultant fine levied on the tribe was extremely onerous and the heavy-handed way in which reparations in cash, labour and livestock were collected from loyal and disloyal headmen alike only served to foster further resentment and extreme hardship. This would be compounded by the drought of 1916, which led to famine, and by the curtailment due to the war of ivory-smuggling across Lake Jipe, to the south of Taveta, into the German colony. The Giriama grudgingly adhered to the peace terms but by 1918, with the government hard-pressed on the war front and anxious to avoid a further conflagration, they were already moving back north of the Sabaki.

In the far west of the country similar 'unrest' also occurred in the early months of the war. The clash between British and German troops at Kisii in September 1914 unleashed lawlessness and looting on a grand scale until action was taken to stop it. This was as swift and decisive as that used to suppress the Giriama revolt: some eighty Gusii lost their lives, hundreds of huts were burnt, and more than 3,000 cattle were confiscated. Thereafter, in the words of one policeman on the punitive patrol, 'the tribe gave no further trouble'[3] – not least because over 20,000 young male Gusii, about half of the total able-bodied male population, were removed from the district to work for the military in the course of the war.

If the action of the Gusii smacked of opportunistic hooliganism in the face of the temporary absence of government officials, the impression was misleading. The British had had to send 'punitive expeditions' against the Gusii in 1904 and 1908; and one of the features of the 1914 uprising – equally evident in that of the Giriama – was the involvement of traditional spirit mediums, cults, and prophets or prophetesses. In the case of the Gusii their sacking of the British *boma* at Kisii was directly attributable to the rising popularity of 'Mumboism', a rejection of all things European in a bid to return to the state of affairs that existed before 'their concepts of peace, good government and life were rudely shattered by colonial rule';* and in that of the Giriama, the prophetess Me Katilili wa Mwadarikola played a central role in fomenting revolt and instigating secret oath-taking among a widely dispersed and decentralised people. A common characteristic of such cults was the dispensing of medicine that would supposedly turn British bullets into water and, despite its obvious inefficacy, adherence to Mumboism grew rapidly in western British East Africa during the war, only abating when, paradoxically, the Gusii blamed the cult for the great famine of 1919.

In western Uganda, there was also a history of resistance to British rule that would become significant in wartime. In Kigezi district an uprising in 1911 was led by the prophetess Muhumuza, she too claiming that British bullets would turn to water when fired at her 'army', and the influence of her *nyabangi* cult lasted beyond her capture and throughout the war. But Kigezi was different in that clan warfare had been endemic for decades before the arrival of Europeans. As one historian of the district put it, 'among the Bakiga, the Basigi fought against the Batimbo, and sometimes against the Baheesi. The Bahundu sometimes fought against the Barihira, and at other times against the Banyangabe. The Bagyeri fought against the Barihira ... The Bainika sometimes fought against the Bagyeyo and at other times against the Bakongwe around Lake Bunyoni. The same was true in other clans.'[4] The war merely exacerbated an already unstable state of affairs, as did the fact that Kigezi's 2,000 square miles were sandwiched between the territories of three colonial powers – Belgian Congo, German Ruanda and British Uganda – and its boundaries had only been demarcated as recently as 1910. Up until then, according to the elders of Kigezi, 'a German called it his, a Belgian also called it his, as well as the English'.[5] Given this situation it is hardly surprising that a further rebellion against British rule occurred in southern Kigezi when Nyindo was told by his half-brother Musinga, the Watusi *Mwami* (sultan) of neighbouring Ruanda who had been armed by the Germans in 1914, that the Germans would soon control his land.

Control of Kigezi was vital to the Allies, as Captain Max Wintgens, the shrewd and highly capable German administrator of Ruanda, well knew. It was through this inaccessible district of lakes, rivers, mountains and forests that the main line of communication ran from British East Africa to the Belgian base at Rutchuru; and he did everything in his power to frustrate the Belgian military build-up – even to the extent of encouraging the

* B. Ogot and W. Ochieng, 'Mumboism – an anti-colonial movement', in Bethwell Ogot (ed.), p. 175. It was paradoxical that the Luo, among whom Mumboism is thought to have originated, offered no armed resistance to the advent of European colonial rule.

anti-European sentiments of the local *nyabangi*. It was no coincidence that Wintgens's visit to Nyindo at the end of 1914 was swiftly followed by the latter attacking 'loyalist' chief Chahafi, and at least one German officer was actually killed assisting with the attack. Nyindo was thwarted and fell back into Ruanda until he reappeared in May 1916 to surrender; but the pro-German Bahorohoro of the Kyogo Valley took up the fight, as did Chief Katuleggi's Batwa pygmies until he too was forced to flee to German East Africa. In central Kigezi as well, a 'usurper' from Belgian territory, Ntokiibiri, fought the Muganda chief Abdulla Muwanika until he fled in 1917. Ten of his accomplices were captured and hanged, but Ntokiibiri was 'to be seen no more'[6] in the district (though he was planning a further incursion when finally captured at the end of 1919). For the first two years of the war a small number of Anglo-Belgian troops were almost constantly occupied in dealing with this turmoil threatening their lines of communication, and the first attempt at collecting hut tax in the district was not surprisingly 'met with resistance and confusion'.[7]

Elsewhere, in the sparsely populated and barren Northern Frontier District of British East Africa, banditry was such a popular local pastime that pre-war government policy was deliberately 'passive'. The administrative infrastructure was non-existent, patrols were sent out infrequently, and 'pacification' was not undertaken until the 1920s. Nevertheless the NFD was so unstable in early 1915 that an expedition was mounted against the Turkana, who took advantage of government preoccupations elsewhere to show, as one senior policeman put it, 'a marked hostility and a mounting spirit of truculence when unsupervised'.[8] A staggering quantity of livestock was confiscated during the six-month operation – more than 19,000 head of cattle, 8,300 camels, 7,000 donkeys and 123,000 sheep and goats – although much of the booty was returned to the Turkana after the claims of neighbouring tribes were met.

Turkey's entry into the war also raised grave concerns in Nairobi about the possibility of an incursion into British territory by Muslim Abyssinians and Somalis. No such incursion occurred until 1916, but when it did it coincided with a number of desertions and incidents of self-mutilation among Muslim soldiers in some of the Indian regiments posted to East Africa, and also turned into 'a very real and costly war'.[9] In February 1916, just as British troops were making the final preparations for their invasion of German East Africa, some 500 Aulihan from Somaliland stormed the British fort at Serenli, killing the British officer and sixty-five men of the garrison. The principal British post in the north-east, Wajir, had to be abandoned, and it took two years before Serenli was reoccupied and the Aulihan were defeated. Throughout the war trouble simmered in the north as anyone and everyone in British East Africa's desolate borderlands sought to 'take every advantage of the situation resulting from the war'.[10]

These uprisings and incursions were certainly time-consuming for Belfield's government. But to draw the conclusion that British East Africa was engulfed by strife, or that 'native uprisings' necessitated the diversion of troops from the front line with German East Africa, would be erroneous. The vast majority of the indigenous population bore the arrival of the war as stoically as they had invariably borne intrusions by 'foreigners', whether African or British; and many on the German East African border, such as the coastal Wadigo, 'begged [the British administration] to have patrols sent out to counteract the effect of the enemy'[11] when raids by German troops carried off their stock, women and impressed men into the ranks of their 'Arab' corps. The man charged with their protection in late 1914 was Major Hawthorn of the KAR who, ironically, had been responsible for the suppression of the Giriama uprising just months before; and in return the Wadigo provided 788 men for service as British carriers during the war from an adult male population numbering no more than 2,000 – a striking contrast to the reticence with which the Giriama treated calls for volunteers.

To say, as did Provincial Commissioner Charles Hobley, that British East Africa's indigenous population 'made no demur to the numerous restrictions which a war imposes on the people involved'[12] was fanciful, even during the first eighteen months of the war when those 'restrictions' were not so onerous. By the end of 1915 there was no community in eastern and southern Africa in which everyday life had not been disrupted to some degree, and the response of each varied enormously. There was some insurrection, but more typical were the displays of collusion. In British East Africa, for example, the Luo chose not to follow the example of their ethnic 'cousins', the Gusii, by using the circumstances of the war as an opportunity to demonstrate against British rule; the Nandi, a tribe which had been one of the fiercest opponents of British rule and had been subjected to five major 'punitive expeditions' in the first decade of the century, was to provide a higher percentage of its adult male population for the KAR and other military units than any other tribe in the protectorate;* and the Kamba provided manpower aplenty to the military authorities from the outset. Indeed the only apparent anomaly among the larger tribes of British East Africa, given their warlike reputation, was the conduct of the Masai, who 'declined to take to military discipline',[13] but provided invaluable intelligence services along the border (as did their brethren on the other side of the border for the Germans). Perhaps, as German East Africa's leading journalist alleged, the explanation for this reticence was that the Masai 'had grown to know the English . . . as still greater cattle-thieves than they themselves'.[14]

---

* Lewis Greenstein (2), p. v; about ten per cent of the adult male Nandi population, 1,197 men, served in the KAR and a further 500 worked in some other 'war-related occupation'.

If these were examples of straightforward collusion, or expedience, there were also numerous expressions of genuine and unstinting loyalty on the part of chiefs and their subjects. Among the former, Daudi Chwa, the Bagandan *Kabaka*, was determined that his people should play their part in the defence of Uganda, and placed his personal 'army' at the disposal of the British authorities, as well as providing porters for IEF 'B' and Tighe's Umba Valley operations in December 1914 and personally directing the formation of the Uganda Transport Corps and Stretcher Bearer Corps from what was described as 'the flower of the educated youth' of the country. Among the latter, the war was perceived by many as offering possibilities of advancement and adventure unimaginable in peacetime. Many a soldier with the King's African Rifles had been decorated by the end of 1915, and stories of the heroics of Sergeants Woldemariam, Miyoiyou, Williams and Sumani not only filtered back to any young African keen to escape the often rigid confines of their tribe but were a recruiter's dream. By the same token, those who had joined missions found that the war brought new opportunities: as a child Adrien Atiman had been taken as a slave from his home near Timbuctu, was rescued by the missionary White Fathers, and now found himself a respected medical orderly for the Belgians; and Ezera Kabali's account of his experiences as a headman in the Carrier Corps not only tells a tale of hardship but displays considerable pride in a job well done. For some, like M'Ithiria Mukaria from Meru district, one of the last surviving veterans of the campaign, enticements such as receiving a uniform, the opportunity to 'select cattle from other peoples' when in the field, and learning Swahili, were sufficiently alluring to prompt them to sign up with enthusiasm.[*] Others, like Aibu Chikwenga, found that recruits were 'treated very well'. 'I enjoyed myself,' he later recounted, '[and] I particularly liked target practice.'[15]

These were not, as has sometimes been suggested, men whose loyalty belied some deep-seated anti-European grudge. The degree of 'oppression' the average African experienced in daily life at the hands of British 'government' was arguably no greater than that experienced by the average 'Tommy' who chose to join Kitchener's Volunteer Army; and the decision to sign up was often motivated by exactly the same sentiments as those expressed by a young British soldier of Belgian parentage who wrote of his choice to embark on a military career in the following words: 'war was in my blood. I was determined to fight and I didn't mind who or what . . . Causes, politics and ideologies are better left to historians.'[16] Such bellicose sentiment translated into Swahili as *tunakwenda tunashinda* – 'we fight, we march'. Coercion

[*] Author's interview with M'Ithiria Mukaria, formerly of 3/3KAR, in Isiolo (February 2003).

was simply not necessary to maintain an escalating supply of soldiers until much later in the war (and even then to no greater extent than it was required in Britain); and it wasn't even necessary in the early months of the war for the recruitment of sufficient porters to keep the British forces supplied. But that would change, with devastating results.

In addition to those who reacted to the war with conspicuous loyalty or outright dissent there were many Africans, perhaps even a majority, whose reactions were best described either as fatalistic – *amri ya mungu* ('it is the will of God') – or confused. The consequences of war induced similar reactions in Europe, but in eastern Africa it was even more pronounced due to the unfamiliarity with the paraphernalia that war seemed to bring with it. 'The African' wrote Ndabaningi Sithole, a founder member of the Zimbabwe African National Union in the 1960s, many years later, 'was overwhelmed, overawed, puzzled, perplexed, mystified and dazzled ... Motor cars, motor cycles, bicycles, gramophones, telegraphy, glittering Western clothes, new ways of ploughing and planting, added to the African's sense of curiosity and novelty. Never before had the African seen such things. They were beyond his comprehension; they were outside the realm of his experience.'[17] This would change too, as it became apparent that what was occurring in Africa was rather more inclusive than the 'White Man's War' that racially conscious European governments had envisaged at the outset.

There was one rebellion in eastern Africa which caused serious alarm, as opposed to minor inconvenience, in British official circles in 1915. It occurred in Nyasaland, the 'Cinderella' of the British protectorates and the domain of missionaries galore. Nyasaland's administration was reputedly 'benign', but in reality it was a good deal less benign than that of Britain's more northerly protectorates. In 1899 Lewis Bandawe began his education at Blantyre Mission, but his home was in Lomweland, three days' journey away in Portuguese East Africa. He was therefore in a rare position to be able to compare the administration of British Nyasaland with that of the infamously 'rapacious' Portuguese. Bandawe readily acknowledged that his people's traditional life had always involved 'indulging in petty tribal wars, in destruction of life and property and in slavery' and that such activities were severely curtailed by the Portuguese occupation after 1897. But then slave-dealing became the preserve of the Portuguese *cipais* (policemen), taxes and forced labour were imposed, and finally there came an order for everyone to start growing cotton. Punishments for non-co-operation were severe and the Lomwe started to migrate into nearby British territory.

Bandawe was one such migrant. Far from finding the British authorities any different from the Portuguese, however, he soon observed that 'the

[British] *boma* was a terror to all people'. 'What depressed me most,' he later wrote, 'was when I once saw of a gang of prisoners. They marched in two's bound by big irons; some four or six prisoners had iron collars round their necks, with a long chain which was passed in loops through each iron collar and attached to each prisoner ... This reminded me of the slaves with their slave sticks round their necks ... I found no difference between such Europeans and my people who owned slaves and were selling them to the coastal people at such places as Quelimane, Angoche and other places.'* Bandawe also described the extreme antipathy to paying hut taxes. The treatment of prisoners was, of course, not markedly different to the way prisoners were treated in Britain's prisons; and taxes are universally unpopular. But the fact that the *boma* was a 'terror to all people' flew in the face of the 'civilising mission ideology', as did the humiliation meted out to the indigenous population. 'To go to the *boma* for any transaction was no pleasure,' wrote Bandawe, 'every African was obliged to take off his hat for any European, whether government or not ... [and] every European, with the exception of the missionaries, had a *chikoti* – a whip made of hippo's hide – which he used on his domestic servants or labourers.'[18] The agents of government, such as the African police force, were equally feared: 'the *boma* knew that the *askari* were pure barbarians, and would do brutality on the villagers, yet allowed them to trouble the villagers as much as they could'.[19] Such was the background, intensified by escalating wartime demands by the government for labour and foodstuffs, to the 'Chilembwe Rebellion' of 1915 – which coincided almost to the day with the arrival of the ubiquitous Major Hawthorn to command 1/KAR in Nyasaland.

John Chilembwe was the founder of the Providence Industrial Mission at Chiradzulu. Born in the 1860s, he had been educated at the Church of Scotland Mission in Blantyre and, unusually for the time, in the United States at Virginia Theological College. According to Bandawe, Chilembwe had been planning a potent demonstration of his increasingly anti-European sentiments even before the outbreak of war and the war simply galvanised him into action. In November 1914, Chilembwe launched his opening salvo, writing the following words to the *Nyasaland Times*: 'It is too late now to talk of what might or might not have been. Whatsoever be the reasons we are invited to join in the war, the fact remains, we are invited to die for Nyasaland. We leave all for the consideration of the Government, we hope in the Mercy of Almighty God, that some day things will turn out well and that Government will

* Bandawe was the first Malawian to receive the MBE. His observations about the prisoners is poignant: it was in Nyasaland that one of the most concerted anti-slavery campaigns had been fought by the British.

recognise our indispensability, and that justice will prevail.'* Chilembwe's very public protest was in stark contrast to the more localised discontent in British East Africa, and his use of a newspaper as a vehicle of dissent was more sophisticated than armed rampage. Alarm bells did not, however, ring immediately in official circles; and as a result, when Chilembwe went a step further and acted on his grievances, colonial officials in Nyasaland were more taken aback than their counterparts in British East Africa ever were by their uprisings.

On the night of 22 January 1915 John Chilembwe's adherents left the church at Mbombwe, some for European estates to the north, some for Blantyre and Limbe, and some to the estates to the east of Magomero belonging to the Bruce family. Three Europeans were murdered on the Bruce Estates, the telegraph line between Zomba and Blantyre was cut, and in the ensuing panic all Europeans in outlying areas were called in to Zomba and Blantyre for their own protection. For a short time the situation 'looked very black', according to one KAR officer, 'and it was thought that a general native rising had taken place'.[20] But Chilembwe's men in the south and north failed to act decisively and the rebellion was quickly suppressed by the Nyasaland Volunteer Force, African 'loyalists', and troops sent from Portuguese East Africa.

Chilembwe himself was killed on 4 February 1915. At least one ringleader experienced terminal sentencing by a 'hasty court'[21] in the field, and by the end of March some forty rebels had been tried and executed and over 300 imprisoned. Battery Quartermaster Sergeant Maker, newly arrived in the country from South Africa, witnessed the aftermath: 'These hangings were more strangulations than anything and the bodies, at first, were left hanging from sun-up to sun-down as a warning to others of the penalty of rebellion. The love of a gamble,' he added, 'is so deeply rooted in the human that bets were even made on which of the bodies would give the last kick'; and the very short, bandy-legged hangman, 'a down and out blown in from the *bundu*',[†] was paid *per capita* and became rich overnight.

Some dismissed Chilembwe's rebellion as an 'insane project',[22] a suicidal grand gesture on the part of a man who had become unhinged. On the other hand, Lieutenant Masters of the KAR was one of many who thought that '[Chilembwe's] plans, if they had been carried out, were good, and if his leaders had had a little more enterprise it would have been a sad affair for the white men in this country'.[23] Whether the colonial government might

* *Nyasaland Times*, No. 48, 26 November 1914. This edition of an organ whose circulation was less than 200 was suppressed by the authorities. Lewis Bandawe, a contemporary observer whose family knew Chilembwe well, later recalled that 'some measure of planning had already taken place ... as early as November, 1914' (Bandawe, p. 62).

† Maker, p. 31. The hangman subsequently commanded a unit of carriers and was described as 'short, ugly and a gorilla of a man ... [who] used the *sjambok* unsparingly' (Haussmann, p. 47).

conceivably have been overthrown was a moot point; what really unnerved even the sceptics was that – as had been true of the 1896 Ndebele Rebellion in Southern Rhodesia – 'there was not the smallest doubt that most [local Africans] knew about [the rebellion]'[24] beforehand and had not warned about it. This brought the strength of the British administration, or lack of it, into very stark relief and was proof positive that the defence of just 800 Europeans in a country of one million Africans was all but impossible against an opponent determined to target supposedly 'innocent' civilians rather than government *bomas*.

Such conduct was deemed 'unsporting', especially by a missionary, during wartime: 'this attempt to stick us in the back came at a rather disconcerting moment', wrote one official, 'and it caused us a great deal of trouble'.[25] Everyone was familiar with John Buchan's *Prester John*, published in 1910, and the book suddenly seemed alarmingly prescient. Chilembwe did not come close to realising missionary 'Prester John' Laputa's vision of a liberated 'Africa for the Africans', but he had done enough to earn himself in later years the soubriquet of 'the first Malawian martyr in the cause of African freedom'.[26]

Chilembwe did not succeed in securing the support from German East Africa that he had hoped for, and a German officer by the name of Weltheim, who had been captured at Karonga in August 1914 and was a POW at Mlanje, even played a major role in preparing the *boma* for defence against the rebels. Given Captain Wintgens's unrestrained efforts to promote anti-British insurrection in Ruanda and Kigezi, Weltheim's conduct may seem anomalous. But it was Wintgens's conduct that was the exception, not the rule. The 'rule' among the colonial powers in East Africa was 'if you are rash enough to start "frightfulness" among black men it may recoil on yourself in the end'.[27] Schnee was extremely concerned about the possibility of 'unrest' in his own colony and was as chary as the British of the consequences of Africans coming 'to realise the physical disabilities of the Europeans and their vulnerability'.[28] He was also dedicated to re-establishing Germany's fitness to rule in Africa in the aftermath of the extraordinarily brutal suppression of large rebellions in South-West Africa and German East Africa during the first decade of the century.

In German East Africa it was claimed that 'not a single tribe rose against our rule [during the war] … nowhere was it necessary to divert a single squad to keep down rebellions'.[29] In fact this was manifestly untrue. There was a good deal more trouble than would ever be admitted by Schnee and von Lettow-Vorbeck, and their fears even prompted them to allow the small Boer population, concentrated in the north-east of the colony, to retain arms in spite of the fact that their own loyalty was considered suspect. Rebellion simmered in the Makonde Highlands in the south-east of the colony right through to 1917; and unrest in many other parts of the colony, although usually dismissed in terms such as 'the usual cattle-raiding exploits on the part of the Ruanda', was more or less continuous. No rising had occurred on a scale that the German administration had initially feared for good reason. German rule had been established and consolidated with a degree of brutality that was unthinkable to British soldiers and colonial officials, and only exceeded by King Leopold's regime in the Belgian Congo in the final decades of the previous century. In other words, if von Lettow-Vorbeck and Schnee were able to conduct the military campaign relatively untroubled by such unrest as sporadically occurred in British East Africa and Nyasaland, it was only because German colonial forces had, in suppressing the 1905–7 Maji-Maji rebellion, imposed what has appositely been called 'the peace of the graveyard'.[30] More than twenty tribes had taken part in the revolt, which had spread over an area of more than 100,000 square miles; and more than 200,000 Africans had perished in battle and as a consequence of the 'scorched earth' tactics employed by the Germans. Furthermore, even six years after the rebellion had petered out German police *askari* were still pursuing survivors of the rebel forces and hanging them, and in so doing sent a stark reminder of the dangers of non-compliance with the German administration to Africans all over the colony. It was a message that was not forgotten during what became known as the 'War of Fourteen–Eighteen'.

PART THREE

1916

THE LAST SURVIVOR: 'Oh, where is the great fleet of my Fatherland?'

[Of all Germany's overseas possessions, German East Africa only remains under the German flag.]

A Recitation (German East)

A well damned land is German East,
Accursed alike by man and beast,
A land of rain – till comes a spell
When nights and days are hot as hell;
From Base to Base in quest of foe,
We blooming 'fed-ups' come and go,
With scrubby cheeks and blistered knees,
Our toe-nails food for jigger fleas.
In dirty huts the lizards crawl,
With other vermin, great and small,
While 'croc' infest the streams of mud,
And while mosquitoes suck our blood,
Till fever gnaws at throat and spine,
Instead of rum we get quinine.
Let poets sing, but not for me,
That 'Hell's pup' of a country.

Private Sam Naishtad

FOURTEEN

The Build-up

The four 'regiments' comprising the 1st South African Mounted Brigade, commanded by Colonel Jakobus 'Jaap' van Deventer,* arrived in East Africa on 30 December 1915. A great bear of a man, van Deventer had been Smuts's second-in-command during the Anglo-South African War, and he inspired respect bordering on devotion among his Boer mounted troops. Indeed many of them would have refused to fight for the *Engelse* had it not been for van Deventer's presence. When his father had been killed in action in South Africa trooper Eugene Duplesis, for example, had sworn that he 'would fight against the *verdomde rooineks* whenever I got the chance'; now, a dozen years later, he had decided that if Botha and Smuts believed that South Africa's interests were best served by supporting the British Empire, that was 'good enough'[1] for him. On the other hand 'A' squadron of the 1st South African Horse was entirely British in composition, and a majority of the troopers of Colonel Eliott's 4th South African Horse were British. For some Indian Army officers the mixture of former adversaries in van Deventer's brigade was a source of concern, the more so as their commander insisted on conversing, very gruffly, only in the Afrikaans *taal* (though he understood English perfectly well); but whatever their reservations, there could be no denying that the arrival of fresh, healthy troops provided a much-needed boost to morale.

The South African mounted troops were sent straight to Kajiado on the Longido front, where the open ground was considered more appropriate for cavalry manoeuvres than the thick bush and forest around Taveta. As they only numbered 2,500 Tighe was still far short of the 10,000 men that he had requested in order to execute an 'offensive defensive' to clear all enemy troops from the border between German and British East Africa. But 'Von Splosh' – as van Deventer was soon nicknamed in the British ranks – was only the

---

* 'Jaap' or 'Jaapie' was a familiar name for Jakobus, but it was also used as a term equivalent to 'hick' or 'country boy'; the latter would soon represent the opinion of many a British Staff officer about van Deventer.

vanguard. With each passing week the news of the progress of the recruiting campaign in South Africa became more encouraging, and before the end of January the War Office knew that six infantry battalions and five batteries of regular artillery had also been promised by Botha. When the number of infantry battalions was subsequently increased to nine it appeared that Botha and Smuts had worked a miracle in the space of just two months, and the size of the force amassing in East Africa was further bolstered by the arrival of the 40th Pathans (the 'Forty Thieves') and the 129th Baluchis from France.* Although both regiments were somewhat depleted in strength by their experiences on the Western Front, the fact that they were battle-hardened 'regulars' was thought likely to balance the relative inexperience of most of the South African troops, and in Colonel Hannyngton, the commanding officer of the 129th Baluchis, the East Africa force was gaining a veteran of colonial warfare in Africa with a fine reputation.

At the end of January the troops already in, or en route to, British East Africa exceeded 27,000 in number; and with the realisation that he would soon have at his disposal a meaningful 'combatant force', equipped with eighty machine-guns and fifty field guns, Tighe's despatches began to adopt a more optimistic tone. The decisive 'scrap' with von Lettow-Vorbeck that he had so desperately hoped for since the disappointments of Tanga and Jasin at last seemed to be in the offing. The occupation of Longido without a fight on 21 January 1916 appeared to confirm his optimism, as did a foray twenty-five miles into German territory by a squadron of the 17th Cavalry from Longido and the increasingly effective patrol work undertaken by no fewer than eight battalions endeavouring to protect the Uganda Railway either side of Voi and the new branch line extending from Voi towards Taveta.

The protection of the railways, in particular, was of critical importance to the military build-up. When responsibility for their management had been assumed by the military authorities in November 1915 it was found that thirty-five locomotives – double the number that serviced German East Africa's Northern Railway – were awaiting repairs to damage wrought by von Lettow-Vorbeck's saboteurs; and every locomotive in the country would be required if the vast tonnage of supplies and new troops arriving at Mombasa were to be deployed in a timely and orderly fashion. The dearth of water between Voi and Taveta created a further logistical strain. A pipeline built from Bura to Mbuyuni to supply the British troops on the Taveta front with 40,000 gallons

---

* The 129th Baluchis, closely followed by the 57th Rifles (who would also see action in East Africa), was the first unit of the Indian Corps to be engaged on the Western Front in 1914 and the first unit to attack German troops (at Hollebeke). To Sepoy Khudadad Khan of this battalion belonged the distinction of receiving the first Victoria Cross of the war.

of water per day was repeatedly sabotaged by German patrols; and even a tripling of the number of train miles run on the line between November and February had failed to eliminate the water supply problem. For the Indian troops arriving from France the lack of water was just one unfamiliar feature of their new surroundings. As the 129th Baluchis' official historian pointed out, it was hard to imagine a 'greater contrast . . . than that between Flanders and East Africa': in the former 'the men had suffered from too much rain and mud' while conditions in the latter seemed to be characterised 'by an excess of drought and dust'.[2]

Despite the palpable sense of relief that something positive was being achieved after the interminable and debilitating months on the defensive, many of Tighe's senior officers were wary of the unbridled confidence displayed by the newly arrived South African troops, the more so when it began to spread through the ranks of their own battalions. Such over-confidence had preceded Tanga, and after reading the intelligence reports for January one veteran of that disaster – Colonel Jourdain of the 2nd Loyal North Lancs – expressed his surprise that they created 'the impression . . . that the German *askaris* want to give in'. 'This *may* be so', he noted in his diary, 'but it is not the impression that should be allowed to get about.' At the beginning of February Jourdain and other battalion commanders met to remind themselves – and the South Africans – that it was quite possible that 3,500 Europeans and 21,500 *askari* were under arms in German East Africa, of whom no fewer than 15,000 could be rapidly moved to oppose the Allied advance on the Taveta front; and that it was 'stupid to think that the Germans cannot look after their own men or that they will not do their best to prolong the war in East Africa'.[3]

The estimates of German troop strength were higher than those subsequently admitted to by von Lettow-Vorbeck, who would claim that a shortage of NCOs precluded him from expanding his force beyond the sixty companies, comprising 2,998 Europeans and 11,300 *askari*, raised by the end of 1915. However the official German account of the campaign put the maximum strength of the *Schutztruppe* at a figure fully one quarter higher than that given by their commander-in-chief; and a plethora of other German sources indicate that in early 1916 von Lettow-Vorbeck was able to muster 15,000–20,000 trained troops. Jourdain's misgivings were therefore well founded: von Lettow-Vorbeck was not outnumbered by as great a factor as the British optimists or the German commander-in-chief wanted – for very different reasons – to believe, and he was most certainly not entertaining any ideas of 'giving in'. Tanga had been just the opener; now, with the arrival of the South Africans and even regiments from France, his strategy of creating a costly diversion in East Africa could begin in earnest. As one German official in Washington remarked at the time: 'nothing more to our liking could have been done if we had had the ordering of the Allies' military movements ourselves. They – and especially Britain – are expending men and money and shipping ... to conquer regions which can give them nothing they do not already have in abundance, and which we will take from them – in Paris, or wherever the Peace Treaty chances to be signed – by a stroke of a pen.'[4]

Von Lettow-Vorbeck's principal concern was not that he was outnumbered, but that the 6,000 troops he claimed were stationed in the north-east would probably have to counter more than one British advance at the same time. If that were to happen he considered it 'very doubtful' that he could inflict defeats 'in succession', but he was determined to cause as much chaos as he could in the attempt and his force was backed by thirty-seven machine-guns and sixteen field guns. The key would be his ability to move his companies 'with lightning rapidity' on interior lines; and with that as his goal 'the necessary preparations were made'.

The Kilimanjaro front remained, as it had always been, the focus of von Lettow-Vorbeck's attention. Having decided to make his stand in the north-east there was not a great deal he could do about the situation in the west and south other than encourage his local commanders to resist the simultaneous preparations for Allied advances in those regions. In the west, the resolve of the Belgian High Command to conduct its own independent campaign remained as firm as ever. Relations with their ally were still strained, as Tighe and Spicer-Simson could attest to, and British suspicions of Belgium's ambitions in Africa were undiminished. But by January 1916 the Committee of Imperial Defence was prepared to put such differences aside, and even to admit that Britain had '[blown] hot and cold on the Belgians'. Belgian troops had proved instrumental in shoring up the British defences of Northern Rhodesia and Uganda; they had taken to the field against the Germans in the campaign in the Cameroons, in West Africa; and now they had succeeded in amassing a force that was sufficiently well armed and well supplied to take advantage of Spicer-Simson's success on Lake Tanganyika and overrun German East Africa from the west. Simple expedience therefore determined that the *froideur* which had characterised Anglo-Belgian relations during the latter half of 1915 should be dispelled, and with that in mind the Committee of Imperial Defence called for the issue of renewed co-operation to be 'thrashed out thoroughly'.[5]

The creation of Belgium's colonial army in a single year was a remarkable feat of logistics. The *askari* were largely raised from the ranks of the 15,000-strong paramilitary *Force Publique*, and led by over 600 officers and NCOs most of whom had been sent from Europe. Recruitment, however, had been the easy part of the process. Supplying them had proved more problematic:

15,500 Gras rifles, 1,000 Mauser rifles, 112 machine-guns, 42 million cartridges and 115,000 artillery shells, field hospitals for each new battalion – all this was shipped easily enough to Mombasa or Boma, on the Atlantic coast. But from Boma to the Rutchuru Valley, where the Belgian Army was concentrating for its offensive, was a journey of over 2,000 miles. Rail and river routes could be used as far as Stanleyville but after that porters – 50,000 of them at any one time – were the only 'vehicle' capable of reaching the posts of the *Brigade Nord*, a journey of six weeks' duration. Over 60,000 loads were transported by such means in 1915 and a similar number in the first quarter of 1916 in order to ensure the battle-readiness of just 12,500 combat troops.[*]

The sheer scale of the operation attested to the ever-increasing importance placed on the campaign by Belgium. It was less than a decade since the Congo had been wrested from King Leopold's grasp by international outcry and placed under direct control of the Belgian government. Criticism of the grisly conduct of Leopold's regime still cast a long shadow over Belgium's presence in Africa, fostering a determination to refute what were regarded as 'the calumnies against the Belgian people of the traitor Casement and Morel'[6] – the two men whose 'Red Rubber' campaign had caused the outcry – by demonstrating not only that Belgium's African colonies were considered an integral part of the homeland but also that Belgium was as fit to rule in Africa as any other colonial power. As was true for Portugal, the war in Africa and the war in Europe were indivisible, and the longer the war continued the more the 'African dog' wagged the 'European tail' for the simple reason that both countries were aware that in any post-war negotiations between the European Powers their African possessions – including any territory seized from Germany – might be the only guarantee of their very survival as nation states.

There were many Britons for whom Belgium's single-minded espousal of the war in Africa was puzzling, especially as Belgian participation in the war in Europe was widely regarded as having fallen far short of what had been expected after the loss of Belgium itself; and the reticence with which the suggestion of increased Anglo-Belgian co-operation was received fuelled the

---

[*] According to Hordern (p. 400 note 4), Tombeur's troop dispositions after withdrawing his Katanga troops from the Northern Rhodesia front were as follows: *Brigade Nord* (Colonel Molitor), north of Lake Kivu (5,200 men); *Brigade Sud* (Major Olsen) on the Rusisi front, south of Lake Kivu (2,500 men); Lake Tanganyika (Colonel Moulaert) (2,200 men); Kigezi front (Major Bataille) (450 men); River Congo Reserve (800 men). Total including support services 11,150 men with sixty-four guns and sixty-five machine-guns. Armaments shipped from Le Havre between August 1914 and December 1916 for the advance included four batteries each of four 70mm howitzers, eight 75mm guns, 16,500 rifles, 27,000 Mills bombs, 115,000 rounds of howitzer and field gun ammunition and 118 machine-guns. The Belgian Official History gives a figure of 11,698 troops and 719 European officers and NCOs.

suspicions of those who accused Belgium of being excessively self-interested and liable at any time to conclude a separate peace with Germany. Charles Tombeur, the Belgian commander-in-chief in the Congo, remained adamant that he was leading an *independent* army acting in concert with, but not subordinate to, the British High Command; and that if the British wanted something he would not consider obliging if there was a hint of command in the request. Even before the equally headstrong Smuts had arrived to lead the British forces such obstinacy had caused myriad problems, and when Ewart Grogan was again entrusted with the job of acting as Liaison Officer with the Belgian troops in January 1916 he soon found that Belgian co-operation came at a price. At a conference at Lutobo, in Uganda, the Belgian High Command stated that they could – or would – only advance if the British supplied 5,000 porters, 100 ox-carts and a medical establishment to accompany the *Brigade Nord* into German East Africa. Their wish-list was not extensive, and it was granted; but to Grogan and many others it smacked of the most cynical opportunism. In effect Tombeur was saying that if his allies wanted him on German soil then they would have to provide all the logistical support. Congolese porters (more than a quarter of a million of whom would be employed before the end of the war), ox-carts and field hospitals were all available – but they were staying firmly on Belgian soil.

Britain did gain something from the bargain. The offensive capability of the Belgian troops was far greater than their number appeared to indicate. Fighting on both the Kivu and Rusisi fronts during 1915 had been almost continuous, providing valuable training for the Belgian *askari* and their officers; and even before the war Congolese *askari* had possessed a fearsome reputation. Many were recruited from the Wamanyema tribe (to which was attached an infamy for cannibalistic proclivities); and they were also the only Allied troops able to move at a comparable speed to von Lettow-Vorbeck's field companies. The Belgian method of colonial warfare precluded the use of supply lines in the field, the *askari* having to rely for survival on their locust-like looting abilities. British field commanders, and their political masters, were rather squeamish about the effect that this inevitably had on its victims and chose instead to have their rate of advance determined by the speed with which supplies could be brought up to any front. But no one denied the efficacy and results of the Belgian *modus operandi*, and British commanders were to prove more than happy to exploit its advantages over the next eighteen months. A further gain was Belgium's agreement that 'in view of [Britain's] major contribution' to the military build-up in the Congo '[its government] would proffer no territorial claims at the end of the war'.[7] Grogan was not at all sure that this promise would be kept, but it was accepted at face value in

Whitehall and he was left lamenting that his 'good friend Henry' had been superseded by Tombeur, whom he regarded as 'negative' and simply 'a pet of the Belgian court, nominated to reap glory'.[8]

To the south, the preparations for an offensive were also proceeding apace. It was a peculiarity of the campaign that responsibility for the advance from Nyasaland and Northern Rhodesia remained not under the authority of the War Office but of the Colonial Office. But at least someone somewhere selected the right man to lead this force after the unfortunate demise of a less-than-popular previous commander when giving a demonstration of how to throw grenades that went disastrously wrong. Brigadier-General Edward Northey would become one of the few British generals to distinguish himself in East Africa. A short man with a military moustache and monocle, he had fought at Mons, the Marne and the Aisne with the King's Royal Rifles; and while recovering from a wound sustained when commanding the 15th Infantry Brigade in June 1915 he was notified that his services were next required in East Africa.

Northey arrived at his new post in January 1916 and proceeded to cover 550 miles in three months to discover what he had inherited on his 200-mile front. The western section was held by about 400 men from the Northern Rhodesia Police and British South Africa Police, most of whom had simply sat at their border posts for six months. The eastern section was manned by the 1st King's African Rifles under Colonel Hawthorn and about 1,300 officers and men of the 1st and 2nd South African Rifles, many of whom had proceeded straight to Nyasaland after serving in German South-West Africa. Although the police units contained many veterans of previous conflicts in Africa, the KAR were the only regular soldiers in the whole force.

Northey found very poor morale among the police, and was astonished that there was no unified chain of command on his front. A BSAP sergeant described 'the tremendous feeling of discontent' among volunteers who were itching for a fight rather than loitering on a diet of bully beef and biscuits in their 'Swiss chalet' grass huts, as Northey referred to them. In this general atmosphere of discontent verging on mutiny the troops manning the western section of the British defences vented their spleen on their commanding officer, Colonel Ronald Murray, formerly of the Bulawayo police. Murray was regarded as 'a stern, unbending sort of chap . . . rather given to parading the men and haranguing them for what he thought were their shortcomings'; and any man falling sick he derided as a 'scrimshanker'. There was no question but that Murray, whose very dark hair and eyebrows invited comparisons with a beetle, and whose swarthy features earned him the nickname 'Kaffir', was decidedly 'unpopular' – but in time he, like Northey, was to gain the respect and admiration of all those who served under him.

In the course of Northey's three-month tour he boosted morale immensely. He commenced proper training operations, authorised raids across the German border which immediately curtailed German activity along the front, and imbued his men with a sense of purpose. The troops soon discovered that he was also the most approachable leader any could imagine – a 'true gentleman' and 'very ordinary, preferring to wear shorts like the rest of the men'[9] – and he ensured that all his men were kept informed of what was happening in the wider war. Sergeant van der Spuy of the South African Mounted Rifles Battery wrote after listening to one of Northey's talks:

It was very interesting, very explicit and was told by one of the original expeditionary force, who has taken part in most of the big battles from Mons onwards, as well as having been wounded twice. He proved a splendid lecturer and by the aid of blackboard diagrams explained things from the very beginning. Many things we did not know or understand were fully dealt with and made quite plain, and it was not till we heard from him the truth of what the western front is like that we realised the grandness and terrors of it, and from what we heard, if [the soldiers there] plumbed the depths of misery and despair, they have also risen superior to them by unsurpassable human courage and endurance.[10]

Northey's aim was to counter the feeling of isolation among his men and dispel any doubts about whether 'their' war mattered. This was important, because his men would soon need 'unsurpassable human courage and endurance' in equal measure when confronted by campaign conditions every bit as testing as those of the war in Europe. As one officer serving under Northey wrote:

Africa could be cruel as well as beautiful. She flayed her children with the whip of fear and greed, and balanced reckless reproduction with orgies of destruction. Everywhere was strife; a frenzied struggle for survival. I recalled the wrestling of tree and creeper, eternally at one another's throat for a place in the sun; the jostling of bushes for a share of the sustaining soil. I could not forget that the lion, hunter of antelope and zebra, could be brought to a slow and painful death by the tiny *chigre*, the burrowing flea that is barely visible to the naked eye. And Man, intruder into Nature's own preserve, could never be at peace. He entered at his peril; ceaseless struggle was the toll he had to pay.[11]

FIFTEEN

The 'First Salaita Show'

M onsignor le Roy, a Catholic missionary who alighted on Taveta in 1890, described the place as 'un Éden africain ... une Arcadie'; and he was not at all surprised that the handful of Europeans who had preceded him had all left feeling 'une sympathie marquée' towards its inhabitants. The Wataveta, two or three thousand in number, were drawn from a number of different tribes. Most had moved to the 'exuberantly' fertile area to seek refuge from enemies (or hardship) in and around the 5,500-acre forest, where banana cultivation soon became the bedrock of society. The menfolk mostly dressed like the Masai (but spoke Swahili); polygamy was the norm; everyone worked the land, but 'not very hard' as it was so fertile; and the Wataveta's government of two assemblies – one for the old and one for the young – resembled 'a republic without a president'.[1] Three decades after le Roy's visit, the Wataveta's 'Éden africain' was no more: after eighteen months of German occupation, those of its inhabitants who had not fled elsewhere found themselves right in the path of the imminent British advance.

The 4,000 or so volunteers of the 2nd South African (Infantry) Brigade, comprising the 5th, 6th, 7th and 8th South African Infantry, began arriving in East Africa on 14 January 1916 and were immediately sent to the rapidly expanding camp at Mbuyuni. Many of the officers had seen action in the Boer War, as had some of their men; but most of the latter were hastily recruited and virtually untrained teenagers and there was a marked shortage of experienced NCOs. These were very much 'scratch' battalions and it was a tall order for their officers to meld them into effective fighting units in a matter of weeks. Furthermore, the Africa in which the South African troops now found them-selves was very different from *their* Africa, and it was decided that the best form of training would be to put the men into the field as soon as possible.

On 3 February, 5/SAI and 6/SAI were detailed to support the 2nd Loyal North Lancs in carrying out a reconnaissance from Serengeti camp towards 'Observation Ridge', from which two batteries opened fire on the small German fort on Salaita Hill; and at the same time the 2nd Rhodesia Regiment and 130th Baluchis demonstrated in force towards the hill. The conclusion drawn from the exercise was that Salaita was held in 'considerable strength',[2] and during a further foray by 6/SAI two days later 300 enemy *askari* were spotted occupying their former positions on Observation Ridge. Shots were exchanged, but there were no casualties until someone tripped on a mine on the west bank of the Njoro riverbed on the way back to camp, throwing Colonel Molyneux to the ground and injuring one private. On 9 February the entire South African Brigade was again ordered off to demonstrate in front of Salaita while the 61st Pioneers searched the Njoro drift and the old caravan road for more mines, and as it deployed before the 'first line of fortifications round [Salaita's] Eastern slopes' about 200 German *askari* and a number of Europeans were seen 'bolting for the entrenchments'. Despite their best efforts, the South African troops 'failed to draw fire from the enemy'[3] and were ordered to torch the long grass either side of the main track running past Salaita to Taveta in preparation for the main attack. The force then retired, reaching Mbuyuni by 2.30 p.m., and a week of manoeuvres – which constituted the brigade's only training in the field – came to an end.

At dawn on 12 February the South African troops received their orders from General Malleson for a 'reconnaissance in force' of Salaita. There were no doubts about what this meant: the British High Command intended to clear the way for a full-scale advance on Taveta. 'We were told', wrote one trooper, 'to carry one blanket each, bandolier-fashion over our shoulders and take one day's ration ... We were informed that we would be sleeping on Salaita that night.'[4] Morale was high. In their short stay the South Africans had, like Mgr le Roy before them, found the nights 'delightfully cool' and the scenery 'splendid'. To the west rose snow-clad Kilimanjaro, to the south lay Lake Jipe and the Pare Mountains, and the ground between the British lines and the Taveta forest in places resembled 'home park-land'.[5] The night before, thirty-three-year-old Sergeant Lane of the South African Medical Corps, a scout-master and civil servant in peacetime, noted in his diary that 'it makes one feel a man to be marching along with all those thousands of troops ... the next twenty-four hours should produce some excitement. I wonder what I shall write in these pages for tomorrow we fight. Hurrah!'[6] Young Victor Morton also recorded that 'the men moved out as cheery as youngsters going to a football match ... we were ordered to cover our helmets in grass and [chaffed] one another at the quaint appearance.'[7]

Brigadier-General Percival Scott Beves, commanding the South African Brigade, was not quite so cocksure and had voiced his doubts to General Malleson. An enthusiastic butterfly collector and musician, the well-liked Beves was particularly concerned that after a week of demonstrations towards Salaita the attack would hardly come as a surprise to von Lettow-Vorbeck, especially as the nine planes of the RNAS and the recently arrived 26th (South

African) Squadron of the Royal Flying Corps had also been busy overhead; and he argued that there was no way of knowing how many German troops were garrisoned at Taveta waiting to reinforce Salaita Hill at a moment's notice. He also complained at being denied the use of 8/SAI, the fourth battalion in his brigade, half of whom had arrived at Mbuyuni two days earlier. Malleson dismissed all these issues, pointing out that adequate artillery preparation and a force of 6,000 South African and British troops would suffice to overwhelm any opposition that von Lettow-Vorbeck could muster. Beves was assured that the intelligence gathered during the past week – both on the ground and from the air – indicated that the garrison on Salaita Hill would be held by no more than 300 rifles, with two machine-guns and no artillery; and that 'the assault would be over before any forces could reach the scene from Taveta'.[8] If German reinforcements did begin to appear then Belfield's Scouts, a volunteer mounted unit detailed to reconnoitre to the north-west beyond Salaita, would be able to warn of their approach in good time.

Malleson's confidence was unsurprising given his apparent numerical advantage. But he was a Staff officer by training, and one who had not inspired widespread confidence since his arrival with IEF 'B' in November 1914. Most of his forays into the field had ended badly, the arrogance he had displayed during two visits in the company of Ewart Grogan to the Belgian High Command had greatly exacerbated tensions on that front, and he had earned a reputation for being 'clever as a monkey but hopelessly unreliable'.[9] Malleson's orders from Tighe were to take Salaita by frontal assault, thereby 'expelling the enemy from British territory';[10] and he was not going to let Beves – whom he considered over-cautious – stand in his way. Had he listened to Beves, or not dismissed 'the Boer method of making wide and unexpectedly rapid flanking manoeuvres favoured by South African troops as rather a vulgar form of warfare and not suitable for English officers and gentlemen',[11] the attack might have fared very differently. Indeed had Malleson displayed the foresight simply to disrupt the train of donkey-carts which supplied Salaita with water, the German stronghold would, by von Lettow-Vorbeck's own admission, have become 'untenable'.[12] Most unfortunate of all, however, and reminiscent of Tanga, was the fact that British intelligence about German troop dispositions was woefully inadequate, and consequently the chances of Malleson's chosen method of attack succeeding were no better than Aitken's had been.

Von Lettow-Vorbeck was kept fully informed by his Chief Scout, ironically a Boer resident of German East Africa by the name of Piet Nieuwenhuizen, as his enemy 'frequently showed considerable bodies of troops' in front of Salaita during the first week in February; and he and Major Kraut, commanding the German troops in the Kilimanjaro area, became increasingly certain that a major attack was imminent. Three companies were moved up from Taveta to reinforce Salaita, a further three under Captain Schulz were deployed between Taveta and Salaita, and Taveta itself was reinforced from troops stationed at the nearby New Steglitz Plantation. *If* the opportunity arose Kraut was therefore in a position to counter-attack in force: altogether he had 1,300–1,400 men on, or reinforcing, the 'almost impregnable'[13] defences on Salaita, supported by no fewer than twelve machine-guns, a 7-pdr field gun, and two light 'pom-pom' guns.

The 2nd South African Brigade and the 1st East African Brigade – 6,000 men with eighteen guns and forty-one machine guns – moved out independently but simultaneously on 12 February.* The first of Beves's force to leave Serengeti camp in a north-westerly direction were the sixty mounted Belfield's Scouts who rode off to scout beyond Salaita Hill for signs of German reinforcements; they were not seen again until the battle was all but over. In their wake, one company of 7/SAI and a double company of the 61st Pioneers (whom Aitken had dismissed after Tanga as being 'fit only as labourers') formed the advance guard, followed by the rest of 7/SAI, the 28th Mountain Battery, two double companies of 61st Pioneers, two armoured cars of the RNAS under Lieutenant-Commander Whittall, 5/SAI and 6/SAI, the Volunteer Maxim Company and the ammunition column. Meanwhile the East African Brigade moved due west towards Salaita.

At 6.45 a.m. both brigades had reached the Njoro riverbed and were about one and a half miles apart. Here they were issued with the orders for the attack. Malleson intended 'enveloping Salaita from the north' with 'Belfield's Scouts and 2 armoured cars to watch right flank … mounted infantry and 2 armoured cars to cover left flank'. Leaving the Pioneers at the dry riverbed 'to improve ramps and search for mines',[14] an hour later the men of Colonel Freeth's 7/SAI – a battalion composed almost entirely of Australians and New Zealanders resident in South Africa – had struggled through the dense bush north of the Salaita–Serengeti track until they reached a position on the edge of a patch of open ground 1,000 yards from the base of Salaita Hill. Although it was remarked that the South Africans had gone up 'in beautiful style',[15] all were extremely thirsty by now as the watercarts had been left in the rear; and progress through the dense scrub had proved unduly strenuous due to Beves's insistence on moving in massed battalions. To the right Colonel Molyneux's

* The 1st East African Brigade comprised the 2nd Loyal North Lancs, 2nd Rhodesia Regiment and the 130th Baluchis. The 2nd South African Brigade comprised 5/SAI, 6/SAI, 7/SAI. Divisional troops: 2nd Loyal North Lancs Mounted Infantry; Belfield's Scouts; 28th Mountain Battery; No. 1 Light Battery (two 12-pdrs); Calcutta Volunteer Battery (six 12-pdrs); No. 3 Heavy Battery (two 4-inch naval guns from HMS *Pegasus*); No. 4 Heavy Battery (two 5-inch howitzers); four RNAS armoured cars; Volunteer Maxim Company; and the 61st Pioneers.

6/SAI, supported by the two RNAS armoured cars and the Volunteer Maxims guarding the battalion's open right flank, had also reached the position from which it was to attack, as had Colonel Byron's 5/SAI on the left. Far from 'enveloping' Salaita, as Malleson described the movement, these three South African battalions had in fact done nothing more than deploy in such a way as to launch a frontal attack on the north side of the hill.

From the Njoro drift two 'Peggies', 4-inch naval guns salvaged from HMS *Pegasus*, opened fire on Salaita at 9 a.m., and this was the signal for the 4th Battery, positioned east of the drift, and the 5-inch howitzers and sundry other batteries which had moved up behind the South African left to commence their bombardment as well. But as Colonel Freeth pushed his battalion on under cover of the bombardment to within 300 yards of the closest German entrenchments he began to notice that all was not as he had been led to expect: the bombardment was not making the slightest difference and enemy rifle fire was 'going along merrily ... while [their] machine-guns were rattling furiously'. Worse still, it was not only obvious that the German defenders had artillery and machine-guns in greater quantities than Malleson had predicted, but their main entrenchments were around the foot of the hill – not on the slopes being 'thoroughly searched'[16] by the British guns. At 9.45 a.m. Captain Collas of the 2nd Loyal North Lancs's Mounted Infantry reached the same conclusion on the east side of the hill, but a message sent back to the guns prompted no alteration in their pattern of fire until well after noon. Fearful of hitting the South African troops, many of whom were within a few hundred yards of the German trenches at the foot of Salaita, the gunners continued to fire at the hill-top fort, where the German and Mahommedan flags still flew defiantly, and its surrounding trenches.

Despite the unexpectedly ferocious, and persistent, response from Salaita's defenders, the South African battalions pressed on with their attack and casualties were surprisingly light. 'It was difficult to see any enemy, and only occasionally was a black head seen for a second',[17] noted one South African; and the German machine-gunners had similar difficulties in picking out targets in the thick bush beyond their cleared fields of fire. To the right of the South African line, Colonel Molyneux, on approaching one such cleared area, requested permission from Beves to open 6/SAI's formation. It was refused, with the result that when crossing the 100-yard strip the battalion came under concentrated German artillery fire. Like 7/SAI to their left, the battalion made it to the relative safety of the bush beyond the clearing and overran a German trench extending due north from Salaita; but in so doing the men were no longer in a position where they could be contacted by Belfield's Scouts if they sent a messenger to warn of German reinforcements moving up from Taveta.

Molyneux's success in clearing even one German entrenchment was a considerable achievement: all the enemy trenches were 'at least six feet deep, with steps up the sides to enable the riflemen to shoot through portholes, and thorn bush was stacked up in front to make a formidable barricade against the advancing troops'. Furthermore, as Sergeant Jones of 7/SAI observed, 'between the lines of trenches the enemy had dug deep pits. The earth removed had been scattered around to hide all traces of digging, and each pit was covered by reeds and light sticks with a thin covering of grass laid on top of the whole. In the bottom of the pit, spiked stakes had been firmly driven, and barbed wire was entwined around the stakes, so that if a man happened to walk over this trap he would be precipitated into the pit and either staked or disembowelled.'[18] The achievement of 6/SAI was not matched by the other South African battalions. Although 5/SAI and 7/SAI were within just a few hundred yards of the enemy they were pinned down by increasingly ferocious fire. Bullets 'came sounding through the air like a swarm of bees', and one 'particularly annoying machine-gun [being] fired from the back of a mule [was] standing in a pit and covered over with bush and grass'. It was 'practically impossible to locate him', one soldier remarked, 'but finally our armoured motor cars came to the rescue and, serving bursts of fire in likely directions, drove the mule out of its lair, the appearance of this strange "Jack-in-the-Green" being greeted with shouts of laughter by our troops'.[19] Less amusing was the realisation that snipers, cleverly concealed as the South Africans had advanced past them, were now even firing at them from trees and anthills in their rear. At 11 a.m., with South African casualties mounting rapidly, Beves gave the order for 5/SAI and 7/SAI to fall back and Malleson ordered the East African Brigade, the General Reserve, to attack. Although the brigade was formed only from troops with plenty of experience of the conditions confronting them, its advance fared no better on the eastern face of Salaita. The 2nd Rhodesia Regiment's attack was repulsed just before noon, the 2nd Loyal North Lancs were equally unsuccessful in their attempt to cross 500 yards of open ground in front of the German trenches, and soon after noon it was clear that neither battalion would be able to make any further progress – or to relieve the pressure on the South Africans to the north of Salaita.

Von Lettow-Vorbeck was in constant touch with Kraut by phone as the battle unfolded, and even before the East African Brigade had launched their attack he had decided, just as he had done at Tanga, that 'the favourable opportunity' he sought 'now presented itself'.[20] By the time he arrived at the front from Moshi, Schulz's 6/FK, 9/FK and 24/FK had advanced from their positions between Salaita and Taveta and past the rear of a detachment of 15/FK to the west of the hill. In doing so, they outflanked Molyneux's 6/SAI and all four of the German companies then began their counter-attack in earnest. No warning of this move from Belfield's Scouts had been received by

Molyneux and to the South African troops Schulz's three companies seemed to have materialised out of thin air. Total confusion and disorder ensued as Molyneux, whose orders were to cover the withdrawal of 5/SAI and 7/SAI, found his battalion bearing the brunt of Schulz's attack. It would never be clearly established whether Beves's command to withdraw was issued before or after Schulz's counter-attack began; what was certain was that it was a 'very anxious time'[21] for the South Africans, especially when recrossing tracts of open ground; and by the time von Lettow-Vorbeck arrived on the scene by car the entire South African Brigade had been put to flight. Their supporting artillery units simply had to 'get out as best as they could'. In contrast to the bizarre eightsome reel being executed by the infantry as each battalion fought to counter attacks on the others, the guns at least pulled back 'splendidly'.[22] 'I don't know how we got out',[23] was the simple conclusion of a trooper with 7/SAI.

In the first instance it was Lieutenant-Commander Whittall's armoured cars – nicknamed *kifaru* (rhinos) by Africans who observed them for the first time – which saved the situation. Although for years after the battle von Lettow-Vorbeck dismissed reports of their presence on the battlefield as pure fantasy,* if the armoured cars had not been present the last stages of the battle 'would have been a massacre'.[24] The 1st East African Brigade was also instrumental in preventing the retreat from turning into a rout. At 1 p.m. they were ordered to move north to cover the South Africans and the 2nd Loyal North Lancs, led by Colonel Jourdain, and the 130th Baluchis, led by Major Dyke, did so in determined fashion. The 130th Baluchis stood firm in the face of a German bayonet charge, and Schulz's counter-attack was stopped in its tracks. Malleson's entire force then began to pull back towards Njoro drift, skirmishing all the way and skilfully covered by a light battery of two 12-pdrs and the 28th Mountain Battery. The last troops reached the drift at 6.15 p.m., and only then did 'Heinie's *askari*', as they were referred to by the South African troops, relent.

As daylight gave way to what was indisputably 'a lovely cloudless night', Sergeant Lane attended to the wounded and countless cases of sunstroke back at Serengeti camp. No one had eaten anything except a few biscuits before dawn, and the bedraggled men were hoarse from having had no water except the little they each carried to see them through an entire day of marching, fighting and retreating chaotically in the searing heat preceding the rainy

---

* See Lettow-Vorbeck (1), pp. 103–4: 'The troops at New Steglitz advanced to Taveta, where some fantastic reports came in about hostile armoured cars, which were alleged to be moving through the thorn-bush desert. The imagination of the natives, to whom these armoured cars were something altogether new and surprising, had made them see ghosts.'

season. 'Our evening meal was not a jovial one,' Lane remarked; 'we were told to expect an attack.'[25]

February 12 1916 was the South Africans' Tanga, its 'welcome to East Africa' from von Lettow-Vorbeck. Like the Indian Expeditionary Force fifteen months earlier, the 2nd South African Brigade had now had their own experience of assaulting a heavily defended position, deadly sniping from front and rear, and rapid counter-attack. With only one stretcher per company and the nearest dressing station 1,000 yards east of Njoro drift, 7/SAI was forced to leave thirty casualties in the field, and von Lettow-Vorbeck claimed his troops buried sixty men – just under half the South African Brigade's 138 casualties. In military terms, even when the thirty-four casualties among the East African Brigade were included, the loss of life was not disastrously high. But in political terms it was a catastrophe for Smuts: in this single 'reconnaissance in force', which he had been led to believe would be virtually unopposed, one third as many South Africans had been killed and wounded as in the entire German South-West Africa campaign.* To add indignity to injury, Freeth's 7/SAI had also lost 100 rifles during its retreat as well as a mass of kit and thousands of rounds of ammunition; and the day after the 'First Salaita Show' it was the 130th Baluchis and 2nd Loyal North Lancs who were sent out to retrieve as much South African equipment from the battlefield as they could find.

'The despatch dealing with this attack on Salaita', wrote one regimental historian, 'is a model which might well be adopted by the Staff College when training its future Generals on how to gloss over unpleasant defeats.' It read: 'the enemy was found to be in force and counter-attacked vigorously. General Malleson was compelled to withdraw to Serengeti, but much useful information had been gained and the South Africans had learned some valuable lessons in bush fighting, and been given the opportunity of estimating the fighting qualities of the enemy'.[26] More prosaically, and a full year after the battle, the South African Forces' magazine remarked that 'to say . . . the Salaita hill fight created a painful impression in South Africa is but mildly to express it, especially as it was many weeks before details were allowed to come through'.[27] 'Far from Salaita I want to be / Where German snipers can't snipe at me' became a familiar ditty around South African campfires in East Africa; and it was four months before the Johannesburg *Star* carried any detailed news of 'an action the story of which will never be told in its entirety'. 'The

---

* Rather unusually, the number of awards presented to South African troops in the German South-West Africa campaign (496) exceeded the number of casualties (424); the number of DSOs (112) alone equalled the number killed (113). See D.R. Forsyth, 'Rewards For War Services: German South-West Africa Campaign 1914–1915', in *Journal of the Military Medal Society of South Africa*, Vol. 29, August 1987.

Salvaging the cargo of the German blockade-runner *Kronborg* in Mansa Bay

One of the starboard gun crews of HMAS *Pioneer* with their mascot, Ben

HMS *Mersey* passes HMS *Severn* during the second attack on the *Königsberg* in the Rufiji delta, July 1915

Examining the wreckage of the *Königsberg*

29th Punjabis and
25th Battalion
Royal Fusiliers
embark for
Bukoba, June 1915

King's African Rifles' machine-gun position overlooking Bukoba

Looff addresses the crewmen of the *Königsberg* as they prepare to join von Lettow-Vorbeck's land forces

German control of Lake Tanganyika, and therefore of the whole western theatre, rested on the presence of the *Goetzen*

The *Daily Mirror* hails the remarkable achievements of Commander Spicer-Simson's 'Lake Tanganyika Expedition'

Spicer-Simson (inset) signalling from the
deck of the Belgian vessel *Netta*

HMS *Fifi* at anchor

A German column makes its way across the *pori*

One of the *Königsberg*'s guns being manhandled into position (the gun is out of picture left)

1st King's
African Rifles
occupying
Longido early
in 1916

The 2nd
Rhodesia
Regiment
entrains

Von Lettow-
Vorbeck observing
British troop
movements on
the Kilimanjaro
front, March 1916

loss in human life was small,' the editor conceded, and there were individual 'incidents in [the action] which redeemed a generally dark day'.[28] But the damage to morale at home and in the ranks was substantial. The myth of invincibility which had accompanied victory in German South-West Africa – the fledgling Union of South Africa's first war – lay in ruins.

The recriminations began immediately. There were plenty among the British and Indian troops who found some vindication of the shame of Tanga in seeing the newly arrived, some thought cocky, South Africans 'run like so many sheep'[29] for want of discipline;* and even Vere Stent, editor of the *Pretoria News*, agreed. While pointing out that 'a retirement in the face of a pursuant and victorious enemy is the most trying task that can be imposed even upon veteran soldiers', he conceded that 'the South Africans retreated with unnecessary hurry'.[30] For this, Beves's reputation as a cautious commander lay in tatters: for the rest of the war he would frequently stand accused of recklessness, and his battalion commanders were bitterly critical of his decision to make them advance in massed ranks as if he were repeating his successful 230-mile march from Karibi to Otavifontein during the campaign in German South-West Africa (a feat accomplished in just sixteen days, but over *open* ground). The 'reconnaissance in force' was of course not of Beves's devising; and, in his defence, he had correctly identified many of its potential short-comings, made it clear that he thought he was a battalion short, and was compromised by a bombardment that had been 'wrongly directed, and was therefore quite ineffective'.[31] Nor was Malleson's woeful under-estimation of the strength of the enemy any fault of Beves's; and Malleson, of all people, should have known how quickly and effectively von Lettow-Vorbeck could counter-attack after witnessing the disaster at Tanga.

As for Mickey Tighe, he had been desperate to seize Salaita and to present it as a trophy to Smuts. Given the numerical advantage of his force, victory *should* have been attainable. But even eighteen months after Tanga too little had seemingly been learnt about von Lettow-Vorbeck's tactics and capability, British commanders continued to adhere too rigidly to inappropriate field regulations, and in choosing Malleson to command the attack, because of rank not record, Tighe made a fateful error. As a result of Salaita Malleson became universally condemned as a man who, whatever his abilities as a Staff officer, 'ought never to have been given a command in the field'[32] – yet within a month he was inexplicably to be given another chance (with equally disastrous consequences). In the meantime Tighe, as if in as great a state of shock as the battered South African troops, waited four whole days before

---

* 'Nobody can get up quite the same enthusiasm for a South African that the South African can' observed one British trooper with the EAMR (see RH/Drury).

informing the War Office of the outcome of the battle. The response from Kitchener, whose attention at the time was first and foremost on the desperate defence of Verdun, was predictably censorious: 'I hope that the necessity of not undertaking premature operations, unless circumstances *absolutely* compel you, is realized by you.'[33]

SIXTEEN

The 'Robbers' Raid'[1]

———◆◆———

J an Smuts arrived in Mombasa on 19 February 1916, and was not best pleased
with the news that greeted him. In November the two South African officers
sent to Nairobi to study the situation in East Africa had come to the conclusion
that the campaign could easily be finished in 'a few months';[2] and the capitulation of German troops in the Cameroons on 15 February had briefly seemed
like a favourable portent. But as he boarded the train in Mombasa station the
full details emerged of how Tighe and Malleson had landed him with a defeat
before he'd even arrived in the country. The effect on the morale of his
volunteer army and the political situation back home was little short of
disastrous.

Smuts immediately set off on a tour of both the Longido and Taveta fronts,
and made one important change to the troop dispositions by moving van
Deventer's Mounted Brigade from the former to the latter. Smuts wanted his
old comrade 'Jaap' close at hand, and was sure that he could be a great deal
more useful in turning German positions around Kilimanjaro, no matter how
difficult the terrain, than crossing the open steppe between Longido and Mt
Meru; and he knew that the advance against Taveta would be the most
important element of his invasion plan. In all other respects he adhered to the
plan agreed between Smith-Dorrien and the War Office, though he dismissed
the option of launching a coastal 'demonstration' by the Royal Navy at the
same time as unfeasible. This was understandable: Smuts had no experience
of naval landings, Tanga had proved an object lesson in their potential shortcomings, and he was desperately short of time if he wanted to strike a major
blow against his opponent before the rainy season. But his decision was
fortunate for von Lettow-Vorbeck, who feared a simultaneous attack on Dar-
es-Salaam or Tanga more than anything.

By 23 February Smuts reported that he was confident of 'turning the enemy
out of the Kilimanjaro and Meru areas'[3] before the rains, and the following
day his plans were duly approved by the War Office. (See Appendix Three.)
His gamble with the weather would have backfired disastrously had the rains
arrived early, but it was still dry ten days later and, with the arrival of the Cape

Corps and the 3rd South African Infantry Brigade, his forces were complete and at the ready on 4 March. The next day General Stewart began his advance with the 1st Division from Longido, traversing thirty-three waterless miles at night to reach the swamp at Engare Nanyuki by dawn on 6 March, and later the same day Nagasseni Hill was occupied by Stewart's mounted column. It was a considerable achievement, reaching his first objective a day earlier than he had agreed with Smuts to leave Longido. But its effect on Stewart's troops was to have important consequences. The regimental historian of the 129th Baluchis described how

> this march ... over semi-desert country, in a tropical sun, in column and on a strictly limited water supply, was an extremely exhausting task requiring good march discipline. All the troops, except a small number in the advance guards and on the flanks, were enveloped in a thick haze of dust from the moment the march started until the halt, at the end of the day. Only those who have done such marches know what they mean. It is one thing to picture war in terms of smartly aligned columns marching on good roads, it is another to see the reality – columns of filthy, sweating men, staggering with fatigue, at the end of such a march, and with parched mouths gasping for water. And to see these troops, in such a condition, pull themselves together for battle with an entrenched enemy, is to see real soldiers and to know the meaning of discipline.[4]

On the Taveta front, van Deventer's Mounted Brigade and the 3rd South African Infantry Brigade – Smuts's 'Flanking Force' – were despatched north-west at dusk on 7 March in a wide turning movement towards Lake Chala which, it was hoped, would dislodge German troops from Salaita Hill without a repetition of the previous month's fiasco; and Tighe, with the all-British 2nd Division, was detailed to march past Salaita, clearing it of any remaining defenders, and on to the Lumi River to the east of Taveta. At dawn on 8 March the South African troops were at the Lumi, which was bridged by the 61st Pioneers, and most of the infantry were across by midday while the mounted troops moved against German positions to the north of Lake Chala. Little resistance was offered to either as the German troops fell back on Taveta, and that same afternoon Tighe unleashed 'a hurricane of artillery fire' on Salaita Hill. There was to be no second battle there. On 9 March Tighe's troops found the hill unoccupied, and without any detectable trace of irony he wrote that had it been otherwise, this 'truly formidable [position] ... would have cost us 1,500 men'.[5] Smuts's turning movement had worked, although it was unfortunate that the retreat from the hill by 1,000 German troops was not intercepted, and on the morning of 10 March Kraut also withdrew from

Taveta through the forest to two hills commanding a *nek* through which ran the main track from Taveta into German East Africa.

To Smuts's intense and mounting frustration, Stewart's progress to the west of Kilimanjaro was no longer proceeding quite so rapidly. His problems were threefold. Intelligence reports indicated that at least five German companies under Major Fischer were in front of him, but there was still little sign of them by the time he reached Geragua, in the wooded western foothills of Kilimanjaro, on 8 March. Secondly, he had crossed terrain infinitely more exacting than that over which the South African troops were advancing in the east, and his men were suffering badly from thirst and heat exhaustion. Thirdly, he had no railway line to support him and his lines of communication were completely exposed not only to opportunistic raids by the enemy but also to the daily deluges that now presaged the arrival of the rains. In these circumstances, Stewart began to exercise a degree of caution about his continued advance. He chose to press on through the foothills with his infantry leaving the guns and mounted troops, whose effectiveness in such country was limited, to follow. By dusk on 11 March Stewart's vanguard had reached an intact bridge over the Sanya River near Boma Ngombe – an advance of just twenty miles in three days – and Smuts's messages to him became increasingly irascible.

Stewart was in an unenviable position. On 10 March his mounted troops had 'bumped' two of Fischer's companies and after a vicious fight had been forced to return, with the artillery, whence they had started their day's trek. In the opinion of their commander this battle vindicated his decision to advance cautiously, but Smuts took the opposing view and was astonished that Stewart had allowed his infantry to become cut off from the cavalry and heavy guns. The situation was rectified when the 29th Punjabis were sent back to escort the latter forward, and the advance was able to resume. But once across the Sanya River the danger of ambush was even greater and the whereabouts of Fischer's troops remained unknown. It was at this juncture that Smuts began to suspect that Kraut was retiring from the Taveta front due west towards Moshi – and Stewart – and not, as he had expected, straight down the Northern Railway.

At Taveta, Smuts was also confronted with having to clear the *nek* between the Latema and Reata Hills before he could press on towards Moshi. The terrain precluded a flanking movement such as had proved successful in prising the Germans off Salaita Hill, so a frontal assault was deemed the only option. This was an unusual decision for a man who was wont to declare that 'British generals seem to take a fortified position as a personal affront and attack it head on. We believe in going round it.'[6] If the objective had not been so important, Smuts's choice of commander – General Malleson – would have seemed like a ploy almost guaranteed to get rid of the man once and for all. Kraut was known to be holding the *nek* in force and dislodging him meant taking the hills, which rose about 700 feet above the plain on either side and were densely covered in bush and boulders. Dark mutterings about Spion Kop and other Boer War battles in which British troops had failed to take elevated positions began to circulate in the ranks as Malleson ordered forward 1,500 men of the 2nd Rhodesia Regiment, the 130th Baluchis and Colonel Graham's 3/KAR at noon on 11 March. But Graham, for one, was jovial and optimistic, having eluded a 'conviction amounting to a certainty'[7] that he would be killed in the earlier advance on Salaita.

At the foot of the hills the King's African Rifles and the Baluchis soon found themselves pinned down by coruscating fire from above, and at 2.30 p.m. Malleson left the field, ostensibly suffering from 'dysentery'. It was his final 'contribution' to the war in East Africa, and Tighe himself was forced to take over command of the attack. It took him some time to ascertain exactly what was happening on Latema and Reata, but it was clear that progress by his two battalions was minimal, prompting him to throw in his reserve – the 2nd Rhodesians – and immediately to request reinforcements from Smuts. Failure, after waiting seventeen months for the opportunity to eject German troops from British soil, was simply unimaginable to Tighe; and in tackling the hills he would, by his own admission, take 'grave risks'.[8] As Colonel Capell's 2nd Rhodesians moved through their 'chummy' battalions, the latter had been pinned down for five hours in searing heat and 3/KAR had tragically lost their commanding officer, shot through the head by a pom-pom shell. Graham's death was universally regarded as a 'terrible loss' as he was 'not only a most accomplished and gallant soldier, but ... regarded with an almost unique devotion by the KAR'.[9] In no time the Rhodesians were also stopped in their tracks, then forced back by a determined counter-attack at 6 p.m. When darkness descended most of the battalion was back on the plain with the other British troops and 5/SAI and 7/SAI, the reinforcements sent from Chala by Smuts.

Tighe, who had been greatly buoyed by the ease with which he had taken Salaita, was not about to admit defeat. Colonel Byron's 5/SAI, anxious to lose its soubriquet 'The Runaway Fifth' earned in the February attack on Salaita, and Colonel Freeth's 7/SAI were ordered to fix bayonets and assault the hills in the dark; and so great was the determination with which they advanced that they almost succeeded in carrying the attack. At least one third of Freeth's battalion made it to the ridges, as did Byron with about forty of his battalion. But having seen half his men killed, when Byron was himself wounded he reluctantly instructed the remainder to withdraw. In the dark, confusion now reigned both on the hills and down below. At 1.30 a.m. Tighe ordered the

130th Baluchis to fix bayonets and advance, but on meeting Byron's retreating troops they too pulled back, believing that the attack had been cancelled. Tighe judged it inadvisable to try again in the dark; and at 4.30 a.m. Smuts told him to withdraw his whole force by dawn, in the hope that an advance that day by van Deventer's mounted troops to the north would force the Germans to evacuate Latema and Reata.

Soon after daylight the truth began to dawn. A large number of the troops listed as missing from the 2nd Rhodesia Regiment and 7/SAI, as well as a few *askari* of 3/KAR of whom Graham would have been proud, had never withdrawn off the hills. On Latema Colonel Freeth had hung on grimly with eighteen men from his battalion and a handful of Rhodesians and KAR; while Major Thompson and a party of 170 had spent the night on Reata in positions intermingled with those of the enemy. As soon as he learnt that these troops were still on the hills Tighe immediately ordered Colonel Taylor's 8/SAI – the 'Jammy Eighth' – and an artillery battery to rush forward in cars from Taveta and by the time Taylor's battalion reached the ridges the Germans were in full flight. Tighe wrote that 'the behaviour of the 5th and 7th SA taken all round was very fine and the men who held on to the ridge all night and then turned the captured German machine-guns on to the demoralised Boches were men to be proud of. They saved the situation and turned the scale.' Freeth and Thompson were immediately awarded the first DSOs to be won by South Africans in the campaign, and despite the severity of the fighting the toll was deemed 'acceptable'. Casualties among the three British battalions amounted to 169, and among the South Africans to a further 100 or so. Kraut's troops, estimated to number about 1,000, were thought to have suffered equally heavily. They were not pursued, and by dawn had disappeared into the dense forest between the hills and Kahe.

Had the attack on Latema-Reata failed, Tighe was certain that the 'bloodsome' battle which had 'cooked'[10] all the men of the South African 2nd Division and most of the Force Reserve would have cost him his command. More importantly, it forced von Lettow-Vorbeck to cancel an attack by nine skilfully deployed and heavily armed companies on van Deventer's 'Flanking Force' as it moved forward from Taveta towards Himo. The outcome of this contest would almost certainly have been disastrous for van Deventer's mounted troops, who only outnumbered their opponents by one third and would have been advancing across unfamiliar terrain. As it was the German force, commanded by the experienced Schulz and Stemmermann, was ordered to withdraw south to join Kraut's detachment at Kahe and Smuts's route to Moshi, the railhead of the Northern Railway, lay open. On 14 March van Deventer's advance guard entered the town unopposed and established contact with the advance guard of Stewart's 1st Division.

On 12 March Smuts, ever the politician, declared the 'first phase' of the campaign to be over. It was a half-truth only. German troops had been cleared from the border and pushed back into German East Africa, but they had not been brought to battle and were massing around Kahe and along the Ruwu River. If Smuts had ever entertained the notion that the first phase would be the only phase, it was abundantly clear that he had failed. For this, Stewart took most of the blame. Smuts had repeatedly lambasted him for not moving quickly enough to cut off the German retreat from Taveta at Moshi, but it was actually Smuts's decision to send van Deventer's mounted troops haring through to Moshi that had forced von Lettow-Vorbeck to order his troops to reconcentrate around Kahe, to the south of their former positions, and not at Moshi. Furthermore, Smuts also blamed Stewart for not reaching Kahe in time to cut *that* line of retreat. This was Smuts at his most arrogant: he was certain that Stewart had not pushed his men hard enough and made no allowance for the difficulties encountered during the advance from Longido. Even had he done so, Smuts simply would not accept that von Lettow-Vorbeck's success in slipping the noose could only be attributed to the actions of his troops on the Taveta front.

On 15 March Smuts wrote to the War Office that Stewart should have been at Kahe by 11 March – within five days of his departure from Longido – and, had that been so, 'there would have been a fair chance of concluding the whole campaign within the next few weeks'.[11] It was an outrageous slur given the eighty miles of terrain across which he had to advance, and the fact that to reach Kahe Stewart needed not only to deal with Fischer's companies but also to outflank von Lettow-Vorbeck's main force. Furthermore Smuts had not made it clear to Stewart at the outset that Kahe was even his objective. 'It is not easy to say what would have happened *had our Division been directed on Kahe*', wrote one officer in the East African Mounted Rifles; 'in all probability we could have reached there before the main German force . . . but so important a point as Kahe must have been held in some strength . . . and our Division was not so strong a fighting force as it appeared on paper'.[12]

It was true that Stewart's troops could have taken Moshi on 14 March (the day that van Deventer did so unopposed). But communications with Smuts's HQ were poor, and Stewart was still expecting to face the retreat of the main German force from around Taveta – so opted to remain holding the bridge over the Sanya River in compliance with his original orders to hold the Moshi–Arusha road and block any German troops retreating westwards. He did, however, also detach a 1,500-strong column under Colonel Sheppard to *try* and fulfil his latest order to cut off the German troops at Kahe, ten miles to the south-east. This order was, at best, a disingenuous move calculated to make Stewart a scapegoat. Rain was now pouring down, and the vast majority of Kraut's troops were gathered around Kahe before Stewart even received the order. In order to reach Kahe they had only had to withdraw ten miles, under no threat whatsoever, from the Latema-Reata *nek*; and for Captain Stemmermann's last troops withdrawing from Himo, von Lettow-Vorbeck's former HQ, the distance was even less. The final indignity wrought on Stewart occurred when the bulk of his division did move the last few miles from the Sanya River to Moshi on 14 March: its advance guard was fired on by van Deventer's mounted troops, who were unable to tell the difference between the uniforms of the King's African Rifles and those of the German *askari*.

In the aftermath of the 'first phase' Smuts was unable to prevent Malleson from being promoted Major-General, as had been recommended by Tighe before his arrival, but he had no hesitation in dismissing him for 'defective leadership in the field'.[13] This caused no great surprise and, in time-honoured fashion, did not appear to impede Malleson's subsequent career.[*] However his dismissal of Stewart, a highly respected officer with a long and distinguished career with the 5th Gurkha Rifles behind him, was an altogether more contentious move. Stewart may not have been the most brilliant soldier, but he was 'safe' and had done exactly what was expected of him since arriving in East Africa in 1914. Smuts, though himself a man who combined caution with sporadic recklessness, quite simply did not want cautious commanders; and in heaping vitriol on Stewart, he earned few friends among British officers. Malleson was a 'viper'; Stewart was universally liked, trusted and admired. In the opinion of many, 'hard things were spoken, and indeed written [about Stewart]', and an 'injustice was done.'[14] in condemning him to command the garrison at Aden for most of the rest of the war. At least his fate was better than that of Major Fischer, who had found his task of holding up Stewart's advance as testing as Stewart had found the presence of Fischer's companies: Fischer was handed a revolver by von Lettow-Vorbeck on arrival at New Steglitz Plantation and shot himself.

Stewart's principal mistake was to have argued with Smuts. When Smuts had first inspected the Longido front Stewart had highlighted all the factors which made an advance on Moshi at the speed required by Smuts unviable, and he had requested a two-day start over the force advancing from the east if he were to attain that objective. Smuts had interpreted this as tantamount to insubordination, and it was from that moment that suspicions arose among

---

* After his dismissal Malleson went to London, where he took up residence in the Naval & Military Club for his defence against what he termed 'lying and scurrilous paper accounts [of his performance] from the Cape'. In 1918, with the rank of Major-General, he was sent by Military Intelligence on the 'Transcaspia Expedition', countering the Bolshevik penetration of Persia and Afghanistan. Once again he courted controversy: the huge cost of the expedition became a public scandal.

many British officers that none of the South African commanders appeared to have 'the slightest idea of the climatic and health difficulties [that confronted them], [nor] had they any experience of fighting in thick bush'.* Furthermore Smuts refused to contemplate that he might be faced with a protracted campaign, despite the fact that Smith-Dorrien had warned him of such a possibility and even some of his own Staff officers were of the opinion that 'campaigning in a country like this was going to be far more difficult than in German West'.[15] 'Cheer up boys, I'm going to work you hard for six weeks – and them',[16] was Smuts's straightforward, and arguably naïve, message to his troops at the start of the offensive.

Amid the recriminations there was still the question of what to do about von Lettow-Vorbeck's concentration around Kahe. If he was not evicted from his positions before the rains began in earnest his troops would be in a position to harry the British lines of communication and frustrate Smuts's preparations for a new offensive when the rains abated. It was therefore of 'vital importance ... for the enemy to be driven south of the [Ruwu] river',[17] and on 18 March Smuts ordered a further advance. He was warned by Pretorius, who after his service in the Rufiji delta was now Smuts's Chief Scout, that von Lettow-Vorbeck was prepared to make a stand at Kahe and had a *Königsberg* gun in his defences. Five days of heavy fighting ensued at places identifiable only by their most proximate feature – 'Masai Kraal', 'Store', 'Euphorbien Hill' and so forth – as the advance encountered stern resistance. Casualties ran as high as 300 men among the 29th Punjabis, 129th Baluchis and the 2nd South African Infantry Brigade, but on 21 March von Lettow-Vorbeck withdrew from his positions around Kahe; and the following night German troops abandoned the entire Ruwu line and began to retreat south-east through the dense bush flanking the Northern Railway.

Smuts was not sure how far south von Lettow-Vorbeck would retire, but correctly guessed that he would have to turn south from the Northern Railway at Mombo if he wanted to reach the Central Railway. On 23 March he reported to the War Office that his subsidiary operation had been 'a complete success',[18] despite the fierce resistance it had met, and the onset of the rains precluded any further advance for the time being. The pause in hostilities enabled Smuts to turn his attention to consolidating his lines of communication and to reorganising his forces. A new 1st Division included all the non-South African troops and 4/SAH, the sole 'British' unit among the South African mounted troops, and was placed under Tighe's command; while van Deventer and

---

* Meinertzhagen, p. 163. Stewart was equally struck by 'the very indifferent view that [many South African officers] took of the African and Indian soldiers. To them they were just "niggers" or "coolies"' (see Gurkha Museum/Stewart Papers/5RGR/Appxi/14 p. 64).

Oom – 'Uncle' – Coen Brits were promoted Major-General and were given the 2nd and 3rd Divisions respectively. (See Appendix Four.) Smuts did not tinker with Smith-Dorrien's headquarters appointees but rather circumvented them by appointing his own parallel staff. This included Brigadier-General Collyer as his Chief of Staff and, lower down the ranks, men like 'Tottie' Krige (his brother-in-law), Manie Botha (the Premier's son), and old comrades Piet van der Byl and Deneys Reitz (son of the former President of the Free State). Piet Pretorius was confirmed in his post as Chief Scout, having been recognised by Smuts as being 'completely fearless' and 'utterly ruthless',[19] and was destined to spend most of the rest of his war operating far behind German lines, engaging in his own 'Great Game' against a fellow Boer, Piet Nieuwenhuizen, von Lettow-Vorbeck's Chief Scout.

Just as Smuts began his sweeping reorganisation he was informed by the War Office that Tighe's services were required back in India (where he became Inspector of Infantry).[*] As Stewart and Malleson were departing at the same time, Smuts was keen to ensure that he was not tarred with the same brush. For almost a year Tighe had done all that could realistically have been expected of him under the most frustrating circumstances, and Smuts was fulsome in his praise of 'all the preliminary work done by General Tighe in the direction of organization and preparation for offensive measures'.[20] Tighe's command passed to the capable and highly respected pre-war Inspector-General of the King's African Rifles, Reginald Hoskins, rather than a South African, but there was no disguising the fact that Smuts's new command structure was more South African in character than the overall composition of the troops in East Africa. In addition to the 18,000 combat troops which had taken part in the March offensive, there were a further 9,000 Indian troops manning the lines of communication, and the total ration strength of Smuts's force at the end of the month amounted to 45,000. The message was clear: Smuts was intent on turning the handling of the campaign into a South African 'family affair' and expected South Africa to gain the lion's share of the credit for the victory which he was certain would soon be his. It was symptomatic of this development that the East African Mounted Rifles, the settler regiment which had proved so indispensable during the early months of the war, found so many of its men being removed for 'subsidiary duties connected with supply and transport'[21] that its strength was reduced to a single squadron; and after its horses had been requisitioned by South African mounted units it was an unmounted squadron. In time, as one of its officers put it, the regiment would 'like an old soldier' simply 'fade away'.[22]

---

[*] Tighe retired in 1920 with the rank of Lieutenant-General. Somewhat appropriately for a bustling commander who hated inaction, he died while running for a bus in 1925.

As early as 4 April Smuts, with optimism redolent of Belfield and Aitken, requested instructions from the War Office as to how conquered German East Africa was to be administered, although he rather cleverly expressed a concern that 'the conquest of German East Africa with my present forces is going to be a most formidable undertaking'.[23] Not all South Africans shared Smuts's overarching confidence. Captain A.J. Molloy, of 5/SAI, wrote home on 7 April, highlighting the 'points which struck [him] most forcibly':

1. That we have a lot to learn in the way of bush fighting from our black enemies, and that in spite of all talk to the contrary, we have found them an enemy to be fully reckoned with. He is resourceful, brave and well trained for this kind of fighting. I have heard he is a bad shot, but the casualties prove the opposite.
2. That the Germans can teach us something in the art of concealment and defence.
3. That this campaign has been an eye-opener to our German South-West warriors. They have seen more here in one day than occurred in the whole German South-West campaign.
4. That India can produce soldiers worthy of that name, who have maintained the best traditions of the British Army in German East Africa.
5. The KAR, a native regiment, have proved themselves to be excellent soldiers, and deserve every praise
6. That with trained troops, we would not have suffered half the casualties we did.[24]

Smuts may or may not have drawn similar conclusions at the end of March 1916. But even if he did he could not afford to dwell on what had gone, or might yet go, wrong: a rapid victory was vital not only for his own reputation but for the political stability of South Africa. Von Lettow-Vorbeck, on the other hand, had no such concerns. It was true that he had been forced to abandon the border with British East Africa but the casualties inflicted on his twenty-seven companies in the north-east were not unduly onerous and his force had executed a successful fighting withdrawal intact. Furthermore, he had long anticipated 'the possibility of the country through which the Northern Railway passed . . . falling into the hands of the enemy',[25] and had already moved his major supply depots and hospitals southwards in readiness for Smuts's next attempt to bring him to heel.

SEVENTEEN

Opsaal! Saddle-up!

———•———

Smuts was impatient to press on with his offensive, despite the gathering clouds and sweltering daytime heat which accompanied the onset of the rains. He knew that it was vital not to let von Lettow-Vorbeck's troops settle in the corridor either side of the Northern Railway. If that happened any advance along the 220-mile line towards Tanga would be bloodier than he could afford as it would traverse terrain that his opponent had had eighteen months to prepare. One German company – 5/SchK – was even lurking around Lake Jipe, within striking distance of Taveta; and with German artillery skilfully deployed in the Usambara and Pare Mountains on his left, not to mention strategic positions like Baumann's Hill on the plains to his right, the likelihood of sustaining huge casualties was so high as to be almost a certainty. It was not a prospect that Smuts relished, and he cast around for diversions that might improve his chances of clearing the Northern Railway with his forces relatively intact.

Smuts recognised that it would be impossible for any force advancing down the Northern Railway to encircle von Lettow-Vorbeck's units, or even to block their line of retreat towards the Central Railway. For the second time he briefly contemplated ordering landings in force from the sea – the strategy that von Lettow-Vorbeck most feared – but again dismissed this possibility, and that of dramatically speeding up the joint Anglo-Belgian advance in the west, as unfeasible at such short notice. The solution he chose instead was a very South African one – an outflanking manoeuvre to the west by van Deventer's mounted troops, followed by an advance up the Northern Railway as soon as the rains abated. This dual strategy had several advantages. Not only would it come as a surprise to von Lettow-Vorbeck, but it would also force him to decide whether to ignore van Deventer (and risk having the Central Railway seized at its midpoint by the South African mounted troops) or to meet the threat (at the cost of a depletion of his forces along, and south of, the Northern Railway). In theory it was a sound plan, which would certainly jeopardise any retreat by the German troops in the north-east along the Central Railway towards Tabora. But its successful execution relied heavily on the intelligence gleaned from 'loyal' Boers living in Arusha district that the rains were never as plentiful to the south and west of Kilimanjaro as they were to the east; and it was also based on the premise that German troops would only be able to counter van Deventer's move by using the Central Railway rather than crossing the wide and waterless tract of country known as the 'Masai Steppe'.

By the end of March Smuts had almost completed the concentration at Arusha of his new 2nd Division, the troops detailed for the flanking movement to the west.* He believed that he could rely implicitly on van Deventer, who had plenty of experience in executing the manoeuvre required of him, to carry the advance no matter what obstacles confronted him. Van Deventer was also lucky. Smuts knew that, van Deventer's men knew that, and luck was going to be needed in great quantities. His plan made British Staff officers at GHQ extremely nervous.

Van Deventer set off with his mounted troops and guns on 3 April, the infantry being ordered to follow as soon as it had completed mustering at Arusha. The first objective was Lol Kissale, a steep mountain with a six-mile circumference at its base which rose from the plains at a point some thirty-five miles south-west of Arusha. Captain Paul Rothert, a former officer of the 15th Infantry Regiment who had served with the *Schutztruppe* since 1907, held this isolated stronghold with 28/FK and sundry other troops – some 500 in all – and at dawn on 4 April he awoke to discover that one squadron of van Deventer's mounted troops had ridden fifty miles overnight to cut off his line of retreat to the south. Soon afterwards the main body of South African troops arrived, dismounting 3,000 yards away from Lol Kissale, and by 9.30 a.m. their guns were brought into action. It was the signal for van Deventer's men to begin their assault on the mountain, and in temperatures rising to as much as 120°F they scrapped their way upwards through the boulders and bush towards the German positions. The fighting lasted all day and by dawn on 5 April thirst had become a serious problem. The Germans, although Lol Kissale was now surrounded, held access to all water on the mountain and neither man nor beast among the attackers had watered since leaving Arusha. But van Deventer's luck held. When Rothert was injured, and was spirited away through the enemy cordon, command of the mountain fell to government secretary Alexander Herrgott who surrendered at dawn on 6 April. Seventeen Germans, 414 *askari* and two machine-guns were captured. Von Lettow-Vorbeck was not impressed when he heard the news, and concluded that Herrgott had 'not properly appreciated'[1] how dire the enemy's lack of water had become.

---

* The 2nd Division consisted of 1st SA Mounted Brigade (Manie Botha) and 3rd SA Infantry Brigade (Berrangé) with 2nd and 4th Batteries SAFA, 28th Mountain Battery, and 12th Howitzer Brigade.

Smuts regarded the speed with which van Deventer had advanced on, and taken, Lol Kissale as exactly what he had demanded – and failed to get – from Stewart; and he ordered him to press on immediately on Kondoa-Irangi, the strategic centre of the plateau rising to the west of the Masai Steppe. After Lol Kissale, however, von Lettow-Vorbeck knew exactly what Smuts was intending, and took rapid steps to ensure that van Deventer would neither take Kondoa-Irangi nor be able to proceed from there to cut the Central Railway. Three companies led by Captain Klinghardt were ordered to leave the Kivu front for Kondoa, a journey of almost 1,000 miles, while the 'good and well-tried'[2] 13/FK, veterans of Tanga and Jasin, were despatched from the Northern Railway on a forced march straight across the Masai Steppe to the same destination. Kondoa was 13/FK's peacetime garrison, and on 18 April Captain Peter Langen, the company commander, was able to report that his unit had successfully completed the 150-mile journey to Kondoa, across terrain thought by Smuts to be 'practically impassable to troops', in just ten days. While this remarkable feat was under way von Lettow-Vorbeck also began the withdrawal of fifteen full companies and two mounted companies from the Northern Railway to the Central Railway, whence they too would march on Kondoa to block van Deventer's advance. Major Kraut, who had organised the dogged defence of Salaita in February and of Latema-Reata in March, was left in charge of just eight companies with which to oppose Smuts's inevitable advance down the Northern Railway. Von Lettow-Vorbeck's redeployment was on a scale, and of an audacity, that Smuts had never contemplated. His hope, as it had been during the 'first phase' of Smuts's advance, was that he might have the opportunity to attack both British thrusts in succession. It was a strategy that, as the German commander admitted, 'involved some risk'; but it was a risk which he was convinced 'had to be run'.[3]

A South African motorcycle despatch rider, who had joined van Deventer at Lol Kissale, remembered the moment when his commander set his sights on the next objective. 'Ry kerels ry', van Deventer barked in Afrikaans – 'ride, boys, ride' – and 'off moved [the mounted troops] with the General himself and a roar of hoof-beats following'.[4] Four days later, on 12 April, they had reached the deserted German *boma* and mission station at Ufiome. From there they struggled on up to Pienaar's Heights, liberating 100 Boer farmers and their families from a prison camp, and then skirmished their way along the old slaving route across the Irangi plateau. The column was often above the clouds, winding its way through a dense forest with the Masai Steppe far below to the left; while to the right lay range upon range of hills as far as the eye could see. Next came a rapid descent into what was usually a sandy desert but was now a swamp; then a further ascent; and on 17 April, the day before Langen's arrival, van Deventer's advance troops were camped just six miles north of Kondoa. By then it was already obvious that Smuts's meteorological intelligence had let him down: rain was bucketing down intermittently and the whole district had been transformed into a quagmire. Had van Deventer started out a week – or even just days – later his troops would never have made it to Kondoa at all; as it was, he found himself almost completely cut off. All the way back down the line it was a similar story. In Voi, British East Africa's main supply depot for the front, Captain Routh was staggered by the spectacle of 'a storm of unprecedented violence' in which nearly seven inches of rain fell in three hours, leaving 'the Ordnance depot ... submerged by a muddy stream from two to three feet deep'; while in Arusha the rain even 'carried a box of axe heads weighing about one cwt some 60 yards'.[5] Van Deventer's luck had enabled him to reach his objective, but in such conditions the outlook for his stranded troops was decidedly bleak.

As Kondoa was a lot harder to defend than the hills overlooking it to the south, Langen's 400 troops evacuated the town the day after they arrived, having offered stern but only brief resistance to van Deventer's final push. Van Deventer's 'victory' was a combination of bravado and bluff: believing Kondoa to be defended by as many as 1,400 rifles, he ordered great fires lit along a broad front north of the town the night before the final advance. The aim was to deceive Langen as to the size of his force, but in the end the decisive factor, apart from the fifty casualties inflicted on 13/FK, was the presence of the eight guns of the 2nd and 4th South African Field Artillery, which had miraculously managed to keep up with the mounted troops despite regularly sinking up to their traces in the mud while crossing the Irangi plateau. Kondoa was exposed, as Langen well knew, and no place in which to be subjected to a bombardment; and to make it even less welcoming Langen torched the *boma* and huge quantities of supplies as his men streamed out of the town towards the Burungi Heights, five miles distant.

When van Deventer cast his eyes over the sandy mica-strewn ground of Kondoa, the Bubu stream running through it, and the smouldering wrecks of its buildings, he had good reason to feel some satisfaction in spite of the rain. His flanks were secure, there was little chance of anyone repeating Langen's feat of crossing the Masai Steppe now the rains had begun, and to the west 10/SAI and the 28th Mountain Battery had seen off an enemy detachment, 200-strong, holding Iraku Ridge and Fort Mbulu on the western scarp of the Rift Valley, eventually forcing it to retire all the way to Tabora. But in less than two weeks his mounted troops had been reduced in number from 1,200 to fewer than 600 as malaria and tsetse took its toll on man and beast; and, unable to advance any further, he now faced the unwelcome prospect of being subjected to an attack from the hills to the south. Among many senior British officers at GHQ the 'nerves' of early April turned to near-panic as the first ominous intelligence reports arrived indicating that fighting to the last on the Central Railway 'was not [von Lettow-Vorbeck's] idea and never had been'.[6] Instead he had moved in force to oppose van Deventer, and it appeared as though Smuts had delivered van Deventer straight into von Lettow-Vorbeck's hands.

For ten days over Easter, which fell on 23 April, the supply situation facing van Deventer became increasingly desperate. Some cattle were captured outside the town and twenty pigs were discovered in a pen, only to be deemed inedible after they consumed forty donkeys that were billeted with them for the night. A few undamaged comestibles were also rooted out among the ruins of Kondoa, but breakfast never consisted of anything more substantial than a piece of sugar cane or half a cup of rice (and was universally referred to as 'Broke Fast'). 'There was no question of starvation',[7] wrote one artillery officer; and had he known the extent of the ordeal being suffered by the stragglers still making their way to Kondoa his words might not have sounded quite so hollow.

In the early part of their 'Great Trek' from the Northern Railway the 2nd Division's infantry were cajoled into twenty-mile overnight marches. After passing Ufiome, however, they were reduced to covering a few miles a day along tracks that were submerged in a giant swamp. Rations were limited to a quarter, and the rain was so unrelenting that at night the men were unable even to light fires. Some were only saved from drowning in their sleep or being taken by lions by the intervention of attentive comrades; and by day many lay by the wayside nursing feet too sore to continue or shivering in the grips of fever, unprotected by greatcoat or blanket. An unholy stench hung permanently in the air, emanating from the carcases of horses, mules and oxen on which lions and hyaenas grew increasingly fat. For the survivors of this nightmare, the last half-mile up to the heights amid which Kondoa nestled was the worst, often taking as much as six hours as oxen were outspanned from wagons and men struggled in their place. On 30 April, however, the first dribs and drabs of General Berrangé's 3rd Infantry Brigade – 9/SAI, 11/SAI and 12/SAI – started to arrive, accompanied by a howitzer battery and the East African Volunteer Machine-gun Company. A private in 11/SAI described his comrades as a 'a discrepit band of haggard faced men, their tattered clothing hanging loosely on skinny frames'. Fewer than half of his company had completed the 'fearful' 250-mile trek and for them Kondoa, for all its shortcomings, was truly a 'cheerful sight'.[8]

The withdrawal of von Lettow-Vorbeck's troops from the Northern Railway did not run entirely smoothly either. There was only one track along which the fifteen infantry and two mounted companies could cover the 125 miles from Korogwe to Kimamba on the Central Railway and congestion was acute. Worse still, the Central Railway still seemed to be running to some sort of peacetime schedule, a deficiency for which Schnee was blamed by von Lettow-Vorbeck. But just as the South African infantry were arriving in desolate Kondoa the detachments led by von Kornatzki, Otto, Stemmermann and Colonel Heinrich Freiherr von Bock were finally completing their own arduous journey and, with supplies plentiful on the Central Railway, were in considerably better fighting condition than their opponents. Efficient lines of communication were set up by Major von Stuemer – the commander of Bukoba during its assault in 1915 – in spite of the teeming rain; and, greatly assisted by a brand new map of Kondoa-Irangi prepared by its administrator and left, when he departed the district, with a local chief for safekeeping, von Lettow-Vorbeck planned his attack in minutest detail. He began with daily bombardments from the Burungi Heights by two naval guns, one from the *Königsberg* and one landed by the blockade-runner *Kronborg*, in an attempt to 'soften up' the South African defences; and with so many troops deployed against him, van Deventer was forced to curtail his daily patrols south of the town. It was clear that the South African troops were about to face an attack on a much larger scale than had been anticipated, and one for which they were singularly ill-prepared. By 9 May all van Deventer's picquets had been pulled in and his men braced themselves as best they could around small hills along a five-mile defensive front.

At 4 p.m. on 9 May the German guns again began their 'Daily Hate', the stupendous noise of each boom reverberating around the hills that enclosed Kondoa. Only this time, at dusk, von Lettow-Vorbeck ordered his infantry down from the Burungi Heights. Lieutenant Martin Faure of 12/SAI had been as surprised as anyone to discover German naval guns deployed against Kondoa, and was relieved that he was 'not as scared as I thought I would be'. But as the full force of the German attack fell on the town he also thought 'once or twice how nice it would be to be lying in my bed at home'. Under the circumstances he was as snug as could be expected in the din of the night attack: 11/SAI and 12/SAI were well entrenched, and time after time the German *askari* threw themselves at the South African lines only to be beaten back. At about 10.30 p.m. von Lettow-Vorbeck changed tack, attempting an assault on the left flank. For 12/SAI 'everything was suddenly hustle and bustle' as they moved along the trenches to counter it. Major Humphrey of 11/SAI, his unlit pipe upside down in his mouth, stood directing the defence while his men 'shot it out', and as midnight approached, he declared during a brief lull: 'Boys, the moon is getting low, and they may want to charge again. I want you all to stand shoulder to shoulder and show that you are better than any soldiers born.' Twenty seconds later he was shot by a sniper. 'Dear old' Lieutenant Perks then rose to his feet, but to any soldier who did likewise he muttered 'Get down, you have no brains.'[9]

By 3 a.m. four full attacks on the South African lines had been repelled when silence finally fell on Kondoa. At dawn some sixty Germans and *askari* were found dead on the battlefield, many with empty bottles 'smelling of *dop*'[10] in their haversacks, and the figure rose during the day to eighty-five. The South African infantry had held firm, sustaining less than thirty casualties and earning five immediate MCs and 3 DCMs; and the crews of the eight South African 13-pdr guns had excelled themselves in the defence of the town.

The failure of the night attack was self-evidently a disaster for von Lettow-Vorbeck, who had personally accompanied the advance patrols down from the heights and satisfied himself that the low hills in front of Kondoa were unoccupied. What had, astonishingly, not been realised – even with the commanding view from the heights and the assistance of what he called his 'perfectly new and excellent map'[11] – was that a second line of small hillocks ran behind the first and it was along these that the South Africans were entrenched. Given that 13/FK had spearheaded the attack on what was their peacetime garrison the error was all the more inexplicable, and the roles of the 'First Salaita Show' had seemingly been reversed. Von Lettow-Vorbeck had detected the error at about 11 p.m. from the unexpected line of 'flashes . . . of rifles and machine guns' in the darkness and, as the wind shifted, the noise of stout defence. But by then it was too late to abort the attack.

Von Lettow-Vorbeck was not wont to flinch at a setback, but one can deduce that his disappointment was extreme from his unusually inaccurate statement about the cost of the error. He did not conceal the fact that von Bock, a retired infantryman who farmed near Arusha, had been severely wounded in the attack or that Friedrich von Kornatzki, one of his best officers, was dead. But in estimating his casualties at 'about fifty killed and wounded' out of an attacking force of 'about 400 rifles', he was being conservative on two counts. German casualties included at least 128 *dead*, as was alluded to in a German newspaper soon afterwards, and his claim that the attack was merely a probe does not ring true in the light of what happened next. His patrols no doubt did detect 'considerable bodies marching from Arusha', and he was absolutely right that Kondoa's defenders 'did not seem to be in great strength as yet': they numbered no more than 1,000 all told. But in concluding that any successful attack on them 'would have to be made over open ground against defences which with our few guns we could not sufficiently neutralise', that he was bound to 'suffer considerable and irreplaceable losses' in such an attack, and that he therefore 'decided to refrain from a general attack',[12] von Lettow-Vorbeck was being disingenuous (and commenting with the benefit of hindsight). His usually faultless intelligence and the familiarity of many senior German officers with the area had, after all, decided his shift of almost twenty companies to Kondoa-Irangi – an immensely complicated and risky manoeuvre executed at speed. And the South African force opposite him numbered no more than 600 rifles until the week before his opening attack. For von Lettow-Vorbeck to claim, as did one British Staff officer on his behalf, that he 'had made a miscalculation'[13] was equally disingenuous in the light of odds of about four to one in his favour. The mauling he received on that night of 9 May was a massive setback which completely derailed his well-laid plans.

The battle had been 'touch and go' for van Deventer, who throughout the night had kept 'his personal transport wagon inspanned and ready to flit'[14] (and had the attack been launched just three days earlier Smuts himself, on a morale-boosting visit to the 'discrepit' men at Kondoa, might have been captured). Van Deventer's legendary luck had held once again, but the stalemate now existing on his front was hardly the result that Smuts had wished for. In the ranks no one knew quite what to expect next, though there was jubilation on the morning of 10 May. That day an artillery duel occurred but the night was quiet. On 12 May 9/SAI and some mounted troops fought an engagement on the right flank, and the next day 12/SAI were ordered to prepare to attack, Lieutenant Faure wishing by now that he 'could get a good rest – this game is very trying as we get very little sleep'. At 11 a.m. the regiment evacuated its trenches and moved to attack German positions on the left flank frontally. 'Quite a decent bombardment' began and a detachment was sent out to draw fire, but with mounted troops baulking at a simultaneous attack on the German right the attack was cancelled at the last minute. This was fortunate for the South African troops. Similar probing manoeuvres continued over the next few days, by the end of which it seemed unlikely that von Lettow-Vorbeck would press again. By mid May Kondoa, and the whole of the Irangi plain, stank of rotting horse flesh; only 300 of van Deventer's force of 2,000 were fully fit (and even the fit were described as being 'none too bright');[15] the two brigade doctors had worked themselves into an early grave; and even after the first valiant carriers arrived on 14 May rations were one cup of flour, one cup of rice, and a little tea, sugar and salt per man per day.

Ten days later van Deventer's supply situation finally began to improve, though food would remain 'practically *non est*'[16] for some time to come, and much-needed reinforcements began to trickle in. As the rains eased a little, 7/SAI and 8/SAI covered the 120 miles from Arusha in twelve days, reaching Kondoa on 24 May (Empire Day), but the motorcyclists of Colonel Fairweather's South African Motor Cycle Corps still found it impossible to cross the Irangi plateau at an average speed any greater than 3 mph. However, on 31 May – Union Day – the troops received a huge morale boost when the first South African biplanes 'buzzed' Kondoa (a feat in itself, as the town was at an altitude that aviators on Europe's Western Front considered safe from anti-aircraft fire); and news arrived that the advance down the Northern Railway against Kraut's force had begun. A visit from the Bishop of Pretoria in early June was also well received, the more so as he described van Deventer's thrust at Kondoa as 'as fine a bit of work as has been done up here, and worthy to rank among the big marches of any previous campaign anywhere'.[17]

In truth, Kondoa had been a miraculous escape that could have temporarily ended Smuts's political career as surely as the Dardanelles had Churchill's; and it would be months before he could consider advancing against the Central Railway from Kondoa.

EIGHTEEN

The Advance down the Northern Railway

———•———

From his lookout post in the North Pare Mountains a young German sailor observed as Smuts's troops assembled for the advance down the Northern Railway. 'When I saw how strong they were,' he wrote, 'it made me feel quite sick: I could scarcely count the brutes.'[1] Von Lettow-Vorbeck's diversion of troops to Kondoa meant that Kraut had just nine companies at his disposal between Kahe and Tanga, no more than 1,750 troops in all.* But he had prepared every mile of ground for a fighting retreat, and nine guns, commanded by the indomitable explosives expert Werner Schönfeld, were deployed along the railway and in the hills to the north.

Smuts divided his force into three columns: Sheppard's to follow the Pangani River, Hannyngton's in the centre, and Fitzgerald's on the left – a total of about 7,500 rifles.† He was expecting stern resistance, which may have partly explained his decision to keep the battered 5/SAI and 7/SAI – the heroes of Latema-Reata – in reserve. But there was also mounting discontent among the South African infantry on this front. For two months they had been at a standstill in a 'fever belt' and, as many refused either to take quinine or use their mosquito nets, the toll had been great. In just two weeks in early April 2,000 South African troops had been admitted to the field hospital at Taveta, and even the ranks of the medical staff were decimated: at another hospital on the slopes of Kilimanjaro in mid April one in seven of the 172 patients were ambulance staff. British Army regulations were also experienced by the South African troops for the first time, and were hugely unpopular. Instead of

---

* German dispositions: 1/FK, 3/FK, 17/FK, 'W'/K, 5/SchK, 7/SchK facing the advance; 30/FK (von Heyden-Linden) at the Pangani River; 26/FK (Naumann) at Same; 17/FK (Kempner) at Tanga. See Boell (1), p.189.

† 'River Column' (Brigadier-General Sheppard): squadron 17th Cavalry, 2nd Rhodesia Regiment, 130th Baluchis, composite battalion of 2nd and 3rd Kashmir Rifles, No. 5 Battery SAFA, 27th Mountain Battery, double company 61st Pioneers; 'Centre Column' (Brigadier-General Hannyngton): 40th Pathans, EAMR detachment, 129th Baluchis, half-battalion 2nd Kashmir Rifles, Nos 6 and 7 Field Batteries, section EA Pioneers; 'Eastern Column' (Lieutenant-Colonel Fitzgerald): one company KAR MI; 3/KAR, one section 27th Mountain Battery.

being given extra fatigues as a punishment for misdemeanours, a trooper was liable to be tied to a tree for hours on end. For many, however, it was the 'jiggers' – fleas which burrow under the toenails to lay their eggs – that caused the greatest suffering during the lay-up and, together with the miseries of malaria, blackwater, and the impossibility of moving through the thick black cotton soil, led to the realisation that this was going to be 'pre-eminently a campaign against Nature'.[2]

On 18 May, two months after the capture of Kahe, Smuts's three columns resumed the offensive in the north-east. Three days later they crossed the Ruwu River largely unopposed, and by 29 May had advanced more than 100 miles through dense bush and in blistering heat. The capture of Mombo forced Kraut to turn south towards Handeni, using the specially constructed trolley-line that had for so long been a key link in the line of communication between the Northern and Central Railways, and the sole German company defending Tanga also withdrew southwards down the coast leaving the Northern Railway in British hands. But despite the loss of the railway German resistance stiffened the further south Kraut retreated. Soon fierce rearguard actions became commonplace, most notably at Mkalamo on 9 June, where the British and South African troops crossed the Pangani River; and at Kangata, where 5/SAI were ambushed on 20 June and sustained twenty per cent casualties (rendering the battalion inactive until October). By then Smuts's men were subsisting on two biscuits a day; had realised the extent to which the German *askari* 'barefooted, and therefore silent in the bush, was a dangerous opponent';[3] and had, as one trooper put it, 'met every animal except the jabberwok'.[4] Most serious of all, however, was the growing sick-list. Of the 1,500 troops for whom the 2nd South African Field Ambulance was responsible, one third were sick. The ranks of the 2nd Rhodesia Regiment and Driscoll's Frontiersmen were reduced by half; of the Indian battalions none mustered more than 350 rifles; and even the now 'seasoned' 2nd Loyal North Lancs had to be ordered to Cape Town for three months' recuperation.

The six-week advance, during which the three columns 'marched and fought, counter-marched and fought again'[5] almost continually, again showed that Smuts's strategy of executing 'long turning movements in the hope of encircling the enemy forces'[6] had not met with resounding success. But the offensive did at least end on a high note. On 24 June a German detachment at the Lukigura River was forced to fight by a sizeable mobile column led by Major-General Hoskins, and a bayonet charge by the Frontiersmen and the Kashmir Rifles secured a decisive victory. Thirty-four men of Captain Döring's three-company detachment were killed and more than fifty captured. Here Smuts finally called a halt, having advanced 250 miles in six weeks, while scouts reconnoitred for a suitable camp to the east of the Nguru Mountains.

It was time to let his lines of communication catch up, and for the troops – many of whom had suffered half a dozen bouts of malaria en route – to rest.

The supply situation remained dire. In April, in a staggering feat of engineering, the railway companies and sappers had managed to push a railway through from Taveta to Moshi just four days before supplies on the front line would have run out altogether, and the line had just managed to keep functioning through the rains. 'In one place,' an officer noted, 'the line went through a flat which the rains had turned into a swamp. The sleepers floated and had to be held in place till the rails were laid on them. After the first train had passed, the whole line disappeared beneath the mud, and soon the rails were as much as 6in out of level. The sight of a train creeping through what appeared to be a sea of mud, with every vehicle tilted to a different angle was not one easily forgotten.'[7] In April and May two more railway companies arrived from India to complete a railway battalion. They were sorely needed. A branch line was laid in the direction of Kondoa and the huge task of repairing the Northern Railway, wrecked by the retreating Germans, was begun even before the Royal Navy and land troops secured Tanga on 7 July – twenty months after the first ill-fated attempt – with a ferocious bombardment. The captured diary of Tanga's Chief Coastguard recorded its effects: 'our bombproof shelter proved ineffective and I, with several other people, found a drain for protection and the air was very stifling. 12-inch shells poured into the town for nine hours. All large and important buildings were wrecked. A shell fell right on my house, blowing all my belongings to glory. I last saw my bed go flying into the air having been driven straight through two stone walls. Such a fine bed too! It was a good job I was not lying in it.' The account concluded 'my God what savages these English are'.[8]

The capture of Tanga was a considerable boost to morale on board the ships of the blockading fleet. As one young officer wrote, 'to say that we were weary of wandering up and down the coast for nearly two years occasionally bombarding objects of offence would be a slight exaggeration for there is always some excitement to be had out of big gun firing, but the arrival of some shell coming at us [from Tanga] undoubtedly added a zest to the pastime'.[9] Just two weeks later the first train ran through Korogwe, and Botha had arrived from South Africa to assess Smuts's progress.

The Royal Navy's role in the capture of Tanga followed hard on the heels of an episode of which it was rather less proud (and which greatly augmented von Lettow-Vorbeck's ability to prolong his resistance to the Allied invasion of German East Africa). In late 1915, in response to a plea from Schnee smuggled out through Portuguese East Africa, Berlin decided to risk sending a second blockade-breaking ship to East Africa. *Sperrbrecher 15* was a veteran of twenty journeys out of Wilhelmshaven into the North Sea. Her Frisian skipper, Lieutenant Conrad Sorenson, and crew were therefore certainly experienced but a journey right out into the Atlantic, round the Cape and thence to a small bay in southern German East Africa was an altogether different proposition. Rechristened the *Marie*, the vessel left Hamburg on 16 January 1916 with instructions to maintain complete wireless silence for the whole voyage. Two months later, on 15 March, she steamed past the northern shores of Portuguese East Africa and made a mockery of the East African naval blockade by slipping into Sudi Bay, a small inlet on German East Africa's south coast, about halfway between Lindi and Mikindani. Her crew had no idea what sort of welcoming committee the shore might provide at this prearranged destination. They had heard no news for two months and the question on all their minds was whether British troops had already seized the south coast ports. As she neared the coast gunfire rang out, but a rapid exchange of signals with the shore soon established that the *Marie*'s voyage was not in vain.

Sudi Bay lay at the mouth of a small river. Its narrow entrance led directly inland for a short distance before dog-legging to port through a succession of sandbanks, and it was overlooked by German watchposts and two artillery positions; as an extra precaution mines were laid across the entrance by the *Marie*. Once inside the bay she became invisible to prying British ships, hidden on the seaward side by a wooded spit over the top of which only the very tips of her mast were visible from the Indian Ocean. It was a near-perfect hiding place for the time that it would take to unload her 1,500 tons of cargo. The crew were greeted on shore by elderly reservist Asmuth, who apologised profusely for mistaking the *Marie* for an enemy ship. The following day Lieutenant Hinrichs, formerly First Officer of the *Königsberg* and now District Commander in Lindi, arrived by bicycle to extend a formal welcome. He was accompanied by Captain Kaiser, a 'decidedly dashing and obviously highly respected officer', who immediately arranged for a huge consignment of fruit for the crew which 'tasted particularly good ... after the long sea trip'.

Kaiser and Sorenson quickly busied themselves planning the unloading operation, and in no time the normally tranquil bay became a hive of activity. There was no lifting equipment so floats were built from shore to ship and all around the steamer while carriers cut a path inland so that the cargo could be spirited away. One crew member, Knud Knudsen, marvelled at the scene as everyone 'set about hauling the guns one after another, the boxes one after the other, off board and onto the rafts; the Africans, some of them incredibly large and strong people, set to work and dragged everything via the connecting float onto land, where others took over from them and brought the loads to Sudi village via the newly constructed path'. Work continued for eight days and nights, and only when it was completed did everyone become aware just how much vital materiel the *Marie* carried. By the time she was fully emptied, ten days later, the excitement among crew, German officers and *askari* was almost uncontainable. In the village were four of the most modern 10.5cm howitzers, two 7.5cm mountain guns, 2,000 modern rifles, three million rounds of ammunition and some 50,000 porter loads prepacked with medicine, uniforms, food and equipment of every conceivable description (including 200kgs of precious quinine). 'One old African black NCO from a machine-gun regiment', Knudsen noticed, 'kept on going up to the beautiful, shining, new machine guns and stroking the barrels and laying himself down aiming with all of them. Others stood by the heavy howitzers and looked down the barrel to admire the interior.' 'It was certainly worth all the fuss,' was his resounding verdict; 'and if our brave brothers remain undefeated, and Smuts and his people gradually find less and less pleasure in this war in Africa, then my heart will laugh with joy and I'll say to myself: "We too contributed to that. We from the *Marie*!".'

Their task complete, the crew were given shore leave and their first taste of African life.

> We particularly liked going to Ssudi village in the evening [Knudsen wrote], where the carriers and the soldiers of the *Schutztruppe*, the *askari*, were camped. It made a very romantic picture. The actual village was only very small – a few huts, which were grouped around the open square in which the village wells were to be found. But around the village there was a beautiful and relatively high palm tree forest. The women had built tents for their husbands and were preparing the food over the fire. The men do nothing. They are simply warriors. Even when marching he takes only his rifle and his rucksack. Everything else is woman's work. She and the children carry the tent and the man's tools as they follow behind him.

As news of the *Marie* spread Germans flocked to the village to inspect the cargo and ascertain if there was any news from Europe. The crew, now celebrities, distributed magazines and newspapers from home which were eagerly devoured. But then HMS *Hyacinth* appeared offshore.

The state of the tide was instrumental in saving the *Marie*. As it was low the ship lay on her side, but she 'resembled a sieve' all the same having sustained five major, and over 100 minor, hits during *Hyacinth*'s bombardment. The engine room and boiler room were untouched, however, and after ten days of non-stop repair work the crew was satisfied that although she 'wouldn't be the prettiest of ships, at least she could sail'. On 11 April six British warships returned and in a further, three-hour bombardment fired in excess of 300 shells. On shore the *askari* were on standby to repel a landing from the whalers *Childers* and *Echo*, but none was attempted and the latter in particular received a severe mauling, being holed by three 4.1-inch shells. The Navy reckoned to have put at least six 6-inch shells into the *Marie*, but to the amazement of her crew an inspection showed that she had not been hit once. Casualties among the crew amounted to four men killed and four wounded. On 23 April she was ready to sail and under cover of darkness slipped out of Sudi Bay, turned north and steamed as close to the shore as possible to avoid presenting the Royal Navy's warships with a silhouette. Smoking was forbidden and when one African crew member lit up he was given 'such a slap by one of the mates that the cigarette flew straight out of his mouth and was no longer able to give away our position'.[10] Confronted by two very shallow areas, Hinrichs and Lieutenant Sprockhoff, formerly of the *Königsberg*, sailed ahead in a dhow and guided the *Marie* out into deeper water. By morning she was away, leaving the watching British ships behind and setting a course that after three weeks would bring her to safety in the neutral Dutch port of Batavia, in Java. Only Captain Roland von Kaltenborn-Stachau, an artillery expert sent by Berlin who had taken charge of von Lettow-Vorbeck's artillery during the battle for Kondoa, was left behind. Meanwhile the *Marie*'s precious cargo was already on its way to Dar-es-Salaam and other destinations around the colony on the shoulders of more than 100,000 carriers.

The resounding success of the *Marie*'s mission was a disastrous setback for the Allies. Her supplies and armaments were the last to reach German East Africa from Europe; thereafter von Lettow-Vorbeck's troops were to be wholly dependent on what they could grow and manufacture locally, or capture from the enemy. After the war von Lettow-Vorbeck was 'emphatic that [the Allies'] greatest defeat was [their] failure to destroy'[11] the *Marie* and the *Kronborg*, the first blockade-runner; and as he first heard of the former's arrival within days of establishing his new headquarters at New Steglitz Plantation, outside Kahe, the knowledge that her cargo would replenish his dwindling stocks of arms and materiel may well have been the catalyst for his ill-fated manoeuvre against Kondoa-Irangi. In addition, the *Marie* brought the Iron Cross, 1st and 2nd Class, for von Lettow-Vorbeck – the most encouraging forty-sixth birthday present he could have imagined.

NINETEEN

The Crescent Flag

—◆—

By the time the *Marie*'s cargo was deployed through German East Africa a further concern had begun to preoccupy British Intelligence officers in Whitehall and Egypt, and it was a concern which considerably increased the importance of the campaign against German East Africa. Early in the war Count Leon Ostrorog, a former Polish adviser to the Ottoman government who was said to have 'a more intimate knowledge of Mahomedan law than any man living', had warned the Foreign Office that he 'did not think it would be an exaggeration to assert that for Great Britain the most important fact at issue in the present world war is this position of Great Britain towards Islam';[1] and by 1916 Germany appeared confident of finding 'allies ... in Abyssinia and in Mohammedan freedom movements' who might not only bolster von Lettow-Vorbeck's position but also 'make the employment of black troops against our European frontiers impossible'. German East Africa had, in the eyes of many in Berlin, become the key to the 'balance of power in the East and in Africa'.[2]

The first reports that German agents were actively preaching a Holy War, and 'endeavouring to stir things up generally' in Portuguese East Africa, reached Lisbon in October 1915. Five Africans, bearing a 'Muslim flag'[3] and a large quantity of dynamite, had been caught en route to blow up the Portuguese frontier post at M'tengula. At much the same time a strong rumour began to circulate in German East Africa to the effect that a Muslim Abyssinian army, led by Ernst von Mecklenburg, had invaded Uganda. Meanwhile all German forts in East Africa were under strict instructions from Schnee to fly the crescent flag, and concern about a possible Muslim uprising in British East Africa grew daily.

The trigger for these concerns occurred in November 1914 when, just as the landings at Tanga failed, Turkey entered the war and proclaimed *jihad* against the Entente Powers. In British East Africa, the Aga Khan's instructions to his Ismaili followers were clear: 'the Mohammedan religion commands its adherents to be loyal to their sovereign and by this is meant the British Raj'; and even the Somali of British East Africa's province of Jubaland, on the border with

Italian Somaliland, declared an end to their 1913 *fitna* against the British and asked 'should not the Somali fight for the British also?'. A few months later, when some followers of the Mbaruk and el Mazrui slaving dynasties, in exile in German East Africa, were known to have joined the German 'Arab Corps', the Sultan of Zanzibar publicly denounced them for their hostility to 'our Good Friend and Protector, His Majesty King George V'.[4] Such signs of loyalty were reassuring, but they were local. General Wapshare, for one, was under no illusions that his orders to remain on the defensive in early 1915 were partly attributable to mounting unease about 'Muslim hordes', and that reinforcements would remain unavailable until 'Turkey [was] done for'.[5]

Turkey's support was central to Germany's strategy of *Drang nach Osten* ('the Drive to the East'), and as soon as the Ottoman Empire declared its allegiance German agents were sent eastwards to spread the word that the Kaiser had secretly become a Muslim, and to instigate a vigorous propaganda campaign publicising German victories on the Western Front. The result was just as intended – the ignition of a 'new and more sinister version of the old "Great Game"'[*] that had not so long ago pitted Britain against Russia in a contest for control of Central Asia. This time the 'Great Game' rapidly became not only more sinister but considerably more deadly: beginning in 1915, an estimated one and a half million 'infidel' Armenians died at the hands of Turkish and Kurdish soldiers when they were expelled to Syria and Mesopotamia. Although this horrifying spectacle was not an intended consequence of German policy, it demonstrated emphatically just how powerful a tool the Kaiser's Holy War, aimed at eclipsing British and Russian power in the Middle East, might become.

Tackling the Muslim threat in Central Asia was treated by the British as an absolute priority, of equal importance to holding the Western Front. If Britain lost its influence in a region considered to be 'the natural connecting link between the three continents of Europe, Asia and Africa',[6] then there could, quite simply, be no further resistance to Germany in Europe. By the middle of 1915 not only had the Indian military refused Kitchener any further troops for Europe, thereby forcing the War Office to increase its reliance on untrained British civilians, but internal security had become as big a concern as the defence of India's northern borders. Islamic militancy had grave implications for an army so dependent on Muslim recruits, and incidents like the desertion of Mahsuds and Mohmands of the 129th Punjabis and the mutiny in four companies of the 5th (Native) Light Infantry in Singapore – two regiments which were subsequently sent to East Africa – created a predicament that was

---

[*] See Hopkirk, p. 2; the efforts of Indian defence chiefs to counter the threat of German intrigues in Persia and Afghanistan are described as redolent of a game of 'hunt the slipper' by Hopkirk (p. 120) in his authoritative account of this 'Great Game', a not dissimilar predicament to that which would soon confront the Allies in their pursuit of von Lettow-Vorbeck.

regarded as truly 'the stuff of nightmares'.[7] Furthermore, a plot by Indian Nationalists and Sikh Ghadarites led by Ram Chandra to create an independent Punjabi state was only narrowly thwarted in February 1915, and demonstrated that the threat to India's internal security was not confined to Islamic revolutionaries.

Having lit the fire under 'the East', German attention firmly alighted on the possibilities for deploying its new 'weapon' in Africa. There can be no doubting the deadly intent of what the British regarded as the combination of 'Germany's evil counsels' and 'Turkish despotism'.[8] A *Reichskolonialamt* memo dated 29 December 1915 described it in the following terms:

> It is clear that the necessary requirements to instigate an insurgence are to be found in Sudan and also in the areas of Somalia that belong to British East Africa and in British Somalia. Such an uprising could, after initial success, take on a greater magnitude in Sudan and in any case could force the English to mobilise disproportionately large masses of troops to enter the area in order to suppress it ... If the insurgence of the Mohammedan tribes on the north, west and south borders of Abyssinia is successful the ... English will be forced to deploy considerable numbers of troops, which would mean both that the Egyptian troops would be weakened and the pressure on the German East African troops would be relieved ... The effect of these plans will become clearer if we begin acting them out immediately. We have the months of May or June 1916 in mind which would at the same time be when a comprehensive attack by the enemy on German East Africa would be most favourable for them.

Britain was not jumping at shadows.

Even at the height of the Anglo-South African war in 1900, many had warned that the rise of 'the Moslem menace' in the north of the continent was a far greater threat to the British Empire in the medium term than war in the south. By mid 1915 this Cassandra prophecy was proving correct: the greatest threat of all was to British security in Egypt and control of the Suez Canal. Just to the west of Egypt the Sanusi, an order of Sufis founded in 1837 whose adherents had waged guerrilla warfare against the Italians since the latters' defeat of the Turks in Cyrenaica in 1912, found themselves in an increasingly parlous position after the outbreak of war. Famine was rife, and after Italy's entry into the war the Allied blockade of the North African coast to safeguard Italian Cyrenaica prevented vital supplies from Turkey from reaching the Sanusi. Relations between the British and the Sanusi were initially 'cordial': Sayyid Ahmad, the Grand Sanusi, could not afford for them to be otherwise until he could be certain that his German and Turkish allies found the means with which to supply him. He did not have to wait long. Both

Enver Pasha, the Turkish Minister of War, and Kemal Atatürk had served with the Sanusi during their war with the Italians; and the continuing importance attached to the Sanusi by the Ottoman Empire was demonstrated when Enver Pasha sent his own brother, Nuri Bey, to assist Sayyid Ahmad. By mid September 1915 Nuri Bey and his fellow military adviser Jafar Pasha Al-Askari had ensured the despatch of a submarine bearing significant quantities of arms and ammunition to Port Sulaiman, and more successful blockade-breaking was to follow.*

It was obvious even to their twenty or so Ottoman advisers that the 'religious zeal' with which the Sanusi pursued the ensuing *jihad* against the British was rooted in their resolutely secular desire to mount a 'justifiable defence of their homelands, and to prevent themselves being treated like cattle by foreign invaders and having their lands and property expropriated'.[9] The Sanusi had refused to join the *jihad* of the Sudanese Mahdists against the British twenty-five years earlier; and their brand of Islam was very different from that of an Iraqi like Jafar or that of the other Ottomans in their camp. For their part, the Ottomans' aims were identical to those of von Lettow-Vorbeck further south: they sought 'to engage as many British troops as possible along a front extending all the way from the Mediterranean to the south of Darfur',[10] and, as was true of von Lettow-Vorbeck before Tanga, were 'only too conscious of the fragility of our situation, and pessimistic about our chances of achieving anything by our military operations'.[11]

The different and sometimes divergent views of the Sanusi and their Ottoman allies were reflected in vacillation on the part of Sayyid Ahmad. But finally he was 'persuaded' by his Ottoman advisers that offence was the only course of action open to him. In early 1916, 5,000 Sanusi tribesmen, the Ottoman military advisers, and the odd stranded German officer invaded Egypt from the west, and shockwaves spread throughout British north-east Africa. On the coast, the Egyptian border was some 300 miles from Alexandria; but the Sanusi stronghold around the oasis of Siwa, 160 miles inland, was just 100 miles west of the Nile. If that were threatened then British control of Egypt, and of the Suez Canal, was in jeopardy. Furthermore, Jafar Pasha's hope that other tribes living adjacent to, or in, British administered territories 'would join our forces [and] stage internal revolts'[12] was almost immediately fulfilled when Ali Dinar, the Sultan of Darfur in western Sudan, staged a simultaneous rebellion.

It was to South Africa – her 'agent' in Africa – that Britain turned for help in countering the Sanusi threat in the Western Desert, just as she had done in East Africa. As was also the case with East Africa, South African troops became

---

* Von Lettow-Vorbeck was aware of the Turkish-Sanusi alliance, and prospect of an imminent uprising against the British, as early as March 1915 (according to entries in his personal diary).

available after the surrender of German South-West Africa. But the 1st South African Infantry Brigade, comprising 5,648 men and 160 officers under Brigadier-General Lukin, were already in England awaiting deployment on the Western Front and had to be hurriedly shipped back to Africa to face the Sanusi. Lukin's troops began their campaign to reoccupy the territory overrun by the Sanusi just as Smuts was forging his way into German East Africa in March 1916. Both forces made use of new weaponry in the form of armoured cars and aircraft; both were operating in the most trying of conditions; and for both 'victory' hardly seemed an appropriate word to describe the capture of border posts as unprepossessing as Taveta and Solûm. Indeed, there were many in the South African ranks who considered that the deployment of over 30,000 of their countrymen in these two theatres of war, at a time when the need for trained men was as great as ever on the Western Front, was proof positive of the absurdity of war.

Lukin's troops, unlike Smuts's, were not detained for long. By the end of March 1916, having rapidly and efficiently secured Egypt's borders, they were once again on their way to Europe (where their numbers would be decimated at Delville Wood).* The Sanusi were not completely defeated, and the campaign dragged on in desultory fashion until pro-British Sayyid Idris succeeded his cousin Sayyid Ahmad as Grand Sanusi in 1917 and concluded a truce with the British and Italians. Meanwhile, in Darfur, Ali Dinar was defeated by the British 'Western Frontier Force' at Beringia and was killed in November 1916 near Juba. With Jafar Pasha persuaded by his British captors (and the hanging of Arab nationalists by the Turks in Damascus in May 1916) to change sides, Sayyid Idris so pro-British that in the next world war he would raise five battalions of Sanusi for the Allies, and the flight of Sayyid Ahmad to Turkey in a submarine, the situation appeared rather more stable. Unrest continued to simmer beneath the surface but, mercifully for the War Office, it was not until after the war that a nationalist revolt in Egypt secured nominal independence and, as it had done in 1916, triggered revolt in Sudan. In eastern Africa, however, concerns in the Colonial Office about 'the Mussulman problem' had reached as near fever pitch as was possible for its august officials. Indeed it threatened to dwarf the challenges already faced by the Allies in trying to bring von Lettow-Vorbeck's *Schutztruppe* to heel.

* Delville Wood was taken by Lukin's brigade on 15 July 1916. Three days later German artillery opened fire on them from three sides. During this ferocious bombardment it was estimated that seven shells fell per second, and that 20,000 shells fell on one square mile alone. The South Africans' orders were to hold the wood at all costs. On 20 July fewer than 159 men emerged from the wood out of almost 3,200 who had entered it. Including the wounded in the wood, there were just 755 survivors. By the end of the war the brigade had suffered casualties equal to three times their initial draft.

In British Somaliland, the Islamic threat came in Salihiyah rather than Sufi form (though the distinction was of secondary interest to those watching religious militancy spread like a virus towards British East Africa). Sayyid Mohammed Abdille Hassan, the 'Mad Mullah', was one of the longest-standing and most successful opponents of the British in Africa. A man described as possessing 'immense charisma, a master of desert and guerrilla warfare ... a man of cruel and merciless temperament indifferent to human suffering', the Sayyid had resisted European (and Abyssinian) encroachment into his domain since the late 1890s. In March 1914 forty of his Dervishes had ridden 150 miles to shoot up Berbera, the capital of British Somaliland, at dawn and cause total panic. In November the Somaliland Field Force, comprising a Camel Corps of 600 Somalis and 650 Indian troops, dislodged a substantial force from three forts at Shimber Berris only to have to return to do the job again in February 1915. With that the British Commissioner had pragmatically decided, given the limited resources at his command, to cordon off the Sayyid's 6,000 adherents in the east of the territory in the hope that most would either desert or be executed by their volatile leader. This is exactly what happened, but British prestige, indeed her very claims on Somaliland, were dependent on preventing further incursions into what was regarded as 'friendly' Somali territory and on containing 'unrest' in British East Africa's borderlands among tribes inspired by the 'Mad Mullah's' defiance.

The policy of containment was only partially successful. By 1916 it was not the 'Mad Mullah' who posed the greatest challenge to peace in north-eastern Africa, however, but events in Abyssinia. Seventeen-year-old Lij Iyasu had acceded to the imperial throne in 1913 following the death of his grandfather Menelik II and proceeded to drop a bombshell on his kingdom by allegedly announcing his conversion to Islam. There remains considerable uncertainty about whether this apostasy was genuine, and even if it took place. It was certainly a charge that clung to Lij Iyasu tenaciously as rivals sought to unseat him and, given the climate of general concern about Islamic-inspired threats, the charge itself was sufficient evidence of danger for British officials.[*] Lij Iyasu certainly had Muslim ancestry, and if he, as ruler of a population that was at least half Muslim, declared a *jihad* then the potential existed for the Horn of Africa and Sudan to be engulfed by a Muslim 'horde'. If that happened, then what was to stop the 'horde' moving southwards in support of von Lettow-Vorbeck? Such suspicions on the part of the British, and indeed the Italians, may sound fanciful in hindsight; but they were to prove well grounded.

---

[*] Braukämpfer (p. 54) asserts that Lij Iyasu's 'final conversion to the Muslim faith did not occur before 1916'.

Although remarkably little is known about Lij Iyasu – as if a polity which had been Christian since the fourth century later wished to erase an acutely embarrassing memory – his behaviour certainly became increasingly eccentric as the war went on. After his fellow Abyssinian potentates refused to crown him *Negus Negusti* (the 'King of Kings') Lij Iyasu had taken to wearing the dress of Abyssinian Muslims and was reputed to have displayed great enthusiasm for acquiring additional 'wives'. But in 1915 what might have been dismissed as a fit of pique on the part of a headstrong teenager began to assume the trappings of something more sinister: Lij Iyasu began spending most of his time in Harar and the Ogaden, in the Muslim east of the country, and even gave the order for the demolition of the Coptic church in Harar. 'Unstable and self-indulgent, ambitious yet lacking both the energy to achieve his ambitions and the personal magnetism or charm which would induce others to sacrifice themselves for him'[13] was the official verdict of the British Consul in southern Abyssinia on Lij Iyasu, coupled with disapproval of his 'devotion to Venus and Bacchus'.[14] But behind this dismissive 'school report' lay a genuine concern about Lij Iyasu's friendly overtures to the 'Mad Mullah' and rumours that German skulduggery was afoot in Addis Ababa, the Abyssinian capital since 1889.

The new capital, as the nexus of Abyssinia's assorted feudal warlords, was renowned for intrigue. Isolation was one key ingredient, as were unrelenting internal political rivalry and antipathy to any outside incursion into the empire's affairs. The effect was a replication of the bizarre and bewildering world of *Alice in Wonderland*. To an outsider, Addis was – and would remain – a 'politically watertight compartment, with distorting mirrors at every turn';* and the Abyssinian empire was an unwieldy agglomeration of disparate groups, the most powerful of which were still organised along resolutely feudal lines. But there were at least three constant determinants in the empire's labyrinthine history: a determination to preserve a high degree of territorial integrity and to combat any foreign control of its affairs, and the preservation of its Christian heritage. Such was the background against which the European colonial powers had for decades jockeyed for position.

Wilfred Thesiger, the British Minister, was a diplomat from the same mould as Errol MacDonell, his counterpart in Portuguese East Africa. Mindful of the possibility of severe unrest in Abyssinia following the death of Menelik II, he had sensibly incorporated various design features into his newly constructed official residence that were aimed at withstanding siege conditions. It was the

* R. Kaplan, *Surrender Or Starve* (Vintage Books, 2003), p. 32. In similar vein Edward Gibbon famously observed: 'encompassed by the enemies of their religion, the Ethiopians slept for near a thousand years, forgetful of the world by whom they were forgotten'.

marked improvement in Abyssinia's pre-war relations with Germany that most concerned Thesiger. Menelik II had once suggested that Germany might like to send a million German settlers to Abyssinia, an overture clearly aimed at counterbalancing Anglo-French influence in Abyssinia's neighbouring territories; and in 1902 consideration was given to a proposal by Karl Inger, an Austro-Hungarian convert to Islam who styled himself Emir Abdullahi Ibn Suleyman Inger, to set up his own sultanate in the Somali-Danakil borderlands of eastern Abyssinia. With Menelik having also declared his intention to 'restore the ancient frontiers of Ethiopia as far as Khartum and Lake Nyanza',[15] both well inside British Africa, the prospects for Germany's most daring attempt to stir up a *jihad* were, on the face of it, not entirely inauspicious; and Britain had to bear in mind that Abyssinia could field over 100,000 armed men, as it had done less than two decades earlier when Menelik II had routed the Italians at Adua (inflicting over 11,000 casualties in the process). With the Ottomans in control of the entire Arabian Peninsula opposite the Horn of Africa except the Aden Protectorate, Abyssinia was most certainly not a power that Britain wished to see as a new and islamicised enemy dancing to a German tune.

The man approved by the German General Staff to foment unrest in Abyssinia was Leo Frobenius, a prominent rather than eminent African scholar (and personal friend of the Kaiser) of whom Britain was intensely suspicious. In pre-war years, Frobenius had been labelled 'a thieving scoundrel'[16] in Whitehall for having removed important artefacts from West African chiefs during an expedition, and although he had agreed to return them after an official enquiry into his conduct he was thereafter branded as 'one of those scientific Germans to whom the word "Hun" can be applied without controversy'.[17] The plan was for Frobenius to carry top-secret documents to the German Legation in Addis Ababa ordering von Syburg, the German Consul, 'to [incite] the Abyssinians to invade Anglo-Egyptian Sudan and to annex territories in the Blue Nile region'.[18] Von Syburg was also authorised to contact the 'Mad Mullah' in Somaliland and encourage him to pursue further insurrection against the British. In Cairo, Allied Intelligence were quickly on to the 'Frobenius Mission' and urged 'the extreme importance of preventing this mission from reaching Abyssinia where they will find a fertile soil for the sowing of intrigues and will almost inevitably raise serious trouble in the Sudan and East Africa'.[19] Ras Mikael, standing in for the absent Lij Iyasu, appeared to be 'not very anxious for the arrival of the mission'. But Thesiger was far from sure where the real sympathies of Abyssinia's elite now lay; and he agreed wholeheartedly with the view of British Intelligence that Frobenius be sent home the minute he arrived in the Horn without being given 'any opportunity of observing the [Suez] Canal's defences'.[20]

After many travails en route from Istanbul, the five Europeans and thirteen Turks and Arabs of Frobenius's 'Fourth German Inner-African Research Expedition' were duly thwarted in their mission by Anglo-Italian vigilance. The Italian authorities in Eritrea were particularly suspicious of 'scientific' expeditions emanating from Germany, and forbade Frobenius from proceeding any further than Asmara, Eritrea's highland capital. Frobenius had no choice but to head back to Germany,[*] and was put on the British Colonial Office's blacklist for being a man 'whose reputation for decent behaviour seems to be as second-rate as his scientific reputation'.[21] But one of his party, Solomon Hall, the son of a German missionary and an Ethiopian mother, made another attempt to reach Abyssinia later in 1915 'carrying secret documents on his body by a special device'.[22] Once again he was intercepted by the Italians in Eritrea and languished in prison there for three years, to the great relief of British Intelligence and Wilfred Thesiger at the British Legation in Addis Ababa. Somehow the 'documents' did reach Addis Ababa by October, because a reply from von Syburg was received in Berlin in March 1916 indicating that Lij Iyasu was making 'military preparations' and had even agreed to destroy Italian wireless stations in Asmara and Massawa, in Italian Eritrea, and Mogadishu, in Italian Somaliland.[23]

In Berlin, the *Reichskolonialamt* remained adamant that 'in the interest of relief of German East Africa an insurrection in the Sudan is very important and urgent',[24] and its hopes of unleashing a *jihad* in East Africa received a colossal boost when General Townshend's army, 10,000-strong, was forced to surrender after a five-month siege to the Turks at Kut, in Mesopotamia, in April 1916. Kut was a disastrous setback for the British attempt to counter 'the Mussulman problem'. In trying to relieve Townshend, the Allies incurred 21,000 casualties; more importantly, the plan to capture Baghdad as a crucial counter to German pro-Islamic posturing lay in ruins. In East Africa the outlook was once again decidedly bleak after the initial success in stymieing German scheming. As one official put it, Kut had 'queered the local pitch pretty badly'.[25]

But just at the moment when Lij Iyasu, Berlin's 'trump card' in the Horn of Africa, might have fulfilled German hopes he was to prove their undoing. Powerful forces, both religious and secular, began gathering in the Abyssinian Highlands (from which Iyasu was increasingly and conspicuously absent). The religious duality of his flirtation with Islam and foreigners may have been

---

[*] The opportunism of Frobenius's mission to secure Abyssinian assistance in eastern Africa was highlighted when, after the war, he published *Der Völkerzirkus unserer Feinde* ('The people's circus of our enemies'), in which he mocked the Allies' use of black soldiers, portraying the latter as circus animals. See Jan Nederveen Pieterse, *White on Black: Images of Africa and Blacks in Western Popular Culture* (Yale University Press, 1992).

reminiscent of Emperor Dawit II's close ties with the Portuguese and 'western' Christianity in the sixteenth century (which were aimed at countering Islamic incursions), or Emperor Fasilidas's with Islam in the seventeenth century (which were aimed at countering Portuguese and Jesuit influence). But by 1916 those who saw him as having overstepped the mark were in the ascendant. To them Lij Iyasu was not engaging in some delicate balancing act between foreign powers for the good of Abyssinia, but invoking the enduring and horrific memories of its abasement at the hands of the Muslim 'Galla hordes' of Ahmed Gragn four centuries earlier – an event which 'went down in the collective awareness of the [Abyssinians] as the single most traumatic event in their history'.[26] The nemesis of German machinations was therefore a seemingly naïve miscalculation: to highland Abyssinians any 'campaign to Arabize the Muslims of the Horn', whom they regarded as their 'inferiors', was 'tantamount to an effort to destroy their country'.[27]

In August 1916, it was widely believed that Lij Iyasu was about to launch his joint Abyssinian-Dervish invasion of Somaliland (and marry the Sayyid's daughter). Britain, France and – somewhat incongruously – Germany reacted to the rumours by sending a message of protest to the Abyssinian government. A revolution in Addis Ababa ensued, an occurrence which is generally regarded as having been 'a direct result of the combined Turkish-German attempt to get Ethiopia on their side',[28] and Lij Iyasu was deposed *in absentia*. After an inconclusive initial battle, Shoan 'loyalists' decisively defeated Iyasu's father at Sagale on 27 October – a battle in which more than 100,000 men were involved – and Menelik's daughter Zauditu was crowned Empress. Neither Germany nor Turkey was represented at the coronation. Zauditu's twenty-four-year-old cousin, Ras Tafari Makonnen (later Haile Selassie) was nominated as her successor.

Iyasu, who had never been formally crowned, was excommunicated by the Coptic Church. He avoided capture in the eastern lowlands until 1921 but German hopes that he might seize back the throne, or that at the very least Ras Tafari Makonnen would be unable to establish a strong government, came to naught. As was its wont, Abyssinia – which had been notably successful in maintaining its independence while the rest of the continent succumbed to European colonisation, and whose feudal rulers were not chary of approaching internal affairs with a brutality matching that of the worst excesses of European colonialism – then turned back in on itself. Ras Tafari Makonnen performed a skilful balancing act, not wishing to commit Abyssinia one way or the other, especially while the war in Europe still raged on into 1917, the Allies' so-called 'year of crises' . But with a Christian back on the imperial throne the greatest potential threat to the flanks of British East Africa finally started to recede.

'All's well that ends well'[29] was the phlegmatic verdict of the British Consul to southern Abyssinia when Lij Iyasu was toppled. While this may have seemed a correct judgement of the situation in his own parish, British Intelligence did not rest on its laurels even after the 1916 Arab Revolt against Ottoman suzerainty which pitted Muslim against Muslim. Lij Iyasu, the Sayyid, the Sultan of Darfur and the Sanusi had caused considerable embarrassment and the neutralisation of each threat had required considerable ingenuity on the part both of local officials and of Brigadier-General Gilbert Clayton's Arab Bureau in Khartoum. There was no way of determining the exact mix of religious zeal and other factors, both internal and external, that had provoked the various *jihad*s. What was certain was the gravity of the threat and the realisation that it was necessary 'to take steps to counteract a Mohammedan proselytising movement before it can actually take place'.[30] As evidence of this new proactive approach, the British Minister in Somaliland even resorted to despatching a group of Somali elders to Egypt in 1916 in order to impress them with 'the full might of the British Empire'[31] in the form of warships, railways and POW camps packed with German and Turkish soldiers.

In East Africa, though it was realised that 'a Turkish *jehad*' had not caught on, 'an African *jehad*' remained, in the eyes of British Intelligence, 'not an improbability'; and the 'chief danger zone in this respect' was thought to be German East Africa, where the war had created fertile ground for 'a conjunction of Islamic propaganda with the cry of "Africa for the African"'.[32] The old Arab slaving routes inland from the coast had brought about much greater Islamic influence in German East Africa than was the case with its neighbours, a fact of which the Germans were well aware. A marked surge in 'the Islamic spirit' had followed the Maji-Maji Rebellion, with many former *askari* to the fore as active participants and propagandists; and the 'Makka Letter Affair' of 1908, centred on the rumoured discovery of a powerful and apocalyptic text at Medina, had caused huge disquiet among the colony's coastal population (not to mention their colonial administrators).[33] It was therefore unsurprising that the outbreak of war between the Ottoman Empire and the Allies had caused an equally huge stir. The diary of a missionary of the White Fathers in Ruanda, Père Lecoindre, records just how far this penetrated. On 11 January 1915 he visited Kigali and found 'the Muslims, excited by the news of the Holy War, [pleading] for news of it at the *boma*'. A week later, a German official visited his mission and seemed 'preoccupied by the excitement of the Muslims, provoked by the rumours of the Holy War'. And two days after that, Lecoindre noticed 'a great hubbub among the Muslims during the night'. That night 'the moon refused to go down and stayed red'; and there was 'fire in the direction of Bugesera'. But, symptomatic of the different reactions of Muslims throughout the Islamic world, many took this to be 'a sign that Allah is displeased with the [Ruandan] sultan who is allied to the Germans';[34] and the authorities responded by giving each *askari* an immediate bonus, and further money to buy *pombe* and meat (ostensibly to celebrate the Kaiser's birthday on 27 January). It would therefore seem that it was not only the British who were alarmed at the potential of the Islamic 'powder-keg', and that Schnee's decision to fly the crescent flag above all German *bomas* was prompted as much by fear as opportunism.

An astonishing German circular fell into British hands when Moshi was captured in March 1916, providing not only further evidence of Schnee's disquiet but a valuable piece of propaganda for the British campaign to 'counteract' the rise of any enmity on the part of East African Muslims. Addressed by Schnee to his district commissioners, the circular read:

> To all stations. You are requested to send out within three months from the date of receipt a report stating what can be done by means of Government servants and teachers to counteract the spread of Islamic propaganda. Do you consider that it is possible to make regulations prohibiting Islam altogether? ... German experts recommend the encouragement of pig-breeding among the natives as an effective means of preventing the spread of Islam in German East Africa. You must consider this point also.

By May 1916 the circular had been distributed by the Allies throughout the Islamic world, although its effect was not wholly as desired. In Egypt, Cairenes considered its contents so outrageous that it was suspected of being 'a pure invention of British diplomacy'; while in East Africa its publication was said 'to have fallen rather flat'.[35] In fact the document was considered genuine enough by many – it was publicly denounced in September 1916 in Mombasa by the Mullah of Moshi himself at a *baraza* attended by more than 5,000 Muslims – and its importance lies not so much in the preposterous questions it raised but in what it reveals about German naïvety in seeking to foster the 'Holy War' against the Allies. Islam was not a monolithic religion to be deployed as the Kaiser and his servants saw fit; and the grievances of Muslims were as heterogeneous as those of disparate peoples anywhere. This is not to say that the threat to Britain was illusory, and could have been dismissed out of hand. It was real enough. But Germany's 'evil counsels' simply lacked the finesse which might have guaranteed a more widespread, momentous and threatening *jihad* in Africa. Instead, as von Lettow-Vorbeck battled his way southwards, the cloak-and-dagger initiatives of Berlin and Istanbul could offer him no immediate encouragement.

TWENTY

'The Cannibals'

———◆———

Allied troops in the field in East Africa were rather more concerned with the German, rather than 'Mussulman', enemy in 1916, and the week after van Deventer reached Kondoa in mid April the Belgian advance into Ruanda finally began, in torrential rain. Control of Lake Kivu had already been secured with the capture of Kwidjwi Island; and the arrival of more than 7,000 carriers from Uganda and Major Grogan's 100 ox-carts provided the necessary transport for the Belgian troops from Kivu district demanded by General Tombeur.

The first priority was to outmanoeuvre Captain Max Wintgens from his base at Kissenyi. For almost two years Wintgens had been a major thorn in the side of the Belgians and the approach to Kissenyi, through the volcanic Mfumbiro region, had proved the undoing of many a Belgian patrol. But in mid April von Lettow-Vorbeck had withdrawn three companies from Ruanda for the attack on van Deventer at Kondoa, leaving Wintgens with insufficient troops with which to continue his stubborn opposition to the Belgians.[*] Colonel Molitor entered Ruanda from the north, crossing the belt of open country south of Lutobo and pushed straight for Kigali, the Ruandan capital. To the west, Major Rouling's guns opened fire from the Sebea River to keep Wintgens's men tied down in their mountain posts overlooking the river. South of Lake Kivu the Rusisi River, with its precipitous mountain backdrop, was in spate. Two battalions under Major Olsen, Tombeur's former *chef militaire* in Katanga who had so ably assisted with the defence of Northern Rhodesia, demonstrated on the river, while Major Muller's 1st Regiment forced its way across the Rusisi just south of Lake Kivu and established a bridgehead at Shangugu. On 3 May Muller turned north-east towards Kigali, taking the

---

[*] German troop dispositions in the far west and north-west were as follows: in Ruanda, three companies under Captain Wintgens (26/FK, Ruanda 'A' and 'B' companies) – fifty-five Europeans, 600 *askari* with five machine-guns and three artillery pieces; in Urundi, Major von Langenn-Steinkeller's *Abteilung* (thirty-six Europeans, 250 *askari*, 100 levies, with three machine-guns and two artillery pieces); in Kigoma, two companies under Captain Zimmer (145 Europeans and 165 *askari* with one machine-gun and nine artillery pieces).

capital two weeks later, and by 21 May the Belgian troops had cleared Ruanda of enemy troops and Chief Musinga submitted to the new colonial power in his land.

The only disappointment was that the appalling weather conditions had enabled Wintgens's force of fifty-five Germans and 600 *askari* to slip the Belgian noose. In June the same happened in Urundi where Major von Langenn-Steinkeller with thirty-six Germans and 250 *askari* evaded capture by Muller. Kitega, Urundi's capital, was occupied on 17 June. But Muller then had to halt for three weeks in order to resupply and recruit sufficient porters for a resumption of his advance. His regiment had only 600 regular porters – fewer than one per *askari* – and three-quarters of them were already sick by the time he had crossed the Rusisi.

When the Belgians were ready to move again, their next objective was to roll up the Germans between Ruanda and Bukoba, on Lake Victoria. Smuts failed to understand why the Belgians had to halt at all after their capture of Ruanda and Urundi, and was frustrated that they had not reached the south-west corner of Lake Victoria a month earlier. If they had set out before the rains, as Smuts had requested, this would have been achievable – but in the absence of transport Smuts's expectations were unrealistic. A week-long naval operation at the end of April had, however, kept Captain Eberhard Gudowius's troops in Bukoba occupied. On the 28th a feint landing was carried out by the 98th Infantry on board *Winifred* and *Nyanza*, followed by a similar feint at Namirembe Bay and the intermittent bombardment of German positions on the western shore of Lake Victoria. These certainly prevented Gudowius from moving troops to assist Wintgens and von Langenn-Steinkeller, but it was not until 9 June that Colonel Adye, commanding the British 'Lake Force', was able to order troops to cross the Kagera line in an attempt to capture Bukoba and drive the German garrison onto the advancing Belgians.

It is doubtful that Gudowius ever even contemplated sending troops towards Ruanda and Urundi. After a disastrous foray across the Kagera line in February which had resulted in the deaths of four Germans and fifty-three *askari*, the Bukoba garrison was very much on the defensive. Furthermore, as Belgian and British troops edged closer to Lake Victoria, the more it became apparent that the enemy had no intention of trying to maintain a foothold in the north-west corner of their colony. Their aim was to retire first on Mwanza and then on Tabora, causing as much discomfort to their pursuers as they could. In the second week of June the Lake Victoria fleet landed Colonel Adye on Ukerewe Island, off Mwanza, at the head of a combined force of 4/KAR, Baganda Rifles, 98th Infantry and Major Drought's 'Skin Corps' (Nandi Scouts who wore little clothing), and met with scant resistance. Eight Germans, two guns and an extraordinary home-crafted torpedo canoe were captured. Then, on 23 June, Gudowius abandoned Bukoba and led his troops southwards. The only real 'prize' from these operations was the capture of the huge rice crop, the staple diet of von Lettow-Vorbeck's Wasukuma *askari*, on Ukerewe Island.

Smuts's principal concern about Anglo-Belgian co-operation remained more political than military. In his opinion, and that of many in Whitehall, it was no coincidence that the Belgian advance had begun in the very week that France followed Britain's lead, given in January, and agreed that 'Belgian colonial rule of the Congo would not be sacrificed in a peace settlement [with Germany]'.[1] Belgium was boxing clever, and much though Smuts needed the Belgians to converge on the Central Railway from the west, he remained wary of their ambitions and did not want them to gain so much as a toehold on Lake Victoria. Belgium already occupied fertile Ruanda and Urundi, the most populous districts of German East Africa, and if they reached the southern shore of the lake before British troops he suspected they might also lay claim to the 6,000 square miles of Karagwe district, to the west of Bukoba, in any post-war settlement. The thought of Belgium straddling a British 'Cape-to-Cairo' corridor was anathema to Smuts, and on 18 June he appointed Charles Crewe, an old political confidant who was the proprietor of South Africa's *Daily Despatch*, to take command of the lake operations and protect British (and South African) strategic interests.[*]

By the time Crewe took command there was, in fact, nothing he could do to stop the Belgians reaching the south-west corner of Lake Victoria first. When they resumed their advance they did so at speed. Major Huyghé's column of the *Brigade Nord* made the 120-mile trek from Kigali to Biaramulo in two weeks, effecting perilous crossings of both the Kagera and Ruvuvu Rivers, sidestepping Wintgens, and struggling through a bush fire on the utterly desolate plains of lower Karagwe en route. To the south Major Rouling pushed westwards equally quickly to converge with Huyghé. On 24 June Biaramulo was occupied by the Belgians and six days later their advance guard reached Namirembe Bay to hoist the Belgian flag on Lake Victoria. The first British troops only arrived there three days later but, to Crewe's relief, the Belgians withdrew back to Biaramulo, a few miles inland, leaving Lake Victoria to the British. Considering all the criticism that Smuts had thrown at Tombeur for not advancing fast enough, it was a gesture of considerable goodwill.

For a week after the Belgians reached Biaramulo it was unclear whether

---

[*] Belgian concerns about its ally's intention were seemingly as justified as vice versa. On 8 February 1916 Colonel House, Woodrow Wilson's closest confidant, had informed King Albert that 'England and France would accept the idea of a vast German colony made up of Belgian, Portuguese and other countries' possessions to the north of South Africa' in return for a US-brokered peace agreement in Europe. Albert was said to be 'profoundly offended' by the suggestion. (See Leonard P. Ayres, *The War with Germany* (Washington, 1919), *passim*.)

Gudowius's 800 troops were still to the north or whether they had slipped round the lake to reinforce Mwanza. On 3 July, however, Major Rouling's detachment at Kato, twenty miles from the south-western corner of Lake Victoria, discovered his whereabouts. During a vicious close-quarters engagement lasting over two hours Gudowius's main force, 300-strong, inflicted substantial casualties on Rouling's. Rouling himself was shot five times, once through the face. But his troops carried the day. Gudowius, thirteen Germans, and his field hospital were captured and most of his troops were rounded up in the next few days. It was an exemplary *coup de filet*. Rouling had achieved something that few other Allied commanders would in the campaign: he had succeeded in confronting and destroying his enemy before he could slip away. Even von Lettow-Vorbeck tacitly recognised this feat, by commenting that 'the engagement went badly for us and cost us heavy losses';[2] and the Belgians scored another success by capturing a detachment led by Captain Zimmerman while it was endeavouring to collect his wife from Katoke Mission.

On 7 July a Belgian patrol also ascertained the whereabouts of Wintgens and von Langenn-Steinkeller. They had taken up positions centred on the Mariahilf Mission, on high ground to the south, where they ignored an order from von Lettow-Vorbeck to attack Biaramulo as being no longer practicable but prepared to block any further Belgian or British advance in the direction of Tabora. On 14 July, Huyghé finally attacked them at Diobahika with five battalions, and a battle raged for thirty-six hours before both sides withdrew. That same day, 2,000 British troops converged cautiously on Mwanza.[*] It was deemed unwise to attempt a landing from the lake because of the presence in the port of a *Königsberg* gun and the likelihood of the harbour being mined. But the approach from the landward side was also fraught with problems: Mwanza was surrounded by hills whose passes were all perfect for setting ambushes. Fortunately, Captain Udo von Chappuis's garrison, 600-strong, had overestimated the size of the approaching British force, and was unnerved by the possibility of a simultaneous attack by the Belgians. When the first British troops reached the outskirts of the port it was found to have been abandoned. Some had escaped down the Tabora road, others by small craft; the wireless transmitter had been blown up and the *Königsberg* gun disabled. Although Lake Victoria was now clear of Germans, a great opportunity had been lost partly through Crewe's caution and partly through his failure to send sufficient troops south to block the road from Mwanza to Tabora.

* 'Lake Force' was split between Namirembe Bay and Ukerewe Island and consisted of: 98th Infantry (three officers and 200 other ranks), 4/KAR (twenty-seven officers and 730 other ranks), Uganda Police Service Battalion (eleven officers and 400 other ranks), Baganda Rifles (ten officers and 350 other ranks), and the Nandi Scouts (seven officers and 230 other ranks).

The Times wrote that 'nothing in the East African campaign has been so encouraging as the triumphal advance of the Belgian columns before whom the Germans bowed their heads; it augurs well for future developments in Europe'.[3] The South African press also conceded that 'it was something like poetic justice that Belgium, which had been so cruelly treated by Germany in Europe, should have the opportunity of taking part in the conquest of the bully's pet colony'; and King Albert personally congratulated Tombeur on his 'brilliant feat of arms'.[4] But the plaudits masked a deepening antipathy between the Belgian and South African High Commands. On the one hand, there could be no denying that the Belgian *askari* had lived up to their reputation as exceptional soldiers who would be more than useful in clearing western German East Africa of enemy troops. On the other hand, even General Wahle, commanding the *Westtruppen* from Tabora, was under no illusions that Smuts 'wanted to vanquish the colony [himself] and have no accomplices'.[5]

A heated propaganda battle ensued between Belgium and Britain – one that would last longer than the war itself. The Belgian *askari* were accused of 'stealing everything, from women to cattle and poultry', and of 'cannibalism'; while their officers were charged with being 'brutal in their treatment of [their] African soldiers'[6] and the Ugandan porters provided by the British. Crewe maintained that the Belgian troops' predilection for 'wholesale ravage, theft and rape is so serious a matter that it is certain to become known in Europe with what effect I leave others to judge'.[7] The Belgians vigorously denied all such allegations. 'During the whole campaign, not a single woman was the object of outrages', was the official line, coupled with assertions that although the troops had largely had to live off the land they had always paid for the food they needed. The *Étoile du Congo* trumpeted that 'white and black, each outrivalled the other in spirit and endurance'.[8]

So politically charged was the Anglo-Belgian operation in German East Africa that the truth would never be unearthed. British missionaries secured testimonies that suited their own expansionist ambitions, British politicians recalled Leopold's colonial regime as proof of Belgium's unfitness to be a colonial power, Belgians reacted indignantly to every accusation. Few sources were untarnished, but arguably the most plausible are the records of the 'neutral' White Fathers' Missions in Ruanda, Urundi and north-west German East Africa. They attest to the widespread fear among local populations as the Belgians advanced, and to their *askari*'s propensity to appropriate all food and anything else not bolted down. At Marienthal, they took all Frau Hammerstein's lingerie, part of her *literie*, and her *vaisselle*; and they behaved 'very grossly' towards Father Martin for protecting an African girl. But rumours that Frau Hammerstein's children had been 'hurled on the ground and cruelly killed' were manifestly untrue, and the mission's diary rejects the possibility that Belgian 'discipline could be so lax'.[9] A civilian commandant was *in situ* in Kigali within one week of the arrival of the Belgians; the telegraph line reached the Ruandan capital four days later and a new post office opened; the President of the Belgian War Council and journalists came to inspect; and Musinga's sub-chiefs answered calls for provisions and porters in a seemingly orderly fashion. All in all the exactions wrought on both the civilian population and the missions by the Belgians seem to have been no harder (nor any easier) than those of the departing Germans.[10] Both gave their *askari* a considerably freer rein than British officers thought appropriate, and Whitehall and Pretoria sought to capitalise on this to as great an extent as possible.

The immediate consequence of the propaganda war between Britain and Belgium was a squabble about Belgian participation in the advance on Tabora, the administrative capital of German East Africa, 150 miles south of Mwanza. While that was being resolved, the final episode in Lake Tanganyika's war was also being played out. As the Belgians progressed through Ruanda, the indomitable Geoffrey Spicer-Simson, who had left Lake Tanganyika in February, returned on 12 May and announced that he had succeeded in finding a suitable British steamer to tackle the *Goetzen* in the event that the Belgian *Baron Dhanis* was never to be completed. It was the *George*, the British Consul's boat at Leopoldville, and it was at that very moment being shipped in pieces for reassembly on the lake complete with crew and torpedo-dropping gear. Although measuring 110 feet by 21 feet she could muster 15 knots, putting her speed in the same class as *Mimi* and *Toutou*. Once again Spicer-Simson had demonstrated extraordinary resourcefulness and patience. But at Lukuga, the Belgian lakeshore HQ, he too witnessed the increasingly sour atmosphere between Belgium and Britain.

By the end of May Tombeur had ordered Moulaert, his local commander on the lake, to act independently. Spicer-Simson was certainly not going to tolerate subordinating his flotilla to a man who did not appreciate his having departed the lake in the first place and who might not have its best interests in mind. On 17 May he agreed to take a look at the German fortress at Kigoma and check on the *Goetzen*. But he refused to launch an attack on the port, and announced at the end of the month that he would be moving his command south to Kituta, in Northern Rhodesia. Commandant Goor, the Belgian naval commander and Spicer-Simson's great ally in his ongoing battle against Belgian authority, was one of many who privately expressed regret at seeing his expedition leave and the manner in which this occurred.

British assistance on Lake Tanganyika did not cease completely. Four Short 827 seaplanes were provided for an ambitious Belgian plan to finish off German resistance in Kigoma from the air. Commandant de Bueger, the senior Belgian pilot, soon found – as had Spicer-Simson six months previously – that Belgian ambitions were not always matched by a realistic appraisal of the situation on the ground. De Bueger had envisaged that Tanganyika was a placid lake when he set out from Europe, not an inland sea covering 12,500 square miles, with an area of average depth of more than 1,500 feet. It was impossible to launch his aircraft from Lukuga, where conditions were either too rough or too calm for his seaplanes to 'unstick', so a base had to be constructed at nearby Lake Tungwe, from which a channel was built to the lake proper to facilitate supply from Lukuga. Undeterred by the colossal difficulties confronting him, de Bueger succeeded in putting a plane in the air before the end of May. It was a courageous, even miraculous, aviation record for Central Africa: the altitude at Lake Tungwe was more than 2,500 feet above sea level.

'Unplanned' landings and wreckages were commonplace occurrences, but on 10 June one plane managed to fly the eighty miles to Kigoma to drop two 65lb rifle grenades on the *Goetzen* from 500 feet. It was a hair-raising exploit: the German shore defences began firing when the plane was still two miles away and with a top speed of 61mph evasion depended on luck alone. A month later, Lieutenant Orta succeeded in taking excellent photographs of the shore defences at Kigoma and on 23 July the Belgian pilots launched another bombing raid. Unbeknownst to the pilots this was all wasted effort. Captain Zimmer had been ordered to remove the 4.1-inch *Königsberg* gun from the *Goetzen* and send it east to von Lettow-Vorbeck, together with the *Möwe*'s 22-pdr raft-mounted gun; and the guns had been replaced by wooden dummies to deceive the seaplane pilots and any other snoopers. The *Goetzen* was left with just a single pom-pom 'for defence against aircraft', and Zimmer took the decision that 'an action with [Spicer-Simson's] fast motor boats could not be thought of'.[11] In mid July, as Olsen's Belgian troops threatened Gottorp, sixty miles from Kigoma, Zimmer and his men were ordered back to Tabora by General Wahle. With the Central Railway already straddled by Belgian troops the *Wami* took them south to the Malagarasi River and was then blown up. The *Goetzen*, the symbol of the Kaiser's ambitions in Central Africa, was scuttled before departure.*

The *Baron Dhanis* was finally launched by the Belgians in November 1916, a year too late to play any part in what had become known as the 'The Battle of the Lake'. But her launch was not without significance. It enabled vital supplies to be ferried across the lake to Belgian troops in German East Africa, and it was of considerable symbolic importance. Four days earlier, to Spicer-Simson's immense satisfaction, HMS *George* had also been launched, an

---

* The *Graf Goetzen* was salvaged by the British in 1924. She had been so thoroughly greased prior to her scuttling that she was in almost perfect working order. Relaunched in 1927, she still plies the shores of the lake today as the *Liemba*.

event the Belgian government wished to trump. Anglo-Belgian relations were deteriorating still further, with Belgium suspecting Britain of being prepared to accept further German expansion in Africa – at Belgium's and Portugal's expense – as part of a peace plan, and Britain suspecting Belgium of being on the brink of concluding a separate peace with Germany.

TWENTY-ONE

The 'Ubiquitous Rhodesians'

———◆———

The end of the rains came later on the southern front than in the west, but as soon as movement was possible, and all his drafts had arrived, General Northey issued the orders for the offensive from Nyasaland. On 25 May, as the Belgians overran Ruanda and van Deventer languished at Kondoa, Northey's 2,600-strong force launched its bold thrust to meet the latter on the Central Railway.* The first objective was to capture the principal German border forts. Northey's right wing, consisting of columns led by Colonel Hawthorn (1/KAR), and Colonel Rodger and Major Flindt of the 2nd South African Rifles were to attack Ipiana (twenty-five miles north of Karonga), Luwiwa (fifteen miles north-east of Fife), and Igamba (a dozen miles north-east of Fort Hill) respectively. His left wing, six companies of BSAP and NRP commanded by Colonel Murray and soon to be christened 'the ubiquitous Rhodesians', was ordered simultaneously to capture Namema, fifteen miles north of Saisi, and then to converge with the right wing at Neu Langenburg, the centre of the principal wheat-growing district of German East Africa. The German troops opposing Northey were thought to number no more than 1,500 and to include only one regular *Schutztruppe* company – Captain Falkenstein's 5/FK at Ipiana.

As Murray's force set out he predicted that it 'would be back in Abercorn in two weeks'.[1] But Namema was the most formidable of all the forts in Northey's sights. Built on a rise, with 15-foot-high walls, it resembled an impregnable medieval castle with extensive exterior earthworks. One Rhodesian soldier ruefully described it as possessing a 'beautiful, beautiful situ-

---

* British troop dispositions: Murray's Column – two companies BSAP (260 rifles), four companies NRP (540 rifles); Hawthorn's Column – one squadron, 1/SAR (200 rifles), four coys 1/KAR (600 rifles); Flindt's Column – one squadron 2/SAR (170 rifles) and two coys 1/KAR (223 rifles); Rodger's Column – 2/SAR less one squadron (462 rifles), one coy NRP (138 rifles). Total: 2,593 rifles, with twenty-six machine-guns and fourteen field guns (Hordern, p. 486). South Africa had provided seventy-four officers and 1,265 other ranks for this front by March 1916. The total strength of 1/SAR and 2/SAR would eventually rise to ninety-nine officers and 1,772 other ranks. They became known as South Africa's 'Forgotten Army'.

ation'.[2] The bush had been cleared for 2,000 yards on all sides by reservist Lieutenant Gotthold Franken and his *askari* of 29/FK, creating a perfect field of fire (which was also thought to have been mined). Murray's field guns, among them an 8-pdr named the 'May Jackson' (after one of Salisbury's most beautiful barmaids), made little impression on the defences or the defenders. Two advanced posts were captured, however, and Franken was fatally wounded during a sortie to probe Murray's encirclement on the bitterly cold night of 28 May.[*] But during the night of 2 June the garrison managed to slip between Murray's lines on a 'pitch-dark night'[3] and escape. It was an unfortunate start to the offensive. Murray was 'very, very angry',[4] and set off in pursuit of his enemy towards Lake Tanganyika – which was not at all what Northey wanted. He sent a message to Murray telling him 'Bismarckburg [on Lake Tanganyika] is merely a place which naturally falls', and that he would be 'very disappointed indeed if you lose touch with the [main body of the] enemy'.[5] But Murray never received the telegram and not only 'lost touch with the enemy' but also decided to capture Bismarckburg.

Murray's luck worsened the further he advanced. He arrived in striking distance of Bismarckburg a day earlier than he had told Spicer-Simson he would, so there was no support from the lake for an attack on the port; and Lieutenant Hasslacher's small garrison and some of the fugitives from Namema – the majority of whom had fled north-east towards Lake Rungwe – escaped from the *boma* in boats. It was a chaotic situation. Many of Murray's men accused their commander of dashing to Bismarckburg 'without any orders at all' which, strictly speaking, was true; and Northey was 'very disappointed'[6] that *two* German contingents had been allowed to escape.

It was somehow appropriate that it was amid such controversy that the Lake Tanganyika Naval Expedition was finally disbanded. Spicer-Simson had told Northey that his 'naval ratings [were] impossible to replace' and that he would not 'dare [to] expose them more than necessary'[7] in supporting Northey's offensive. Landing a detachment of NRP at Mpimpwe, north of Kirando, was therefore the flotilla's swan-song. There, Spicer-Simson handed over *Mimi, Toutou* and *Fifi* to Commander Thornley, and his force dispersed, their 'naval action in miniature'[8] at an end. Spicer-Simson was invalided home suffering from 'acute nervous debility'. But he could draw some satisfaction from the fact that even the Belgians credited him in public with a feat 'unique in British history', and complimented him with the observation that 'rarely indeed have officers and men of the Royal Navy worked in an environment

---

[*] Franken was shot by Lieutenant 'Acid Guts' Bryce Hendrie who then found Murray's Intelligence officer's notebook in Franken's pocket. 'How it got there I have never heard explained' Murray remarked (see IWM/ Hopkins).

so foreign or met conditions of greater difficulty with more complete ultimate success'.[9] In London, *The Illustrated London News* had already splashed the story across its covers, Magee filed his scoop with *The Daily Mirror*, and his more detailed account would merit thirty-one pages in *National Geographic* in 1922. Spicer-Simson, after recovering from his ordeal, returned to work as Assistant Director of Naval Intelligence, was awarded the DSO, and made a Commander of the Order of the Crown by King Albert; while Lieutenant Wainwright, Lieutenant Dudley and Dr Hanschell won the DSC, and twelve members of the expedition won the DSM. Such was the official recognition given to this extraordinary expedition, and in 1918 Spicer-Simson's first lecture on the campaign was endorsed by the First Sea Lord, Sir Henry Jackson. Soon afterwards he was invited to be one of the Admiralty's delegates at the Peace Conference at Versailles.*

On Northey's right wing his commanders fared little better than Murray after crossing the Songwe River into the district known as 'the Switzerland of German East Africa'. Captain Aumann's 'L' police company escaped from Colonel Rodger's clutches at Luwiwa, after Rodger fluffed what Northey termed 'a chance such as a commander seldom gets in war';[10] Flindt, a former 17th Lancer who was now a planter in Zululand, was held up by his guns and found the sugar-loaf mountain position of Igamba deserted; and Hawthorn found Ipiana also deserted and sped forward to the German mission station at Utengule without a fight. Not a single German detachment had been brought to battle on Northey's right, and when his troops approached Neu Langenburg Falkenstein and Aumann were both found to have slipped away over the Poroto Mountains.

There was 'legitimate disappointment'[11] at the failure to finish off the campaign in the south within a couple of weeks. The enemy, whose numbers were only half those estimated by Northey's intelligence service at the outset, had simply taken advantage of the vast spaces available to retreat until such time as they chose to fight; and in the meantime Northey's troops were

---

* In 1921 Spicer-Simson was elected the first Secretary-General of the new International Hydrographic Bureau, a position he held until his retirement in 1937; among those who unequivocally elected him to the post in 1921 was none other than his Belgian opposite number during the Tanganyika campaign, Commandant Goor. Geoffrey Spicer-Simson died in British Columbia in 1947 leaving a widow, Amy, but unfortunately no offspring to defend him against the publication in 1968 of Peter Shankland's *The Phantom Flotilla*. A 'lurid and often inaccurate' account (Mackenzie (1), p. 410), this was largely based on the tale as woven by the expedition's doctor. Not only did he not like Spicer-Simson, but he was manifestly an outsider on an expedition governed by naval rules and regulations. The result was a rather grotesque caricature of Spicer-Simson which was perpetuated by other subsequent accounts that drew uncritically on Shankland as a source.

introduced to campaign conditions that had proved more onerous than any of them had imagined. The terrain over which they had advanced was, as one BSAP private wrote in his diary, 'all up hill and down dale over the mountains. Sometimes ascending many thousands of feet and descending into the valleys beyond – only to again commence climbing. Struggling through deep *dongas* with the guns. Everyone dead beat. The *tenga* boys [carriers] dropping out all along the line. Many of them made their last journey this time.'[12] An inspection of the German defences at Neu Langenburg also gave an indication of what lay ahead as and when the enemy decided to stand and fight: one gunner with the South African Mounted Rifles was unnerved to discover that 'in front of the perimeter large hollows had been excavated and these then filled with sharpened sticks hardened by fire, some about waist high, with shorter ones in front, and graded down to those of an inch or so high, to catch the barefooted *askari*. There were thousands of these sticks closely planted, like a garden.'[13] Range discs had also been set up in the bush, cleared to make a field of fire.

Although Northey's opponents remained as elusive as ever, communications between his units were proving hopelessly unreliable, and the toll on soldiers and carriers mounted daily, he was able to draw some consolation from the fact that his advance had brought 20,000 square miles of German East Africa under British control. Furthermore, his troops had been 'blooded', and the enemy were seemingly caught between them and the Central Railway, towards which van Deventer would soon begin to advance. Northey therefore remained optimistic, announcing that 'everything has so far gone very well' and, after consulting with Smuts, he ordered his commanders to 'press on for all you are worth' to Iringa 'and strike as long as there is anything left [of the enemy]'.[14] Murray's column, by now thoroughly inured to campaign conditions, covered the 250 mostly mountainous miles from Bismarckburg back to Neu Langenburg and the centre of operations in just seventeen days.

By early July Hawthorn and Flindt, the latter described by his men as a 'weird old man'[15] on account of his habit of talking incessantly, had converged at the dazzling white fort of Njombe, at the junction of the routes to Lupembe and Iringa. Progress remained difficult. A rapid movement by Hawthorn's 1/KAR to Iringa was thwarted by continuing rainfall and supply problems; and Flindt's guns had had to be hauled right over the Livingstone Mountains, harried all the way by German stragglers. But at least Northey's two wings were now forty miles from each other to the south of Malangali; and news began to filter back that the enemy meant to make a stand on a line between Malangali and Madibira, these two posts commanding the main route to Iringa. Two hundred Germans, half of whom were *Königsberg* men rushed south from Iringa by Captain Braunschweig, were thought to hold Malangali;

while 700–800 *askari* of 2/FK, 5/FK 10/FK and at least one *Königsberg* gun were thought to be at Madibira.

On 24 July, while Murray executed a feint to tie down the garrison at Madibira, Rodger attacked the long rocky ridge of Malangali and a further ridge to the right of the road which covered it. When his troops were just 2,000 yards away a huge explosion, soon followed by another and two thunderous crashes, confirmed the presence of a 'big gun', scaring witless the column's porters and many of the rank and file. At about 11 a.m. Hawthorn's 1/KAR had worked around the rear of the ridge, however, and repelled a determined counter-attack at the point of bayonets. The German gun was then shifted from its emplacement in the *boma*, opening fire on Hawthorn's men from a range of just 900 yards. The action became even more ferocious on this eastern side of Malangali and Rodger moved to the west side of the hill and began to advance up the rocky spurs. In the afternoon four of the South African Mounted Rifles's mountain guns, 75mm QF guns captured in German South-West Africa, were unlimbered and a duel between two well-drilled artillery teams commenced. At one point a shell from the German gun fell right next to a mountain gun but failed to explode, another wiped out a Maxim team, and the SAMR guns had constantly to shift their positions to avoid being obliterated during the three-hour engagement.

Fierce fighting continued after dark, but when Rodger reached the summit the Germans had gone, leaving on the Iringa road the 'big gun' which had shed a wheel. It was not from the *Königsberg* but one of the modern Krupp quick-firing howitzers that had been landed by the *Marie* at Sudi Bay in April. Firing 44-pdr high-explosive shrapnel with a range of six miles, the gun should have enabled Braunschweig to hold Malangali, but the unflinching opposition of Hawthorn's column and his fear, once Rodger's force started to move to the west, that he might be surrounded, decided him otherwise. His force had also sustained 150 casualties, thirty Germans being found dead on the battlefield, and Braunschweig was unnerved to hear in the midst of the baffle that the Wahehe chief in the territory over which he would have to retreat had declared his support for the British. With Malangali captured, the German troops at Madibira hastily abandoned their exposed positions to Murray, and Northey issued orders to all his column commanders 'to pursue and annihilate'.[16]

The victory at Malangali confirmed the fighting ability of Northey's force but his intelligence scouts, thrown out across a vast area, now started to report unsettling 'goings-on'. Forty miles to the north-west Captain 'Jock' Fair observed a German soldier organising supplies at a crossing of the Great Ruaha River at Kiganga; and scouts from Hawthorn's column sent 100 miles to the east to check on the large mission station at Lupembe found that a detachment of 1/KAR that had successfully seized the mission station from the Germans – killing Dr Stier, the former Governor of Neu Langenburg in the process – was now itself surrounded by Captain Falkenstein and some 600 *askari*. On 19 August Hawthorn's column arrived at Lupembe and forced Falkenstein to retreat back across the Ruhudje River, where the column experienced one of the occasional wondrous, as opposed to murderous, spectacles that war in the African bush could offer. 'As we approached the river, just about dawn,' Sergeant Maker of the SAMR recalled, 'something caused me to stop dead still, which also brought the patrol to a halt. There was no talking allowed so everything was done by signs. Nothing happened. The signal was given to advance and, at that moment the whole countryside appeared to move! As far as one could see there were eland: males, females and calves. They slowly moved off up the river … I often wonder, with the advance of civilization, if a sight like this will ever be seen again.'[17] Hawthorn's column crossed the river and drove Falkenstein off hills with commanding views over the river towards Songea. In his new position astride the Ruhudje River, he looked to have outflanked any German troops intent on retreating from Iringa down the river to the southern end of the Mahenge plateau.

Northey's position at the end of August was a difficult one. He could either stay put and be drawn into a debilitating game of 'ring-a-roses' with German detachments, many of which were not what he called the '*original* enemy'; or he could press on now that his supply situation was improved by the cessation of the rains and attack Iringa. He chose, at Smuts's behest, the more decisive option. Whatever the dangers of this strategy, to link up with van Deventer at Iringa and threaten von Lettow-Vorbeck's left flank might just force a German surrender.

Northey's advance on Iringa was rapid, but once again the 'annihilation' of the enemy proved an elusive goal. The terrain south of Iringa was thickly wooded, with steep hills and narrow valleys providing perfect cover for ambushes. Snipers seemed to be everywhere, further stretching the nerves of the British troops. On one afternoon a bathing parade of the SAMR was taken by surprise and had to man their guns naked. But on 29 August 'Murray's Rhodesians' entered Iringa. After the unfortunate start to his campaign, Murray's men had warmed to their commander, developing a 'sneaking regard for him as a fighter'[18] as they scrapped their way north through so many encounters that they were remembered only by names like 'Bamboos' or 'Blue Gums'. The cool of the highlands was also welcome relief after the furnace-like temperatures down at Madibira and Malangali and the men enjoyed being in something that resembled a proper town. There were gardens galore, Indian traders, even – to everyone's great surprise – 100 Chinese labourers. In the German officers' mess, however, a life-sized portrait of an *askari* reminded them that their task was probably not over. To the east of Iringa Rodger's column, despite harrying Braunschweig's retreating troops for days, were unable to stop them retiring out of reach onto the Mahenge plateau.

In taking Iringa Northey had achieved his objective with a hard-fought advance of over 200 miles. But his men were spread very thin on the ground and dependent on extraordinarily long supply lines. At Iringa, they were once again on quarter rations – ¼ tin of bully beef and one biscuit per day. Most were 'hardened colonials' who, as one of their number put it, 'would have vandalised Valhalla [or] smoked strong Boer tobacco in the corridors of the Vatican'.[19] But soon it would become apparent just how exposed they were. Northey would have to fight tooth and nail for the territory he had captured, and the very survival of his columns.

TWENTY-TWO

'Abso-Damn-Lutely Fed Up'

At Kondoa, 200 miles north of Iringa, a 'long period of enforced inactivity' had followed von Lettow-Vorbeck's unsuccessful attack in May. Conditions had remained almost as appalling as before for van Deventer's force. 'Food was scarce and sometimes lacking altogether,' wrote one South African officer, 'and cold, biting rains, varied by oppressive heat, prevailed much of the time. The Germans were before us in the ravines and gorges, but in such rough country it was difficult to know exactly where their front line ran. Often bullets whipped around our ears from some unexpected quarter, and it was but rarely that we caught more than a fleeting glimpse of the enemy'.[1] There were *some* improvements. By mid June the South Africans, all of whom were 'abso-damn-lutely fed up', were able to change their shirts for the first time in two months, and small quantities of delicacies like jam, bacon and currants trickled in. 'The shock nearly killed us,' wrote one private in 9/SAI, particularly grateful that a dependence on locally grown tobacco – 'one draw for sixteen coughs'[2] – was briefly mitigated by the arrival of a small consignment of real tobacco.

On 24 June the 'Daily Hate' – bombardment by the German guns from the heights to the south of the town – suddenly ceased, and two days later the German troops simply disappeared. Von Lettow-Vorbeck could 'not abide situations where you sit about and pot at each other for days on end'[3] and he had decided to withdraw the majority of his troops from Kondoa district eastwards to cover Kraut's retreat from the Northern Railway. By the end of the month the first troops from Kondoa reached Morogoro, and the German rearguard was instructed to pull back towards the Central Railway and then to the fertile district around Mahenge. Unfortunately, van Deventer's Division was in no position to mount an effective pursuit of the rearguard until almost a month later: sickness was rife among his men, with 12/SAI alone having lost forty per cent of its effective strength in May.

By the time van Deventer's columns had crossed 100 waterless miles to capture Dodoma and get astride the Central Railway at the end of July, his lines of communication were in a highly precarious state. 'Since we left

Kondoa-Irangi,' wrote one mounted trooper, 'we have been out in the blue, chasing the Huns over *kopjes* and deserts. A glance at the map will give you some idea of the country through which we have passed – wild, uninhabited, barren, and God-Forsaken. How we managed it we cannot remember, but we did ... General van Deventer has taken huge risks, but all along our fellows have obeyed his orders with willingness and alacrity, never questioning the wisdom of the move, although at times it seemed suicidal.'[4] A two-week pause was necessary before van Deventer could press on eastwards along the railway to effect a junction with Smuts. When he did so his advance met almost daily opposition from Captain Otto, a bespectacled maestro of rearguard actions, who stood between van Deventer and Smuts with five companies. But Mpapua was taken on 12 August, Kilossa (and its rum distillery) ten days later, and van Deventer's troops – after five months – were within fifty miles of Smuts's. (See Appendix Five.)

Smuts's simultaneous advance through the Nguru Mountains was equally torrid. Although the eleven infantry battalions and four mounted regiments in his two divisions outnumbered the detachments of Kraut, Schulz, Stemmermann and von Heyden-Linden by a factor of two, they proved woefully inadequate for the task of encircling the enemy. Like Otto to the west, the German detachments all successfully extricated themselves from the mountains and in one action in particular – at the Wami River on 17 August 1916 – inflicted 120 casualties on General Sheppard's 1st Brigade. On 26 August, after three weeks of vicious scrapping Smuts's advance guard lay awake 'in pouring rain about six miles from [Morogoro] and heard the crashes and saw the flames as the Germans ran their engines and rolling stock from both sides of a destroyed bridge over a deep gorge'. The next day Morogoro, with its broad avenues, Sailer's Hotel, and acre upon acre of mango and palm trees, was taken. It was, as one British officer put it, 'really an insignificant little town, but it was the first we had seen for three hundred miles and so most exciting'.[5]

As was the case with all captured towns, the arrival of British troops on the Central Railway was not a boon for every inhabitant. The Greek and Indian traders were certainly keen to see the restoration of order, but for looters it was a different story. A gunner from Hull described the scene which confronted him on his entry to the town: 'I found a big crowd there, so I went to see what was happening ... [A looter] had been condemned to death and after having dug his own grave, he had been brought to be shot. The culprit stood against a wall. After the volley was fired, he stood long enough for me to think that the whole party had missed him. Then his knees crumpled and he slowly collapsed. I thought this rather peculiar. I had seen men hit but if it was serious they went down in a hurry. Apparently this is not so in all cases.'[6]

Local Africans were not the only ones keen on looting. It was an activity at which Boer troops also 'excelled'. Tensions were mounting between Briton and Boer, and the thieving proclivities of many of the latter compounded a worsening reputation. 'They have not the least discipline' was a common judgement, and there was widespread disgust among British troops at their 'filthy camp habits'. 'No sanitary arrangements are made by them,' the gunner from Hull wrote; 'every night they will sing and pray for an hour or so, then they will gamble and blaspheme for hours. As soon as they are on active service, they never shave, very seldom wash or even think of putting a stitch in their clothing. It is easy to imagine,' he concluded, 'that in a very short time, a more ragged or more disreputable crowd would be very hard to find.'[7] He would soon be proved correct, as Smuts set his sights on cornering von Lettow-Vorbeck in the Uluguru Mountains to the south of Morogoro.

For over a month, rumours of impending peace had circulated throughout the South African ranks. As Smuts's and van Deventer's forces approached the Central Railway these grew stronger, probably as a result of the visit to East Africa by Botha (travelling incognito as 'Colonel Campbell') and Smuts's belief that the capture of the Central Railway 'would be the end of the campaign'.[8] Sergeant Lane of the South African Field Ambulance was so confident that he bet that 'peace will be declared on August 8th'. 'I don't think I will be very far wrong,'[9] he wrote confidently, and certain Boer commanders even began to confirm that 'peace will shortly be declared'.[10] It was wishful thinking. Smuts's flanking manoeuvres had completely failed to inflict any meaningful damage on his opponent, and the performance of Enslin's 2nd Mounted Brigade in the Nguru Mountains was singled out for particular criticism by British and German alike. In the words of one senior British Staff officer, 'von Lettow-Vorbeck should have been brought to a standstill, and forced to fight it out, on more than one occasion' during July and August; instead he managed to retire both from Kondoa and the Nguru Mountains. The bush, the black cotton soil, and the climate all favoured him but there was no denying that he had executed his withdrawal 'with the greatest skill'.[11] The German commander remained confident that, even if all his troops were pushed south of the railway, he could 'continue the war for a long time to come'.[12] By now 'von Lettow Fallback', as he was often referred to, had become an almost mythical figure; in the British ranks stories abounded of him personally carrying wounded *askari* from the battlefield, and even of training himself to go barefoot in readiness for the day when he would have no boots.

More than 100 miles to the south-west of Morogoro, a threat to Northey's hard-pressed and thinly spread troops was emerging from a completely unexpected direction. In early August Crewe's 'Lake Force', 2,250-strong with fifteen machine-guns, began their advance on Tabora from Mwanza. After much diplomatic wrangling, further Belgian co-operation had been secured, with the result that the joint advance turned into a race. Before the British and Belgian troops, Wahle's companies were deployed along a fifty-mile defensive front to the north of Tabora and the lion's share of the fighting required to dislodge them fell, once again, to the Belgians. At the end of the first week in September, all the Belgian commanders scored victories against Wahle's forward positions; and for two weeks thereafter their columns fought daily battles of increasing intensity in stifling heat. Finally, at 10.30 a.m. on 19 September, three lieutenants hoisted the Belgian flag above Tabora, releasing some 200 POWs in the process. Crewe only learnt this humiliating news five days later.

As the Belgian troops closed in and Crewe looked set to cut the Central Railway to the east General Wahle had recognised that Tabora, 'a long town like a hand towel' and the largest in the colony, was quite impossible to defend. On three sides it was ringed with hills which gave a perfect field of fire for enemy artillery; and Wahle had to consider the presence of two sizeable hospitals – and the German women and children in the town – as well as the fact that the railway might not provide the means of a quick flight for much longer. Furthermore, his casualties in September amounted to fifty Germans dead, 150 taken prisoner and over 300 *askari* dead or wounded; and as Tombeur's troops approached Tabora the intelligence that could be gleaned from the local population began to dry up and a distinct air of unease descended on the district. On 18 September he was forced to order the abandonment of the town, and sent a fifty-strong decoy force down the railway towards Kilimatinde while keeping the true direction of his withdrawal a closely guarded secret. Huge quantities of supplies were destroyed and four guns disabled as the German troops departed.

Wahle's feint in the direction of Kilimatinde, 150 miles west of Tabora, was a complete success. Crewe ordered 4/KAR to converge on the railway at Igalula and to sweep westwards supported by an advance by 8/SAI and a squadron of 4/SAH from van Deventer's force, but they were all too late to forestall Wahle. At the stations at Malongwe and Igalula he mustered his 2,000 battle-hardened troops in the first week of October and divided them into columns led by von Langenn-Steinkeller and Lieutenant Joseph Zingel, former Administrator of Bismarckburg. Zimmer's *Möwe* company, for so long the masters of Lake Tanganyika, was disbanded and its men redistributed. A third column, Max Wintgens's, was positioned south of Tabora, ready to oppose any further

Belgian advance. At this juncture, Wahle revealed his plan to his commanders: he intended to march their eleven companies straight across the barren waste-land south-west of Tabora, judged by his opponents to be 'no country for the movement of troops',[13] and recapture Iringa. His 'venture into the unknown' was, as he recognised, a 'very high-risk strategy indeed'.[14] But after ten days the crafty old general discovered that the Belgians had pursued him no further than Sikonge, and that Crewe's Lake Force was a busted flush in the process of being disbanded.

Tabora was as far as Tombeur could, or would, go. His troops had marched some 1,300 miles since April, and of the 8,500 troops he had started out with from Lake Victoria only 5,850 were still fit for action. The guns of two of his three artillery batteries had been lost or destroyed, and with the expiry of the contracts of the Ugandan porters (among whom cerebro-spinal meningitis had broken out) he was desperately short of transport. Furthermore, the Germans had pursued a rigorous scorched earth strategy in their retreat to Tabora, stripping the whole area of foodstuffs. 'There was no one who did not regret this forced stop,' Tombeur wrote, 'but there was also no one who, at this point, believed that we could recommence the offensive the day after our entry to Tabora.'[15]

This was not how Smuts interpreted Tombeur's decision. His seeming intransigence was regarded as further evidence of escalating Belgian ambitions in Central Africa, and when Tombeur subsequently refused to budge from Tabora Smuts accused him of '[taking] advantage of our necessities to claim that their original offer of evacuation had lapsed', despite alluding 'in ambiguous terms to gradual withdrawal'.[16] That politicking was afoot there was no doubt. Even when the rains were imminent, Tombeur could have withdrawn his troops on the Central Railway to Lake Tanganyika. But he was ordered not to by the Belgian government, and as Smuts had no troops with which to garrison Tabora his hand was weak. What most irked Smuts, however, was the failure – as he saw it – of Tombeur and Crewe to round up Wahle's *West-truppen*; and as Crewe was an old friend, it was Tombeur alone that he blamed.

Out on the barren steppe south-west of Tabora, marked on the map with nothing but a white blob, Wahle's *Westtruppen* found the conditions even more arduous than he had imagined.* He finally ordered a day's rest at Kiromo, in Itumba district, where von Langenn-Steinkeller's and Zingel's columns

---

* The *Westtruppen* now comprised: *Abteilung* Zingel (with General Wahle) – 26/FK, 7/ResK (Kalman), 'Bukoba' *Kompanie* (Ralph Wahle), and *Batterie* Vogel; *Abteilung* von Langenn-Steinkeller – 7/FK (Wentzel), Muansa 'A' and 'D' *Kompanie* (Günzert), and munitions column (Dannert); *Abteilung* Wintgens – Ruanda 'B' *Kompanie* (Bockmann), Ruanda 'A' *Kompanie* (Langen), 29/FK (Siebel), machine-gun company (Besch) and 3.7cm *Batterie* (Vortag). Attached to Wintgens was the main artillery column, *Abteilung* Hübener: 22/FK and a naval howitzer.

converged; and it was there that considerable friction arose between Wahle and one of Schnee's officials when it emerged that the latter had failed to keep together all the porters recruited in Malongwe, and had consequently burnt huge quantities of precious supplies. He had also brought insufficient money to pay the *askari*, all of whom were now forced to accept the general's 'credit'. Equally perturbing was that there was no word of Wintgens's detachment, accompanied by Colonel Hübener's and one of the 10.5cm howitzers from the *Marie*. Unbeknownst to Wahle, Wintgens had in fact reached Isunuka, seventy miles south-west of Wahle, but the trek had exacted a heavy toll: forty-three Germans and forty-four *askari* had already been abandoned to an uncertain fate along the way.

Despite the mounting difficulties Wahle pressed on. Each night the porters would straggle into camp after midnight only to be up at dawn for the next day's march. Many were simply abandoned, too weak to continue, others died from sheer exhaustion. The 500 cattle accompanying the columns dwindled to fewer than 100; and as rations began to run out the porters' maize ration was cut by a third and they began to 'visibly reduce in size'.[17] Water was so scarce that they were even forbidden to cook. For men on the march for eight hours each day in unbearable heat, this was a drastic measure. 'What it actually means not to cook and to subsist on raw or ground maize morning noon and night can only be appreciated by someone who has been forced to endure such a hardship,' wrote Wahle; 'many nights I prayed that we would find some provisions the next day . . . the deprivations suffered by us on that march were the most extreme I experienced in the whole campaign.'[18]

The further south Wahle's columns progressed, the more vigilant they had to be. They were still some way from making contact with any of Northey's troops but had entered an area in which Germans of any description were extremely unpopular. The Wahehe had been 'pacified' in 1898 following a four-year campaign by Tom von Prince (the colonial veteran who had been killed at Tanga in 1914); but more recently, embittered at the loss of control over their territory, the Wahehe had participated in the ill-fated Maji-Maji Rebellion and still retained large quantities of rifles. Seeing an opportunity to settle old scores, Wahehe warriors therefore harried Wahle's columns every step of the way, and were undeterred by the hangings carried out on any of their number who fell into German hands.

With all three of Smuts's divisions astride the Central Railway at the end of August, the fall of Dar-es-Salaam was only a matter of time. The Royal Navy had not rested on its laurels since capturing Tanga in July. Although the fleet was not quite as large as the one assembled to destroy the *Königsberg* a year earlier, it still constituted a significant naval presence. Admiral 'Ned' Charlton, who had succeeded King-Hall as commander-in-chief of the Cape Station in August 1915, flew his flag from HMS *Vengeance* (while *Hyacinth* underwent a refit), and he had the light cruisers *Challenger, Talbot* and *Pioneer* at his disposal. Alongside them remained many vessels whose functions were symptomatic of the versatility still required in maintaining a blockade. The monitors *Mersey* and *Severn* remained on station with their mother ship *Trent,* as did the gunboats *Echo, Childers, Pickle, Fly, Thistle* and *Helmuth.* HMS *Manica,* the Navy's first kite-balloon ship which had seen action at the Dardanelles, provided an observation platform for the bombardment of onshore positions; and *Himalaya* supported the RNAS's seaplanes. After Tanga had fallen, Pangani and Sadani to the south were also taken in joint operations without encountering much opposition, and Charlton was asked by Smuts to capture Bagamoyo, between Sadani and Dar-es-Salaam, without assistance from the land forces.

Although Charlton was told that the old slaving port of Bagamoyo was only held by ten Germans and about forty *askari,* and a bombardment by *Vengeance*'s 12-inch guns on 5 August failed to draw any response, he was determined not to take any chances and to use every single rating and bluejacket available. When his force began their landing before dawn on 15 August his caution proved justified: Bagamoyo was protected by a *Königsberg* gun, a five-barrelled pom-pom and a garrison over 400-strong – fully one third larger than the naval force – with at least two machine-guns. But Charlton's plans were well laid. *Mersey* and *Severn* drew fire from the *Königsberg* gun while lighters put the naval force ashore and the *Helmuth* and a picket boat then closed to within 500 yards of the gun, peppering it with 3-pdr fire. With the naval ratings on the beach below it, this 'seriously discomposed' the German gunners, who abandoned their gun. A seaplane then began bombing the German trenches in concert with a full-scale bombardment from the ships offshore. By 6.30 a.m. Captain von Bodecker had ordered his men to retreat back towards the Holy Ghost Fathers' Mission at the rear of the town and when he and Captain Bock von Wülfingen – who had commanded the attack on Kisii two years earlier – were both killed, 'all initiative on the part of the enemy was lost'. The operation was altogether a 'most remarkable piece of work'[19] by the Navy, although it cost the life of Royal Marine Captain Thomas, a decorated veteran of Gallipoli who led the landings, and there was jubilation in the ranks at being the first to capture a *Königsberg* gun intact. So celebratory was the mood that an abandoned baby hippo found during the attack was sent as a gift to the Sultan of Zanzibar, whom the Navy considered their patron as well as host to the RNAS's aerodrome. The Sultan wrote to Charlton thanking him 'from the very bottom of my heart' for his new pet, and for 'freeing us from the barbarism of our common enemy'.[20]

With Bagamoyo in British hands, the Navy set its sights on Dar-es-Salaam. On 21 August HMS *Challenger* bombarded the railway station at night as a prelude to joint operations, and in the succeeding days planes joined in the bombing of the port. Tension mounted daily among the inhabitants. Nis Kock, from the blockade-runner *Kronborg*, was charged with spiriting away the munitions that could be moved and wrote: 'the town was like a whole community in dissolution. Troops on the march passed through hardly making a pause. The white soldiers flung themselves on the hotels' good food like starving beasts, and often they were utterly played out. Long columns of bearers [also] passed through, going north or south, and white women and children poured in from every point of the compass.' Two years after the outbreak of war, it was clear that 'the good days in Dar-es-Salaam were over', and that 'the country was finally up against it'.[21]

By 3 September Colonel Price's coastal column of 1,900 men had advanced from Bagamoyo on three separate objectives: the Mabibo Heights overlooking Dar-es-Salaam, Ruvu station (forty miles inland) and Ngerengere station (eighty miles inland). At each the only sign of the enemy was a few stragglers. On the morning of 4 September, with *Challenger, Vengeance, Mersey, Severn* and various smaller craft lying inshore, Dar-es-Salaam finally surrendered. Recently promoted Commander Charlewood, a veteran of almost all the major naval actions since 1914, was given the honour of receiving the surrender. It was a Pyrrhic victory, although the capture of the port's wireless station did mean that direct contact with Berlin finally ceased. The troops had rarely encountered the enemy during their advance, but the damage wrought on the Central Railway by the retreating Germans was immense. Rolling-stock had been driven off the line into ravines and all bridges had been blown. Nothing remained intact on the Central Railway, once the very symbol of German ambitions for its East Africa colony. In the capital itself only 380 civilians remained, and eighty sick and wounded in the hospital. A young 'bluejacket' observed that 'many of the female citizens were in tears on our entry and the majority were sulky and sullen whereas most of the menfolk kept out of sight'. The indigenous population on the other hand, sensing that the arrival of the British might mean an end to bombardments and deprivation, 'received [them] with delight'.[22] Work began immediately to try and restore both the harbour and railway to some semblance of working order. It would prove to be a mammoth undertaking – sixty bridges had been destroyed between the coast and Dodoma – but by the first week in October the line was open for limited traffic.

On 31 August Smuts sent a message to the War Office which read: 'I would submit that on occupation of Central Railway it will be advisable to make a serious effort to effect the surrender of the German forces without running the risk and expense of protracted guerrilla operations in the far south of their territory.' With the short rains only weeks away, and von Lettow-Vorbeck's troops all dug in south of the railway, Smuts's chances of saving 'millions of expenditure'[23] and convincing his opponent that further resistance was futile were slim. But he opted for one more push in the hope that 'if [von Lettow-Vorbeck] were given no rest, he would give in'. This was not the news that most of his field commanders, and certainly not those endeavouring to keep them supplied, wanted to hear. As one of the latter wrote, 'the country was bare of supplies ... and the transport stretched to the furthest limit. The effects of the climate were being felt more and more [and] the camps along the railway were full of sick and worn-out men'.[24]

Smuts's plan looked straightforward enough on paper. He was convinced that the enemy was 'now worn out, having been pursued without intermission for hundreds of miles', and that 'his morale has gone, and his numbers are diminishing rapidly on account of sickness, captures and, most of all desertions'.[25] With that in mind he ordered van Deventer to push south to Kidatu on the Ruaha River, thereby blocking von Lettow-Vorbeck's route to the Mahenge plateau, while his own force encircled the German positions in the Uluguru Mountains, south of Morogoro. General Hoskins's 1st Division, comprising Sheppard's and Hannyngton's brigades, was to advance along the eastern side of the Ulugurus while Coen Brits tackled the west with Beves's 5/SAI and 6/SAI and Enslin's 2nd Mounted Brigade, assisted by Nussey's 1st Mounted Brigade which Smuts had detached from van Deventer. Execution of the plan was a different matter. One third of the 1st Division's ration strength of 9,400 men were on the sick-list and Driscoll's 'Frontiersmen', for example, could only put 100 men in the field. Similarly, when Nussey's brigade completed a thirty-three-mile ride to its start point for the offensive, only 900 of its 1,413 men were fit enough to continue. Opposing the offensive were five German detachments – at least 3,500 troops with more than forty machine-guns – led by Otto, Schulz, Liebermann, Tafel and Stemmermann. They were among von Lettow-Vorbeck's most experienced commanders, and they held the high ground.[*]

The operations in and around the Uluguru Mountains proved to be, in Smuts's own words, 'among the most difficult of the whole campaign'[26] and

---

* The German companies were: Otto (23/FK, 24/FK, 6/SchK, 14/ResK); Schulz (4/FK, 9/FK, 13/FK, 21/FK); von Lieberman (11/FK, 27/FK, 'W' *Kompanie*); Tafel (1/FK, 17/FK, 30/FK, 1/SchK) and Stemmermann (3/FK, 14/FK, 18/FK, 22/FK, 4/SchK).

were conducted in weather which alternated almost hourly between raging heat and torrential rain. German resistance was stubborn, ferocious and unpredictable. The detachments in positions in the heights overlooking Morogoro were not forced down to the plains, as Smuts intended, but succeeded in retiring straight through the mountains, 'the wildest and most impassable in East Africa ... with sheer precipices falling to yawning gorges, swampy valleys and thick jungles'. As they began to arrive in Kissaki, to the south of the Ulugurus, all the German troops 'showed signs of the retreat', malaria was rife, and uniforms were 'faded and tattered'. But they had again achieved a feat that had been considered impossible by Smuts, defying conditions of 'constant misery and torture'.[27]

Even a timely convergence at the southern end of the Ulugurus of Smuts's two flanking manoeuvres proved impossible. When Enslin and Beves were just eight miles west of Kissaki on 5 September, Hoskins's troops were still over forty miles away to the north-east; and instead of waiting for the British Division the South African commanders launched an attack that was mauled by Otto. Nussey also had to withdraw when he confronted Tafel north of Kissaki, and the consequence of these 'two isolated efforts' leading to a 'double retirement'[28] was that von Lettow-Vorbeck was able to withdraw his entire force to Duthumi, where he fought yet another rearguard action, and then over the Mgeta River to safety. It was here that Nis Kock first set eyes on his commander-in-chief:

> He didn't look much as I'd imagined him, his clothes were shabbier than those of most officers and he wore no badge of rank. He had on a rather dilapidated sun-helmet, riding breeches and puttees, and a pair of exceedingly well-worn riding boots. Judging by all this he was not a man who thought much about appearances ... But his face struck one as remarkable. It was no typical army chief's face, a little moustache was the only military thing about it, and there was a hovering smile at the corners of his mouth. I had imagined something much more brusque and unapproachable; but his whole bearing was intrepid and self-assured.[29]

When Hoskins's troops, shattered and famished, finally converged on Kissaki the German troops were already entrenched on the other side of the Mgeta River. Five German naval guns and 500 4.1-inch shells had been captured during the advance, but they were scant consolation. Smuts's plan to 'bottle up' von Lettow-Vorbeck around Morogoro had, like his plan to cut him off north of the Central Railway, failed; and with rain now falling heavily, and many of his troops having advanced 200 miles in six weeks, it was impossible for Smuts to consider launching an immediate offensive south of the Mgeta. To the west the situation was no better. Van Deventer's advance from the Central Railway towards Mahenge was also brought to a standstill by the rain on 10 September, by which time half the men in his division were sick. In total, more than 6,000 British troops were in hospital at the end of the month, and Brits's 3rd Division had ceased to be an effective unit.

On the southern front it was not only the first rumours of Wahle's approach, and the fact that van Deventer's troops were still separated by 100 miles of unholy terrain from Iringa, that made Northey's position start to look 'distinctly grave'[30] in early October. Mindful of his need to hold the main food-growing districts south of the Central Railway by the advent of the rainy season, von Lettow-Vorbeck had begun shifting his troop dispositions in August. Holding the Mahenge plateau would give him command of the rice-growing district in the Kilombero (Ulanga) Valley, a resource all the more precious since the fall of Mwanza, and he had sent the trusted Kraut from Kilossa to reinforce Braunschweig on the plateau in August. The combined force of about 2,500 troops with twenty-four machine-guns and six field guns now defending the Mahenge plateau soon proved a considerable obstacle to Smuts's plan for Northey to occupy it; and while Northey watched for Wahle's approach from the west, he suddenly heard that in the east Kraut was personally leading a substantial force of ten or eleven companies to attack Hawthorn's column on the Ruhudje River.* The first inkling of this 'scarcely believable' threat was brought by runner to Hawthorn in late September. Patrols were immediately sent out and, as one trooper attested, 'sure enough back came our patrol closely followed by the enemy'.

Kraut's attack on Hawthorn's positions began in the afternoon of 28 September, with the SAMR guns subjected to a heavy bombardment from Kraut's artillery. They answered with double explosive shells which 'made terrific double reports in the drum-like air of the forest',[31] and Hawthorn's troops held firm – killing forty-two and wounding more than eighty of Kraut's attackers (including eleven Germans). Sniping continued all night, making everyone jumpy and relieved to receive the order the following morning to pull back through elephant grass taller than a man to the Ruhudje, which was crossed in darkness. Once across the river the column dug in around Mkapira and was joined there by Murray's 'ubiquitous Rhodesians', who were fortuitously completing their march all the way from Iringa, harrying German troops

* Kraut's force included 2/FK, 5/FK, 10/FK, 15/FK, 16/FK, 19/FK, 25/FK, 5/SchK, 8/SchK and 'L' *Kompanie*.

through the mountainous country around Muhanga Mission and right down the sweltering Ruhudje Valley by way of Makua.

It was now fully apparent that an entire new front had opened up to Northey's east, stretching 200 miles from Iringa to Songea, and in order to try and arrest the general drift of the campaign southwards, Admiral Charlton continued his subjugation of the German ports. On 7 September Kilwa Kivinje surrendered to *Vengeance* and Kilwa Kisiwani to *Talbot* and *Challenger.* Six days later Kiswere was occupied by the Royal Marines without a fight and Sudi Bay, the *Marie's* former hideout, and Lindi followed. By 18 September the whole of German East Africa's coastline was in British hands. It was over two years since the naval operations against German East Africa had commenced, yet the work of the four cruisers and fleet of smaller vessels was still not at an end. To the south the Portuguese, who had formally entered the war in March, were finally advancing across the Rovuma into German East Africa, and it was tacitly recognised that on past form this might well involve a need for support.

In early May, Smuts had written to Admiral Charlton that 'we will have to see our mission through whatever proportion of sickness we may have'.[32] Less than six months later, however, he was forced to contemplate the possibility that he had been stymied by a combination of disease, natural obstacles and the tactics of his elusive and determined opponent. Smuts's response was characteristically optimistic. At the end of September he informed the War Office that the operations he planned for October and November would be 'final'. They had to be: the War Office was pressing for as many as possible of the 50,000 or so British, Indian and South African troops tied down in East Africa to be made available for other fronts; and Botha and Smuts had already decided to begin repatriating the remains of their most depleted units. Among the first to leave was Byron's 5/SAI, which could only muster 118 fit men, and embarkation orders were also received by – among others – 9/SAI (reduced to 116 men from its original strength of 1,135 all ranks) and by 1/SAH and 2/SAH (among whose original officers only one – Captain Bagenal – had not been hospitalised). Among the Indian Army and other British units the story was the same: even the 57th (Wilde's) Rifles could only field one in five of its men after just three months in Africa.

Smuts would later write that 'it may be that I expected too much of my men' in calling for a further advance at this juncture, 'that I imposed too hard a task on them under the awful conditions of this tropical campaign'. But his response to this question was resolute: 'I do not think so ... It is true that efforts like these cannot be made without inflicting the greatest hardships on all, but it is equally true that the Commander who shrinks from such efforts should stay at home.' He knew that he would be unable to destroy all of von Lettow-Vorbeck's detachments – the main force between the Mgeta and Rufiji Rivers, Kraut's strong force on the Mahenge plateau, and Wahle's – in succession before the end of the year. But the encirclement of the main body might still be feasible, and Smuts even thought that there was an outside possibility that the enemy might seek to surrender.

At the end of September Smuts wrote to Schnee in the following terms:

> It is unnecessary for me to point out that on your Excellency and Colonel von Lettow rests the responsibility for the welfare of the helpless people of this Colony, who are cut off from all hope of succour from abroad and have already been called upon to make such efforts and sacrifices for more than two years. A continuation of the campaign even for a short while longer at this season of the year and in the deadly country to which your forces are now confined must mean untold suffering and complete ruin for them and at the end there will be no alternative to unconditional surrender. Under these circumstances I would impress upon Your Excellency that the time has come for you and Colonel von Lettow to consider very seriously whether this useless resistance should not now cease in a manner honourable to yourselves.[33]

His overture was a judicious mix of bluff and blackmail, and Schnee 'declined the proposal'.[34]

Von Lettow-Vorbeck regarded Smuts's missive as confirmation that his opponent's 'blow had failed', that he was 'at the end of his resources'.[35] He still had 1,500 Germans and 7,500 *askari* in the field, and had succeeded in moving huge quantities of supplies and munitions – including several thousand cattle – from Kissaki before abandoning the town. To say that all was well, however, would be an overstatement. In the retreat from Morogoro, *askari* whose homes were north of the railway had deserted and even switched sides in considerable numbers; and many of the European troops viewed the prospect of further 'desperate resistance quite without hope'[36] with no great enthusiasm. As was true of their pursuers, there was an increasing realisation that the campaign was not, as some in Europe believed, 'a sightseeing tour arranged by Cooks',[37] and that 'if you are told to "live on the country" and the country has not got it, well you have had it'.[38]

TWENTY-THREE

Smuts's 'Final Phase'

————◆————

At Mkapira, forty miles west of Mahenge, Murray and Hawthorn dug in after their initial 'bump' with Kraut at the end of September. Their position, on a slope with forest on three sides and the swampy banks of the Ruhudje on the fourth, was an exposed one; but observation posts on 'Picquet' Hill to the north would warn of any attack on the network of gun pits and trenches constructed by the British troops. At the centre of the camp the South African Mounted Rifles' guns afforded further protection, and for three weeks Kraut, keen to make quite certain that his second attack was successful, also remained on the defensive while he awaited the arrival of further troops from the Mahenge plateau.

During the early hours of 20 October, two days before Northey was warned by van Deventer that Kraut had fully ten or eleven companies at his disposal, British scouts at Mkapira warned Hawthorn that an attack was imminent and the camp was put on full alert. At dawn the lookouts were driven off Picquet Hill by German troops, and within minutes it became clear that Mkapira was surrounded and its lines of communication with Lupembe had been cut. Only two of Kraut's companies remained east of the Ruhudje River while two had crossed to seize Picquet Hill, three occupied another hill to the south of Mkapira, and another had taken up a position at nearby Mudikula. All the river crossings for miles were held by German detachments, and at 8 a.m. concentrated fire from the German artillery and more than a dozen machine-guns was directed against the British camp. The barrage went unanswered until mid afternoon, when the SAMR guns were briefly called on to assist in repelling an attack against Murray's trenches on the higher ground to the north of the camp. But after the attack was beaten off the British guns again fell silent for fear of giving away their positions, and for three days Kraut continued his bombardment unopposed as he endeavoured to soften up a foe whose strength he estimated at just three or four companies.

On 29 October Mkapira's defenders repelled another determined German attack and, as many in the camp were now suffering from dysentery and the effects of an acute shortage of foodstuffs, Hawthorn and Murray decided that the time had come to attempt to break the siege. The counter-attack was 'a brilliant piece of work'.[1] Hawthorn's troops beat back the two German companies to the north of the camp, Murray's Rhodesians and a company of 1/KAR attacked two others to the south-west and a KAR detachment moved up from Kasinga, fifteen miles west of Mkapira, in support. Before light Murray's BSAP charged 10/FK's picquets with the bayonet and did not stop until they were right into the enemy trenches, and all around Mkapira German troops were forced out of their offensive positions. Freiherr Louis von Schrötter, who had just a month earlier received the Iron Cross 2nd Class, lost two of 10/FK's three machine-guns to Murray; Hawthorn's KAR also captured a machine-gun and a small field gun in their attack; and a barrage laid down by the SAMR guns to the west was of such ferocity that the German companies holding the road to Lupembe were unable to move in support of those being attacked nearer Mkapira.

Kraut appeared to have been taken completely by surprise by the counter-attack, and many of his troops fought through the early stages of the battle in a state of semi-undress. In a few hours it was all over. German casualties amounted to almost fifty killed and eighty-one captured, whereas British casualties numbered just twenty-five. In addition to the three machine-guns and the field gun, documents summarising Kraut's movements up to 26 October were captured. These revealed that Kraut's intention had been to starve Mkapira's defenders into surrender, thereby securing the Mahenge plateau from any further threat from the south-west. Instead he was routed. Von Lettow-Vorbeck acknowledged a 'partial disaster' and somewhat disingenuously claimed that Kraut – who had a superiority of about four to one – had 'insufficient resources . . . to take [Mkapira] by force'.[2]

After Mkapira, Murray's demeanour was said to soften. His men had finally proved themselves up to his exacting standards, and they in turn now acknowledged him to be 'a commander that one was proud to serve'.[3] But no sooner had the dead been buried than news was received at Mkapira that Lupembe was being heavily attacked and Hawthorn left to relieve the mission as fast as possible. He found the route clear because Kraut, mistakenly thinking that the din emanating from the west indicated that his own 25/FK was under attack on the Lupembe road, pulled those of his mauled troops who remained on the west bank of the Ruhudje back over the river. But after a while Kraut, who had no knowledge of the whereabouts of Wahle's *Westtruppen*, became increasingly uncertain of the veracity of his belief that 25/FK was engaged with British troops to the west.

When the first news of fighting around Lupembe reached von Lettow-Vorbeck he too considered it a 'riddle', and one that 'was not solved until later'.[4] Unbeknownst to both of them, while Kraut had been advancing from the Mahenge plateau to Mkapira Wahle's advance troops had had their first contact with Northey's force. On 17 October scouts operating from Njombe, Northey's HQ, reported a large enemy force to the north and it was subsequently identified as Wintgens's column, which was making for the mountain stronghold of Ngominyi, thirty-five miles south-west of Iringa. As was his wont, Wintgens was operating entirely independently: Wahle had in effect lost him, and only after Wintgens crossed the Great Ruaha River in the fourth week in October did Wahle's son finally locate him. On 23 October, before communication was established with Wahle, 'Captain Winkins', as Allied reports referred to Wintgens, sent out Zingel's 26/FK to ambush a column led by Colonel Baxendale which had escorted an SAMR battery forward from Malangali to Iringa and was returning via Ngominyi. Baxendale was killed, his column of fifty Northern Rhodesia Police suffered thirty-three casualties, and Wintgens then turned his attention to Ngominyi itself, which was held by Captain Clarke with two 12-pdr naval guns and fifty men. After a siege lasting six days, during which even the sick and wounded were forced to remain in the trenches, the depot surrendered. The last time Clarke was seen alive he was hurling his empty revolver at a German *askari*, and in addition to Clarke and Lieutenant Bones thirty of Ngominyi's garrison were killed and the naval guns and a wireless fell into Wintgens's hands.

Having arrived from Iringa a day too late to relieve Ngominyi, a column led by Colonel Rodger was the next British unit to encounter Wintgens. Two days of fierce fighting ensued, in which Rodger found his SAMR battery so completely outgunned by Wintgens's artillery that he had to order them to withdraw; and only after the arrival of reinforcements from Iringa did Wintgens disengage and head for the mission station at Madibira. There he left 150 sick and wounded men and cast around for his next target, unaware of the extent to which his attack on Ngominyi had compromised Wahle's plans. Wahle had intended for all his columns to attack Iringa, and was forced by Wintgens's absence at Ngominyi to launch it without the assistance of his most audacious commander. The result, to Wahle's considerable annoyance, was 'costly and without success'[5] because on 26 October, the advance guard of troops sent by van Deventer – comprising Colonel Freeth's 7/SAI, a detachment of 4/SAH under Captain Walker, Colonel Fairweather's motorcyclists, and a section of mountain guns – finally arrived in Iringa.

Some of the South African troops were immediately despatched to rescue Rodger from Wintgens's clutches and the remainder prepared to oppose Major von Langenn-Steinkeller's attack from the north, but the likelihood of Iringa being held appeared remote. Freeth's 'Fighting Seventh' had completed the last seventy-two miles of its forced march in just seventy-four hours, Walker's 'mounted' troops arrived with only ten horses after a 170-mile trek, there were just twenty-one fit men among the town's existing garrison, and there was no reserve. However Walker's troopers succeeded in inflicting more than 100 casualties on von Langenn-Steinkeller's column and Wahle was forced to admit that his attack on Iringa 'didn't work'.[6] Had Wintgens not dallied at Ngominyi the outcome might have been very different; and even as it was the South African troops which had saved Iringa were in no state to remain in the field for much longer. Given their sorry state, the arrival of van Deventer to take command of operations in the vicinity of Iringa was not quite the boon that Northey had envisaged.

Although Kraut's appearance on the Ruhudje River, which required Northey to deploy Hawthorn and Murray against him, had not facilitated the capture of Iringa by Wahle, it did enhance the *Westtruppen*'s freedom of movement. After the failure to take Iringa Wahle and von Langenn-Steinkeller made straight for Malangali, vacated by Braunschweig in July, and on 8 November bombarded its defences with one of the 12-pdr British naval guns captured by Wintgens at Ngominyi. Over the next four days three attempts to storm Malangali, manned by only 100 *askari* of Colonel Tomlinson's newly formed Rhodesia Native Regiment, were beaten off; and only on 12 November did Wahle reluctantly withdraw when Murray's 'ubiquitous Rhodesians' arrived on the scene, having been rushed 120 miles by lorry and car from Mkapira. Wahle's rearguard was routed by Murray, and a plane was used to break up his force as it retired east towards Lupembe. Two MCs, a DSO and six DCMs were awarded on the spot to Murray's men, while Captain Marriott of 2/SAR also won the DSO for his handling of the Rhodesia Native Regiment's recruits in the trenches.

Wahle knew that he had stirred up a hornet's nest, and that breaking through Northey's lines would be all the more difficult now that the enemy's mobility had been greatly enhanced by the ability to use vehicles in the hot, dry November conditions. He was even more worried, however, by his supply situation. Still unaware of Kraut's proximity the other side of the Ruhudje River, Wahle recognised that he had to settle somewhere with abundant provisions before the rains began. The Mahenge plateau was his destination of choice, but his stocks of food were so depleted that he needed more supplies in order to reach it. With that in mind he had sent Wintgens ahead to Lupembe Mission to see if its rice-growing district was in British or German hands while he invested Malangali. As a result, Northey had been forced by the appearance of Wahle's troops amid his lines (and their regular attacks on his convoys) to order Hawthorn to the relief of Lupembe and Murray to the relief of Malangali. It was therefore Wahle's appearance that explained 'the riddle' perplexing Kraut: it was not his 25/FK which was under attack, but Lupembe that was being shelled by Wintgens, prompting the withdrawal of many of the British who had so successfully thwarted his attack on Mkapira.

At Malangali Wahle had given strict orders to Wintgens, whom he considered to be 'an excellent soldier and leader' but 'always ambitious',[7] not to attack Lupembe before the arrival of the *Westtruppen* main force. But once again the opportunistic Wintgens could not (or would not) resist the temptation. Lupembe Mission was on a high plateau, 5,000 feet above sea level, and to the east the ground dropped away sharply to swampy 'buffalo and elephant country' which extended sixty miles to the escarpment leading to the Mahenge plateau. It was defended by sixty Europeans and 250 new Awemba recruits to 1/KAR led by Captain Wyatt; and the garrison possessed just four machine-guns and two old muzzle-loading 7-pdrs (which belched black powder when fired). No attack had been expected – eighty German prisoners and the families of the Awemba recruits were living in and around the grounds of the mission – but morale was high and Lupembe's defences had been carefully constructed.

Wintgens's 400 *askari* were mostly Baganda and Nubians who had served with him for years, and his column had eight machine-guns and three field guns with which to launch his attack in mid November. But for six days the defences held firm, as the Awemba recruits sang and made 'not particularly polite remarks' about the German *askari* to bolster their morale. In one of three major assaults Wintgens's *askari* drove cattle ahead of them into the British trenches, on another occasion they attacked in the failing light at dusk, and just before dawn on 14 November they charged the east side of the mission (an assault which was said to be 'the worst of the lot'). Like the previous attacks it was repulsed and this time, despite having lost two of their machine-gun officers, the British troops 'had the idea that we had given the Germans such a knock that they would probably not try it again'. In daylight, while Wintgens collected his dead and wounded under a flag of truce, a message arrived to say that Hawthorn was approaching with the relief force from Mkapira; but that night was 'as sleepless as ever' as a final assault by Wintgens was anticipated. At 9 a.m. on 15 November, however, Wintgens's field hospital could be seen withdrawing under 'an immense Red Cross flag'.[8] The siege was over, and at 5 p.m. Hawthorn's first troops arrived at Lupembe from the east while Murray's men, rushed in cars from Malangali, attacked Wintgens's rearguard to the west.

Père Paradis, one of two missionaries of the White Fathers attached to the British forces at Lupembe, had baptised ninety-four Awemba recruits during the week's fighting;[*] and he had buried six Germans and forty-one *askari*. In

---

[*] See WF/Petit Écho/1917. Another White Father, Père Mazé, was a prisoner of Wintgens and managed to escape during his retreat and join Père Paradis at Lupembe.

fact Wintgens's column had suffered more than 300 casualties, half of whom lay in the mission's tiny hospital; and the naval gun seized by Wintgens at Ngominyi was recaptured. Captain Wyatt and machine-gunner Lieutenant Slattery were both recommended for instant awards; but all the European troops at Lupembe recognised that it was to the Awemba recruits that the victory really belonged.

Wintgens may have intended to attack again on the night of 14 November, but when Wahle arrived from Malangali with Murray hard on his heels the possibility of a further assault was immediately dismissed. Wahle was once again livid that his orders had been ignored by Wintgens, and that as a result the whole area around Lupembe was swarming with British troops blocking his path towards the Mahenge plateau. Worse still, when Wahle attempted to reorganise the *Westtruppen* at M'frika, a few miles east of Lupembe, he discovered that Colonel Franz Hübener's column, with its 10.5cm howitzer from the blockade-runner *Marie*, was missing. Wahle had ordered Wintgens never to leave Hübener, but the order had seemingly not been received and Wintgens had assumed that after the abortive attack on Iringa Hübener must have linked up with Wahle. In fact Hübener was still west of Malangali, and on 18 November Wahle sent a runner to him with a message informing him 'Break through Malangali now impossible. Ubena Lupembe strongly fortified and garrisoned. Try to march south-eastwards via Mufindi to Mpanga Kiganga where I shall try to effect a junction with Kraut.'[9]

It did not take Northey long to discover Hübener's whereabouts and a mixed force of NRP, RNR and BSAP led by Murray took to vehicles for a dash to Ilembule, forty miles north-west of Lupembe. So great was the importance attached to preventing Hübener from rejoining Wahle that this relatively small force possessed no fewer than fifteen machine-guns, and when Hübener's column appeared on 26 November he realised that his path eastwards was well and truly blocked by a determined and well-armed enemy. After loosing off more than 250 howitzer rounds at Murray's entrenchments around the mission station, Hübener surrendered on the condition that he could blow up the howitzer, that his *askari* were to be taken to Nyasaland and not used as carriers, and that his carriers were to be paid what was owed to them and sent home. Northey agreed to the terms and sixty-eight Germans and 249 *askari* were taken prisoner, among them Captain Albrecht Hering, who had commanded von Lettow-Vorbeck's artillery at Tanga and in the north-east in the first year of the war. The capture of the German column was deemed a 'very satisfactory enterprise'[10] by Northey, and compensated in part for the disasters that had overtaken Baxendale and Clarke in recent months.

Despite the loss of Hübener and the failure of Wintgens's attack on Lupembe, Wahle's *Westtruppen* were not beaten. One hundred and twenty-nine Germans and 619 *askari* had been killed, captured or wounded since the first engagements with Northey's troops at the end of October, but Wahle remained as determined as ever to break through with the 750 survivors to the Mahenge plateau. From M'frika he sent out patrols to the east and within days one returned with the news that there were German troops – Kraut's force – on the Ruhudje River. In the fourth week of November Kraut, who had heard nothing from Wahle since July, and Wahle finally linked up. It was an astonishing feat of 'determination and aptitude'[11] by the elderly general and, even though his trek from Tabora 'had cost [the *Westtruppen*] dear',[*] Northey was bitterly disappointed when he learnt that Kraut and Wahle had succeeded in joining forces.

While Northey was fighting Wahle and Kraut in the south during October and November, Smuts's plan for a final push against the main German force was thwarted by the rain and von Lettow-Vorbeck in equal measure. After Schnee and von Lettow-Vorbeck had refused his invitation to surrender he hoped that the enemy might stand and fight north of the Rufiji River, and with that in mind he made enquiries of the War Office about the feasibility of using gas against the *Schutztruppe*.[12] This was an extraordinary initiative, quite out of keeping with the impression both sides sought to maintain of a 'chivalrous campaign',[†] and showed how desperate to end the campaign Smuts had become. The idea came to naught. Smuts was advised that the scrub and long grass would render gas ineffective at a range of over 200 yards, but that if he still wanted to proceed 3,000 50lb cylinders – sufficient to attack a single 1,400-yard front – could be made available in two months' time. Time, however, was a luxury Smuts felt he could ill afford; he declined the offer.

By the end of October von Lettow-Vorbeck had withdrawn half his troops over the Rufiji, and instead of forcing him to fight north of the river Smuts had to consider the best means of preventing his retreat further southwards. In order to do so he needed to reinforce the units holding Kilwa, on the coast, and Kibata, a huge white *boma* north-west of Kilwa on a plain encircled by

---

* Crowe, p. 239. Boell put the Western Command strength at the start of the Belgian offensive at 3,400 troops, armed with nineteen machine-guns and twenty-two guns. Losses up to the junction with Kraut are enumerated as follows: 115 killed in action, nine dead, 859 captured, 208 missing, 548 left behind, 916 deserted (mostly the Mwanza garrison's local *askari*), a total of 2,655 casualties which reduced Wahle's strength to 745 rifles (see Boell (1), p. 296).

† See, for example, Lettow-Vorbeck (1), p. 170: 'the mutual personal esteem and chivalry which existed throughout in spite of the exhausting warfare carried out on both sides'.

the Matumbi Hills – and this required a further reorganisation of his forces. A new 1st Division, commanded by General Hoskins and comprising Hannyngton's and O'Grady's brigades, was despatched to Kilwa; while only Sheppard's brigade remained north of the Rufiji facing the eight companies under Captain Otto's command that von Lettow-Vorbeck had left as his new rearguard.[*]

Within days of the withdrawal of half of his force from north of the Rufiji, it became apparent that von Lettow-Vorbeck had anticipated that Smuts might seek to cut him off to the south when two companies commanded by Captain Schulz probed the defences of Kibata on 7 November. But it took weeks for von Lettow-Vorbeck to transfer nine companies from the Rufiji to Kibata as well, and by early December Hannyngton's brigade had reinforced the British defences there and O'Grady's brigade occupied the Matandu Valley to the west of the Matumbi Hills. On 6 December the battle that Smuts had hoped would occur north of the Rufiji commenced around Kibata, but with the roles reversed: it was the British troops, not von Lettow-Vorbeck's, who found themselves in danger of encirclement as Lieutenant Apel of the *Königsberg* began a ferocious bombardment of the *boma* with one of his former ship's guns, a howitzer and two mountain guns. In getting artillery up into the Matumbi Hills undetected von Lettow-Vorbeck had once again done 'the impossible';[13] and as Hoskins despatched reinforcements from Kilwa to Kibata and ordered O'Grady's brigade into the Matumbi Hills Smuts's plans for an advance inland to Liwale lay in tatters.

The battle around Kibata raged more or less continuously throughout December 1916, and rapidly dispelled any impression in the British ranks that von Lettow-Vorbeck's resolve might be diminishing. On a single day the recently arrived Gold Coast Regiment sustained casualties of fifteen per cent in its ranks, and fifty per cent among its officers; and von Lettow-Vorbeck estimated total British casualties at about 400. On Boxing Day 1916 Major Harold Lewis of the 129th Baluchis wrote to his mother with the following account of his experiences at Kibata:

We have had a very hard time, and really for some days it was touch and go whether we should be able to hold our own against the Huns. However, thanks to our men, we did it. My double Company has had two great stunts. The first was when the Boche first appeared against us and we (less

* Sheppard's 1st East African Brigade comprised: 25th Royal Fusiliers, 30th Punjabis, 130th Baluchis, 3rd Kashmir Rifles, half double company 61st Pioneers. Hannyngton's 2nd East African Brigade: 57th Rifles, Gold Coast Regiment, 1/3 and 2/3KAR. O'Grady's 3rd East African Brigade: 2nd Loyal North Lancs, 129th Baluchis, 40th Pathans, 1/2 and 2/2KAR.

than half the regiment) and [1/2 KAR], were in an isolated post. My men were in the place most violently attacked; all day long my left picquet was subjected to desultory bombardment from several guns, and also from heavy machine-gun fire. An hour before dark, this developed into an intense bombardment, and except for the size of the shells, I never experienced such a hot one, even in France ... We lost heavily in the redoubt ... however our men stuck it like heroes, though there was little left of the trenches.

Despite this repulse the German *askari* had gained a foothold on the end of the spur of Picquet Hill onto which the 129th Baluchis and KAR were clinging, and they were told 'to retake it'. Lewis's letter continued:

our fellows, as usual, got right up to the Hun trenches at night, and if they had been supported would have got through. But they were not supported. Poor little Bunny was killed right on their trenches ... and they gave me the job with full powers to make any arrangement I liked. So I fixed up a stunt with bombs and various machine-guns in flanking positions to co-operate. We planned it so as to leave our trenches, and creep up to the Huns in the inky blackness, and to have moonlight as soon as we had taken the trenches. Accordingly at 11 p.m. the line of bombers crept over the parapet and formed up in line in the darkness. They were followed by the first line, also with bombs who formed up behind. Then the second line crept out and formed to the right to guard against counter-attacks. The third line took their place in our trenches, and waited to push up to help the first line. Ayub Khan, of course, led the bombing line and his first bomb, which hit the German sentry in the chest, was the signal. Bombs were thrown, the guns and machine-guns opened and the still black night became a pandemonium. The German machine-guns on the lodgement poured a stream of bullets on to our trenches over the heads of our men, who lay on their stomachs, throwing bombs and pulling up the Hun stakes and obstacles. After about ten minutes, the Hun machine-gun stopped and the third line left our trenches and rushed forward and, yelling wildly, got into the Hun trenches and killed the survivors. All the time the Sepoys were getting through the obstacles. They were cheering and shouting, and nothing could have stopped them, and once in the trenches nothing could live. They were like a crowd of furies, and I have never seen anything equal to their dash. This action relieved the situation enormously, and practically put an end to the Huns' offensive and now no-one can speak too highly of the 129th DCO Baluchis ... Ayub, during the night attack, was shot through his handsome face, but I am pretty sure he will live to fight another day. He is the bravest man I ever knew.*

Von Lettow-Vorbeck was as disappointed by the failure to inflict a resounding defeat on the enemy at Kibata as he had been at Kondoa, but he still regarded his situation as 'remarkably favourable'. He was in no doubt that he could 'contemplate the continuation of the war for a considerable time',[14] and was greatly encouraged in his task by the news that the Kaiser had awarded him the *Pour le Mérite*.[†]

While the main British and German forces fought around Kibata, Northey moved his HQ forward to Lupembe and prepared for an offensive against Kraut and Wahle. Smuts had visited the southern front at the end of November and he, Northey and van Deventer had decided that it would be impossible, given that only 2,000 troops were fit for combat on a front which was almost 300 miles long, to push across the Ruhudje and Ulanga Rivers and onto the Mahenge plateau; and that a much larger force would be required to clear the plateau after the rains. But in the meantime a 'demonstration' against Wahle and Kraut by van Deventer's troops (at Iringa) and Northey's (further south) was considered to be an attractive compromise. Even if it failed to persuade von Lettow-Vorbeck that his left flank was in danger of collapse, it would at least clear the enemy from the lowlands to the west of the plateau and cause considerable congestion on the plateau itself.

Wahle's reappearance had swelled Kraut's ranks by about a third, and forced Northey to withdraw the small garrison left at Mkapira for fear that it might fall victim to a joint attack by Wahle and Kraut, but it was something of a mixed blessing. When Wahle's 3,000 carriers were included, the arrival of the *Westtruppen* meant 4,000 extra mouths to feed during the rainy season. A huge area, stretching as far south as Songea, was being planted by the local population but until the harvest the troops on the plateau would have to survive as best they could. There was no prospect of assistance from von

---

* IWM/Lewis: letter to his mother, 26 December 1916. This was one of the first times that Mills bombs were used in the campaign.
† Smuts's letter of 7 November 1916 conveying the news of his award to von Lettow-Vorbeck read: 'May I hope that, though we are unfortunately compelled to oppose each other, an expression of my sincere congratulations on your richly deserved distinction may not be distasteful to you.'

Lettow-Vorbeck's main force, with whom even the most rapid communication took anything up to a week.

By Christmas Eve 1916 Wahle had moved his headquarters from M'frika to a rubber plantation at Tanganika, about halfway between Lupembe and Mkapira, and closer to Kraut's troops on the Ruhudje. The nightmare of the trek from Tabora was swiftly forgotten as his troops enjoyed luxuries from the *Marie's* cargo sent to them by Kraut. The first news from home that any of Wahle's officers or NCOs had received in many months was a further distraction from their recent travails, and he, Wintgens, von Langenn-Steinkeller and Zingel all learnt that they, like Kraut, had been awarded the Iron Cross 2nd Class in September. The German East Africa campaign had not been forgotten by Berlin.

Northey's Christmas offensive soon put paid to the festivities. The rains had arrived early, and as his troops assembled in the pouring rain and pitch dark they could not muster much enthusiasm for carols extolling the virtues of 'peace on earth and good will to all men'. Murray's Rhodesians swept down the Ruhudje Valley with the intention of seizing the crops around Ifinga, fifty miles south-east of Mkapira, and soon Wahle was pushed back to the Ruhudje. The conditions were grim, with rain falling almost continuously, and the British soldiers were required to subsist on little more than a biscuit a day. As they advanced they were sniped at continuously at all hours of the day and night.

By the middle of January 1917 Wahle had been pushed back over the Ruhudje at Mkapira and then assumed command of all German troops concentrated on the Mahenge plateau. On 24 January Kraut's companies abandoned their positions, narrowly avoiding encirclement by Murray, and they retired onto the plateau around Gumbiro before being ordered by Wahle to occupy the region between Ifinga and Mpepo, on the lower Ruhudje. Meanwhile Wintgens was sent south to Kitanda, near the source of the Luwegu River. The defeat at Mkapira in October had, in the opinion of his opponents, caused Kraut, von Lettow-Vorbeck's principal commander in the defence of the north-east earlier in the year, to lose his nerve. As one officer later recalled, 'his force was now thoroughly demoralised, and would not face us at any cost'.[15] In his new position, the impending harvest would at least enable his troops to survive while the opportunistic Wintgens could reconnoitre the possibility of raiding British convoys on the Songea–Wiedhafen road, or even attacking Songea itself.

At the north end of the plateau, van Deventer's advance against Lincke, the former Deputy Chief of the colony's police, was equally indecisive. As an officer with the remnants of 4/SAH remarked, 'the capture of [Lincke] looked easy enough on paper, and ... van Deventer had the enemy surrounded on the map with a ring of indelible pencil. But having seen the forest, the deep gorges, and the size of the country in which we were to operate, I was not so sure.'[16] The aim was to get in the rear of Lincke's three companies at Muhanga Mission. Lincke, however, proved 'too clever for that' and any further pursuit was mitigated by an acute shortage of rations. The South African troops were ordered back to Dodoma and received their ticket home. 'We were glad to go,' wrote the mounted officer. 'The campaign had degenerated into something like searching for a needle in a haystack, with a handful of Germans hidden in thousands of square miles of bush. They had made a splendid stand, but they were not the real enemy. The real enemy were the deadly climate, the wild regions, and the swamps and forests, and scrub'.[17] Meanwhile, Lincke and Aumann remained on the loose at the north end of the plateau, and Northey was forced by the rains to call off the pursuit of Wahle and withdraw all his units to the western side of the rapidly rising Ruhudje River.

The temporary respite was welcomed by Wahle but the shortage of food-stuffs on the plateau soon became acute. Furthermore, his decision to send Wintgens to forage around Kitanda and seize the new harvest when it was ready involved a good deal of risk. The rains did not prevent Northey from operating to the south of the plateau, and just as Wintgens set out for Kitanda, British troops advanced against Major von Grawert's 7/FK and 12/FK, which had been sent by Kraut to Songea district in October and, after failing to support an unsuccessful attack by Falkenstein's 5/FK against Songea *boma* in November, had remained near Likuyu ever since – von Grawert being unable or unwilling to oppose Colonel Byron's 5/SAI, which had been reconstituted in South Africa and sent to garrison Songea. Von Grawert was an experienced soldier from the Reuss principalities in eastern Thuringia, and knew Mahenge district better than anyone, having served there for fifteen years. But when, on 22 January 1917, he found himself surrounded by a 500-strong force of 5/SAI, RNR and sundry levies led by Major J.J. McCarthy of the NRP he surrendered without a fight. It was an astonishing decision, considering his local knowledge and the fact that his force was only outnumbered by McCarthy's by a factor of less than two, but von Grawert had decided that his supply situation was hopeless. Von Lettow-Vorbeck subsequently accused von Grawert of 'exaggerating the difficulties of supply', and reminded him that 'there is almost always a way out, even of an apparently hopeless position, if the leader makes up his mind to face the risks'.[18] Von Grawert had clearly had enough, and as a result would carry the stigma of having *kapituliert* on his service record until his death in 1941.

When Wahle first heard the news he assumed that von Grawert's men must have been all 'more or less ill' to have surrendered. A message soon reached him, however, that eighty men, led by Sergeant-Major Winzer, had refused 'to give themselves up so shamefully' and had escaped southwards towards Likuyu. This made the capture of 230 officers and *askari*, two machine-guns, and a valuable naval anti-aircraft gun even more unpalatable. For Northey, on the other hand, it was the best news since the capture of Hübener's detachment, and McCarthy's success had prevented a link-up between Wintgens and von Grawert which would have threatened Songea. He was also encouraged by Murray's simultaneous capture of Ifinga, which made the position of Kraut's four companies on the lower Ruhudje untenable and forced him north-east towards Mpepo.

Northey's relentless pressure, exerted despite the pouring rain, unnerved Wahle. The Mahenge plateau was protected to the west by the rising rivers but to the south the path was open for 'an easy march towards Mahenge [and] the heart of the *Westtruppen*'[19] after the rains – unless Northey was stopped. Two companies under Captain Lincke were immediately 'rushed' from Muhanga on a forced march lasting two weeks to the southern end of the plateau; and Kraut was ordered to Gumbiro district where he would be in touch with Wintgens, whose column had become isolated after the surrender of von Grawert. In the coming month the actions of their two columns would preclude any assault on the plateau from the south, and just as Northey seemed to have Wahle and Kraut hemmed in on the plateau, his well-laid plans to bring them to battle would lie in ruins.

During these first eight months of Northey's campaign the men of Hawthorn's 1/KAR were never on full rations for more than two to three days at a time, and newspapers and letters took three to four months to arrive at the front. The reason for this was simple: Northey's supply lines were judged to be 'the most precarious and difficult [of the campaign]', and 'were certainly the longest communications with which any British force was involved during the course of the war'.[20] They began in South Africa. Most supplies were first shipped from Durban to Beira, then transferred onto smaller steamers for the eighty-mile journey to Chinde, then onto river boats for the journey up the Zambezi to Chiromo, then on to the railway to Blantyre, then overland to Lake Nyasa – and another 200-mile trip on the lake steamers. A subsidiary line originated in the docks at Cape Town. From here a 700-mile trip by rail to Livingstone was followed by a further 700-miles by carrier and canoe through Northern Rhodesia to Fife. But these only brought the supplies to the *rear* of Northey's field of operations, the point from which he had started in May 1916. From the borders of Nyasaland and Northern Rhodesia carriers had to negotiate distances of up to 200 miles over mountains and through dense bush into German East Africa.

More than 70,000 Africans had already been employed in this capacity by the end of the first phase in February 1917, a sobering figure as Nyasaland's total population was no greater than one million. Most convoys were led by missionaries belonging to British missions or the White Fathers in a well-meant (though futile) attempt to ensure the welfare of the carriers; but nothing could protect them from the ravages of disease and, after Wahle's appearance from the west, the danger of attack. 'I would award the palm of merit to the *tenga-tenga* [porters]',[21] was Northey's verdict on these largely unwilling participants in the war. When the question of committing their story to paper was raised after the war, however, the verdict in the Colonial Office was the less said about it the better.

Maintaining communication between his columns was another Herculean challenge for Northey, the more so after the appearance of Wahle's *Westtruppen*. Telephone and telegraph lines were frequently cut and often runners or motorcyclists were the most reliable means of transmitting messages, though they were slow in relative terms and, worst of all, could be captured. The construction of a durable surface on the Stevenson 'Road', previously little more than a track running for 300 miles from Lake Nyasa to Lake Tanganyika, opened this lateral route to motor transport and improved matters considerably; and during 1916 South African engineers (two-thirds of whom were invalided from any further war duty) also organised the construction of roads to Madibira, Malangali, Lupembe, Songea and Tandala. By early 1917, some 1,500 miles of motor road had been constructed, saving many combatant and carrier lives in the process. But the rains necessitated a repetition of much of the work and caused commensurately higher casualties among conscripted labourers.

Given the problems confronting him, and the constant changes to his objectives caused by Wahle and Kraut, Northey's achievements were considerable. His troops, with whom he was required to clear the enemy from a corridor measuring approximately 200 miles by 100, numbered fewer than 3,000 at the outset. That they succeeded at all was due to Northey's leadership. He was a commander who would insist on a stranded despatch rider joining him in the back of his Staff car. He would visit the sick in the hospital at Njombe, his headquarters, every Sunday morning and sit on the men's beds for a chat. On many occasions he sent his own car to pick up wounded. Such things were greatly appreciated and, whatever the hardships, Northey was recognised as a general who 'would see to it that his troops were properly cared for'.[22] He also had two outstanding commanders serving him. Hawthorn was indomitable and, after the early debacle at Namema, Murray was considered by Northey to be 'one of the finest soldiers I have ever come across'.[23] As for Northey's scouts, once met they were never forgotten. Often operating far behind the German lines and even mixing with German troops, these men 'were considered quite reckless and completely mad', and were wont to send messages such as 'Encountered [German] patrol with mg [machine-gun] crossing river stop what shall I do with mg stop'.[24] With the assistance of troops such as these Northey had, like Wahle, achieved the seemingly impossible in late 1916.

Smuts, on the other hand, was facing mounting criticism in South Africa as early as the summer of 1916, and this reached a crescendo as the first 8,000 South African troops returned home in November with hair-raising tales of the conditions they had endured. One sergeant remarked, as he watched two South African infantry battalions begin their journey home from the front: 'it was a long drawn out crowd and they reminded me of the picture of Napoleon's retreat from Moscow. The men were all done in – pale, fever stricken, many in rags ... how different they were a year ago when full of life and fun. Now they are listless and worn out. The men are plucky enough but the fever finishes them and they struggle along – chins on their chests – dragging one foot after the other.'[25] 'I'm afraid,' he added, 'that many mothers won't recognise their young sons.'[26] Smuts the politician needed an urgent answer to his predicament every bit as much as Smuts the soldier. His plans to corner von Lettow-Vorbeck's main force lay in tatters, and on 4 December 1916 news had reached him that a long-awaited Portuguese advance into southern German East Africa had met with disaster. The name Newala meant little to any British troops. But it was a name that would never be easily forgotten in Portugal.

TWENTY-FOUR

'The Condemned'

The rumours circulating in late 1915 of an impending invasion of Portuguese East Africa by German troops had quickly dissipated when South African troops began arriving in British East Africa. From then on it was clear that von Lettow-Vorbeck was going to be fully occupied far to the north. Relative calm was restored, but not for long. In Lisbon the government of General Joaquim Pimenta de Castro had been overthrown in a violent revolution in May 1915 and by the end of the year elections had put Afonso da Costa's democrats in power. In order to try and tackle the ongoing instability in Portuguese politics, the new government had decreed that no criticism could be directed at the armed forces. This was 'a perilous tactic'.[1] But, after Portugal had found (or been found) a suitable pretext to provoke Germany to declare war on 9 March 1916, it paved the way for further action on the border between Portuguese and German East Africa.

Lisbon set its sights on the Kionga Triangle, north of Palma, as a suitable target. It covered 215 square miles and had been a bone of contention between the Portuguese and German colonies for more than two decades. Seized by a German gunboat in 1894, a move which had forced the Portuguese to withdraw to Cape Delgado, it was a potent symbol of Portuguese fears for its future as a colonial power. Patriotic pride demanded its recapture, as did strategic necessity. Without a foothold on the Rovuma delta military operations upriver, between the sea and Nhica, would be virtually impossible; and the cross-border smuggling by the Germans which so irked Britain would remain a fact of life. In April 1916, Major da Silveira assembled a force 400-strong at Palma, ten miles south of the frontier, and advanced on Kionga. There were only a few border guards standing between him and his objective, and on 10 April the reoccupation of Kionga was achieved without difficulty. It was to prove the high point of Portugal's involvement in the campaign in East Africa.

Despite having already lost nearly a quarter of the Second Expeditionary Force to sickness, the hapless Major Mendes's suggestion that garrisoning Kionga would best be undertaken by indigenous troops was overruled by Álvaro de Castro, the Governor-General. Flush with success, Castro also ordered Mendes to prepare to clear the north bank of the Rovuma delta of German troops. The Governor-General himself took command of this operation, but the task proved too formidable even with an overwhelming superiority in numbers. On 21 May a small force of Marines crossed the 2,000-yard-wide Rovuma to land near 'Fábrica', a German sugar factory on the north bank and, supported by a bombardment from the cruiser *Adamastor* and gunboat *Chaimite*, burnt everything they could find. Six days later, a larger force left Namiranga and Namaca with the intention of permanently occupying the north bank. But this time naval reservist Lieutenant Sprockhoff, commander of the Kilwa *Abteilung*, had prepared a reception. He had set out from Kilwa on 23 April, Easter Day, to counter the Portuguese threat and his 100 rifles and two machine-guns now waited, 'with unbelievable audacity',[2] until the Portuguese landing was well under way before strafing the enemy with machine-gun fire. Two Portuguese gunboats were captured and the landing force abandoned its mission in ignominy, no more able to achieve their limited objective than were the Portuguese to defend the Tagus. Thirty-three men died in the 'Battle of Namiranga' on 27 May, twenty-four were wounded and eight, including the captain of the *Chaimite*, were taken prisoner.[3] A senior British Intelligence officer described the landings as 'a smaller and worse edition of the Tanga fiasco'.[4]

In Lisbon, the battle was overlooked. The recapture of Kionga, executed in the grand *tradição de heroismo*, was all that mattered. As *The Times History of the War* succinctly put it, 'the laurels gathered' in Lisbon, and a new issue of Kionga stamps was produced in Lourenço Marques, even though 'the results obtained ... did not in fact correspond to the effort made'.[5] More than ever, 'the issue of Portugal's attitude to the war [was] inseparable from party and political interests'[6] at home, and the men sent out by Lisbon 'without science or conscience'[7] were soon simply referred to as *os condenados* – 'the condemned'.

On the Rovuma delta, three-quarters of the 'condemned' men in da Silveira's command were sick by July 1916 on account of the 'ignorance and stupidity of the soldiers'[8] in not boiling their water or taking quinine, and a huge number had to be shipped away from the horrifically insalubrious stretch of coast and out of the colony. Those who remained had to confront persistent attacks launched across the Rovuma by Sprockhoff. All were repulsed but, as one Portuguese captain lamented,

the exhausting life on the swampy bank of the Rovuma, with the deleterious effect of an unforgiving climate, the nervous depression caused by the proximity of the enemy, without the compensation of good and regular food drained the strength of almost all the troops, who were reduced to the most abject physical state. By night, in the trenches and posts and lookouts, there was the humidity, the haze of the *cacimbo* season, and the cold; by day, shaking with fever, unable to rest because of the searing heat in the tents, everywhere became a veritable hell.[9]

By the end of June all available vessels were ferrying the sick from Kionga. It was a 'tragic sight'.[10] Of the 1,000 men of the 21st Infantry Regiment (3rd Battalion) which had formed the backbone of the Second Expeditionary Force, casualties had risen to 102 deaths and more than 600 sick and 'missing' in various hospitals around the colony. Within these totals, combat accounted for just nineteen of the casualties. The expedition's medical officer, Captain Sá Teixeira, made the situation abundantly clear to Lisbon: in his opinion Europeans simply could not be expected to survive for long in this corner of Africa. But his warnings went unheeded. Even as the 'Battle of Namiranga' (or of Namaca, no one was quite sure of its name) was taking place a decree was passed in Lisbon, framed in the usual bombastic and curiously anachronistic language, which authorised the despatch of yet another expeditionary force to Portuguese East Africa.

The size of Portugal's Third Expeditionary Force,[*] 5,000-strong, showed that Lisbon was as ambitious as ever to play its full part in the offensive against von Lettow-Vorbeck as Smuts pushed the main German force south towards Portuguese East Africa. The expedition was the initiative of the *Union Sagrada* government formed in March 1916, and its ill-trained troops began embarking on 29 May. By early July the elderly General Ferreira Gil, another political appointee whose most recent post was that of director of Lisbon's *Colégio Militar*, had reached Palma. His orders were vague, but the general intention was ambitious: an advance across the Rovuma to Mikindani and Lindi was envisaged, followed by a sweep west towards Tabora and the advancing Belgians. The Governor-General reckoned that it would take just three months to capture the whole south-eastern region of German East Africa.

Unfortunately, Lisbon's obsession with upholding the 'prestige' of the Republic, and fear that the war in East Africa might end without it even having set foot in German territory, was matched only by the total inability of its forces to fulfil Portuguese ambitions. Insufficient transport and the immediate debilitation of his troops by disease meant that Gil felt he was in no position to accede to the wishes of his superiors let alone those of Smuts, who supported the idea of a Portuguese advance on Liwale. Gil's immediate

---

[*] The Third Expeditionary Force comprised 1st, 2nd and 4th Mountain Batteries, three battalions from *Regimento* 23 (Coimbra), *Regimento* 24 (Aveiro) and *Regimento* 28 (Figueira da Foz), three QF batteries from *Grupo* 4, 5, and 8. Total strength: 211 officers and 5,985 men with 1,378 horses and 159 vehicles.

preoccupation was to try to move his headquarters to Mocímboa da Rovuma, 100 miles upriver, in the hope of improving the health of his men by abandoning the base at Palma. But as his troops arrived in the colony in dribs and drabs, the last as late as September 1916, Gil could not contemplate an offensive for months after his own arrival. In the meantime all he could do was reinforce the border posts along the Rovuma, and create a strategic reserve at Negomano (which was successfully defended against a German cross-border raid on 28 August).

Once Gil's force was complete, the pressure from Lisbon to advance mounted still further. Telegram after telegram exhorted him to act. 'Our prestige as a belligerent nation will be considerably diminished and our interests as a colonial nation prejudiced if an offensive against the Germans be not at once undertaken by the decided invasion of the territory beyond the Rovuma', read one; while another informed him 'the government assume the responsibility of affirming that at the present time it is better to face a difficult and dangerous action than to remain inactive'.[11] As early as July Smuts had also pressed his ally 'not to run the risk of arriving late or of [rendering] our operations useless'; a 'rapid offensive'[12] was urgently required of him. Had Gil been able to fulfil the grandiose ambitions of Lisbon, his advance could theoretically have helped to end the war by September. In practice, however, it was absurdly unrealistic for either Smuts or the Portuguese government to have expected that 6,000 Portuguese troops and ten companies of *askari* could have swept up the 3,500 German troops who were, by September, in the vast south-east quadrant of German East Africa.

By the middle of September, even though the most recent troops to arrive had undergone no training whatsoever, Gil could dither no longer. His initial plan had already been superseded by the arrival of the Royal Navy and British troops at the German port of Mikindani, but it was nevertheless towards Mikindani that three of Gil's columns advanced from Nhica on 18 September. A week later he established his HQ at the port, enabling him to tell his political masters that he had at least linked up with his British allies; and another column, mostly comprising *askari* employed by the *Companhia do Niassa*, garrisoned posts along the Rovuma between Mocímboa da Rovuma and Lake Nyasa. Smuts, whose patience with Gil was almost exhausted, suggested a Portuguese advance through Newala and Masasi to Liwale, a considerable modification of Gil's earlier ambitions to link up with the Belgians. If successful it would help in cornering Kraut and Wahle on the Mahenge plateau. But Gil took fright at Smuts's plan and agreed only to advance through Newala, on the Makonde plateau, as far as Masasi and the Lukuledi River. It was not an overly taxing objective.

As soon as 'strong forces of Portuguese' crossed the Rovuma and 'invaded the highlands of Makonde' von Lettow-Vorbeck guessed what was happening. 'A report came in,' he wrote, 'which caused me to suppose that the landing of strong enemy forces at Kilwa, and the appearance of hostile detachments which, coming from the west towards Liwale, had arrived on the Mbaranganda River, formed part of a big convergent movement by the enemy against Liwale'. Apart from Sprockhoff's small detachment, which had continually harassed the Portuguese since the failure of their attempt to cross into German East Africa in May, von Lettow-Vorbeck now had three new companies of *askari* stationed inland of Lindi. But these two forces, in his opinion, were 'rather too weak to enable [us] to turn against the Portuguese ... with any prospect of a rapid and decisive success'.[13] A larger force had to be cobbled together. At Mpotora, fifty miles north-east of Liwale, was von Boemcken's detachment of two companies and Lieutenant Häuser's *Königsberg* gun from Dar-es-Salaam. Captain Rothe was despatched to lead this force against the Portuguese, and Looff, who had successfully commanded land troops since the destruction of his cruiser, was ordered from the Rufiji delta to take overall charge of the offensive.

This was the first time that von Lettow-Vorbeck had paid any attention to the Portuguese. He had little respect for what his officers called Britain's 'vassal state',[14] nor for what his *askari* called the *shenzi ulaia* – their 'trashy soldiers'. But he did not want any enemy troops, even Portuguese soldiers, threatening him from the Makonde plateau. As a future location for supply dumps the high ground of the plateau offered many advantages, so Looff had to ensure that 'it should not remain in the hands of the Portuguese'.[15] But there was another motive, about which von Lettow-Vorbeck subsequently remained much more silent, for sending 1,000 troops south: the Makonde in German East Africa needed 'pacifying', and when Looff had dealt with the Portuguese he was told to restore order on the plateau.

It took Looff, marching at the head of three companies, three weeks to reach his rendezvous with Rothe's *Abteilung*. Much of it was through unmapped territory but Looff was guided by retired Major Gaston Schlobach, who kept him entertained with stories of living on his farm in Kilimanjaro district and hunting. After the vicissitudes of living on the Rufiji, and the capture of Dar-es-Salaam, Looff's German companions were glad to escape the north, where 'the enemy, the war and misery' dominated every conversation. Living as best they could according to Schlobach's motto 'early to bed, early to rise, makes a man healthy, wealthy and wise', they felt more like 'colonial pioneers'[16] than soldiers. On the other hand Major Stemmermann, who succeeded Looff as commander on the Rufiji, offered odds of 100–1 in favour of the capture of the column in its attempt to slip past the Allied troops at Kilwa. Although at times the enemy positions inland of Kilwa were clearly visible, Stemmermann lost his money and Looff's column pressed on southwards.

Looff's objective was simple enough: to deny the key Portuguese positions access to water, which was scarce on the Makonde plateau. With the British in the coastal ports, however, he also had to be sure to guard his left flank against them and protect supply dumps in which Hinrichs had secreted much of the precious cargo from the *Marie*. Looff decided that the British would be best squared by a feint executed from the Kaiser Plantation at Mtama in the direction of Lindi. Captain Kaiser, a retired colonial soldier, knew every inch of his district and harassed the British first on one side and then the other of the Lukuledi River. The impression thus created was of a large force and the British ceased to send patrols too far inland, leaving Looff free to concentrate on the Portuguese. On 14 November he arrived at Masasi Mission for his rendezvous with Rothe, and with Hinrichs and Sprockhoff already in action on the plateau, Looff and Rothe set off to reconnoitre the old German *boma* at Newala, perched on the south-western rim of the Makonde plateau.

The Portuguese 'invasion' of the Makonde plateau had not been easy. This strikingly beautiful massif rising 3,000 feet above sea level was criss-crossed by seasonal streams and dense *miombo* woodland, making the movement of troops difficult. It was perfect terrain for setting ambushes and, as early as 4 October, Sprockhoff had inflicted a heavy defeat on a column led by Captain Francisco Curado at Maúta. The Portuguese had, however, achieved their objective of occupying Newala and their left flank was seemingly secured by the garrison at Negomano, at the confluence of the Rovuma and Lujenda Rivers. The ejection of the tiny German force at Newala had occurred with hardly a shot being fired, though Gil's increasingly self-congratulatory reports sent back to Lisbon referred to a 'a fierce combat'.[17] A column sent out to occupy Masasi, as agreed with Smuts, was less fortunate: intercepted by Rothe on the Kivambo Heights on 8 November, it was beaten back with serious losses, including that of the Portuguese commander, Major Leopoldo da Silva. This then was the position when Looff arrived: Masasi was still in German hands and the Portuguese were licking their wounds back at Newala.

Newala was a well-constructed *boma* set right on the edge of the Makonde plateau. Its twenty-foot-high sloping walls made it almost impregnable, but its one weakness was serious. The fort only contained a small cistern and was reliant for water on wells one and a half miles away down the escarpment. This was Looff's first target. On 22 November Rothe's 4/SchK and Tanga/K attacked the wells at dawn. The 1,000 Portuguese troops defending Ribeira de Newala were well entrenched and put up a fierce resistance for twelve hours, killing three German officers in the process. At dusk, Rothe ordered his *askari* to fix bayonets and the Portuguese were finally dislodged, leaving sixty dead on the battlefield. Some of the survivors fled south to the Rovuma, others withdrew up the escarpment to the fort. The next day it was surrounded and Looff unleashed a furious bombardment from Häuser's *Königsberg* gun, a captured English 4.7-inch cannon and other smaller artillery pieces. Looff knew that thirst would eventually compel the Portuguese to surrender and the only threat to his encirclement would be the despatch of a column to relieve the fort.

Captain Benedito de Azevedo's relief column did not turn out to be a formidable threat. This hotch-potch, mostly sick force of 230 rifles and two mountain guns cobbled together from Maúta, Ntchichira, Sicumbiriro and Nangade was intercepted by Hinrichs's 20/FK a mile from Newala on 28 November and retired on Maúta, whence it had come. That night the Portuguese troops at Newala, fed up with their 'black and bitter'[18] occupation of the *boma* and believing themselves to be surrounded by a force 2,000-strong, knew there was now no prospect of further outside help. The next night a pea-soup fog descended on the plateau – so thick that Looff was concerned about the agitation in his own *askari*'s ranks – and decided against a night offensive. At dawn, when he did advance, Newala was no longer occupied. The Portuguese troops – thirty officers, 810 other ranks and 400 porters – had fled in the night. Looff was livid, but Newala offered compensation aplenty. The departing troops had left everything behind, including vehicles, horses, mules, 100,000 rounds of ammunition, and a staggering quantity of provisions, rifles, and medical supplies. It was, in Looff's opinion, 'the biggest haul from the enemy [during the campaign]', and he concluded that 'the English had supplied their ally well'.[19]

While some of Looff's troops guarded the booty and prepared to move it as fast as possible, detachments were sent to chase the fleeing Portuguese. But only the rearguard of a total of some 2,500 men from Newala and its supporting posts on both sides of the border could be seen when they reached the Rovuma, heading in disarray for Mocímboa da Rovuma and Nangade 'without even saying goodbye'. The chase was abandoned, Looff remarking that he was unable 'to run all the way to the Cape'.[20] Gil's offensive lay in ruins, and von Lettow-Vorbeck ordered Rothe's troops back to the Kilwa front to face the British while Looff completed a clearing-up operation on the Rovuma.

In the ensuing days, all posts except Fábrica, north of the Kionga Triangle, were cleared of Portuguese troops. On 1 December Francisco Curado's garrison at Nangade was bombarded by the *Königsberg* gun at a range of six miles, and turned tail. Mocímboa da Rovuma, Major Azambuja Martins's HQ for the Masasi offensive, was burnt to the ground on 6 December. Even the 150 Portuguese troops at Negomano, who had distinguished themselves in August, decided that the best course of action was to march all the way back to the coast. Two weeks later the rains began and the Rovuma started to rise. Von Lettow-Vorbeck's southern flank was now securely sealed, and the Makonde plateau was once again quiet.

Even before the fall of Newala General Gil, languishing in Palma with 'marsh anaemia' since the middle of October, had asked to be relieved of his command. The Governor-General, Álvaro de Castro, took charge and ordered the reoccupation of the posts south of the Rovuma with what remained of Gil's troops. A hundred and fifty Portuguese officers and 3,400 other ranks were now on the sick-list and, fearing a German attack on Palma, Castro ordered an evacuation of the port. The 'Newala Campaign' was over and Portugal had 'learnt a bitter lesson about War'.[21]

Politicians in Lisbon were unable to deny that Portugal's troops had been put to flight, but the defeat was subjected to a radical revision. Great emphasis was placed on lauding 'the heroic' Leopoldo da Silva, who had lost his life in 'one of the great actions of the colonial campaigns'[22] at Kivambo. Much was also made of the 'indomitable spirit of camaraderie'[23] displayed by the *Coluna de Sacrifício* in trying to rescue Newala; for good measure Benedito de Azevedo and a Sergeant Machado were both awarded the *Cruz de Guerra* 2nd class. As for the flight from Newala – described by one participant as the 'Epic of the Damned'* – it was recast as a 'brilliant' retirement. Even the Portuguese *askari* were found a place in this myth, and Corporal Ali was awarded the *Cruz de Guerra* for his conduct at Ribeira de Newala on 22 November. This was the extent to which the campaign had, as Gil's Chief of Staff put it, 'assumed a major importance for the nation in order to save its colonies'.[24]

It was with some astonishment that Errol MacDonell, the British Consul, read his copy of the *Lourenço Marques Guardian* on Boxing Day 1916. There, in black and white, he saw that Portugal's latest president, Bernardino Machado, claimed to have 'at present 15,000 splendidly trained troops' in Portuguese East Africa who 'were holding the Rovuma River from the Indian Ocean to Nyasa'; and that 'six thousand additional troops were proceeding there from Portugal'. In a memo to the Foreign Office MacDonell remarked that 'I can only state that President Machado must have been ill-informed in so far as the Luso-German frontier is concerned. Had the Portuguese taken up a line as suggested in this Press Article ... the German East African campaign would now have ended.'[25] Correlating information from his many agents, MacDonell concluded that the Portuguese had lost 800 rifles, fourteen machine-guns and two artillery pieces at Newala alone. Although it would be many months

---

* *Epopeia Maldita*, the title of combatant Antonio de Cértima's book, published in 1924; Newala was also referred to as 'The Palace of Good Fortune' by another disillusioned soldier (Selvagem, p. 200).

before von Lettow-Vorbeck dropped his visiting card on Portuguese East Africa in earnest, the situation at the end of the year was such that 'the Germans could enter the [Portuguese] Nyassa territories any time they wished';* and, with the Kaiser publishing his peace terms in Europe, rumours began to circulate that von Lettow-Vorbeck would soon be 'making a dash for Portuguese East Africa, whence [he] may trust to luck to get away by boat'.[26]

Smuts evinced no concern at the Portuguese failure to seal the southern border of German East Africa. By the autumn of 1916 he had completely lost patience with his ally to the south after repeatedly being accused of perfidy by General Gil, the latter casting around for any excuse for his total non-performance on the battlefield. At the end of October Gil had even refused to receive Smuts's Political Officer, Major Hayes Sadler, on the basis that Lisbon was yet to confirm acceptance of his appointment (a hesitancy undoubtedly born of Gil's – and Lisbon's – 'anxiety to conceal [Gil's] incompetency, inefficiency, and mal-organization').[27] Gil's propensity, one he shared with the Belgians, to squabble about who would administer any territory captured in German East Africa was also regarded by Smuts as absurdly tiresome.

The catastrophic defeat at Newala had put an end to Gil's shenanigans and, even at home, he was fiercely criticised in Lisbon's political inferno for his leadership of an expedition which had been 'disastrous for the country and shameful for the Portuguese Army'.[28] Had Gil's offensive succeeded, however, it would have had a very marked effect on German morale. As long as enough territory was held to dump supplies further south, von Lettow-Vorbeck could continue to believe that a fighting withdrawal was possible – even eluding Hannyngton and O'Grady's troops inland from Kilwa; but if the Portuguese had successfully established a cordon stretching from the Makonde plateau to Liwale his supply situation, already precarious, might have been severely compromised.

Smuts's response to the Portuguese failure was an attempt to cut off von Lettow-Vorbeck's rearguard in the north – Otto's five companies on the Mgeta River – before the February rains, and to force the surrender of the nine companies led by von Lettow-Vorbeck and Schulz which faced Kibata. In the north, he decided to send Beves's South African infantry from the west to attempt to get behind Otto's positions, while the rest of the force launched a

* TNA/FO/929/7. The 'Nyassa territories' refer to an area controlled by the *Companhia do Niassa* in the north of Portuguese East Africa.

'holding attack' from the Mgeta River. In the view of many a British commander such a strategy had by now been shown to be seriously flawed. 'In
bush country,' wrote one, 'where it is easy for bodies of troops to slip away, it
is necessary for success that the centre of an attacking force should press the
enemy's front vigorously while the wings should press in the enemy's flanks,
rather than that the outflanking columns should move wide round and hope
for the enemy to be driven back on them. To commit a central column as at
the Mgeta to a "holding attack" is to achieve nothing.'[29]

On New Year's Day half of General Cunliffe's Nigerian Brigade, whose four
infantry battalions and battery of artillery had arrived in East Africa in
December, duly began their advance from the Mgeta in concert with the 2nd
Nigeria Battalion and the 2nd Kashmiris under Colonel Lyall and Colonel
Dyke's 130th Baluchis. Smuts had assumed that Otto would stand and fight,
perhaps near Beho-Beho, twenty miles south of the Mgeta. But he had no
intention of so doing and, having fought a number of rearguard actions,
withdrew at speed to the Rufiji, which he crossed at Kibambawe on 5 January,
destroying the bridge behind him. The 'holding attack' thus 'achieved nothing', and the 1st and 4th Nigeria Battalions were even withdrawn after just
four days' fighting.

To the west Smuts had ordered Beves's South African infantry to make a
wide detour, screened by Sheppard's column, and cross the Rufiji at Kipenio,
fifteen miles upstream of Kibambawe. Once across the river they were so
exhausted and so far ahead of their supply lines that they could not press
against Otto from the south. Their state of paralysis 'wrecked Smuts's hopes',[30]
but their advance did at least cause von Lettow-Vorbeck some inconvenience.
Six companies were hurriedly despatched from the Kibata front to Lake
Utungi to cover Otto's withdrawal (leaving Schulz with just three companies
at Kibata); Tafel's three companies, guarding supply dumps south of the Rufiji,
were recalled to the Rufiji under the command of von Chappuis; and two
companies at Kissangire, towards the coast, were also ordered to march inland.
Some fifteen companies were therefore concentrating near Otto's 1,000 troops
armed with fourteen machine-guns.

As Colonel Sheppard's column crossed the Rufiji at Kibambawe Colonel
O'Grady marched north from Kibata, pushing back Schulz's weakened detachment, to occupy Mohoro and Utete downstream of Otto, and the 1st and 3rd
Nigerians reinforced Beves at Kipenio. On 20 January, as the eightsome reel
of British columns about the Rufiji reached some semblance of an orderly
conclusion, an encirclement of von Lettow-Vorbeck's main force seemed a
possibility, albeit a remote one. Four days later the 3rd Nigeria Battalion and
one company of the 4th advanced with artillery against Otto's rearguard at
Ngwembe. Fierce fighting raged all day, three British officers being awarded

the Military Cross, and Otto was wounded. But for some inexplicable reason the attack was broken off. One officer with the Nigerian Brigade wrote 'at this crisis of the campaign it is quite possible that if the British had got through [Ngwembe] the whole campaign might have taken very different lines, and possibly been greatly curtailed'.[31] The Nigerian battalions had certainly been 'blooded' by Otto, sustaining almost 100 casualties, but their officers were in no doubt that a further attack could have been pressed if adequate reinforcements had been sent forward. In fact no thought had been given to providing the Nigerians with a reserve. Intelligence reports had indicated that Ngwembe was held by just two German companies, whereas there were three, with two in reserve; and behind them lay von Lettow-Vorbeck's main force. On 25 January the rains began, precluding a resumption of the offensive. Once again Smuts had gambled – both with the weather and the size of the force deployed to 'clear out' Otto – and lost as his *final* final offensive ground to halt.

By then, however, Smuts was already on a ship bound for England and a seat at the Imperial War Conference convened by David Lloyd George with a view to ensuring that representatives of the British Dominions were given a greater say in the conduct of the war and other 'commonwealth' matters. On the Rufiji he left his troops in what one gunner described as 'the most deadly place we have yet struck. Mosquitoes, tsetse fly and all other crawling insects are here by the million. At night the yelping and howling of wild beasts keeps us awake. We are having a bad time with fever. The gun can only be fired with help of two cooks and a servant.'[32]

TWENTY-FIVE

The 'Suicidal System of Supply'[1]

In May 1916 Major Routh, the endlessly inventive British officer charged with organising British East Africa's Ordnance Department, felt that most difficulties with which he had been confronted since 1914 were 'on the point of being surmounted'.[2] His task had been immense. In addition to dealing with the eight East African governments and five ministries in London, the heterogeneous force which the War Office had cobbled together for the invasion of German East Africa from the north had myriad differing requirements – and its troops were strung out along nearly 1,500 miles of 'front', nearly three times the distance from Calais to Nice. If the German troop dispositions were 'like planets ... ours were like the Milky Way',[3] lamented Routh.

When Routh had arrived from India with IEF 'B' in November 1914 there had been no recognisable ordnance or supply system in place. Newly arrived regular soldiers had been appalled at having to buy things locally as required, and with the influx of thousands of under-equipped troops from India and elsewhere inflation had become rampant. Mr Jacobs at 'The Dustpan' in Nairobi sold 1,000 water bottles to the East African Mounted Rifles for Rs12 (rupees) each, more than double the usual price, and such profiteering was the norm as storekeepers sought to milk the government. Ensuring that such items were sourced and distributed on a more efficient, and less costly, basis was not Routh's remit; but with a staff of just two fellow-officers and nine NCOs Routh had worked through prolonged bouts of insomnia and attacks of malaria to put his own department on a more regular footing.

By early 1916 his establishment was handling an inventory comparable in size to that of the divisional arsenal at Allahabad – which had three times the number of staff for the task – and the challenges it confronted on a daily basis were considerably more complex. The four armed vessels on Lake Victoria all mounted different guns; Maxim guns had to be refitted with longer legs (for use in long grass) and shields (due to the close-quarter nature of much of the fighting); a consignment of .303 bullets were found to fall out of the muzzles of some of the rifles issued to the KAR if the rifles were aimed downwards;

and so the list went on. Then, in late 1915, Routh's 'belt-and-braces' operation suddenly had to cope with the impending arrival of the South African troops: 'You can imagine my feelings,' he wrote, 'we knew first only of a Brigade and five batteries. Then a Cavalry Brigade. Then two more Brigades, eventually six. We'd no idea what rifles they were armed with ... we didn't know what their guns were, nor if there was any ammunition with the batteries, or fire control instruments ... we had no knowledge of the saddlery they were using ... I put it to you, two unknown divisions arriving in an undeveloped country. What hope on earth had we of fixing them up?'[4] For some of his staff the strain was simply too much: one NCO had to be sent back to India suffering from acute 'melancholia', or depression. 'There's a limit', Routh noted, 'and this poor devil has reached it.'[5]

By the time Routh was transferred to Mesopotamia in mid 1916, and the Army Service Corps took over responsibility for all supplies, including ordnance, the situation was much improved; but transport had become a well-nigh insoluble problem. On arrival in East Africa, Major Hazleton, the new officer in charge of Supply and Transport, was told that Smuts's main advance into German East Africa would not take place until after the rains; and even in that timeframe he knew that he would not be able to guarantee to support the advance while also converting Routh's Indian Army organisation to his own British Army methods. Worse still, the distances covered by Smuts's troops in the initial operations of March and April 1916 were far greater than he had envisaged, with the result that some units were operating in German East Africa without even first-line transport. To many it had seemed as though Smuts had forgotten his reputation for 'halving the time allowed for a task but doubling or quadrupling the facilities'[6] and had simply set off as if he were replicating his famous raid into the Cape during the Boer War.

By June the vehicles Hazleton had ordered from the War Office had arrived from England, but by then the campaign was being fought in conditions which rendered them useless and Hazleton was forced to cobble together an ox transport system as best he could. But van Deventer's advance to Kondoa-Irangi 'knocked to smithereens' his efforts: even when the rains eased in May the journey from the railhead at Taveta, which took fifteen days, was so arduous that almost all oxen died along the way; and after the rains disease spread rapidly along the route to Kondoa. As late as July only seven wagons arrived in Kondoa out of a convoy of twenty-eight carrying supplies from a depot just fifteen miles to the north of the town; and by then it was obvious that the combination of disease, overwork and enemy artillery fire had produced 'heart-breaking results for the transport arrangements'.[7] Livestock seemed to be as ineffective as vehicles and, having lost 30,000 oxen in the first months of the advance, Hazleton had to admit that his transport system 'never quite caught up'[*] with the troops.

Hazleton was sharply critical of what he perceived to be the unorthodox, or 'gung-ho', character of the South African thrust into German East Africa. In his opinion there were 'too many troops for the transport available'; van Deventer's lunge at Kondoa had caused a serious 'leak'[8] in the transport system; and the failure to launch a diversionary attack against Dar-es-Salaam was a serious oversight. His was the view of a British supply officer. On the other hand, Smuts was adamant that the tail should not wag the dog, that the transport and supply arrangements 'should not be permitted to dominate'. He made it quite clear that he was aware that 'efforts like these cannot be made without inflicting the greatest hardships on all'.[9] But when von Lettow-Vorbeck was not brought to heel within weeks – which would have justified his tactics – Smuts found himself in a predicament with grave implications not only for the campaign but for his political career. When he arrived to inspect the situation at Kondoa in early May he was seen to be visibly shocked at the appearance of van Deventer's mounted troops; and criticism began to spread even to the South African support units as the realisation dawned that campaigning conditions in East Africa were 'far beyond the capabilities of a fledgling army' and would have to be fought out in 'one of the inner circles of a quartermaster's hell'.[10]

As Smuts confronted the possibility of the campaign degenerating into a repeat of the Boer War – in which his heavily outnumbered fellow-Boers had held out for two years longer than seemed even remotely possible in the spring of 1900 – with the roles reversed, only one means of transport existed which might prevent mass casualties among his troops due to starvation. Vehicles were no use, oxen were no use. The only beast of burden seemingly in plentiful supply was human, and if porterage had not become the bedrock of his transport system after the initial advance of March–May 1916 the campaign, in the words of its official history, 'could never have been fought at all'.[11]

The story of how almost every able-bodied African male civilian in the

---

[*] Hazleton, p. 230. Between September and November 1916 10,000 horses, 11,000 oxen and 2,500 donkeys expired in the field, and livestock wastage rates for the year were running at nearly 300 per cent (as against sixteen per cent in 1914 and sixty-seven per cent in 1915). One Australian with the South African Veterinary Corps, C.C. Doak, was so distressed by this that he took his own life with an overdose of morphia. By the end of 1918 a total of 31,000 horses, 33,000 mules and 34,000 donkeys had perished. *The Official History of the War: Veterinary Services* described the campaign as 'a chamber of horrors in so far as animal life was concerned' (p. 417). Von Lettow-Vorbeck tried to maximise the difficulties of using animal transport. He frequently sent his veterinary officer, Dr Friedrich Huber, to survey possible lines of retreat with a view to choosing one that would be most deadly for Allied livestock.

'The Girls They Left Behind' – King's African Rifles recruits leave for the war

Portuguese troops embarking at Lisbon for East Africa

Allied troops prepare to advance, March 1916

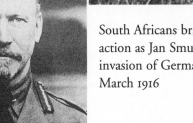

South Africans bring their guns into action as Jan Smuts (inset) orders the invasion of German East Africa in March 1916

Königsberg gun during the German retreat down the Usambara Railway

German prisoners being led into captivity; and at a concert hall performance at the Fort Napier prison camp in South Africa

Sylvester Cabaret Fort-Napier 1916 -17.

In the north-west Belgian troops commanded by Charles Tombeur (inset) advance towards Tabora, capturing the town in September 1916; while in the south-west General Northey's troops capture Fort Namema before converging on Iringa

German attempts to stir up an anti-British *jihad* in Abyssinia and elsewhere in north-east Africa were finally frustrated at the end of 1916 with the defeat of emperor Lij Iyasu and his replacement by Ras Tafari (centre), seen here flanked by the British Consul-General in Addis Ababa Wilfred Thesiger (right) . . .

. . . but in German East Africa there was no let-up in the fighting

German *askari* play cards, and Nigerian gunners wrestle, in their camps; but discipline for malefactors was harsh

The naval campaign continued unabated throughout 1916; ratings, such as these stokers ('clinker-knockers') on the *Kinfauns Castle*, toiled under appalling conditions

HMS *Hyacinth* tilted to fire inland at German positions along the Lukuledi River

British territories neighbouring German East Africa, and in German East Africa itself, became involved in the conflict is one of the greatest tragedies of World War I. In the first months of the war African carriers were not employed in great numbers, and volunteers were easily found for specific projects. Fewer than 10,000 men, recruited from Uganda and British East Africa, were sent to Mombasa in September and October 1914 to work for the two Indian Expeditionary Forces; about 2,000 Wateita were recruited to work on the construction of the new military railway from Voi towards Taveta in early 1915; and 5,000 Africans from the coast supported Tighe's Umba Valley operations in January 1915. In relative terms all these men were reasonably well paid, receiving Rs15 per month plus their food, a figure which was three times an individual's annual hut tax payment (and compared to a wage of Rs25 for an *askari* in the King's African Rifles, Rs30 for a good interpreter, or Rs50 for hard, seasonal agricultural work); moreover, the conditions under which they were employed were strictly monitored by government officials. It was realised that without proper sanitary measures and medical attention there would be a 'great danger of epidemics of malaria and dysentery', and that 'if such should unfortunately occur apart from the decrease in the labour force the work will get a bad name'.[12] The results of such vigilance varied. The inspection reports of the railway labour camps at Voi River and Mwatate in March 1915, for example, showed that only fourteen out of 1,690 Wateita were on the sick-list on the days of the inspections and that there were no deaths either through disease or accident.[13] On the other hand, disease caused significant casualties among the carriers supporting the Umba Valley operations.

If the labour requirements during the first six months of the war appeared relatively undemanding, as they subsequently would, the situation changed markedly during 1915. Although the campaign was, with the exception of 'affairs' such as Bukoba, a stalemate the arrival of more and more troops was accompanied by the need to create a suitable military infrastructure with which to support them – a task which was dependent upon increasing numbers of carriers and other labourers. The Military Labour Bureau, later renamed the Carrier Corps, was formed to oversee this development. Commanded by Lieutenant-Colonel Oscar Watkins, a well-respected government official, its approach was paternalistic; but by the autumn of 1915 Watkins's porterage system, devised in the belief that the war would only last a few months, began to creak at the seams. So great was the need for manpower that the Carrier Corps had expanded from 25,000 to 45,000 men and, with only a small staff and a rank that precluded him from dealing with generals on equal terms, Watkins became less able to ensure the proper treatment of his men; and at the same time legislative measures were passed which were to have very unfavourable consequences for those employed by the Carrier Corps.

By mid 1915 the expense of the war was a matter of grave concern to Belfield's government, and to Whitehall, and as labour was increasingly drained by the Carrier Corps and the docks in Mombasa the prospects for recruiting sufficient manpower at an acceptable cost looked bleaker by the month. This problem was exacerbated by the fact that although the Carrier Corps's wages were fixed, those of the dock workers in Mombasa were not; and the latter took advantage of the scarcity of semi-skilled labour to demand an increase in wages from Rs25 to Rs30 per month and the abolition of the existing monthly contract system (which left dock labourers free, if they so desired, to take advantage of the rising wages secured by casual day labourers). All wartime attempts to formalise dock labour were thwarted; and only by tolerating high rates of pay and a low degree of control could Belfield's government ensure that Mombasa continued to meet the escalating demands of the military at the same time as handling booming exports of cotton from Uganda, and coffee and sisal from British East Africa.

But if the dockers and other skilled workers offered no prospect of cost-savings to the government, the Carrier Corps was a different matter. It only required unskilled labour, and as its recruitment 'pool' was the whole of British East Africa rather than one town the bargaining power of carriers and casual labourers was precarious. The result was the 1915 Native Followers Recruitment Ordinance, which sought to exploit this weakness to the full. It stipulated that service in the Carrier Corps could now be enforced through conscription, and that wages were to be fixed at one third of the prevailing level – Rs5 per month plus food, rising to Rs6 after three months' service. This was a derisory level of remuneration, barely exceeding the *daily* wage of the settler volunteers in 1914; the metal identification tags with which each carrier was issued cost Rs2, and a blanket typically cost Rs3/50. Furthermore the ration scale for carriers' rations did not reach parity with those of *askari* in the KAR until 1917, despite the extremely onerous nature of carrier work. It is impossible to avoid the suspicion that payment might have been waived altogether were it not for a universal fear of accusations of slavery; and although 'specialists' like machine-gun porters would continue to be paid higher rates, the Carrier Corps had, despite all Watkins's good intentions, become little more than a press gang justified by 'the exigencies of war'.

It was ironic that just as the carriers' terms of employment were undergoing this radical revision, facilitated by a supposedly unlimited supply of unskilled labour, there were already signs that certain communities had been squeezed dry of recruits, and that no amount of coercion was likely to produce more carriers. In early 1915 one third of the 1,500 Wakamba men working outside their home district of Machakos were being employed by the military in Nairobi; one year later a further 2,000 had been called up by the Carrier Corps, quadrupling the number of men employed by the military and increasing to one in ten the number of adult males working away from home. The repercussions of such extensive labour migration were considerable, the more so as it was accompanied by an increasing demand for foodstuffs. As one enlightened official put it, 'astounded villagers saw their menfolk taken from them in thousands ... their grain-bins emptied, [and] their cattle driven away'. Cash was always paid by the authorities for supplies, but cash was of little use in many districts; and before long many tribes found that not even 'their own exertions [could] replace what the troops consumed, for with the departure of the able-bodied men hardly any but old people and women remained in the villages, so that there was never enough labour to till the fields'.[14] In the case of many tribes the deleterious consequences of their involvement in the war were also compounded by recent history. The Wateita, for example, had experienced terrible droughts and famines in the 1880s and 1890s which had wrecked the land and decimated the population; the misguided excision of large tracts of their best land for European sisal plantations; and the establishment on their land of a European coffee plantation and a mission for the Holy Ghost Fathers.

Many young men fled their homes to the towns in an increasingly futile attempt to avoid being caught up in the war; and for those who stayed put the consequences were often worse than being recruited for the Carrier Corps. The Wakasigau, for example, were blamed by the military authorities when Captain Doering's detachment of *Schutztruppe* captured the mountain of Kasigau in August 1915; and when it was recaptured they found themselves 'convicted' en mass of disloyalty, it being deemed 'absolutely impossible for the enemy to have attacked without knowledge and active assistance [of the] local natives'.[15] Eleven men were arrested, three were executed, and more than 700 members of the tribe were deported to Malindi district. That was not all. Their huts were burnt down by the KAR, their goats slaughtered and cattle 'placed' with 'loyals', and the inhabitants of two villages were heavily fined. Within two months of their deportation to the coast one third of the exiles were suffering from malaria.

By the end of 1916 there was not a single community in British East Africa that had not suffered in some form from the effects of the war. Tribes on the border with German East Africa lived in constant fear of having their loyalty questioned, stocks of foodstuffs had been reduced to a bare minimum, and men taken for carrier duty were paid less while being required to serve for longer in conditions more strenuous than had ever been envisaged in the early days of the Military Labour Bureau. Worst of all, however, was that there appeared to be no end in sight – either to the fighting or the demands of the Carrier Corps. Seventy-two thousand Africans had been called up in British East Africa for non-combatant military service in the eighteen months leading up to Smuts's offensive in March 1916; by the end of the year that number had doubled – and more than 4,000 fatalities had already occurred in the Carrier Corps, a considerably greater number than among the combatant troops.

The predicament of civilians recruited for carrier work in other British territories was no better than that of their comrades in British East Africa. In late 1915 and early 1916 120,000 Ugandan carriers were required to transport the Belgian supplies and armaments shipped from Europe to the Belgian HQ in Kivu district, and when Tombeur was finally ready to advance into German East Africa he had made it clear that he would only do so if his troops were supported by British first-line carriers. The Belgian government's decision that Congolese carriers, 260,000 of whom manned its colony's internal lines of communication during the war, could not serve in German East Africa resulted in the onus once again falling on Uganda; and once again the Bagandan *Lukiiko* (parliament) responded positively by authorising the creation of 'CARBEL', a carrier unit whose 7,238 men mustered at Mbarara in April 1916 for the Belgian advance.

CARBEL was commanded by Captain Anderson and sundry other officers who were settlers or government officials in peacetime. A nightmare lay ahead. The first seventy miles of the advance towards Kigali took place in almost continual, torrential rain and freezing cold. Several rivers in spate had to be forded en route, and with usable firewood a scarcity there was no way for the men to dry at night, let alone cook. After a pause of almost a month in Ruanda, Tombeur's advance recommenced in early June and three weeks later the Belgians had reached Lake Victoria. Six hundred sick porters were sent home from here, and new drafts arrived to take their place for the final 220-mile advance on Tabora, undertaken in searing heat. There the five-month assignment ended. But there was scarcely enough food in Tabora to provision CARBEL for the return journey and by the time its survivors reached Mwanza, and the ships that would take the carriers home, many were on the brink of starvation. In all 789 men out of a force 8,429-strong had died, and 402 were missing (and presumed dead). All four interpreters, nine sub-chiefs and forty-nine headmen returned safely to Uganda, but the senior *Ssaza* (district) chief did not. His body was buried in Mwanza with full military honours.

The death of one in seven of CARBEL's carriers may seem alarming, but it was not an untypical mortality rate and, given the conditions encountered during the Belgian advance, it could easily have been many times greater. The fact that CARBEL was officered by men with a genuine concern for the welfare of their charges, and that it was accompanied by two doctors with adequate medical supplies, also helped to keep casualties to a 'minimum' and brought out the best in the men. Praise was heaped upon them by Captain Fenning, who succeeded Anderson as commanding officer after he was taken sick, particularly for their conduct when required to march 'for 17 days without rest' during the final advance on Tabora, when – as often happened – they had 'to turn out for a long night march just after having settled down from the day's march', and when they came under fire. On one occasion 'a batch of carriers transporting trench mortars' came under concentrated artillery fire but 'continued their way towards danger until they were ordered to halt; on another Carrier No. 693 (Nasanairi Kalibwani) 'refused to leave a Belgian *sous-officier* who was working a machine-gun, taking an active part in keeping him supplied with ammunition and eventually, when the enemy fire became too hot, assisting in the evacuation of this gun'.

CARBEL's 'most praiseworthy conduct'[16] would be matched by many other carrier units during the war, especially those that were led by knowledgeable, sympathetic officers (many of whom were missionaries). It was unusual, however, in that it furnished historians with accounts written not only by its European officers but also by one of its African participants; and that he, Ezera Kabali, wrote to the *Kabaka* of Uganda after his return 'assuring him that, in spite of [CARBEL's] great loss, the Baganda would continue to give whole-hearted service to the British'.[*] In general the lot of the carrier was such that enthusiasm for further service was muted, and one glimpse of their columns, comprising mile upon mile of men carrying loads of fifty or sixty pounds on their heads, trudging through the mud and across the rivers, was enough to make most Allied soldiers realise why this was so. Furthermore, although there were plenty of 'bad apples' in positions of responsibility with carrier units throughout East Africa, there were many conscientious men on whom the carriers' plight had a profound effect.[†] Captain W. Hillbrook, a medical officer with CARBEL, was one such man – and the trauma caused by his unit's experience was so great that he was sent to an asylum in Nairobi , 'talking and shouting in an incoherent manner' and suffering from 'fleeting delusions, mistaking the identity of those around him'. The diagnosis was that 'exhaustion bordering on collapse' had caused 'acute confusional insanity', and Hillbrook's doctor found it impossible to 'induce sleep ... or quiet his

---

* Welbourn, p. 225; Kabali's testimony was subsequently instrumental in securing an official reprimand of seven Belgian officers and NCOs for the mistreatment of carriers.

† Private Rowland, a Frontiersman from Bury, Lancashire, wrote of the 'Kavirondo' headman of his carrier column: 'On the first occasion that I met him ... I shook his hand and those of his friendly team. Whenever our paths crossed they would come to greet me with hand outstretched and broad smiles across their shining black faces. I count it among my happiest memories to have known them' (Liddle/Rowland).

struggling'.[17] Hillbrook died in as troubled a state as a carrier abandoned by the side of the road, his case of insanity the most acute of its kind that the doctor had ever experienced.

CARBEL's very existence, like that of other British carrier units, was symptomatic of a singular dilemma confronting Smuts in his attempt to encircle von Lettow-Vorbeck's troops. Belgian officers expected their troops to live off the land, and among their units combat troops usually outnumbered carriers. But this was a *modus operandi* which found no favour with British colonial governments on account of its consequences for local populations. Even if a system of paying a fair price for supplies was in place it would inevitably be open to all sorts of abuse, and it was thought counter-productive to plunder the inhabitants of a German colony which would soon be under British administration. The logic was laudable in theory, and if Tombeur had not requested the services of Ugandan carriers the British military authorities may well have insisted on providing such support, but ultimately it was counter-productive: as British carriers had to carry their own supplies as well as those of the troops to whom they were attached a huge number of men, many of whom would die or suffer permanent impairment due to disease, had to be employed. The mathematics were sobering. For example, in order to maintain troops 450 miles from the railhead in Northern Rhodesia 16,500 carriers were needed to transport a single ton of supplies – enough to feed 1,000 *askari* and their camp-followers for just one day – for the simple reason that 14,000 men were required to carry the food for the 2,500 who carried the troops' supplies.

By Christmas 1916 the 'human cargo' transport system chosen by British forces had, for all its good intentions, involved the recruitment of considerably more Africans than the 100,000 pressed into military labour during the Anglo-South African War. It even exceeded the 180,000 black Americans enlisted in the segregated regiments of the Union during the American Civil War. Yet, with no prospect of an imminent end to the hostilities, the tragedy was only just beginning. Carrier units were still multiplying, like hydra, the toll wrought by disease and inadequate or inappropriate diets was escalating daily, and even the carriers' already measly pay was so devalued by high prices in German East Africa that their monthly stipend wasn't even sufficient to buy a packet of ten cigarettes. 'A carrier is one of the lowest forms of life,' wrote one motor transport officer, not without some sympathy, 'and he is always more or less in a state of misery, as well he may be, for his job is to carry forty pounds' weight on his head, and as he takes no interest in the war, he does not find this very amusing.'[18]

At the same time it became increasingly difficult for an individual to evade labour recruiters. Chiefs and headmen complied, often with suspicious alacrity, with the authorities under threat of imprisonment or heavy fines; and even for pastoral people there was a singular dearth of places to hide. For a few it was still possible to secure civilian work in Nairobi and Mombasa or to evade the system by 'squatting' on the farms of Europeans. For those already in the ranks desertion was possible, but less so the further they were led from home. Even hopes of 'getting it over with' evaporated when the terms of service lengthened from three months to nine, and soon there would be no African family in the British colonies neighbouring German East Africa which did not see some – or all – of its menfolk led off to war.

The fate of civilians coerced in vast numbers into carrier service in German East Africa, particularly those who lived in the north-east, was similar to that of their counterparts in British territories – but the way in which they were employed differed significantly. On the one hand they seldom found themselves working far from their homes, which enabled them to return quickly to plant or harvest crops and reduced the likelihood of contact with diseases to which they were not naturally immune. On the other hand carriers not directly employed as 'professionals' by a *Feldkompanie* were not paid for their labours, and women and children were recruited on a scale which, in British eyes, constituted an outrage. Furthermore, no attempt was made to keep proper records for 'casual' labour – a surprising oversight which belied the reputation for thoroughness attributed to German colonial governments. The explanation for such an oversight was simple. Schnee and von Lettow-Vorbeck had fewer qualms about the use of forced labour than their British counterparts, and do not appear to have recognised that their actions might expose them to accusations of condoning slavery.

Schnee's failure to keep proper administrative records conveniently made it impossible to compute with any degree of precision the number of Africans employed in supporting the German war effort. Records of sorts *were* compiled for the paid carriers who were an integral part of a *Feldkompanie*, each of which had a standard complement of 322 porters (approximately two men or boys to carry the equipment of each *askari*) plus thirty to fifty 'specialists' responsible for machine-guns and other heavy materiel; and these records formed the basis for an 'official' figure of just 14,000 carriers having been employed during the entire war. This was a risibly implausible estimate, even for the number of 'professional' carriers; and it ignores completely the recruitment of carriers for work on von Lettow-Vorbeck's lines of communication and specific wartime projects. The accounts of German combatants indicate that 8,000 carriers were used to establish a network of supply dumps in the north-east in 1914; and that 100,000 – in Looff's words – 'happily undertook'[19] the task of distributing the cargo of the blockade-runner *Marie* in 1916. By the same token, when van Deventer sought to recruit 15,000 carriers in Irangi district for his advance towards the Central Railway in mid

1916, he was only able to gather half that number because the retreating German force which had invested Kondoa had scoured the district before him; and when German troops retreated through the Uluguru Mountains Hans Stache, their transport officer, was said by a fellow combatant to have 'shanghaied any [African] he could lay his hands on, and was prepared to commit any crime to get them'.[20] The carriers attached to each *Feldkompanie* were, in other words, but a fraction of a total headcount of those who 'worked for the troops'. Even von Lettow-Vorbeck admitted that the number of *Landschaftsträger* – 'casual' labourers – ran into 'hundreds of thousands';[21] and subsequent estimates put the figure at 350,000 or more.[22] No record of fatalities, let alone casualties, was kept by German officials.

As von Lettow-Vorbeck's supplies diminished the districts still under German control were denuded of all available foodstuffs as well as carriers; and only in quite exceptional cases was payment offered for either. Such 'total disregard for the barest needs of the native population' was, in the opinion of British officers, the principal factor underpinning von Lettow-Vorbeck's 'ability to keep a large army in the field'; and the 'wholesale seizure of every vestige of foodstuff throughout the country' was to have dire consequences. 'What of those unfortunates who were of no military value – the old men, the old women, and the young children?' asked a young British lieutenant who advanced through the Ulugurus in the wake of the retreating German troops, before concluding that 'their lot was a desolate village and starvation'.[23]

Before the end of 1917 more than 300,000 Africans were to die in German East Africa from the famine caused by war. This represented a death toll of one in twenty of the colony's *total* African population; among the populations most affected by the fighting the casualty rate was far higher. Meanwhile, there was no diminution in the numbers seized for military labour, nor in the numbers of fatalities. 'Our road is paved with the corpses of the natives we have been obliged to kill',[24] wrote one of Wintgens's officers; and those who survived faced the gruesome prospect of being pounced on by recruiters from the advancing Allied forces. For many it was as if the days when Arab slave-raiders would descend on the tribes of the interior had returned; and even though they were paid, and less frequently roped together or beaten, when serving in British carrier units their duties and the conditions they encountered remained equally repugnant.

'Can you wonder that [the carriers] suffered,' wrote one British government official, 'and suffered terribly? Of course they did. These poor, spiritless, ragged creatures had to hump their heavy packs and follow some of the most active and hardy troops that ever took to the field, over fearfully difficult country, through one of the most prolonged and rapid wars of movement ever known.'[25]

Such expressions of sympathy for the 'many thousand of blacks who suffered in uninterpretable silence'[26] did little to ameliorate the lot of the carrier. But they were at least common among British troops and civilian administrators. The accounts of German combatants, on the other hand, while universally fulsome in their praise for the 'loyalty' of the indigenous population, scarcely express even so much as a fleeting realisation of the consequences – or questionable morality – of the way in which they exploited their colonial subjects. In 1919, at the Versailles Peace Conference, this apparent absence of any vestige of guilt was to have far-reaching ramifications and played directly into the hands of those seeking to establish that 'in the German colonies ... the same militaristic system prevailed as in Germany itself'.[*] It was an accusation which von Lettow-Vorbeck brushed aside with a simple *tu quoque*: 'No doubt, in a long war cases of brutality and inhumanity do occur. But that happens on both sides.'[27]

There were *some* Africans for whom service in a carrier unit was an adventure of sorts. Those fortunate enough to own canoes on the Lukulu River, in Northern Rhodesia, were paid five shillings for each run upriver with supplies for the frontline troops, plus six shillings for food and a sixpence bonus for each load reaching its destination intact; the caretaker of the carrier cemetery at Voi earned four times the amount paid to carriers in the field; and literacy could secure a desk job in a labour bureau which might carry a wage up to thirty times that of a carrier in the field. 'Specialists', such as carriers attached to a mechanical transport unit or stretcher-bearers, were also far better rewarded, better looked after, and less likely to succumb to disease; and they learnt skills which would, for better or worse, secure them employment in the post-war colonial economy. Mobility also brought the opportunity for those from inland communities to learn Swahili, the language of commerce, and in so doing a whole new vocabulary was spawned including words like *daktari*, *kuli* (dockyards), *sigara*, and *papa* (literally a shark, and therefore a submarine).

Somewhat surprisingly, in view of the hardships of carrier service, 'black' humour was also every bit as evident in the field as in the trenches in Europe. When Korombo, a farm worker, returned to Nanyuki after nearly two years in the Carrier Corps he declared to his employer that the food had been 'abominable' and the work 'heart-breaking'; but one of his most abiding memories was of the occasion when Belgian *askari* had set eyes on his substantial frame and shouted '*nyama!* Food!'. Korombo had, he said, not felt 'very nice when troops of this kind were quartered nearby' and assured anyone

---

[*] Beer, p. 270. George Beer was the Chief of the Colonial Division of the American delegation at Versailles.

who doubted his tale that 'those jackals were hungry, I tell you'.[28] Those who could laugh at their experiences or who gained something from their period of service must, however, have been a very small minority. For the majority the advent in eastern Africa of 'total war' brought misery on a scale that was unimaginable for all but the most beleaguered civilians in Europe.

PART FOUR

1917

DESIGN FOR A TANK FOR THE RUFIJI FRONT

(Patent applied for in the British Empire, France, Russia, USA, Italy, Japan, Belgium, Portugal, Roumania, Serbia, Montenegro, Cuba and San Marino)

'My average rate of retreat has been 15 miles a day, and we hope to exceed that shortly. I have been on the verge of collapse, but a bottle or two of Hock in the evening and then I see things through Hock coloured spectacles ... when the war is over we shall institute an annual marathon from Kilimanjaro to Mt Kenia, and I bet we beat all-comers every time.'

'Interview' with 'von Lettow Fallback',
The Leader, 21 April 1917

TWENTY-SIX

Unfinished Business

The convening of the Imperial War Conference in London in early 1917 could not have come at a better time for Botha and Smuts. The political situation in South Africa was as tense as at any time since the start of the war: another Boer rebellion was thwarted during 1916, and it was generally believed that South Africa's involvement in the war had become unpopular with a majority of even the moderates among the Afrikaans-speaking population. In December *De Volkstem* captured the prevailing mood when it stated that 'the development of the situation in German East must necessarily become a question of guerrilla fighting in the woods for which a man of the calibre of General Smuts is not required', and urging that 'the sooner he returns the more welcome he will be'.[1] As criticism of Botha's loyalty to the British Empire mounted, his dilemma had become acute: if Smuts returned home leaving the East Africa campaign unfinished his return would smack of defeat and the reputations (and ambitions) of both men would suffer at home and abroad. The Imperial War Conference was therefore a 'heaven-sent opportunity',[2] enabling Botha to send Smuts to London as South Africa's representative (thereby creating the impression that his departure from East Africa was forced by the need to attend to even weightier imperial matters than the campaign against von Lettow-Vorbeck), while Botha dealt with the domestic strife at home.

In order to safeguard his reputation, and bolster morale in South Africa, Smuts – ever the *slim* (cunning) politician – marked his withdrawal from the fray with a declaration of victory in East Africa. It was certainly the case that his decisive leadership in the field, and his willingness to take risks, had wrested more than one million square miles of German territory from the Kaiser; and that this territorial gain was sufficiently secure to enable Walter Long, the British Colonial Secretary, to declare that German East Africa, Ruanda and Urundi would never now be returned to Germany. But von Lettow-Vorbeck and Schnee remained undefeated in the field, and when the arrival of the rains led to some of the most desperate fighting of the war, particularly on the Rufiji front, it became abundantly obvious that they were no more likely to surrender than they had been when invited to do so in September 1916. Military, as opposed to political, victory remained as elusive as ever.

Smuts was fulsome in his praise of his troops, declaring himself 'eternally proud' of them and publicly stating that 'in the story of human endurance the campaign deserves a very special place, and the heroes who went through it uncomplainingly, doggedly, are entitled to all recognition and reverence'.[3] But his words did not silence his critics and for every soldier – South African, British or Indian – who regarded Smuts as 'the catalyst' who ensured that 'the muddied waters crystallised into some sort of war purpose'[4] there was one who lambasted his reliance on wide turning movements for being a strategy that was bound to fail in the open spaces of German East Africa; and for every admirer of his 'natural simplicity' and 'ruthless determination', which many considered to be a refreshing and 'striking contrast with the mannerisms of the British regular officer',[5] there were those who considered him to have been outrageously autocratic. 'He would stand no opposition', 'he would have his own way absolutely and in detail', 'all opposition to him was a personal affront', 'he did not understand teamwork',[6] were common enough opinions among Staff officers who had found themselves serving under 'Oom Jannie'; and many of the disease-ridden, exhausted South African troopers were quick to voice their disgust at what they perceived as the unnecessary hardships they had been forced to endure. Stories of mutinous behaviour soon began to circulate in the South African press, and the allegations levelled at Smuts by Colonel Kirkpatrick, the commanding officer of 9/SAI, were of sufficient gravity to merit the convening of an official Court of Enquiry.*

Smuts's rebuttal of what he called the 'grumblings of a few thoughtless or malcontent mischief-makers' was forthright. His view was that 'under the extraordinary difficulties with which I was confronted in this campaign, I had the choice of either doing nothing or doing the job as it has been done'; and that 'even Moses himself in the desert had not such a commissariat situation as faced me'.[7] There was a good deal of truth in both statements, but with anti-British propaganda increasingly rife in a South Africa in which the cost of living had risen dramatically on account of its involvement in the war, Smuts's prickliness did little to endear him to the public. That the Hertzogites should seize on every opportunity to attack him was no surprise; but soon the

---

* See *The Daily Mail*, Durban, 21 November 1916. It also emerged that 2/SAH had been on the verge of mutiny in September when Captain Lee wrote to Colonel de Jager, 'I wish to bring to your notice that ninety per cent of the men returned as unfit since leaving Kondoa-Irangi were rendered unfit by insufficient rations'. Lee's letter contained an implicit threat that his men would only advance when better and more plentiful rations were received (SANMMH/A/416/3: Lee to de Jager, 16 September 1916).

outcry spread to supporters of the predominantly British-speaking members of the Labour Party, many of whom had served in the infantry battalions sent to East Africa and were unable to find work when they returned home.

The atmosphere of unease was not confined to the white population. Just as the war had led to increasing repression in British East Africa (where a War Council comprising three officials, two settlers and the general manager of the Standard Bank had ruled by *diktat* since the introduction of conscription in late 1915 and led to a considerable strengthening of the political and economic power enjoyed by the white settler population), so too did the outlook for South Africa's three and a half million non-whites worsen with each year that failed to witness an end to the conflict. By the end of the war the ranks of white miners in the gold mines of the Rand would have swelled to such an extent that they accounted for more than half the workforce, and their increasing political power secured more and more preferential terms of employment to those of their black counterparts; while in the countryside the decision of African political activists to suspend for the duration of the war their opposition to the 1913 Land Act – which sought to prohibit Africans from owning land outside designated reserves which encompassed only a tenth of the country – began to look like a gesture that was unlikely to be rewarded. Racial paranoia and the white population's desire to impose greater segregation dominated South African politics, and although black leaders voiced their objections with a degree of sophistication and persistence that would not be matched in East and Central Africa for decades to come, their efforts were in vain. In March 1917, Botha publicly praised South Africa's 'natives' and other 'non-whites' for their loyalty; but by then it was clear that the likelihood of their leaders ensuring 'fair play' had been severely compromised by the intensification of South Africa's war effort.

Despite Botha's praise for the loyalty of South Africa's indigenous population, he would not countenance its participation in anything other than a non-combatant capacity. Boer and Briton alike considered the involvement of more than 100,000 Africans in the Anglo-South African War to have been an embarrassing (and potentially dangerous) expedient that should not be repeated at any cost. Indian bearer companies and 20,000 African labourers were sent to the East African campaign, and Native Labour Contingents served in German South-West Africa and France. But so great were the fears of the potential consequences of arming Africans that Smuts publicly censured Germany's rumoured intention to mobilise 'vast native armies . . . in the next great war';[*] and the only non-white South Africans allowed to bear arms were

---

[*] Smuts, p. 141. The comment was attributed to General von Freytag, Deputy Chief of the German General Staff.

the 'coloureds' of the Cape Corps. Even in their case only one tenth of the 80,000 or so volunteers were actually put into the field.

Expressions of loyalty to the British Empire among Africans, 'coloureds' and Indians were almost universal, not least because of the enduring belief that in Whitehall lay the only hope of blocking the Land Act and other discriminatory legislation, and as a result the ban on 'natives' participating in combat roles was extremely unpopular. 'Fancy refusing native assistance ... on the ground of colour,'[8] wrote the South African National Native Council's Solomon Plaatje; 'it would seem that the South African government is so deeply in love with the natives that they are scrupulously careful lest the natives should singe so much as a hair in the present struggle, and that white men alone may shoot and kill one another.'[9] The irony of South African racial policy did not escape Plaatje. While Botha and Smuts would not allow 'the militarization of the natives' in South Africa, as early as April 1916 Smuts had pressed for the expansion of the King's African Rifles; and by the end of the year he had been dependent on the arrival of substantial numbers of troops from West Africa in order to withdraw white South Africans from the fray.[*]

Smuts's policy smacked of hypocrisy: East and West Africans were allowed to distinguish themselves, and win awards, in the field – but black South Africans were not. The explanation for this seeming anomaly, as Plaatje well knew, was simple. Contributing to the war effort could potentially be regarded as deserving of reward, and a cursory glance at what was happening in India was enough to show Botha and Smuts that times were changing. By the end of the Great War more than 1.4 million Indians had served in the armed forces, a majority of them as combatants; and the Punjab alone, whose Pathan and Baluch battalions fought in East Africa, contributed more than a third of the one million Indian troops who were sent overseas. This was a colossal contribution, matched by an equally huge bestowal of supplies, livestock, and cash; and it was a significant factor, amid increasing unrest and a marked rise in politicisation in India, in deciding Lord Montagu, the Secretary of State for India, to announce in 1917 a 'gradual development of self-governing institutions with a view to the progressive realisation of responsible government' in India.

The reforms did not constitute a major weakening of Britain's power in India, but they were quite sufficient to alarm white South Africans; and that alarm would soon increase exponentially when rumours began to circulate of a further reward for India: German East Africa. The message to Botha, and

---

[*] Smuts, p. 144. Smuts had first called for an additional three battalions of KAR to be formed in April 1916. This possibility had, however, been under consideration ever since Wapshare's command, and the reformation of the previously disbanded 2/KAR was approved by the Chief of the Imperial General Staff on 4 March 1916 (two weeks after Smuts's arrival in East Africa).

all white South Africans, was clear: securing the future of a white-dominated South Africa, and the lion's share of any reward for the many tens of millions of pounds that the war was costing their country, was dependent on ensuring that the indigenous population were excluded from contributing in any combatant capacity. Given the determination to achieve this outcome, it is unsurprising that the fact that almost as many black South African labourers died in the East Africa campaign (1,188 men) as white South African troops (1,599 men) was not widely publicised.

'Smuts's War' may have proved immensely unpopular in South Africa, but in Britain he was received as a hero of the highest order. Prime Minister Lloyd George guffed his appreciation of 'one of the most brilliant generals in this war'; Churchill called him 'an altogether extraordinary man'; and Andrew Bonar Law, leader of the Conservative Party, praised the fact that two South African politicians had been responsible for 'two of the most notable achievements [of the war] so far'[10] in conquering German South-West and German East Africa. The esteem in which Smuts was held was so universal – at a time of numerous crises for Britain's war effort in Europe – that it was even suggested that he should be given command of the Egyptian Expeditionary Force in Palestine. Smuts did not take to the field again, but was persuaded to stay in Britain after the Imperial War Conference and spent the rest of the war working hand in glove with Field Marshal Sir Douglas Haig and Lord Milner – the creation of the Royal Air Force being just one among a plethora of projects with which he was intimately involved. Smuts's secondment to Whitehall suited Botha well. Although it robbed the South African Premier of the presence of his most trusted adviser and confidant, he could be certain that Smuts would defend South Africa's interests to the hilt in London at a time when his unpopularity at home was a political liability. It was also expedient for Smuts's reputation that he was 'able to quit the scene' for a while and stifle the allegations emanating from Africa that it was 'very far from being the case' that he had 'all but finished the job'[11] there.

Back in East Africa, Smuts's sudden departure and the withdrawal of almost all of the South African troops from the campaign caused utter chaos. The remaining troops, a bewilderingly heterogeneous collection of soldiery, had been decimated by the advances of 1916 and the stalemate on the Rufiji front, and the 'very unthankful and heart-breaking task'[12] of restoring their morale and fighting capacity fell to Major-General Hoskins, Inspector-General of the King's African Rifles. Among the logistical services his appointment 'immediately [ensured that] a more normal set of conditions prevailed'. Major Hazleton, the senior Supply and Transport officer, noticed that his staff set about their task with 'a new zest', and were able to '[start] afresh to calculate our requirements on organised lines with more or less cut and dried facts as to numbers of forces and the extent and object of their operations'.[13]

The state of the combat troops was more troubling, however, and Hoskins's initial reaction was to request renewed assistance from South Africa. He was a popular figure in the south, and his reconciliatory conduct when serving on the Military Governor's Staff in Pretoria at the end of the Anglo-South African war had earned him many friends in high places, but his appeal met with only limited success. Botha wanted to draw a line under the campaign, and told Hoskins that he was 'much concerned' about the reaction of his electorate if any troops were sent back to East Africa. In March, 6/SAI, 7/SAI and 8/SAI were declared unavailable as 'the larger proportion of the men of these regiments' were deemed 'physically unfit to return'; and replacing them with fresh drafts was said to be 'out of the question' while recruiting was under way for more troops for the war in Europe. A 'strong feeling' of reluctance to serve in East Africa had resulted from the tales of returning soldiers, leaving Botha no option but to discount the possibility of a 'renewed employment of white Union troops . . . on grounds of health, transport and expense'.[14]

Botha's reaction put Hoskins in a quandary. Two battalions of infantry – 7/SAI and 8/SAI – did eventually return to East Africa during 1917; Colonel Morris's Cape Corps, whose men had shown themselves to be indefatigable and resourceful soldiers, remained in the field; and a few hundred South African troops stayed on with Northey's force. But to all intents and purposes 'the big South African Expeditionary Force' had 'melted like butter in the sun',[15] leaving Hoskins with an acute manpower crisis. The loss of the South African mounted troops – known locally as the *Kabure* – was particularly serious: without cavalry of some description no further advance was possible. In time, the KAR Mounted Infantry and Indian 25th Cavalry would show that they were more effective (and disciplined) than the Boer irregulars, but at the beginning of 1917 Hoskins had no reason to believe that time was a luxury that the War Office would allow him. The declaration of victory made by 'that damned fellow Smuts'[16] – as many of Hoskins's officers referred to their former commander-in-chief – had prompted the War Office to request that he release eight infantry battalions, five artillery batteries, his armoured cars and the planes and pilots of 26th Squadron (Royal Flying Corps) for deployment elsewhere, and it took Hoskins weeks to convince his superiors that the situation was not quite as his predecessor claimed.*

---

* An officer with the 40th Pathans wrote the following words to his sister in March 1917: 'I do wish to goodness that they would not say that the show is all but over. It is not. It is easy enough to advance through a country where the enemy do not intend to stand. The real difficulty is when he has got down to an area he has decided to stand in, and where he knows every inch of ground and you know none . . . Do believe me when I say that *all* our difficulties are ahead of us.' (IWM/Thornton.)

On 1 March Hoskins informed the War Office that although the military establishment in East Africa still exceeded 40,000 troops on paper, the ration strength of units that were considered reliable was only 24,000 rifles – and fewer than half that number were fit for combat. This completely precluded defeating an enemy of similar size, given the vastness of the territory through which von Lettow-Vorbeck could retreat; and, as Hoskins warned, if the enemy chose to withdraw into Portuguese East Africa there would be nothing he could do to stop such a move. The only possible solution lay in continuing to draw on India, to give a prominent role to the recently arrived Gold Coast Regiment and the Nigerian Brigade, and to speed up the expansion of the King's African Rifles. Indeed so desperate was the search for any available manpower that troops from the West Indies – the 2nd West India Regiment, who had fought in the Cameroons, and the volunteers of the British West Indies Regiment – were to find themselves posted to East Africa.

It was fortunate that Hoskins knew what he was doing in increasing the regiment's expansion rate. By the end of the war its establishment rose to twenty-two battalions; and British soldiers who fought alongside the KAR were unanimous in describing almost all of its battalions as 'rippers' who were 'fit to fight against or alongside any troops in the world'.[17] The same was true of the Gold Coast Regiment, 'of whose behaviour', wrote one signals officer, 'it is impossible to speak too highly: they fight like heroes ... [and there are] no better comrades in a scrap';[18] and also of the Nigerians. The recruitment of so many African troops was not an entirely smooth process. In Nigeria there was widespread opposition, the more so as its troops had already participated in the Cameroons campaign; and most of the KAR recruits in 1918 were former German *askari*. But military service was infinitely more attractive than service with a carrier unit, and many a willing volunteer took to it with alacrity. Joining the KAR was not only regarded as 'one of the most lucrative and prestigious forms of employment open to unskilled Africans'[19] but also, as was true for young Britons who had rushed to join 'Kitchener's Army', an *adventure* – complete with smart uniforms, brass bands, dance societies, and the opportunity to learn new skills. Furthermore, volunteers knew that if they survived they would return home comparatively rich, able to marry well, and respected (or even envied); indeed many tribes, such as the Yao of Nyasaland and the Nandi of British East Africa, responded to such incentives by providing disproportionately high numbers of recruits.

The recruitment *en masse* of African soldiery was a source of concern in Whitehall as well as South Africa, and it was never taken to the extremes suggested by the 'Million Black Army Movement' (or by France). But whatever the fears of humanitarian groups and racial supremacists alike, the fact remained that such soldiers were cheap, courageous, and available in large numbers – and alternatives there were none. Even Smuts had realised this when he called for the recruitment of three new battalions of KAR just two months after his arrival in East Africa in February 1916; but by declaring victory prematurely he had sought to make quite sure that African soldiers would not be given the credit for succeeding where he and his white South African troops had failed.

While the expansion of the KAR proceeded apace the death toll among carriers, particularly on the Rufiji front, rose to alarming proportions and Hoskins realised that unless a mass levy raised the number of carriers recruited by the Carrier Corps since the start of the war to 160,000 his new troops would never become mobile. Dar-es-Salaam had been put on a proper footing as Base; Kilwa had become a sizeable port; extensive tram-lines were being built inland from Kilwa and Lindi; and the nightmare of obtaining the necessary provisions for battalions whose diets were radically different was almost solved. But without a full-strength Carrier Corps all these improvements would count for nothing. At the end of April 1917, Hoskins could finally see light at the end of the tunnel and informed Whitehall that he would be able to advance in two months' time. It was not quick enough for his military superiors. Smuts had let it be known that he thought Hoskins was dawdling, and so great was his influence in Whitehall that his successor was 'reassigned' to Mesopotamia in May.

The news of their commander-in-chief's dismissal (on the grounds of 'the consequent strain of prolonged service'[20] in East Africa) was received with dismay by British officers in East Africa, all of whom thought that Hoskins had not been given a real chance. Hoskins was widely regarded as 'one of the most gifted soldiers of the campaign' and 'certainly the most popular';[21] and there was no doubting that his demise had been hastened by what one member of the Committee of Imperial Defence called his refusal 'to regard operations [in German East Africa] as a sort of picnic' – an approach which had exposed gaping flaws in the myth of Smuts's 'victory'. Over the coming months Hoskins's caution would be 'proved right',[22] however, and at the end of the war many would voice the opinion that 'had he remained in charge ... there would have been no campaign in 1918'.[23]

The identity of Hoskins's successor further illustrated the extent of Smuts's influence in London (and his keenness to ensure that the myth of his victory should not unravel any further): 'Jaap' van Deventer was recalled from South Africa, and Colonel Sheppard was selected as his Chief of Staff. Both men had reputations as 'fighters'. Indeed van Deventer's ride to Kondoa had shown him to be enterprising almost to the point of recklessness: while Sheppard, the Army rackets champion, was considered to be 'one of the very few men who really enjoyed fighting' and was usually referred to by his soubriquet 'Ha Ha

Splendid' (on account of his catchphrase 'Ha Ha Splendid! Lots of fighting and lots of fun!').[24] Equally important, both men were popular; and it was hoped that this would enable them to extract the best from the handful of other generals who had proved their worth in East Africa – in particular Northey, and the Irishmen Hannyngton and O'Grady (who was said to be 'brave as a lion ... a man who, like the German leader himself, appealed personally to [African] troops').[25]

The position that van Deventer inherited was as follows. Tafel had succeeded Wahle as commander of the 3,000 German troops on the Mahenge plateau, while von Lettow-Vorbeck's main force of 5,000 rifles occupied a vast swathe of territory inland from Kilwa and Lindi. The plan was to dislodge Tafel and then surround, or bring to a decisive battle, all the enemy's troops in the south-east. No thought was given to securing some sort of 'peace without victory', as had been advocated in Europe by Woodrow Wilson in April: von Lettow-Vorbeck was to be defeated outright and the rest of the German colony seized. But the pressure from London to finish the campaign quickly, combined with van Deventer's predilection for 'action', resulted in an advance being attempted 'a month too soon' for the supply and transport services and attracted a familiar lament from Major Hazleton: 'When would we learn not to advance until ready in every detail?'[26] Only half the mechanised transport he had ordered had arrived in East Africa, ambulances were almost non-existent, and the mass levy of carriers had fallen far short of its target.

Worse still, while Hoskins was valiantly struggling to reorganise his force, the rainy season caused severe hardship for the troops in the field. On the Rufiji front, the failure to encircle the retiring German forces in January had appalling consequences for the British troops, in particular those from Nigeria who had only arrived a month before, and the Carrier Corps. Within two days of the start of the rains on 25 January the 120 miles of road from the railhead at Mikesse that had been so painstakingly constructed during the dry season were washed away and the entire Rufiji area became 'a vast lake'. This meant that supplies could only be brought forward by carrier convoys – 12,000 men to feed 3,000 troops – which had to brave infestations of crocodiles (in the wet) and lions (on the dry ground). No fresh meat ever got through, and the Nigerian troops seldom received more than 13oz of foodstuffs per day. In desperation, they took to digging up roots and even the corpses of dead animals 'with disastrous results on many occasions'.[27] Hides used on bridges were removed and boiled up in soup, theft became commonplace, and delicacies such as bush rat pie and monkey's brains on ration biscuits began to appear on the mess tables. February, March and April were described as 'black months for the Nigerian Brigade' by its officers, as their men 'got terribly thin and wretched, till they became almost unfit to take the field in any active operations'. 'The hardships passed,' they concluded, 'must be unparalleled in military operations of our time. Our condition could not have been worse even if we had been in a siege.'[28]

Patrol work did continue throughout the deluge from Mkindu, the Nigerian Brigade's main camp, and, to the south, from an outpost at Kibongo, facing Ngwembe (the forward position of Otto's five companies based at Kibambawe). Canoes were sometimes used but more often than not the patrols necessitated wading for miles through water waist-high (and sometimes neck-deep). An attack on Ngwembe planned for the second week in March had to be abandoned due to the critical shortage of supplies, and after Kibongo was attacked Hoskins decided that only 2nd and 4th Nigeria Battalions should remain at Mkindu while the others withdrew to Mpangas. Despite the appalling conditions they were attacked en route and in this 'very unpleasant little show'[29] the loss of the column's guns and loads was only averted by the bravery of two young lieutenants who were awarded the Military Cross. This ambush on a track generally thought to be 'as safe as any country road in England' was subsequently judged to have had the intention of capturing General Cunliffe and the Staff of the Nigerian Brigade, who had fortuitously moved along the same route the day before. Such boldness on the part of the enemy stretched nerves to the limit. So too did the wildlife: the noise of a herd of hartebeest moving past Kibongo at night was indistinguishable from that which might be made by a German patrol.

By mid April 1917 the situation was so bad, and disease so prevalent, that the 1st and 4th Nigeria Battalions and the regimental battery were ordered back to the railway. While this was 'the most cheerful news' that any of the men had heard for months, what lay ahead was a trek never to be forgotten. A hippo attacked the ferry across the Rufiji, drowning eleven soldiers; crocodiles lay in wait in the swampland that constituted the track north, and 'dead mules and donkeys and even dead carriers littered the road in various degrees of putrefaction'.[30] The stretch from Duthumi to Tulo, a distance of just twelve miles, took eight and a half hours to traverse, and by the time Mikesse was reached more than one third of the troops had been abandoned along the way. It seemed 'little less than a miracle'[31] to those who struggled into the town that any supplies, let alone the single mail, had reached Mkindu at all during the rains.

Van Deventer had no idea of the extent of the damage inflicted on his troops during the rains when he first arrived from South Africa and ordered them to prepare for an advance 'a month too soon'. Within weeks, however, he admitted that the state of half his troops was 'not altogether satisfactory'. Disease had decimated the ranks of the West African troops on the Rufiji front, and among the Indian battalions the 40th Pathans were only fit for duty on the lines of communication, the 130th Baluchis were 'worn out', the 57th Rifles and 129th Baluchis could barely muster 100 men each, and the Cape Corps had evacuated two-thirds of its men. 'What wouldn't one give for the food alone in France,' wrote an officer with the 40th Pathans who had served on the Western Front, 'for the clothing and equipment! For the climate, wet or fine, and above all for the fighting where one knows one is up against the real thing. I am perfectly ready to be killed,' he added, 'but if that is to happen, please, I want to die a strong man, with all my faculties intact, not a half-starved weakling.'[32]

In fact only three battalions of Indian troops were thought to be 'in a state to fight',[33] and it was this desperate situation that enabled van Deventer to persuade a reluctant Botha to send back some, at least, of the South African infantry regiments. There was one thing that Botha dreaded more than further casualties being inflicted on South African troops, and that was the prospect of van Deventer being humiliated and the myth of Smuts's victory being unravelled. If such a calamity occurred South Africa's war effort would have been in vain, and might even plunge the country into civil war.

The troops and carriers were not the only ones to suffer from the rainy season stalemate: the rains had also presented the Royal Navy, and the RNAS pilots, with a plethora of new challenges – and brought a tragedy whose effects were keenly felt throughout the blockading fleet. In early January Flight Lieutenant Moon's seaplane came down in the Rufiji delta during an attempt to reconnoitre German troops dispositions inland and, after three days of trying to struggle to safety, without food or water, he was captured. His observer, Commander Bridgeman, was less fortunate: despite valiant attempts by Moon to save him, he drowned. The crews of the *Mersey*, the transport *Bajune* and the small cargo vessel *Mafia* also suffered terribly in their ultimately successful attempt to supply British troops cut off at Utete, seventy-five to eighty miles up the Rufiji, and in Mohoro district, from the sea. Without their efforts the troops would undoubtedly have starved, but almost every seaman involved in the operation was struck down by frequent attacks of malaria. More than a dozen vessels remained on the East Africa Station, and any hopes that the destruction of the *Königsberg* and the capture of all of German East Africa's ports might have brought an end to their involvement in the campaign had long since evaporated.

The knowledge that the plight of von Lettow-Vorbeck's troops was no better than their own was of little consolation to British troops as they prepared as best they could for van Deventer's advance. On the Rufiji front the German *askari* subsisted for months on half-rations, and were often forced to succumb to the same desperate measures as British troops eating roots and hippo meat; while the death rate among carriers was as high as one in five. At any one time eighty per cent of the European troops were sick with malaria or dysentery, and supplies of quinine ran perilously low after one third of the total German stock fell into the hands of Nigerian troops when a mobile medical depot was captured near Mkindu in March. More fatal even than malaria was the prevalence of blackwater, which had accounted for almost two-thirds of all German fatalities caused by disease (as opposed to combat) in the period up to June 1917.

Many a German prisoner captured at this time maintained that von Lettow-Vorbeck could not possibly hold out for longer than a couple of months. That he was able to do so was partly due to the efficiency and careful planning of his medical officers. There were no fewer than sixty-three doctors in German East Africa at the start of the war, a figure that dwarfed the number of medical practitioners in British East Africa and was attributable in part to a pre-war campaign against sleeping-sickness. Under the supervision of Dr Meixner and his team of experienced doctors the network of field hospitals and laboratories established in the north-east had been moved southwards, as von Lettow-Vorbeck retreated, with a minimum of disruption. The resources at their disposal had certainly dwindled, but the 200kgs of quinine brought by the blockade-runner *Marie* had sufficed for 1916 and thereafter improvisation made up for shortages. 'Lettow Schnapps' – the 'home-made' quinine distilled from the bark of the *cinchona* tree – was still being produced; bandages were fashioned from bark; and stocks of a typhoid treatment manufactured at an institute in Dar-es-Salaam had been spirited out of the city before its capture. Per capita, the medical resource available to the German troops was far greater than that of the Allies right until mid 1917, when the rising death toll due to disease – particularly among carriers – finally forced the latter to pay serious attention to the expansion of their medical services.

Further inventive solutions were also used by the beleaguered Germans to tackle the shortages of basic foodstuffs and other consumables. Before it fell into British hands the research institute at Amani, in the Usambara Mountains, had produced substitutes for everything from toothpaste to candles to tobacco. 'Whisky' and a 'petrol' of sorts were manufactured in small quantities; honey was substituted for sugar; salt was produced by evaporating sea water after the saltworks at Gottorp were captured by the Belgians; hippo fat was used for cooking; and bread was made from other grains (and even from sweet potatoes) when wheat was scarce. The result of all this improvisation was that the German troops were, in many respects, better off than most of the British front-line troops. For them, medical attention was always nearer to hand; and many of the *ersatz* provisions would have been regarded as luxuries by British troops always at the furthest extent of their lines of communication.

The measures undertaken by Schnee and von Lettow-Vorbeck to combat shortages enabled them to confound the sceptical opinions voiced by some of the German prisoners who had fallen into British hands on the Rufiji front. No matter how great the hardships confronted by his men, von Lettow-Vorbeck remained as determined as ever to fight on. His troops were not dying in large numbers for want of food or medical attention, and he was certain that the dry season was sure to bring new opportunities. It *might* even bring another blockade-runner from Germany; and in the meantime his tactics would continue to confer certain important advantages. These were not underestimated by the British troops who had spent the rainy season on the Rufiji, and the historian of the Gold Coast Regiment succinctly described the challenge facing van Deventer in the following words:

> the enemy, who alone knows his plans and his objectives, and whose movements are designed to avoid rather than seek contact with his pursuers, unless he can attack or sustain attack in circumstances favourable to himself, possesses throughout the immense advantage of the initiative. If he elects to retreat, the pursuer must plod after him, whither he knows not, through country which is not of his choice, and with the character of which he has had no opportunity of rendering himself familiar. If the enemy resolves to make a stand, it is almost invariably in a position which he has selected on account of the advantages it affords him; and when in due course he has been ejected from it, the pursuit through The Unknown of an elusive and usually invisible enemy begins *ab novo*, in circumstances which the apparent success has done nothing material to improve. These facts combine to render a campaign in the bush a heart-breaking and nerve-racking experience.[34]

TWENTY-SEVEN

The Raiders

———◆———

On Northey's front the rainy season precluded operations against the Mahenge plateau itself, but south of the plateau there was no respite for his exhausted troops. Von Grawert's decision to surrender near Likuyu was a significant boost to morale, as was Murray's capture of General Wahle's son. But the presence of detachments led by Kraut, Wintgens and Lincke in the fertile territory between Songea and Wiedhafen, on Lake Nyasa, could not be ignored.

Wintgens was the first to cause a disturbance. En route to link up with Kraut in January 1917, he could not resist targeting Colonel Tomlinson's Rhodesia Native Regiment at Kitanda, twenty-five miles east of the lake. It was a main supply depot for Gumbiro district, in which 12,000lbs of 'German' corn had been seized during the operation against von Grawert, and Wintgens meant to recapture these vital foodstuffs. For two weeks Tomlinson withstood the siege and was eventually relieved on 30 January by a force led by Major McCarthy which was composed of two companies of 5/SAI and one of the Rhodesia Native Regiment. A few days later, Wintgens withdrew in search of easier pickings elsewhere, having inflicted forty per cent casualties on Tomlinson's garrison of 230. Wintgens was within reach of Kraut, but either because of a disagreement or his preference for independent action, their columns did not remain in the same area for long.

Kraut – whom Wahle had instructed to forge as far south as he thought necessary – found few supplies around Songea; so he marched south to Tunduru and then crossed the Rovuma on 11 April to relieve the Portuguese garrison at Mitomoni of their provisions. From there he sent Willibald von Stuemer south and Heinrich Freiherr von Bock eastwards, while he remained near the Rovuma to secure the next harvest. The presence of at least seven German companies within striking distance of Lake Nyasa forced Northey to move his HQ to Zomba to cover the possibility that Kraut might try and invade Nyasaland; and 5/SAI, with their distinctive diamond-shaped flash of white and green halves worn on each side of their 'Wolseley' helmets, were converted into a mounted regiment patrolling the Nyasaland-Portuguese East

Africa border on mules. Not until July was Kraut forced back over the Rovuma into German territory, after which he sent his three companies, under the command of Lieutenant Krüger, to Lindi district while he made his way to rejoin von Lettow-Vorbeck.

The first indication that Wintgens's column, which was 500-strong and armed with no fewer than eleven machine-guns, was not following Kraut south was provided when one of his patrols attacked Milow Mission, thirty miles north of Wiedhafen, and another was encountered still further north. Their location made it clear that Wintgens was either creating a diversion while withdrawing back on to the Mahenge plateau, or that he meant to cross Northey's lines between the lake and Northey's HQ, which at the time was still at Njombe. If the latter, it was a threat which Northey could not afford to ignore, and he wasted no time in rushing 1/1KAR from Lupembe to Tandala, on the north-east corner of Lake Nyasa, and ordering Murray to lead two companies of his 'ubiquitous Rhodesians' in pursuit of Wintgens. Northey's worst fears were confirmed at dawn on 18 February when Wintgens duly attacked Tandala in freezing rain. But after two days of heavy fighting Wintgens withdrew, and by 25 February his detachment had disappeared in a north-westerly direction.

Wintgens's courage and unpredictability had earned him a considerable respect among Northey's troops (and among the Belgians before them). 'We all formed the opinion', wrote one, 'that he was a very fine officer, not only a good soldier with plenty of initiative.'[1] Why he decided to fight his way straight across Northey's lines, rather than retreat to the Mahenge plateau or follow Kraut southwards, remains a mystery. Post-war legends, perhaps founded on the desertion of twenty of his *askari* during the battle at Tandala, suggested that he had decided to take his men back to their homes in the north-west of the colony; a number of German sources would claim otherwise – that Wintgens initially intended only to forage for supplies on Northey's lines of communication and along the border between German East Africa and Northern Rhodesia. In the absence of any comprehensive account penned by Wintgens himself neither explanation can be verified. His aims may well have changed, and his attacks in 1916 on Ngominyi and Lupembe demonstrate that he was a commander who liked to act spontaneously, unexpectedly, and often in defiance of orders from his superiors. Whatever his thought processes, their consequences were catastrophic for Northey: for three months after his break from Kraut, 'Winkins' was destined to lead 'Murray's Rhodesians' a merry dance that took many of them, including their commander, to breaking point. The 'Wintgens Raid' had begun.

In the estimation of his fellow-officers Murray was considered to be 'the only man in the field at the time who looked in the least likely to be able to deal with [Wintgens] if he could only come to grips with him'.[2] It was something of a miracle, however, that Murray, who by now was himself almost constantly sick, still had a fighting force at all. At Christmas 1916 he had even witnessed a mutiny among the ranks of the men of 'A' Company of the British South Africa Police who had had enough of their commander 'volunteering for everything' – an occurrence which Murray handled in characteristically forthright fashion. He called the mutineers together and told them that he was 'ashamed of [their] mutinous action', adding that it would be a 'terrible shock' to No they as he had 'such a high regard' for the BSAP. He then told them that if any man refused to march he would have them shot by an *askari*. The mutiny ended as quickly as it had started, but for a long time afterwards the transgressors would offer inducements to the bearers of the *machila* in which Murray was often forced to travel to dump him every time they crossed a river. Murray was wise to this ploy and, 'gripping his walking stick', he always 'girded up his loins and battled on up the next mountain without further assistance'.[3] As had been true from the outset, he meant to lead from the front, but the longer he and his men remained in the field the more their numbers dwindled.

By the time he was ordered to pursue Wintgens, the sickness rate among Murray's troops was so high that nothing seemed able to counter it. At the Base hospital in Zomba even the diligence of 'Calamity Kate' and 'Hellfire Jane', the senior (and rather elderly) nursing sisters, was not sufficient to combat a 'state of chaos' which patients described as 'unforgettable'. 'The wards', wrote one, 'were overflowing and the beds were in no kind of order. They lay in haphazard positions like a gigantic unsolved jigsaw puzzle. The mosquito nets, so small they looked more like shrouds, were propped up off the beds by sticks and bits of string, and in the sweltering atmosphere many patients were nearly suffocated.' In addition to those suffering from the ravages of malaria or dysentery, there were many with grisly wounds. One KAR officer, for example, had been 'hit by a bullet in his left eye, [which] traversed the nasal cavity, emerged through the side of his face and re-entered the body to shatter his right shoulder and sever his arm'. Then there were the suicide cases, watched over by the 'conscientious Afrikaner' Foulkes; and the huge number of blackwater cases about which the medical staff were, by their own admission, 'abysmally ignorant', and whose victims were often discharged prematurely only to drop dead before they reached the railhead; and the German patients, including the 'kindly elderly doctor with carcinoma of the liver [who] sent for his wife in Dar but died before she could get to Zomba';[4] and even a number of men who missed their loved ones to such an extent that they had 'gone all peculiar' (and found that being told to 'do what a little boy does and do it twice a week'[5] did little to alleviate their depression).

In the middle of March Wintgens's force reappeared at Neu Utengule, thirty miles north of Lake Nyasa, and Murray closed in on him while the Northern Rhodesia border posts were reinforced in case Wintgens broke south. On 15 March, Murray drove Wintgens's rearguard out of their positions and it soon became apparent that his next destination was not the Northern Rhodesia border but the mission station at St Moritz, below which was the only ford across the Songwe River that wasn't covered by floodwater many feet deep. Once again Murray rushed to cut off his enemy, but on 20 March Colonel Tomlinson committed his Rhodesia Native Regiment and one company of the Northern Rhodesia Police, which had arrived before Murray, to a premature attack. As had happened before when Wintgens met Tomlinson it was the latter who came off second best. Tomlinson quickly found his troops surrounded by Wintgens, losing three machine-guns in the process, and then had to hang on grimly until Murray and Major Baxter's 1/1KAR broke through to relieve him a week later. Even with the arrival of these reinforcements Wintgens did not immediately turn tail. Only on 31 March did he finally cross the river and make for the St Boniface Mission on the Saisi River. Tomlinson, who by then was suffering from blood poisoning, did not get another command and was heavily criticised for having dug in on the plain below the mission rather than in the hills further south, a decision which arguably cost the lives of more than sixty of his men.

Hoskins, who was still commander-in-chief in East Africa when Wintgens set off on his raid, was seriously alarmed by the break-out and told Northey that 'the rounding up of Wintgens is now of greater importance than anything else in the campaign'.[6] But in the ensuing month, as Wintgens traversed the hilly, wooded country north-west of the St Moritz Mission and then set off across the desolate *pori* towards Tabora for the second time in six months, he evaded all attempts by Murray to outflank him. The toll on both forces was colossal. By the end of April one in ten of Murray's 2,500 first-line carriers had died, one in seven had been sent back sick, and the troops had advanced far beyond the furthest point to which Northey's supply lines would stretch; while Wintgens was only able to maintain his fighting strength by arming an increasing number of his carriers. By the third week in May Wintgens himself had contracted typhus and was finally forced to surrender to the Belgian Major Bataille at a village on the Ugala River, three days' march from Tabora. Any euphoria in the Allied ranks was short-lived: although the Belgians had captured the man they considered to be their 'most terrible enemy',[7] Wintgens's surrender did not encompass the surrender of his force and his officers all decided to fight on.[*]

---

[*] Wintgens was awarded the *Pour le Mérite* for his record in the campaign, as was his brother Kurt, an airman on the Western Front. Only 214 such awards were made to field officers in the Great War and this was the only case of brothers winning the distinction.

'Murray's Rhodesians' had covered 350 miles in just fourteen weeks in their pursuit of Wintgens, an average of twenty-five miles a day in blistering heat on minimal rations, and could go no further. By 14 June 1917 they had made their way back to Northey, and then, almost without respite, they were despatched to Songea to prepare for an offensive against the German troops which had remained on the Mahenge plateau under the command of Tafel. The failure to catch the man who in many ways was their own commander's *Doppelgänger* was a huge disappointment to Murray's troops, and was only partly mitigated by Sergeant Booth of the British South Africa Police being awarded one of only four VCs of the campaign for his gallantry during an engagement at Johannesbruck, on the Songea–Wiedhafen road on 12 February. Worse still, Ronald Murray's health, mental and physical, had been broken by the strain of twelve months in the field. He relinquished command of the NRP and the fifty-six BSAP troopers still fit for duty to Major Fair at the end of June, and although he would return to the field once again he was eventually invalided to South Africa, shipped back to England, and died soon after the war. Although Murray was undoubtedly a strict disciplinarian, and obsessively determined, his officers and men were unanimous in regarding him as 'a gallant leader and a fine soldier'[8] whose achievements were never fully recognised; and twelve months later, as the campaign entered its most desperate phase, theirs was not the only voice to lament the fact that there was no Murray to unleash on von Lettow-Vorbeck. In the meantime, Hoskins, far from being rid of the threat posed by Wintgens's raid, was forced to deploy 3,000 troops to hunt for Wintgens's detachment and to request the assistance of six Belgian battalions.[*] In stating that news of Wintgens's break-out was received 'too late for me to interfere'[9] von Lettow-Vorbeck failed to do justice to the enormity of the inconvenience caused by his subordinate just at a time when Hoskins was battling to reorganise his troops for a major offensive after the rains.

Command of Wintgens's troops, of whom about 500 had survived their second traverse of the *pori* south of Tabora, passed to Captain Heinrich Naumann. Six feet two inches tall, with jet-black hair and 'stern, eagle-like eyes',[10] Naumann had – like Wintgens – been awarded the Iron Cross 1st and 2nd Class in September 1916 and was considered to be every bit as dangerous an opponent. In contrast to Wintgens, however, Naumann's initial instinct

---

[*] 'Edforce' comprised contingents from 30th Punjabs (550 rifles), 1st Cape Corps (980 rifles), 1/6KAR (990 rifles), 4th Nigeria Battalion (220 rifles), and a mountain battery. Colonel Dyke's 130th Baluchis, 4/3KAR, and the KAR Mounted Infantry – who had been sent to cut off Wintgens from the north and west during April – were withdrawn at the same time as Murray's Rhodesians. The Belgian pursuit battalions were IV, VI, XI and XIII (each *c.* 500 rifles) under the command of Colonel Thomas.

was to reunite his troops with Tafel on the Mahenge plateau. Quite how he might have intended to do this is uncertain: crossing the *pori* a third time would have been unthinkable given that he was desperately short of provisions and that Murray's troops could have turned to face him instead of continuing on their way back to Northey. In any case, his first priority was to break loose from the British and Belgian units closing in on him – and that could only be done by heading further north rather than south. Within days of Wintgens's surrender, Naumann had simply slipped through the Anglo-Belgian encirclement and led his troops across the Central Railway fifty miles to the east of Tabora – a feat which was the first of many indignities to be inflicted on 'Edforce', the troops of General W.F.S. Edwards now charged with capturing Naumann, and their Belgian allies.

By the end of the first week in June Naumann had traversed 100 miles of dense 'elephant bush' to Mkalama, north-east of Tabora. His rearguard was briefly 'bumped' during his escape by the Belgian 4th *Bataillon* and Colonel Sargent's 4th Nigeria Battalion, but soon afterwards the opportunity of forcing him to stand and fight was lost and Naumann compounded the problem facing his pursuers by sending off small detachments in all directions like so many sparks from a Verey light. Sergeant Müller's column overran Singida, to the west, another column captured a herd of 600 cattle from the British supply lines and Naumann's main force simply disappeared. It was thought that Naumann's principal options were to break north-west to Lake Victoria, or to head north-east towards the former heartland of German settlement around Kilimanjaro; and both potential destinations caused extreme disquiet to the Allies because they had been under British administration for a year, and the consequences of Naumann 'stirring up the natives' in districts providing immense quantities of foodstuffs and recruits to the war effort were likely to be calamitous. In the end Naumann chose the first option for an extraordinary reason: he had heard a local rumour that an invasion force of 'Somalis' were just three days' march north of Nairobi, and by moving north-west he could, if he chose, enter British East Africa by a route that was unlikely to be guarded as closely as any running close to Mt Kilimanjaro. Naumann's gullibility in attaching any credence to the rumour may seem extraordinary. But he had been in the wilds for months, and supporting a Somali 'invasion' by making as big a nuisance of himself as possible – and possibly even linking up with the invaders – was a more attractive course of action at the time than seeking to fight his way back through the British troops guarding the Central Railway.

As soon as Naumann's approximate position was ascertained, the authorities in Mwanza, on the shores of Lake Victoria, were told to expect an attack at any moment. On 15 June Major Warwick, the garrison's commanding officer, ordered all specie removed to the *Winifred* and instructed the port's many

Indian traders to pack up their stock and prepare for a rapid departure. If this smacked of panic, it was justifiable under the circumstances: Warwick had absolutely no idea of the whereabouts of any of the British, let alone Belgian, columns pursuing Naumann, and intelligence reports indicated that the German force descending on him might be as strong as 1,500 rifles. Furthermore, any defence would have to rest principally on Major Drought's 'Skin Corps', armed scouts who had played a prominent role in all fighting around the lake since the start of the war but could hardly be described as 'regular' troops in any sense of the word. Warwick issued orders for the corps to prepare its main defensive position near Mwanza's gaol; but Drought, as was his wont, decided his own dispositions after concluding that there were 'easier means of committing suicide than drawing up in main street'.[11] Furthermore, Drought was convinced that the 4th Nigeria Battalion and the Belgian 4th *Bataillon*, which had been sent to relieve Mwanza from the west, could not be far away; and he was equally certain that there was 'absolutely no object in the Hun going to Mwanza as they must reckon on forces being landed from our steamers to cut them off'. Fortunately for the residents of Mwanza – and British prestige on the lakeshore – Drought's reading of the situation proved correct. Only one German patrol reached Lake Victoria, at Guta, where it was immediately put to flight when the Belgian 6th *Bataillon* were landed there by steamers of the British lake flotilla.

Although Mwanza itself had escaped attack, Naumann's main force appeared – yet again – to have disappeared into thin air. The task of finding him was entrusted to Drought, who immediately sent out famous elephant-hunter Lieutenant Sutherland with 100 levies and four local Boer farmers as guides to patrol towards Ikoma, closely followed by the 'Skin Corps' and the Belgian 6th *Bataillon* and 13th *Bataillon*. Their mission was a difficult one, given the vast area Naumann had at his disposal; and it needed to be executed with caution as 'Edforce', whose pursuit of Naumann had been labelled 'a great failure',[12] was withdrawn from the fray at this juncture so that its troops could be rested before taking part in van Deventer's imminent advance against von Lettow-Vorbeck's main force.

After leaving Mkalama Naumann's main force had in fact marched over 100 miles through Wasukuma territory – once a major recruiting ground for German *askari* and carriers – to Schanoa; and ten days after that, having recruited 100 former German *askari*, he'd covered a further 100 miles to arrive, as Major Drought suspected, at Ikoma. The small British garrison manning Ikoma's fort, a pre-war outpost of 14/FK, proved no obstacle to Naumann, who then prepared to confront the Anglo-Belgian force from Mwanza. He did not have long to wait. On 29 June Major Larsen's 13th *Bataillon* caught up with Sutherland's patrol near Ikoma and, despite having been instructed to await the arrival of the 6th *Bataillon* and Drought's 'Skin Corps', proceeded to launch an attack on the fort. In so doing Naumann's carefully laid trap was sprung: the fort itself was only held by a handful of *askari* and the bulk of Naumann's troops were deployed some distance away. No sooner had the attack begun than Naumann ordered them forward and in no time Larsen's and Sutherland's troops were surrounded. The consequences were horrific, and provided a graphic demonstration of Naumann's ruthlessness. One quarter of the 450 Allied soldiers were killed, including a large proportion of the wounded and captured, and only half the force escaped the envelopment unscathed. German casualties, on the other hand, could be counted on one hand; and an entire machine-gun company, 138 rifles, and 25,000 rounds of ammunition fell into Naumann's hands.[*] It was the worst defeat inflicted on Belgian troops in the entire campaign, and when Drought arrived to take command of the remnants of Belgian and British troops Larsen was led off to face a Belgian court-martial. Of Lieutenant Sutherland, last seen being led into the fort by two German *askari*, nothing was ever heard again.

The unusually high percentage of Allied soldiers killed during the attack was regarded with considerable suspicion in the immediate aftermath of the battle, as was Naumann's message, replying to an enquiry by Drought, that he had never come across Lieutenant Sutherland. Officers captured by either side had seldom just disappeared in a campaign that had witnessed few atrocities, and as Naumann marched off in the direction of Lake Natron many of the Allied officers at Ikoma came to the conclusion that they were pursuing a psychopath rather than another Wintgens. As he left the scene of the battle, it was Drought who was the first to think the unthinkable – that Naumann might even be intending 'to threaten Nairobi'.[13] If that was indeed his plan when he left Ikoma, Naumann changed his mind when he neared the border with British East Africa and learnt the truth about the Somali 'invasion': the rumour had been started by nothing more than a Somali incursion on the Jubaland border, 'sixteen to twenty days' march north of Nairobi'.[14] This put paid to any further thoughts of entering British East Africa, and Naumann decided that the time had come to turn south in the hope of breaking through the British troops on the Central Railway to rejoin Tafel or von Lettow-Vorbeck.

By the end of July 1917 Naumann had marched hundreds of miles through Ngorongoro and Ufiome districts to arrive within striking distance of Kondoa,

---

[*] See Boell, p. 329. Belgian casualties: sixty *askari* dead, eleven wounded, forty-one captured; and two Belgians captured. British casualties: three Europeans killed and one missing, seventy *askari* dead. German casualties: one *askari* and one carrier killed; one German and two *askari* wounded.

the scene of van Deventer's stand fourteen months earlier. British posts throughout the north-east were put on a state of high alert, but there was not much they could do in the event of attack: almost all fit and reliable troops had been moved south for the advance against von Lettow-Vorbeck, leaving little more than pocketfuls of long-suffering Indian Imperial Service Troops like the Kapurthalas and Rampurs in the rear. This placed van Deventer in a dilemma: Naumann could not be allowed to rampage across his lines of communication. He had to be caught, and the task of cornering him once and for all fell to Colonel Dyke and a detachment comprising the 1st Cape Corps, the KAR Mounted Infantry, the 4th Nigeria Battalion and 10/SAH (the only unit of South African mounted troops to have returned to the campaign). The prospect of success seemed remote; and as van Deventer prepared to advance in the south and from the coast he was frequently reminded, to his considerable annoyance, that if a greater number of South African mounted troops had returned to the campaign in early 1917 'this particular foe' might not have been so successful in eluding 'all attempts to round him up during the last six months'.[15]

To the great surprise – and relief – of the handful of troops garrisoning Kondoa, Naumann bypassed the town, choosing to trek across the Masai Steppe to the Nguru Mountains and Handeni instead. Then, rather, than marching towards the Central Railway, he suddenly turned north again and split his force into several detachments. Naumann had seemingly decided that the Central Railway would be too heavily defended, and that wreaking havoc in the former heartland of German settlement would constitute a more effective contribution to the German war effort. Not all his commanders appeared to agree with his decision: Lieutenant Zingel and the remnants of 26/FK, about 100 men, made little effort to escape encirclement by the Cape Corps at Kakera and the column surrendered on 2 September. On the other hand Walther Bockmann, the *Königsberg's* Second Engineer, brazenly led a detachment of a similar size to Kahe, on the Northern Railway, where he captured the British Administrator and destroyed two trains laden with supplies for the Allied build-up further south.

With the KAR Mounted Infantry, eighty de Jager's Scouts, the Cape Corps, 500 KAR from Nairobi, and 10/SAH hard on his heels Naumann led his own column back into the Nguru Mountains, and at Loita Hill, seventy-five miles south-east of Kondoa, his luck – and ammunition – finally ran out. On 2 October he surrendered with fourteen European officers and NCOs, 159 *askari* and about 350 carriers; a week later Bockmann's detachment of three officers and fifty-three *askari* surrendered to the KAR Mounted Infantry on the slopes of Mt Oldeani, a volcanic crater north of Lake Eyasu; and one German patrol was even captured halfway up the slopes of Mt Kilimanjaro. The total haul amounted to about 400 troops, a further 170 having been killed, captured or wounded during their six-month rampage, and at last the 'Naumann Stunt' was at an end.*

If Wintgens really had intended to return his *askari* to their homes in the north, which is doubtful, Naumann did not carry out his wish; nor did he make any real attempt to rejoin von Lettow-Vorbeck or Tafel; and von Lettow-Vorbeck deemed it unfortunate that 'this operation, carried out with so much initiative and determination, became separated so far from the main theatre of war as to be of little use'.[16] He had, however, caused chaos right across the north-east, disrupting the efforts of British officials to create a wartime administration in occupied territory and raiding the British lines of communication just at a time when supplies and troops were being moved south for a new advance against von Lettow-Vorbeck; and he plausibly claimed that as many as 10,000 British and Belgian troops had leen diverted from their duties elsewhere to pursue him, and that the intrepid pilots of the seven serviceable British biplanes had spent countless flying hours searching for him. Furthermore, Hoskins's inability to corner Naumann in May 1917 had been sharply criticised by Smuts and may have contributed to his dismissal.

Naumann's achievement was, by any standards, considerable. But he did not earn the respect from his opponents that was accorded to Wintgens because he, and some of his officers, were deemed not to have 'played the game'. In June 1917 two of the latter had raped villagers near Lake Victoria, and Naumann himself was regarded as the very personification of the 'hydra-headed monster of Prussian militarism', a man who 'swaggered about with a look of indifference'[17] as he committed atrocities against African and Allied soldier alike. In 1918 he earned the dubious distinction of being the only German participant in the campaign sent to stand trial in England for the murder of Lieutenant Sutherland at Ikoma and 'cruelty to native women'. He was sentenced to death, commuted to seven years' imprisonment, but was returned to Germany in November 1919.

* When Naumann finally surrendered to the Cape Corps the latter had covered 1,100 miles in two and a half months in pursuit of their quarry, seventy-five per cent of it on foot.

TWENTY-EIGHT

The Allies

———•———

The participation of Belgian troops in the pursuit of Wintgens and Naumann was symptomatic of a thaw in Anglo-Belgian relations. In September 1916 General Tombeur – or Baron Tombeur of Tabora, as he was newly styled by the Belgian government – had told Smuts that his initial offer to evacuate Tabora before the rainy season had lapsed; and, although he continued to refer to a gradual withdrawal, Belgian troops had remained in occupation ever since. This seeming intransigence greatly exacerbated Smuts's – and Britain's – fears that the Belgian government had decided to renege on the assurances given at the start of the war that it had no intention of pursuing territorial gains in East Africa, and that it was seeking to use its occupation of Ruanda, Urundi and western German East Africa as a bargaining counter in secret negotiations for a separate peace with Germany. The formal appointment of a civilian government for the occupied territories, led by Colonel Malfeyt, was also regarded with suspicion, and when Malfeyt refused to allow Smuts to recruit carriers from the west Anglo-Belgian relations sank to an all-time low.

The Belgian government was not wholly to blame for the worsening state of affairs. Smuts was wont to treat his ally in high-handed fashion, demanding rather than requesting further assistance, and was loath to give the Belgian commanders (and *askari*) the credit they were due for their advance to Tabora. Furthermore, Smuts was in no position to demand the immediate withdrawal of Belgian troops from German East Africa when he was unable to provide sufficient troops or civilian administrators to replace them. When Hoskins succeeded Smuts, the extent to which personal animosity between Smuts and Tombeur had undermined further co-operation was immediately apparent: no sooner had Smuts left East Africa for the Imperial War Conference in London than the first Belgian troops began to leave Tabora and make their way back to Lake Tanganyika and the Congo. At this juncture, however, Wintgens had set out on his raid towards Tabora, forcing Hoskins to appeal for Belgian assistance. Having done so, renewed co-operation was secured without much difficulty and Hoskins soon developed a close rapport with

Tombeur's capable and respected successor, Colonel Huyghé. At a conference at Ujiji in the third week of April, at which the plan for the operations against Wintgens and Naumann was agreed, Huyghé even agreed that Hoskins should be in overall command; and at two further conferences, at Dodoma in mid June and Dar-es-Salaam in July, van Deventer and Huyghé were also able to agree on the basis for a Belgian advance from the Central Railway to Mahenge. This was a very significant development, facilitated in part by a £3m loan (£105m in today's money) from Britain to Belgium for 'colonial development', and it greatly improved van Deventer's chances of cornering von Lettow-Vorbeck.

Belgium's return to the fray was eased by Hoskins's focus on military, as opposed to political, matters; and van Deventer was equally pragmatic in his dealings with his Belgian counterparts. But in London and Le Havre the politicking which had characterised Smuts's time in East Africa continued. There was a realisation that a new phase in the 'Scramble for Africa' was under way, and that it might be the last phase. Belgian suspicions that Britain might seek to dispossess her ally of a colonial presence in Africa altogether remained acute; while in Britain criticism of Belgium's record in Africa and her 'colonial methods' showed no sign of diminishing. The renewed involvement of Belgian troops was also regarded as a double-edged sword: no one denied their effectiveness or ability to advance more rapidly than most British troops, but their commanders' insistence that the troops live off the land was scarcely conducive to good relations with the long-suffering inhabitants of any territory through which they advanced. So great were the fears on this score that van Deventer – at Whitehall's behest – proposed creating a chain of supply dumps to support the Belgian advance to the Mahenge plateau, and as Huyghé knew that Tafel's troops would pick the plateau clean before retreating he gladly accepted the offer.

Tombeur's prolonged occupation of Tabora caused alarm in East Africa as well as in Europe, and the forthright views expressed by Ewart Grogan, for example, the former Liaison Officer with the Belgian troops and a member of British East Africa's War Council, were more or less common currency by mid 1917. On the one hand, Grogan was deeply suspicious of Belgium's motives; and as Lord Milner's adviser on African boundary questions at the Versailles Peace Conference in 1919 he would roundly dismiss Belgian claims that Ruandans and Urundians expressly desired Belgian rule as absurd. 'No natives in all Central Africa would on their own initiative do anything of the kind', he told Milner, adding that 'Billygee, the native name for the Belgians, is the synonym for "Bogeyman" – mothers use it to horrify their babes'.[1] On the other hand, Grogan's admiration of the Belgian *askari* knew no bounds, and having agreed to van Deventer's request that he resume his duties as Liaison

Officer he penned an emotional tribute to Huyghé's troops as they massed on the shores of Lake Tanganyika prior to the advance on Mahenge. 'It was a dark night,' he wrote, 'and we took our stand midway to take the salute. In the rising dust and smoky glare of the torches the impression was of some immense, half-seen submarine coming out of the depths. Except for an occasional word of command there was no other sound than ... the soft pad, in perfect unison, of thousands of naked feet. The only clearly visible feature of this monster was the glaring white eyeballs and glistening white teeth as it passed the saluting point. I was stirred to the depths.'[2] The Belgian Congo army, however mercenary the intentions of the Belgian government, was on the march again.

While Anglo-Belgian relations in the field were steadily improving, Anglo-Portuguese relations took another turn for the worse. In Europe, negotiations between Britain, France and Portugal regarding the possibility of Portuguese troops being sent to the Western Front only served to reaffirm Portuguese suspicions that 'the lot of the smaller nation inexorably caught up at this crucial time in the concerns of the larger one was ... not a happy one';[3] and soon after the first troops of a 55,000-strong Portuguese Brigade disembarked in France in February 1917 Lisbon was plunged into yet another political crisis. Opposition to the war, both in parliament and on the streets, reached fever pitch as strikes broke out all across the country, martial law was imposed, and General Pereira d'Eça was subjected to an enquiry into atrocities committed in the wake of a German incursion into Portuguese West Africa in 1915. In April, the *Union Sagrada* government fell.

General Gil's simultaneous return from Portuguese East Africa after the disaster at Newala in December 1916 only served to strengthen the hand of the anti-war and anti-British lobbies. But no Portuguese government was willing to abandon the fight, either in Europe or Africa, because to do so would be an admission of failure that would further damage Portugal's *brio nacional* – its national pride – as well as its chances of retaining its colonies when the war was over. Errol MacDonell, who was appointed to the unenviable position of Liaison Officer with the Portuguese forces in March 1917, explained the Portuguese dilemma in the following words: 'though many [Portuguese] know that at present they have made a hopeless fiasco of the German East campaign, if anyone says so in public he would incur the obloquy of the military, the press and the public'. Such obfuscation on the part of the Portuguese did not bode well for the future of Anglo-Portuguese co-operation on the Western Front or in East Africa; nor did MacDonell's despatch to the War Office which reiterated an opinion prevalent in Whitehall that 'the Portuguese hate and suspect all foreigners, and ... they hate the British most of all because they fear them'.[4]

Von Lettow-Vorbeck's officers were well aware of this antagonism. After his victory at Newala one of them wrote that 'morale was positive' among the German troops, whereas the same 'could not be said of the Allies';[5] and, according to Looff, the victor at Newala, British officers in Lindi 'could not stop themselves from expressing their delight that their less-than-esteemed allies, the "Pork-and-Beans", had been comprehensively walloped'.* At the end of the rainy season German troops immediately began to take advantage of the breakdown of Anglo-Portuguese co-operation on the Rovuma front. In February 1917, repeated raids were launched against Negomano and Portuguese frontier posts; and, further west, Kraut marched into Portuguese East Africa in April, sending von Stuemer towards Lake Nyasa while von Bock foraged so far to the east that it was feared he might attack Porto Amelia on the coast.

Such brazenness was hardly reassuring for van Deventer as he prepared to push von Lettow-Vorbeck's main force towards the border with Portuguese East Africa, and by July 1917 it was estimated that more than 40,000 square miles of the colony was devoid of any Portuguese presence, civilian or military. Meanwhile, von Stuemer and von Bock promised local Yao and Makua chiefs that taxation and forced labour would not be imposed when Germany gained control of the Portuguese colony, and as a result their officers were able to crow that 'the natives of the whole area were almost without exception on our side. Although we came to demand food and porter services, and could no longer pay real money, they abandoned the Portuguese nonetheless and offered every assistance'.[6] When one of von Stuemer's patrols was spotted in July near Fort Johnston, on the shores of Lake Nyasa, Northey sent Colonel Shorthose's 1/4KAR to attack his base at Mwembe, and by the end of August von Stuemer had retired back across the Rovuma with his 700 troops. Two months later there were no German troops remaining in Portuguese East Africa. But by then von Lettow-Vorbeck had been informed by von Stuemer that the area around Mwembe was exceptionally fertile, that the local population 'had no real fear'[7] of Germans, and that he had even been able to buy quinine and other medical supplies from a number of Portuguese officials whose sympathies lay with Germany. In time this information would prove invaluable.

The activities of von Stuemer and von Bock were a severe embarrassment to the Portuguese government, and 'German intrigues' in Portuguese East Africa were blamed for yet another disaster to befall their colony in what was without doubt 'an evil year for the Portuguese'.[8] The truth lay much closer to home. The war had greatly increased the harshness of Portuguese colonial

* In German POW camps, to be sent to the Portuguese barracks was a punishment reserved only for British soldiers unpopular with their compatriots.

rule, which Britain had criticised for years as being characterised by 'revolting practices'. 'No regard whatsoever was paid to native rights,' wrote one former British Consul, 'the chief reason being that natives were not considered as possessing any.'[9] Since 1914 forced labour had become increasingly widespread, local populations being coerced *en masse* by undisciplined and ruthless press gangs without even being offered the derisory remuneration paid to British carriers and labourers. The sick and old were not exempt, young women were 'ravished' at will, and by the end of 1916 increasing numbers of young men fled to the mines of Southern Rhodesia and the Transvaal to escape the Portuguese *cipais* and earn a wage. Meanwhile, the predicament of those left behind was so bad that when the *cipais* set about the task of levying 5,000 additional carriers in Barue, a centuries-old kingdom that had been incorporated into Tete district and only 'pacified' as recently as 1902, a full-scale rebellion ensued.

The Barue revolt shared with the rebellions in British East Africa in the early part of the war the durability of ancient traditions, the vital role played by spirit mediums, and the belief in 'medicine' that would turn Portuguese bullets to water. But there the similarities largely ended. It was on an altogether larger and unprecedented scale and, like the Maji-Maji Rebellion in German East Africa a decade earlier, it succeeded in uniting as co-combatants an impressive array of ethnic groups. Two rivals for the title of Makombe of the Wabarue fought independently – Nongwenongwe in the north and Makosa in the south – and their influence increasingly secured support from neighbouring leaders and *chicundas* – bandits – in the Zambezi Valley after the start of hostilities in March 1917; it was even claimed by one loyalist chief that two Portuguese officials joined the rebellion.[10] By the end of April the rebels had thrashed a Portuguese force sent to restore order and reached the outskirts of Tete, the provincial capital; and the British in Nyasaland were forced to play host to Senhor Lino, the Portuguese Administrator at Zumbo, who fled across the Luangwa River to the British post at Feira accompanied by sundry followers and his portable commode. By early May several thousand rebels were on the rampage, 'happy as ever', as Captain Molyneux at Feira put it, 'to capture (and probably murder) any loyalists they can',[11] and extinguish any trace of Portuguese overlordship in Zambezia Province.

MacDonell judged the situation in Zambezia to be 'critical', not least because the fighting forced more than 100,000 refugees to flee over the border into Nyasaland and the Rhodesias. But British sympathy for their ally was limited. There was a strong sense that the Portuguese were getting no more than they deserved and, despite the fact that the Portuguese had provided the British with troops during the Chilembwe Rebellion in Nyasaland, the British refused to reciprocate (although arms and ammunition were sent). To the huge disgust of the Portuguese, the British also refused to close their borders to refugees and rebel leaders; and such limited co-operation as was offered was thought to be motivated solely by a concern for the safety of the railway to Beira from Southern Rhodesia and other routes to the coast.

Portuguese troops tackled the rebellion in a rather more determined fashion than they had ever opposed German troops. When forced to provide a refuge for Senhor Lino, Captain Molyneux cynically predicted that 'when the Portuguese Expeditionary Force turns up from Tete (perhaps next year) we may see some excitement'[12] – and 'excitement' was exactly what followed. In May Captain de Melo and a force of Angoni levies began the suppression of the rebellion in earnest, and the consequences were horrific: thousands were killed, women were enslaved by the Angoni and the whole territory was plundered. By November, what has been described as 'the last of the great rebellions of Central and Southern Africa', and 'the most important African reaction against the demands of the Great War'[13] was broken, and both claimants to the Makombeship fled to Southern Rhodesia. Portuguese celebrations were muted for the simple reason that the Barue revolt, which witnessed that last deployment of a traditional Angoni *impi*, was not an isolated incident. In June Major Neutel d'Abreu led thousands of Portuguese troops and 2,000 Makua levies against the Makonde on the Mvua plateau. Here too the weakness of Portuguese rule had been exposed by the war and the *Companhia do Niassa*, the company administering the district, had long been infamous for '[committing] every variety of irregularity and illegality imaginable'.[14]

The forceful manner with which both these rebellions were suppressed was evidence that the Portuguese, though not prepared to admit as much, were panic-stricken that their status as a colonial power in Africa would be severely compromised if hostilities in Europe suddenly halted at a time when they were not even in control of their colonies. Such fears explained Portugal's insistence on sending troops to France as well as three expeditionary forces to East Africa; and during 1917 they were exacerbated by increasingly public expressions of German territorial ambitions in Africa. 'The role of Portugal will end; we are the natural inheritors in Africa'[15] had become the mantra of the *Kolonische Zeitung*, which proposed that 'in the South, leaving the frontier in the middle of Mozambique, [Germany] should drive through Rhodesia to German West Africa, including Angola' and, worse still for the Portuguese, that 'this dominion should be joined to the [Portuguese] islands of the west – Azores, Madeira, Cabo Verde, Principe, São Tome'. South African ambitions – in particular the desire to annex Delagoa Bay – were equally feared, and Smuts's presence in London guaranteed that his country's objectives would be forcefully pressed. All in all, Portugal was caught between a rock and a hard place, fearing its 'enemies' and its 'allies' alike, and as a result the campaign in East Africa had, no matter how great the objections of a majority of the Portuguese population to their country's involvement in the war, 'assumed a major importance for our nation in order to save its colonies'.[16]

The message sent from Lisbon to the Portuguese High Command in East Africa was clear: *something* had to de done. And as most of its members were political, as opposed to military, appointees – Álvaro de Castro, the Governor-General who had succeeded Gil as commander-in-chief, was a lawyer from Coimbra who had held ministerial positions in Portugal, and Major Cabrito, his Chief of Staff, was regarded by the British as nothing more than a political 'thug' – the political ramifications of failure were not underestimated. This explained the ruthless fashion in which the Barue and Makonde revolts were suppressed, and the feverish activity which followed a conference with the British military authorities in mid 1917. The main Portuguese base was moved from Palma to Mocímboa da Praia, tracks leading to the posts on the Rovuma were greatly improved, permission was even granted for 'Cohen's Scouts' to operate in Portuguese territory (though recruitment of carriers by the British was expressly forbidden), and MacDonell was informed that landing facilities for a new force of 10,000 soldiers and 10,000–15,000 tons of material were being built at Mocímboa da Praia, together with two large hospitals.

The flurry of activity in Portuguese East Africa was certainly welcomed by van Deventer, but he remained sceptical about the outlook for Anglo-Portuguese military co-operation. All the European troops in Portuguese East Africa were known to be suffering from malaria, dysentery, blackwater or syphilis; the Portuguese *askari* went unpaid for months at a time; the carriers were beset by pneumonia and chills as they slept in the open and were seldom given blankets or greatcoats; and few of the Portuguese camps even had proper latrines. By the time the 5,000 troops of a Fourth Expeditionary Force started to arrive it was obvious that few of Castro's initiatives had led to any lasting improvements in the situation; and most of the new troops felt doomed from the moment they set foot on shore. 'The same fate awaits them as the former expedition,' MacDonell warned the War Office, 'that is to say those who do not die of fever or dysentery will return with their health permanently shattered';[17] and as he tried valiantly to assess whether the new force would be of greater use to the British than any of its predecessors his misgivings increased. Its leader, Colonel Tómas de Sousa Rosa, was reputed to be 'one of the most unpopular officers in the army' who had 'the utmost difficulty in getting officers to serve under him'. Furthermore, Sousa Rosa was, like Castro, a staunch republican and MacDonell's interpreter was a royalist – a situation which did little to foster harmonious relations between the British and

Portuguese staffs. But Portugal remained 'convinced that in military and all other matters they are as experienced as any other nation'[18] and, as Sir Edward Grey had predicted, was prepared to 'cling to [her colonies] as Tacitus says the love of dissimulation clung to Tiberius at his last gasp'.[19]

TWENTY-NINE

Into 'The Unknown'

On Northey's front, it was the remnants of 'Murray's Rhodesians' who were given the task of spearheading an advance onto the Mahenge plateau in July (although Murray himself was no longer fit to take to the field with his men). Two companies of NRP led by Major Dickinson were ordered to advance across the Ruhudje River from Lupembe against Aumann's three companies, while Lincke's troops were pushed back from the Likuyu district to Mpondas by a combined force of KAR, 5/SAI, 1/SAR and 2/SAR led by Hawthorn. Aumann did not give up his ground easily: the operation to dislodge him took almost three weeks and it was not until mid August 1917 that Dickinson and Colonel Fair, who had advanced north from Kitanda with 1/RNR and a company of NRP, were able to link up west of Mpepo – where Aumann's 400 men held a heavily entrenched ridge.[*] On 19 August a three-pronged assault attack on his positions was launched, and after ten days of heavy fighting Aumann withdrew to the north-east. Near Litete he turned and fought again, but when almost a third of his troops were killed, wounded or captured, he began a series of forced marches towards Mahenge. Fair chased him to within twenty-five miles of the town, and called on Aumann to surrender. Aumann refused, knowing that Fair could not defeat him with a frontal attack and that his enemy's supply lines must be stretched to breaking-point. The German commander then struck south, having heard that Colonel Huyghé, the Belgian commander-in-chief, had begun his advance from the north towards Mahenge.

There was no panic in the German ranks as Northey and Huyghé began their encirclement of the Mahenge plateau. Tafel, who had been sent by von Lettow-Vorbeck to replace Wahle in May, was a skilful and experienced field commander, and he had able officers in Aumann, the explosives expert Schönfeld (who had organised the Rufiji delta defences and the raids against the Uganda Railway in 1915), and the former policeman Friedrich Lincke.

---

[*] Aumann's three companies were 'L' *Kompanie* (Bauer), 'A' *Kompanie* (Jaeck), and 5/FK (Gutknecht).

Schönfeld had held the northern approaches to Mahenge through the rains, and Lincke the southern approach vacated by Kraut and Wintgens in February.* Furthermore, Tafel's force had been strengthened by the arrival of Captain Otto with his five companies from the Rufiji front, which brought its strength to about 2,500 rifles in fourteen companies. After the rains supplies were also not a problem, and Tafel and von Brandis, his Chief of Staff who spoke English with a Scottish accent, having had a Scottish nanny, had organised a chain of dumps stretching far to the south-east that would feed their troops until December. The only slight concern was how new *askari* recruited during the rains, and carriers who had been 'converted' into *askari*, would fare in battle as Tafel sought to carry out von Lettow-Vorbeck's order to hold the plateau as long as possible, and then hasten to the area between the Mbemkuru and Lukuledi Rivers to link up with his commander-in-chief.

When Northey began his advance from the west Huyghé's four battalions of Belgian troops – some 2,000 rifles – started south from the Central Railway in two groups. The main force of three battalions, led by Major Bataille, started from Kilossa and at the end of the third week of August had pushed Schönfeld out of Kidodi and Tope and crossed the Ruaha River. Bataille then marched on Ifakara and effected a junction with a British column, led by Colonel Tytler, Colonel Hubert's Belgian 12th *Bataillon* (which had advanced from Iringa) and Major Gilly's 10th *Bataillon* (which had started from Dodoma). By the second week in September the territory between the Ruaha and Kilombero Rivers had been cleared of German troops and, after a two-week halt to regroup and resupply, Bataille's troops fought their way up the escarpment on to the Mahenge plateau. On 7 October Mahenge was attacked, and after three days of fierce fighting in pouring rain Tafel slipped away southwards, enabling Major Muller to hoist the Belgian and British flags over the town. Two hundred and fifty wounded Germans and *askari* were taken prisoner.

It was almost exactly a year since Belgian troops had captured Tabora and once again, despite appalling supply difficulties and the desertion of one quarter of the 13,000 first-line carriers supplied by van Deventer, they had done exactly what had been asked of them at a speed that was positively disconcerting to their British allies. But when they entered Mahenge they were so short of supplies that only two battalions, Muller's and Gilly's, were able to pursue Tafel across land stripped bare by the retreating foe. Worse still,

---

* Schönfeld commanded three companies: 2/SchK (Schlawe), *Abteilung* Aruscha, and *Abteilung* Pangani – 300 rifles in all, supported by a *Königsberg* gun. Lincke commanded five companies: 6/FK (Poppe), 7/FK (Kalmann), 15/FK (Lincke), 24/FK (Schülein) and 29/FK (Schroeder) with a battery of artillery (Vogel) – a total of sixty-four Germans and 540 *askari*.

Colonel Fair seemingly made no effort to cut off Tafel's retreat, and Murray relieved him of the command of the NRP for his failure. As Fair took up his new duties as garrison commander at Mahenge, Tafel's force raced southwards in three columns commanded by Otto, Schönfeld and Tafel himself while Aumann was chased by two NRP companies towards Saidi. Northey's chances of cornering Tafel appeared to have evaporated but Hawthorn was sent to shadow Otto's column, which halted at an entrenched position on the Luwegu River; and Colonel Shorthose marched a detachment of 4/KAR all the way from Tunduru, on the border with Portuguese East Africa, to link up with Gilly at Liwale, 200 miles south-east of Mahenge, in the third week of October. These measures were, however, of dubious efficacy: Northey's 3,000 troops were now spread over such a vast area that Tafel was sure to have ample opportunity to break across Northey's lines of communication exactly as Wahle and Wintgens had done before him.

In the east van Deventer, notwithstanding the parlous state of his troops and Naumann's 'stunt' in the north-east, was under strict instructions from the War Office to defeat von Lettow-Vorbeck once and for all in the dry season. Too many British naval and merchant vessels were still employed in supporting the East Africa campaign and their value to the British war effort increased exponentially as German U-boats inflicted ever-increasing losses on British shipping. The revolution in Russia and mutinies among the French troops in Europe also exacerbated Britain's plight, and underscored the importance of ending Germany's resistance in Africa so that men and materiel could be released for service elsewhere (even if only garrison duty in India). But van Deventer's task was far more challenging than he had been led to believe when he had been instructed by Botha and Smuts to 'clear up' in German East Africa.

As soon as the rains – the worst in living memory – had ended in April 1917, von Lettow-Vorbeck had started to withdraw all remaining troops on the Rufiji front to face the threat of British advances inland from Kilwa and Lindi. A new German headquarters was established at Nahungu, and from there von Lettow-Vorbeck directed his units facing the ports. Detachments led by Wahle, Kraut and Looff opposed Lindi, Göring and von Lieberman opposed Kilwa, and von Lettow-Vorbeck himself commanded a reserve of half a dozen companies which could be deployed on either front as and when required. The German forward troops made conditions as uncomfortable as possible for those in the British bridgeheads, vigorously opposing any patrols venturing too far inland and even, on occasion, mounting daring raids deep inside the British lines. Meanwhile a chain of supply dumps was set up stretching far to the south: von Lettow-Vorbeck knew that he would eventually be forced to retreat but he had no intention of doing so in a hurried or disorganised fashion – and he was certain that at some point the opportunity would arise to inflict a substantial defeat on the enemy. A message from the Kaiser reassuring von Lettow-Vorbeck that 'The Heroes of East Africa',[1] who since the arrival of the *Marie* in April 1916 had been required to survive solely on captured and home-fashioned supplies, were not forgotten further stiffened his resolve and, in time, would encourage him to fight the two largest battles of the entire campaign.

On the face of it, the odds were not in favour of prolonging the resistance much longer. The ration strength of British troops in German East Africa still exceeded 50,000 rifles, whereas von Lettow-Vorbeck could count on no more than 9,000 troops (a third of whom were with Tafel on the Mahenge plateau or with Naumann in the north); and the next phase of the campaign would be fought in districts which had played a prominent role in the Maji-Maji uprising a decade earlier (and whose 'loyalty' was therefore questionable). When sickness rates and van Deventer's need to protect his lines of communication were taken into account, however, the disparity between the two sides narrowed dramatically; and the maximum number of troops available for the British advance inland from Kilwa and Lindi was no greater than 13,000. Furthermore, von Lettow-Vorbeck was familiar with the terrain and could move his troops with greater rapidity than the enemy.

The British advance began in early July. (See Appendix Six.) From Kilwa three columns, commanded by General Beves because Hannyngton was sick, were ordered to clear all German troops from the 100-mile front which extended inland from the port to Liwale. Further south, O'Grady, who was regarded by von Lettow-Vorbeck's officers as 'one of the better horses in the British stable', was ordered to force his way inland from Lindi and cut off the German retreat from the Kilwa front. Five months of almost continual fighting in the unhealthiest area of the entire colony lay ahead, the heat intensifying by the week and every water hole – when they could be located – being vigorously defended by the enemy. In many areas the bush was so thick that, as the commander of one of the Kilwa columns put it, 'large bodies of troops [could] pass each other within a mile distance without being aware of the passage of the other';[2] maps were rudimentary, with place names usually referring to an area of twenty square miles or more; violent bush fires frequently raged across the steppeland; and, as ever, it was the terrain and disease which were to prove even more formidable enemies than the German *askari*.

The three columns from Kilwa succeeded in prising the enemy out of its positions overlooking the port within days, an achievement in itself considering the hilly terrain was covered in '*miombo* forest, *miombo* forest, thick bush and then more *miombo* forest'.[3] But with each mile that the German commanders retired south, via Mnindi, their *askari* seemed to fight even more doggedly. By the middle of the month Captain von Lieberman had effected a concentration of a dozen companies – some 2,000 rifles with forty-eight machine-guns and a battery of captured Portuguese artillery – at Narungombe. There he determined to stand and fight: it was the last source of water north of the Mbemkuru River sufficient for a large body of troops, and he urgently needed to regroup after a week of almost constant fighting. Von Lieberman deployed across the track approaching Narungombe, his left flank in thick bush and his right on the swamp, and waited for his foe. His positions were well entrenched, with a cleared field of fire, and the German machine-guns were placed on rising ground either side of the track.

On 19 July the three British columns from Kilwa attacked.[*] Beves's force outnumbered von Lieberman's by a factor of two and had twice as many machine-guns, but von Lettow-Vorbeck was known to be approaching Narungombe with at least four companies. The main attack was frontal, led by the Gold Coast Regiment, a detachment of the 33rd Punjabis and 1/3 KAR, and the battle raged over appalling terrain from just after dawn until dusk. Visibility was seldom more than thirty yards and often less as the bush ignited into a colossal inferno. 'The day got hotter and hotter,' wrote one KAR officer, 'while the smoke from the grass fires, until they burnt themselves out, caused considerable discomfort; water was running short in the waterbottles, while the troops were getting tired.' 'By 3 p.m.,' he continued, 'it was obvious we were getting nowhere, while a strong rumour was going round that von Lettow was only a few miles away with his fresh troops and we were in for a heavy knock.'[4] Four German counter-attacks on the British flanks were beaten off during the day, one of them mauling the inexperienced *askari* of 3/3KAR on the British left, but when 1/3KAR on the right fought its way into the German trenches von Lieberman, thinking that he was being attacked by an enemy many times larger than it actually was, ordered his commanders to retire on Mihambia, a dozen miles to the south, as they were running short of ammunition. The withdrawal came as something of a surprise to many British officers. 'We were badly beaten,' was the general prognosis, 'all the Germans had to do was to press home their attack and he could have taken prisoner what was left of the British forces'.

* No. 1 Column (Colonel Orr): 8/SAI (less two companies), Gold Coast Regiment, 33rd Punjabis (reduced to a machine-gun detachment only), 2/2KAR and 27th Mountain Battery. No. 2 Column (Colonel Ridgway): 7/SAI, 1/3 KAR (Colonel Fitzgerald), 2/3 KAR (Colonel Phillips), 22nd Mountain Battery. No. 3 Column (Colonel Taylor): 8/SAI (two companies), 3/3 KAR (Colonel Dickinson) and 40th Pathans (detachment). German force (Captain von Lieberman): Spangenburg's detachment (21/FK and a 'regiment' of Angoni levies), Kempner's detachment (11/FK, 27/FK, two artillery pieces), Büchsel's detachment (17/FK and 14/ResK), and Steinhäuser's detachment (10/FK, 3/SchK, 10/SchK) – a total of ninety-five Germans and 850 *askari*.

After the German troops had disappeared 'an uncanny silence fell over the battlefield'.[5] Some of the most battle-hardened German company commanders had been in the fray – including Walter Spangenburg, Franz Kempner, Walter Büchsel and Leopold Steinhäuser – and British casualties were severe. Among the 800 men of the Gold Coast Regiment one in five lay dead or wounded; six of the officers of 1/3KAR were killed and 200 of its *askari* killed or wounded; and 8/SAI, which had supported the Gold Coast Regiment, sustained casualties of one third and lost three of its machine-guns to the enemy.

In the immediate aftermath of the battle von Lettow-Vorbeck was livid with von Lieberman for disregarding an order to hold Narungombe until he arrived to 'seal the doom of the enemy's main body'. But when he found out that von Lieberman had only received the order when his withdrawal was already well under way he relented; and when the full extent of the casualties inflicted on Beves's force became apparent von Lieberman was fulsomely praised for his 'brilliant leadership' in dealing such a 'heavy blow'[6] to the enemy. Had von Lettow-Vorbeck arrived on the scene twenty-four hours earlier, the battle at Narungombe would have completely put paid to the Kilwa offensive. As it was, no further advance could be contemplated for almost two months while a scorched earth and blockhouse strategy was adopted to clear a route south.

The battle at Narungombe *seemed* to demonstrate that van Deventer had acted too precipitously, and more carelessly than Hoskins would ever have done, in trying to appease the War Office's desire for a swift end to the campaign. But had he not ordered the offensive the Kilwa troops would probably have been robbed of any offensive capability within weeks. Half the men of 7/SAI, which had returned from South Africa at the end of June with a ration strength of 966 all ranks, had contracted malaria within a month of their arrival at Kilwa (and by November their effective strength would be 158). The only hope of combating such massive sickness rates was to reach higher ground inland; and within weeks O'Grady was also ordered forward from Lindi to Mingoyo. But there too the advance of O'Grady's three columns soon encountered vigorous opposition from Wahle's nine companies,* and British casualties were severe, particularly among the 30th Punjabis (seven of whose eight British officers were wounded, to add to the 250 other ranks killed or wounded). No further move could be attempted until October, and in the meantime there were many among the British ranks who began to wonder if the campaign would only end when they were fighting in the streets of Cape Town.

---

* O'Grady advanced in three columns: 3/2KAR on the right; 25th Royal Fusiliers, 259th (Loyal North Lancs) Machine-gun Company and 3/4KAR on the left; and 30th Punjabis in the centre.

In October, van Deventer was ready to order a resumption of the advance. General Hannyngton, who had returned from hospital, took charge of the Kilwa force, Beves moved south to assume command of the Lindi force, and this time the pressure exerted on the enemy was better co-ordinated. From the north Hannyngton ordered the Nigerian Brigade and Colonel Orr's column, backed by three new battalions of Indian troops,* to converge on Bweho Chini, forcing the enemy to retire south from Mihambia and Ndessa towards Nahungu, leaving behind more than 100 dead. On 27 September Nahungu, von Lettow-Vorbeck's HQ, was surrounded but he had already fled and Franz Köhl succeeded in eluding the British encirclement with six companies which now constituted the rearguard of the main German force. It soon became clear that the general line of the German retreat was towards the Lukuledi River, and not inland towards Liwale, so the Nigerian Brigade were sent still further south to the Lukuledi to sandwich Wahle and von Lettow-Vorbeck between Mahiwa and Lindi while Hannyngton cleared Captain Köhl's detachment from the area around Ruponda. (See Appendix Seven.)

In the south, Beves divided the Lindi force into two columns, led by O'Grady and Tytler, which began to advance up the Lukuledi River towards Nyangao in early October.† As Wahle's troops retreated inland he suddenly found that two of the three Nigerian battalions sent south by Hannyngton had arrived at Mahiwa cotton plantation to cut off his line of retreat, but his concerns were soon dispelled by the simultaneous appearance of von Lettow-Vorbeck's reserve near Mahiwa. Over the next four days the battle that ensued around Mahiwa and Nyangao, three or four miles apart, proved to be the most costly – to both sides – of the campaign. Repeated efforts by O'Grady and Tytler to relieve the Nigerian troops around Mahiwa were thwarted by Wahle while behind his positions detachments led by Göring, Köhl, and Walther von Ruckteschell (an artist of some repute who had been visiting the colony on a painting trip when war broke out) launched attack after attack against the Nigerian defences. On 17 October, the third day of the battle, Tytler ordered 3/4KAR to attack Wahle's positions on a ridge two miles

---

* 55th (Coke's) Rifles, 127th Baluchis and 25th Cavalry commanded by Colonel Dyke.
† British troops' strengths on 6 October were as follows: Lindi Force (Beves): No. 3 Column (O'Grady) 1/2KAR, 3/2KAR, Bharatpur Infantry – 1,100 rifles, No. 4 Column (Tytler) 3/4KAR, 30th Punjabis, 25th Royal Fusiliers, 259th Machine-gun Company – 1,100 rifles, Reserve – 400 rifles, Lines of Communication – 1,000 rifles. Kilwa Force (Hannyngton): No. 1 Column (Orr) 1/3KAR, 2/2KAR, 27th Mountain Battery – 1,200 rifles, No. 2 Column (Ridgway) 2/3KAR – 2,200 rifles, Reserve – (Dyke) 55th Rifles, 127th Baluchis – 1,400 rifles, 25th Cavalry – 600 rifles, Lines of Communication – 1,100 rifles. Nigerian Brigade (Mann) – 2,000 rifles. After Naumann's surrender Colonel Breytenbach's 10/SAH and Colonel Morris's 1st Cape Corps proceeded to Kilwa and 4/4KAR to Lindi.

south-west of Nyangao while O'Grady moved the Bharatpur Infantry and 1/2KAR up on his right. Bit by bit the British troops began to dislodge the German *askari* from their entrenchments, but in the late afternoon a ferocious counter-attack was launched which pushed the whole British line back. An hour later O'Grady attacked again, and at nightfall there was still no let-up in the intensity of the fighting.

Soon after dawn on 18 October O'Grady finally broke through to the beleaguered Nigerians, 3/2KAR in the vanguard, but when Tytler was again counter-attacked Beves was forced to throw in his reserve while the remnants of the 'Frontiersmen', now in their third year of campaigning, endeavoured to fill the gaps which had emerged between Tytler's and O'Grady's columns. It was the battalion's last action of the war, one which saw their strength reduced from 120 men to fewer than fifty as Wahle kept up the pressure on the Lindi columns until nightfall. Meanwhile, as the battle neared its climax, Colonel Orr's column arrived from Ruponda and marched against the two or three German companies, part of Kraut's force, which held the Lukuledi Mission. A 'sharp fight' took place, forcing Kraut to abandon the mission and, after the appearance of this new force thirty miles west of Mahiwa and Nyangao, von Lettow-Vorbeck's and Wahle's troops finally began to abandon their positions. On 19 October the battlefield was quiet.

At Mahiwa and Nyangao the ranks of the Nigerian battalions and Beves's columns, 5,000 troops in all, were decimated: total casualties were estimated at between one third and a half. At Nyangao, on 17 October, Colonel Giffard's 1/2KAR lost half its British officers and NCOs and a third of its *askari*; at Mahiwa, on 16 October alone, the surrounded 1st, 2nd and 4th Nigerians lost more than 300 killed and wounded; and, when Kraut launched a counter-attack against Orr's column at Lukuledi Mission on 21 October, 1/3KAR incurred equally severe casualties before Kraut called off the attack and led his six companies off to join von Lettow-Vorbeck in the vicinity of Ndanda, twenty miles to the east of the mission. As the German troops moved to new positions south of the Lukuledi River it was far from certain what the substantial loss of life had achieved. On the one hand, the timely appearance of Orr's column at Lukuledi Mission had undoubtedly robbed von Lettow-Vorbeck of the option of retiring on Masasi, a dozen miles south of the mission; and Beves's assault on Wahle's positions had forced the enemy to abandon the Lukuledi River altogether. On the other hand, Orr's advance had made him reliant on supply lines almost 400 miles long – a situation which forced him to return to Ruponda, whence he had started, while arrangements were made for his troops to be supplied from Lindi rather than Kilwa; and Beves's determination had seemingly robbed O'Grady and Tytler's troops of any offensive capability whatsoever. Beves, who had arrived in East Africa for the 'First Salaita Show' with a reputation as a 'cautious' soldier (and avid butterfly collector), broke down under the strain and was relieved of his command for repeatedly pressing the attack from the east in spite of the mounting casualties. This was arguably just the strategy that Smuts should have used more often; but it ended with the near-annihilation of his force, a price that van Deventer was no more prepared to pay than Smuts before him.

Although the British troops had been badly mauled, and needed rest and recuperation before van Deventer could contemplate attempting to finish the enemy between the Lukuledi River and the Makonde plateau before the rains, the fighting around Mahiwa and Nyangao could not be described as a decisive victory for von Lettow-Vorbeck. Nine machine-guns, a field gun and 200,000 rounds of ammunition had been captured – but at a considerable cost in irreplaceable men and materiel. More than 500 German troops lay dead or wounded, including a third of Wahle's complement, and over 850,000 rounds of ammunition were expended during the four days' fighting; desertion was also rampant, and those supply dumps that had not fallen into the hands of the marauding 25th Cavalry or other British troops would only support the remaining troops for a maximum of six weeks. Von Lettow-Vorbeck's problems did not end there. All German troops (with the exception of those retreating from the Mahenge plateau with Tafel) were now boxed up in 100 square miles of the south-eastern corner of the colony; there was no information about the whereabouts of Tafel, who – so it was thought – had most probably been cut off by British and Belgian troops from Liwale or British troops from Tunduru and Songea; and van Deventer's troops, though severely battered, were likely to resume their offensive as soon as practicable. This was the situation when, on 24 October 1917, von Lettow-Vorbeck called a conference with Schnee. The prognosis of the Governor of German East Africa, whom von Lettow-Vorbeck now referred to ironically as 'the Governor of Chiwata', was bleak; but his commander-in-chief, who was rumoured to have donned his full regimental dress for the first time in the campaign at Nyangao, made it quite clear that the war 'could and must be carried on'.[7] After all, Major Schulz and two German companies held the *boma* at Newala on the Makonde plateau, recaptured from the Portuguese in December 1916, and from Newala it was but a short hop into territory where further pursuit by the British might be thwarted: von Lettow-Vorbeck had begun to set his sights on Portuguese East Africa.

On 6 November the British advance recommenced and van Deventer, mindful of the general direction of von Lettow-Vorbeck's line of retreat, requested the Portuguese High Command to concentrate its troops at Mocímboa da Rovuma, Chomba and Negomano with a view to opposing any incursions to Portuguese territory by German troops being driven south. From the east General Cunliffe, who had succeeded Beves, and whose Lindi troops now included his own Nigerian Brigade, pushed Wahle's seven companies further down the south bank of the Lukuledi River towards Nangoo and Ndanda; and Hannyngton's Kilwa troops also converged on Ndanda from the north. On 10 November the two forces linked up, capturing nearly 200 Germans and *askari* in the process, while a detachment of Colonel Breytenbach's mounted troops – 10/SAH, the 25th Cavalry and the KAR Mounted Infantry – swooped on Masasi, seizing a similar number of prisoners and making quite certain that the option of retreating south-west, as opposed to due south, remained closed to von Lettow-Vorbeck. To the great relief of the advancing columns Cunliffe's men also captured a naval gun, and when another was found disabled at Masasi they continued on their way towards the Makonde plateau reassured by the knowledge that none of the *Königsberg's* armaments remained in enemy hands to bombard them from the heights to the south. With the mounted troops proving increasingly effective, and with fresh troops like the Cape Corps now on the front, morale lifted still further and there was a widespread belief that an engagement around Chiwata might well prove decisive.

Despite Schnee's doubts about the merits of continuing the fight, von Lettow-Vorbeck was certain that as the enemy completed 'the concentric march of his columns', those columns would become 'helplessly crowded on a narrow area', thereby presenting him with the opportunity either to counter-attack or to 'march where I liked'.[8] Wahle's remaining troops still had plenty of fight in them, having vigorously opposed Cunliffe's advance until the capture of Ndanda Mission threatened them in the rear; and even then they had retreated in an orderly fashion up onto the Makonde plateau assisted by the equally assured troops of von Lieberman's detachment. But von Lettow-Vorbeck was thwarted, on at least two occasions, by the fact that he only had ammunition sufficient to put one third of his troops into battle at any one time and by the need to ensure that his last remaining supply dump was safely withdrawn from Chiwata.

By 15 November it was obvious to van Deventer that his opponent would not, or could not, stand and fight at Chiwata, that he was falling back on Lutshemi; and when Chiwata was taken 100 Germans and more than 400 *askari*, all sick or too wounded to be moved, fell into British hands. Meanwhile the plight of those able to fight on worsened. Three days of fierce, and continual, fighting accompanied their retreat through the Lutshemi Valley towards Nambindinga; and as a further 300 Germans and 700 *askari* were captured one of the few remaining sources of hope for von Lettow-Vorbeck's commanders lay in the possibility, remote though it seemed as no word had been heard from Tafel since early October, of the remnants of the *Westtruppen* appearing from the north-west to throw the British advance off-balance.

Although Tafel had initially shown no sign of urgency in his retreat from Mahenge, he had upped the pace considerably after British and Belgian troops captured Liwale in the third week in October: British and Belgian columns appeared to be in close pursuit, and a larger Belgian force was known to be marching inland from Kilwa to ensure that he could not break north-east across the lines of communication of Hannyngton's Kilwa troops. On 12 November, Tafel's three columns* – led by Otto, Schönfeld and Tafel himself – crossed the Liwale–Songea track, heading south-east, and he knew that he was at last within reach of a link-up with von Lettow-Vorbeck and Wahle. A patrol was sent ahead to ascertain the location of von Lettow-Vorbeck's HQ and as darkness fell on 15 November Tafel arrived in the vicinity of Abdullah Kwa Nanga, fifty miles south-west of Liwale. The only British troops in his way were 250 *askari* of Major Hawkins's 2/4KAR, but at dawn the following morning a further 200 of Colonel Shorthose's 1/4KAR arrived from Tunduru to rescue Hawkins. Tafel could simply have sidestepped the British troops; but he chose to take them on, knowing that if they were resoundingly defeated they would be unable to pursue him as he marched on towards von Lettow-Vorbeck. Just two hours after its arrival on the high ground to the south of the village Shorthose's relief column was set upon by Otto's detachment, forcing it to withdraw after incurring heavy losses, and within hours Schönfeld's column descended on Hawkins. The attack lasted all day, but at nightfall Tafel ordered his commanders to press on south-eastwards (with four serviceable machine-guns captured from the enemy). The *Westtruppen*, comprising some 1,750 officers and *askari* and equipped with as many as a dozen machine-guns and over half a million rounds of ammunition, had broken through.

Although British reinforcements from the Liwale–Songea track and Belgian reinforcements from Liwale arrived on the scene too late to prevent Tafel from moving on, there was a glimmer of hope in the British ranks. By their own admission, their opponents 'looked terrible' as they disappeared out of sight. 'The immensely long retreat had left them pretty well dead-beat,' wrote one German officer, 'and their uniforms hung around them in rags. Some of the *askari* had given up trying to keep the bits together, and carried on in their shorts, and with a machine-gun belt slung across their shoulders, or a captured English or Belgian bandolier. Not all of them had boots, and if they had, it was a pair of English or Belgian ones, dragged from a corpse after a fight.'[9]

---

* Tafel's column (10 November 1917): 5/FK, 22/FK, *Abteilung* Pangani and 'L' *Kompanie*. Schönfeld's column: 23/FK, 24/FK, 1/SchK and 3/SchK. Otto's column: 1/FK, 6/FK, 7/FK, 15/FK, 29/FK. Total strength: 181 Europeans, 1,558 *askari* and 3,732 carriers and followers.

Furthermore, a Belgian patrol succeeded in catching up with Tafel's rearguard, killing Lieutenant Niemir, capturing Captain Bauer and seizing all Tafel's documents; and on 18 November the patrol sent by Tafel to gain touch with von Lettow-Vorbeck at Nambindinga fell into British hands. Successful though their escape from Mahenge had undoubtedly been, the questions on the minds of all Tafel's officers as they sped towards the Makonde plateau were: 'How long can it go on? Have we not been through enough for East Africa?'[10]

Liwale was as far as Colonel Huyghé's Belgian troops could, or would, go and Belgium played no further active part in the campaign. Their involvement had cost the lives of more than 2,000 officers and *askari*, a death toll equivalent to one in seven of the force which had invaded Ruanda and Urundi and swept down to Tabora the previous year, and it had been characterised by an ability to march vast distances at speed, to make do with the most precarious supply arrangements imaginable, and a predilection for undertaking frontal assaults which was the envy of many a British officer. Political wrangling may have accompanied every phase of Anglo-Belgian co-operation, but few who had encountered the Belgian *askari* sought to deny that they had proved every bit as effective as 'Murray's Rhodesians', the West African battalions, the Indian mountain gunners, and the pre-war battalions of the King's African Rifles. The Belgian Congo had also provided Britain with more than half of its wartime requirement for copal (for the munitions industry), and about five per cent of its requirement for copper, palm oil and rubber. As von Lettow-Vorbeck and Tafel trudged their way ever closer to Portuguese East Africa, the likelihood of Belgium's contribution being matched by Britain's other ally looked slim.

THIRTY

The German Pimpernel

V on Lettow-Vorbeck's escape from encirclement at Chiwata and in the Lutshemi Valley was acknowledged by his adversaries as 'a notable achievement, in great measure due to the skilful work of his rearguard commanders'.[1] But it left his force in desperate straits. At Chiwata, ninety-eight Germans and 425 *askari* had surrendered to the British, and more men and field guns had been captured as his remaining companies were harried every inch of the way up the Lutshemi Valley. On the face of it, his offensive capability was negligible; and requisitioning sufficient supplies for his men was well-nigh impossible. Stocks of quinine for the Europeans would only keep them on their feet for less than a month, and after they were exhausted von Lettow-Vorbeck knew that it would be 'madness to go on with the fighting'. As his bedraggled troops fought their way towards the wooded high ground around Nambindinga, he hoped to reorganise and even, if Tafel reappeared, to ensure that 'those who had begun fighting in the Belgian Congo and those from the Kenya frontier could hear the sound of each others' rifles'[2] for the first time. But he knew that he would also be forced to effect 'a drastic reduction of strength'[3] if the struggle were to continue.

On 17 November, von Lettow-Vorbeck announced his 'fateful decision'.[4] All of his troops, including the 1,000 or so Europeans, were to undergo a medical examination – and those who were not fully fit would be left behind. Seven hundred Europeans and 2,000 *askari* failed the test; for some the news came as a relief, but for others it was a bitter disappointment. Fever-ridden Nis Kock, from the blockade-runner *Kronborg*, was one of those for whom 'it was world-shaking'* to be told that he must remain at Nambindinga; and lying nearby was the badly wounded Captain von Lieberman, who had led the German troops at Narungombe in July and commanded the defence of Ndanda during the withdrawal onto the Makonde plateau. When dusk descended, Kock watched as 'fire upon fire was lighted ... not bold, flaring

---

* Kock p. 250 and p. 253. See also Lettow-Vorbeck (1), p. 221: 'the majority ... were bitterly disappointed at having to remain'.

soldiers' fires, but little sparks of light in the darkness', around which 'the men who were to stay behind' huddled:

> More and more wounded kept coming in from the fight that had raged round the camp all day, machine-gun firing was still to be heard about the camp, but the intervals between bursts got longer and longer and at last a few *Askari* companies came in: they had been holding up the English advance as long as it was light, and moving slowly and heavily they disappeared among the trees. But then, as if they had sprung out of the ground, still more companies took shape out of the pitchy darkness. This was the German East African Army, marching towards the frontier river, the Rovuma. The camp-fires gleamed on fantastic shapes, black and white side by side, carrying rifles over their shoulders, butt pointing backwards ... More came by, and still more.[5]

Von Lettow-Vorbeck's determination to press on with the troops fit enough to do so was remarkable, and even those who were glad to be left behind felt a 'shuddering admiration' for their 'implacable, unwearying'[6] commander. In a single month, he had lost a further eight of the thirty-three commissioned officers with whom he had started the war; and his 'new' army consisted of just thirteen or fourteen companies, armed with thirty-seven machine-guns and two artillery pieces (commanded by the wooden-footed *Königsberg* officer Richard Wenig). Leaving waterless Nambindinga, and their comrades, to the British these troops began their march across the inhospitable Makonde plateau right away; and on 18 November the vanguard reached Kitangari, where Max Looff, whose naval guns and sailors had contributed so much to the German war effort, was judged too sick to continue. It was over two and a half years since the former captain of the *Königsberg* had abandoned his ship for the land war, and had he been able to march for just two more days he would have found himself back at Newala, the scene of his victory over the Portuguese almost exactly a year earlier.

After weeding out the last of the sick troops at Newala von Lettow-Vorbeck, newly promoted by Berlin to the rank of Major-General, marched down off the plateau on 21 November at the head of a force comprising 278 Europeans, 1,700 *askari* and 3,000 porters and followers commanded by naval Lieutenant Besch, the column's quartermaster.* That night the Germans camped at Mpili, on the Rovuma, having routed a very surprised mounted detachment of

---

* Göring puts the figure of carriers at as high as 7,000 plus 1,000 family followers (p. 150). Boell (1), p. 399 states 3,900 carriers, 470 *askaris*' boys, and 1,300 women and children. Both are higher than von Lettow-Vorbeck's estimate of 3,000, and attest to the fact that reliable records were not kept for carriers.

10/SAH who were watering their horses at the river. The prisoners were sent back north to the British, but horses were kept by von Lettow-Vorbeck 'as a possible addition to rations'.[7] Meanwhile the 55th (Coke's) Rifles arrived at Newala as the advance guard of No. 1 Column less than twenty-four hours after the departing enemy. With his back to the escarpment von Lettow-Vorbeck would have been hard-pressed in daylight to emulate the Portuguese feat of 1916 of 'disappearing' from this cliff-top redoubt, the more so if adequate forces had been in position on the north bank of the Rovuma; and, as the regiment's official historian lamented, if the column had arrived one day earlier 'whatever the fortunes of the fight which would certainly have taken place, it must have had a marked effect on von Lettow's further retreat'.[*] Instead, on 22 November, an unimpeded von Lettow-Vorbeck led the bulk of his troops west along the Rovuma towards the Portuguese garrison at Negomano, at the confluence between the Rovuma and Lujenda Rivers, while Karl Göring was despatched due south towards another garrison at Nasombe with three companies.

As they made their way along the Rovuma there was little jubilation in the German ranks. Köhl's five-company vanguard, von Ruckteschell's rearguard of two companies, and Wahle's central column of three companies were spread out over a considerable area: everyone knew that British troops would be in hot pursuit, that 'the battle against the wolves'[8] would continue, and all the officers were in the grip of a 'great fear ... about provisions'. For old General Wahle, who had started his military career in 1867, three years before von Lettow-Vorbeck was even born, it was 'the third time such a situation had arisen [during the war]', but he resolved to 'grit [his] teeth and bear it even if it meant starving to death'. The dearth of provisions was not the only problem: with the rainy season approaching the temperature rarely fell below 39°C in the shade – the 'most insane heat'[9] that Wahle had experienced in the whole campaign. Even the capture of a small British supply column failed to alleviate the misery, and with each passing day the only thing sustaining the troops was von Lettow-Vorbeck's certainty, resulting from the intelligence gleaned from von Stuemer and von Bock after their incursion into Portuguese East Africa earlier in the year, that 'something might be done'[10] at Negomano.

A little before dawn on 25 November the main German force began its crossing of the Rovuma a little above the confluence with the Lujenda. The river was only about 700 yards wide at this point, being the dry season, but men still found themselves up to their chests in the water at times and even the horses captured from 10/SAH were unsure of their footing. Wahle noticed

---

[*] Wylly (2), p. 133; he added acerbically that 'it was also believed that more energetic action by the SA mounted columns [on the Rovuma] might have produced better results'.

that 'many eyes were filled with tears' as the troops left German East Africa, but the crossing was successfully completed without incident and on the south side of the river everyone stripped off to dry. Within an hour the sombre mood changed to one of *allgemeine Würchtigkeit* – 'absolute callousness'[11] – as von Lettow-Vorbeck announced his plan.

Since his arrival in September Colonel Tómas de Sousa Rosa, the new Portuguese commander-in-chief, had repeatedly assured van Deventer that the border with German East Africa was held by the 6,500 Portuguese troops and nineteen companies of *askari* pushed inland from the coast. By early November, however, he had begun to renege on his suggestion that they should also 'demonstrate' north of the Rovuma for fear that it would weaken his defences in the event of a German attack somewhere to the west of Mocímboa da Rovuma; and when MacDonell informed van Deventer that Captain Mena of the Portuguese General Staff had privately voiced his 'entire disagreement with the commander-in-chief and his colleagues', van Deventer was forced to agree to the abandonment of a Portuguese advance 'for the time being'. Indeed Mena's doubts about Sousa Rosa's abilities were framed in terms which were 'so exact' and 'so incontrovertible'[12] that van Deventer was unable to offer any reassurance to Northey and other commanders who repeatedly warned him that it was 'essential to close [the Portuguese] door firmly';[13] and by the time von Lettow-Vorbeck led his troops off the Makonde plateau Sousa Rosa had still failed to fulfil a promise to strip the territory south of the Rovuma of any surplus foodstuffs even though it had become increasingly obvious to British Intelligence officers 'what von Lettow's last move would and must be' if he was not cornered on the Makonde plateau.

At 7 a.m. on 25 November Negomano, which was occupied by a 'large Portuguese force with great supplies of arms and ammunition' but 'totally unsupported by any British troops',[14] received a warning from Major Cohen, MacDonell's Intelligence officer, that an attack by von Lettow-Vorbeck was imminent. The warning was to no avail. Six companies in two detachments led by von Ruckteschell and Köhl threw themselves at the Portuguese defences with a ferocity unequalled in three years of campaigning, and after twenty-four hours of continual fighting Major Quaresma, the garrison commander, surrendered. The Portuguese accounts of the battle told of great heroism, a fight against insuperable odds, and of eventually running out of ammunition. There were undoubtedly examples of individual bravery among the defenders, who were divided between Negomano itself and its nearby water supply, but a subsequent inspection of Negomano by British Intelligence officers also revealed that the garrison had only been entrenched according to the Portuguese military's understanding of the word and that, far from having rations for a siege of up to six days as Sousa Rosa subsequently claimed, the troops were on the brink of starvation. By the same token Quaresma, a political appointee who was only in command by dint of the fact that he was the oldest of the majors and therefore senior to Major Teixeira Pinto, a veteran of African bush-fighting, claimed three-quarters of the garrison escaped during the night, leaving 'only' twenty-two Portuguese officers and a couple of hundred *askari* dead on the battlefield; whereas von Lettow-Vorbeck was certain that 'scarcely more than 200 of the enemy force, about 1,000 strong, can have survived'.* The truth probably lay somewhere between the two estimates. What is certain is that a garrison of 1,200 Portuguese troops was overrun and a quarter of a million rounds of ammunition, six machine-guns and several hundred modern rifles were captured – a disaster for van Deventer, who on receiving the news was heard to mutter 'dit lyk soos verraaiery' ('it looks like treason').

'With one blow,' wrote von Lettow-Vorbeck, 'we had freed ourselves of a great part of our difficulties',[15] while British officers expressed their disgust that 'in spite of the example and fate of the Port force at Newala a year before, a large Port force with great supplies of arms and ammunition, but totally unsupported by any British troops, was allowed to collect at Negomano at the junction of the Rovuma and Lugenda rivers'.[16] The huge haul of arms and ammunition, European foodstuffs and medical supplies was certainly a boon, but the dearth of suitable provisions for von Lettow-Vorbeck's starving *askari* forced him to leave Negomano as soon as possible and march upriver in search of further pickings. By 28 November even von Ruckteschell's rearguard companies, 2/FK and 21/FK, had abandoned the Portuguese garrison, leaving Sousa Rosa to ponder where von Lettow-Vorbeck would strike next. The loss of Negomano caused panic in the Portuguese High Command, a situation which was exacerbated when British planes, flying in low cloud, bombed Mocímboa da Rovuma in the mistaken belief that Göring's detachment had taken the garrison; and in his confused state Sousa Rosa insisted that the 'main attack' was yet to come, and would be directed against Chomba and then Mocímboa da Praia, on the coast. As the main Portuguese supply base, Mocímboa da Praia was certainly a tempting target. But it was over 200 miles from Negomano, and it was very unrealistic for Sousa Rosa to claim that von Lettow-Vorbeck could cover that distance before the arrival of the rainy season. His assessment of the danger to the coastal bases was mere fantasy, rooted in a disingenuous attempt to pretend that Negomano had simply been a local

---

* Lettow-Vorbeck (1), p. 231. This was clearly an exaggeration, indeed on the next page von Lettow-Vorbeck contradicts himself by saying that 'about 200 enemy dead' were buried, 'about 150 Europeans' were released on parole, and 'several hundred *askari*' were taken prisoner. Schnee's estimates were probably more accurate: he claimed that twenty-five Portuguese officers and soldiers and 162 *askari* were killed, and 490 prisoners were taken (Schnee (1), p. 310).

setback, and reports sent to van Deventer claiming that large German detachments were raiding villages south of Porto Amelia grossly exaggerated the truth.

As von Lettow-Vorbeck proceeded west along the Rovuma, rather than east towards the coast, the fate of Tafel's fourteen companies preoccupied him every bit as much as the search for food. Unbeknownst to his commander-in-chief, after breaking through the British lines at Abdullah Kwa Nanga Tafel had reached Mt Rondo, from which he could see the Indian Ocean to the east and the Makonde plateau to the south-east. Lack of water and increasing indiscipline in the ranks were his major sources of concern, but on 21 November Tafel could hear artillery fire to the east and two days later he was told by locals that Newala was still in German hands. Approaching the main force would, he realised, need to be carefully executed and was best done from the south-western edge of the plateau directly below Newala.

From the British point of view, Tafel's last known position was thirty miles south-west of Masasi on the Bangalla River. Stopping him effecting a junction with von Lettow-Vorbeck was vital, and all available troops were sent to hunt him down. On 26 November, Captain Max Poppe, at the head of 6/FK and 7/FK, 'bumped' a detachment of the 129th Baluchis, which had not received a warning of Tafel's approach (and sustained casualties of twenty per cent among its 250 men in what was to be the battalion's final action after two and a half years in East Africa); and that night all of Tafel's columns converged near Luatala. There it was decided to jettison thirty-two Europeans, 180 *askari* and 1,330 carriers and women before crossing the Rovuma the following morning in the hope of stumbling across a patrol from the main German force.

Once across the river Tafel's troops were on the track south that Göring had followed five days earlier towards Nasombe; indeed during the afternoon they were just hours from one of Göring's patrols. But finding no sign of his compatriots Tafel reluctantly reached the conclusion that he would have to surrender, and on the afternoon of 28 November he destroyed half a million rounds of ammunition and led his troops back across the Rovuma. At the confluence with the Bangalla River, the officers of the 55th (Coke's) Rifles and Gold Coast Regiment awaited them, and Tafel's 1,371 surviving troops were taken prisoner.[*]

When news of Tafel's surrender reached von Lettow-Vorbeck, he admitted

---

* See Boell's figures (1), p. 397: No. 1 Column took the surrender of nineteen German officers, ninety-two German NCOs and others, 1,260 *askari*, 2,093 carriers and 227 followers. Van Deventer put the total Allied 'haul' during November 1917 at 1,115 Europeans, 3,382 *askari* and six artillery pieces in working order.

that it was 'the greatest disappointment'[17] of his war. He was denied not only the valuable ammunition but the services of troops, many of whom had fought their way diagonally right across German East Africa, that would have doubled the size of his force. As it was, only Captain Otto, fourteen fellow-Germans and twenty-three *askari* – a patrol which Tafel had allowed to continue the search for their commander south of the Rovuma – succeeded in locating Göring; and after raiding various Portuguese posts between Negomano and Mocímboa da Rovuma both commanders joined von Lettow-Vorbeck before Christmas. Tafel's surrender was some compensation to the men of Coke's Rifles for so narrowly missing von Lettow-Vorbeck at Newala, the more so as Tafel, Lincke, Aumann and Schönfeld were among the most skilled and respected enemy officers. But as the prisoners were marched off to the sea, every British soldier knew that Tafel's command was very much second prize.[*]

Meanwhile the task of pursuing von Lettow-Vorbeck's main force was undertaken by the Indian 25th Cavalry, a KAR Mounted Infantry detachment, and the Nigerian Brigade, while the Gold Coast Regiment and two battalions of KAR occupied Negomano. Their trail led the mounted troops through 'a more desolate and depressing tract of bush [than] ... it would be hard to conceive' for 'hard and laborious days' on end. Rations were 'continually running out'; sickness reached epidemic proportions; and although a motor road was rapidly opened from the Rovuma to Negomano there was an ever-present fear that the river would soon start to rise and turn thousands of square miles into a 'huge sweltering swamp'.[18] Within days of the sacking of Negomano Major Cohen's scouts also discovered how futile further pursuit would be: von Lettow-Vorbeck and Wahle had decided that 'two generals at the head of our tiny band was excessive'[†] and that the search for food would be easier if they split up. With that, the main force divided and any vestigial hopes of surrounding it evaporated.

Wahle led his detachment in a westerly direction along the Chiulesi River towards the Mkula Hills, where von Stuemer's troops had sojourned between April and August, and after three days of fighting overran a Portuguese post at Puchapucha which yielded a further 300 rifles. For once genuine resistance

---

[*] Theodor Tafel was one of only four of von Lettow-Vorbeck's senior officers to take to the field again in World War II (the other three being Franz Köhl, Alfred Gutknecht and Heinrich Naumann). Tafel commanded Infantry Regiment 435 for the first three years of the war, and was then appointed Commandant of Stalag XX B; he ended the war with the rank of Major-General and was awarded the German Cross in Gold for his conduct on the Eastern Front in 1941.

[†] Wahle, p. 48. Only seven out of thirty-three of von Lettow-Vorbeck's senior regular officers of 1914 were still in the field with him: Kraut, Schulz, Stemmermann, Göring, Otto, von Chappuis and Köhl.

was put up by the Portuguese troops – half of whom died on the battlefield – and officers Francisco Curado and Viriato de Lacerda became heroes at home; but Portuguese accounts of 'the most brilliant action of the campaign' were characteristically exaggerated and, in claiming that it 'compensated honourably for the disaster at Negomano',[19] deluded. Meanwhile Oizulo also fell to Stemmermann's 3/SchK on the night of 26/27 November, and von Lettow-Vorbeck marched his companies up the Lujenda River at a rate of twenty miles per day. On 2 December Kempner's 11/FK were sent forward to Nanguar and its well-fortified *boma* was captured without encountering resistance. Here, at last, 850 packs of 'native' food fell into von Lettow-Vorbeck's hands, as well as 300,000 rounds of ammunition.

An *embarras de richesses* followed the fall of Nanguar. Three days later Köhl's five companies,* with Schnee in tow, were ordered east towards Montepuez and Medo district; and from there raiding parties set out for the coast (thereby transforming Sousa Rosa's panic-stricken reports of the previous month into prophecies). Another detachment, led by Otto von Scherbening, a planter from Lindi, disappeared south and was away for months, eventually reaching the Lurio River via Mtenda and Mahua before continuing on up the Malema River and capturing Malema *boma* itself, fifty miles south of the Lurio, in mid February 1918; and in time shopkeeper Ernst Wolfram's patrol reached the coast well to the south of Porto Amelia. As Köhl's troops foraged far and wide, Köhl himself stayed in contact with the main German force through a relay system of couriers despite the fact that by Christmas von Lettow-Vorbeck had marched as far as Matarica, a station of the Portuguese *Companhia do Niassa*.

In just three weeks von Lettow-Vorbeck and Wahle had seized eighteen tons of foodstuffs from Portuguese garrisons, averting what Schnee feared 'might well have been a catastrophe',[20] and were well out of reach of any British troops when torrential downpours heralded the start of the rains. Furthermore, all of the troops in the north-west had reached suitable destinations in which to sit out the rains. Von Lettow-Vorbeck was at Matarica which, with its massive buildings, gardens, fruit and vegetables, and ample supply of pigs and 'native' food, provided everything he could have wished for; Wahle was equally comfortable at the prosperous *Companhia do Niassa* station at Mwembe in the Mkula Hills; and five companies led by Otto and Göring were settled near the confluence of the Lujenda and Luambala Rivers. They were not destined to spend the New Year in German East Africa, as many had boasted they would to captured Portuguese officers at Negomano; but all the troops were well provisioned, and a million rounds of ammunition

* Köhl's detachment comprised 3/FK, 10/FK, 11/FK, 17/FK and 6/SchK, accompanied by Sabath's field gun.

and eleven machine-guns had been captured in Portuguese East Africa – even more booty than had been captured from the British at Tanga in November 1914.

As the level of the Rovuma rose, the only British troops left in Portuguese territory were those sent with Colonel Rose to strengthen Porto Amelia (the Gold Coast Regiment, 4/4 KAR and an Indian Mountain Battery), and Colonel Clayton's 2nd Cape Corps, which had been raised in mid 1917 for service in Nyasaland and was moved forward by Northey to M'tengula to guard against any move by von Lettow-Vorbeck towards the eastern shores of Lake Nyasa. Portuguese troops still garrisoned Chomba and Mocímboa da Rovuma as well, but they were under strict instructions not to venture out. It was no wonder, given this state of inaction among the Allies, that one German soldier recorded in his diary that 'never have we fared so well during the last four years'.[21]

As if to compound van Deventer's dilemma another revolution took place in Lisbon in December 1917. Not only did this have the effect of paralysing both the civilian and military authorities in Portuguese East Africa, but the new premier, Sidónio Pais, a former Portuguese Ambassador to Berlin, was rumoured to be pro-German. Ominous chatter in the Portuguese ranks suggested the possibility of an early cessation of hostilities through the conclusion of a separate peace with Germany by Pais; and at the same time van Deventer was forced by the War Office to release all Indian troops with the exception of two mountain batteries.[*] The end of the Indian Army's three-year involvement in the campaign – prompted by 'considerable anxiety'[22] in India, revolution in Afghanistan, and Germany's peace agreement with the Bolsheviks – could not have come at a worse time; and it was accompanied by the departure of the Nigerian Brigade, who had by universal acclaim 'made for themselves in East Africa a reputation second to none'.[23] None of this would become evident to von Lettow-Vorbeck for months. But he was right in concluding that his invasion of Portuguese territory 'had put [van Deventer] at his wits' end';[24] and as he had just received news that the oakleaves had been added to his *Pour le Mérite*, won in 1916, he saw no reason to answer van Deventer's optimistic invitation to surrender.

Van Deventer attracted sharp criticism in certain quarters for allowing von Lettow-Vorbeck to escape, and Sergeant Castle, the senior typist at Allied GHQ, was well placed to assess the prevailing mood. On 1 December he

---

* 'I shook the dust of EA off my feet. May I never return there,' wrote an officer of the 40th Pathans. During his regiment's two years in Africa one third of its original complement had been killed or wounded and nearly one and a half times its original complement evacuated to India due to sickness (IWM/Thornton).

wrote in his diary 'Von Splosh wired [the War Office] that all Germans were out of GEA and that the show was over – bar, of course, the shouting. We (who do not believe everything we are told) have ideas of our own.' The similarities with Smuts's declaration of 'victory' at the start of 1917 were 'somewhat startling'. The only difference this time was that van Deventer had to stay to face the consequences – a decision on the part of the War Office which attracted further criticism. On 10 December, having heard that van Deventer had been awarded the KCMG, Castle wrote '*Sir* Von Splosh – to our great disgust and disappointment – stays on. No doubt he is averse to losing the huge salary he gets (£3,500 per year). Thus we again see the evil of Political Influence. Here is a man of no education and no knowledge of up-to-date military matters controlling a force of all parts of the empire and not being in sympathy nor understanding with more than one contingent i.e. his own countrymen from South Africa. He hardly speaks English and has to guide him Lt Col van Velden (an awful shit).'[25] For his part, van Deventer's view of British Staff officers was evidenced by his instructions to George Brink and all the other ADCs who served him during the war: 'Oppas dat hulle my nie vernenk nie' – 'make sure they do not cheat me'.[26]

Castle's forthright opinions were typical of many of the Staff originally selected by Smith-Dorrien who had found themselves required to serve successive South African 'masters' instead; and among van Deventer's field commanders there were also many who had wished 'for such a man as Hoskins or Northey to be in charge'[27] of the operations in 1917, and considered that 'it should have been a bobby's job to pick off'[28] the enemy's troops after they crossed the Rovuma. But a majority of field officers recognised that without any meaningful effort on the part of the Portuguese to defend their border, or even their garrisons, van Deventer's attempt to encircle von Lettow-Vorbeck on the Makonde plateau had been doomed from the outset. Van Deventer's gruff, no-nonsense manner also made him popular in the ranks, whereas a new commander would have to earn a similar level of respect and would almost certainly take time to appraise the situation, and the War Office gave barely a second thought to the possibility of replacing him. Time was of the essence, and the campaign was entering what looked likely to be as taxing a phase as any that had preceded it.

A shortage of fit and experienced troops was one problem. At the beginning of December the ration strength of van Deventer's force still exceeded fifty-five thousand,* but after the withdrawal of the Indian and Nigerian battalions,

---

* IWM/Castle: British and South African troops: 2,322 officers and 18,029 other ranks; Indian troops: 258 officers and 12,383 other ranks; African troops: twenty officers and 23,485 other ranks. Total ration strength: 56,477 rifles.

the need to garrison German East Africa, and the prevalence of sickness were taken into account this number was reduced by two-thirds. Equally serious was the shortage of carriers, without whom the troops would be unable to move. 'Many carriers fall and die, exhausted by the weight of their pack, and the excessive rain', wrote one officer on the supply lines in Nyasaland at the end of November; 'they lie on a bed of withered ferns by the roadside where the jackal and vulture devour them – each one a hero, though unknown to them.'[29] By the end of 1917 more than a million Africans from the British colonies and German East Africa had been recruited for carrier duty with the British forces since the start of the war, and the mass levy commenced earlier in the year had had to be suspended when officials everywhere warned that the indigenous population had been squeezed dry. Yet if British troops were to advance into northern Portuguese East Africa after the rains a further 75,000 carriers would have to be found to man the supply lines. Finally, the terrain and the Portuguese (whom van Deventer considered to be 'so incompetent as to be positively dangerous')[30] were every bit as worrying as his manpower shortage; and his only option under such challenging circumstances was to try and keep Portuguese involvement to an absolute minimum, to make his strategy and supply arrangements as flexible and adaptable as those of the enemy, and to hope that the luck for which he was famed had not deserted him altogether.

At the end of 1917 the Allies were in a position 'more dangerous than at any time since the first weeks of the war', and continuing to fight the campaign in eastern Africa seemed to many to be a futile waste of resources. But Lloyd George made it clear that the retention of Germany's African colonies remained a fundamental war aim, even if such a policy invited criticism of Britain for harbouring 'imperialistic designs'.[31] The message was clear: the outcome of the campaign in Portuguese East Africa *mattered*; and, even though it had proved 'impossible to round up a mobile enemy' during the previous two years, van Deventer was authorised to pursue a strategy of 'virtual extinction' in the hope of inducing von Lettow-Vorbeck to surrender. 'I ordered my commanders to miss no chance of fighting', he wrote, 'and thus cause the enemy casualties, whatever the risk.'[32]

THIRTY-ONE

The 'China Affair'

As von Lettow-Vorbeck retreated from the Lukuledi River towards the Makonde plateau persistent rumours about a German submarine operating off the East African coast began to circulate in the British ranks. The rumour was prompted by the havoc wreaked off Cape Town by U-155, which sank nineteen British vessels in 1917, but in East Africa it was through the air, not beneath the waves, that Berlin planned to send assistance to von Lettow-Vorbeck's beleaguered troops.

This astonishingly audacious plan was the brainchild of Max Zupitza, who had been repatriated from Togo in a prisoner exchange in 1916. Zupitza was a former head of the medical corps in German South-West Africa who also knew German East Africa well; and when he read an article in the *Wilnaer Zeitung* in June 1917 that stated that the wartime development of airship technology had been so rapid that a transatlantic flight might soon be possible, his mind turned to the possibility of using that technology to help his stranded compatriots in East Africa. Several weeks later airship LZ120 spent 101 hours aloft over the Baltic, and for Zupitza this amounted to conclusive 'proof that an airship could remain aloft to accomplish the voyage to Africa'. Without further delay he then set himself up as champion of what was destined to become 'one of the most daring feats of the whole war'.[1]

The *streng geheim* – 'Top Secret' – mission to airlift vital arms, ammunition and medical supplies for von Lettow-Vorbeck to the Makonde plateau was codenamed the 'China Affair'; and the high-level support that Zupitza attracted without difficulty was evidence of the extent to which the outcome of the war in East Africa mattered to Berlin. Every available airship was being used for bombing raids on Britain at the time. Yet Zupitza managed to secure the use of L57, as well as the unstinting support and co-operation of Dr Walter Förster (Germany's leading meteorologist), Hugo Eckener (who had assumed responsibility for Germany's airship programme after Count Zeppelin's death), and Admiral von Capelle (the Navy Minister). Captain Peter Strasser, Germany's commander of airship operations, was equally effusive in his praise for the project, writing that 'completion of the operation will not only provide immediate assistance for the brave Protectorate troops, but will be an event that will once more enthuse the German people and arouse admiration throughout the world'.[2] The ultimate stamp of approval was provided by the Kaiser himself.

The 'China Affair' did not start auspiciously. L57 accidentally blew up outside her shed at Jüterborg the day before setting out for Jamboli in Bulgaria, the intended launch point for the expedition. But a replacement was immediately made available by von Capelle and on 3 November L59 left Staaken for Jamboli, powered by five 240hp Maybach engines. Her voyage was also not without incident: in dense fog the steering cables of both the rudder and reserve rudder broke, but running repairs enabled her to reach Bulgaria in twenty-eight hours. By then the possibility of further technical problems was not the overriding concern of Zupitza's team: news of van Deventer's latest advance had reached Berlin, and everyone feared that the Makonde plateau might soon be occupied by British, rather than German, troops. Time was of the essence, and L59 needed substantial modification before setting off on her mission. At Staaken she had already been lengthened to 226.5m, making her the largest airship ever built, but other work had to be carried out to render her as useful as possible. By the time it was completed every component of L59 was earmarked for a specific purpose: the muslin envelope would be made into bandages, the duralumin ribs would be converted into wireless mast and stretchers, the canvas could be used for tents and clothing, and the catwalks were covered with leather for making boots. In addition, L59's lifting capacity enabled her to carry fifteen tons of cargo including thirty machine-guns and more than 400,000 rounds of ammunition. If the voyage was successfully completed there was no doubt that it would greatly enhance von Lettow-Vorbeck's offensive capability, and the arrival of a large consignment of mail from home – the first for more than two years – was thought likely to provide a further boost to the morale of the European soldiers.[*]

On 13 November L59, Zupitza and the twenty-two hand-picked crew members were finally ready for their 3,600-mile journey and Captain Bockholt gave the command to cast off. Within hours, however, L59 was fired on by Turkish soldiers when passing over Smyrna and then ran into weather so atrocious that Bockholt was forced to jettison a ton of his precious cargo before reluctantly turning back to Jamboli. On 13 November the western

---

[*] Goebel and Förster, p. 50. The inventory listed the cargo as comprising 311,100 rounds of ammunition; 230 machine-gun belts holding 57,500 cartridges; fifty-four machine-gun ammunition boxes containing 13,500 cartridges; thirty machine-guns; four rifles for the crew in the event of emergency; nine spare machine-gun barrels; sixty-one sacks of medical supplies; binoculars, rifle-bolts, knives and spare radio parts.

reaches of the Makonde plateau were still in German hands; but a week later, when the weather cleared and Bockholt set off on his second attempt, von Lettow-Vorbeck was only clinging on to Newala district. As L59 passed Crete, reaching speeds as high as 65mph, Bockholt had no way of knowing this, and wound in his wireless antenna as he pressed on through another storm undeterred by the St Elmo's fire crackling around the 2.5 million cubic feet of hydrogen keeping L59 aloft.

At dawn on 21 November L59 passed over the Egyptian coast and Bockholt set a course for the Makonde plateau. By noon the following day Farafah oasis could be spotted far below, and that night Wadi Halfa and the Nile were just visible through the darkness. Everything seemed to be going to plan, but unbeknownst to Bockholt his superiors had been making repeated attempts to contact him while L59's wireless antenna was wound in. Soon after midnight the message was finally received, and to Bockholt's astonishment it read: 'Break off operation. Return. Enemy has seized greater part of Makonde Highlands, already holds Kitangari, Portuguese are attacking remainder of Protectorate forces in the south.'[3] At 2.30 a.m. on 24 November, just as von Lettow-Vorbeck's troops were making their way along the north bank of the Rovuma towards the Portuguese garrison at Negomano, Zupitza recorded that 'with heavy heart the commander hove to for the return'.[4] The buoyant spirits of the airmen plummeted as most of the cargo was thrown overboard; and during the night of 24/25 November L59 left Africa at Solûm, scene of the Allied defeat of the Sanusi in 1916.

By the time L59 touched down at Jamboli the crew were in a terrible condition. Frozen to the core and exhausted, some were in the grips of a fever while others had chronic headaches caused by oxygen deprivation. As they set foot on land everyone 'staggered as if they were still in the heaving gondolas of the airship';[5] and the knowledge that L59 was the first dirigible to cross the Tropic of Cancer, and had completed a record-breaking journey of 4,340 miles in ninety-five hours, was scant consolation. Bockholt was immediately awarded the *Pour le Mérite*, but his efforts to secure permission for another attempt to reach von Lettow-Vorbeck were unsuccessful. Just months later, he and his crew perished when L59 exploded and came down in the Mediterranean near Otranto. Only Zupitza and Hans Schedelmann, a crewman on leave, survived to see their feat praised for being not only 'unique in the annals of aeronautics' but for '[paving] the way for the intercontinental services to come'.[6]

For many years conspiracy theories about the abrupt recall of L59 abounded. Some claimed that the message was a dupe sent from England or Khartoum; some that the message from Berlin was genuine enough but that it was the result of a bogus message from British Intelligence purporting to originate from von Lettow-Vorbeck.[7] Smuts's former ADC, Piet van der Byl, even peddled a fantastic story involving spies in Spain and intelligence masterstrokes by Smuts and an Intelligence officer who had long since left the campaign; and he claimed that L59's mission was 'to pick up von Lettow and spirit him away', thereby 'increasing German prestige among the African population who looked upon von Lettow with so much awe that they would never refer to him by name'.[8] Such hogwash may have derived from the first book to mention L59, Edwin Woodhall's *Spies of the Great War*. Woodhall was a veteran of Scotland Yard and British Intelligence who was single-handedly responsible for the wartime capture of Percy Topliss, the infamous 'Monocled Mutineer'. In his account a British agent named Tony Mortimer, known to Woodhall 'by personal association',[9] returned from Vienna in September 1917 with the news that a 'super-Zeppelin' was about to leave for East Africa, a story that prompted his superiors to send 'a bogus message ... to Berlin, purporting to emanate from von Lettow-Vorbeck'.[10]

Bogus wireless messages aside, what is certain is that British Intelligence was aware of Bockholt's mission before L59 even left Staaken for Jamboli. Van Deventer informed MacDonell of it in a despatch dated 10 November, and the following day all British troops pursuing von Lettow-Vorbeck towards the Makonde plateau were instructed to be on the alert for 'a Zeppelin [coming] to East Africa from Palestine'. Aeroplanes were put on standby and two mountain guns were 'dug in for [L59's] reception'[11] at Kilelo Hill on the Makonde plateau. But the mission had to be aborted due to the bad weather over the Mediterranean, and by the time Bockholt began his second attempt von Lettow-Vorbeck was leading the troops not left behind at Nambindinga towards Newala.

After the war von Lettow-Vorbeck 'stoutly denied ever having heard of [the mission] except by vague rumour among the natives near Lindi, to which [he] gave no credence'.[*] Schnee, when he too was first informed by British officers of L59's attempt to reach the Makonde plateau, also dismissed it as fantasy. And Max Looff, when questioned in captivity about 'the proposed landing place of the Zeppelin', thought the whole thing was either a tremendous joke or some cunning ruse on the part of his captors. Sucking reflectively on his pipe, he eventually replied 'I can tell you, in the strictest confidence, that two Zeppelins were to come, one to bomb Lindi and the other Tabora'.[12]

---

[*] Von Lettow-Vorbeck to Colonel Brian Hawkins (see W. Lloyd-Jones, p. 200); 'even when told that it had reached Khartoum they laughed at the idea as being impossible and impracticable'.

THIRTY-TWO

The Propaganda War

———•———

L 59's ill-fated mission to relieve von Lettow-Vorbeck demonstrated the extent to which his continued resistance was regarded by Berlin as being of the utmost importance at the end of 1917. The year had witnessed innumerable setbacks to the Allied war effort, and when victory on the battlefield or at the negotiating table was eventually secured the presence of undefeated German troops on African soil would, so it was thought, facilitate the immediate return of all former colonies to the Reich. On the other hand Britain's views on the matter hardened during the year. As early as February Walter Long, the Colonial Secretary, had publicly declared that no one should think that the struggle in Africa had been in vain because he had no intention of ever returning Germany's colonies. With that, the battle lines were drawn for a ferocious propaganda war in which Britain sought to counter German territorial ambitions with increasingly forthright criticism of the past conduct of 'the spiked helmet in Africa'.

The propaganda war marked a dramatic change to the pre-war status quo. Before the war Dr Solf, the German Colonial Secretary, had thought that Germany's interests, as a latecomer to the 'Scramble for Africa', would be best served by assuming the role of 'England's junior partner';[1] and as his counterpart, Lord Harcourt, was as germanophile as Solf was anglophile, Britain and Germany had had no difficulty in conducting a series of secret negotiations with a view to carving up the colonies of Portugal and Belgium after their 'inevitable' demise as colonial powers. By the summer of 1914 the broad terms of an agreement had been approved, giving the mineral-rich Belgian province of Katanga and Portuguese East Africa south of the Zambezi to Britain; while Portuguese West Africa (Angola), Portuguese East Africa north of the Zambezi, and most of the Belgian Congo (subject to France's assent) were assigned to Germany. The agreement was never signed for reasons which, on the part of Britain, included the reluctance of the Foreign Office to use Africa as a means of promoting détente, suspicions about Germany's intentions in Europe, and a reluctance to undermine Portugal; and, on the part of Germany, a nervousness about the likely consequences of the publication of such a formal agreement. The events of August 1914 inevitably precluded any further discussions, but Germany's appetite for territorial aggrandisement had been whetted and Solf's enthusiasm for the creation of a German *Mittelafrika*, stretching from the Indian Ocean to the Atlantic, remained undimmed.

On the face of it the negotiations, and Solf's ambitions, were incongruous. In the immediate aftermath of unification Bismarck had demonstrated no great zeal for securing 'a place in the sun' for Germany, but like the equally sceptical Gladstone he soon found that the activities of sundry 'romantics, dreamers and vagabonds'[2] in Africa could no longer be ignored. By 1890 'German' Africa already encompassed an area considerably larger than the *Reich* itself and Bismarck found himself increasingly drawn into the debate on the merits of colonial expansion by his need to maintain his support among National Liberal and Conservative enthusiasts in the Reichstag, and by the vigorous lobbying of the newly formed Pan-German League, which sought to arouse 'patriotic self-consciousness at home … and, above all, to carry forward the German colonial movement to tangible results'.[3] For the young Kaiser Wilhelm II, however, Bismarck's stance on the colonial issue was not sufficiently proactive and the Heligoland-Zanzibar Treaty, demarcating Britain's and Germany's respective 'spheres of interest' in East Africa, attracted criticism from pro-colonialists for compromising the furtherance of Germany's national interests. In 1890 Bismarck was dismissed, his lack of enthusiasm for colonial ventures being cited by the Kaiser as one of the reasons prompting his decision.

By the mid 1890s Germany's colonial project had foundered and Bismarck's successor, Leo von Caprivi, shared his opinion that 'the less Africa, the better'. The wayward actions of Carl Peters, 'Germany's Rhodes' in East Africa and a man referred to by Africans as *mkono wa damu* ('blood on his hands'), played a significant part in creating a crisis of confidence, as did the fact that Germany's million square miles of Africa were proving a continual drain on funds. They had also failed to fulfil their promise as potential outlets for Germany's burgeoning population, were widely considered to be a military liability which required continual 'maintenance' by the Imperial Navy, and, worse still, were a source of friction with other European Powers. In 1904 an article in the *Freisinnige Zeitung* encapsulated the general mood in Germany: 'our power has not been strengthened [by our colonies], our prosperity has not been increased, in short not a single one of the purposes for which colonial possessions were acquired and maintained has been fulfilled'.[4]

Within two years of the publication of the *Freisinnige Zeitung*'s article full-scale rebellions in German South-West Africa and German East Africa threatened radically to undermine German 'prestige' at home and abroad. But colonial enthusiasts were not prepared to admit defeat, however discredited the methods of some of Germany's 'romantics, dreamers and vagabonds', and the Kaiser's pursuit of *Weltpolitik* precluded even contemplating such a thing. In 1906, a programme of 'reform' was instigated by Bernhard Dernburg, the Colonial Secretary, and his department was separated from the Foreign Office as a first step towards putting Germany's colonial house in order. Dernburg was, above all, determined to counter widespread accusations that Germany looked upon its colonies as little more than pools of slave labour; and in German East Africa, Solf (Dernburg's successor) and von Rechenberg (Schnee's predecessor) set about replacing a preoccupation with 'pacification' with one of 'development'. There was no attendant resurgence in political or public enthusiasm for colonies in the years immediately preceding the outbreak of war, but it did at least seem as though the colony's strife-torn past had been put behind it, and that German East Africa's economy might be poised on the brink of a prosperous future. Sisal exports were booming, the 'native' economy was growing rapidly, over 1,000 miles of railway were already complete, and millions of Marks had been spent on administrative expansion. The other side of the continent, German South-West Africa also looked set fair, and was producing one quarter of the world's diamonds.

By the second year of the war Solf finally began to attract greater support for his colonial 'experiment' as the mood in Germany became increasingly nationalistic. The desirability of further overseas expansion and the need to combat raw material shortages were issues that had risen to the top of the political agenda, and Germany's existing colonies seemed to offer the beginnings of a solution to both 'problems'.* As a result the pro-colonial lobby was able to count on greater popularity in the Reichstag than ever before; and when Solf organised a huge colonial rally in June 1916 he won the endorsement of not only the National Liberals and Conservatives but also the Social Democrats (who had always opposed colonialism in the past). With that, Solf's concept of a German *Mittelafrika*, a counterpoint to Chancellor Theobald von Bethmann-Hollweg's *Mitteleuropa*, became 'the decisive objective of colonial expansion beside Turkey';⁵ and, spurred on by the Kaiser and Hindenburg, Solf began to cast his eye over more than just Africa's *Mittel.* The two billion Marks (£100m, or *c.* £5.5bn in today's money) of German taxpayers' money spent in the colonies between 1884 and 1914 may have yielded little return thus far, but if the Portuguese territories in East and West Africa, Belgian Congo and French Equatorial Africa – possibly even some of the British possessions in West Africa – were annexed after Germany's victory in the war, Africa could become 'Germany's India', its 'Second Fatherland'.†

---

* The resurgent appeal of colonies led to the publication of such influential works as Emil Zimmermann's *The German Empire of Central Africa as the Basis of a New German World Policy.*
† The title of a contemporary poem by Dr Ernst Marshall.

Britain's response to Germany's ill-concealed and mounting ambitions was to launch 'a vast propagandist gas-attack'[6] against her 'colonial methods' and fitness to rule in Africa. Germany's regular and unrestrained use of brute force in the colonies in the years immediately after the Anglo-South African War had never, for obvious reasons, attracted much criticism from Britain; and it was conveniently overlooked once again during the negotiations between Harcourt and Solf. But the war prompted a radical reappraisal of Germany's colonial past, and when South African troops discovered certain 'secret documents' during the conquest of German South-West Africa in 1915 Botha wasted no time in publishing their contents. In the aftermath of the suppression of the Herero Rebellion in 1904–6 Dernburg had admitted that 75,000 Hereros and Ovambos had died as a result of Colonel Lothar von Trotha's *Vernichtungsbefehl* ('extermination order'), and he had gone to great lengths to emphasise that von Trotha's brutal conduct of the campaign was not sanctioned by the government. But the 'secret documents' revealed the death toll to have been as high as 150,000–200,000 – between half and two-thirds of German South-West Africa's entire indigenous population – thereby establishing that the scale of the atrocity was far greater than Dernburg had claimed. This was not quite the revelation it purported to be: it was common knowledge, whatever the claims of British propagandists, that Germany had been economical with the truth and the staggering cost of the campaign – £23m (*c.* £1.3bn in today's money) and the lives of 2,000 German troops – was definitive proof of the full connivance of the German government. The significance of the 'secret documents', which were selectively published in a 1916 South African Blue Book, was that they presented the British government with the perfect pretext for expressing outrage at a tragedy to which it had previously turned a blind eye.[*]

Britain needed no device to revisit the German suppression of the simultaneous Maji-Maji Rebellion in German East Africa, even though this had also failed to attract any official censure at the time, because the Reichstag *had* publicly sanctioned the actions of the *Schutztruppe* and there was no way of disguising what Schnee subsequently called 'a relatively large sacrifice of native life'.[7] In fact by the time the rebellion was finally scotched in 1907 as many as a quarter of a million Africans had died, the vast majority of them from starvation and disease caused by the *Schutztruppe*'s scorched earth tactics, and

---

[*] See, for example, Freeman (1), pp. 10–11: 'Practically all news from Germany's African colonies underwent a censorship . . . the world heard much of "Congo Atrocities" and nothing whatever of the indescribable inhumanities practised by the Germans. Even the details of Germany's unspeakable campaign against the Hereros did not find their way to the outside world until Botha discovered archives bearing on them.'

this further tragedy had finally forced Germany to admit that its colonial policy was flawed (and to instigate Dernburg's reforms). The irony of Britain's belated condemnation of German brutality was that her forces were now engaged in a struggle in East Africa with an enemy which had successfully blended the tactics favoured by the Maji-Maji rebels (a combination of pitched battles and guerrilla warfare) with the scorched earth tactics that had eventually defeated them, and which was commanded by a German general who had himself been a member of von Trotha's staff in German South-West Africa – von Lettow-Vorbeck.

The second target of British propaganda was Germany's administrative, as opposed to punitive, practices. In the decade before the war Dernburg's reforms were considered to have drawn a line under the unsavoury goings-on during the rebellions in Germany's African colonies, and the administration of her colonies had earned a good deal of respect for its efficiency; but when Germany's future as a colonial power began to be called into question Dernburg's reforms were swiftly forgotten. By 1916 the prevailing view in Whitehall, and among those sections of the British public with an interest in Africa, was that 'the African world was a book that the Germans had never opened'[8] and that, as latecomers to the continent, 'whatever talents the Germans as a nation possessed, the control of subject races was not one of them'.[9] Brute force, not efficiency, was now said to be the cornerstone of German administration: one treatise on the subject concluded that 'in the German colonies, as in Germany herself, the militaristic system prevailed',[10] while another declared that even after Dernburg's reforms there was 'far more of the mailed fist in German civil administration than ... may at first sight appear'.[11]

Accusations that Germany still condoned domestic slavery in East Africa resurfaced, Carl Peters's objectionable views and deeds were widely publicised (greatly assisting his rehabilitation in the eyes of the German public),[*] and evidence was gathered from Africans in occupied territory regarding their views on the 'People of 15' (fifteen lashes being the standard punishment for even the most minor infractions against German administration). Documentary evidence that Schnee had considered whether to encourage pig-breeding as a means of stemming the rising popularity of Islam was circulated not only to the administrators of occupied German East Africa but also

---

[*] See, for example, 'Africanus', *The Prussian Lash*, p. 86, quoting from a speech by Peters in 1902: 'The English system pampers the blacks to such an extent as to make the country impossible for the whites ... To me the most advantageous system seems to be one in which the negro is forced, following the example laid down by military law, to devote some twelve years of his life to working for the Govt.'

to mosques throughout the country, and British officials were given strict instructions only to follow 'German ordinances and regulations ... *when they were not repugnant to British law*'.[12] A senior official was even commissioned by the Colonial Office to write a history of German East Africa which sought to establish once and for all Germany's unfitness to rule in Africa.[13]

The German response to British accusations of degeneracy and brutality was forthright. The atrocities committed against the Herero and Maji-Maji rebels were portrayed as being ancient history, and already atoned for; and Britain's colonial methods were decried as feeble. Ada Schnee encapsulated the German view when she wrote that the 'weak point' of British administration 'is that it gives in to the natives too much. Because of this they become insolent and lazy which is not permitted under German doctrine'.[14] Theodor Gunzert, the former Administrator of Mwanza, echoed her sentiments, asserting that Africans 'needed the enlightened, ruthlessly effective and harsh Absolutism of seventeenth and eighteenth century Europe';[15] and his colleagues took pride in perceiving themselves to be regarded by their subjects as *wakali lakini wenye haki* – 'hard, but fair'.[16] The definitive proof of the fairness of German rule was said to be the unstinting loyalty of the civilian population during the war, and although the truth of the matter was that Schnee and von Lettow-Vorbeck resorted to methods even more repressive than those of the British military authorities to strip German East Africa of all available foodstuffs and labour, and seldom paid for either, and that as many as 300,000 African civilians died as a result of their scorched earth policy, this was destined to become the central myth of all German accounts of the war.

The most forceful rebuttal of British propaganda was directed at accusations that Germany was guilty of war crimes in East Africa, the third arrow in the British quiver. The conduct of *askari* did not cause much of a stir, and only a handful of British writings endeavoured to draw distinctions between the German *Schutztruppe* and African troops fighting for the British (not least because by 1917 many former German *askari* had enlisted in the King's African Rifles);* nor, with one or two notable exceptions such as Heinrich Naumann,

---

* One such account was P.C. Wren's fictional *Cupid in Africa* (Heath Cranton, 1944) which included the following passage: 'Sergeant Simba was what he looked, every inch a soldier, and a fine honourable fighting-man, brave as the lion he was named after; a subordinate who would obey and follow his white officer to certain death, without questioning or wavering; a leader who would carry his men with him by force of his personality, courage and leadership ... Beside Sergeant Simba, the average German soldier is a cur, a barbarian, and a filthy brute, for never in all the twenty years of his "savage" warfare has Sergeant Simba butchered a child, tortured a woman, murdered wounded enemies, abused (nor used) the white flag, fired on the Red Cross, turned captured dwelling-places into pig-styes and latrines in demonstration of his *kultur.*'

did the conduct in battle of their European officers; and details of the plight of African civilians in German and British territory were either yet to emerge or deemed best ignored. But the atrocities alleged to have been committed against European POWs in German East Africa who were freed during the advances in 1916 and who published accounts of their experiences in a number of books, newspapers and journals soon afterwards, were deemed scandalous.

These accounts, and those of German POWs shipped to India, South Africa, Egypt and even Malta, show that although the conditions in POW camps were hard and irksome, they were rarely life-threatening. Hardship, however, was not the real issue. It was the 'prestige' of the European in Africa that was perceived as having been undermined by incarceration: Allied prisoners were unanimous in their condemnation of being forced to undertake menial tasks, such as cleaning latrines, in front of African guards. Germany responded to allegations of deliberately 'humiliating' prisoners in this way by claiming that the consequences of the Allies' deployment of 'coloured tribes' on the Western Front were equally 'humiliating', and a vituperative Reichstag Command Paper on the subject declared that in 'wars between civilised nations' it was illegal to use African troops against Europeans if they were not 'kept under a discipline which excludes the violation of the customs of warfare among civilised people'. The very public airing of racial, or racist, views concerning the wartime threat to European 'prestige' contrasted markedly with what had occurred during the Anglo-South African War – when both sides sought to downplay, or even deny, their use of 'native' combatants – and the propaganda battle outlasted the fighting: in 1919, when French troops from West Africa were stationed in the occupied Rhineland, the public outcry in Germany reached fever pitch when the soldiers were discovered to be pursuing such 'barbarous practices'[17] as consorting with German girls.

Britain seized the high ground in the war of words rather more successfully than on the battlefields of East Africa. No slaughter on a remotely comparable scale to that perpetrated not once, but twice, by Germany had ever been committed in the name of the British Empire in Africa. But it was harder to draw such a clear-cut distinction between the two countries' administrative methods. In more peaceful times many a British settler, and the overwhelming majority of South Africans, had always held the 'efficiency' and 'discipline' of German colonial rule in high esteem. Moreover, when British and South African administrators took over the government of captured territory in German East Africa, they found fewer differences between British and German rule than their political masters considered helpful; and they were hardly in a position to decry the severity of German labour practices, for example, when they were themselves being required to coerce Africans by the thousand to act as carriers for the military (even though a token wage was paid to 'British' carriers). It also became abundantly clear that German overlordship was as popular with many chiefs as was true in British colonies: in both cases alliances with colonial officials could be used to great advantage in securing privileges or settling old scores. Equivocation on the question of the respective merits of British and German rule abounded in official reports;[18] and no less a figure than Edmund Morel, whose 'Red Rubber' campaign had exposed the appalling atrocities committed in the name of King Leopold in the Congo at the turn of the century, realised that 'it would be quite impossible for a case to be presented to an international tribunal against the exercise of German sovereign rights in Africa, on the plea of German ill-treatment of natives'. The presentation of such a case, wrote Morel, 'would invite not only a damaging and unanswerable *tu quoque*, but a citation of much British evidence in praise of German administration in Africa'.[19]

Many British commentators who aired such views were quickly silenced. Morel himself was imprisoned in 1917 under the Defence of the Realm Act and other dissenters, such as Percy Molteno of the Anti-Slavery and Aborigines Protection Society, who challenged the Under-Secretary of State for War to clarify 'whether the system of recruiting carriers is voluntary or compulsory' and confirm the veracity of rumours that casualties in the Carrier Corps were running at 'an average of ten thousand carriers per month',[20] immediately found themselves branded 'unpatriotic'. By the third year of the war the national mood in Britain was as uncompromising as that in Germany, and the stakes in Africa were, in the eyes of 'old Africa hands', as high as they were in Europe. The outcome of the war would, after all, decide the final phase of the colonial 'Scramble for Africa'.

In the field, even the more enlightened government officials who found that judging 'the relative popularity among the natives of the Huns and ourselves' was 'by no means an easy question to answer',[21] and who disliked being instructed to enforce onerous increases in the taxes paid by their African charges during the war, or troopers who had witnessed a carrier rolling over during punishment and having his genitals accidentally whipped off by the next blow of the *sjambok*, sensed what was at stake; and in almost every case they subscribed to the view that although German rule may have been efficient, it was built on a degree of authoritarianism that they found unacceptable. Missionaries, who were competing for post-war access to millions of souls formerly administered to by German missions, also threw their weight wholeheartedly behind the British propaganda campaign: a war was being fought for the future of 'civilisation', and if the enemy was painted 'blacker than he deserved'[22] then so be it. As for the damage the conduct of the war might inflict on British 'prestige', that could be dealt with later: as one KAR officer wrote in an open letter to all Provincial Commissioners in British East Africa, there would be 'a real necessity for the undertaking of propaganda work ... which will help to obliterate the memory of the hardships incurred by the natives in the course of the war'.[23]

PART FIVE

1918

THE VICTOR

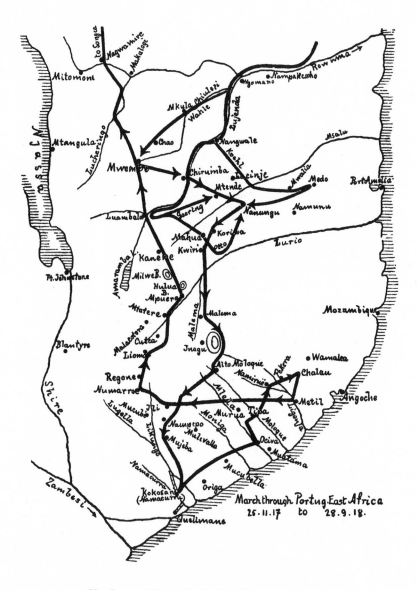

Von Lettow-Vorbeck's sketch of his route through
Portuguese East Africa, 1918

THIRTY-THREE

The Hunt Begins

In September 1917 van Deventer had offered Colonel Tómas de Sousa Rosa assistance with holding the 250-mile 'Rovuma line' should von Lettow-Vorbeck attempt to invade Portuguese East Africa. The offer had been declined, and MacDonell had advised that 'the presence of a British force in Portuguese territory would be highly unwelcome as the Portuguese would take it as a serious reflection on their military efficiency'.[1] The consequences were disastrous, and by the time van Deventer secured permission to send British troops over the Rovuma von Lettow-Vorbeck had already disappeared into the blue.

The surrender of numerous Portuguese garrisons placed van Deventer in a very awkward position. On the one hand Sousa Rosa was a political appointee, as opposed to a soldier, who had not only let him down in spades but was also, in MacDonell's opinion, 'most impulsive', 'unrestrained in his language', and possessed of a 'distressing peculiarity of changing his mind at least three times before arriving at a decision'.[2] But on the other hand the Portuguese commander-in-chief had at least spent much of 1917 as the sole Democratic voice to decry the Portuguese conduct of the war in Lisbon's Chamber of Deputies (at a time when criticism of the military was illegal); and since his arrival in Portuguese East Africa he had demonstrated an extremely authoritarian approach to lapses of discipline among his troops. In the aftermath of Negomano a variety of punishments for laziness – including beatings – were meted out to a major, eight captains, and dozens of lieutenants; while thirty-one officers captured by von Lettow-Vorbeck but released on parole were arrested and imprisoned indefinitely in the fortress at Mocímboa da Praia. Such conduct reinforced MacDonell's belief that Sousa Rosa, whatever his personal shortcomings, would do as much to help 'terminate the campaign' as his 'limited and indifferent forces [would] permit';[3] and Sousa Rosa was at least pro-British, whereas if he were replaced by Sidónio Pais's new government in Lisbon his successor might prove fatally unco-operative.

The threat posed to the future of Anglo-Portuguese co-operation in Africa by the revolution in Lisbon cannot be overstated. Republican politics had exacerbated the fractures between church and state, town and country, and within the trades unions in Portugal, and Pais's government was confronted by an urgent need to restore public order and counter the mounting shame at the lamentable performance of Portuguese troops on the battlefields of Europe and East Africa. As the unpopularity of the war plumbed new depths in Portugal Sir Lancelot Carnegie, the British Minister in Lisbon, compounded Pais's parlous situation by warning him of 'the possibility of a grave disaster involving heavy losses of men and materiel' in East Africa, one that would constitute an even more 'serious risk to the prestige of Portugal in Africa'[4] than Negomano.

Britain's strategy of appealing to Portuguese *brio nacional* was fraught with risk: it might have driven Pais to try to reassert Portuguese neutrality or, worse still, to enter into negotiations for a separate peace with Germany. But the response from Pais reassured those who had feared that his sympathies lay with Germany. He confirmed that the 50,000 Portuguese troops in Europe (who were paid by Britain) should remain under Anglo-French command; and he agreed that van Deventer should control operations in Portuguese East Africa. Sousa Rosa, at Carnegie's behest, was promoted General as a vote of confidence, and Massano de Amorim, who had commanded the First Expeditionary Force in 1914–15, returned to Portuguese East Africa to replace Álvaro de Castro as Governor-General of the colony.

MacDonell welcomed the appointment of a soldier, rather than a politician, as Governor-General but soon found himself engulfed by yet another political storm. The 'War Aims' of the British Labour Party, published in November 1917, appeared – to the Portuguese at least – to advocate the confiscation of their African colonies,[*] and no sooner had MacDonell dealt with Portuguese ire at that than a major scandal broke in the South African newspapers. It was alleged that a 'woman market' was operated by many Portuguese officials in East Africa, who would – for a fee – rubber-stamp the purchase of (very) young concubines for Europeans. The Portuguese government threatened a libel action against this slur and, though there was a good deal of truth in the allegations, an official apology had to be issued by the South African government before the matter was allowed to drop. So raw was the atmosphere created between Britain and Portugal by these events that MacDonell had to insist on returning to his post as Consul in Lourenço Marques in January 1918.

---

[*] A statement was made in the House of Commons in November 1917 affirming that Britain 'has no desire to deprive [Portugal] of her colonies', but on 28 December the Portuguese Minister in London wrote that the Labour Party's document 'profoundly hurts the feelings of my country' (see MNE/ *Portugal Na Primeira Guerra Mundial,* document 645, pp. 217–18).

Van Deventer was fulsome in his praise for the resourcefulness shown by MacDonell during his prolonged stint in the field: 'the Portuguese are by no means easy to deal with,' he wrote, 'and MacDonell's task has been no sinecure'.[5] His resumption of diplomatic duties left a gaping hole at the front, but van Deventer was fortunate in being able to call on Major 'Sos' Cohen, MacDonell's very capable Intelligence officer, to fill his shoes as Liaison Officer with the Portuguese forces. In the coming months Cohen would be driven to the 'verge of a nervous breakdown'.[6] British carrier recruiters found their job impossible due to the non-co-operation of Portuguese officials, and van Deventer was soon forced to lodge an official complaint at the total lack of assistance given by the officials of the *Companhia do Niassa* (which was owned by a German consortium) to the British troops stationed at Porto Amelia.

By the end of January 1918 the prospects for renewed military co-operation between British and Portuguese troops after the rainy season began to look decidedly bleak. On the diplomatic front MacDonell had once again rendered the Portuguese administration in Lourenço Marques 'quite tame',[7] but the truculence of many Portuguese officials in the north and the state of the Portuguese troops were worrying. When MacDonell had inspected the troops at the main coastal base of Mocímboa da Praia in December 1917 he found the camp sanitation to be execrable, discipline non-existent, and the 'crass ignorance and inexperience of campaigning in Africa'[8] to be all-pervasive. In February 1918, when van Deventer went to make a further assessment, he found the situation unaltered and pronounced the Portuguese troops 'totally unfit to take the field against the Germans'. Their health was 'pitiable', sanitation 'did not exist', sick Africans weren't even treated, syphilis was (inevitably) as endemic as in Portugal, and few Portuguese officers spoke any local language.* All the troops were keen to return home, with many feigning sickness and resorting to self-harm to secure their passage; and in an almost risible twist, convict soldiers selected from those who supported the wrong side in the December revolution were starting to arrive as 'reinforcements' of the most useless kind. In effect their punishment amounted to a death sentence for many: in one unit of 340 mutineers from the Portuguese Navy eighty-five men were to die from disease in 1918. Meanwhile, the attitude of the senior Portuguese officers remained as dualistic and 'curious' as ever: 'in public', van Deventer noted, 'they expressed much confidence in themselves and their troops, affected eagerness to take to the field, and appeared to resent being

---

* The frequent assertion by British and German troops that most of the Portuguese soldiers were afflicted with venereal diseases of one sort or another provoked outrage in Portugal. See, for example, E.A. Martins (4), p. 65: 'this severe mark against our military *brio* must be remedied'.

kept in the background. But I am certain that they really recognised that their troops were no match for even a tenth of the number of German *askari*. In short there was a good deal of high-flown talk, but very little practical keenness.' The 'real work must be done by British troops' was his unsurprising conclusion.[9]

Van Deventer's options were limited. His Indian troops had almost all been ordered home or to other theatres; the Nigerian Brigade, having sustained casualties of one in three in the six weeks' fighting which culminated in the battle at Mahiwa, returned to West Africa; and most of the British and colonial regiments had either departed or ceased to exist. This left the King's African Rifles, the Gold Coast Regiment, Northey's Rhodesian units and the 2nd Cape Corps with which to pursue his strategy of 'virtual extinction'. As a Boer, van Deventer was as ambivalent as Smuts about the possible political consequences of militarising 'natives' and did not share the opinion of many a British officer that it was 'a thousand pities that instead of three weak battalions [of KAR] we had not a quarter of a million of these splendid black warriors of East and Central Africa when war broke out'.[10] But as the man charged with conducting a campaign over hundreds of thousands of square miles of bush in Portuguese East Africa, he had good reason to be grateful for the massive expansion of the KAR. Without the new battalions he could not possibly have garrisoned British and German East Africa while also fighting in Portuguese territory, and even with them the number of fit and experienced troops who could be deployed in the new campaign barely exceeded 11,000.[*]

Van Deventer's plan was to deploy two columns comprising three battalions of 2/KAR, 4/4KAR and the Gold Coast Regiment in harrying von Lettow-Vorbeck's troops from the east while Northey's troops – two battalions of 4/KAR, three battalions of 1/KAR, the NRP, RNR and Cape Corps – pressed in from Nyasaland and the north. Their task, even at the outset, was formidable. For one thing, although reasonable maps of northern Portuguese East Africa existed in London, the War Office failed to forward them and the troops had to make do with 'an enlargement of a schoolboy atlas';[11] and for another the likely centre of operations was about 1,000 miles from van Deventer's and Northey's headquarters at Dar-es-Salaam and Zomba (in Nyasaland) respectively. Finding sufficient carriers to support the troops also remained a problem, not only on account of the unco-operative attitude of Portuguese officials, but also because carrier work was universally unpopular

---

[*] By 1918 even recruitment to the KAR was not always a smooth process. In August 'tensions became very acute' in the Masai Reserve. The Masai, 'it was generally thought' by the government, 'would be only too pleased' to provide a new company to add to the tribe's existing one. But when recruiting commenced there was great unrest and finally bloodshed, in which fourteen *moran* (warriors) of the Purko and Loita clans were killed. (See RH/Ainsworth/380, pp. 98–9.)

among an indigenous population who had never been paid for such work by the Portuguese. When British recruiters insisted on paying for and adequately provisioning recruits the Portuguese authorities cried foul, objecting 'on the grounds that [this was] putting ideas into the natives' heads'.[12] As for the enemy, even if von Lettow-Vorbeck's detachments did concentrate in one area it was most unlikely that they could be surrounded by a force numbering only 5,000 rifles. They had, in the words of the historian of the Gold Coast Regiment's campaign, 'been transformed from an army in the field into a mobile band of fugitive marauders, whose only objects were to avoid capture, to cause their pursuers and to all connected with them the *maximum* amount of loss and trouble, and simultaneously to maintain themselves by seizing any supplies upon which, from time to time, they could contrive to lay their hands'.[13] In the circumstances, rumours of the presence of a German raiding vessel prowling in East African waters in the hope of lifting von Lettow-Vorbeck and Schnee from the coast were the least of van Deventer's worries.

As a prelude to the operations planned for the dry season the 2nd Cape Corps advanced from Lake Nyasa in early January towards von Lettow-Vorbeck's position at Matarica while Colonel Hawthorn's KAR battalions moved against Göring and Otto in Luambala district. By the end of February all German troops had been cleared from the area west of the Lujenda and the enemy pushed back as far as Mtende. In the east, Colonel Rose simultaneously pushed Gold Coast troops inland from Porto Amelia as fast as they arrived (and sufficient carriers could be found); and by the end of the rains the Porto Amelia Force ('Pamforce') had established a bridgehead around Ankuabe and Meza which would oppose any German advance towards the Indian Ocean. These 2,000 troops were then placed under the direction of General W.F.S. Edwards, formerly Commandant-General of the Uganda Police and Inspector-General of the lines of communication in German East Africa, and divided into two columns: Colonel Rose's 'Rosecol', comprising the Gold Coast Regiment and 4/4KAR; and Colonel Giffard's 'Kartucol', comprising 1/2KAR and 2/2KAR. (See Appendix Eight.) There were no major engagements on this front during the rains, but Pamforce's men were introduced to some alarming characteristics of campaigning in Portuguese territory: due to the effects of Portuguese rule the local population invariably 'witnessed the wholesale destruction of Portuguese *bomas* with ecstatic delight' and regarded British troops as little more than 'hired bravados engaged by the Portuguese to capture their deliverers'.[14] As a result 'deadly boobytraps' caused 'a great deal of trouble' and 'quite a number' of motorcycle despatch riders, in particular, were killed.[15] Despite such hindrances and constant torrential downpours Pamforce's and Northey's manoeuvres did, however, achieve the important objective of securing Nyasaland, Southern Rhodesia and the coastal ports from the indignity that had befallen the Portuguese south of the Rovuma.

In the vast space between Pamforce and Northey's troops von Lettow-Vorbeck's 'band of marauders' proved 'exceptionally resourceful'[16] during the rains. As one of his men succinctly put it, 'necessity ... is the mother of invention, and we grabbed whatever we could to fulfil our requirements'.[17] The German position was advantageous in that von Lettow-Vorbeck had no lines of communication or major supply dumps to defend. But many of the *askari* were becoming 'war weary' and uncertain 'as to where the campaign was going to lead them'. He had been able to count on their loyalty thusfar by the simple expedient of allowing them to bring their women with them across the Rovuma, but knew that to take them too far from their homes and relations might have adverse consequences. 'Small annoyances', he wrote, 'such as ... the persuasion of women and so on', contributed to an increasing number of desertions, but he dismissed these as being 'only a passing phase' after which 'the old lust of battle and the old loyalty returned, even among those who had begun to hang their heads'.[18] In fact the German commander, who just a month earlier used to punish 'misbehaviour' in the ranks with measures as innocuous as making offenders stand on boxes with pumpkins on their heads, had ended the 'passing phase' by shooting or hanging deserters; and part of the justification for splitting up his troops was to counter the possibility of a large-scale mutiny in the ranks (something the British sought to encourage by dropping seditious leaflets from planes). Concentration of his forces had to occur sometime, however, because the captured supplies started to run out. By the end of February von Lettow-Vorbeck, Wahle, Otto and Göring had all moved eastwards, dislodged in torrential rain by Hawthorn's advance from Nyasaland, to the Medo-Msalu-Nanungu area, where Köhl had supervised the planting of crops. At a new HQ at Nanungu, from where von Lettow-Vorbeck ordered a period of rest while patrols were sent out in all directions to reconnoitre enemy troop dispositions, supplies were soon plentiful and the reception of the local inhabitants friendly.

The reconcentration of the German detachments seemed to present van Deventer with an opportunity 'to bring [the enemy] to bay',[19] and it was fortuitous that a new rebellion in Barue district on the border with Southern Rhodesia prevented Sousa Rosa from insisting that Portuguese troops be given a leading role in his plans. At the end of March the British troops were ordered to converge simultaneously on the enemy from the west and east, and a succession of scrappy – but fierce – encounters were fought in the next two months at places which invariably began with the letter 'M': Montepuez, Mahua, Medo, Mriti, Msalu, Matarica and Makoti. The appalling terrain, the vast area involved, and the small number of troops combined to turn the campaign into something akin to a deadly game of ring-a-roses. Von Lettow-Vorbeck, who was forty-eight years old on 20 March, was in buoyant mood when he heard news of Ludendorff's *Kaiserschlacht* Spring Offensive in Europe; and he even began to show signs of being punch-drunk with all the fighting, thinking that it might be possible to turn the tables on his pursuers by manoeuvring them into a trap. When a large British column was 'roughly handled' by 'little more than two hundred'[20] German troops at Mt Kireka, near Makoti, he was exuberant; but victory was only secured by incurring casualties in excess of forty per cent among the attacking force. Such high casualties could not be sustained indefinitely, and van Deventer knew it. The field reports of his commanders began to display an increasing obsession with the number of 'GW' – 'German White' – casualties, hoping that there was a point at which a shortage of officers and NCOs might force a surrender; a bell was rung for each one at the British HQ in Dar-es-Salaam.

One eventuality that van Deventer – whose immense hands seemed to cover an entire map during briefings – had not seriously considered was the possibility that instead of attempting to break out of his encirclement by marching back to German East Africa (where Colonel Fitzgerald's three battalions of 3/KAR awaited him on the Rovuma), von Lettow-Vorbeck might move further south. The logic behind this oversight was sound enough – that mass desertions would take place among the German *askari* if they were led still further from their homes and their route back was blocked – but it was to prove erroneous. Having received news from Otto von Scherbening's detachment that the area around Malema, more than 300 miles to the south, was 'very productive',[21] von Lettow-Vorbeck took the astonishing decision to proceed south towards the Lurio River. The *askari* were 'squared' by the simple expedient of reiterating that German East Africa would be returned to Germany after the war, and that any deserters found thereafter would be hanged. It was a threat which van Deventer, who could not secure permission from the War Office to 'promise chiefs protection after the war', was forced to concede 'had great effect'.[22]

Captain Franz Köhl's seven companies, which were dislodged by Rosecol and Kartucol from Medo district in mid April, became the German rearguard for the move south, and his diary attests to the unceasing and severe nature of the fighting that ensued. In one engagement on 1 May at Mt Koronje, for example, the 22nd Mountain Battery was ambushed in a bamboo thicket by Spangenburg and lost five British officers and twenty-one Indian gunners in a matter of minutes; the battery's two precious guns were only saved from falling into Spangenburg's hands because there were no pack mules left alive. For the next three weeks Köhl clung tenaciously to positions to the north of Mt Koronje, but in the end he was very nearly trapped there. Von

Lettow-Vorbeck, by his own admission, had 'omitted to give [Köhl] definite orders to withdraw ... immediately' as the British simultaneously converged on the mountain and on Korema, twenty-four miles south of Mt Koronje; and on 22 May Köhl's rearguard was ambushed in a narrow pass by Kartucol and Colonel Griffiths's 3/1KAR. Köhl lost his baggage column, including all Schnee's personal effects, all medical stores and 70,000 rounds of ammunition; Schnee came within a whisker of being captured. But Rosecol and the KAR Mounted Infantry, to their bitter disappointment, arrived just too late to prevent Köhl, the Bavarian gunner on whose pugnacity von Lettow-Vorbeck had become increasingly reliant, and Schnee, the Governor-in-exile of German East Africa, from escaping. As it was Köhl's seven companies made their way south to rejoin von Lettow-Vorbeck, harried all the way by Kartucol, Rosecol and the KAR Mounted Infantry through the mountainous country inland from the port of Moçambique.

On 1 June von Lettow-Vorbeck's main force crossed the Lurio River, 300 yards wide and four feet deep, while Captain Erich Müller's advance guard made hell-for-leather for Malema to search for supplies, inflicting severe casualties on a company of 2/4KAR which endeavoured to block his path. After narrowly avoiding disaster at Mt Koronje von Lettow-Vorbeck's demeanour was that of a *verrückte Helmut* – a man who had nothing to lose and would fight to the bitter end – and he set his sights on 'the small hostile garrisons'[23] he expected to find south of the Lurio. The Portuguese *boma* at Malema was the first prize, but altogether more tempting was the large settlement at Alto Molocué and in his determination to sack it von Lettow-Vorbeck marched his troops south at a rate of twenty miles a day for two weeks. An occasional 'holding action'[24] and 'a series of little collisions'[25] enabled him to break clean away from his pursuers, and he evaded a battalion of 1/KAR sent to cut him off to the west of the Inagu Hills by the simple expedient of passing through the eastern rather than western foothills. Thereafter he was gratified to learn that he had reached an area in which his troops had even less reason to fear the reaction of the local African population than usual. As mission-educated Lewis Bandawe put it, his people were incensed at the 'slave-dealing' of Portuguese *cipais*, the wholesale imposition of taxes and forced labour, and the order to grow cotton that had been the salient features of Portuguese rule; and according to him, when Müller's advance guard approached Alto Molocué on 16 June and 'started firing a machine gun near the *boma* ... all the Portuguese authorities and their men ran away leaving everything behind them, which the Germans took possession of'.[26]

Alto Molocué, with its many European houses set on a small rise surrounded by orange trees in full bloom and overlooking hundreds of miles of forest, was as beautiful a place as any that the German troops had come across in

Portuguese East Africa. But it did not yield the vast booty that von Lettow-Vorbeck had hoped for, and its Administrator had removed all ammunition from the *boma* before fleeing. He did leave all his documents behind, however, and from these von Lettow-Vorbeck learnt that Ille, the headquarters of the Lugella Company, lay to the south at the confluence of the Lugella and Likungo Rivers. He ordered his troops to prepare to march on within days and by the time British troops entered Alto Molocué at the end of June they found the place deserted and burnt to the ground.

By crossing the Lurio River and slipping past the British 'cordon' in the Inagu Mountains, von Lettow-Vorbeck had again outwitted van Deventer. What the Germans referred to as 'the Opera War' was beginning, with the Germans stalking isolated Portuguese *bomas* and the British always in hot pursuit. When Schnee asked one *askari* why he never stopped grinning, the reply was '*Mtiti* – "the enemy" – in front. *Mtiti* at the side. That is why I laugh!'[27] There was nothing comical about the situation for van Deventer. Pamforce's fighting advance had taken it more than 250 miles from its coastal base, which necessitated a hasty reorganisation of its lines of communication so that the troops could be supplied from Moçambique rather than Porto Amelia; 1,100 lorries shipped by the War Office to German East Africa were found to be 'the wrong sort for convoy work';[28] and at this crucial juncture he lost the services of the indomitable Gold Coast troops. Their regiment had been more or less continually in combat in East Africa for almost two years, during which time it had incurred casualties equivalent to half its original strength, and it was in dire need of a rest. Leaving only its Mounted Infantry unit behind, the rest of the regiment began the long journey home to West Africa laden with decorations and accolades.*

While making for Ille von Lettow-Vorbeck captured a British carrier column and Spangenburg appropriated a herd of pigs at Nampepo – a rare treat. But the real prize was found at Ille itself after the Portuguese garrison bolted at the first sight of Müller's advance guard. Huge booty fell into German hands, including several machine-guns and much-needed clothing; indeed it was so huge that over 300,000kgs of foodstuffs were burnt before von Lettow-Vorbeck ordered a resumption of the march south towards the Indian Ocean. What van Deventer referred to, through gritted teeth, as a 'new stage of the campaign'[29] had begun in earnest.

---

* Approximately 3,800 officers and men saw service with the Gold Coast Regiment in East Africa, and the regiment sustained casualties of nearly fifty per cent (215 killed in action, 725 wounded, 270 died of disease, 567 invalided, thirteen missing). Fifteen MCs and three DSOs were awarded to British officers; twenty-two DCMs, twenty-four Military Medals and three MSMs were awarded to the African NCOs and other ranks.

THIRTY-FOUR

Nhamacurra

Von Lettow-Vorbeck's escape across the Lurio River had, by his own admission, involved a good deal of luck. Not only had he nearly lost Köhl's rearguard companies in the process of withdrawing southwards, but the river was in spate until only 'a short time before'[1] he needed to cross it. Often his troops had been forced to pitch camp for the night with the fires of the enemy visible no more than 1,000 yards away. But his skill matched his luck in withstanding the extreme pressure exerted on him by his pursuers and, as one South African forces magazine put it, 'German though [von Lettow-Vorbeck] is, we must admit that he has made the utmost of his opportunities'.[2]

By the time the German advance guard reached Ille the strain began to show. Franz Köhl's field diary reveals as much in starkest detail; and Dr Deppe, one of the six German doctors who saw the campaign in Portuguese East Africa through to its conclusion, meticulously recorded ninety-five engagements with the enemy in the second quarter of 1918. Captured documents showed that, far from being able to maraud entirely at will, German commanders were 'just as much disturbed by flanking movements' as the British, and routinely resorted to exaggerating the casualties inflicted in each scrap in the hope that it would boost morale. Furthermore, the German columns were so short of carriers that insufficient food could be carried to sustain the troops during the succession of forced marches which took them south; and caring for the sick and wounded became increasingly problematic. Dr Meixner's field hospitals were often no sooner set up than they would have to be dismantled, making the recuperation of the sick more prolonged and the performance of complex surgery on the severely wounded well-nigh impossible. Stocks of precious quinine also dwindled to just a few kilograms, with the result that one in three of the 276 Europeans who had started the campaign in Portuguese East Africa were left by the wayside during 1918. Most were found by the British, and given appropriate medical attention, but twenty-seven Germans recorded as still 'missing' at the end of the war probably suffered a lonely death in the bush.[3]

As the strain on his troops increased, von Lettow-Vorbeck became even more autocratic. To the mounting annoyance of his detachment commanders, who were given 'the greatest possible freedom of action',[4] he seldom told them where he was heading from day to day and the result was what von Lettow-Vorbeck called a 'lack of caution' on their part which caused 'many unnecessary losses'.[5] He was quite prepared to admit his share of responsibility for this situation, but that did not stop him from continually criticising the actions of others. He blamed Schnee, without justification, for the disaster that had befallen Köhl's baggage column; he was said to 'stare silently' at anyone who showed the slightest hesitation in carrying out his orders 'until that man shrank into a mere fraction of himself and disappeared';[6] and even General Wahle, still struggling on at the head of a detachment despite his considerable age, complained that he 'had a feeling that [von Lettow] just wanted to get rid of me'. When von Lettow-Vorbeck tried to order the ailing Wahle to stay behind, he was told by the latter that the order was 'illegal' because it was tantamount to an order to surrender. 'It was', wrote Wahle, with evident satisfaction, 'the first time that anyone had answered back to him',[7] and for once von Lettow-Vorbeck was forced to back down.

Wahle and Schnee were not alone in feeling that their commander-in-chief wanted rid of them. As van Deventer successfully completed the realignment of his lines of communication so that his troops could be supplied from Moçambique rather than Porto Amelia, Sousa Rosa began to think that it was time for his troops to resume a more active role in the campaign. For a while van Deventer fobbed him off with a variety of excuses, but when Sousa Rosa 'begged' him to give his men 'a chance in the field' the decision to expose his ally 'to the least possible danger'[8] had to be rescinded. Political, rather than military, considerations were still to the fore: Sousa Rosa's renewed enthusiasm had little to do with any improvement in the capability or morale of his troops and everything to do with his political masters in Lisbon. Sidónio Pais's new government had been greatly embarrassed by the lamentable performance of most of the Portuguese troops at the Battle of the Lys during Ludendorff's offensive on the Western Front in April, and that same month some of their comrades had mutinied at their barracks in Horsham. Good news was urgently needed from somewhere, and Lisbon instructed Sousa Rosa to provide it.

The prospects for renewed military co-operation between Sousa Rosa and van Deventer were bleak. A request from the War Office for permission to recruit 3,300 *askari* in Portuguese East Africa for service with a new King's African Rifles brigade in the Middle East had failed to elicit a response; in the port of Beira street fights between British and Portuguese troops were a regular occurrence; in Niassa province the conduct of Colonel Cabrita, the new Acting Governor-General, was so anti-British (and anti-Sousa Rosa) that one of Sousa

Rosa's more loyal officers even challenged him to a duel; and most Europeans in the Portuguese ranks were as sick as ever. The only thing in favour of involving Portuguese troops once again was van Deventer's critical shortage of manpower. The loss of the Gold Coast Regiment meant that he had just 7,500 British troops available for deployment against von Lettow-Vorbeck as he made his way towards the coastal ports of Moçambique province, and even sick Portuguese reinforcements might for once prove better than none at all.*

On 1 June, as von Lettow-Vorbeck made his way across the Lurio River, Sousa Rosa was asked 'to send a garrison and mobile column to Quelimane and to arrange to withdraw all stores and ammunition dumps from outlying posts and places on the coast or to destroy them'. The 'necessity for immediate action'⁹ was made clear by van Deventer. But Sousa Rosa did not begin sending the first troops from Mocímboa da Praia south to Quelimane until two weeks later, and by then Alto Molocué had been ravaged and von Lettow-Vorbeck's path to Quelimane lay open. The news of the fall of Alto Molocué completely unnerved Sousa Rosa, whose response was to request that three companies of 2/3KAR, which had recently been shipped to the port of Moçambique, should be rushed south to help him defend Quelimane immediately. Van Deventer was livid, and sent a scathing report to the War Office: 'The Portuguese have failed me very badly', he wrote on 25 June, 'their advance troops did not reach Quelimane until June 20th. A company was then sent forward to Mocuba and yesterday scattered and ran away from 30 German native soldiers losing two machine-guns. Very little has been done in the way of securing the base; ammunition and supplies at Alto Molocué and Ille were allowed to fall into enemy hands, and no attempt has yet been made to bring into safety the large stocks of supplies which (I am now told) exist at various places on the coast north of Quelimane.'

Within weeks of the renewal of Anglo-Portuguese 'co-operation', all van Deventer's plans seemed to have been stymied by his allies; and the chaos was compounded when, at the exact same time as Sousa Rosa was requesting the assistance of the King's African Rifles at Quelimane, the Governor of Moçambique province flatly refused to authorise the recruitment of carriers to support British troops stationed there. Van Deventer's conclusion was forthright. Political considerations could not be allowed to undermine his conduct of the campaign any further: he informed the War Office that 'the

---

* On 20 June 1918 the ration strength of the British troops committed to the Portuguese East Africa campaign was as follows: Kartucol – 1,400 rifles; 3/2KAR – 850 rifles; Fitzcol – 1,300 rifles; Nyasaland forces – 3,900 rifles; KAR Mounted Infantry and Mounted Howitzer – seventy rifles. Total: 7,520 rifles. In the southern area of operations the Portuguese had twenty-two *askari* companies and five European companies, a total of approximately 5,500 rifles. (See TNA/WO/158/475.)

time has come when the Portuguese authorities must be told the truth, namely that their troops in Portuguese East Africa are totally unreliable and a source of grave danger to their Allies', and suggested that 'the Portuguese role be in future definitely restricted to garrisoning sea bases or other places on coast and dealing with the Barue rebellion'.[10] In the meantime van Deventer was left in the unenviable position of having to consider what might happen to the substantial settlement at Nhamacurra, between Ille and Quelimane. The only hope of preventing von Lettow-Vorbeck from overrunning the Portuguese garrison there appeared to rest on the presence of two companies of Colonel Gore-Browne's 2/3KAR, which had completed a dash from Lindi, 600 miles north in German East Africa, in less time than it had taken Sousa Rosa just to move Portuguese troops from Mocímboa da Praia to Quelimane.

At dusk on 1 July three companies led by Captain Erich Müller, once a 'staffer' but now showing himself to be 'possessed of a very sound tactical judgment and great initiative',[11] fell on the Portuguese-held 'western sector' of Nhamacurra, driving straight between its western flank and the river. At least a quarter of the Portuguese troops were caught asleep at their posts, and two artillery pieces and a Lewis gun were captured by Müller as he drove the enemy out of their poorly prepared positions. The following day saw 'several hours of very severe hand-to-hand fighting'[12] as Müller pressed his attack against the Portuguese central sector while von Lettow-Vorbeck brought up his main force in support. By nightfall most of the 400 Portuguese troops holding Nhamacurra's sisal factory had surrendered, and two more field guns and four machine-guns fell into German hands. This collapse forced Gore-Browne, whose troops were positioned on the eastern fringes of the settlement, to fall back on Nhamacurra's little railway station where he redeployed his men and rallied those Portuguese troops which had not surrendered. Under his command the 21st *Companhia Indigena* and the artillery of Lieutenant Lemonde Macedo distinguished themselves alongside the KAR *askari*, and numerous attacks were beaten off. But at 3 p.m. on 3 July, the third day of the battle, a ferocious assault led by Kempner and von Ruckteschell and backed by a bombardment by the captured guns broke through Gore-Browne's defences to the north-west of the station; and, with that, von Lettow-Vorbeck threw his entire force into the fray.

British and Portuguese troops fought on, side by side, until they found themselves trapped with their backs to an angle in the Nhamacurra River. At dusk, as they tried to swim the ninety yards to safety, Gore-Browne and more than 100 British and Portuguese *askari* drowned; and the number of Allied troops who managed to escape the German envelopment of Nhamacurra was negligible. Three Portuguese battalions and two British companies had been decimated. When news of the disaster reached van Deventer he expressed his disgust to the War Office in no uncertain terms: in his opinion the Portuguese, who had never been anything but 'an incredible drawback' ever since von Lettow-Vorbeck had crossed the Rovuma, had now 'utterly failed' him. The reply from the War Office cautioned him 'to exercise care that no action be taken by you that could be construed as an insult to the Portuguese nation'.*

Von Lettow-Vorbeck 'at last obtained what he sought'[13] at Nhamacurra: sugar galore from the Lugella Company plantation, 3.75kgs of quinine, ten machine-guns, 444 modern rifles and more than 300,000 rounds of ammunition were found in various storehouses or on the battlefield. Most important of all, a further 300,000kgs of foodstuffs were also seized, a haul considerably too large for the number of carriers that could be mustered by a despairing Quartermaster-Lieutenant Besch. As he beetled about organising as best he could the removal of the booty, his comrades' attention was diverted elsewhere: champagne, wine and spirits aplenty had been unearthed – a discovery which led to 'a wholesale jollification'.[14] 'Not a single man black or white [was left] sober', wrote General Wahle, adding that it was 'fortunate that there was no enemy about'.[15] By the time British troops did converge on Nhamacurra the enemy had slipped away eastwards. The only consolation was that von Lettow-Vorbeck had baulked at making use of a river steamer whose skipper, knowing nothing of the recent battle, had inadvertently steered it into Nhamacurra within hours of its capture.

On 4 July Sousa Rosa called a council of war in Quelimane to discuss how the port could be defended. Two companies of KAR were on their way from Lindi and three Portuguese companies had been ordered north from Lourenço Marques, but in the meantime Quelimane's garrison, such as it was, consisted of thirty ratings from the *Adamastor*, a Portuguese light cruiser lying offshore; 112 ratings from Commander Victor Boyes's gunboat *Thistle*; 100 local auxiliaries; and sixty civilian volunteers. Boyes and Major Cohen, the British Liaison Officer, were adamant that Quelimane must be defended to the last man. But they were only supported by a minority of Portuguese officers present; and Sousa Rosa and the Acting Governor of Quelimane district were visibly shaken by the prospect of an imminent attack. 'It was obvious', wrote Boyes in his official report of the conference, 'that the Commander-in-Chief was panic-stricken and had every intention of leaving the town; in support of his policy of not defending the town, he read an excerpt from a book on military strategy wherein it was laid down that an enemy would not sack an undefended town'. The thought of resistance was 'clearly very repugnant' to

---

* TNA/WO/158/476: correspondence of 6 and 8 July 1918. Van Deventer estimated that the Portuguese had lost three field guns, one Hotchkiss gun, twenty machine-guns, 1,000 rifles and more than a million rounds of ammunition in 1918.

British and South
African troops cross
the Ruaha River at
the end of 1916,
while British
airmen celebrate
Christmas in the
hope that the
campaign will soon
be over

The Allied offensive grinds to a halt in early 1917, frustrated by the worst
rains in living memory and von Lettow-Vorbeck's elusive tactics.
General Hoskins (above) paid the price

Askari of 15 *Feldkompanie* in camp

One of von Lettow-Vorbeck's indomitable NCOs

Max Wintgens, though increasingly sick, remained on the loose until mid 1917

Belgian troops
capture
Mahenge in
September 1917

L59, the
airship sent by
Berlin with sup-
plies for the
beleaguered
German troops

Indian troopers of the 25th Cavalry cross the Rovuma River after von
Lettow-Vorbeck's escape into Portuguese East Africa, November 1917

The German High Command on the run in Portuguese East Africa in 1918: von Lettow-Vorbeck and Kraut (left), Governor Schnee (below), and Wahle and Boell (below left)

The Allied officers charged with the final pursuit of von Lettow-Vorbeck:
(left to right) Northey, van Devenber, Sheppard and Errol MacDonnell

Askari of 2/4 KAR
in Portuguese
East Africa

Schnee (centre right) with the remaining German officers after surrender

Schnee, von Lettow-Vorbeck and their men receive a heroes' welcome at the Brandenburg Gate in Berlin, March 1919

M'Ithiria Mukaria, the oldest surviving
veteran of the King's African Rifles, in Isiolo
(photographed by the author, February 2002)

The memorial at the spot near the
Chambezi River where von Lettow-Vorbeck
was informed that the war in Europe was
over

Unveiling of the War Memorial in Nairobi, 1927

Sousa Rosa, and his Chief of Staff was known to have placed all his kit on a launch and shifted his headquarters to the waterside ready to skedaddle on the *Adamastor*. In the end the British officers, fed up with the Portuguese propensity to present von Lettow-Vorbeck with 'convenient Ordnance and Supply dumps', carried the argument and Sousa Rosa, though angry at what he perceived as a challenge to his authority and 'in such a nervous state as to be hardly responsible for his actions',[16] was forced to back down.

It was fortunate for Sousa Rosa, who after the disaster at Nhamacurra decided that he was 'very unwell',[17] that von Lettow-Vorbeck had no way of knowing that Quelimane was to all intents and purposes undefended. Furthermore he was concerned that his troops were too near to the Zambezi, and that they might find themselves trapped between British troops and a river which they had no way of crossing. It was time 'to turn about', but first, rather than attack Quelimane, von Lettow-Vorbeck decided that he wanted 'to cause the enemy anxiety'[18] by moving east towards Moçambique. So he recrossed the Likungo River, with Köhl to the rear and Müller in advance of the main force, and made for Namirrue, a hill-top post held by just a single company of 2/3KAR. For two days in the fourth week of July the garrison succeeded in thwarting Müller's attempts to overrun it, but when a British relief column inadvertently marched straight into von Lettow-Vorbeck's main force it was routed and Namirrue's fate was sealed. This completed a disastrous month for 3/KAR. The one remaining company of 2/3KAR was sent to garrison Quelimane, and the half-company of 3/3KAR that survived the ill-fated attempt to relieve Namirrue was put on lines of communication duty at Lindi for the rest of the war. To van Deventer's consternation, the battles at Nhamacurra and Namirrue had shown that not all KAR units were as seemingly indestructible as Giffard's 2/KAR.

By the beginning of August von Lettow-Vorbeck had moved on to Chalaúa, forty-five miles inland from António Enes at the centre of a 'wide and exceptionally fertile district'. He had retreated the equivalent of the distance between Paris and Leningrad since March 1916 and now, 'free from interference',[19] he was briefly able to rest his troops. While he planned his next move patrols were sent out raiding as far as they wished, and the proximity of German troops triggered yet another rebellion against the Portuguese administration in the coastal province of Angoche. The rebellion was something of a godsend for van Deventer because it forced Massano de Amorim to admit that while his troops tackled the insurrection he would be able to contribute no more to the campaign than defending Portuguese East Africa's ports; equally welcome was the news that Nhamacurra and the Portuguese 'mutiny' at Quelimane had decided Massano de Amorim to sack Sousa Rosa. Portugal's campaign in East Africa was over.

'Was it worth the effort of having fought?' was the question posed by many a Portuguese combatant, to which the answer was invariably: 'It is sad to say, but I think not.'[20] Official statistics show that 19,438 officers and soldiers were sent from Portugal to fight for the *Pátria* in East Africa with the various expeditionary forces, but the veracity of the records on which the statistics are based is at best questionable. The total number of European troops to have served in the campaign may be accurate enough, but in compiling the list of casualties Portuguese officials, in Lisbon and in East Africa, simply told the story they wanted the public to hear – and in so doing produced some startling anomalies. For example, just sixteen Portuguese officers, thirty-eight other ranks, and eighty-eight *askari* were said to have died in combat, whereas 2,145 were said to have died from diseases of one sort or another. The message that Portugal wanted heard was clear: it was nature, not German troops, that had defeated its troops. As for the levies employed by Portugal in the campaign, a total of exactly 8,000 suggests that record-keeping was as non-existent as it was for the '60,000' carriers recruited for service with the Portuguese troops and '30,000' for service with the British troops. It seems that round numbers were good enough for enumerating the participation of the indigenous population, although four 'token' heroes were found among the *askari* and were awarded the *Cruz de Guerra*.

There can be no doubting the magnitude of the trauma inflicted on Portugal by the Great War. The nation was already in 'spasm' on the eve of war; by 1918 it was on the verge of total collapse.* Some of their allies considered it 'a shame to laugh at the Portuguese', that they were 'doing their best';[21] and van Deventer was prevailed upon to compliment the 'brave and efficient Portuguese officers and men' (and to decry their 'native troops' for being 'such poor material')[22] in his final despatch on the subject of Anglo-Portuguese co-operation. Sousa Rosa was predictably exonerated of any misconduct by a Commission of Enquiry in Lisbon, and was even made a Companion of the Bath by Britain in the interests of harmonious relations with the *velha aliada*. But when Portugal sought a reward for its contribution to the war at Versailles, and lodged a claim for war reparations for the suffering inflicted on 153,000 Africans, her allies would decide that enough was enough.

---

* The Governor-General of Portuguese East Africa, Álvaro de Castro, was a prominent participant in the attempted coup of January 1919 which followed the assassination of Sidónio Pais. He was Prime Minister for ten days in November 1920 and for eight months in 1923–4.

THIRTY-FIVE

Tipperary mbali sana sana!*

———◆———

Van Deventer could not afford to let von Lettow-Vorbeck settle indefinitely in Chalaúa district, raiding Portuguese outposts at will and stirring up the local population. During the first week in August, just as the short rains began, he started to redeploy his troops in an arc to the south of a new motor road connecting Moçambique with Nampula and Malema (a *boma* to the north of the Inagu Hills); and he ensured that the ports of Quelimane and Moçambique were reinforced and were supported by gunboats lying offshore. To the west, Hawthorn, who had succeeded Northey as commander-in-chief of the Nyasaland and Rhodesian units, ordered his troops to concentrate between Malokotera and Munevala; and the task of flushing von Lettow-Vorbeck out of Chalaúa district fell to the three battalions of Colonel Giffard's Kartucol and the KAR Mounted Infantry. Van Deventer knew that the only chance of securing victory lay, as ever, in harrying von Lettow-Vorbeck 'until his forces had been so reduced as to be innocuous'.[1] But with fewer than 35,000 troops now available in the whole of East Africa (of whom one in five were sick at any one time) his strategy was becoming increasingly difficult to sustain.

The conditions in which Kartucol advanced in the second week in August were execrable. Pouring rain turned the black cotton soil into a quagmire, and elephant grass taller than a man often restricted vision to a matter of yards. On 13 August, as Giffard's troops finally approached Chalaúa, von Lettow-Vorbeck's main force was thought to be still in the district and the chances of forcing him to fight looked good. But German scouts had warned of Kartucol's imminent arrival and von Lettow-Vorbeck had slipped away south-west to cross the Ligonha and Molocué Rivers just a few miles from the sea. The direction of his withdrawal made the situation 'extremely confused', and briefly raised the possibility that Quelimane might after all be attacked. By the third week in August, however, von Lettow-Vorbeck was known to be heading due north. Kartucol was rushed by a series of forced marches, often

* 'It's a long way to Tipperary', King's African Rifles marching song.

covering more than twenty miles a day in spite of the poor weather, to the Inagu Hills to head him off and was joined there by one of General Hawthorn's columns, comprising 3/1KAR and the NRP. On 24 August a patrol of 2/4KAR stumbled into the German advance guard near the Lugella River, a little south of Numarroe, and was pursued all the way back to the *boma* (whose Portuguese administrator 'professed no knowledge of the approach of the enemy').[2] After a fierce baffle, during which the commanding officer of 2/4KAR was captured and four of his officers and forty-seven *askari* lost their lives, Numarroe was overrun. Twenty miles to the north, the garrison at Regone braced itself for an immediate attack, fortifying the *boma* to such an extent that only a prolonged siege would cause it to fall.

After Numarroe it was clear to van Deventer and Hawthorn that von Lettow-Vorbeck had skilfully shifted his line of advance westwards so as to bypass the Inagu Hills and Kartucol, and with each day van Deventer grew more certain that the German commander-in-chief had finally set his sights on marching all the way back to German East Africa. But von Lettow-Vorbeck's next move provided a reminder, if such were needed, that he was anything but predictable. After dark on 26 August he led his troops straight past Regone and made for Lioma, pursued by 3/4KAR and 'Shortcol' – 1/4KAR and the RNR. Scraps between opposing patrols now became increasingly frequent and increasingly ferocious. After one engagement the German *askari* were so charged that they simply shot all their prisoners, many of whom were former comrades who had swapped sides. Their conduct was motivated as much by fear as by a desire to exact retribution: the enemy's use of German commands and German tactics when deploying former German *askari* in battle was calculated to induce panic, and after eight months of campaigning in Portuguese East Africa sheer exhaustion, hunger and the excessive heat of the time of year intensified the sense of desperation among von Lettow-Vorbeck's troops still further.

Von Lettow-Vorbeck may have confounded van Deventer's well-laid plans by passing well to the west of the British troops in the vicinity of the Inagu Hills, but at Lioma, twenty miles to the north-west of Regone, he meant to fight. On 30 August he attacked Lioma's well-entrenched camp from three sides, wiping out a platoon of 1/1KAR before the first troops of Giffard's Kartucol could reach the embattled garrison. 3/2KAR was the first battalion to arrive, and it immediately launched a counter-attack, driving off the German troops and inflicting heavy casualties in the process. By dawn on 31 August 2/2KAR and 1/2KAR were also on the scene, having marched right through the night from the Inagu Hills, and a day of immensely confused fighting ensued. On the German side Captain Poppe was shot in the chest and Quartermaster-Lieutenant Besch's thigh artery was severed; Lieutenant

Boell and Dr Küdicke's entire field hospital were captured; and Lieutenant von Schrötter, the *Königsberg*'s Lieutenant Freund and three senior NCOs were killed. The loss of these officers was serious, the more so after the recent capture of Major Schulz and Lieutenant Ott and the death of Lieutenant Selke; and when Karl Göring was wounded in mid afternoon von Lettow-Vorbeck was forced to reel in his and Müller's detachments and break off the engagement. As the *Schutztruppe* were pursued north by Kartucol through dense bush and rugged hills towards the Lurio River, von Lettow-Vorbeck knew that the battle at Lioma had been a narrow escape. But unbeknownst to him only Shortcol stood between him and the Lurio River, and it was too weak to arrest his advance; while in his rear Kartucol was flagging after marching 435 miles in the previous month. On 4 and 5 September von Lettow-Vorbeck led his troops across the Lurio without encountering any opposition.

Despite their recent travails two of Kartucol's three battalions unexpectedly outran the enemy at Pere Hills at noon on 6 September; and as a result became cut off from 2/2KAR when it was set upon by Müller's advance guard. Ten machine-guns were deployed against the battalion as it took cover in and around a dry riverbed, and German troops fought their way to within fifty yards of its transport and baggage column; but in the late afternoon Colonel Giffard outflanked Müller with 1/2KAR and 3/2KAR and forced him to withdraw. Throughout the day's fighting the KAR NCOs, particularly those of 2/2KAR on whom the survival of the battalion depended after seven of its British officers were killed or wounded, displayed 'courage, initiative and leadership ... at their best'.[3] Eight DCMs were awarded for the action to add to the sixteen won at Lioma, thereby confirming the reputation that Kartucol had earned for being as effective a unit as any deployed against von Lettow-Vorbeck in the war. It was also the most persistent column, having pursued von Lettow-Vorbeck for 1,600 miles through Portuguese East Africa, crossing twenty-nine large rivers and fighting thirty-two engagements along the way. At the end of September its *askari* were finally sent back to garrisons in German East Africa for a much-needed rest.

Von Lettow-Vorbeck described the fighting at Pere Hills as 'pretty violent'[4] and his considerable respect for Giffard's troops decided him against risking a counter-attack after dark. His casualties in the first week of September were already serious enough: in addition to the thirty-four Germans who had fallen at Lioma, about 200 *askari* had also been killed, wounded or captured there and at Pere Hills. In other words a single week had robbed him of about fifteen per cent of his combatant strength, and two companies, 14/FK and 4/SchK, were so depleted that they had to merge. Worse still, as he marched north towards Mahua, a bronchial virus of exceptional virulence rampaged through his dozen remaining companies (following hard on the heels of an outbreak of cerebro-spinal meningitis). In no time over half the men were affected and, as no more than 100 could be carried at any one time, many of the rest were abandoned to an uncertain fate in the bush.

Schnee's diary for this period reveals the extent of the hardships endured by the *Schutztruppe* during September. As a civilian, and somewhat superfluous, observer what preoccupied him more than the fighting were the sicknesses afflicting all the troops, *askari* wives going into labour, and the loss of individuals whom he counted as friends. When the bronchial virus abated, having killed one in ten of those it struck, he hoped that the suffering might diminish – but then there was an outbreak of smallpox which incapacitated more than fifty *askari* in one company. Schnee's sympathy for the plight of Dr Müller and the staff of the mobile hospital was immense, all the more so when Müller himself succumbed to malaria and had to hand over to Dr Taute. As the *askari* marched on towards the Rovuma, Schnee noticed that even the 'fit' *askari* coughed incessantly, their lungs wracked by respiratory complaints brought on by the combination of freezing cold nights, rain and river-crossings, and searing daytime heat.

When the fast-flowing Lujenda River was forded in mid September, and the mountains to the east of Lake Nyasa came into view, von Lettow-Vorbeck's troops found themselves on the plains leading to the Rovuma – and German East Africa. The easier terrain was certainly welcomed by the *askari*, who had marched for an average of ten hours a day for thirty-five days, but the plight of the carriers worsened. Many had been impressed when the German troops entered Portuguese East Africa ten months earlier, and when a number of them attempted to escape to their homes von Lettow-Vorbeck had their comrades roped together and issued orders that any 'deserters' should be shot on sight. Every night rifle shots rang out through the darkness, but 300 of the 4,000 carriers gathered up since leaving Chalaúa district did manage to evade their guards and slip away southwards. Schnee recorded his rather belated concern that the only 'crime' of these 'innocent people' was 'trying to escape from having been compelled to act as bearers',[5] but at no stage, even when criticising 'the High Command' for 'sacrificing life',[6] does he appear to have considered that any responsibility for the increasing cruelty being meted out on the carriers or the inhabitants of an area that German troops were now raiding for the fourth time in two years, might lie with him. There were hardly any crops worth seizing this time, and most of the local population wisely fled before the advance of von Lettow-Vorbeck's 'army'. Indeed so great was the problem of supplies that at an impromptu auction held among the German officers and NCOs a tin containing a few bits of mouldy chocolate fetched Rs130 – more than two years' wages for a British carrier – and the scrawniest of fowls fetched Rs40–50.

The predicament of van Deventer's troops was no better. His columns had been called upon to perform yet more 'remarkable feats of endurance', often in bush so dense that large hostile patrols could pass within half a mile of each other in total ignorance of the presence of the other; and they too were on very short rations because 'emulating the utterly ruthless German method' of living off the country was deemed 'impossible'[7] by van Deventer. With Kartucol now a busted flush, and Shortcol unable to overhaul the retreating enemy, von Lettow-Vorbeck reached the Rovuma at the end of September. At Mitomoni, near the Rovuma's confluence with the Messinge, he led 172 Germans, 1,260 *askari* and 3,000 carriers and camp-followers back into German East Africa. Van Deventer's indignity could only have been greater if his opponent had, just for old times' sake, sacked Negomano, some 250 miles downriver.*

Less than a week after crossing the Rovuma the *Schutztruppe* were within striking distance of Songea. Von Lettow-Vorbeck's first thought was to head for Tabora, following in Wintgens's footsteps across the desolate steppe northwest of the St Moritz Mission. But after brushing aside attempts by 'Kartufor' – 2/4KAR and the NRP – to block his route on the Songea–Wiedhafen road he decided that his freedom of movement appeared to be wholly unrestricted. By the time he reached Njombe, Northey's former headquarters, in mid October only a single company of Kartufor remained in close pursuit – and it had far outrun its supply lines. It was abundantly clear that van Deventer was flummoxed by the situation confronting him. General Hawthorn's troops were ordered to stay in close contact with the enemy; Kartucol was remobilised and instructed to advance against von Lettow-Vorbeck from Bismarckburg, on Lake Tanganyika, and from Northern Rhodesia; and a protective cordon was established to the south of the Central Railway between Morogoro and Dodoma. But in the meantime, von Lettow-Vorbeck altered his plans: so little pressure was being exerted on him that he decided that Northern Rhodesia presented an altogether more proximate and tempting target than Tabora – and it would not involve leading his troops across the steppe. One of his officers explained his thinking thus: 'the fact that the inner part of Rhodesia had not been affected by the war and hence had enough provisions was one of the main reasons for this decision. What is more, the English would not have reckoned with the Germans heading to Rhodesia and hence would not have been prepared for it. Later from Rhodesia there were many options that opened up for the Germans ... a whole range of possibilities, whose effects were not to be underestimated.'[8] They included a trek right

---

* The size of the area of operations in Portuguese East Africa during 1918 had been about 470 miles north–south by 330 miles east–west – approximately two-thirds the size of France.

through to Portuguese West Africa – today's Angola – and the Atlantic.

One additional factor that almost certainly influenced von Lettow-Vorbeck's decision was the constant stream of deserters from the German ranks, including his own gun-bearer and many of the veteran Angoni carriers who were now within striking distance of their homelands. The gravity of the situation finally seemed to dawn on von Lettow-Vorbeck: in marked contrast to his utter ruthlessness during the last few weeks in Portuguese East Africa he remarked that 'it would after all have been asking too much of human nature to expect that these men, who had not seen their people for years, should now march straight through their native district'.[9] The *askari* were also given a pay rise by the 'High Command', a measure which Schnee regarded as 'obviously hopeless'[10] since the troops had been forced to accept credit for their services for nearly two years. Deserting carriers and *askari* were not the only ones for whom the war ended soon after the crossing of the Rovuma. General Wahle, who had survived being shot through his bush hat at Namirrue, and was now suffering from a double ruptured hernia, was finally forced to request that he be left behind at the mission station at Njombe. He was treated by his captors with huge respect and whisked away to hospital in Iringa by car, so weak that he could barely dress himself. For Wahle, a holiday to visit his son, who was now languishing in a POW camp in Egypt, had turned into four years' active service; during that time he had been awarded the Iron Cross 1st Class, the *Pour le Mérite*, and gained the distinction of being the oldest combatant of the war on either side.

Schnee's pride and fanatical devotion to duty did not allow him to relinquish his post in similar fashion, although he too was an 'utter wreck'.[11] On 9 October the sole remaining German wireless, which could receive but not transmit, was able to pick up fragments of news from Europe for the first time in almost a year and Schnee was greatly encouraged to learn that German troops still held the 'good old Hindenburg Line'.[12] In the following week, however, snippets of news found at abandoned British posts – a telegram here, a Reuter transcript there – were less positive; and at Njombe Schnee came across 'very unfavourable news relating to the Western Front, the Bulgarian armistice, and the capture of Damascus'. All in all Germany's position was 'not conducive to good cheer',[13] and the death of colonial pioneer Carl Peters in September was even interpreted by some German officers as heralding the end of Germany's status as a colonial power in Africa.

Von Lettow-Vorbeck's reaction to the news from other fronts was that it all sounded 'very improbable',[14] and he ordered his troops to push on without giving it a second thought. At one point on the march towards Neu Utengule they had to battle for miles through a bush fire with flames several metres high, but the mission was reached by the end of October. There was still no resistance en route, although the German force was now right in the heart of the territory through which Northey, Hawthorn and Murray had advanced two years previously; and, having outflanked any British troops which might have been guarding the northern tip of Lake Nyasa, von Lettow-Vorbeck was able to turn south and set a course straight for the Northern Rhodesia border. On 1 November 1918 Spangenburg was ordered to attack Fife while Köhl's rearguard turned to face any British troops in close pursuit. Köhl need not have worried, as 1/4KAR was more than thirty miles behind the German force, but Spangenburg's attack showed just how weak the *Schutztruppe's* offensive capability had become. By mid-afternoon on 1 November the *boma* at Fife was strongly held by the dogged Northern Rhodesian Police Service Battalion, which had been rushed up Lake Nyasa from Fort Johnston with only hours to spare; and as von Lettow-Vorbeck's artillery now comprised nothing more than an old Portuguese gun and a trench mortar which blew up, he was unable to make any impression on Fife's defences. Worse still, von Lettow-Vorbeck came within a whisker of being killed and after a few hours he called off the attack and decided to push on in search of easier pickings. Hawthorn expected him to make for Abercorn, and deployed one of the remobilised battalions of Kartucol and troops who had been garrisoning Kasama to block his path. But once again von Lettow-Vorbeck confounded all expectations and made straight for defenceless Kasama. A state of near panic ensued in Northern Rhodesia. The two other remobilised battalions of Kartucol had received their orders to proceed to Northern Rhodesia, but had not even left Lindi; and in their absence only Colonel Hawkins's 1/4KAR, which had marched 1,830 miles in the previous six months and only possessed a map from a schoolboy atlas to guide them in Northern Rhodesia, was in any position to stay in touch with the enemy.

In late October and early November the news from Europe gleaned by Schnee and 'the High Command' from captured sources became ever worse. There was a rumour that Hindenburg was dead, and that peace and an armistice were about to be *imposed* on Germany. 'It seems to me', wrote Schnee, 'that for the main part everyone hopes for peace in the near future, with the deliverance that it will bring us from our situation, which grows ever more unbearable and which consciously or unconsciously will leave its mark permanently on us.' But he was utterly mystified as to 'how our people [could] have deserved such an ending?'[15] This sense of dismay, and of being cruelly wronged, was even more pronounced among the remnants of German East Africa's officer corps than in Germany itself. When the *Schutztruppe* had crossed the Rovuma into Portuguese East Africa a year earlier the Fatherland still seemed to hold all the aces in Europe; now only the two of clubs seemingly remained in the Kaiser's hand.

During the night of 3–4 November hundreds more carriers deserted the *Schutztruppe*, including fifty from Schnee's own column; and on 5 November, when Köhl's rearguard successfully beat off an attack by 1/4 KAR near the White Fathers' Mission at Kayambi, only 3/FK and 10/FK were still able to field more than 100 *askari*. So great was the shortage of officers that three of the eleven German companies were now commanded by a sergeant, an under-paymaster and an 'acting-officer'. Yet von Lettow-Vorbeck, having 'appro-priated' a herd of 400 cattle and six months' stock of quinine from the mission station at Mwenzo, remained as stubborn and optimistic as ever, his courage 'unquenchable',[16] and still believed that it would be possible 'to reach the Zambesi-Congo watershed'.[17] After Fife even Colonel Hawkins, commanding the closest British troops, was of the opinion that von Lettow-Vorbeck had broken clear away; and on 9 November Spangenburg's advance column reached Kasama. Thanks to the foresight of District Officer Hector Croad, who had been warned of the imminent arrival of the *Schutztruppe* on his turf, Spangenburg found the town deserted and stripped of all stocks of desperately needed ammunition. Cigarettes and tobacco were the only comforts left behind, and without halting a moment longer than necessary Spangenburg sped off in pursuit of Croad, who had removed all supplies to a rubber factory on the south side of the Chambezi River.

On 12 November, as Spangenburg reached the Chambezi and started to probe the defences of the rubber factory, von Lettow-Vorbeck arrived at Kasama. Köhl's rearguard had had to fight a fierce four-hour battle with Hawkins's 1/4KAR and been forced to disappear into the bush to the west, but as soon as Spangenburg took the rubber factory – defended only by invalids and convicts released by Croad from Kasama's gaol – he sensed that his route south would be completely open. That day, however, Köhl captured a British despatch rider from whom he learnt of the Armistice in Europe, and von Lettow-Vorbeck set off on a bicycle to inform Spangenburg. Twenty-four hours later he reached the Chambezi just in time to forestall what would undoubtedly have been a decisive attack on the rubber factory. Croad crossed the river to meet the German commander-in-chief. The message that the war was over circulated rapidly among the German *askari* spread out between Kasama and the Chambezi.

Despite all the news from Europe that had filtered through to him in recent weeks, von Lettow-Vorbeck remained 'convinced that the conclusion of hostilities must have been favourable ... to Germany'.[18] Indeed his state of denial was so great that he immediately began preparations to move all his troops across the Chambezi in case the peace proved short-lived; and he refused to believe Croad when he told him that the Kaiser had fled to Holland and that Germany was now a republic. The 'prevailing opinion' among

German officers and NCOs was that Germany must have 'come off fairly well'.[19] But Schnee's reaction was more guarded: he experienced 'no feeling of happiness' at the cessation of hostilities and just hoped that 'everything will end in a fair and honourable way'.[20]

The terms of the Armistice came as a rude shock to von Lettow-Vorbeck and his officers, as did news conveyed by British officers confirming the state of turmoil in Germany, the mutiny of the German fleet, the Kaiser's abdication and Ludendorff's flight to Sweden. Not a single one of them would ever accept the notion that Germany had been the prime aggressor in the war, and extreme bitterness set in when Schnee's 'worst anticipations' were surpassed by the news that Alsace-Lorraine was being wrested from Germany, the Rhineland occupied, and the colonies seized. In Northern Rhodesia, as the rains began in earnest, Schnee, von Lettow-Vorbeck and 153 German colonials finally started to realise that 'only the gods knew what the future holds for Germany'[21] and her African empire.

At 11 a.m. on 25 November 1918, under a stormy rain-filled sky, Brigadier-General W.F.S. Edwards received von Lettow-Vorbeck's surrender at Abercorn. Lieutenant Boell, the official historian of the German campaign, recorded that 'a wrestling match that held the whole world in shock and disbelief, and which was probably unique in the history of the world, had finally drawn to a conclusion'.[22] It was a year to the day since the German commander had invaded Portuguese East Africa, and exactly two weeks after the signing of the Armistice in Europe; 34,000 British troops, supported by 71,000 carriers, remained in the field in East Africa. The guard of honour was provided by *askari* of 1/4KAR and the Northern Rhodesia Police. Interest in the German survivors, who looked 'hard as nails' though they obviously 'felt the surrender keenly',[23] was immense. Colonel Hawkins recorded his first impressions in the following words: 'Von Lettow himself turned out to be a very different man from what we had expected. A little over medium height, and wearing a short pointed beard, with fair hair turning grey, he is a fine-looking man of forty-nine . . . instead of the haughty Prussian one had expected to meet, he turned out to be a most courteous and perfectly mannered man: his behaviour throughout his captivity was a model to anyone in such a position.'[24] Von Lettow-Vorbeck was the first to admit, in conversation with Hawkins, that 'the luck of war' had run in his favour. He also revealed that his worst fear of the whole campaign was that Smuts would effect naval landings at Tanga and Dar-es-Salaam at the same time as his advance against Taveta in March 1916 – a strategy which, in his rush to end the campaign swiftly, Smuts had never seriously contemplated.

The official surrender document was signed by Edwards, von Lettow-Vorbeck, Spangenburg and Captain Anderson, and Edwards politely declined von Lettow-Vorbeck's offer of his sword. German officers were also permitted to retain their swords and revolvers. The fact that Schnee was not a signatory, when Dr Seitz had signed the capitulation of German South-West Africa three years earlier, was indicative of von Lettow-Vorbeck's insistence that the surrender of his troops did not signify a surrender of Germany's control of its East African colony. But it was anomalous: as Governor, Schnee was still technically the supreme commander in German East Africa, and his superior – Colonial Minister Dr Solf – was the supreme commander of all *Schutztruppe*. Whether this lapse in protocol was symptomatic of the pre-eminence over Schnee that von Lettow-Vorbeck had secured in the early months of the war, or merely of the collapse of *Ordnung* and *Protokolle* in Germany itself, is a moot point. The British inventory of men and arms recorded the presence at Abercorn of 155 Germans, and among them were the detachment commanders Otto, Köhl, Müller, Spangenburg, von Ruckteschell, Kempner[*] and von Scherbening and the two surviving artillery officers from the *Königsberg*, Apel and Wenig, who had been so instrumental to von Lettow-Vorbeck's success during the ten months in Portuguese East Africa. These were the remnants of more than 3,000 Europeans who had taken to the field during the campaign, of whom about one in five had been killed in combat, or died from their wounds or disease.[25] To ensure that their sacrifice had not been in vain, von Lettow-Vorbeck – the only German commander to have occupied British soil in the Great War – punctiliously insisted that the *Schutztruppe*'s one remaining field gun, thirty-seven (mostly British) machine-guns, and 1,071 (mostly Portuguese) rifles should count towards the total weaponry surrendered by Germany in Europe.

Interest in the 1,168 German *askari* was equally keen. Only 261 of them had been recruited during the year in Portuguese East Africa, and a majority of the survivors had served in the *Schutztruppe* for periods in excess of fifteen years. Most were Wamanyema, but many Wasukuma carriers had also taken up arms along the way. Of their former comrades, 6,308 had been killed in combat, died from disease, or been listed as missing presumed dead.[26] Three-quarters of the 2,000 remaining carriers, most of whom were Wasukuma, were discovered to have served right through the Portuguese East Africa campaign. For them, as for the *askari* and the 1,101 camp-followers (the wives, children and servants of the *askari*), a return home was finally possible.[†]

The surrender, at van Deventer's behest, was sensitively handled by Edwards. It needed to be. Article XVII of the Armistice agreement had only

---

[*] Franz Kempner was executed in 1944 for his part in the July plot to assassinate Adolf Hitler.
[†] The ration strength of British troops, including carriers, at the time of the surrender was a staggering 111,731.

stipulated that the German forces in East Africa should be 'evacuated', but the War Office had insisted that evacuation could only be effected if 'unconditional surrender and disarmament' took place. This was secured, by van Deventer's own admission, 'by a judicious mix of firmness and bluff'. Von Lettow-Vorbeck sensed that there was trickery afoot but, unable to secure confirmation of his suspicions from Berlin, he accepted the War Office's conditions under official protest. Van Deventer was quite clear in his own mind that 'we had no real right to demand [a surrender] at all'.[27] One consequence of surrender that caused considerable bitterness was that both the German combatants and the *askari* became POWs; equally contentious was the War Office's refusal to lend von Lettow-Vorbeck the two million Marks he owed his *askari* in back pay (a debt that Germany honoured eight years later). However dubious the means by which the surrender had been secured, there was a limit to how conciliatory Britain was prepared to be; and as one observer pointed out, 'there were many other Africans to whom the Germans owed money, but whom they were either unwilling or unable to pay'. Indeed there was no attempt – and never would be – to determine 'what the natives [had] lost[*] as a result of von Lettow-Vorbeck's 'total disregard of the barest needs of the native population' and his 'wholesale seizure of every vestige of food stuff left to them'[28] in both German and Portuguese East Africa. Indian traders were owed an estimated twenty million rupees as well, and no debt to impressed – as opposed to 'regular' – carriers was even recognised by German officers.

Although many British officers felt very strongly about such matters, perhaps surprisingly so, von Lettow-Vorbeck remarked that 'examples of discourtesy ... were absolutely exceptional'.[29] Furthermore, van Deventer insisted that during their voyage home the Germans should be 'granted the honours of war' and treated as ordinary citizens rather than POWs; and as they were transported up Lake Tanganyika to Kigoma on the *George*, and thence by railway to Tabora, British officers along the route were warned to be sensitive to the fact that the journey was likely to 'cause feelings to run high'.[30] At Tabora tears were shed by German and *askari* alike as they were finally separated and the *askari* continued, during a brief internment before being allowed home, to demonstrate haughty contempt for their British counterparts whom they had so often bested. On occasions they were not even averse to disarming and thrashing their camp guards.

* Steer, p. 300. See also p. 264: 'In decrees of 1915 and 1916 the German government had banned cash holdings in excess of business and personal requirements; holders of surplus cash were forced to accept interim 3% notes, which Germany covenanted to pay, and quite naturally did not pay, six months after the war.'

In Dar-es-Salaam, the Germans were received by General Sheppard, van Deventer's Chief of Staff, and in January 1919 von Lettow-Vorbeck and his retinue of German officers and NCOs sailed for Europe on the SS *Transvaal* (formerly the *Feldmarschall*). They were fortunate. Shipping was in desperately short supply and their comrades in POW camps in Egypt and India would, like many Allied troops, have to wait more than a year to be repatriated. As he reached Europe von Lettow-Vorbeck reflected that 'we East Africans know only too well that our achievements cannot be compared with the military deeds and devotion of those in the homeland ... [but] we had come back home unsullied, and that Teutonic sense of loyalty peculiar to us Germans had kept its head high even under the conditions of war in the tropics'.[31] After returning to Berlin he and his men paraded beneath the Brandenburg Gate on 2 March 1919, receiving a heroes' welcome from a populace which had for the most part refused to accept the reality of defeat in the field. But the Germany that von Lettow-Vorbeck knew, and whose nationalism and militarism he embodied, had ceased to exist.

Within a few months of his triumphant return von Lettow-Vorbeck, 'the Hindenburg of Africa', was shot at by a 'revolutionary' after delivering a lecture in the Pomeranian city of Stargard about the victory at Tanga but, undaunted, he soon took to the field again. He was, despite his four years of extreme privation in the African bush, still motivated by the same fanatical single-mindedness, bordering on *Eitelkeit* ('conceit'), when he led a *Freiwilligkorps* onto the streets of Hamburg where – with Kraut, Wintgens and Köhl on his staff – he was charged with suppressing the Spartacist uprising. Then, in March 1920, at the age of fifty, he became a leading figure in the Kapp Putsch, the nationalist revolt against the Social Democrats which sought to install a military dictatorship in anarchic Germany. The coup attempt failed and von Lettow-Vorbeck, fortunate to escape imprisonment, formally retired in May. It was the end of an extraordinary military career, but he and Schnee soon began another campaign which they would never abandon: the fight to secure the return of the German colonies. Both men lived into the 1960s, having survived into their nineties.

Among his former opponents there were many who would always feel nothing but respect for von Lettow-Vorbeck. In 1929 he was even invited as guest of honour to a campaign 'reunion banquet' in London. But there were some who accused him of having a 'brutal heart',[32] of 'wanton ruthlessness'.[33] In their eyes, the whole campaign was caused by German militarism gone mad and the Allies' dogged insistence on countering it at every turn. It could have been otherwise, as one senior colonial administrator in East Africa perceptively pointed out: 'Had we not invaded German East Africa', wrote Charles Dundas, 'it was quite possible that von Lettow-Vorbeck would have been compelled to surrender in order to save his own people, particularly the German women and children, from extreme privation. Instead we relieved him of that burden and left him unencumbered to pursue his tactics of attrition. One wonders at times whether it would not have been more profitable to content ourselves with holding our own borders, leaving the Germans to stew in their own juice', he mused, before concluding that 'in a sense it all seemed so futile . . .'.[34]

'There Came a Darkness'

———•———

The death toll among the 126,972 British troops who had served in the East Africa campaign was officially recorded as 11,189 – a mortality rate of nine per cent – and total casualties, including the wounded and missing, were a little over 22,000. The loss of life among armed combatants was, however, only the tip of the iceberg. By the end of the 1917 mass levy of military carriers, without whom the campaign could never have been fought at all, a majority of adult males in the five British territories bordering German East Africa had been coerced into manning the supply lines. In some areas, such as British East Africa's Teita district, three-quarters of able-bodied men served away from home; in others, in German East Africa, men found themselves impressed first by the Germans and then by the British. The consequence of mobilising manpower on this scale was 'a maelstrom of gigantic proportions',[1] and in August 1917 the Acting Governor of British East Africa had to inform van Deventer that the country's manpower resources were exhausted. By the end of the war more than one million carriers had been recruited by the British in their colonies and in German East Africa, of whom no fewer than 95,000 had died. One third of a small labour contingent recruited in the Seychelles never returned from the war; one in five men in British East Africa's Carrier Corps died; and at least 41,000 Africans conscripted by the British in occupied German East Africa perished – the highest number from any of the recruiting 'pools' in East Africa.

When the death toll among British troops was added to that of the carriers the official 'butcher's bill' in the East Africa campaign exceeded 100,000 souls. The true figure was undoubtedly much higher: as many a British official admitted, 'the full tale of the mortality among [the] native carriers will never be told'.[2] Even 100,000 deaths is a sobering enough figure. It is almost double the number of Australian or Canadian or Indian troops who gave their lives in the Great War; indeed it is equivalent to the combined casualties – the dead *and* wounded – sustained by Indian troops. It is as if *the entire* African workforce employed at the time in the mines of South Africa had been wiped out. Yet the East Africa campaign remains, by and large, a forgotten theatre of war.

The scale of the tragedy was not immediately apparent, either in Europe or in Africa, not least because the compilation of statistics was delayed by 'the many problems of demobilisation'.[3] Even in the summer of 1919 the Chief of the Colonial Division of the American delegation at the Versailles Peace Conference remarked that the number of 'native victims ... may be too long to give to the world and Africa'.[4] He was correct. There were many European combatants who paid tribute to the King's African Rifles, which had earned a reputation for being 'fit to fight against or alongside any troops in the world',[5] and about whose *askari* one colonel wrote 'they do not know what fear means; they have won the war for us in East Africa';[6] and there were many, like General Northey, who awarded the carriers 'the palm of merit'. But when the mortality rate among the latter became common knowledge in Whitehall it was deemed to be a 'bloody tale' that was best ignored, or even suppressed. As one Colonial Office official put it, in particularly unsavoury terms, the conduct of the campaign 'only stopped short of a scandal because the people who suffered most were the carriers – and after all, who cares about native carriers?'[7] This was not entirely fair to the many British soldiers, missionaries and administrators who expressed great concern about the horrors they had witnessed in East Africa in diaries and official reports. But for the most part their opinions did not find their way onto the agenda of politicians and civil servants back home who were preoccupied with 'bigger issues' elsewhere (or with excoriating Germany's colonial credentials).

Many of the deaths, among carriers and troops, could be attributed to another 'scandal' about which little was heard after the war. By the end of 1917 a number of 'whistle-blowers' had alerted the War Office to the lamentable state of the medical establishment in East Africa, and their allegations were too serious to be ignored. In the year ending October 1917 twelve times more soldiers had died of disease than in combat, and there were fewer than 13,000 hospital beds available for carriers – of which half were so far from the front lines as to render them unreachable for those struck down by malaria, dysentery or pneumonia in German East Africa. This, combined with sanitary arrangements which 'courted failure from the first' and inadequate rations, was the principal cause of a rise in the carrier mortality rate to almost thirty per cent in July 1917; and even in Nairobi plague was endemic. When Dr Pike compiled his exhaustive report on the state of the campaign's medical facilities he pulled no punches, concluding that there was 'much to regret in the medical history of this campaign'. The officer in charge of the infectious diseases hospital at Bombo, 4/KAR's home depot in Uganda, was court-martialled; the officer in charge of No. 3 British Hospital in Nairobi was censured for never having visited Kijabe Sanatorium, which was also his responsibility; and the four senior medical officers in East Africa were summoned to face charges 'on the score of discipline or efficiency as the case may be'. But Pike had to qualify his report to avoid it being 'buried', and the price paid for achieving any improvement in the situation was his statement that the blame for the death toll among the carriers, while 'a most regrettable occurrence', should not 'rest with the medical authorities'.[8] The implication was clear: carriers were expendable whereas troops were not. But even when the Court of Enquiry finally convened to consider the charges against the senior medical officers, the accused had all returned to India and were officially exonerated a year later by the Army Council.

The suffering borne by the indigenous populations of East Africa was not confined to those who were recruited for carrier duties. The principal consequence of a drain on manpower unparalleled since the 1870s, when Arab slavers had annually exported 25,000 Africans to the Middle East, was the severe impairment of the capacity for survival of those left behind; and when the rains failed in British East Africa in late 1917 and early 1918 famine reduced those who barely managed to eke out an existence in years of good harvests to a state of total destitution. By mid summer, it was reported that 'the people subsisted in many parts on wild roots and grasses' and there were rumours 'that some of the people had resorted to cannibalism' (rumours which 'were never substantiated' but which the administration had 'good reason to fear ... were true').[9] One European farmer, Llewelyn Powys, described the situation around Nanyuki in the following words:

> famine stalked through the land with Pestilence galling his kibe. Week after week the country lay prostrate under the blank stare of a soulless sun. Month after month the waters of the lake sank lower and lower ... It was as though the earth itself was undergoing some appalling process of putrefaction. The air was tainted, the flaked dusty mould stank. Everywhere one came across the carcasses of animals dead from exhaustion, carcasses with long muddy tongues protruding ... the vultures grew plump as Michaelmas geese ... the sun rose and sank in a blinding heaven, and under its hideous presence all sensitive life trembled and shrank.[10]

Famine and its attendant diseases were not the only calamities to befall the indigenous populations of eastern and southern Africa. In the British colonies the war also brought tax rises and the enactment of increasingly repressive land and labour laws; while in South Africa the white population campaigned relentlessly for greater racial segregation, paving the way for a plethora of discriminatory legislation in the 1920s. At the end of 1918 the South African National Native Council wrote to King George V emphasising the loyalty of Africans during the war and requesting that 'London intervene to lessen their oppression and see that voting rights were extended to the African population',[11] but the plea was ignored; and the *Kabaka* of Uganda and his chiefs beseeched the colonial government to put an end to *kasanvu* labour, which required all young men to work for set periods on government projects, but it took four more years to secure its abolition. Throughout sub-Saharan Africa it seemed, as one enlightened Norwegian resident of British East Africa put it, that '"all" that was wanted from Africans was that they should work for foreigners for a minimum wage without consideration for their betterment in any way';[12] and that African interests, though 'proclaimed in public as the basis of Allied policy' were, in the words of one disenchanted British administrator, 'largely disregarded in private'.[13] When an officer with 5/SAI noted in late 1917 that 'people in South Africa write and tell me they are sick of hearing about the German East Africa campaign,' his appropriate riposte was to say that he was 'sure that these poor natives in East Africa are pretty sick of it too'.[14]

The worst calamity of all was saved for last. For the surviving troops and carriers on both sides, and for the civilian populations prostrated by four years of fighting in East Africa, October 1918 – 'Black October' – brought an even greater disaster than total war. The records of the military and civilian authorities say remarkably little about the advent of the 'Spanish' influenza epidemic, or the 'disease of the wind' as it was referred to in Abyssinia.[*] It was almost as if its effects were beyond their comprehension, and to begin with it was not easy to separate deaths caused by this new scourge from those caused by a host of other ailments besetting combatant and non-combatant alike. Even von Lettow-Vorbeck's surviving doctors, who after four years in the field were well versed in treating almost every affliction known to man, were unable to determine the moment when the 'bronchial virus' which spread like wildfire through the German ranks in September 1918 was replaced by something altogether more horrifying. But within weeks of the Armistice Captain Walter Spangenburg, eleven other Germans, and 279 German *askari* and porters – one in eight of those who had surrendered at Abercorn – had died from the flu, and deaths in the British ranks had soared to four times their level in October. Only then did it become clear that East Africa was in the grip of an epidemic which 'Western' medicine was completely unable to combat, and that peace had brought no respite from the suffering.

Among the civilian population of sub-Saharan Africa this new curse, so virulent that a man could quite simply drop dead while walking home to his *shamba*, was simply beyond imagination. It arrived in Mombasa and South Africa in September, in southern Nyasaland at the beginning of October, and

---

[*] For example H.R. Wallis's *Handbook of Uganda*, published in 1920, failed to the mention the epidemic in its narrative of the Great War, and there was no reference to it in the 1925 *Report of the East Africa Commission*.

in Portuguese East Africa in the third week in October; and the new 'clinical front'[15] rapidly showed itself to be even more fluid than the 'war front' in Portuguese East Africa. It spread along the railways and lake steamer routes (conduits intended for economic development which in the past four years had only brought death and destruction to Africa); it spread along the vast lines of communication supporting the troops; it spread with soldiers and porters returning to their homes as the war reached its final stages; and it spread along labour migration roots, particularly into the mines of southern Africa.

By the time von Lettow-Vorbeck and his German officers reached Dar-es-Salaam the situation was dire. 'In Sea View camp,' wrote a surviving Frontiersman,

> there were very few left standing; the bugles [were] all employed in blowing the last post while the sun was yet high in the heavens. A party of twenty details arrived from Nairobi; in twenty-four hours only one was left. The sick and the dead lay thickly in the hospital beds and on stretchers laid along the passages. New burial grounds were started; native and Indian *fundi* made coffins by lamplight and wondered if they themselves would occupy them ... rumour averred that this was THE END: that a God weary of war had determined to wipe humanity off the world by means of a plague more fatal than man's destructiveness ... Out in the bush even the baboons were dying in their thousands.[16]

He might have added 'out to sea' as well: one in six of the 155 sappers of the 14th Company QVO Sappers died during their voyage back to Bombay in November.

In South Africa one returning soldier described how a 'fear and horror of the dreaded disease hung over the entire country'. Then, in next to no time, 'the disease was suddenly transformed to an epidemic'; then 'it took on the proportions of a national emergency'; and eventually 'it turned out to be a disaster, little less than a national catastrophe'.[17] Among the South African gunners of the South African Mounted Rifles, a unit which had served in Nyasaland since early 1916, eight-four men died in October alone;[18] while in the Transvaal Labour Bureau former combatant Adam Payne described how 'in many cases the reports [of casualties on the mines] did not come in because all the officials of the mine hospital were themselves down with the epidemic'. 'The native patients', he continued, 'were so numerous that they overflowed from the beds to the floor, and from the floor of the hospitals to the compound rooms ... often those attending to the sick themselves collapsed suddenly [and] the ambulances were trotting the streets day and night.'[19] From a staff of thirteen in his Germiston office, only Payne was not struck down. In a matter of a few weeks influenza claimed 250,000–350,000 lives in South Africa; while in some of the mines of Southern Rhodesia the death rate was as high as sixteen per cent, and even in southern Africa's isolated rural areas it was between three and ten per cent.[20]

In British East Africa, the situation was no different. Revd Horace Philp started work as a medical officer on 2 November 1918 at Fort Hall, in Kikuyu province; within eight weeks there were an estimated 17,000 deaths in his district of Nyeri, while the Native Council in Ulu district, centred on Machakos, reported 8,000 deaths among a population of 120,000. By the time the epidemic abated it had killed 70,000 people, one tenth of the population of a province which had already lost a fifth of the 45,000 men sent for carrier duty during the war. For British East Africa as a whole, the official estimate of the death toll was 160,000; but it is unlikely that fewer than 200,000 men, women and children died – a substantially greater loss of life than that caused by the war itself (and almost a tenth of the total population of the protectorate).

The governments of the British colonies in sub-Saharan Africa were powerless in the face of the epidemic, but they did at least instigate emergency relief measures to counter the famine that followed. In occupied German East Africa, however, a country whose most productive areas had been fought over and ravaged by both sides, the skeleton British administration was hard-pressed to arrange sufficient food for the military establishment, let alone civilians; and even had food been available there was no transport. The consequences were appalling, particularly in the outlying areas of a country considerably larger than Germany itself. In 'Kondeland', for example, in the south-west, at least ten per cent of the population died in the epidemic and subsequent famine; and in some districts the death toll was as high as twenty per cent.

African responses to the epidemic varied. Many tribes among whom diseases of one sort or another were endemic, and for whom survival had always been precarious, regarded it with customary resignation: it was simply *shauri ya mungu* – 'the will of God'.[*] Others attributed it to witchcraft. And some of those who suffered the greatest loss of life by dint of their proximity to the war or their close involvement with the colonial economy naturally blamed the 'White Man's Palaver'. One phrase, however, was common to many oral histories: 'there came a darkness'.[21] By the time the epidemic was over 1.5–2 million people are estimated to have died in sub-Saharan Africa – a higher

---

[*] It should be borne in mind that, for example, infant mortality rates in areas as disparate as those of Teita district, the 'Swahili' coast, and Uganda were fifteen to twenty per cent; that bilharzia affected sixty to seventy per cent of the coastal Wadigo; and that respiratory and venereal disease were endemic to eastern and southern African indigenous populations.

death toll than that of French troops in the war. It was the final, diabolical confirmation that the Great War in East Africa was above all a war against nature, and a humanitarian disaster without parallel until the post-Independence era.

The willingness of many British combatants and colonial officials to acknowledge publicly the horrors that war had brought to the people of East and Central Africa may not have been shared by many in Whitehall; but German participants in the campaign experienced no 'war guilt' whatsoever – and the fate of Africans under German rule was even worse than that of those under British rule. It was symptomatic of the German attitude to the civilian populations of Ruanda, Urundi and German East Africa that no attempt was made even to keep records of how many civilians were conscripted for carrier duties, let alone the casualties among them: the campaign's official historian simply noted that 'of the loss of levies, carriers and boys [we could] make no overall count due to the absence of detailed sickness records'.[22] The total was certainly not less than 350,000 men, women and children;[23] and it is inconceivable that the death rate among them was lower than one in seven. Furthermore, in stark contrast to common practice in the British colonies, these carriers were seldom paid anything for their service; and when famine, caused by the wholesale 'theft of food, cattle, and men'[24] by the military authorities, descended on many parts of the country the people were simply left to starve. The people of Ugogo district, for example, between Kilimatinde and Dodoma, were forced to provide some 35,000 carriers for the *Schutztruppe* in 1916 as well as large quantities of grain and cattle; and as a direct result of this, and changes in the pattern of rainfall, a famine the following year killed fully one fifth of the population.[25] At least 300,000 civilians are thought to have perished in Ruanda, Urundi and German East Africa as a direct result of the German authorities' conduct of the war (*excluding* those conscripted for carrier service) – an even higher number of deaths than during the Maji-Maji Rebellion a decade earlier;[26] and by the time British administrators and troops occupied the former German colonies they were already, in effect, little more than slave states.

This was not how German officials and soldiers regarded the state of affairs in their East African colonies. Von Lettow-Vorbeck and Schnee subsequently expressed great pride in the fact that as many as two million Africans had 'served the military in some capacity or another'[27] by providing supplies or services, and for them this constituted definitive proof of the loyalty (rather than suffering) of 'Germany's Africans'. There was not the slightest sign of recognition, either in their accounts or those of any German combatant, that the tragic effects of the war had been compounded by the extreme severity of their regime; and in less than two decades a Nazi publication, *Deutschland braucht Kolonien* ('Germany needs colonies'), would claim that just 1,000 carriers had died supporting the *Schutztruppe*. The sacrifice of hundreds of thousands of Africans had simply been erased from German history, although the myth of their 'loyalty' had not.

There was also a striking absence of any post-war reassessment in Germany of stereotypical views of Africans in the aftermath of the war. The same was certainly true of South Africa as well. But Bishop Willis of Uganda, on the other hand, voiced questions which many a British missionary, colonial official and soldier had shown themselves willing to address during the campaign. In a speech in 1919 he declared that Africans had 'met Europeans, all of different classes, some deeply prejudiced against colour in any form, some entirely free from race prejudice; some who believed in keeping the African in his place, some who equally believed in treating every man with respect. And for the first time Europeans in many cases met Africans in direct and personal contact, marching together, fighting and suffering together ... and many a European reviewed and revised his idea of the African from this contact'.[28] The lesson to be learnt, he asserted, was that 'African and European in Africa need one another'; and he warned that any attempt 'to put the clock back, and arrest the upward progress of these millions of [African] men and women must inevitably bring with it its own terrible nemesis'.[29] The extent to which his words were heeded by cash-strapped British governments during the next decade is a moot point. What is significant is that there was a tacit admission by the Allied colonial powers, even allegedly 'dissolute' Portugal and 'tyrannical' Belgium, that something needed to be done to put their colonial 'houses' in order – whereas in post-war Germany the colonial lobby recognised nothing untoward in the way that Germany had ruled in Africa, or fought in Africa, and only saw what it wanted to see: an unflinching and unquestioning loyalty on the part of millions of contented colonial subjects. *Koloniale Schuld*, 'colonial guilt', was as conspicuously absent as war guilt.

While the populations of sub-Saharan Africa struggled to cope with the aftermath of the influenza pandemic the fate of Germany's colonies was decided at the Versailles Peace Conference. The process was described by Lord Milner as a 'huge scramble' to redraw the colonial map of Africa; and by Major Grogan, the former Liaison Officer with the Belgian forces in East Africa who was his adviser on boundary questions, as 'an astounding [education] into how the great international affairs of state are adjusted'.[30] At one point, when Lloyd George was considering whether to cede Jubaland, 25,000 square miles of north-eastern British East Africa, to Italy, Milner asked Grogan 'where is it, and has it any significance?'. 'Thus,' remarked Grogan, 'are empires made and unmade.'[31]

One particularly influential Belgian report submitted at the conference 'rejected German claims that they had not undertaken military preparations in their colonies and were not responsible for the spread of the war to Africa' and also 'discounted the argument that the performance of Germany's African troops deserved some compensation'. The undoubted success of von Lettow-Vorbeck's opposition to the Allied forces was attributed solely 'to his ability to withdraw and the use of terror to ensure local support'; and the report concluded that Germany had 'proved incapable of understanding and administering colonial populations'.[32] George Beer, Chief of the Colonial Section of the American delegation, was equally damning: the German colonies were not, in his opinion, 'as in the British commonwealth, regarded as parts of one large political aggregate, each of which must be administered partly in its own interest ... [and] were never regarded as ends in themselves, but merely as means to spread *Kultur*, to reinforce prestige and power, and to add to the wealth of Germany'.[33] As a result of these and other equally vituperative submissions Germany was summarily dispossessed of her colonies, and Britain and South Africa emerged from Versailles as the clear 'winners' in eastern and southern Africa: South Africa was handed German South-West Africa, and German East Africa became British Tanganyika. Ruanda and Urundi, to the considerable annoyance of Smuts and Milner, were handed to Belgium (an occurrence which would have been unimaginable ten years earlier, after the revelations concerning King Leopold's murderous regime in the Congo); and Portugal was thrown a scrap in the form of the Kionga Triangle.

Among British imperialists, and South African adherents to the imperial cause, there was a palpable sense of triumph at the outcome of the final phase of the Scramble for Africa. An all-red 'Cape to Cairo' route, sought for a generation by imperialist diehards convinced of its commercial and strategic importance, had become a reality; and from 1919 'Rhodes's Dream' even began to appear in travellers' guide-books. In theory it had become possible to traverse the African continent end to end in just fifty-three days (via 4,456 miles of railway, 2,004 miles on board steamers, and 363 miles of road) without ever setting foot on territory not controlled by the British Empire. The war had been, as von Lettow-Vorbeck had always maintained it would be, 'decided on the fields of battle in Europe',[34] but this was not at all the outcome that he – or his political masters in Berlin – had envisaged.

Although Africa was as important to the colonial powers at Versailles as at any time since the late 1890s, Africans themselves were given no greater voice than 'ordinary' Europeans. Missionaries were deputed to collate and express African views; but they, like the politicians, had their own expansionist agenda and many shaped their submissions accordingly. Furthermore, as one British colonial official pointed out, Africans were 'not so simple as to tell the victor that they preferred to be ruled by the vanquished [and] if the truth be known, the native might have said "a plague on both your houses".[35] Despite the obvious shortcomings of the process Musinga, the paramount chief in Ruanda, obligingly denounced his former allies by declaring that 'the Germans did not pay attention to my affairs ... they left me as a wild animal';[36] and a host of witnesses were found to castigate German 'frightfulness'. Only one major concession to 'African interests' emerged from Versailles: with 'selfish imperialism' of the pre-war variety on trial, and a prevailing sense that Africans 'could no longer be bandied about like so many sheep',[37] Germany's former colonies – at the insistence of America – were not simply handed over to the victors lock, stock and barrel. As 'mandates', described by one historian as 'Imperialism's new clothes',[38] they were supposed to be administered as a 'sacred trust of civilisation' under the auspices of the League of Nations; but for most Africans there would prove to be little distinction between colonies and mandates. In the post-war era the cash was simply not available, even had the political will existed, to turn high-flown ideals and aspirations into reality.

It would take another world war, in which African *askari* would serve with equal distinction, for the politicisation of the indigenous population of East Africa to begin in earnest. But in 1935 fifty chiefs assembled in Machakos to inform Dr Arthurs, a missionary, of their views on the call-up of the King's African Rifles reserves in response to Mussolini's invasion of Abyssinia. 'The position is not the same as in 1914–18', Arthurs was told, 'nor would we assist in any cause which would involve spearing our fellow Africans. You called us to help in the war of Fourteen–Eighteen, and we willingly went, but if you called us now we would ask the reasons and have to be convinced of the justice of the cause before we would go again.'[39] Their suspicions were justified. African colonies were still viewed as valuable bargaining counters in Whitehall, and when the Abyssinian invasion was accompanied by the raising of the swastika by Germans who had been allowed to return to East Africa, British politicians began to explore the possibility of appeasing Hitler by handing back the country that they had seized at such vast expense.

Africa was once again a pawn in the clash between Germany and her European neighbours, so much so that in 1938 Tanganyika was even suggested as a possible outlet for Germany's Jewish population. Hitler's reply was forthright: while he was certainly interested in the return of Germany's colonies, 'he could not be expected to ask the German people to turn over to the Jews ... territories drenched in "the blood of German heroes" where von Lettow-Vorbeck had fought'.[40] The following year he was still articulating colonial demands, although more preoccupied with the *Drang nach Osten*, and just for good measure conferred upon a somewhat ambivalent sixty-nine-year-old von Lettow-Vorbeck the honorary rank of *General der Infanterie*. The wheel had seemingly turned full circle.

'The Lonely Graves'
(To Those Who Fell in East Africa, 1914–1918)

by Malcolm Humphery

Full many suns have gone their ways,
Since you were laid beneath the plains,
To memory belong those days,
And lasting stillness with you reigns.

The tramp of feet, the boom of gun,
The bullet's hiss, and wounded's groan –
Then, when the fighting has been done,
You were left there, dead and alone.

Nought but the wind now bends the grass,
Cicadas o'er you shrill their song,
And through the forest, as they pass,
The lions echo loud and long.

The silent years go drifting by
As clouds, and yet you do not mind,
Lonely, yet not alone, you lie:
You live in hearts of those behind.

APPENDICES

APPENDIX ONE

German East Africa *Schutztruppe*: Dispositions July 1914

Commander: Oberstleutnant P. von Lettow-Vorbeck
Staff Officers: Major A. Kepler, Hptm. G. Kraut, Hptm. T. Tafel
Adjutant: Oberlt K. Göring
Ordnance Officer: Lt E. Müller

Feldkompanie	Garrison	Officers
1/FK	Aruscha	Hptm. Willmann, Lt Boell, Lt Körbling
2/FK	Iringa	Hptm. Styx, Oberlt Falkenstein, Oberlt Aumann (at Ubena)
3/FK	Lindi	Hptm. Doering, Lt Freiherr von Grote, Lt Krüger
4/FK	Kilimatinde	Hptm. Rothert, Lt Kaufmann, Lt Freiherr von Lyncker, Lt Goetz, Oberlt von Linde-Suden (at Ssingida)
5/FK	Neu-Langenburg/ Massoko	Hptm. von Langenn-Steinkeller, Oberlt von Veltheim, Lt Kieckhöfer
6/FK	Udjidji	Hptm. Freiherr von Hammerstein-Gesmold, Lt Poppe, Oberlt Gerlich (at Kasulu)
7/FK	Bukoba	Hptm. Bock von Wülfingen, Lt Bergmann, Lt Bender, Oberlt Freiherr von Haxthausen (at Biaramulo)
8/FK	Tabora	Hptm. Fischer, Lt Bauer, Lt Naumann
9/FK	Usumbura	Hptm. Otto, Oberlt Spalding, Lt Meyer
10/FK	Dar-es-Salaam	Oberlt von Chappuis, Oberlt Henneberger, Lt Gutknecht, Lt Spangenburg
11/FK	Kissenji	Hptm. Stemmermann, Oberlt Köhl, Oberlt von Busse, Lt Erdmann, Lt Freiherr von Stosch
12/FK	Mahenge	Hptm. von Grawert, Lt Walde, Lt Schroeder
13/FK	Kondoa-Irangi	Hptm. Hans Schulz, Lt von Oppen, Lt Langen
14/FK	Muansa	Hptm. Braunschweig, Lt von Kleist, Lt Recke, Oberlt Giehrl (at Ikoma)

Principal recruiting depot (Dar-es-Salaam) – Hptm. P. Baumstark, Lt K. Wolff

Four new companies were formed in 1914 from the police and former *askari*:
15/FK (Moshi)
16/FK (Tanga)
17/FK (Bagamoyo)
18/FK (Dar-es-Salaam)

The following senior officers were transferred from government to military service after the outbreak of war
Hptm. M. Wintgens (resident of Ruanda)
Lt E. von Heyden-Linden (Dr Schnee's adjutant)
Hptm. F. von Kornatzki (Inspector of Police)
Oberlt F. Lincke (Deputy Inspector of Police)
Lt E. von Brandis (Commandant of Police HQ)
Lt W. Schreiner (Police HQ)
Hptm. R. von Kaltenborn-Stachau (artillery expert, arrived on the blockade-runner *Marie* in March 1916)

Former German Army and *Schutztruppe* officers resident in German East Africa

Major G. Schlobach	Hptm. K. Freiherr von Ledebur
Major W. von Stuemer	Hptm. R. Klinghardt
Hptm. F. Richter	Hptm. E. Gudowius
Hptm. T. von Prince	Hptm. K. Schimmer
Hptm. T. von Hassel	Oberlt W. von Debschitz

Active list and retired officers visiting German East Africa at the outbreak of war

Generalmajor K. Wahle	Oberlt W. Vorberg
Hptm. J. von Boemcken	Lt E. von Lieberman

The source for these lists is Ludwig Boell's *Die Operationen in Ostafrika*, p. 21. Certain minor details are contradicted by other leading sources: for example, Maillard and Schröder's *Das Offizierkorps der Schutztruppe für Deutsch-Ostafrika im Weltkrieg 1914–1918* lists brothers named von Busse, but neither were regular army officers with 11/FK. It should also be noted that Boell's list of government officials who transferred to the military during 1914 and his list of former *Schutztruppe* officers resident in German East Africa are incomplete.

Note on the composition of German *Feldkompanien*
1. The average peacetime establishment of a *Feldkompanie* was three German officers, two German NCOs, one medical officer and 160 African NCOs and *askari*. Each self-contained unit was equipped with two to three machine-guns, and was typically supported by thirty to fifty irregulars known as *ruga-ruga* and approximately 250 porters. About two-thirds of the *askari* were recruited in German East Africa and one third in Sudan, Abyssinia and Somalia.
2. According to Boell (1), p. 28 a total of 3,595 Europeans and 14,598 *askari* served in the *Schutztruppe* during the campaign, and the greatest strength was achieved in March 1916 (3,007 Europeans and 12,100 *askari*).

Note on German ranks and their British equivalents

Army

    Generalmajor – Major-General

    Oberst – Colonel

    Oberstleutnant (abbr. Oberstlt) – Lieutenant-Colonel

    Hauptmann (abbr. Hptm.) – Captain

    Oberleutnant (abbr. Oberlt) – First Lieutenant

    Leutnant (abbr. Lt) – Second Lieutenant

    Feldwebel/Vizefeldwebel/Sergeant – Sergeant-Major/Sergeant/Sergeant

    Wachtmeister/Vizewachtmeister – Sergeant (GEA police)

    Zahlmeister/Unterzahlmeister – Paymaster

    Kriegsgerichtsrat – Provost-Marshal

    (Feld-)Intendantur – Quartermaster

Navy

    Kapitän (abbr. Kapt.) – Captain

    Kapitänleutnant (abbr. Kptlt) – Lieutenant-Commander

    Korvettenkapitän (abbr. Kvtkpt.) – Lieutenant-Commander

    Oberleutnant (abbr. Oberlt) – Lieutenant

    Leutnant (abbr. Lt) – Second Lieutenant

    Oberingenieur (abbr. Obering.) – Chief Engineer

APPENDIX TWO

Indian Expeditionary Forces 'B' and 'C': Summarised Orders of Battle 1914

1. INDIAN EXPEDITIONARY FORCE 'B'

General Officer Commanding: Maj.-Gen. A.E. Aitken

27th (Bangalore) Infantry Brigade (Brig.-Gen. R. Wapshare)
    2nd Battalion Loyal North Lancs
    63rd Palamcottah Light Infantry
    98th Infantry
    101st Grenadiers

Imperial Service Infantry Brigade (Brig.-Gen. M.J. Tighe)
    13th Rajputs
    2nd Kashmir Rifles
    3rd Kashmir Rifles (half-battalion)
    3rd Gwalior Rifles (half-battalion)

Force Troops
    61st KGO Pioneers
    28th Mountain Battery (six guns)
    Faridkot Sappers and Miners (one company)
    No. 25 and No. 26 Railway Companies

    Plus ancillary units

    Force strength: 7,972 troops and 2,164 Indian Army followers

2. INDIAN EXPEDITIONARY FORCE 'C'

General Officer Commanding: Brig.-Gen. J.M. Stewart

29th Punjabis
Jhind Imperial Service Infantry (four companies)
Bharatpur Imperial Service Infantry (four companies)
Kapurthala Imperial Service Infantry (four companies)
Rampur Imperial Service Infantry (four companies)
27th Mountain Battery (six guns)
Calcutta Volunteer Battery (six 15-pdrs)
Volunteer Maxim Gun Company (four machine-guns)

Force strength: approximately 3,000 troops and 2,500 followers

APPENDIX THREE

German East Africa *Schutztruppe*:
Order of Battle 5 March 1916

Commander-in-Chief: Oberst P. von Lettow-Vorbeck

I. NORTH-EAST COMMAND

Note: * indicates naval rank

Neu Moschi – Headquarters
  General Staff Officer: Hptm. Tafel
  Adjutant: Oberlt E. Müller
  Ordnance Officer: Oberlt Boell
  Quartermaster: Hptm. Freiherr von Ledebur/Hptm. Richter
  Provost-Marshal: Dr Goorman
  Hptm. Feilke
  Commander of the Northern Railway: Lt Holtz
  Communications Officer: Feldpostdirektor Rothe

  4/FK – Hptm. Göring
  21/FK – Oberlt von Ruckteschell

Kilimanjaro and Taveta district
  A. Lake Jipe (southern end): 5/SchK (Hptm. R. Doering)

  B. Taveta: Abt. Schulz (Hptm. H. Schulz)
  6/FK – Hptm. Vorberg
  9/FK – Hptm. Otto
  15/FK – Hptm. Lincke
  24/FK – Oberlt Schülein
  30/FK – Oberlt Werner
  C73 9cm field gun

  C. Salaita Hill and Rombo: Abt. Kraut (Major G. Kraut)
  18/FK – Hptm. von Kornatzki
  27/FK – Oberlt Osman
  'W' Kompanie – Lt Volkmar*
  Abt. Rombo – Oberstlt Freiherr von Bock
  Feldbatterie Sternheim (three 6cm field guns, one 3.7cm revolver canon) – Oberlt
    Sternheim

Kahe district
  A. Northern Railway
  Abt. Bahnschutz – Lt Kluge
  Linie Kompanie – Hptm. von Bodecker

B. Wilhelmstal: Abt. Wilhelmstal (Hptm. K. Freiherr von Ledebur)
C. Lembeni: Abt. Stemmermann (Hptm. P. Stemmermann)

11/FK – Oberlt von Lieberman
16/FK – Oberlt E. von Brandis

D. Pantzier Hill: Abt. Demuth (Hptm. G. Demuth)
1/FK – Oberlt Merensky
10/FK – Oberlt Steinhaüser
19/FK – Oberlt Freiherr von Unterrichter-Rechtental
6/SchK – Hptm. Kohl
7/SchK – Oberlt Gaehtgens
Feldbatterie Fromme (two 3.7cm field guns, one 4.7cm field gun) – Lt Fromme

E. Himo: Abt. Augar (Hptm. G. Augar)
3/FK – Oberlt von Busse
13/FK – Oberlt Langen
14/FK – Hptm. Freiherr von Haxthausen

Aruscha district: Abt. Fischer (Major E. Fischer)
Abt. Aruscha – Lt Kaempfe
8/SchK (mounted) – Major von Boemcken
8/FK – Hptm. Bauer
9/SchK (mounted) – Oberlt Freiherr von Lyncker
28/FK – Hptm. Rothert

Total strength of North-East Command: approximately 800 Europeans and 5,200 *askari* with forty-seven machine-guns and ten field guns.

2. OTHER *SCHUTZTRUPPE* DISPOSITIONS (NORTH)

Tanga Battalion (Major P. Baumstark)
17/FK – Hptm. Adler
4/SchK – Oberlt Methner
Tanga Kompanie – Oberlt Auracher
Pangani Kompanie – Kptlt Schütt*
'N' Artillery Company – Kvtkpt. Schoenfeld*
Tanga Coastal Patrol – Oberlt Zahn

Muansa Command (Hptm. U. von Chappuis)
'A' Kompanie – Oberlt von Oppen
'B' Kompanie – Lt Gunzert
'D' Kompanie – Lt von Gynz-Rekowski
'E' Kompanie – Unterzahlmeister Rehse
'F' Kompanie – Vizefeldwebel Piorr

Bukoba Command (Hptm. E. Gudowius)
7/ResK – Lt Kalman
'C' Kompanie – Oberlt von Paulssen
Abt. Bukoba – Hptm. L. von Brandis

3. *WESTTRUPPEN* (WESTERN COMMAND) DISPOSITIONS

Commander: Generalmajor K. Wahle

Ruanda Command (Hptm. M. Wintgens)
7/FK – Hptm. Von Linde-Suden
23/FK – Hptm. Klinghardt
25/FK – Oberlt H. Müller
26/FK – Lt Zingel
Ruanda 'A' Kompanie – Oberlt Steffens
Ruanda 'B' Kompanie – Lt Lang

Urundi Command (Major E. von Langenn-Steinkeller)
14/ResK – Hptm. Braunschweig
Abt. Urundi – Lt Wentzel

Lake Tanganyika Command (Kvtkpt G. Zimmer*)
Abt. Möwe – Kptlt Schreiber
Artillerie – Hptm. Hering
Kasulu Post – Lt Meinicke
29/FK – Oberlt Franken

Neu Langenburg Command (Hptm. W. Falkenstein)
5/FK –
'L' K – Hptm. Aumann

Iringa Command (Hptm. E. Styx)
2/FK

Mahenge and Ssongea Command (Major G. von Grawert)
12/FK
Abt. Ssongea – Oberlt Schulz

4. DAR-ES-SALAAM COMMAND

Commander: Kapt. M. Looff*
Adjutant: Oberlt Angel*

22/FK – Kptlt Jantzen*
1/SchK – Hptm. Bock von Wülfingen
2/SchK – Oberlt Altmann
3/SchK – no commander
Landsturmkompanie Dar-es-Salaam – Oberlt Treuge
Abt. *Königsberg* – Kptlt Koch*
Maschinengewehrkorps (Machine-gun Company) – Oberlt Weise
Küstenschutzabt. Dar-es-Salaam (Harbour Defences) – Oberlt Herm*
Küstenartillerie (Coast Artillery) – Kptlt Apel*
Artillerieabt. – Vizewachtmeister Beuse
20/FK (Lindi) – Kptlt Hinrichs*
Abt. Delta – Hptm. von Bomsdorff
Abt. Kilwa – Lt Sprockhoff*
Abt. Bagamoyo – Lt Teichs
Abt. Pangani – Lt Günther

5. LINES OF COMMUNICATION – MOROGORO

Commander: Kapt. M. Looff*
Adjutant: Lt T. Brethauer/Hptm. C. Willmann

Tabora: Major von Stuemer

Central Railway
Dodoma – Vizefeldwebel Kränzlin
Morogoro – Oberlt Horn*
Kigoma – Vizewachtmeister Krenkel
Tabora – Oberlt Brandt
Ssingida – Vizewachtmeister Hoffmeister
Kilimatinde – Lt Coltzau*

Total *Schutztruppe* strength (all districts): sixty companies with ninety-six machine-guns (including seventeen captured from British forces and two from Belgian forces) and forty-nine field guns (including two captured from British forces).

In addition, the following non-combatant establishments had been set up:

Recruitment depots
Tanga district – Kptlt Niemeyer*
Lembeni – Sgt Seubert
Ngulu – Sgt von Zawadsky
Same – Feldwebel Reinhardt
Tabora – Oberstlt Hübener

Principal medical establishments
Generaloberarzt (Surgeon-General): Dr H. Meixner
North-East
Neu Moschi/Alt Moschi – Stabarzt Dr Stolowsky/Stabarzt Dr Marshall/Stabarzt Dr Höring
Mombo – Stabarzt Dr Seyffert (epidemic hospital)/Stabarzt Dr Taute (field laboratory)/Oberapotheker Dörffel (stores)
Wugiri – Oberstabarzt Dr Schörnisch
Korogwe – Stabarzt Dr Müller
Taveta – Stabarzt Dr Wünn
Aruscha – Stabarzt Dr Fickert
Central Railway
Morogoro – Stabarzt Dr Barthels
Dodoma (medical reserve) – Stabsapotheke Dr Schulze
Mpapua – Stabarzt Dr Arning
Tabora – Regierungsarzt Dr Moesta
Kigoma – Regierungsarzt Dr Weitling
Dar-es-Salaam – Oberstabarzt Dr Exner (Government Hospital), Stabarzt Erhart (Sewa-Hadji Hospital), Stabarzt Dr Manteufel (Epidemic Institute)
West
Muansa – Stabarzt Dr Koch
Bukoba – Regierungsarzt Dr Heidsieck
Ruanda – Stabarzt Dr Wolff
Urundi – Stabarzt Dr Grothusen

German medical ranks and their British equivalents

Oberstabarzt – Colonel in Medical Corps

Stabarzt – Captain in Medical Corps

Oberveterinär – Colonel in Veterinary Corps

Veterinär – Captain in Veterinary Corps

Stabapotheke – Staff pharmacist

(Ober-) Apotheke – Pharmacist

Regierungsarzt – Government doctor (i.e. one who had not taken a military rank)

APPENDIX FOUR

British Forces in East Africa:
Summarised Order of Battle 4 April 1916

1. 1ST EAST AFRICAN DIVISION (MAJ.-GEN. A.R. HOSKINS)

1st East African Infantry Brigade (Brig.-Gen. J.A. Hannyngton)
    2nd Loyal North Lancs
    2nd Rhodesia Regiment
    130th Baluchis
    3rd Kashmir Rifles }
    3rd King's African Rifles } Composite Battalion

2nd East African Infantry Brigade (Brig.-Gen. S.A. Sheppard)
    25th Royal Fusiliers
    29th Punjabis
    129th Baluchis
    40th Pathans

Divisional Troops
    17th Indian Cavalry (one squadron)
    East African Mounted Rifles
    King's African Rifles Mounted Infantry (one company)
    East Africa Pioneer Corps (Mounted Section)
    27th Mountain Battery
    5th Battery South African Field Artillery
    No. 6 Battery (four 12-pdr guns, manned by 2nd Loyal North Lancs)
    No. 7 Battery (four 15-pdr guns)
    38th Howitzer Brigade (one section – two 5-inch howitzers)
    Willoughby's Armoured Car Battery
    2nd Loyal North Lancs Machine-gun Company

2. 2ND EAST AFRICAN DIVISION (MAJ.-GEN. J. VAN DEVENTER)

1st South African Mounted Brigade (Brig.-Gen. M. Botha)
    1st SA Horse
    2nd SA Horse
    3rd SA Horse
    8th SA Horse (being formed in South Africa)

3rd South African Infantry Brigade (Brig.-Gen. C. Berrangé)
    9th SA Infantry
    10th SA Infantry
    11th SA Infantry
    12th SA Infantry

Divisional Troops

South African Scout Corps

28th Mounted Battery (six 10-pdrs)

2nd Battery South African Field Artillery (four 13-pdrs)

4th Battery South African Field Artillery (four 13-pdrs)

No. 12 Howitzer Battery (two 5-inch howitzers)

East Africa Volunteer Machine-gun Company

No. 4 Light Armoured Car Battery

3. 3RD EAST AFRICAN DIVISION (MAJ.-GEN. C. BRITS)

2nd South African Mounted Brigade, being formed in South Africa (Brig.-Gen. B. Enslin)

5th SA Horse

6th SA Horse

7th SA Horse

9th SA Horse

2nd South African Infantry Brigade (Brig.-Gen. P. Beves)

5th SA Infantry

6th SA Infantry

7th SA Infantry

8th SA Infantry

Divisional Troops

1st Battery South African Field Artillery (four 13-pdrs)

3rd Battery South African Field Artillery (four 13-pdrs)

38th Howitzer Brigade (one section – two 5-inch howitzers)

No. 8 Battery (six 12-pdrs)

No. 5 Light Armoured Car Battery

4. ARMY TROOPS

4th South African Horse

Belfield's Scouts

2nd Battalion King's African Rifles

61st Pioneers (less one company)

SA Pioneer Company (less four sections)

No. 9 Battery (four 12-pdr naval guns)

No. 10 Heavy Battery (three 4-inch naval guns)

No. 11 Heavy Battery (four 4-inch naval guns)

134th Howitzer Battery (four 5.4-inch howitzers)

38th Howitzer Brigade (four 5-inch howitzers)

Trench Mortar Brigade (twelve trench mortars)

No. 10 (Naval) Light Armoured Car Battery

Royal Flying Corps

1 Squadron RNAS

26th Squadron RFC

Kite Balloon Section

South African Motor Cyclist Corps
East African Intelligence Corps
North-West Railway Volunteer Maxim Gun Section

5. LINES OF COMMUNICATION

5th Indian Light Infantry
17th Indian Infantry
61st Pioneers (one company)
63rd Palamcottah Light Infantry
101st Grenadiers
Bharatpur Imperial Service Troops
Jhind Imperial Service Troops
Kapurthala Imperial Service Troops
3rd Gwalior Imperial Service Troops
Rampur Imperial Service Troops
2nd Kashmir Rifles (four companies)
Cape Corps
Arab Rifles (one company)
East African Pioneer Company

6. DETACHED FORCES AND GARRISONS

i) Lake Detachment and Uganda
   98th Infantry
   4th King's African Rifles
   Baganda Rifles
   Nandi Scouts
   European Machine-gun Section

ii) Nairobi Defence Force

iii) Mombasa Marine Defence Corps

iv) Zanzibar African Rifles (one company)

v) Mafia African Rifles (one company)

Plus ancillary units – Railway Companies, Telegraph Companies, Engineers, Supply &
Transport, Medical, Veterinary, Ordnance etc.

APPENDIX FIVE

British Order of Battle (Main Force), 5 August 1916

1st East African Brigade (Brig.-Gen. S.A. Sheppard)
29th Punjabis
130th Baluchis
2nd Kashmir Rifles
Squadron 17th Cavalry
No. 5 Battery SAFA
No. 6 Field Battery
134th Howitzer Battery
No. 1 LAM (Light Armoured Mobile) Battery
MG detachment 2nd Rhodesia Regiment
One company 61st Pioneers
One section East Africa Pioneers

2nd East African Brigade (Brig.-Gen. J.A. Hannyngton)
57th Wilde's Rifles
3rd Kashmir Rifles
3/King's African Rifles
King's African Rifles Mounted Infantry
27th Mountain Battery
MG detachment 129th Baluchis

Divisional Troops
Squadron East African Mounted Rifles
25th Royal Fusiliers
2nd Rhodesia Regiment
Cape Corps
No. 7 Field Battery
MG company 2nd Loyal North Lancs
One section East Africa Pioneers

3RD DIVISION (MAJ.-GEN. C. BRITS)

2nd South African Mounted Brigade
5th SA Horse
6th SA Horse
7th SA Horse
8th SA Horse

2nd South African Infantry Brigade
5th SA Infantry
6th SA Infantry

Divisional Troops
No. 1 Battery South African Field Artillery
No. 3 Battery South African Field Artillery
No. 8 Field Battery
No. 13 Howitzer Battery
No. 5 LAM Battery
Volunteer MG company

APPENDIX SIX

British Forces in East Africa:
Summarised Order of Battle 30 June 1917

1. 'NORFORCE' (BRIG.-GEN. E. NORTHEY)

Col. R. Murray's Column
Rhodesia Native Regiment
Northern Rhodesia Police (less two companies)
British South African Police

Col. G. Hawthorn's Column
2/1 King's African Rifles
1st South African Rifles
2nd South African Rifles
Northern Rhodesia Police (two companies)

Nyasaland Border Force
5th South African Infantry
1/4 King's African Rifles
King's African Rifles (Zomba Depot)

Force Reserve
1/1 King's African Rifles

Force Troops
South African Motor Cyclist Corps
5th Battery South African Mounted Rifles

2. 'HANFORCE' (BRIG.-GEN. J.A. HANNYNGTON)

No. 1 Column (Col. R. Rose/Col. G. Orr)
7th South African Infantry
33rd Punjabis
Gold Coast Regiment
2/2 King's African Rifles

No. 2 Column (Col. H. Grant/Col. R. Ridgway)
129th Baluchis
1/3 King's African Rifles
2/3 King's African Rifles
3/3 King's African Rifles

Force Reserve
8th South African Infantry

3. LINDI COLUMN (BRIG.-GEN. H. DE C. O'GRADY)

25th Royal Fusiliers
1/2 King's African Rifles
3/2 King's African Rifles
3/4 King's African Rifles
No. 259 Machine-gun Company

4. NIGERIAN BRIGADE (BRIG.-GEN. F.H.B. CUNLIFFE)

1st Battalion, Nigeria Regiment
2nd Battalion, Nigeria Regiment
3rd Battalion, Nigeria Regiment
4th Battalion, Nigeria Regiment
Gambia Company

5. IRINGA COLUMN (COL. W.K. FRASER-TYTLER)

17th Indian Infantry
2/4 King's African Rifles

GENERAL RESERVE

30th Punjabis
Cape Corps
1/6 King's African Rifles

LINES OF COMMUNICATION

130th Baluchis
40th Pathans
5th Light Infantry
British West Indies Regiment
Bharatpur Imperial Service Troops
Jhind Imperial Service Troops
Kapurthala Imperial Service Troops
3rd Gwalior Imperial Service Troops
Rampur Imperial Service Troops
2nd West India Regiment
Arab Rifles

Plus artillery and ancillary units

APPENDIX SEVEN

German East Africa *Schutztruppe*:
Order of Battle 14 October 1917

Commander-in-Chief: Oberst P. von Lettow-Vorbeck

I. MAIN FORCE

Note: * indicates naval rank

Headquarters
    Chief Staff Officer: Hptm. E. Müller
    Ordnance Officers: Lt Vortisch, Lt von Katte
    Quartermaster: Lt Besch*
    Medical Officer: Dr Stolowsky
    Provost-Marshal: Lt Vortisch
    HQ Commandant: Oberveterinär Dr Huber

A. Abteilung Wahle (Generalmajor K. Wahle)
Headquarters
    Staff Officer: Oberlt Boell
    Medical Officer: Stabarzt Dr Mohn
    Legal counsel: Hptm. Schmid
    Post Commander at Mahiwa: Oberstlt Freiherr von Bock
Abt. Rothe (Hptm. W. Rothe)
    Kompanie Tanga – Hptm. W. Rothe
    20/FK – Lt Tietgen
    19/FK – Hptm. Krüger
Abt. von Lieberman (Hptm. E. von Lieberman)
    'S' Kompanie – Oberlt Thiel
    14/ResK – Oberlt Wunderlich*
    3/FK – Lt Ott
'O' Kompanie (Hptm. W. Vorberg)
4/SchK (Oberlt W. Methner)
9/FK (Hptm. U. von Chappuis)

1 Batterie – 10.5cm howitzer (Hptm. von Kaltenborn-Stachau)
5 Artillerieabteilung – 10.5cm field gun, 4.7cm field gun (Oberlt Wenig*)

B. Abteilung von Ruckteschell (Oberlt W. von Ruckteschell)
    21/FK – Oberlt von Ruckteschell
    10/FK – Oberlt von Busse

C. Abteilung Göring (Hptm. K. Göring)
    4/FK – Hptm. Göring
    14/FK – Lt Batzner

13/FK – Lt Brucker
8/SchK – Oberlt Meyer
17/FK – Oberlt Freiherr von Schrötter

2 Batterie: two 7.5cm mountain guns (Vizefeldwebel Sabath)

D. Abteilung Köhl (Oberlt F. Köhl)
6/SchK – Lt Wolfram
18/FK – Kptlt Jantzen*

4 Batterie: Portuguese mountain gun (Vizefeldwebel Eylert)

E. Etappenleitung (HQ) (Hptm. P. Stemmermann)
11/FK – Lt Kempner

F. Abteilung Kraut (Major G. Kraut)
25/FK – Oberlt H. Müller
2/FK – Lt von Scherbening
3/SchK – Oberlt Osman
'I' Kompanie – Hptm. von Gellhorn
Abt. Schultz – Hptm. Schulz
Etappenkompanie – Oberlt Dransfeld
5/SchK – Hptm. Klinghardt

10.5cm field gun (Lt Frankenburg*)

G. Feldintendanturabteilungen (Quartermasters' detachments)
Massassi – Lt Kluge
Lindi/Mahiwa – Lt Vibrans

H. Feldlazarette (Field hospitals)
I – Stabarzt Dr Weck
II – Oberarzt Dr Wolf
IV – Regierungsarzt Dr Thierfelder
V – Stabarzt Dr Greisert
(III – Dr Brühl – had been captured on the Rufiji on 21 April 1917 with sixty German and
140 African patients)

I. Etappenlazarette (Base hospitals)
I – Stabarzt Dr Breuer
II – Stabarzt Dr Müller
Sanitätsreserve – Stabsapotheker Dr Schulze

2. WESTTRUPPEN

Commander: Hptm. T. Tafel

Staff Officer: Hptm. Augar
Adjutant: Lt Dannert
Quartermaster: Hptm. E. von Brandis
Medical Officer: Stabarzt Dr Grothusen
Provost-Marshal: Dr Oeschger

A. Abteilung Schoenfeld (Kvtkpt W. Schoenfeld*)
Abt. Aruscha – Lt Kaempfe
2/SchK – Hptm. Rothert
24/FK – Lt Zeltmann
23/FK – Oberlt Schlawe*

B. Abteilung von Brandis (Hptm. E. von Brandis)
Abt. Pangani – Lt Bohlen
5/FK – Oberlt Gutknecht

C. Abteilung Aumann (Hptm. H. Aumann)
'L' Kompanie – Hptm. Aumann
22/FK – Oberlt Niemir

D. Abteilung Poppe (Hptm. M. Poppe)
6/FK – Hptm. Poppe

E. Abteilung Otto (Hptm. E. Otto)
1/FK – Oberlt Merensky
7/FK – Lt Kalman
15/FK – Hptm. Lincke
29/FK – Oberlt Herm*

C73 9cm field gun (Lt Kühn)
Batterie Vogel (Oberlt Vogel) – 6cm field gun and 3.7cm field gun

F. Abteilung von Heyden (Hptm. E. von Heyden-Linden)
1/SchK – Hptm. von Heyden-Linden
Königsberg Kompanie – Obering. Schilling*

G. Patrol Kloefkorn (Lt H. Kloefkorn*)

H. Feldintendanturabteilung (Quartermaster) Mlembwe (Intend. T. Ehmig)

I. Etappenkommando (HQ) Liwale (Hptm. F. Braunschweig)

K. Feldlazarette (Field hospitals)
VI – Oberstabarzt Dr Exner
VII – Stabarzt Geisler
VIII – Stabarzt Grothusen
IX – Stabarzt Dr Penschke
X – Stabarzt Erhart

Feldsanitätsdepot (Medical stores) – Oberapotheker Dörffel

APPENDIX EIGHT

British Forces in East Africa:
Summarised Order of Battle 31 March 1918

1. 'NORFORCE' (MAJ.-GEN. E. NORTHEY)

Col. G. Hawthorn's Column
2/1 King's African Rifles
3/1 King's African Rifles

Col. C. Clayton's Column
2nd Cape Corps

Independent Battalions
2/4 King's African Rifles
3/4 King's African Rifles

Forces Reserve
1/1 King's African Rifles
1/4 King's African Rifles
4/1 King's African Rifles
Northern Rhodesia Police

2. PORTO AMELIA FORCE – 'PAMFORCE' (BRIG.-GEN. W.F.S. EDWARDS)

Col. R. Rose's Column
Gold Coast Regiment
4/4 King's African Rifles
King's African Rifles Mounted Infantry

Col. G. Giffard's Column
1/2 King's African Rifles
2/2 King's African Rifles

Force Troops
Gold Coast Regiment Mounted Infantry
58th Vaughan's Rifles

3. MOZAMBIQUE FORCE – 'MOBFORCE'

3/2 King's African Rifles

4. GENERAL RESERVE (LINDI)

Col. T. Fitzgerald's Column
    1/3 King's African Rifles
    2/3 King's African Rifles
    3/3 King's African Rifles

5. GARRISON TROOPS

Dar-es-Salaam: 2nd West India Regiment, Arab Rifles, British West Indies Regiment
Coastal Ports: 1/7 King's African Rifles
Tabora: 2/6 King's African Rifles
British East Africa: 1/5 King's African Rifles, 1/6 King's African Rifles

Plus artillery and ancillary units

NOTES

INTRODUCTION [pp. 1–7]

1 Grogan, p. 96
2 Bismarck speech in 1868. See Hans Spellmayer, *Deutsche Kolonialpolitik im Reichstag* (Kohlhammer, Stuttgart, 1931), p. 3
3 *Pall Mall Gazette*'s description of the British Empire, 31 March 1900
4 Pakenham, *The Boer War* (Abacus, 1992), p. 572
5 Adas, p. 40
6 *The Times*, 27 September 1884
7 Hatton, p. 125
8 Duff (2), p. 903
9 Sandes (1), p. 498
10 See Steer, p. 262
11 DuBois, p. 707
12 Smuts, p. 145
13 DuBois, p. 714
14 *African World Annual 1919*, p. 29
15 Beadon, p. 292
16 Gaddis Smith, 'The British Government and the Disposition of the German colonies in Africa, 1914–1918', in Gifford and Louis, p. 275
17 A. Calvert, *The German African Empire* (Laurie, 1916), p. xv
18 *The Leader*, 28 November 1914
19 See, for example, Gary Sheffield's *Forgotten Victory* (Headline Review, 2002), p. 325
20 Sandes (1), p. 498
21 Beck (1), p. 37
22 Northey, p. 85
23 See, for example, *Africa & Orient Review*, September 1920, p. 8
24 *Cape Times*, 3 February 1919
25 See foreword to *Through Swamp and Forest: The British Campaigns in Africa* (privately printed by Harrison, Jehring & Co. Ltd, undated)
26 Sheppard (2), pp. 138–9
27 Difford, pp. 93–4
28 Ibid., p. 93
29 IWM/Lewis: letter to his mother dated 15 April 1916

CHAPTER ONE:

'The Germans Open the Ball'

[pp. 13–25]

1 *The Nongqai* (South African Forces magazine), January 1919, p. 18
2 IWM/Mott
3 Davis and Robertson, pp. 97–8
4 IWM/Ritter
5 IWM/McCall, p. 1
6 Ganz, p. 278
7 TNA/WO/137/3893: Solf to Schnee (23 July 1914)
8 Ada Schnee, p. 15
9 TNA/WO/137/3893: Solf to Schnee (23 July 1914)
10 Ada Schnee, pp. 14–15
11 Schnee (1), p. 35
12 TNA/WO/137/3893: Solf to Schnee (23 July 1914)
13 Schnee (2), p. 42
14 Ada Schnee, p. 43
15 Listowel, p. 55
16 Boell (1), p. 74
17 Solf, p. 89

18 Lettow-Vorbeck (1), p. 3
19 TNA/WO/137/3893: Solf to Schnee (23 July 1914)
20 Lettow-Vorbeck (1), p. 3
21 A. Russell (1), p. 196
22 Lettow-Vorbeck (1), p. 21
23 Ibid., p. 31
24 Ibid., p. 28
25 Ibid., p. 29
26 Ibid.
27 IWM/Mott, p. 3
28 See Charles M. Good, *The Steamer Parish* (University of Chicago Press, 2004)
29 Ransford, p. 238
30 Sanderson, p. 30
31 TNA/WO106/573
32 Calwell (Director of Military Operations at the War Office), p. 177
33 RH/McGregor Ross (Mss. Afr.s. 1876, Vol. 8/1), letters 628 and 629
34 Lettow-Vorbeck (1), p. 21
35 PORT/MNE/C50(a-1)
36 E.A. Martins (2), p. 183
37 This version of events – claiming that the attack was accidental – was directly contradicted by the account of another participant, Otto Pentzel
38 CHAR/13/38/56
39 TNA/CO533/145. Another file note reads: 'Is Mr Hawkin a German agent?'
40 Hansard Vol. LXXV, pp. 1655–6

CHAPTER TWO:

Phoney War [pp. 26–39]

1 Callwell, p. 177
2 RH/Bremner, letter of 20 August 1914
3 TNA/CO/533/140
4 TNA/CO/533/142
5 RH/Bremner, letter of 20 August 1914
6 O'Neill (1), p. 64
7 Lettow-Vorbeck (1), p. 30
8 Ibid., p. 29
9 *The Leader*, 13 March 1915
10 Wallis (1), p. 250
11 IWM/Edwards, W.F.S.
12 RH/Masters: 8 August 1914
13 IWM/Mott

14 O'Sullevan, p. 210
15 TNA/CO/533/141
16 Charlewood, p. 125
17 Looff (1), p. 62
18 Charlewood, p. 125
19 King-Hall, p. 245
20 Sharpe, *Kenya Weekly News*, 4 September 1959, p. 56
21 Lettow-Vorbeck (1), p. 34
22 TNA/ADM/137/3893
23 RH/Covell
24 Sheppard (1), p. 72

CHAPTER THREE:

'The Action of a Lunatic' [pp. 40–58]

1 Remark of Col. Sheppard, GSO1 to IEF 'B' quoted in Sandes (2), p. 537
2 See Sandes (1), p. 499. The logistical troops comprised a company of Faridkot Sappers & Miners, a 'small bridging train' of Bombay Sappers & Miners, a Field Park of the Madras Corps and the 61st Pioneers.
3 RH/Covell. In peacetime the *Homayun* ferried pilgrims bound for Mecca up the Persian Gulf. Its human cargo now comprised the Faridkot Sapper & Miners, a detachment of armoured train personnel, the Ordnance Field Park, Engineer Field Park and the Supply Coolie Corps.
4 R.S. Meikle, *After Big Game* (Laurie, 1918), p. 85. Meikle was a visitor to Tanga in 1914.
5 Lettow-Vorbeck (1), p. 35
6 See NAM/17/FK Field Report
7 Meikle, p. 86
8 IWM/Crampton
9 TNA/CO/533/146
10 Wynn, p. 46
11 NAM/17/FK Field Report
12 Hordern, p.80 note 3
13 NAM/17/FK Field Report
14 IWM/Crampton: account of Capt. H.G. Evans of the *Karmala*
15 IWM/Aitken report
16 Russell (2), p. 105

17 Lettow-Vorbeck (1), pp. 39–41
18 Ibid., p. 40
19 IWM/Dunnington-Jefferson: letter from R. Meinertzhagen
20 NAM/Davidson
21 NAM/Macpherson
22 Hordern, p. 86
23 NAM/Macpherson
24 WO 95/5333: 98th Infantry War Diary
25 TNA/WO/95/5333: Hordern, p. 90
26 IWM/Wapshare
27 Lettow-Vorbeck (1), p. 43
28 Wynn, p. 93
29 Lettow-Vorbeck (1), p. 43
30 Ibid., p. 45
31 Hordern, p. 94
32 IWM/Crampton
33 Charlewood, p. 130
34 NAM/Davidson
35 IWM/Ritter
36 Ada Schnee, p. 19
37 Russell (2), p. 107

CHAPTER FOUR:

The Aftermath [pp. 59–66]

1 Hordern, p. 101
2 Callwell, p. 177, expressing the view of the Committee of Imperial Defence
3 Ada Schnee, p. 40
4 Callwell, p. 177
5 TNA/CO/533/146: Lord Curzon speech, 18 November 1914
6 TNA/CO/533/151
7 TNA/CO/533/146: Lord Curzon speech, 18 November 1914
8 TNA/CO/533/145
9 TNA/CO/533/142
10 TNA/WO/82/5210
11 CHAR/13/38/70
12 CHAR/13/38/74
13 TNA/CO/533/138, dated 3 December
14 TNA/CO/533/151 and 145
15 Wynn, p. 79
16 IWM/Wapshare diary, January 1915
17 Lord Crewe in the House of Lords, 18 November 1914 (see TNA/CO/533/146)
18 TNA/CO/533/151

19 SANMMH/Guy
20 Wylly (1), p. 96
21 RH/McGregor Ross, letter of 10 November 1914
22 TNA/CO/533/142

CHAPTER FIVE:

Marking Time [pp. 67–76]

1 CHAR/13/38/57
2 IWM/Ritter
3 CHAR/13/38/21
4 CHAR/13/38/60
5 IWM/Ritter
6 CHAR/13/38/21
7 IWM/Crampton
8 Ibid.
9 CHAR/13/38/70
10 Lettow-Vorbeck (1), p. 52
11 Charlewood, p. 132
12 Ibid., p. 133
13 CHAR/13/38/114
14 CHAR/13/38/108
15 TNA/CAB/45/10 (Otto Gerlach diary)
16 TNA/CAB/45/43 (Routh, An Ordnance Officer in East Africa, 1914–1918), p. 59
17 TNA/CO/533/142
18 TNA/CAB/45/43 (Routh, An Ordnance Officer in East Africa, 1914–1918), p. 109
19 Ibid., p. 59
20 Ibid., p. 230
21 Ibid., p. 138
22 Ibid., p. 58
23 Ibid., p. 13
24 Ibid., p. 117
25 Ibid., p. 69
26 Davis and Robertson, p. 97 and p. 100
27 The Leader, 28 November 1914
28 Hordern, p. 122
29 Ibid., p. 121
30 The Leader, 28 November 1914

CHAPTER SIX:

The Coast [pp. 79–93]

1 The Leader, 1 January 1915
2 Charlewood, p. 153
3 IWM/Ritter

4 TNA/CAB/45/43 (Routh, *An Ordnance Officer in East Africa, 1914–1918*), p. 103
5 Ibid., p. 54
6 IWM/Crampton
7 Hordern, p. 125
8 Lettow-Vorbeck (1), p. 63
9 Hordern, p. 127
10 Ibid., p. 128
11 Looff (1), p. 58
12 Looff (1), p. 63
13 Liddle/Frank Drury (HMS *Challenger*)
14 King-Hall, p. 262
15 TNA/CAB/45/218: 'RNAS Operations in East Africa' by J.T. Cull
16 TNA/CAB/45/218
17 CHAR/13/69/173
18 Pretorius, p. 6
19 Ibid., p. 131
20 Ibid., p. 16
21 Ibid., p. 19
22 CHAR/13/69/117
23 *The Pioneer Observer* ('Pro Bono Matlow'), First Issue, 9 April 1915, National Library of Australia
24 TNA/ADM/101/357
25 Kock, p .53
26 Ibid., p. 60
27 CHAR/13/69/117
28 CHAR/13/69/52
29 IWM/Murray
30 Kock, p. 96
31 Alliston, p. 50
32 Kock, p. 16
33 TNA/ADM/137/4297
34 King-Hall, p. 266

CHAPTER SEVEN:

The War in the West [pp. 94–101]

1 Hill, p. 355
2 TNA/WO/32/5812
3 Ibid.
4 Royaume de Belgique, *Les Campagnes Coloniales Belges*, Vol. 1, p. 183
5 Quoted in MacKenzie (2), p. 181
6 TNA/DO/119/908
7 Tasker, p. 57

8 Magee, p. 331

CHAPTER EIGHT:

'A Brilliant Affair' [pp. 102–12]

1 IWM/Wapshare
2 See Roger Pocock, p. v
3 Stoneham (1), pp. 66–7
4 Liddle/Shaw
5 See Liddle/Pim
6 Stoneham (1), p. 166
7 IWM/Buchanan
8 TNA/WO/33/858
9 Anon. (2), p. 299
10 *The Leader*, 3 July 1915
11 See WF/*Petit Écho*, pp. 87–8
12 IWM/Buchanan
13 Ibid.
14 Waltermann, p. 30
15 WF/*Rapport Annuel 1915*, pp. 258–60
16 IWM/Ball
17 TNA/WO/33/858
18 Hill, p. 363
19 O'Sullevan, p. 213
20 Lettow-Vorbeck (1), p. 96
21 Wahle, p. 22
22 Hordern, p. 186
23 TNA/DO/119/912
24 'Leviathan', p. 177
25 Tasker, p. 59
26 TNA/DO/119/912
27 Magee, p. 335
28 Ibid., p. 336
29 G. Spicer-Simson (1), p. 759
30 Magee, p. 342
31 Tasker, p. 61

CHAPTER NINE:

The End of the *Königsberg* [pp. 113–24]

1 TNA/CAB/45/218
2 AWM/Alliston, p. 57
3 TNA/CAB/45/218
4 Ibid.
5 IWM/McCall
6 IWM/Wright
7 Pretorius, p. 22
8 Liddle/Brewster, p. 14

9 TNA/ADM/137/4297
10 IWM/Ritter
11 IWM/Crampton
12 IWM/Acheson (account of Cdr Wilson)
13 Charlewood, p. 157
14 IWM/Acheson (account of Cdr Wilson)
15 Charlewood, p. 158
16 TNA/CAB/45/218
17 TNA/ADM 137/4297
18 TNA/ADM1/8427/192
19 IWM/Crampton
20 Pretorius, p. 25
21 IWM/Acheson (account of Cdr Wilson)
22 Pretorius, pp. 25–6
23 IWM/Acheson (account of Cdr Wilson)
24 Looff account quoted in Liddle/Grenfell, p. 91
25 IWM/Ritter
26 Liddle/Grenfell
27 IWM/Acheson (account of Cdr Wilson)
28 IWM/McCall
29 IWM/Crampton
30 Liddle/Grenfell
31 IWM/McCall
32 King-Hall, p. 270
33 Pretorius, p. 27

CHAPTER TEN:
'The Lion and the Springbok'
[pp. 125–35]

1 With grateful acknowledgement to Ronald Hyam and Peter Henshaw, *The Lion and the Springbok* (CUP, 2003)
2 Hyam and Henshaw, p. 101
3 O'Connor, p. 9
4 Haggard, p. 30
5 Blackwell (1), pp. 51, 54, and 55
6 Hyam and Henshaw, p. 30
7 Liddle/Speed
8 King-Hall, p. 249
9 Dundas, p. 95
10 King-Hall, p. 259
11 Ibid., pp. 259–60

12 Callwell, p. 178
13 Macdonald, p. 46
14 Botha speech to the House of Assembly, 28 March 1918, quoted in Buxton, p. 174
15 Hancock, p. 378
16 Capell, p. 30 (Capell was the commanding officer of the 2nd Rhodesia Regiment)
17 Hordern, p. 162
18 Capell, p. 34
19 Schnee (1), p. 45
20 *The Leader*, 17 April 1915
21 *The Leader*, 11 September 1914
22 Meinertzhagen, pp. 151–2
23 King-Hall, p. 260
24 TNA/WO/32/5324
25 TNA/WO/32/5234: Smith-Dorrien appraisal
26 TNA/CAB/17/143: Callwell, 9 November 1915
27 Callwell, p. 178

CHAPTER ELEVEN:
A Velha Aliada – 'The Old Ally'
[pp. 136–44]

1 TNA/FO/371/972, June 1910
2 TNA/FO/371/2105: 'Spain and Portugal', August 1914
3 Ribeiro, p. 150; and for this thesis see Ribeiro, pp. 132–214 *passim*
4 Ribeiro, p. 154
5 Vincent-Smith, pp. 218–19
6 Bessa, p. 147
7 Arning, p. 296
8 Newitt (1), pp. 5–6 and *passim*
9 PORT/MNE/C/23/177/1–2
10 PORT/MNE/C/20/131
11 PORT/MNE/C/20/126/1–3
12 PORT/MNE/C/20/135/2
13 Arning, p. 297
14 TNA/FO/929/1 (MacDonell/Black intelligence), TNA/FO/929/2 (German wireless station in Port Nyasa) and TNA/WO/106/576 (Bohlen Mission)
15 PORT/MNE/C/20/147
16 The cargo manifests of all vessels putting into the coastal ports, which reveal a great

deal about 'suspicious' imports, are listed in PORT/MNE/C/24/181

CHAPTER TWELVE:
'Swallows and Amazons'
[pp. 145–54]

1 Zimmer, p. 656
2 Ibid., p. 657
3 Harding, p. 248
4 Tasker, p. 63
5 Spicer-Simson (1), p. 760
6 Tasker, p. 64
7 Magee, p. 357
8 Zimmer, p. 657
9 ZNA/BC/1/5/1: Tanganyika Expedition papers (transcripts of interrogations)
10 Zimmer, p.659
11 Magee, p. 361
12 Zimmer, p. 660
13 Tasker, p. 66
14 Stiénon (2), p. 67
15 Moulaert, p. 53
16 Callwell, p. 179
17 IWM/Smith-Dorrien: diary entries 23–8 January 1916
18 IWM/Castle
19 Sampson, p. 12
20 The Star, 14 February 1916
21 van der Byl, p. 200
22 Lettow-Vorbeck (1), p. 75

CHAPTER THIRTEEN:
The African War
[pp. 155–65]

1 Charles Dundas quoted in A.J. Temu, 'The Giriama War, 1914–1915', in Ogot (ed.), p. 228
2 Dundas, p. 74
3 'Garibu', p. 386
4 Ngologoza, pp. 22–3
5 Ibid., p. 50
6 Ibid., p .62
7 Ibid., p. 58
8 Foran, p. 47
9 Sharpe, Kenya Weekly News, 4 September
1959, p. 56
10 Foran, p. 49
11 KNA/PC/Coast/1/13/107
12 Hobley, pp. 286–7
13 Lytton, p. 109
14 Poeschel, p. 27 (Poeschel was the Editor of the Deutsch-Ostafrika Zeitung)
15 Chikwenga, p. 17
16 de Wiart, p. 15
17 Ndabaningi Sithole, quoted by Adas, p. 39
18 Bandawe, pp. 70–3
19 Chanock, p. 130
20 RH/Masters
21 Ibid.
22 Duff (1), p. 50
23 RH/Masters
24 Ibid.
25 Duff (1), p. 51
26 See, for example, John McCracken (ed.), Britain and Malawi: A Hundred Years
27 Duff (1), p. 175
28 Hobley, p. 287
29 Poeschel, p. 20
30 Zirkel, p. 103

CHAPTER FOURTEEN:
The Build-up
[pp. 169–76]

1 Duplesis, pp. 1–2
2 Thatcher, p. 74
3 TNA/WO/95/5339
4 Freeman (1), p. 9
5 TNA/CAB/17/143
6 Stiénon, p. 669
7 Grogan, p. 227
8 Ibid., p. 251
9 Haussmann, p. 13
10 See The Nongqai Vol. V (1916), p. 370
11 Wynn, p. 37

CHAPTER FIFTEEN:
The 'First Salaita Show'
[pp. 177–86]

1 Le Roy, pp. 165–7

2 Hordern, p. 230

3 SANMMH/Confidential War Diary of 2nd SA Infantry Brigade (Staff Capt. F.W. Esselen)

4 *Springbok*, July 1974 (account of Victor Morton)

5 Payne, p. 6

6 SANMMH/Lane

7 *Springbok*, July 1974 (account of Victor Morton)

8 Collyer, p. 55

9 Meinertzhagen, p. 108

10 TNA/WO33/858

11 Grogan, p. 219

12 Lettow-Vorbeck (1), pp. 79–80

13 Ibid., p. 103

14 Divisional Operation Order No. 4

15 Sampson, p. 13

16 Ibid.

17 *The Nongqai* Vol. V (1916), p. 361, account of Special Correspondent and dated 23 March 1916

18 *Natal Witness*, 16 February 1929

19 Sampson, p. 14

20 Lettow-Vorbeck (1), p. 103

21 Sampson, p. 14

22 SANMMH/Stephens

23 *The Nongqai* Vol. V (1916), p. 361, account of Special Correspondent, p. 362

24 SANMMH/Lane

25 Ibid.

26 Thatcher, p. 83

27 Sampson, p. 14

28 *The Star*, 2 February 1916

29 RH/Bagenal

30 Stent, Part I

31 Fendall, p. 62

32 Ibid., p. 59

33 TNA/WO/33/858: CIGS to Tighe, 18 February 1916

CHAPTER SIXTEEN:

The 'Robbers' Raid'

1 Poeschel, p. 21

2 Meinertzhagen, p. 163

3 TNA/WO/33/858

4 Thatcher, p. 87

5 IWM/Ewart: Tighe to Maj.-Gen. Richard Ewart, 13 March 1916

6 van der Byl, pp. 204–5

7 Cranworth, p. 215

8 IWM/Ewart: Tighe to Maj.-Gen. Richard Ewart, 13 March 1916

9 Cranworth, p. 216

10 IWM/Ewart: Tighe to Maj.-Gen. Richard Ewart, 13 March 1916

11 TNA/WO/33/858

12 Wilson, p. 74 (author's italics)

13 TNA/WO/141/62, Smuts despatch 15 March 1916

14 Cranworth p. 217

15 Reitz, p. 108

16 SANMMH/Lane

17 Hordern, pp. 251–2

18 TNA/WO/33/858

19 Meinertzhagen, pp. 208–9

20 Smuts quoted in Tighe's obituary, *National Review* Vol. 86 (1926), p. 927

21 Wilson, p. 84

22 Wilson, p. 100

23 TNA/WO33/858

24 See Bisset, p. 59

25 Lettow-Vorbeck (1), p. 80

CHAPTER SEVENTEEN:

Opsaal! Saddle-up!

1 Lettow-Vorbeck (1), p. 126

2 Ibid.

3 Ibid., p. 127

4 SANMMH/Dewey, p. 3

5 TNA/CAB/45/43 (Routh, *An Ordnance Officer in East Africa, 1914–1918*), p. 367

6 Fendall, p. 67

7 Crowe, p. 118

8 SANMMH/Adkins, p. 68

9 *Natal Daily News*, 8 May 1954

10 SANMMH/Faure

11 Lettow-Vorbeck (1), p. 134

12 Ibid., pp. 137–8

13 Fendall, p. 70

14 RH/Bagenal, p. 67
15 Ibid., p. 63
16 SANMMH/Dewey, p. 4
17 Sampson, p. 25–6

CHAPTER EIGHTEEN:

The Advance down the Northern Railway
[pp. 206–11]

1 *The Leader*, 28 October 1916
2 TNA/WO/32/5325
3 van der Byl, p. 201
4 Letter to *The Leader*, 13 May 1916
5 Cranworth, p. 225
6 Maxwell, p. 60
7 Woodhouse, p. 41
8 *The Leader*, 28 October 1916
9 IWM/McCall
10 Knudsen, pp. 14–27
11 W. Lloyd-Jones, p. 199: von Lettow-Vorbeck comment to Col. Brian Hawkins in November 1918

CHAPTER NINETEEN:

The Crescent Flag
[pp. 212–23]

1 TNA/141/786/7530/2
2 Emil Zimmerman, quoted in Smuts, p. 143
3 TNA/FO/929/1
4 TNA/CO/533/142
5 IWM/Wapshare
6 Parfitt, p. 34
7 Hopkirk, p. 116
8 Parfitt, p. 25 and p. 31
9 Jafar Pasha, quoted in Facey, p. 67
10 Facey, p. 69
11 Ibid., p. 65
12 Ibid.
13 Hodson, p. 123
14 Ibid., p. 19
15 Scholler, p. 313
16 TNA/CO/822/3/12
17 TNA/CO/533/621: remark of Lord Harcourt, Secretary of State for Colonies

18 Braukämpfer, p. 555
19 TNA/FO/141/572/2: Lt-Col. Clayton to Sir Milne Cheetham, 24 February 1915
20 TNA/FO/141/572/2
21 TNA/CO/822/3/12
22 Scholler, p. 309
23 See TNA/FO/141/816. By mid 1916 the potash deposits mined by the Italian *Compagnia Mineraria Coloniale* at Dallol on the Abyssinian-Eritrean border were vital to the Allied munitions industry.
24 Scholler, p. 322 note 18
25 Archer, p. 86
26 Ehrlich, p. 636
27 Ibid., p. 632
28 Scholler, p. 304
29 Hodson, p. 130
30 TNA/FO/141/786
31 Beachey, p. 115
32 TNA/FO/141/786: intelligence report of Capt. J.E. Phillips, East African Expeditionary Force, prepared for Lord Milner on 15 July 1917 (pp. 3–4).
33 See C.H. Becker, 'Materials for Understanding Islam in German East Africa', TNR No. 68 (1968), p. 60.
34 WF/Casier 113/Kigali
35 TNA/FO/141/666/ Schnee circular dated December 1913

CHAPTER TWENTY:

'The Cannibals' [pp. 224–31]

1 See Digre, p. 107
2 Lettow-Vorbeck (1), p. 185
3 *The Times*, 15 August 1916
4 Special Supplement by Ernest Henrion in Sampson, p. 48
5 Wahle, p. 35
6 See Welbourn, pp. 223–4
7 Quoted in Digre, p. 103
8 Special Supplement by Ernest Henrion in Sampson, p. 56
9 WF/Casier 183, diary for Marienthal Mission, August 1916
10 See WF/Casier 113 (for Kigali) and WF/Rabeyrin *passim* (for Urundi)
11 Zimmer, p. 660

CHAPTER TWENTY-ONE:

The 'Ubiquitous Rhodesians'

[pp. 232–38]

1 Langham, p. 84
2 Liddle/Messum
3 Bradley, p. 40
4 Liddle/Messum
5 TNA/WO/95/5334
6 Liddle/Messum and TNA/WO/95/5334
7 IWM/Northey
8 Spicer-Simson (1), p. 761
9 Weerd, p. 1461
10 Hordern, p. 466
11 Ibid.
12 Walker, p. 143
13 Maker, p. 39
14 TNA/WO/95/5334
15 RH/Masters
16 Maker, p. 43
17 Ibid., p. 45
18 Liddle/Messum
19 Letcher, p. 20

CHAPTER TWENTY-TWO:

'Abso-Damn-Lutely Fed Up'

[pp. 239–51]

1 Reitz, p. 114
2 SANMMH/Winstanley
3 Kock, p. 127
4 The Nongqai (1916), p. 425
5 Cranworth, p. 230
6 Fewster: 29 August 1916
7 Fewster: 5 September 1916
8 Fendall, p. 67
9 SANMMH/Lane
10 SANMMH/Faure
11 Fendall, p. 73
12 Lettow-Vorbeck (1), p. 141
13 Hordern, p. 507
14 Wahle, p. 33
15 Tombeur, p. 4
16 TNA/WO/106/257
17 Wahle, p. 36
18 Ibid., pp. 34–5
19 Second Supplement to The London Gazette, 15 June 1917: Charlton despatch

of 28 January 1917
20 Urban, p. 143
21 Kock, p. 118 and p. 128
22 Liddle/Parnham
23 TNA/CAB/17/43
24 Fendall, p. 77
25 TNA/WO/33/858
26 Ibid.
27 Kock, pp. 135–6 passim
28 Orr (9), p. 297
29 Kock, p. 155
30 Sampson, p. 63
31 Maker, p. 45
32 See Urban, p. 137, letter dated 6 May 1916
33 Boell (1), p. 234
34 Schnee (1), p. 230
35 Lettow-Vorbeck (1), p. 158
36 Kock, p. 131
37 Fewster: 20 December 1916
38 Liddle/Archdale

CHAPTER TWENTY-THREE:

Smuts's 'Final Phase'

[pp. 252–66]

1 TNA/CAB/45/20 (Report of Capt. L.A. Russell)
2 Lettow-Vorbeck (1), p. 184
3 See, for example, IWM/Hopkins
4 Lettow-Vorbeck (1), p. 184
5 Ibid., p. 187
6 Wahle, p. 33
7 Ibid., p. 36
8 Sampson, p. 67: account of P.C. Young
9 IWM/Hopkins
10 Crowe, p. 238
11 Hordern, p. 459
12 TNA/WO/33/858: Smuts to CIGS, 14 October 1916
13 Thatcher, p. 141
14 Lettow-Vorbeck (1), pp. 170–1
15 TNA/CAB/45/20 (Report of Capt. L.A. Russell)
16 Reitz, p. 152
17 Ibid., p. 155
18 Lettow-Vorbeck (1), p. 188
19 Wahle, p. 38
20 Beadon, p. 323

21 IMW/Northey
22 Liddle/Messum
23 IWM/Northey
24 Liddle/Groves
25 SANMMH/Lane
26 Ibid.

CHAPTER TWENTY-FOUR:

'The Condemned'

[pp. 267–79]

1 Meneses, p. 86
2 Looff (1), p. 151
3 See Major Motta Marques, 'A passagem do Rio Rovuma,' *Revista Militar* (1920), pp. 299–304
4 Meinertzhagen, p. 190
5 *The Times History of the War*, p. 340, quoting Lt-Col. Barbosa, 'O nosso esfôrço em África', in *Revista Militar* (1918), p. 129
6 Vincent-Smith, p. 222
7 Manuel Gomes da Costa, pp. 253–4
8 Silva, p. 37
9 Ibid., p. 73
10 Ibid., p. 75
11 *The Times History of the War*, p. 344
12 Hordern, p. 389
13 Lettow-Vorbeck (1), p. 165
14 Looff (1), p. 150
15 Ibid., p. 152
16 Ibid., p. 155
17 PORT/MNE/*Portugal Na Primeira Guerra Mundial* Vol. II, p. 64, Document 511
18 Selvagem, p. 227
19 Looff (1), p. 164
20 Ibid., p. 163
21 Aragão, p. i
22 See Antonio Mario de Figueredo, 'Rápido Bosquejo da Grande Guerra', *Revista Militar* Vol. 71, No. 6–7, pp. 353–76
23 Tenente Simões da Mota, 'A coluna de socorro a Newala', *Revista Militar* No. 9–10 (1928), pp. 458–67
24 E. A. Martins (1), p. 97

25 TNA/FO/929/7
26 IWM/Castle: diary entry, 14 December 1916
27 TNA/WO/158/477
28 Meneses, p. 90
29 Orr (7), p. 78
30 Ibid., p. 74
31 Downes, p. 80
32 Fewster: 13 January 1917

CHAPTER TWENTY-FIVE:

The 'Suicidal System of Supply'

[pp. 278–90]

1 Beck (1), p. 62
2 TNA/CAB/45/43 (Routh, *An Ordnance Officer in East Africa, 1914–1916*)
3 Ibid., p. 45
4 Ibid., pp. 213–14
5 Ibid., p. 91
6 Trevor, p. 263
7 Hazleton, p. 231
8 Ibid., p. 232
9 Beadon, p. 309 and p. 311
10 Paterson and Levin, p. 74 and p. 85
11 Hordern, p. 23 note 1
12 KNA/PC/Coast/1/9/31: Hobley to Platts (DC Voi), 3 January 1915
13 KNA/PC/Coast/1/13/132: inspection reports of 24/25 March 1915
14 Duff (2), p. 907
15 KNA/PC/Coast/1/3/86: report dated 23 August 1915
16 IWM/Fenning, p. 11
17 KNA/MOH/1/8146: medical report of James H. Thomson, Medical Officer
18 Baily, p. 95
19 Looff (1), p. 131
20 Kock, p. 136
21 Lettow-Vorbeck (1), p. 24
22 See, for example, Helbig (1), p. 145
23 Bovill, pp. 281–2
24 Beer, p. 45
25 Duff (2), p. 910
26 Steer, p. 254
27 Lettow-Vorbeck (1), p. 107
28 Powys, p. 154

CHAPTER TWENTY-SIX:

Unfinished Business

[pp. 293–305]

1 *The Leader*, 23 December 1916
2 Crafford, p. 133
3 Smuts, p. 136
4 Grogan, p. 235
5 '*Ons Jan* is eighty today' by Ewart Grogan, in *The East Africa Standard*, 24 May 1950
6 Armstrong, *passim*
7 Smuts, p. 135
8 Plaatje, pp. 304–5
9 Ibid., p. 307
10 *The Leader*, 31 March 1917
11 Falls, pp. 234–5
12 Wienholt, p. 188
13 Hazleton, p. 233
14 TNA/WO/32/5825
15 Wienholt, p. 188
16 RH/Masters, p. 134
17 W. Lloyd-Jones, p. 160
18 Liddle/Speed
19 Parsons (1), p. 273
20 TNA/WO/33/953
21 Cranworth, p. 220
22 Callwell, p. 176
23 Wienholt, p. 190
24 Cranworth, p. 220
25 Wienholt, pp. 187–8
26 Hazleton, p. 234
27 Downes, p. 89
28 Ibid., p. 90
29 Ibid., p. 100
30 Ibid., p. 109–10
31 Ibid., p. 113–14
32 IWM/Thornton
33 TNA/WO/33/953
34 Clifford, pp. 2–3

CHAPTER TWENTY-SEVEN:

The Raiders

[pp. 306–15]

1 Langham, p. 256
2 IWM/Hopkins
3 ZNA/Oral/LE/2: J.W. Leach

4 RH/Spindler, pp. 91–2
5 Liddle/Pratt
6 TNA/CAB/44/8
7 Daye (2), p. 54
8 See, for example, Langham, p. 267
9 Lettow-Vorbeck (1), p. 189
10 IWM/Bowden
11 TNA/CAB/45/48 (Drought Papers)
12 IWM/Castle
13 TNA/CAB/45/48 (Drought Papers)
14 Boell (1), p. 329
15 TNA/WO/158/481: telegram from Gen. Edwards to GHQ, 21 July 1917
16 Lettow-Vorbeck (1), p. 189
17 IWM/Bowden

CHAPTER TWENTY-EIGHT:

The Allies

[pp. 316–23]

1 BOD/Milner Papers: Grogan letter, 5 June 1919
2 Grogan, p. 246
3 Vincent-Smith, p. 238
4 TNA/WO/158/477: MacDonell to War Office, 20 March 1917
5 Selig, p. 204
6 Arning, pp. 301–2
7 Ibid.
8 Lima, p. 340
9 Maugham, p. 233 and p. 231
10 See Warhurst thesis, p. 185
11 Hobson, p. 461
12 Ibid.
13 Ranger (1), p. 80
14 TNA/WO/158/477: MacDonell to War Office, 20 March 1917
15 Quoted by Ferreira Martins, 'Verdades Esquecidas E Ignoradas: Portugal Na Guerra De 1914–18', in *Republica*, 31 March 1956
16 E.A. Martins (1), p. 97
17 TNA/WO/158/477: MacDonell to War Office, 20 March 1917
18 Ibid.
19 TNA/FO/800/61: December 1911, Sir Edward Grey to British Ambassador in Berlin, quoted in Langhorne (p. 369)

CHAPTER TWENTY-NINE:

Into 'The Unknown'

[pp. 324–35]

1 *Kriegsdepeschen aus ruhmreicher Zeit, Band 6 (1/1/1917–31/7/1917)*: despatch of 31 July 1917
2 Ridgway, p. 247
3 Lieberman in Zache, p. 437
4 RH/Gethin
5 Ibid.
6 Lettow-Vorbeck (1), p. 202
7 Ibid., p. 216
8 Ibid., p. 220
9 Kock, p. 212
10 Ibid., p. 215

CHAPTER THIRTY:

The German Pimpernel

[pp. 336–46]

1 Orr (2), p. 56
2 Kock, pp. 248–9
3 Lettow-Vorbeck (1), p. 221
4 Ibid., p. 220
5 Kock, p. 253–4
6 Ibid., p. 253
7 Lettow-Vorbeck (1), p. 225
8 Looff (1), pp. 176–7
9 Wahle, p. 48
10 Lettow-Vorbeck (1), p. 225
11 Ibid., p. 229
12 TNA/WO/106/587
13 TNA/WO/158/478
14 Wienholt, p. 203
15 Lettow-Vorbeck (1), p. 232
16 Wienholt, p. 213
17 See W. Lloyd-Jones, p. 199
18 TNA/CAB/45/19 (E. St C. Stobart Papers)
19 See, for example, E.A. Martins (2), p. 66
20 Schnee (1), p. 124
21 Wienholt, p. 217
22 Maxwell, p. 66
23 TNA/CAB/45/19 (E. St C. Stobart Papers)

24 Lettow-Vorbeck (1), pp. 235–6
25 IWM/Castle
26 Birkby, p. 60
27 IWM/Castle
28 Liddle/Smith
29 ZNA/Williams, p. 227
30 TNA/WO/33/953
31 See Gaddis-Smith, 'The British Government and the Disposition of the German Colonies in Africa, 1914–1918', in Gifford and Louis, p. 292
32 *The London Gazette*, Fourth Supplement, 13 December 1918

CHAPTER THIRTY-ONE:

The 'China Affair'

[pp. 347–50]

1 Marben, p. 180–81
2 Strasser, 16 September 1917, quoted in Robinson (2), p. 111
3 Ibid., p. 118; Robinson's thorough account is based on L59's official war diary in the 'Tambach' Archives, among other sources
4 Maximilian Zupitza, in Langsdorff, p. 334
5 Robinson (2), p. 119
6 See, for example, Henry Villard, *Cross & Cockade* Vol. 23, No. 2 (1992), p. 75. Schedelmann wrote a short account of L59's mission in the 12 January 1919 edition of *Luftpost*.
7 See Marben, p. 198 and Woodhall, p. 171
8 van der Byl, p. 232
9 Woodhall, p. 170
10 Ibid., p. 171
11 See Maker, p. 50
12 Looff (1), p. 179

CHAPTER THIRTY-TWO:

The Propaganda War

[pp. 351–59]

1 Hatton, p. 125
2 Koponen, p. 77
3 Ganz thesis, p. 39

4 Quoted by Ganz, p. 203
5 Stoecker, p. 262
6 Poeschel, p. 10
7 Schnee (1), pp. 116–17
8 Listowel, p. 48
9 Popkess, p. 94
10 Beer, p. 270
11 Joelson (1), p. 247
12 RH/Hollis; author's italics
13 Charles Dundas's *History of German East Africa* was eventually published in 1923
14 Ada Schnee, p. 27
15 Gunzert, p. 176
16 Listowel, p. 52
17 *Employment, contrary to International Law, of Colored troops upon the European Arena of War by England and France*, Berlin, 30 July 1915, pp. 1–2
18 See for example the Feetham Report (TNA/CO/691/20) and its Addendum; and Cd. 9210, *Correspondence Relating To The Wishes Of The German Colonies As To Their Future Government*
19 Morel quoted in 'Africanus', *Audiatur et altera pars: An Appeal for Fair Play* (M. Graser, Cape Town, *c.* 1921)
20 Speech of Percy Molteno, MP for Dumfriesshire, to the House of Commons, 17 July 1917
21 Payne, p. 126
22 Ibid., p. 127
23 KNA/DC/MKS/10B/6/1: letter of Major Foster (KAR) to Provincial Commissioners in British East Africa, 5 March 1918

CHAPTER THIRTY-THREE:

The Hunt Begins

[pp. 363–71]

1 TNA/WO/158/478
2 Ibid.
3 Ibid.
4 PORT/MNE, document 653, pp. 224–5
5 TNA/WO/158/478
6 TNA/WO/158/479
7 Ibid.
8 TNA/WO/158/475: MacDonell report, 8 January 1918
9 WO158/475: van Deventer memo, 1 October 1918
10 W. Lloyd-Jones, p. 160
11 Liddle/Smith
12 Britten, p. 432
13 Clifford, p. 212
14 Ibid., p. 284
15 Liddle/Groves, p. 66
16 Britten, p. 432
17 Selig, p. 204
18 Lettow-Vorbeck (1), pp. 243–4
19 TNA/WO/158/476
20 Lettow-Vorbeck (1), p. 254
21 Ibid., p. 250
22 TNA/WO/158/474: van Deventer memo, 16 May 1918
23 Lettow-Vorbeck (1), p. 263
24 Ibid., pp. 262–3
25 Ibid., p. 264
26 Bandawe, p. 48
27 TNA/WO/106/1460: Schnee War Diary, p. 22
28 TNA/WO/158/475
29 TNA/WO/158/476

CHAPTER THIRTY-FOUR:

Nhamacurra

[pp. 372–8]

1 Lettow-Vorbeck (1), p. 260
2 *The Nongqai*, January 1919, p. 17
3 See Deppe (1), p. 156 for a breakdown of the casualty statistics for the year in Portuguese East Africa
4 Lettow-Vorbeck (1), p. 270
5 Ibid., p. 264
6 Lieberman in Zache, p. 436
7 Wahle, p. 51
8 TNA/WO/158/476: van Deventer to War Office, 25 June 1918
9 TNA/WO/158/475
10 TNA/WO/158/476
11 Lettow-Vorbeck (1), p. 271
12 Ibid., p. 273
13 Moyse-Bartlett, p. 401
14 Lettow-Vorbeck (1), p. 277

15 Wahle, p. 51
16 TNA/WO/158/474; see also Boyes account in IWM/Misc 80/Item 1228
17 TNA/WO/33/953
18 Lettow-Vorbeck (1), p. 279
19 Ibid., p. 287
20 Cértima, p. 280
21 Vere Stent, *The Great Safari*, No. 11
22 TNA/WO/158/476: von Deventer to War Office, 9 July 1918

26 Boell (1), p. 427
27 TNA/WO/158/907
28 Bovill, p. 279
29 Lettow-Vorbeck (1), p. 322
30 TNA/WO/158/907
31 Lettow-Vorbeck (1), p. 326
32 Helbig, p. 214
33 Joelson (2), p. 237
34 Dundas, pp. 104–5

CHAPTER THIRTY-FIVE:

Tipperary mbali sana sana!

[pp. 379–91]

1 *The London Gazette*, Fourth Supplement, 13 December 1918
2 Moyse-Bartlett, p. 405
3 Ibid., p. 408
4 Lettow-Vorbeck (1), p. 300
5 TNA/WO/106/1460: Schnee War Diary, p. 27
6 Ibid., p. 32
7 TNA/WO/33/953
8 Boell (2), p. 325
9 Lettow-Vorbeck (1), p. 305
10 TNA/WO/106/1460: Schnee War Diary, p. 50
11 Ibid., p. 46
12 Ibid., p. 55
13 Ibid., p. 75
14 Lettow-Vorbeck (1), p. 318
15 TNA/WO/106/1460: Schnee War Diary, p. 81
16 Sandes (1), p. 498
17 Lettow-Vorbeck (1), pp. 311–12
18 Ibid., p. 316
19 TNA/WO/106/1460: Schnee War Diary, p. 95
20 Ibid., p. 81
21 Ibid., p. 97
22 Boell (2), p. 324
23 Bradley, p. 61
24 See W. Lloyd-Jones, pp. 196–7. Von Lettow-Vorbeck was in fact still forty-eight.
25 Deppe (1), p. 156 lists 577 deaths, Boell (1), p. 427, 734 deaths

EPILOGUE:

'There Came a Darkness'

[pp. 392–402]

1 Melvin E. Page (1), p. 1
2 Duff (2), p. 909
3 KNA/CA/12/4: letter from Oscar Watkins, commanding the Carrier Corps, to all Provincial Commissioners, 16 February 1930
4 See Steer, p. 262
5 W. Lloyd-Jones, p. 160
6 See RH/Matson 5/14, p. 159
7 TNA/CO/820/17
8 See TNA/WO/141/31: Pike Report and Court of Enquiry Papers
9 KNA/PC/CP/1/1/2: Short History of Kikuyu Province 1911–27
10 Powys, p. 154
11 Digre, p. 126
12 RH/Johansen, p. 30
13 Dundas, p. 196
14 Lt Rice in *The Nongqai*, October 1917, p. 205
15 Patterson and Pyle, p. 1302
16 Stoneham (1), p. 44
17 Kloppers, pp. 22–3
18 *The Nongqai*, November 1918, p. 508
19 Payne, p. 132
20 See Ranger (2), p. 175
21 Ellison, p. 221
22 Boell (1), p. 427
23 See Helbig (1), p. 145
24 Maddox, p. 197
25 Ibid., *passim*
26 Helbig (1), p. 145
27 Lettow-Vorbeck (1), p. 77

28 See RH/Matson 5/14, p. 159

29 Ibid., p. 160

30 Grogan, p. 250

31 Ewart Grogan, 'Sixty Years in East and Central Africa', in *Rhodesia and East Africa* (1958), p. 56

32 See Digre (pp. 147–8), quoting Terrier's *Les Ambitions coloniales de l'Allemagne*, p. 69

33 Beer, pp 36–7

34 Lettow-Vorbeck (1), p. 3

35 Dundas, p. 80

36 Digre, p. 156

37 Dundas, p. 80

38 See Digre's excellent study, *Imperialism's New Clothes: The Repartition of Tropical Africa, 1914–1919*

39 KNA/DC/MKA/10B/6/1

40 See Jonny Moser, *Nisko: The First Experiment in Jewish Deportation*, Simon Wiesenthal Center Annual 2 (1985), Ch. 1, p. 1. The suggestion was, somewhat ironically, put to Hitler by Oswald Pirow, the South African Minister of Defence.

BIBLIOGRAPHY

I. PRINTED SOURCES

Abbreviations for those periodicals most commonly referred to:

EAMJ	– *East African Medical Journal*
GJ	– *Geographical Journal*
JAH	– *Journal of African History*
JAS	– *Journal of the African Society*
JCH	– *Journal of Contemporary History*
JICH	– *Journal of Imperial and Commonwealth History*
JMAS	– *Journal of Modern African Studies*
JRA	– *Journal of the Royal Artillery*
JRAS	– *Journal of the Royal African Society*
JRUSI	– *Journal of the Royal Services Institution*
JSAHR	– *Journal of the Society for Army Historical Research*
JSAMHS	– *Journal of the South African Military History Society*
JUSII	– *Journal of the United Services Institution of India*
MHQ	– *Military History Quarterly*
NJ	– *Nyasaland Journal*
NRJ	– *Northern Rhodesia Journal*
OMRS	– *Journal of the Orders and Medals Research Society*
SAHJ	– *South African Historical Journal*
SARH	– *South African Railways and Harbours Magazine*
TNR	– *Tanganyika Notes and Records*
UJ	– *Uganda Journal*

The Nongqai – The South African Services Magazine
The Leader of British East Africa

– Military and other ranks have not been included
– Publication in the United Kingdom unless otherwise stated

Achilles, Albert, *Erinnerungen aus meiner Kriegsgefangenschaft, 1914–20* (Traditionsverband ehemaliger Schutz- und Überseetruppen, 1977)
Adas, Michael, 'Contested Hegemony: The Great War and the Afro-Asian Assault on the Civilizing Mission Ideology' *Journal of World History* (March 2004), pp. 31–63

Adler, F.B., Lorch, A.E. and Curson, H.H., *The South African Field Artillery: German East Africa and Palestine 1915–1919* (J.L. Van Schaik, Pretoria), 1958

'Africanus' (1), *The Prussian Lash in Africa* (Hodder & Stoughton, 1918)

'Africanus' (2), *Audiatur et altera pars: An Appeal for Fair Play* (M. Graser, Cape Province, n.d.)

Alberto, Manuel Simões, *Condenados* (Tip. Lusítânia, Aveiro, 1933)

Alexandre, Valentim, *O Império Áfricano: Séculos XIX e XX* (Colibri, Lisbon, 2002)

Alliston, John M., *The African River Wars 1914–1916* (The Naval Historical Society of Australia Inc., 2000)

Anderson, R. (1), *The Battle of Tanga* (Tempus, 2002)

Anderson, R. (2), 'The Battle of Tanga', *War In History* Vol. 8, No. 3 (2001), pp. 294–322

Anderson, R. (3), *The Forgotten Front* (Tempus, 2004)

Anderson-Morshead, A.E.M., *The Building of the 'Chauncy Maples'* (UMCA, 1903)

Anon. (1), 'Extracts from the diary of an officer of the Königsberg', *JRUSI* Vol. 63 (1918), pp. 235–40

Anon. (2), 'A Backwater: Lake Victoria Nyanza During The Campaign Against German East Africa', *Naval Review* Vol. 9 (1921), pp. 287–317

Aragão, Francisco, *Tropas Negras* (Seara Nova, Lisbon, 1926)

Archer, Geoffrey, *Personal and Historical Memoirs of an East African Administrator* (Oliver & Boyd, 1963)

Armstrong, F.C., *Grey Steel: J.C. Smuts, A Study in Arrogance* (The Book Club, 1937)

Arning, Wilhelm, *Kampf um Deutsch-Ostafrika: Vier Jahre Weltkrieg in Deutsch-Ostafrika* (Verlag von Gebrüder Jänecke, Hanover, n.d.)

Arnold, John, *The African DCM* (OMRS, Devon, 1998)

Ashete, Aleme, 'European Adventurers in Ethiopia at the Turn of the 20th Century', *Journal of Ethiopian Studies* Vol. 12, No. 1 (1974), pp. 1–17

Ashley, F.J., *With a Motor Bike in the Bush* (Blackie & Son, n.d.)

Atiman, Adrien, 'By Himself', *TNR* Vol. 21 (June 1946), pp. 46–76

Augar, Georg, 'Auf Sprengpatrouille gegen die Ugandabahn', in *Kampf um Kolonien* (Deutscher Wille, Berlin, n.d.)

Baily, F.E., *Twenty-Nine Years Hard Labour* (Hutchinson, n.d.)

Baiõa, Manuel et al., 'The Political History of Twentieth-Century Portugal', *e-Journal of Portuguese History* Vol. 1, No. 2 (Winter 2003)

Bandawe, Lewis Mataka, *Memoirs of a Malawian* (CLAIM, Blantyre, 1971)

Barbosa, Col. E., 'O Nosso Esforço Militar Em Africa', *Revista Militar* Vol. 70 (1918), pp. 129–134

'Ba-Ture' (1), 'Beho-Chini', *Blackwood's Magazine* Vol. 203 (1918), pp. 324–34

'Ba-Ture' (2), 'A Nigerian Column', *Blackwood's Magazine* Vol. 203 (1918), pp. 779–94

Beachey, Ray, *The Horn Aflame* (Bellew Publishing Company, 1990)

Beadon, R.H., *The Royal Army Service Corps* Vol. II (Cambridge University Press, 1931)

Beck, Ann (1), 'Medicine and Society in Tanganyika, 1890–1930', *Transactions of the American Philosophical Society* Vol. 67, No. 3 (April 1977)

Beck, Ann (2), *A History of the British Medical Administration of East Africa, 1900–1950* (Harvard University Press, 1970)

Beer, G.L., *African Questions at the Paris Peace Conference* (Macmillan, 1923)

Beinart, William, *Twentieth Century South Africa* (Oxford University Press, 2001)

Belien, Paul, 'Surrender Monkeys', *The Spectator*, 31/7/2004

Beringe, Major von, 'Mit L59 Kurs Deutsch-Ostafrika', *Köhlers Kolonialkalendar* (1939), pp. 90–95

Bessa, Carlos Gomes, *O Combate de Muíte: Aspectos Relacionados Com A Participação Portuguesa na Guerra de 1914–18 em Moçambique*, Academia Portuguesa Da História, Anais II Serie Vol. 31 (1986), pp. 135–270

Birkby, Carel, *Uncle George* (Jonathan Ball, Johannesburg, 1987)

Bisset, W.M., 'Unexplored Aspects Of South Africa's First World War History,' *Militaria* Vol. 6, No. 3 (1976), pp. 55–61

Blackwell, Leslie (1), *Blackwell Remembers* (Bailey Bros & Swinfen, 1971)

Blackwell, Leslie (2), *African Occasions* (Hutchinson, 1938)

Blumberg, H.E., *Britain's Sea Soldiers: A Record of the Royal Marines During the War 1914–1919* (Swiss & Co., Devonport, 1927)

Boell, Ludwig (1), *Die Operationen in Ostafrika* (privately published, Hamburg, 1951)

Boell, Ludwig (2), 'Der Waffenstillstand 1918 und die ostafrikanische Schutztruppe', in *Wehrwissenschaftliche Rundschau* Vol. 14 (1964), pp. 324–36

Botelho, José Justino Teixeira, *História Militar e Política dos Portugueses em Moçambique* (Centro Tip. Colonial, Lisbon, 1936)

Bourquin, S., 'Heia Safari!', JSAMHS Vol. 7, No. 1 (June 1986), pp. 34–43

Bovill, E.W., 'Notes From East Africa: The Uluguru Mountains and the Rufiji Plain', GJ Vol. 50, No. 4 (October 1917), pp. 277–83

Bradley, K., 'The Northern Rhodesian Regiment', *The African Observer*, Vol. 6, No. 6 (April 1937), pp. 34–43; and Vol. 7, No. 1 (May 1937), pp. 53–63

Brantley, Cynthia, *The Giriama and Colonial Resistance in Kenya, 1800–1920* (University of California Press, 1981)

Braukämpfer, Ulrich, 'Frobenius as Political Agent: Journey to Eritrea in 1915', in Marcus, H.G. (ed.), *New Trends in Ethiopian Studies* (The Red Sea Press, New Jersey, 1994), pp. 553–61

Braun-Stade, K., 'Die Ersatztoffe im Kriege in Deutsch-Ostafrika', *Tropenpflanzer* Vol. 29 (1926), pp. 307–16 and pp. 350–61

Bravman, Bill, *Making Ethnic Ways: Communities and their Transformation in Taita, Kenya 1800–1950* (James Currey, Oxford, 1998)

Brelsford, W.V. (ed.), *The Story of the Northern Rhodesia Regiment* (Galago Publishing, 1990)

Britten, W.E., 'GEA – War Recollections', *The Royal Engineers Journal* Vol. 49 (1935), pp. 430–44

Brode, H., *British and German East Africa: Their Economic and Commercial Relations* (Edward Arnold, 1911)

Brown, J.H., *A Missionary In The Making* (privately published, n.d.)

Brown, Judith, 'War and the Colonial Relationship: Britain, India and the War of 1914–18', Chapter 6 of *War and Society* (ed. Foot, M.R.D.) (Paul Elek, 1973)

Buchanan, Angus, *Three Years of War in East Africa* (John Murray, 1919)

Buhrer, J., *L'Afrique Orientale Allemande et la guerre de 1914–1918* (L. Fournier, Paris, 1922)

Bull, G.G.C., *A History of the 4th Battalion, 19th Hyderabad Regiment* (Gale & Polden, 1933)

Burg, Paul, *Forscher, Kaufherren und Soldaten: Deutschlands Bahnbrecher in Afrika* (Köhler Verlag, Leipzig, 1936)

Buxton, S.C., *General Botha* (John Murray, 1924)

Byl, Piet van der, *From Playgrounds to Battlefields* (Howard Timmins, Cape Town, 1971)

Callwell, Charles, *Experiences of a Dug-Out* (Constable, 1920)

Campbell, Charles, *Chapters from a Soldier's Life* (privately published, 1941)

Campbell, W.W., *East Africa by Motor Lorry* (John Murray, 1928)

Cana, Frank R., 'Frontiers of German East Africa', GJ Vol. 47, No. 4 (April 1916), pp. 297–303

Cann, John P., 'Mozambique, German East Africa and the Great War', *Small Wars & Insurgencies* Vol. 12, No. 1 (Spring 2001), pp. 114–43

Capell, A.E., *The 2nd Rhodesia Regiment in East Africa* (Simson & Co., 1923)

Caroselli, F.S., *L'Affrica nella Guerra e nella pace d'Europe* (Fratelli Treves Editori, Milan, 1918)

Carvalho, Filipe Ribeiro de, 'A Campanha Na Africa Oriental (a incursão alemã no distrito de Quelimane em Junho de 1918)', *Revista Militar* Vol. 88 (1936), pp. 652–68

Cato, Conrad, *The Navy Everywhere: Royal Overseas Operations in World War I* (The Battery Press, Nashville, 2002)

Cayen, A. (1), *Les Campagnes belges d'Afrique 1914–1917* (Ministère des Colonies de Belgique, Paris, n.d.)

Cayen, A. (2), *Au Service de la Colonie* (Librairie de la Grand Place, Brussels 1938)

Cértima, António de, *Epopeia Maldita* (Portugal-Brasil Depositária, Lisbon, 1924)

Chanock, M. (1), *Unconsummated Union: Britain, Rhodesia and South Africa, 1900–45* (Manchester University Press, 1977)

Chanock, M. (2), *Law, Custom and Social Order: The Colonial Experience in Malawi and Zambia* (Heinemann, New Hampshire, 1998)

Charbonneau, Jean, *On se bat sous l'Équateur* (Charles-Lavauzelle & Cie., Paris, 1933)

Charlewood, C.J., 'Naval Actions on the Tanganyika Coast, 1914–1917', TNR Vol. 54 (1960), pp. 121–38, and Vol. 55 (1960), pp. 153–80

Chikwenga, Aibu, 'An Autobiography', *Society of Malawi Journal* Vol. 25, No. 2 (1972), pp. 11–21

Christiansen, Carl (1), *Blockadebrecher nach Deutsch-Ostafrika* (C. Bertelsmann Verlag, Gütersloh, n.d.)

Christiansen, Carl (2), *Durch! Mit Kriegsmaterial zu Lettow-Vorbeck* (Verlag für Volkskunst, Stuttgart, 1918)

Clarke, Peter, *West Africans at War* (Ethnographica, 1986)

Clayton, A. and Savage, D.C., *Government and Labour in Kenya, 1895–1963* (Frank Cass, 1974)

Clifford, Hugh, *The Gold Coast Regiment in the East Africa Campaign* (John Murray, 1920)

Clyde, D.F., *History of the Medical Services of Tanganyika* (Government Press, Dar-es-Salaam, 1962)

Collyer, J.J., *The South Africans with General Smuts in German East Africa 1916* (The Government Printer, Pretoria, 1939)

Cooper, Frederick, 'African Workers and Imperial Designs', in *The Oxford History of the British Empire* (OUP, 1999), pp. 286–316

Corbett, J. and Newbolt, H., *History of The Great War: Naval Operations* Vol. IV (Longmans, Green & Co., 1928)

Cory, H., *Historia Ya Wilaya Bukoba* (Lake Printing Works, Mwanza, n.d.)

Costa, Manuel Gomes da, *Portugal na Guerra: A Guerra nas Colónias* (Arthur Brandão, Lisbon, 1925)

Costa, Mário (1), *É o inimigo que fala – Subsídios inéditos para o estudo da Campanha da África Oriental 1914–1918* (Imprensa Nacional, Lourenço Marques, 1932)

Costa, Mario (2), 'Grande Guerra em Moçambique', *Revista Militar* Vol. 82, Nos 3–4 (1930), pp. 161–75 and pp. 298–307

Costa, Mario (3), 'A Grande Guerra Na África Oriental Portuguesa', *Revista Militar* Vol. 80 (1928), pp. 483–90

Costa, Victorino Gomes da, 'A Marinha Portuguesa Na Ultima Guerra', *Revista Militar* Vol. 71 (1919)

Crafford, F.S., *Jan Smuts* (George Allen & Unwin, 1945)

Cranworth, Lord, *Kenya Chronicles* (Macmillan, 1939)

Cripwell, H.A., 'Operations around Mpepo, German East Africa, 1917', *Rhodesiana* Vol. 10 (1964), pp. 54–79

Crowe, J.H.V., *General Smuts' Campaign in East Africa* (John Murray, 1918)

Cuddeford, D.W.J., *And All For What?* (Heath Cranton, 1933)

Cundall, Frank, *Jamaica's Part in the Great War* (Institute of Jamaica, London, 1925)

Curry, George, 'Woodrow Wilson, Jan Smuts, and the Versailles Settlement', *American Historical Review* Vol. 66 (1961), pp. 968–86

Däbritz, C., *Zwischen Kilimandscharo und Uganda-Bahn* (Verlag Dr Hermann Eichenhagen, Breslau, 1936)

Davidson, F.H.N., 'The War Effort of the British Empire in the World War, 1914–1918', Lecture to the Swiss Officers' Society (War Office, 1935)

Davis, A. and Robertson, H.J., *Chronicles of Kenya* (Cecil Palmer, 1928)

Daye, Pierre (1), *Les Conquêtes Africaines de Belges* (Librarie Militaire Berger-Levrault, Paris, 1918)

Daye, Pierre (2), *Avec les vainqueurs de Tabora* (Les Editions Rex, Brussels, 1935)

Demhardt, Imre Josef, *Deutsche Kolonialgesellschaft, 1888–1918* (privately published, Wiesbaden, 2002)

Demuth, Georg, 'Gegen den Kasigau-Berg', in *Kampf um Kolonien* (Deutscher Wille, Berlin, n.d.)

Dennis, L.G., *The Lake Steamers of East Africa* (Runnymede Malthouse, Egham, 1996)

Deppe, Ludwig (1), *Mit Lettow-Vorbeck Durch Afrika* (Verlag August Scherl, Berlin, 1919)

Deppe, Ludwig and Charlotte (2), *Um Ostafrika* (Verlag. E. Beutelspacher, Dresden, 1925)

Deroover, Marcel, 'The Belgian Lines of Communication up to Tabora', *South African Railways and Harbours Magazine* Vol. 12 (1918), pp. 235–9 and pp. 315–19

Desmore, A., *With The 2nd Cape Corps Thro' Central Africa* (Citadel Press, Cape Town, 1920)'

Difford, Ivor, *The Story of The First Battalion Cape Corps, 1915–1919* (Cape Town, 1920)

Digre, Brian, *Imperialism's New Clothes: The Repartition of Tropical Africa 1914–1919* (Peter Lang, New York, 1990)

Dolbey, Robert, *Sketches of the East Africa Campaign* (John Murray, 1918)

Downes, W.D., *With the Nigerians in German East Africa* (Methuen, 1919)

Duarte, António, 'Esboço para uma Leitura Estratégica sobre a Campanha de Moçambique (1914–1918)', *Revista Militar,* Aug–Sept 1998, pp. 675–704

DuBois, W.E. Burghardt, *The African Roots of War,* Mary Dunlop Maclean Memorial Fund Publication No. 3 (1915), pp. 707–15

Duff, Hector (1), *African Small Chop* (Hodder & Stoughton, 1932)

Duff, Hector (2), 'White Men's Wars in Black Men's Countries', *National Review* Vol. 84 (1925), pp. 902–11

Dundas, Charles, *African Crossroads* (Macmillan, 1955)

Duplesis, E., *The Cohort of The Damned* (Sampson Low Marston, n.d.)

Dyde, Brian, *The Empty Sleeve: The Story of the West India Regiments of the British Army* (Hansib Caribbean, 1997)

Eckart, P., *Blockade-Brecher 'Marie'* (Verlag Ullstein, Berlin, 1937)

Eckhart, Wolfgang U., 'The Colony as laboratory: German sleeping sickness campaigns in German East Africa and in Togo, 1900–1914', *History & Philosophy of the Life Sciences* Vol. 24, No. 1 (March 2002), pp. 69–89

Ehrlich, Haggai, 'Ethiopia and the Middle East: Rethinking History', in Marcus, H.G. (ed.), *New Trends in Ethiopian Studies* (The Red Sea Press, New Jersey, 1994), pp. 631–41

Eichstadt, J., 'Der Sanitätsdienst in DOA während des erstes Weltkrieges', *Wehermedezinische Monatschrift* (1983), pp. 207–10

Ellinwood, Dewitt C. and Pradhan, S.D. (eds), *India and World War I* (Manohar, New Delhi, 1978)

Ellison, James G., 'A Fierce Hunger: Tracing Impacts of the 1918-19 Influenza Epidemic in Southwest Tanzania', in Phillips, Howard and Killingray, David (eds), *The Spanish Influenza Pandemic of 1918–19* (Routledge, 2003), pp. 221–9

Facey, W. (ed.), *A Soldier's Story: The Memoirs of Jafar Pasha Al-Askari* (Arabian Publishing, 2003)

Falls, Cyril, *The First World War* (Longmans, Green & Co., 1960)

Faria, Eduardo de, *Expedicionários* (Lisbon, 1931)

'F.C.', *On Safari: Experiences of a Gunner in the East African Campaign* (J.C. Juta & Co., Cape Town, 1917)

Fendall, C.P., *The East African Fighting Force* (The Battery Press, Nashville, 1992)

Fernandes, Paolo Jorge, 'The Political History of Nineteeth Century Portugal', *e-Journal of Portuguese History* Vol. 1, No. 1 (Summer 2003)

Fewster, 'Dan', 'A Hull Sergeant's Great War Diary' (ed. Robert B. Sylvester, 1999), The South African Military History Society, 1999

Feyver, W.H., *The Distinguished Service Medal 1914–1920* (J.B. Hayward & Son, 1982)

Fitzpatrick, Percy, *The Origins, Causes and Objects of the War* (T. Maskew Miller, Cape Town, n.d.)

Foran, W.R., *The Kenya Police 1887–1960* (Robert Hale, 1962)

Forster, Kent, 'The Quest for East African Neutrality in 1914', *African Studies Review* Vol. 22, No. 1 (1979), pp. 77–82

Fosbrooke, H.A., *Chagga Forts and Bolt Holes*, TNR pp. 115–29

Frankland, A., *The 101st Grenadiers* (Gale & Polden, 1927)

Fraser-Tytler, W.K., 'Cavalry in Bush Warfare', *Cavalry Journal* Vol. 15 (1925), pp. 501–13

Freeman, Lewis R. (1), 'End of German Power in Africa', *Land & Water* (Sept 1916) pp. 9–11

Freeman, Lewis R. (2), 'Rhodes's "All Red" Route: The War's Effect upon the Cape-to-Cairo Railway', *World's Work* Vol. 27, pp. 159–77

Frontera, Ann, *Persistence and Change: A History of Taveta* (Crossroads Press, 1978)

Gardner, Brian, *German East* (Cassell, 1963)

'Garibu' (Inspector Johnson, EA Police), 'Early Days of a Sideshow', JRA Vol. 64 (1937), pp. 375–85

Garson, N., 'South Africa and World War I', JICH Vol. 8 (1979), pp. 68—85

Geyser, O., *Jan Smuts and his International Contemporaries* (Covos Day, South Africa, 2001)

Gibson, Ashley, *Postscript To Adventure* (J.M. Dent, 1930)

Gifford, Prosser and Louis, Wm Roger, *Britain and Germany in Africa: Imperial Rivalry and Colonial Rule* (Yale University Press, 1967)

Gil, Fereira, 'A invasão da Africa Oriental Alemã pelos portugueses. O esfôrço da espedição de 1916', *Revista Militar* Vol. 71 (1919), pp. 331–52

Gleeson, I., *The Unknown Force* (Ashanti Publishing, Johannesburg, 1994)

Goebel, F. and Förster, W., *Afrika zu unsern Füssen: 40,000km Zeppelin-Kriegsfahrten* (von Hase & Koehler Verlag, Leipzig, 1925)

Gogarty, H.A., *Kilima-njaro: An East African Vicariate* (Society for the Propagation of the Faith, New York, 1927)

Gómez, Hipólito De La Torre, *El Imperio del Rey: Alfonso XIII, Portugal y los ingleses (1907–1916)* (Mérida, Madrid, 2002)

Göring, Karl, *Deutsch Ostafrika: Kriegserlebnisse, 1914–20* (Erfurt, 1925)

Graham, C.A.L., *The History of the Indian Mountain Artillery* (Gale & Polden, 1957)

Grant, F.A., Bidgood, W.H. and Saint Hubert, C. de, 'Belgian Air Operations Over Lake Tanganyika 1915–16', *Naval Notebook* Vol. 3 (1979), pp. 1–4

Greenstein, Lewis, 'The Impact of Military Service in World War I on Africans: The Nandi of Kenya', JMAS Vol 16 (1979), pp. 495–507

Grogan, Ewart, 'Musings Of A Nonagenarian' (unpublished manuscript, 1963)

Groves, C.P., *The Planting of Christianity in Africa* (Lutterworth, 1957)

Grundlingh, Albert, *Fighting Their Own War: South African Blacks and the First World War* (Ravan Press, Johannesburg, 1987)

Guedes, A.N., *Nótulas de um expedicionário* (Beira, 1963)

Guingand, Francis, *African Assignment* (Hodder & Stoughton, 1953)

Gunzert, Theodor, 'Memoirs of a German District Commissioner in Mwanza 1907–16, TNR Vol. 66 (1966), pp. 171–82

Gürich, G., *Während des Krieges in Deutsch-Ostafrika und Südafrika* (Dietrich Reimer, Berlin, 1916)

Haas, Rudolf de (1), *Im Sattel für Deutsch-Ost* (Brunnen Verlag/Karl Winkler, Berlin, 1927)

Haas, Rudolf de (2), *Die Meuterer* (Hesse & Becker Verlag, Leipzig, 1927)

Haggard, H. Rider, *Diary Of An African Journey (1914)* (Hurst & Company, 2001)

Halton, E.C., 'The Battle of Tanga, East Africa', *The Lancashire Lad* Vol 4. (1953), pp. 238–42

Hammerstein, H., 'Die deutschen Frauen während des Krieges in Ostafrika', *Tropenpflanzer* Vol. 22 (1919), pp. 8–17

Hamshere, C.E., 'The Campaign in German East Africa', *History Today* Vol. 15 (1965), pp. 249–58

Hancock, W.K., *Smuts – The Sanguine Years, 1870–1919* (Cambridge University Press, 1962)

Harding, Colin, *Frontier Patrols: A History of the British South African Police and other Rhodesian Forces* (G. Bell & Sons Ltd, 1937)

Harrison, Mark, 'Medicine and the Culture of Command: The Case of Malaria Control in the British Army during the two World Wars', *Medical History* Vol. 40 (1996), pp. 437–52

Harvey, R.J., 'Mirambo', TNR Vol. 28 (1950), pp. 10–28

Hassforther, E.E., 'An Account of a Journey Through NW German East Africa in 1913–14', TNR Vol. 61 (1963), pp. 209–15

Hatchell, G.W. (1), 'The East African Campaign: 1914–1919', TNR Vol. 21 (1946), pp. 39–45

Hatchell, G.W. (2), 'The British Occupation of the South-Western Area of Tanganyika Territory, 1914–1918', TNR Vol. 51 (1958), pp. 131–55

Hatton, P.H.S., 'The Search for an Anglo-German Understanding through Africa, 1912–14', *European Studies Review* Vol. 1, No. 2 (1971), pp. 123–45

Hauer, August, 'Vor zwanzig Jahren: als Frontarzt im Zuge', in *Deutsche medizinische Wochenschrift* Vol. 60 (1934), pp. 1852–6

Haupt, Werner, *Die Deutsche Schutztruppe, 1889–1918* (Nebel Verlag, Utting, 1988)

Haussmann, Leon (ed. Martin, Colin), *Corporal Haussmann Goes To War* (Kenilworth, South Africa, 2000)

Hayes, G.D., 'Lake Nyasa and the 1914–18 War', NJ Vol. 17, No. 2 (1964), pp. 17–24

Haywood, A. and Clarke, F., *The History of the Royal West African Frontier Force* (Gale & Polden, 1964)

Hazleton, P.O., 'East African Campaign', *Royal Army Service Corps Quarterly* (October 1920), pp. 225–37

Head, Michael, *The Naval Campaign of East Africa*, The Naval Historical Society of Australia Monograph 175 (2001)

Heathcote, T.A., *The Military in British India* (Manchester University Press, 1995)

Helbig, Klaus (1), 'Die deutsche Kriegführung in Ostafrika, 1914–18', *Militargeschichte* Vol. 28 (1989), pp. 134–45

Helbig, Klaus (2), 'Der ostafrikanische Widerstandskampf während des ersten Weltkrieges', in Büttner, Kurt and Loth, Heinrich (eds), *Philosophie der Eroberer und koloniale Wirklichkeit* (Akademie-Verlag, Berlin, 1981), pp. 303-49

Henderson, W.H., 'The War Economy of German East Africa, 1914–17', *Economic History Review* Vol. 13 (1942), pp. 104–10

Herm, Walther, 'Die letzte Reise der "Somali"', in Schmidt, Fred, *Kapitäne berichten* (Dietrich Reimer Verlag, Berlin, 1936), pp. 165–87

Hess, Robert L., 'Italy and Africa: Colonial Ambitions in the First World War', JAH Vol. 4, No. 1 (1963), pp. 105–26

Heuchling, Jürgen, 'Deutsch-Ostafrika im Ersten Weltkrieg (Teil I),' *Deutsches Soldatenjahrbuch* Vol. 42 (1994), pp. 37–48

Heye, A., *Vitani* (Verlag Grunow, Leipzig, 1926)

Hildesheim, Erik (transl.), 'From Bulgaria To East Africa' (orig. by Schedelmann, Hans), in *The Aeroplane* (January 1919), pp. 466-466A

Hill, M.F., *The Permanent Way* (East African Railways and Harbours Board, Nairobi, 1950)

Hobley, Charles, *Bantu beliefs and magic; with particular reference to the Kikuyu and Kamba tribes of Kenya colony; together with some reflections on East Africa after the war* (H.F. & G. Witherby, 1922)

Hobson, Dick, 'The Feira Affair', NRJ Vol. 4 (1961), pp. 454–61

Hodges, G.W.T. (1), *The Carrier Corps* (Greenwood Press, Connecticut, 1986)

Hodges, G.W.T. (2), 'African Manpower Statistics for the British Forces in East Africa, 1914-1918', JAH Vol. 19, No. 1 (1978), pp. 101–16

Hodson, A., *Seven Years in Southern Abyssinia: 1914–1927* (T. Fisher Unwin, 1927)

Hoffman, Ali, 'Deutsch-Ostafrika im Weltkriege', in *Kampf um Kolonien* (Deutscher Wille, Berlin, n.d.)

Hoffman, Regis, *WWI in East Africa: Civil Censorship* (Charvil Press, 2001)

Holland, Robert, 'The British Empire and the Great War, 1914–1918', *The Oxford History of the British Empire*, Vol. IV (OUP, 1999), pp. 114–37

Holtom, E.C., *Two Years' Captivity in German East Africa* (Hutchinson, 1918)

Hopkirk, Peter, *Like Hidden Fire* (John Murray, 1994)

Hordern, Charles, *Military Operations East Africa* (Vol. I), *August 1914–Sept 1916* (The Battery Press, Nashville, 1990)

Horwitz, S., 'The Non-European War Record in South Africa', *Handbook On Race Relations In South Africa* (OUP, 1949), pp. 534–8

Houart, Victor, 'The Battle of the Lake', *Royal Air Force Flying Review* Vol. 16, No. 2 (1960), pp. 35–6, and 44

Howe, Glenford, *Race, War and Nationalism: A Social History of West Indians in the First World War* (James Currey, 2002)

Hoyt, Edwin, *Guerilla: Colonel von Lettow-Vorbeck and Germany's East African Empire* (Macmillan, 1981)

Hulten, Ida Pipping van, *An Episode of Colonial History: The German Press in Tanzania, 1901–1914*, The Scandinavian Institute of African Studies (Research Report No. 22) (Uppsala, 1974)

Hurren, B.J., *Perchance: A Short History of Naval Aviation* (Nicholson & Watson, 1949)

Hyam, Ronald, *The Failure of South African Expansion, 1900–1948* (Macmillan, 1972)

Hyam, Ronald and Henshaw, Peter, *The Lion and the Springbok* (Cambridge University Press, 2003)

Iliffe, John (1), *A Modern History of Tanganyika* (Cambridge University Press, 1979)

Iliffe, John (2), *Tanganyika under German Rule* (Cambridge University Press, 1969)

Iliffe, John (3), *East African Doctors* (Cambridge University Press, 1998)

Ingham, Kenneth (1), *A History of East Africa* (Longmans, Green & Co., 1962)

Ingham, Kenneth (2), *Jan Christian Smuts* (Weidenfeld & Nicolson, 1986)

Inhülsen, Otto, *Wir ritten für Deutsch-Ostafrika* (von Hase & Koehler Verlag, Leipzig, 1926)

Isaacman, Allen F., *The Tradition of Resistance in Mozambique* (University of California Press, 1976)

Iseghem, A. van, 'Le transport d'une marine à travers la brousse africaine en temps de guerre', *Bulletin Société Belges D'Études Coloniales* (1923), pp. 125–42

Jacquenin, H., 'Operations Navales Sur Le Lac Tanganika Au Cours De La Première Guerre Mondiale', *Neptunus* (1965), pp. 24–37

Jadot, Albert, 'Une batterie de montagne des troupes coloniales belges dans l'Est Africain allemande en 1915–16', *Bulletin Belge Des Sciences Militaires* Vol. 5, No. 1 (1924), pp. 529–60

'Jini Yake', 'Another Side-Show', *Blackwood's Magazine* (October 1917), pp. 446–54

Joelson, F.S. (1), *The Tanganyika Territory* (T. Fisher Unwin, 1920)

Joelson, F.S. (2), *Germany's Claims to Colonies* (Hurst & Blackett, 1939)

Johnston, Harry (1), *The Black Man's Part in the War* (Simpkin, Marshall, Hamilton, Kent & Co., London, 1917)

Johnston, Harry (2), 'The Political Geography of Africa Before and After the War', *East Africa Standard*, April 1915, p. 2

Jones, H.A., *The War in the Air*, Vol. III (Clarendon Press, 1931)

Joseph, C.L., 'The British West Indies Regiment, 1914–18', *Journal of Caribbean History* Vol. 2 (1971), pp. 94–124

Jungblut, Carl, *Vierzig Jahre Afrika* (Spiegel Verlag Paul Lippa, Berlin, 1941)

Kakwenzaire, P.K., 'Sayyid Muhammed Abdille Hassan, Lij Yasu and World War I Politics: 1914–1916', *Transafrican Journal of History* Vol. 14 (1985), pp. 36–45

Kálmán, Géza, *Miaka Ile: Peace and War with Black People* (Budapest, 1923)

Kankelheit, Marie, 'Wie es mir in Ostafrika erging', *Deutsche Kolonialzeitung* Vol. 35 (1919), pp. 23ff.

Katzenellenbogen, S.E., 'Southern Africa and the War of 1914–18', Chapter 7 of *War and Society* (ed. Foot, M.R.D.) (Paul Elek, London, 1973)

Keane, G.J. and Tomblings, D.G., *African Native Medical Corps in the East African Campaign* (Richard Clay & Sons, 1920)

Kearton, Cherry, *Adventures with Animals and Men* (Longmans, Green & Co., 1935)

Keith, Arthur, *War Government of the British Dominions* (Clarendon Press, 1921)

Killingray, D. (1), 'African Voices from Two World Wars', *Historical Research* Vol. 74 (2001), pp. 425–43

Killingray, D. (2), 'Labour Exploitation for Military Campaigns in British Colonial Africa 1870–1945', *Journal of Contemporary History* Vol. 24 (1989), pp. 483–501

Killingray, D. (3), 'The Idea of a British Imperial African Army', JAH Vol. 20, No. 3 (1979), pp. 421–36

Killingray, D. (4), 'Race and Rank in the British Army in the Twentieth Century', *Ethnic and Racial Studies* Vol. 10, No. 3 (July 1987), pp. 276–90

Killingray D. and Mathews, J. (5), 'Beasts of Burden: British West African Carriers in The First World War', *Canadian Journal of African Studies* Vol. 13 (1979), pp. 7–23

Killingray, D. (6), '"A Swift Agent of Government": Air Power in British Colonial Africa, 1916–39', JAH Vol. 25 (1984), pp. 429–44

King, Norman, 'Mafia', GJ Vol. 50, No. 2 (August 1917), pp. 117–25

King-Hall, Herbert, *Naval Memories and Traditions* (Hutchinson, 1926)

Kloppers, Hannes, *Game-Ranger* (Juta & Co., South Africa, n.d.)

Knight, E.F., *The Union-Castle and the War, 1914–1919* (The Union-Castle Mail Steamship Co., 1920)

Knudsen, Knud, *Fahrt nach Ostafrika* (Otto Lenz, Leipzig, 1918)

Kock, Nis (ed. Christensen, Christen P.), *Blockade and Jungle* (Robert Hale, n.d.)

Köhl, Franz (1), *Der Kampf um Deutsch Ostafrika* (Verlag Kameradschaft, Berlin, 1919)

Köhl, Franz (2), 'Der Durchbruch nach Portugiesich Ostafrika in Jahre 1917', *Köhlers Kolonialkalendar* (1939), pp. 38–42

Koponen, Juhani, *Development for Exploitation: German Colonial Policies in Mainland Tanzania, 1884–1914* (Lit Verlag, Helsinki/Hamburg, 1995)

Koppe, Bruno, 'Hauptmann Wintgens's Rückzug von Ruanda nach Tabora und die Kämpfe um Tabora', *Koloniale Rundschau* (1919), pp. 175–95

Krech, Hans, *Die Kampfhandlungen in den ehemaligen deutschen Kolonien in Afrika während des I. Weltkrieges (1914–1918)* (Verlag Dr Köster, Berlin, 1999)

Kyle, Steven, 'Portugal and the Curse of Riches', *Portuguese Studies Reviews* Vol. 10, No. 2 (2003), pp. 101–25

Lang, Franz, 'Spionage am Kilimandjaro', *Kolonial-Post* Vol. 33 (1939), pp. 139–40

Langham, R.M.W., 'Memories of the 1914–1918 Campaign with Northern Rhodesian Forces', NRJ Vol. 2, No. 1 (1953), pp. 49–60; Vol. 2, No. 4 (1954), pp. 79–92; Vol. 3 (1956–9), pp. 253–67; Vol. 4 (1959–61), pp. 166–79

Langhorne, Richard, 'Anglo-German Negotiations Concerning the Future of the Portuguese Colonies, 1911–1914', *The Historical Journal* Vol. 16, No. 2 (1973), pp. 361–87

Langmaid, Kenneth, *Beat to Quarters* (Jarrolds, 1968)

Langsdorff, Werner von (ed.), *Deutsche Flagge über Sand und Palmen*, (C. Bertelsmann, Gütersloh, n.d.)

Lawford, J.P., *30th Punjabis* (Osprey, 1972)

Lawford, J.P. and Catto, W.E., *Solah Punjab: The History of the 16th Punjab Regiment* (Gale & Polden, 1967)

Layman, R.D., *Naval Aviation in the First World War* (Chatham Publishing, 1996)

Leconte, Louis, *Les Ancêtres De Notre Force Navale* (Ministère De La Défense Nationale, Brussels, 1952)

Letcher, Owen, *Cohort of the Tropics* (privately published, 1931)

Lettow-Vorbeck, Paul von (1), *My Reminiscences of East Africa* (Battery Press, Nashville, 1990)

Lettow-Vorbeck, Paul von (2), *Ostafrika* (Koehler Verlag, Leipzig, 1920)

Lettow-Vorbeck, Paul von (3), *Heia Safari!* (Koehler Verlag, Leipzig, 1952)

Lettow-Vorbeck, Paul von (4), *Mein Leben* (Koehler Verlag, Leipzig, 1957)

Lettow-Vorbeck, Paul von (5), *Afrika wie ich es wiedersah* (J.F. Lehmanns Verlag, Munich, 1955)

Lettow-Vorbeck, Paul von (6), *Was mir die Engländer über Ostafrika erzählten* (Verlag Koehler, Berlin, n.d.)

Lettow-Vorbeck, Paul von (7), *Tagebuch 7/9/1914–18/3/1915* (privately published)

'Leviathan', 'The Battle of the Lake', *Blackwood's Magazine* (August 1917), pp. 176–87

Lewin, Evans, *The Germans and Africa* (Cassell, 1939)

Lewis, G.E., 'An East African War Diary', *Quarterly Bulletin of the South African Library* Vol. 27 (1973), pp. 98–119

Lima, Américo Pires de (1), *Na Costa d'África – mémorias de um médico expedicionário a Moçambique* (Gaia, Lisbon, 1933)

Lima, Américo Pires de (2), *Aspectos Sanitários Da Expedição A Moçambique Em 1916* (Primeiro Congresso Militar Colonial, Porto, 1934), pp. 340–7

Listowel, Judith, *The Making of Tanganyika* (Chatto & Windus, 1965)

Little, David Shaw, *Letters* (privately published, Edinburgh, 1952)

Lloyd, A.W., *Jambo or With Jannie in the Jungle* (African Publications, London, 1920)

Lloyd-Jones, Stewart, 'The Slow Death of the First Republic', *Portuguese Studies Review* Vol. 10, No. 2 (2003), pp. 81–100

Lloyd-Jones, W., *K.A.R.* (J.W. Arrowsmith, 1926)

Lochner, R.K., *Kampf im Rufiji-Delta* (Wilhelm Heyne, Munich, 1987)

Looff, Max (1), *Les marins du Koenigsberg au combat sur la mer et dans la brousse* (Payot, Paris, 1933)

Looff, Max (2), *Deutsche Kolonie in Not* (Verlag von Anton Bertinetti, Berlin, 1928)

Loth, Heinrich, *Griff nach Ostafrika: Politik des deutschen Imperialismus und antikolonialer Kampf, Legende und Wirklichkeit* (Deutscher Verlag der Wissenschaften, Berlin, 1968)

Louis, Wm Roger (1), *Ruanda-Urundi* (Clarendon Press, 1963)

Louis, Wm Roger (2), 'Great Britain and the African Peace Settlement of 1919', *American Historical Review* LXXI, No. 3, pp. 875–92

Louvers, Octave (1), *La campagne d'africaine de la Belgique et ses résultats politiques* (Société anonyme M. Weissenbruch, Brussels, 1921)

Louvers, Octave (2), 'La Conquête du Ruanda-Urundi', *Bulletin des Séances* Vol. 6 (1935), pp. 167–78 and 372–8

Lovering, Timothy, 'African Women and the Colonial Army in Nyasaland, 1891–1964', in *Twentieth Century Malawi* (eds McCracken; J; Lovering, T.J; and Chalamanda, Fiona), University of Sterling Occasional Paper No. 7 (2001), pp. 5–20

Lucas, Charles, *The Empire At War*, Vol. IV (OUP, 1925)

Lüthy, Herbert, 'India and East Africa: Imperial Partnership at the End of the First World War', JCH Vol. 6 (1971), pp. 55–85

Lutteroth, Ascan, *Tunakwenda* (Verlag Broscheck & Co., Hamburg, 1938)

Lytton, The Earl of, *The Desert and the Green* (Macdonald, 1957)

Macaulay, Neil, *Mandates* (Methuen, 1937)

Macdonald, Tom, *Ouma Smuts, The First Lady of South Africa* (Hurst & Blackett, n.d.)

Macedo, Carlos Lemonde de, *Nhamacurra, Caderno de Guerra e de Paz* (Lisbon, 1982)

MacKenzie, John (1), 'The Tanganyika Naval Expedition', *Mariner's Mirror* Vol. 70 (1984), pp. 397–410

MacKenzie, John (2), 'The Naval Campaigns on Lakes Victoria and Nyasa', *Mariner's Mirror* Vol. 71 (1985), pp. 169–82

Mackinney, Herbert, *Cartoons of the Great War* (Cape Times, 1916–1919)

Maddox, Gregory, 'Mtunya: Famine in Central Tanzania, 1917–20, JAH Vol. 31 (1990), pp. 181–97

Mader, F.W. (1), *Die Schlacht bei Tanga* (C. Bertelsmann Verlag, Gütersloh, n.d.)

Mader, F.W. (2), *Am Kilimandjaro* (Union Deutsche Verlag, Berlin, 1927)

Mader, F.W. (3), *Vom Pangani zum Rovuma* (Union Deutsche Verlag, Berlin, n.d.)

Maercker, Fritz, 'Die erste Marine-Expedition und das erste Seegefecht auf dem Tanganjikasee', *Deutsche Kolonialzeitung* Vol. 35 (1918), pp. 34–6

Magee, Frank, 'Transporting a Navy Through the Jungles of Africa in War Time', *National Geographic Magazine* Vol. 42, No. 4 (1922), pp. 331–62

Mahony, D., 'Pat', *Parodies* (Standard Press, Cape Town, n.d.)

Maillard, W.-E. and Schröder, J., *Das Offizierkorps der Schutztruppe für Deutsch-Ostafrika im Weltkrieg 1914–1918* (Traditionsverband ehemaliger Schutz- und Überseetruppen, 2003)

Maker, J.G., 'A Narrative of the Right Section, 5th Mountain Battery, South African Mounted Riflemen, Central African Imperial Service Contingent, Nyasaland, 1915–18', JSAMHS Vol. 4, No. 1, pp. 30–33, and No. 2, pp. 39–53

Mann, Erick J., *Mikono ya damu: 'Hands of Blood', African Mercenaries and the Politics of Conflict in German East Africa, 1888–1904* (Peter Lang, Frankfurt am Main, 2002)

Marben, Rolf, *Zeppelin Adventures* (John Hamilton, 1932)

Marjomaa, Risto, 'The Martial Spirit: Yao Soldiers in British Service in Nyasaland, 1895–1939', JAH Vol. 44, No. 3 (2003), pp. 413–32

Martin, A.C., *The Durban Light Infantry*, Vol. I (Durban, 1969)

Martins, E. Azambuja (1), *Nevala* (Famalicão, Lisbon, 1935)

Martins, E. Azambuja (2), 'A Campanha de Moçambique', in Martins, Ferreira (1), pp. 183–9

Martins, E. Azambuja (3), *Expedições Militares no Barué 1917: Seus Precedentes e Ensinamentos* (Lisbon, 1937)

Martins, E. Azambuja (4), 'O Comando Alemão Na África Oriental', *Revista Militar* Vol. 74, No. 2 (1922), pp. 58–66

Martins, Ferreira (1), *Portugal na Grande Guerra*, Vol. II (Lisbon, 1938)

Martins, Ferreira (2), *A Cooperação Anglo-Portuguesa na Grande Guerra de 1914–1918* (British Embassy, Lisbon, 1942)

Martins, Ferreira (3), 'Verdades Esquecidas E Ignoradas: Portugal Na Guerra De 1914–1918', *Republica* (March 1956), pp. 3–8

Matson, A.T. (1), *Nandi Resistance to British Rule, 1890–1906* (East Africa Publishing House, Nairobi, 1972)

Matson, A.T. (2), 'Wireless Interception on Lake Victoria', UJ Vol. 35 (1971), pp. 43–8

Maugham, R.C.T., *Africa As I Have Known It* (John Murray, 1929)

Maylam, Paul, *South Africa's Racial Past* (Ashgate, 2001)

Maxwell, W.E., *Capital Campaigners* (Gale & Polden, 1948)

Mazet, Horace S., 'Germany's Secret Project "China Matter"', *Military History* (June 1986), pp. 12–17 and pp. 55–7

McDonald, Donald, *Surgeons Twoe And A Barber* (William Heinemann, 1950)

Meighörner-Schardt, Wolfgang, *Wegbereiter des Weltluftverkehre wider Willen: Die Geschichte des Zeppelins-Luftshifftyps 'w'* (Zeppelin-Museum, Friedrichshafen, 1992)

Meinertzhagen, Richard, *Army Diary 1899–1926* (Oliver & Boyd, 1960)

Meneses, Filipe Ribeiro de, 'Too Serious a Matter to be Left to the Generals? Parliament and the Army in Wartime Portugal, 1914–18', *Journal of Contemporary History* Vol. 33, No. 1 (1998), pp. 85–96

Menezes, José de Magalhães e, *A acção dos irregulars nas campanhas de Moçambique*, pp. 280–302 (Varia: Primeiro Congresso Militar Colonial, Porto, 1934)

Methner, Wilhelm, *Unter Drei Gouverneuren* (Korn Verlag, Breslau, 1938)

Michel, P., 'In Dienst des roten Kreuzes in Deutsch-Ostafrika', *Evangelisch-Lutherisches Missionblatt* Vol. 75 (1920), pp. 16–29, 41–4, 63–8, 88–91, 107–15

Mielke, Otto (1), *Schleichfahrt nach Ostafrika* (Arthur Moewig Verlag, Munich, 1955)

Mielke, Otto (2), *In die Enge getrieben* (Arthur Moewig Verlag, Munich, n.d.)

'Miles', *Jules Renkin et la Conquête Africaine* (G. Van Oest et Cie, Paris, 1917)

Miller, Charles, *Battle for the Bundu* (Macmillan, 1974)

Mirão, Cardoso, *Kináni (quem vive?) – Crónica de Guerra no Norte de Moçambique 1917–1918* (Livros Horizonte, Lisbon, 2001)

Moberly, G.K., *A Square Deal* (Shuter and Shooter, Pietermaritzburg, 1946)

Moesta, K., 'Die Einwirkungen des Krieges auf die Eingeborenbevölkerung in Deutsch Ostafrika', *Koloniale Rundschau* (1919), pp. 5–25

Monson, Jamie, 'Relocating Maji-Maji: The Politics of Allaince and Authority in the Southern Highlands of Tanzania, 1870–1918', JAH Vol. 39 (1998), pp. 95–120

Monteiro, H., 'A Grande Guerra Na Africa Portuguesa', *Revista Militar* Vol. 75 (1923), pp. 456–73

Moore, Major W.G., *Early Bird* (Putnam, 1963)

Moreira, Alberto de Laura, *Os Serviços Administratavos na Expedição A Moçambique Em 1916* (Varia: Primeiro Congresso Militar Colonial, Porto), pp. 295–302

Moser, J. (ed.), *Der Weltkrieg 1914–1918 in Seiner Rauhen Wirklichkeit* (Justin Moser Verlag, Munich, n.d.)

Moskopp, Revd S.J., 'The PEA Rebellion of 1917', NRJ Vol. 5, No. 2 (1962), pp. 154–60

Mosley, Leonard, *Duel For Kilimanjaro* (Weidenfeld & Nicolson, 1963)

Mota, Simões da, 'A coluna de socorro a Newala', *Revista Militar* Vol. 80 (1928), pp. 458–67

Moulaert, G., *La Campagne du Tanganyika, 1916–1917* (L'Édition Universelle, Brussels, 1934)

Moyse-Bartlett, H., *The King's African Rifles* (Naval & Military Press, n.d.)

Muller, Emmanuel, *Les Troupes du Katanga et les Campagnes d'Afrique 1914–1918* (Établissements Généraux D'Imprimerie, Brussels, 1935)

Müller, Herman, *Kriegserinnerungen aus DOA* (privately published; original in Privatarchiv Christain Baust, Monheim, n.d.)

Mumby, Frank, *The Great World War*, Vol VI (The Gresham Publishing Co., n.d.)

Munro, J. Forbes and Savage, Donald, 'Carrier Corps Recruitment in the British East Africa Protectorate, 1914–1918', JAH Vol. 7, No. 2 (1966), pp. 313–42

Naishtad, Sam, *The Great War Parodies* (privately published, South Africa, n.d.)

Nasson, Bill, 'A Great Divide: Popular Responses to the Great War in South Africa', *War and Society* Vol. 12, No. 1 (May 1994), pp. 47–64

Newitt, Malyn (1), *Portuguese Warfare in Africa* (www.cphrc.org.uk, n.d.)

Newitt, Malyn (2), *A History of Mozambique* (Hurst, 1995)

Ngologoza, P., *Kigezi and its People* (East African Literature Bureau, Nairobi, 1969)

Nigmann, Ernst, *German Schutztruppe in East Africa, 1889–1911* (Mittler, Berlin, 1911)

Northey, Edward, 'The East African Campaign', JAS Vol 18 (1920), pp. 81–7

Nuhn, Walter, *Flammen über Deutsch-Ostafrika* (Bernard & Graefe, Bonn, 1998)

Ochieng, William, *The Battle of Kisii* (Staff Seminar, Kenyatta University, 1979)

O'Connor, J.K., *The Afrikander Rebellion* (George Allen & Unwin, 1915)

Ofcansky, T. (1), 'A Bibliography of the East African Campaign, 1914–1918', *Africana Journal* Vol. 12, No. 4 (1981), pp. 338–51

Ofcansky, T. (2), 'The East African Campaign in the "Rhodesian Herald"', *History in Africa* Vol. 13 (1987), pp. 283–93

Ofcansky, T. (3), 'The British Medical Administration During The East Africa Campaign, 1914–1918', Adler Museum Vol. 12, No. 2 (1986), pp. 12–17

Ogot, Bethwell (ed.), *War and Society in Africa* (Frank Cass, 2001)

O'Neill, H.C. (1), *The War in Africa (1914–1917) and the Far East (1914)* (Longmans, Green & Co., 1918)

O'Neill, H.C. (2), *The Royal Fusiliers in the Great War* (William Heinemann, 1922)

Onslow, John, 'Hard Voyage To Battle', *Army Quarterly* Vol. 103 (1973), pp. 480–89

Orr, G.M. (1), '1914–1915 in East Africa', JUSII Vol. 56 (1926), pp. 58–86

Orr, G.M. (2), 'Von Lettow's Escape into Portuguese East Africa, 1917', *Army Quarterly* Vol. 13 (1926), pp. 50–59

Orr, G.M. (3), 'Random Recollections of East Africa, 1914–1918', *Army Quarterly* Vol. 11 (1926), pp. 282–93

Orr, G.M. (4), 'Some Afterthoughts of the War in East Africa,' JRUSI Vol. 69 (1924), pp. 693–702

Orr, G.M. (5), 'From Rumbo to the Rovuma: The Odyssey of "One" Column in East Africa', *Army Quarterly* Vol. 7 (1923), pp. 109–29

Orr, G.M. (6), 'A Remarkable Raid', JRUSI Vol. 71 (1926), pp. 73–80

Orr, G.M. (7), 'The Winter Campaign of 1916 in East Africa', JUSII Vol. 60 (1930), pp. 69–78

Orr, G.M. (8), 'Operations on Interior Lines in Bush Warfare', JRUSI Vol. 70 (1925), pp. 127–33

Orr, G.M. (9), 'Smuts v Lettow: A Critical Phase in East Africa, August to September 1916', *Army Quarterly* Vol. 9 (1925), pp. 287–99

O'Sullevan, J.J., 'Campaign on German East Africa-Rhodesian Border', JAS Vol. 15 (1916), pp. 209–15

Osuntokun, Akinjide, *Nigeria in the First World War* (Humanities Press, New Jersey, 1979)

Overton, John, 'War and Economic Development: Settlers in Kenya, 1914–1918', JAH Vol. 27 (1986), pp. 79–103

Page, Malcolm, *KAR* (Leo Cooper, 1998)

Page, Melvin E. (ed.) (1), *Africa and the First World War* (St Martin's Press, New York, 1987)

Page, Melvin E. (2), 'The War of "Thangata"', in JAH Vol. 19, No. 1 (1978), pp. 87–100

Page, Melvin E. (3), *The Chiwaya War: Malawians and the First World War* (Westview Press, 2000)

Page, Melvin E. (4), '"With Jannie in the Jungle": European Humor in an East African Campaign, 1914–1918', *The International Journal of African Historical Studies* Vol. 13, No. 3 (1981), pp. 466–81

Parfitt, Canon J.T., *Mesopotamia: The Key to the Future* (Hodder & Stoughton, 1917)

Parsons, Timothy (1), 'African Participation in the British Empire', *Black Experience and the Empire* (OUP, 2004), pp. 257–85

Parsons, Timothy (2), 'All askaris are family men: sex, domesticity and discipline in the King's African Rifles, 1902–1964', in Killingray, David and Omissi, David (eds), *Guardians of Empire* (Manchester University Press, 1999), pp. 157–78

Parsons, Timothy (3), '"Wakamba Warriors are Soldiers of the Queen": The Evolution of the Kamba as a Martial Race, 1890–1970', *Ethnohistory* Vol. 46, No. 4 (1999), pp. 671–701

Paterson, H. and Levin, M., *Through Desert, Veld and Mud* (privately published, Durban, 2002)

Patience, Kevin, *Königsberg: A German East African Raider* (Zanzibar Publications, 2001)

Patterson, David and Pyle, Gerald, 'The Diffusion of Influenza in Sub-Saharan Africa During the 1918–19 Pandemic', *Social Science and Medicine* Vol. 17 (1983), pp. 1299–1307

Payne, Adam, *Blow, Blow The Winds of Change* (PENS, Johannesburg, 1989)

Pélissier, René (1), *Naissance du Mozambique* (Pélissier/Centre de la Recherche Scientifique, Orgeval, 1984)

Pélissier, René (2), *História de Moçambique*, Vol. II (Editorial Estampa, Lisbon, 2000)

Pencz, Rudolf, *Marschmusik und Schutzgebiete* (Traditionsverband ehemaliger Schutz- und Überseetruppen, 2005)

Pentzel, Otto, *Buschkampf in Ostafrika* (Thienemanns Verlag, Stuttgart, n.d.)

Peperkorn, Albert, 'Die Funkentelegraphie in Deutsch-Ostafrika während des Krieges', *Afrika Nachrichten* Vol. 6 (1925), pp. 107–8 and pp. 130–31

Perry, F.W., *The Commonwealth Armies: Manpower and Organisation in Two World Wars* (Manchester University Press, 1988)

Phillips, C.J., *Uganda Volunteers and The War* (A.D. Cameron, Uganda, 1917)

Phillips, Howard, *Black October: The Impact of the Spanish Influenza Epidemic of 1918 on South Africa* (Government Printer, Pretoria, 1990)

Pineau, Arthur, *Le Vicariat du Tanganyika Durant la Guerre 1914–1918* (privately published)

Plaatje, Solomon, *Native Life in South Africa* (Ravan Press, Johannesburg, 1982)

Pocock, Geoffrey, *One Hundred Years of The Legion of Frontiersmen* (Phillimore, 2004)

Pocock, Roger (ed.), *The Frontiersman's Pocket-Book* (John Murray, 1909)

Poeschel, Hans, *The Voice of German East Africa* (August Scherl, Berlin, 1919)

Ponte, Nunes da, *Notas da Campanha de Moçambique (1917–1918)*, *Revista Militar* Supplement (Lisbon, 1940)

Popkess, Athelstan, *Sweat In My Eyes* (Edgar Backus, 1952)

Powys, Llewelyn, *Black Laughter* (Harcourt, Brace, New York, 1924)

Praval, K.C., *Valour Triumphs: A History of the Kumaon Regiment* (Thomson Press (India), 1976)

Pretorius, P.J., *Jungle Man* (George G. Harrap, 1947)

Pritchard, H.L. (ed.), *History of the Royal Corps of Engineers*, Vol. VII (The Institution of Royal Engineers, Chatham, 1952)

Prüsse, Albert, *Zwanzig Jahre Ansiedler in Deutsch-Ostafrika* (Strecker und Schroder Verlag, Stuttgart, 1929)

Raeder, Erich (ed.), *Der Krieg zur See: Der Kreuzerkrieg in den ausländern Gewässern*, Band 2 (E.S. Mittler & Sohn, Berlin, 1923)

Ranger, Terence (1), *Revolt in Portuguese East Africa: The Makombe Rising of 1917* (St Antony's Papers No. 15, Southern Illinois University Press, 1963)

Ranger, Terence (2), 'The Influenza Pandemic in Southern Rhodesia: A Crisis of Comprehension', in Arnold, David (ed.), *Imperial Medicine and Indigenous Societies* (Manchester University Press, 1988), pp. 172–88

Ranger, Terence (3), *Dance and Society in Eastern Africa* (University of California Press, 1975)

Ransford, Oliver, *Livingstone's Lake* (Thomas Y. Crowell, New York, 1967)

Raum, O.F., *Der Beitrag der Schutztruppenoffiziere zur Völkerkunde von Deutsch-Ostafrika* (Berlin, 1988)

Reck, Hans, *Buschteufel* (Dietrich Reimer/Ernst Vohsen Verlag, Berlin, 1926)

Reitz, Deneys, *Trekking On* (Faber & Faber, 1933)

Ribeiro, Margarida Calafate, 'Empire, Colonial Wars and Post-Colonialism', *Portuguese Studies* Vol. 18 (2002), pp. 132–214

Richardson, Anthony, *The Crowded Hours: The Story of 'Sos' Cohen* (Max Parrish, 1952)

Ridgway, Brig.-General R.T., 'With No. 2 Column, German East Africa 1917', *Army Quarterly* Vol. 5 (1922), pp. 12-28, and Vol. 6 (1923), pp. 247–63

Ritchie, Eric Moore, *The Unfinished War* (Eyre & Spottiswoode, 1940)

Robinson, Douglas (1), *The Zeppelin In Combat* (G.T. Foulis, 1962)

Robinson, Douglas (2), *The Flight of the German Naval Airship L59*, American Aviation Historical Society, Vol. 4, No. 2, 1959

Roehl, Kurt (1), *Ostafrikas Heldenkampf* (M. Warneck, Berlin, 1918)

Roehl, Kurt (2), 'Ruanda-Erinnerungen: zum Gedächtnis an Major Wintgens', *Koloniale Rundschau* (1925), pp. 289–98

Rosas, Álvaro, *Terras Negras: impressões duma campanha* (Porto, 1935)

Rothe, W., 'Der Einfall der Portugiesen in Deutsch-Ostafrika 1916', *Deutsche Kolonialzeitung* Vol. 5 (1920), pp. 40–43 and pp. 50–51

Roy, Alexandre le, *Au Kilima-ndjaro* (Paris, 1914)

Royaume de Belgique, *Les Campagnes Coloniales Belges 1914–1918* (Ministry of Defence, Brussels, 1927–9, three volumes)

Ruhland, O., 'Die Verwendung von Schiffsgeschützen im Ostafrikanischen Feldzuge 1941–1918', *Marine-Rundschau* Vol. 32 (1927), pp. 97–108

Russell, A. (1), 'War Comes To Tanganyika – 1914', TNR Vol. 57 (1961), pp. 195–8

Russell, A. (2), 'The Landing At Tanga 1914', TNR Vol. 58 (1962), pp. 103–7

Russell, L.A., 'The Last Phase of the East African Campaign', *Rhodesiana* Vol. 17 (1967), pp. 41–55

Rutherford, Alan (ed.), *Kaputala – The Diary of Arthur Beagle and the East African Campaign 1916–18* (Hand Over Fist Press, Bishops Cleeve, 2001)

Sampson, Philip J., *The Conquest of German East* (Special Commemoration Number of *The Nongqai*, Pretoria, 1917)

Sanderson, G.M., 'Gunfire On Nyasa', NJ Vol. 14, No. 2, pp. 13–26

Sandes, E.W.C. (1), *The Military Engineer In India* (The Institution Of Royal Engineers, 1933)

Sandes, E.W.C. (2), *The Indian Sappers and Miners* (The Institution of Royal Engineers, 1948)

Santos, Ernesto Moreira dos, *Combate De Negomano* (Guimarães, 1961)

Sarmento, José Alberto, *A Expansão Alemã* (Lisbon, 1919)

Schnee, Ada (transl. Sam E. Edelstein Jnr), *Bibi Mkuba* (Borgo Press, California, 1995)

Schnee, Dr H. (1), *Deutsch-Ostafrika im Weltkriege* (Verlag Quelle und Meyer, Leipzig, 1919)

Schnee, Dr H. (2), *German Colonization Past and Future* (George Allen & Unwin, 1926)

Schnee, Dr H. (ed.) (3), *Deutsches Kolonial-Lexicon* (Verlag Quelle & Meyer, Leipzig, 1920)

Schneider, Hannes, *Die Eisenbahnen in den ehemaligen deutschen Schutzgebieten in Afrika* (Traditionsverband ehemaliger Schutz- und Überseetruppen, 2005)

Schoen, Walter von, *Auf Vorposten für Deutschland: unsere Kolonien im Weltkrieg* (Ullstein, Berlin, 1937)

Scholler, H., 'German World War I Aims in Ethiopia: The Frobenius-Hall Mission', in Tubiana, J. (ed.), *Modern Ethiopia from the Accession of Menelik II to the Present* (A.A. Balkema, Rotterdam, 1980), pp. 303–26

Schuffenhauer, Ida, *Komm wieder Bwana* (Süsseroth Verlag, Berlin, 1940)

Schulke, R., 'Arzneiversorgung und Ersatzmittelbescaffung während des Feldzuges in Deutsch-Ostafrika', *Pharmazeutische Zentralle für Deutschland*, Vol. 60 (1919), pp. 333–6 and pp. 347–51

Selig, P. (ed.), *Auf Jagd- und Kriegspfaden in Ostafrika: Erlebnisse des Afrikareisenden W. Bode in den Jahren 1901–1920* (Fulda, 1925)

Selow-Serman, K., *Blockade-Brecher* (August Scherl, Berlin, 1917)

Selvagem, Carlos (Colonel Carlos Tavares Andrade dos Santos), *Tropa D'África* (Aillaud e Bertrand, Porto, 1924)

Shackleton, C.W., *East African Experiences, 1916* (Knox, Durban, 1941)

Shankland, P., *The Phantom Flotilla* (Collins, 1968)

Sharpe, H.B., 'Memories of the East African Campaign', serialised in *Kenya Weekly News*, 1959

Sheppard, S.H. (1), 'The East African Campaign, 1914–16', in JRUSI (February 1942), pp. 71–6

Sheppard, S.H. (2), 'Some Notes on Tactics in the East African Campaign', JUSII Vol. 48 (1919), pp. 138–57

Shepperson, G. and Price, T., *Independent African: John Chilembwe and the Origins, Setting and Significance of the Nyasaland Native Rising of 1915* (Edinburgh University Press, 1958)

Shorthose, Capt. W.T., *Sport and Adventure in Africa* (Seeley Service & Co., 1923)

Silva, Júlio Rodrigues da, *Monografia do 3° Batalhão expedicionário do RI n.° 21 à Província de Moçambique em 1915* (Imprensa Beleza, Lisbon, n.d.)

Smuts, J., 'East Africa', GJ Vol. 51, No. 3 (March 1918), pp. 129–49

Solf, W.H., 'Schnee und Lettow-Vorbeck', *Die Deutsche Nation* Vol. 2 (1920), pp. 87–95

Soper, G., 'Our War Elephants', *Wide World* Vol. 43, pp. 309–11

Spaulding, Jay and Kapteijns, Lidwien, *An Islamic Alliance: Ali Dinar and the Sanussiya, 1900–1916* (Northwestern University Press, Illinois, 1994)

Speed, Neil, *Born To Fight: Major Charles Joseph Ross DSO* (The Caps and Flints Press, Melbourne, Australia, 2002)

Spencer, Ian, 'The First World War and the Origins of the Dual Policy of Development in Kenya 1914–1922', *World Development* Vol. 9, No. 8 (1981), pp. 735–48

Spicer-Simson, Geoffrey (1), 'Operations on Lake Tanganyika in 1915', JRUSI Vol. 79 (1934), pp. 750–64

Spicer-Simson, Geoffrey (2), 'Naval Operations in Central Africa', *United Empire* (June 1918), pp. 287–91

Spicer-Simson, Theodore, *A Collection of Characters* (University of Miami Press, 1962)

Spies, S., 'The Outbreak of the First World War and the Botha Government', in SAHJ Vol. 1 (1969), pp. 47–57

Spuy, Kenneth van der, *Chasing The Wind* (Books of Africa, Cape Town, 1966)

Standaert, Eugène, *A Belgian Mission to the Boers* (Hodder & Stoughton, 1917)

Stapleton, Tim, 'The Composition of the Rhodesia Native Regiment During the First World War: A Look at the Evidence', *History in Africa* Vol. 30 (2003), pp. 283–95

Steer, G.L., *Judgment on German Africa* (Hodder & Stoughton, 1939)

Stent, Vere, *The Great Safari*, collected articles for the *Pretoria News*, 1914–1919

Steward, Keith, 'An African Hero Who Deserved the Victoria Cross: Colour Sergeant George Williams', OMRS (March 2005), pp. 19–26

Stiénon, Charles (1), 'L'Effondrement Colonial De L'Allemagne', *Revue des deux mondes* (April 1917), pp. 645–84

Stiénon, Charles (2), *La Campagne Anglo-Belge de L'Afrique Orientale Allemande* (Berger-Livrault, Paris, 1918)

Stoecker, Helmuth, *German Imperialism in Africa* (Hurst, 1986)

Stoneham, C.T. (1), *Africa All Over* (Hutchinson, 1934)

Stoneham, C.T. (2), *From Hobo To Hunter* (John Long, 1956)

Strachan, Hew (1), *The First World War in Africa* (Oxford University Press, 2004)

Strachan, Hew (2), *The First World War: To Arms* (Oxford University Press, 2001)

Stratford, D.O., 'Naval Ships Move Overland Up Africa', JSAMHS Vol. 1, No. 4 (June 1969), pp. 28–30

Stuemer, Willibald von, 'Die Kaiserliche Schutztruppe für Deutsch-Ostafrika', lecture to the II *Seebataillon Infanterie-Regiment 69* on 5 February 1937

Stürmer, Michael, *The German Empire 1871–1919* (Phoenix Press, 2001)

Sunseri, Thaddeus, *Vilimani: Labor Migration and Rural Change in Early Colonial Tanzania* (James Currey, 2002)

Swan, Jon, 'The Final Solution in South West Africa', *Military History Quarterly* (Summer 1991), pp. 36–55

Tafel, Theodor, 'The German East Africa Native Troops', JRAS Vol. 14 (1914–15), pp. 82–90

Tasker, George, 'Naval Occasions on Lake Tanganyika in the 1914–18 War', NRJ Vol. 3 (1956–9), pp. 57–68

Taute, M. (1), 'Ärztliches aus dem Kriege in Deutsch-Ostafrika', *Archiv für Schiffs- und Tropenhygiene* Vol. 23 (1919), pp. 523–44

Teixeira, Nuno Severiano (1), '1914–1918: To Die For One's Country?! Why Did Portugal Go To War?', *Portuguese Studies Review* Vol. 6, No. 1 (1997), pp. 16–25

Teixeira, Nuno Severiano (ed.) (2), *Portugal E A Guerra* (Colibri, Lisbon, 1998)

Teixeira, Nuno Severiano (3), *O Poder e a Guerra 1914–1918* (Editorial Estampa, Lisbon, 1996)

Telo, António José, *A marinha e o apoio ao império, Diário de Notícias Portugal E A Grande Guerra* (Supplement 23), Lisbon, 2003, pp. 273–4

Terlinden, C., 'Les Campagnes Belges Dans L'Est Africain Allemand (1914–1917)', *Revue d'histoire des colonies* (1932), pp. 77–98

Terrell, W.E., *With the Motor Transport in British East Africa* (Headley Brothers, n.d.)

Thatcher, W.S., *The 4th Battalion DCO Tenth Baluch Regiment in The Great War (129th Baluchis)* (Cambridge Univesity Press, 1932)

Thomas, H.B. (1), 'The Kionga Triangle', TNR Vol. 31 (July 1951), pp. 47–50

Thomas, H.B. (2), 'Kigezi Operations 1914–1917', UJ Vol. 30, No. 2 (1966), pp. 165–73

Thomas, Roger, 'Military Recruitment in the Gold Coast During WWI', *Cahier D'Études Africains* Vol. 15 (1975), pp. 57–83

Thompson, E.S., 'A Machine Gunner's Odyssey Through German East Africa, January 1916–February 1917', JSAMHS Vol. 7, Nos 3–6

Thompson, Richard H., 'The Rise and Fall of the Monitor, 1862–1973', *Mariner's Mirror* Vol. 60, No. 3 (1974), pp. 293–310

Toit, Brian du, *The Boers in East Africa* (Bergin & Garvey, 1998)

Tombeur, Charles, 'Après Tabora', *La Revue Coloniale Belge* Ann. 1, No . 14 (1946), pp. 4–7

Tomkins, Sandra M., 'Colonial Administration in British Africa during the Influenza Epidemic of 1918–1919', *Canadian Journal of African Studies* Vol. 28, No. 1 (1994), pp. 60–83

Tõrres, José, *A Campanha Da África Oriental* (Imprensa Nacional, Lourenço Marques, 1919)

Trevor, Tudor, *Forty Years in Africa* (Hurst & Blackett, 1932)

Tylden, G. *The Armed Forces of South Africa* (City of Johannesburg Africana Museum, 1954)

Twain, Mark, *King Leopold's Soliloquy* (Seven Seas Books, Berlin, 1961)

Union of South Africa, General Staff, Defence Headquarters, *The Union of South Africa and The Great War, 1914–18: Official History* (Pretoria, 1922)

Urban, Frank, *Ned's Navy: The Private Letters of Admiral Sir Edward Charlton, KCB, KCM* (Airlife Publishing, Shrewsbury, 1998)

Viehweg, Rudolf, *Unter Schwarz-Weiss-Rot in fernen Zonen: Erlebnisse eines Matrosen auf dem Kreuzer 'Königsberg'* (privately published, Leipzig, 1933)

Viera, Josef (1), *Die Tangaschlacht* (Ensslin & Laiblin, Reutlingen, n.d.)

Viera, Josef (2), *Deutsch-Ostafrika lebt* (Loewes Verlag, Stuttgart, 1936)

Viera, Josef (3), *Ein Kontinent rückt Näher* (Verlag Hugendubel, 1942)

Viera, Josef (4), *Mit Lettow-Vorbeck im Busch* (Loewes Verlag, Stuttgart, 1937)

Vincent-Smith, John, 'Britain, Portugal, and the First World War, 1914–16', *European Studies Review* Vol. 3 (1974), pp. 207–38

Wahle, Kurt, *Erinnerungen an meine Kriegsjahre in Deutsch-Ostafrika* (privately published, 1920)

Walker, W.H.J. (ed. Wright, T.B.), 'The East African Diary Of A271 Private WHJ Walker, Southern Rhodesia Column, 1916', JSAHR Vol. 81 (2003), pp. 132–51

Wallis, H. (1), *Handbook of Uganda* (Kampala, 1920)

Wallis, H. (2), 'The War in Uganda', *National Review* Vol. 79 (1919), pp. 556-61

Waltermann, K., 'Bukoba im Kriege', *Nachrichten aus der Ostafrikanischen Mission* Vol. 32 (1919), pp. 25–31

Warhurst, Philip, 'Smuts and Africa: A study in sub-imperialism', SAHJ Vol. 16 (1984), pp. 82–100

Waters, R.S., *History of the 5th Battalion (Pathans) 14th Punjab Regiment* (John Bain, 1936)

Watkins, Elizabeth, *Oscar From Africa* (Radcliffe Press, 1995)

458

Webb, F., 'North Nyasa District and the War, 1914–1918', NJ Vol. 17, No. 1 (1964), pp. 16–23

Weber, B.E.M., 'Influence Des Facteurs Politiques Sur La Conduite De La Guerre En Afrique Orientale Allemande', *Bulletin Belge Des Sciences Militaires* Vol. 7, No. 1 (1926), pp. 174–91

Weeks, J.H., '*n Jong soldaat: Ervarings en herinneringe* (Potchefstroom Herald, 1969)

Weerd, H.A. de, 'The Tanganyika Expedition', *Proceedings of the US Naval Institute* (October 1932), pp. 1461–3

Welbourn, Revd F.B., 'Ezera Kabali's Diary Of The 1916 War', UJ Vol. 27, No. 2 (1963), pp. 223–6

Wenig, Richard (1), *In Monsun und Pori* (Safari-Verlag, Berlin, 1922)

Wenig, Richard (2), *Kriegs-Safari* (Verlag Scherl, Berlin, 1920)

Westerman, Percy F., *Wilmshurst of the Frontier Force: A Story of the Conquest of German East Africa* (S.W. Partridge, 1918)

Westgate, T.H., *In the Grip of the German* (Belfast, 1918)

Whittall, W., *With Botha and Smuts in Africa* (Cassell, 1917)

Wiart, Adrian Carton de, *Happy Odyssey* (Pan Books, 1955)

Wienholt, Arnold, *The Story of a Lion Hunt* (Andrew Melrose, 1922)

Wilde, A.T., *Regimental History of the 4th Battalion, 13th Frontier Force Rifles (Wilde's)* (privately published, 1932)

Williams, F. Lukyn, 'Nuwa Mbaguta, Nganzi of Ankole', UJ Vol. 10 (1946), pp. 124–35

Williams, G.A., 'First British Army Air Ambulance From Nyasaland', *The Society of Malawi Journal* Vol. 35, No. 1, p. 76

Wilson, C.J., *The Story of the East African Mounted Rifles* (The East African Standard, 1938)

Wood, Gordon, *I Was There* (Arthur H. Stockwell, Devon, 1984)

Woodhall, Edwin T., *Spies of the Great War* (John Long, 1932)

Woodhouse, H.L., 'Notes on Railway Work in East Africa, 1914–1918', *Royal Engineers Journal* Vol. 37 (1923), pp. 37–46

Woodward, David, 'The Imperial Strategist: Jan Christiaan Smuts and British Military Policy, 1917–1918', JSAMHS Vol. 5, No. 4

Wren, P.C., *Cupid In Africa* (Heath Cranton, 1944)

Wright, Tim, *The History of the Northern Rhodesia Police* (BECM Press, Bristol, 2001)

Wrigley, G.M., 'The Military Campaigns Against Germany's African Colonies', *Geographical Review* Vol. 5 (1918), pp. 44-65

Wyllie, W.L., Sea *Fights of the Great War* (Cassell, 1918)

Wylly, H.C. (1), *The Loyal North Lancashire Regiment* (The Royal United Service Institution, 1933)

Wylly, H.C. (2), *The History of Coke's Rifles* (Gale & Polden, 1930)

Wynn, W.E., *Ambush* (Hutchinson, 1937)

Yeats-Brown, F.C.C., *The Star and Crescent: Being the Story of the 17th Cavalry From 1858–1922* (Pioneer Press, Allahabad, 1927)

Young, Francis Brett, *Marching On Tanga* (E.P. Dutton, New York, *c.*1917)

Young, T. Cullen, 'The Battle of Karonga', NJ Vol. 8, No. 2 (1955), pp. 27–30

*Zache, Hans (ed.), *Das deutsche Kolonialbuch* (Wilhelm Andermann Verlag, Berlin, 1925)

Zimmer, Gustav, 'The Crew of the Möwe on Lake Tanganyika', *Naval Review* Vol. 10 (1922), pp. 650–60

Zimmermann, Emil, *The German Empire of Central Africa* (Longman, 1918)

Zirkel, Kirsten, 'Military Power in German Colonial Policy: The Schutztruppen and their leaders in East and South-West Africa, 1888-1918', in Killingray, David and Omissi, David (eds), *Guardians of Empire* (Manchester University Press, 1999), pp. 91–113

Zupitza, Max, 'Die Hilfsexpedition für die DOA Schutztruppe auf dem Luftwege', *Deutsche Kolonialzeitung* Vol. 36 (1920), pp. 29–32

*Hans Zache's *Das deutsche Kolonialbuch* contains the following articles (listed in sequential order):
Lettow-Vorbeck, Paul von, 'Tanga', pp. 418–21
Kempner, Franz, 'Der Sieg von Tanga', pp. 422–5
Arning, Wilhelm, 'Der Ruhmestag von Tanga', pp. 426–7
Looff, Max, 'SMS Königsberg im Rufiflusse', pp. 428–35
Lieberman, Eberhard von, 'Das Gefecht von Narungombe (19.7.1917)', pp. 436–49
Tafel, Theodor, 'Die letzten Kämpfe der Westruppen und ihr Marsch zum Rovuma (1917)', pp. 450–55
Naumann, Heinrich, 'Sechs Monate hinter den englischen Linien in Deutsch-Ostafrika', pp. 456–9

2. ARCHIVAL SOURCES

Australian War Memorial, Canberra (AWM/)
MSS 1232: Alliston, John M, *The Riddle of the Delta*

National Archives of Australia
MP1185/6–1919/8917: *An account of the movements of HMAS Pioneer during the Great War* by Surgeon-Lt Melville Anderson

Bodleian Library, Oxford (BOD/)
Ms Harcourt
Ms Milner

Bodleian Library of Commonwealth and African Studies at Rhodes House (RH/)
Ainsworth, J. (Mss.Afr.s.379 and 382)
Anti-Slavery and Aborigines Protection Society (Mss.Brit.Emp.s.22/G133)
Bagenal, Q.J. (Mss.Afr. s.2351)
Bremner, B.H. (Mss.Afr.s. 1372)
British East Africa Native Carriers (Mss.Brit.Emp.s.22/G133)
Clearkin, Peter (Mss.Afr.r.4)
Coryndon, R. (Mss.Afr.s.633)
Covell, Gordon (Mss.Afr.s.385-7)
Dobbs, C. (Mss.Afr.s.504)
Drury, N.C. (Mss.Afr.s.1625)
Elkington, Jim (Mss.Afr.s.1558)
Elliot, Jim (Mss.Afr.s.1179)
Gethin, Jim (Mss.Afr.s.1277 and 1747)
Grier, Selwyn (Mss.Afr.s.1379 – *A Record of the Doings of the Oversea Contingent, Nigeria Regiment, During The Campaign in German East Africa*)
Hollis, A. C. (Mss.Brit.Emp.s.295-7)
Johansen, Alfred (Mss.Afr.s.1792/5/11: Matson Papers)
Markus, Otto (Mss.Afr.s.1764)
Masters, A. C. (Mss.Afr.s.1997)

McGregor Ross, W. (Mss.Afr.s.1876, Vol. 8 – letters)
McGregor Ross, W. (Mss.Afr.s.2305 – diaries)
Millar-Smith, R. (Mss.Afr.s. 1213)
Miller-Sterling, C. (Mss.Afr.s.2051)
Overseas Nursing Association (Mss.Brit.Emp. s.400)
Spindler, Miss F (USPG/X Series/item 632)
Watkins, O. (Mss.Afr.s.1408)
Willis, J. J. (Mss.Afr. s.1792/5/14: Matson Papers)

Churchill Archives Centre, Cambridge (CHAR/)
Churchill Papers

Imperial War Museum, London (IWM/)
Acheson, Patrick (P160)
Aitken, A.E. (80/13/1)
Arnold, H. (77/171/1)
Ball, R.W. (CONS. SHELF)
Beves, P.S. (80/23/1)
Bowden, A.F. (P393)
Buchanan, A. (82/25/1)
Castle, E.W. (83/5/1)
Charlewood, C.J. (98/1/1)
Cooke, Gerald (P80-86)
Crampton, D. (71/29/2)
Croxton, F.C. (01/38/1)
Derby, V.E. (82/25/1)
Drury, Frank (91/11/1)
Dunnington-Jefferson, J. (66/155/1)
Edwards, W.F.S. (67/115/1-2)
Elliott, J. (67/256/1)
Ewart, R. (73/88/1)
Fenning, E.G. (P252)
Gardner, A.A. ([40])
Johnson, F.S. (P473)
Johnson, G.S. (77/109/1)
Hamill, J.S. (92/18/1)
Hawkins, E.B.B. (P126)
Hopkins, F. (94/28/1)
Hopper, H.H. (68/27/1)
Kellie, G. (P252)
Kemp, A.E. (91/3/1)
King, Norman (PP/Micr/150)
Kirke, E. (82/28/1)
Lettow-Vorbeck, Paul (323.61)
Lewis, H.V. (74/48/1)
Lyall, R.A. (72/28/6)
McCall, Henry (86/31/1)
Captain Bertie Maxwell (77/147/1)
Miller, A.S. (P15)

Mott, A.C. (99/16/1)
Mountfort, R.D. (CONS. SHELF)
Murray, R.G. (P281)
Nichols, A.W. (83/31/1)
Northey, E. (P5)
Pinder, H.S. ([303])
Rigby, S. (99/15/1)
Ritter, P. (Germ. Misc. 16)
Rowland, F.D. (74/98/1)
Russell, L.A. (02/6/1)
Smith-Dorrien, H. (87/47/10)
Turner, C. (74/155/1)
Turner, R.B. (P252)
Vernon, W.F. (76/202/2)
Wapshare, Richard (88/61/1)
Watkins, H. (74/88/1)
Wedgwood, J.C. (PP/MCR/104)
Weld-Forrester, W. (P261)
Willby, G.F. (78/31/1)
Wright, A.J. (96/47/1)

Misc 80 (1228): Nhamacurra Conference, July 1918
Misc. 164 (2541): Diary of an unidentified stoker on HMS *Weymouth*, 1914–16

The Gurkha Museum
Stewart Papers (5RGR/Appx1/9 and 14)

Kenya National Archives (KNA/)
Attorney- General Series (AG/)
District Commissioner Kwale Series (DC/KWL)
District Commissioner Machakos Series (DC/MKS)
District Commissioner Taita Series (DC/Taita)
District Commissioner Voi Series (DC/Voi)
District Officer Taveta Series (DO/Taveta)
Ministry of Health Series (MOH)
Provincial Commissioner Coast Series (PC/Coast)
Provincial Commissioner Nyanza Series (PC/Nyanza)

Missionari d'Africa ('The White Fathers') Archives, Rome (WF/)
Société des Missionaires d'Afrique *Rapports Annuels* 1914–18
Casiers
Petit Écho 1914–18
Grand Lacs

Les Missionaires dans l'Afrique Équatoriale pendant la guerre, 1914–19
Les Pères Blancs des Missions Équatoriales pendant et aprés la guerre, 1914–22
Léonard, H., 'Les Missions De L'Est-Africain Pendant La Guerre (1914–1916)', *Rapport Annuel 1916 (Supplément)*, pp. 65–103
Mazé, Joseph, *Vicariats de Mwanza et de Bukoba*

Rabeyrin, Claudius, *Les Missionaires dim Burundi durant la guerre des gentilshommes en Afrique Orientale, 1914–18* (1978)

The National Archives, London (TNA/)
ADM (Admiralty) series
AIR (Air Department) series
CAB (Cabinet Papers) series
CO (Colonial Office) series
FO (Foreign Office) series
WO (War Office) series

National Army Museum, London (NAM/)
Barton, W. (7807-23-3/4-MFN)
Cooper, P.R. (6506-16: misc. KAR documents)
Davidson, F. (6112-661)
Dobbs, C. (8103-76)
Hawkins, E.B. (8205-103)
Hawkins, E.B. (6806-21)
Macpherson, R.G. (6012-409)
McCarthy, V. (6707-10: documents relating to General Sir J.M. Stewart)
Moyse-Bartlett, H. (6705-60)
Williams, G.A. (6909-46)

6506-16: Collection of documents relating to East Africa campaign
6506-16: 17/FK Field Reports

Peter Liddle Collection, Brotherton Library, University of Leeds (LIDDLE/)
Archdale, F.A. (AFE03)
Brewster, B.T. (RNMN)
Bridgeman, Hon. R.O.B. (AFE05)
Brown, L.O. (AIR 054)
Cameron, Alexander (AFE07)
Cooke, Gerald (AFE08)
Faber, S.E. (AIR110)
Falconer, J. (RNMN)
Grenfell, C.H. (RNMN)
Groves, A.V. (AFE11)
McCall, H. (RNMN)
Messum, A.L. (AFE17)
Parnham, W.J. (RNMN)
Pearson, B. (AFE21)
Phillips, C.G. (AFE22)
Pim, G.A. (AFE24)
Pratt, H.B. (AFE25)
Saunders, H.W.L. (AIR274)
Seager, J.H. (AFE26/AR277)
Seddon, W. (AFE27)
Shaw, C. (AFE28)
Speed, E. (AFE31)

Wedgwood, J.C. (DF135)
Wilkinson, J.S. (AFE37)

Portuguese Archives (PORT/)
Arquivo Histórico Militar (ATTM/)
Gil, Ferreira, *Relatório*
Rosa, Tómas de Sousa, *Relatório das operacoes contra os alemaes no Leste Africano*
Militar Relatórios da Expedição a Moçambique
Relatório do Coronel Massano de Amorim
Relatório original do Governador Carvalho Araujo sobre Inhambane Repartição Militar, 1914–1919
Arquivo Histórico-Diplomático do Ministério dos Negócios Estrangeiros (MNE/)
Servico Biblioteca e Documentaças Diplomática do MNF
Portugal Na Primeira Guerra Mundial (1914-1918): As Negociações Diplomáticas E A Acção Militar Na Europa E Em África, Vol. II (Ministério Dos Negócios Estrangeiros, Lisbon, 1997)

Preussischer Staatsbibliothek zu Berlin
Preussischer Kulturbesitz

E. Gudowius (Nachl. 300)

Royal Commonwealth Society Collection, Cambridge University (RCS/)
Carrier Corps (Mss.468: Papers of Capt Harold Beken Thomas)
Paice, Arnold

South African National Museum of Military History (SANMMH/)
Adkins, G.E.
Berrangé, C.
Brink, Andries
Brits, C.E.G.
Brits, C.J.
Campion, Edwin
Dawson, William
Deventer, Jacobus van
Dewey, H.R.
Faure, Martin
Green, Ted
Guy, Graham
Jackson, F.E.
Jager, G.J.W. de
James, J.C.
Lane, William
Makin, David
Mapham, Walter
Miller, R.
Payne, J.H.A.
Stephens, F.G.W.
Stuart-Findlay, A.

Winstanley, W.

Unit Papers:
2nd East African Brigade
2nd South African Infantry Brigade
5th Battery South African Field Artillery
7th South African Infantry Regiment
8th South African Infantry Regiment

Blake, Arthur, 'Report on the Outstanding Historical Injustice Suffered by Members of South African Labour Units Who Served in World War One'

Zimbabwe National Archives (ZNA/)
Lake Tanganyika Naval Expedition 1915–16 Papers
Leach Papers
Hugh Williams Papers

3. THESES

East, John, 'The campaign in East Africa, 1914–18. A Select Annotated Bibliography' (thesis submitted for Fellowship of the Library Association, 1987)
Ganz, Albert H., 'The Role of the Imperial German Navy in Colonial Affairs' (Ohio State University, 1972)
Greenstein, Lewis, 'Africans in a European War: the First World War in East Africa with special reference to the Nandi of Kenya' (Indiana University, 1975)
Helbig, Klaus, 'Legende und Wahrheit: Der Erste Weltkrieg in Ostafrika und die Rolle des Generals Lettow-Vorbeck' (Leipzig University, 1968)
Lever, A.W., 'The British Empire and the German Colonies' (University of Wisconsin, 1963)
Lovering, T.J., 'Authority and Identity: Malawian Soldiers in Britain's Colonial Army, 1890— 1964' (Stirling University, 2002)
Reigel, Corey W., 'The First World War in East Africa: A Reinterpretation' (Temple University, 1990)
Warhurst, Philip, 'Rhodesia and her neighbours, 1900–23' (Oxford University, 1970)
Yorke, E.J., 'A Crisis of Control: War and Authority in Northern Rhodesia, 1914–1919' (Cambridge University, 1984)

INDEX